Brill's Companion to the Reception of Presocratic Natural Philosophy in Later Classical Thought

Brill's Companions to Philosophy

Ancient Philosophy

VOLUME 6

The titles published in this series are listed at *brill.com/bcpa*

Brill's Companion to the Reception of Presocratic Natural Philosophy in Later Classical Thought

Edited by

Chelsea C. Harry and Justin Habash

BRILL

LEIDEN | BOSTON

Cover illustration: Christopher Walsh. Untitled abstraction of nature (2014); oil on canvas 8x10 in.; Courtesy of Christopher Walsh.

The Library of Congress Cataloging-in-Publication Data

Names: Harry, Chelsea C., editor. | Habash, Justin, editor.

Title: Brill's companion to the reception of presocratic natural philosophy in later classical thought / edited by Chelsea C. Harry and Justin Habash.

Description: Leiden ; Boston : Brill, [2020]. | Series: Brill companions to philosophy. Ancient philosophy, 2588-7823 ; volume 6 | Includes index. | Summary: "In Brill's Companion to the Reception of Presocratic Natural Philosophy in Later Classical Thought, contributions by Gottfried Heinemann, Andrew Gregory, Justin Habash, Daniel W. Graham, Oliver Primavesi, Owen Goldin, Omar D. Álvarez Salas, Christopher Kurfess, Dirk L. Couprie, Tiberiu Popa, Timothy J. Crowley, Liliana Carolina Sánchez Castro, Iakovos Vasiliou, Barbara Sattler, Rosemary Wright, and a foreword by Patricia Curd explore the influences of early Greek science (6-4th c. BCE) on the philosophical works of Plato, Aristotle, and the Hippocratics. Rather than presenting an unified narrative, the volume supports various ways to understand the development of the concept of nature, the emergence of science, and the historical context of topics such as elements, principles, soul, organization, causation, purpose, and cosmos in ancient Greek philosophy"– Provided by publisher.

Identifiers: LCCN 2020037965 (print) | LCCN 2020037966 (ebook) | ISBN 9789004318175 (hardback) | ISBN 9789004443358 (ebook)

Subjects: LCSH: Philosophy, Ancient. | Science, Ancient–History. | Pre-Socratic philosophers. | Philosophy of nature.

Classification: LCC B187.S32 B75 2020 (print) | LCC B187.S32 (ebook) | DDC 182–dc23

LC record available at https://lccn.loc.gov/2020037965

LC ebook record available at https://lccn.loc.gov/2020037966

Typeface for the Latin, Greek, and Cyrillic scripts: "Brill". See and download: brill.com/brill-typeface.

ISSN 2588-7823
ISBN 978-90-04-31817-5 (hardback)
ISBN 978-90-04-44335-8 (e-book)

Copyright 2021 by Koninklijke Brill NV, Leiden, The Netherlands.
Koninklijke Brill NV incorporates the imprints Brill, Brill Hes & De Graaf, Brill Nijhoff, Brill Rodopi, Brill Sense, Hotei Publishing, mentis Verlag, Verlag Ferdinand Schöningh and Wilhelm Fink Verlag.
All rights reserved. No part of this publication may be reproduced, translated, stored in a retrieval system, or transmitted in any form or by any means, electronic, mechanical, photocopying, recording or otherwise, without prior written permission from the publisher. Requests for re-use and/or translations must be addressed to Koninklijke Brill NV via brill.com or copyright.com.

This book is printed on acid-free paper and produced in a sustainable manner.

Contents

Foreword: Some Thoughts on Interpreting the Presocratics and Their Reception   VII
  Patrica Curd
Oxford Classical Dictionary – Abbreviations List   XII
List of Figures   XIII
Notes on Contributors   XIV

Introduction   1

PART 1
Reception: Methodology and Grounding Concepts

1   *Peri Phuseôs*: Physics, Physicists, and *Phusis* in Aristotle   13
    Gottfried Heinemann

2   Plato's Reception of Presocratic Natural Philosophy   44
    Andrew D. Gregory

3   Presocratic Echoes: The Reception of Purposive Nature in Classical Greek Thought   71
    Justin Habash

4   The Reception of Early Greek Astronomy   91
    Daniel W. Graham

PART 2
Hidden Reception: Exploring Sources and Developing Themes

5   Pythagorean Ratios in Empedocles' Physics   113
    Oliver Primavesi

6   Pythagoreanism and the History of Demonstration   193
    Owen Goldin

7   Aristotle's Outlook on Pythagoras and the (So-Called) Pythagoreans   221
    Omar D. Álvarez Salas

8	Eleatic *Archai* in Aristotle: *A Dependence on Theophrastus'* Natural History? 261 *Christopher Kurfess*	
9	The Reception of Presocratic Flat Earth Cosmology in Aristotle, the Doxography, and Beyond 289 *Dirk L. Couprie*	
10	Elements and Their Forms: The Fortunes of a Presocratic Idea 323 *Tiberiu Popa*	
11	Aristotle, Empedocles, and the Reception of the Four Elements Hypothesis 352 *Timothy J. Crowley*	
12	The Aristotelian Reception Of Heraclitus' Conception of the Soul 377 *Liliana Carolina Sánchez Castro*	
13	Mixing Minds: Anaxagoras and Plato's *Phaedo* 404 *Iakovos Vasiliou*	
14	Platonic Reception – Atomism and the Atomists in Plato's *Timaeus* 429 *Barbara Sattler*	
15	Presocratic Cosmology and Platonic Myth 453 *Rosemary Wright*	
	Index 483	

Foreword: Some Thoughts on Interpreting the Presocratics and Their Reception

Patricia Curd

One way to think about the reception of a philosophical thinker is to consider the influence of that philosopher on another, or the use that the later writer makes of the work of the earlier. Thus, we can discuss how Descartes's work influenced Spinoza, or how John Rawls made use of both Aristotle and Kant in developing *A Theory of Justice*. Sometimes the influence is seen as direct: How does Spinoza respond to the questions that Descartes asked and develop his own answers to them? Sometimes the influence is less direct: Rawls took care to talk about an Aristotelian principle, claiming to capture something about what Aristotle saw about ethical theory without claiming to be giving "Aristotle's view." In these examples, readers have (or can have) the advantage of having the texts of Descartes, Spinoza, Aristotle, and Rawls in front of them, and can judge to what extent the responders have quoted correctly, or whether the interpretive response is more or less consistent with what one reads in the original. Are we getting Descartes' own view, or a Cartesian theory?

When the subject (as here) is *The Reception of Presocratic Natural Philosophy in Later Classical Thought* a special problem arises. What remains to us of early Greek philosophy is (literally) fragmented.[1] In some cases, we have have only a word or two, or a few lines. In other cases (Thales, for example), there is good reason to think that nothing that Thales himself wrote has been preserved in the writing of another author. For some others (Parmenides and Empedocles), although we have larger segments of text, we can be sure that much is missing. The problem becomes more complicated because, in many cases, the sources of the Presocratic fragments are the very people (among

---

1 The standard collection of texts has been *Die Fragmente der Vorsokratiker*, 6th edition (H. Diels; rev. W. Kranz). It was Diels who introduced the now widely-used numbering system for identifying Presocratic authors, the fragments (supposed by Diels to be authentic quotations), and the testimonia about them. There are now a number of alternative collections that both improve on DK and provide translations of DK's Greek and Latin texts (DK provide German translations of only the B-sections, the fragments). See for instance, D. Graham, *The Texts of Early Greek Philosophy* (Two Volumes), Cambridge University Press 2010; and A. Laks and G. Most, *Early Greek Philosophy*, Loeb Classical Press, seven volumes, 2016. For the moment, the DK numberings are still the customary way to refer to these texts.

others: Plato and Aristotle in 4th C. BCE; Simplicius in the 6th C. CE) who are using and interpreting these texts to make their own points. Moreover, by the time we get to a number of valuable sources for our early philosophers (e.g., Simplicius, who is the only source for some of the most important fragments of Parmenides), the materials that they are using are old, rare, and sometimes in tatters. The problems involved are intertwined: we must rely on our sources to reconstruct the the thought of the first philosophers, but we need to have an interpretation of that thought in order to evaluate the responses of those who are our sources. Imagine that all or most of Plato's works are lost to us, and try to reconstruct his views using the remarks about them in Aristotle, and information drawn from the ancient commentators on Aristotle. (This is actually the case with Zeno of Elea's four paradoxes of motion. We have no original texts, only Aristotle's names for and proposed solutions to the paradoxes in *Physics* 6.9.)[2] So, how do we read and study the Presocratics and how do we think about their influence? Although there are difficulties, complete pessimism is misplaced. We can always wish that we had more textual and doxographical evidence, but there is enough general agreement among scholars about enough material to make Presocratic studies lively and interesting; nevertheless most who work on early Greek philosophy understand that a certain level of humility in the face of the evidence should prevail: As in the case of Empedocles and the Strasbourg Papyrus, more new material may yet come to light that will require reconsideration and revision of previous interpretations.[3]

Recently, there has been discussion of the proper term for referring to the group that we are discussing.[4] *Presocratic* goes back to the nineteenth century, and originally implied that Socrates marks a break in the development of philosophy because of his interest in ethics. Some scholars now prefer the use

---

2 There is a similar problem with the texts of Presocratic atomism: C.C.W. Taylor, the editor of the Phoenix/Toronto volume on Leucippus and Democritus puts it in his preface to the volume, "the evidence for the atomists presents the peculiar difficulty that, while the number of purported fragments is large, very few fragments deal with the atomists' central doctrines, for which we are almost wholly reliant on doxographical evidence." *The Atomists: Leucippus and Democritus*, Toronto: University of Toronto Press, 1999 (p. xi).

3 For Empedocles, see Martin and Primavesi, *L'Empédocle de Strasbourg*, Berlin: Walter de Gruyter, 1999. There is also the fascinating case of the Derveni Papyrus: see Gábor Betegh, *The Derveni Papyrus: Cosmology, Theology and Interpretation*, Cambridge University Press, 2004.

4 See, for instance, *The Cambridge Companion to Early Greek Philosophy* (A.A. Long, ed.) Cambridge University Press, 1999; *The Oxford Handbook of Presocratic Philosophy* (P. Curd and D. Graham, eds.) Oxford University Press, 2018; and A. Laks, *The Concept of Presocratic Philosophy: Its Origin, Development, and Significance* (Translated by G.W. Most), Princeton University Press, 2018.

FOREWORD

IX

of "early Greek philosophy/philosophers." Because of the ubiquity of the older term and because it now seems clear that there was no real break between the Presocratics and the philosophers of the classical Athenian period, the name "Presocratic" is more often a neutral label used to refer to a group of thinkers (who themselves are often classified as early Presocratic or later Presocratic). There is also the irony that Socrates himself wrote nothing, and so there is no evidence for his supposed single-minded interest in ethics other than the depictions of Socrates by Plato and other authors. There is even counter-evidence in Plato: the Socrates of the *Phaedo* reports his early interest in the theories of Anaxagoras.

Careful study of the extant fragments and testimonia can help us build accounts and interpretations of the earliest Greek philosophers. In some cases, we can disentangle text and interpretation by paying attention to language: Archaic dialect and language usage can confirm that we have a genuine text rather than a later report, summary, or outright forgery. Since some Presocratics wrote in verse (Xenophanes, Parmenides, and Empedocles), paying attention to poetic meter can sometimes help connect passages that are reported in different sources. Simplicius occasionally comments on the archaic or poetic language of passages he quotes. For example, in what is now fragment B2, he notes that Anaximander "said that the indefinite (*to apeiron*) is both principle (*archē*) and element (*stoicheion*) of the things that are, and he was the first to introduce this name of the principle." Later in the same passage he observes that Anaximander "speaks in rather poetical language." The vocabulary of early Greek thought presents difficulties of its own. In the Anaximander fragment from Simplicius, it is unclear just which word it is that Anaximander is said to have been the first to use (*apeiron* or *archē*) and there have been disagreements among interpreters about this. One thing does seem clear, though: *Stoicheion* with its technical meaning of *element* as Simplicius uses it here, is an Aristotelian coinage, and it would not have been used in this sense by Anaximander himself. The same goes for such Aristotelian terms as "matter" and "substance." While post-Aristotelian commentators and philosophers can happily use these words and know what they mean by them, using them to explain Presocratic views can be seriously misleading. Thus, many who work on early Greek philosophy talk about *stuff* rather than *matter*. This is not a case of being overly fastidious, for to speak of matter invites talk of form, and the form-matter distinction is Aristotle's important solution to complicated physical and metaphysical problems that can be traced back through Plato to the Presocratics. The same caveat goes for translations and understandings of the various forms of the Greek verb *einai* (to be). It is a mistake to think that the fundamental notion here is *existence*. Rather, the being of a thing is what it is to be that sort of thing (its nature, or as Aristotle would say, its essence).[5] Parmenides' account of "Truth" (frs. B1.26–28 to B8.51) is not concerned with what exists (grass, grasshoppers, numbers, pains, etc.) but with what counts as a metaphysically fundamental entity in any account of how things are. Only such a being can be a genuine object of knowledge and serve as an explanatory foundation.[6] This notion of a basic being continues through later Presocratic thought and in Plato, e.g., in the *Phaedo*, only the Forms can be said genuinely to be; and in the central books of the *Republic*, Parmenidean assumptions about what it is to be are provide the starting points for the arguments that the Forms are the only objects of knowledge. This progression culminates in Aristotle's radical and problem-solving assertion in *Metaphysics* Z.1 that "being is said in many ways" and the fundamental way of being is to be a substance (*ousia*).

Yet we might ask: in what sense are these early Greek thinkers *philosophers*? Clearly they did not think of themselves as such. While in fragment 35 (from Clement) we find that "according to Heraclitus, men who are lovers of wisdom (*philosophoi*) must be inquirers into many things," the extent of the actual quotation is open to question: Is the word *philosophoi* part of the original text? In an important sense it makes no difference; the presence or absence of a particular word is not relevant in determining whether these thinkers were engaged in what we would now call philosophizing, and Heraclitus was certainly interested in wisdom and the criteria for claiming to know or understand how things are. While we should be careful to avoid anachronism in attributing later philosophical meanings to the terms that they use, the Presocratics can and did use traditional language in new ways, and invented new words.[7] The fact that a word has a particular meaning (or range of meanings) in Homer or Hesiod or other early texts does not entail that the same word cannot have a novel or extended meaning in Heraclitus. Thus, for instance, arguments about how we should understand Heraclitus' notion of *logos* cannot be solved simply by canvassing its uses in Homer. The notion of nature (*physis*) in early Greek philosophy is another subject about which scholars have disagreed vigorously. It seems clear that many of the Presocratics (if not all – and the question of who belongs on the list remains open) were indeed interested in questions about the possibility and structure of human knowledge, in worries about how that which can be known must be in order to be knowable, and the roles that

---

5   See especially C. Kahn, "Why Existence does not Emerge as a Distinct Concept in Greek Philosophy," *Archiv für Geschichte der Philosophie* 58 (1978) pp. 323–334.

6   Anything that is real in the Parmenidean sense will exist, but that follows from its nature as metaphysically basic, and is the foundation of an acceptable explanation.

7   Empedocles in particular uses a number of words that occur in no other ancient texts.

FOREWORD

can or cannot be played by sense perception and thinking in answering such questions. Not only are what we would call first-order scientific, metaphysical and epistemological problems considered, but ideas about the proper structure of the accounts (or theories) that would solve these problems are being developed. Another important point is that the Presocratics were discussing and responding to one another. Heraclitus names some of those with whom he disagrees. In other cases, linguistic resonances and word choices indicate that Parmenides was aware of earlier views about the nature of the cosmos, and that both Anaxagoras and Empedocles are constructing accounts that take seriously Parmenides' strictures on the nature of what-is and the possibility of knowledge.

Thus, borrowings and influence (acknowledged and unacknowledged) and responses (both positive and negative) are already present in the Presocratics themselves. In addition, many of the philosophical questions and range of philosophical topics that engrossed and were developed in new ways by Plato, Aristotle, and those who came after them began with the Presocratics. As the contents of this volume demonstrate, when we consider the reception of Presocratic philosophy, we see that the earliest Greek thinkers set the agenda for those who followed.

Patricia Curd

Oxford Classical Dictionary – Abbreviations List

Arist.	Aristotle
Cra.	Cratylus
De an.	De anima
DK	H. Diels and W. Kranz, Fragmente der Vorsokratiker
Gen. corr.	De generatione et corruptione
Grg.	Gorgias
Int.	De interpretatione
Metaph.	Metaphysics
Mete.	Meteorologica
[*Mund.*]	De mundo
Ph.	Physica
Phd.	Phaedo
Phlb.	Philebus
Pl.	Plato
Plt.	Politicus
Prm.	Parmenides
Prt.	Protagoras
Resp.	De respiratione
Resp.	Respublica
Sens.	De sensu
Soph.	Sophista
Tht.	Theaetetus
Ti.	Timaeus
Top.	Topica

Figures

5.1 The seven phases of the cosmic cycle 161

5.2 The basic structure of the cosmic time-table as deduced from the Florentine scholia by Rashed 2014 168

5.3 The subdivision of the cosmic time-table in accordance with the proportions of the double *tetraktys* 171

5.4 The seven phases of the cosmic cycle in accordance with the proportions of the double *tetraktys* 175

5.5 The 40 time units of the *Sphairos* as embedded both in the *tetraktys* of Love and in that of Strife 178

9.1 Falling on a flat earth 291

9.2 Alleged "centrifocal dynamics" on a flat earth (after Rovelli) 292

9.3 Measuring the height of a pyramid and the height of the sun on a flat earth (drawing not to scale) 298

9.4 On a flat earth, the sun is nearby and rather small 299

9.5 Anaxagoras' proof that the earth is flat 303

9.6 Seen from far above the earth's surface, the horizon that cuts the sun is curved irrespective of whether the earth is spherical or a flat disk 304

9.7 The tilt of the heavens 305

9.8 The daily paths of the heavenly bodies before and after the tilt of the heavens 306

9.9 The tilt of a spherical earth equals the obliquity of the ecliptic 310

9.10 Before and after the supposed tilt of the earth 311

9.11 The circular flat earth 314

9.12 The position of the celestial pole on a flat earth 315

9.13 The shadow of the earth causing the Milky Way 319

Notes on Contributors

Omar D. Álvarez Salas

is Professor of Classics and Ancient Philosophy at the Universidad Nacional Autónoma de México (UNAM) and Researcher at the Center for Classical Studies of the Institute of Philological Research (IIFL) of the UNAM. He is the co-author of *El libro de Heráclito 2500 años después* with Livio Rossetti, Thomas M. Robinson *et al.* (2015), which he also co-edited with Enrique Hülsz. Currently, he is engaged in the study of philosophical pseudepigraphy with a focus on the *Pseudopythagorica*. He has published articles and contributed chapters on ideological interactions among Western Greek intellectuals and poets in the VI–V centuries B.C. as well as on the reception of Presocratic thought in comedy writers of the Greek West and in Plato.

Timothy J. Crowley

is College Lecturer in the School of Philosophy at University College Dublin. He received his DPhil at the University of Oxford. His thesis, a study of Aristotle's elements, was awarded the 2010 Conington Prize, awarded triennially by the Faculty of Philosophy at Oxford for the best dissertation in the field of Ancient Philosophy and Ideas. His work has been published in *Oxford Studies in Ancient Philosophy*, *Phronesis*, *The Classical Quarterly*, and *Archai*.

Dirk L. Couprie

studied philosophy in Groningen and Leiden (1959–1965), where he became associated professor and published on Kant and Wittgenstein. From 1971 to 1986, he worked in university- and higher education administration. After that, he returned to the study of philosophy, wrote a dissertation on Anaximander in 1989 and became an independent scholar. From 2014 to 2017 he was leader of two projects on Presocratic philosophy at the university of West Bohemia in Pilsen. He wrote mainly on Presocratic cosmology. His last book was *When the Earth Was Flat: Studies in Ancient Greek and Chinese Cosmology*. New York: Springer 2018.

Patricia Curd

is Professor of Philosophy Emerita, Purdue University. Her books include *The Legacy of Parmenides: Eleatic Monism and Later Presocratic Thought* (Princeton University Press) and *Anaxagoras of Clazomenae: Fragments; Text and Translation with Notes and Essays* (University of Toronto Press). She is co-editor (with Daniel Graham) of *The Oxford Handbook of Presocratic Philosophy;* and the author of journal and anthology articles on Early Greek philosophy and on Plato. Her research has been supported by grants from the Center for Hellenic Studies, The National Humanities Center, The National Endowment for the Humanities, Clare Hall (Cambridge University), the John Simon Guggenheim Foundation, and Purdue University.

Owen Goldin

is Professor of Philosophy at Marquette University. He has written mostly on ancient philosophy. He is the author of *Explaining an Eclipse: Aristotle's Posterior Analytics 2 8-10* (University of Michigan Press, 1996), and a number of articles on the Presocratics, Plato, Aristotle, and Hellenistic philosophers. He is the translator of *Philoponus (?): On Aristotle, Posterior Analytics 2* (London, Duckworth Press, 2009), and, with Marije Martijn, of *Philoponus: On Aristotle, Posterior Analytics I. 19–31,* (Bristol, Bristol Classical Press), 2012.

Daniel W. Graham

is Abraham Owen Smoot Professor of Philosophy at Brigham Young University. He has an MA in classics from Brigham Young University and a PhD in philosophy from the University of Texas at Austin. He is past president of the International Association for Presocratic Studies. His books include *Aristotle's Two* Systems (1987); Explaining *the Cosmos* (2006); (with co-editor Patricia Curd) *The Oxford Handbook of Presocratic Philosophy* (2008); *The Texts of Early Greek Philosophy*, 2 vols. (2010); and *Science Before Socrates* (2013). He has been a visiting fellow at Clare Hall, Cambridge, and a visiting professor at Yale University.

Andrew D. Gregory

is Professor of History and Philosophy of Science in the Department of Science and Technology Studies at University College London. He has written extensively on ancient philosophy and science, especially on Plato and on the Presocratic tradition and his books include *Plato's Philosophy of Science, Ancient Cosmogony, The Presocratics and the Supernatural,* and *Anaximander: A Re-Assessment.* He is currently working on a book on Early Greek Philosophies of Nature.

Justin Habash

is Assistant Dean for Teaching and Learning in the Carey Business School at Johns Hopkins University. His work in ancient philosophy focuses on the differences in the theories of nature among the Presocratics, and the reception of these ideas in the natural and political philosophies of Plato and Aristotle.

Gottfried Heinemann

born 1949, holds a doctoral degree in mathematics (Kassel 1977) and a habilitation degree in philosophy (Kassel 1981). He has taught philosophy at the University of Kassel since 1981. His books include: *Zeitbegriffe* (ed., 1986), *Studien zum griechischen Naturbegriff, Teil I: Philosophische Grundlegung: Der Naturbegriff und die "Natur"* (2001), *Aristoteles und die moderne Biologie* (ed., with R. Timme, 2016); articles on Greek concepts of nature and of philosophy, on Aristotle's *Physics*, on Whitehead, etc.

Christopher Kurfess

received his Ph.D. in Classics, Philosophy and Ancient Science from the University of Pittsburgh. He is the author of articles on the Presocratics, Aristotle, and their later reception, and has taught in departments of Classics and Philosophy at the University of West Virginia, Gettysburg College, and McDaniel College. His current research focuses include Parmenides and Aristotle's biological works, particularly the *Historia Animalium* and the *Parva Naturalia*.

Tiberiu Popa

who earned his doctorate at the University of Pittsburgh, is Professor of Philosophy at Butler University (Indianapolis, USA). His recent publications deal, among other things, with Aristotle's science and philosophy of science and with topics of philosophical interest in the Hippocratic Corpus. His current research is devoted in part to the history of the idea of a law of nature.

Oliver Primavesi

born 1961, holds the chair of Greek (I) at the Ludwig-Maximilians-Universität Munich. His research has been devoted mainly to Aristotle and to the Presocratics, in particular to Empedocles. His books include *Die Aristotelische Topik* (1996), and *Empedocles: Physika* I (2008). He has co-authored, with Alain Martin, *L'Empédocle de Strasbourg* (1999) and with Jaap Mansfeld, *Die Vorsokratiker Griechisch/Deutsch* (2011), he has edited with Katharina Luchner, *The Presocratics from the Latin Middle Ages to Hermann Diels* (2011), and contributed new critical editions of Aristotle's *Metaphysics A* (2012) and *De motu animalium* (forthcoming) to the respective volumes of the *Symposium Aristotelicum* series.

Liliana Carolina Sánchez Castro

is professor of the University of Cartagena in Colombia. She received her Ph.D. in Philosophy in 2014, with a dissertation on the Early Greek doctrines on the soul gathered by Aristotle in the first book of the *De Anima*, that afterwards became the book *Traditio Animae: la recepción aristotélica de las doctrinas presocráticas del alma.* She is currently working in the reception of Presocratic thought in Late Antiquity, especially in the tradition initiated by Aristotle's *De Anima.*

Barbara Sattler

is professor for ancient and medieval philosophy at the Ruhr-Universität Bochum, having taught at St. Andrews University, Yale University and the University of Illinois at Urbana-Champaign before. She is the author of The Concept of Motion in Ancient Greek Thought - Foundations in Logic, Method, and Mathematics, CUP 2020, and has published more broadly on the metaphysics and natural philosophy of the Presocratics, Plato, and Aristotle.

Iakovos Vasiliou

is currently Professor of Philosophy at The Graduate Center, City University of New York. His research focuses primarily on ancient philosophy, in particular on ethics, moral psychology, epistemology, and philosophy of mind. He is the author of *Aiming at Virtue in Plato* (Cambridge University Press, 2008), the editor of *Moral Motivation* (Oxford University Press, 2016), and has published a number of articles on Plato and Aristotle.

Rosemary Wright

is Emeritus Professor of Classics at the University of Wales. She graduated from London and Oxford, and has held posts as Lecturer (Queensland and Aberystwyth), Fellow (Harvard Hellenic Center), Senior Lecturer (Aberystwyth and Reading), and Professor and Head of Department (University of Wales, Lampeter). She has written and reviewed extensively in Greek Philosophy (mainly Presocratics and Plato), but she also has an online Dictionary of Mythology at the University of Patras. Her main publications are: *Empedocles, The Extant Fragments; Cosmology in Antiquity; Cicero, On Stoic Good and Evil; Introducing Greek Philosophy*, and (ed.) *Reason and Necessity in Plato's* Timaeus. (Details on web-site: wrightclassics.org)

Introduction

Plato and Aristotle, together with the Hippocratic thinkers, are the most celebrated and prolific contributors to a period of ancient Greek thought that we will refer to here as "later classical." This name and designation is partially bounded by time, ca. 5th–4th centuries BCE. But, more importantly, it means thinkers that form a sort of "second wave" in ancient Greek thought. This is to suggest that in Plato, Aristotle, and the Hippocratics, we see not only new ideas and novel arguments, but also dialectical arguments, responses to previous positions, and even syntheses of previous ideas. These syntheses, in turn, create new ideas, and even paradigms in early philosophy and science. Those whom we will consider here as a more or less "first wave" of thinkers, given their status as interlocutors to the later classical thinkers, are more commonly known as the "Presocratics," or as Aristotle called them, the φυσιολόγοι (*physiologoi*). This "first wave" of thinkers spans a longer time in history, ca. 6th–4th century BCE, as well as a far more diverse geography, from modern day western Turkey to modern day southern Italy. What is more, they represent different philosophical schools. Nevertheless, we group them together because we have the sense that they made a collective, if not directly related, effort that effactually began ancient Greek philosophy and science with various enquiries into nature.

This volume takes for granted that both Plato and Aristotle were profoundly influenced by these "first wave" philosophical forebears. For, despite Plato's Socrates's well-known account of his own turning away from natural philosophy in the *Phaedo*,[1] ideas about the concept of nature inform Platonic philosophy across Plato's corpus. Thus we see discussions of "nature" not only in Plato's *Timaeus*, his singular work on cosmogony and cosmology, but also in works like the *Republic*, a foundational text of political theory, which also takes up the nature of *human* being. Aristotle, often considered the first scientist in the West because of his profound contributions to the foundations of biology and zoology, was also the first philosopher to develop a method by which to undertake and proliferate a complete *phuseôs epistêmês*,[2] or science of nature. While Aristotle's negative accounts almost alway reply to commonly held theories of his time (*endoxa*), these theories are often treated anonymously and not considered in their own right. The

---

1 Plato *Phaedo* 96a ff.
2 Aristotle *Physics* i.1.

endoxa to which Aristotle replies nevertheless come from a rich historical tradition of investigation into the greatest mysteries of nature and being, which though perhaps not methodological in compilation and scope, certainly aimed at the same target as Aristotle: truth. As John Burnet put it, curiosity was the common denominator,[3] and Jonathan Barnes famously argued that it was reason.[4]

Despite centuries of excellent philological and philosophical scholarship produced on these early Greek thinkers,[5] they remain lesser known to most than the later classical thinkers. This may be due in part to a lack of extant literature we have from them today. Whereas a figure like Empedocles might present an anomaly to this generalization because we have more extant from him than most, in other cases, e.g., Thales, we have only a few lines of testimony on which to rely. So, even when Plato or Aristotle allude to these first wave thinkers, we face the challenge of sometimes having no other real source to cross-reference, and thus needing to rely on these allusions in order to know the Presocratic thinkers at all. Of course, the fact that we have the allusions indicates for us the relative importance they had for the later classical thinkers; and, yet, the lack of extant material whence we could examine, confirm, or deny certain attributions can make any effort to know these early Greek thinkers better seem speculative at best.

This leads us to a question of reception. While to scholars familiar with both of these waves of thinkers, it is undisputed that the later classical thinkers "received" many ideas (*endoxa*), formulations, and arguments from the early Greek thinkers, the details and force of the reception is still not widely understood. Consequently, what exactly served as theoretical catalysts for the second wave of ancient Greek thought, in what capacity, and to what end, is a topic for ongoing examination.[6] The purview of the present volume is to address, as reasonably as possible, the reception of first wave natural philosophy by the second wave thinkers. By 'natural philosophy,' we mean discussions of what some today might consider early or proto-scientific concepts of elements,

---

3   John Burnett. (1920) *Early Greek Philosophy* 3rd edition. London: A&C Black, page 13.

4   Johnathan Barnes. (1982) *The Presocratic Philosophers*. London: Routledge, page 2 ff.

5   The most recent of which is Patricia Curd and Daniel Graham's 2008 volume, *Oxford Handbook on Presocratic Philosophy*, which includes new interpretations of age-old debates about the Presocratics.

6   See again Curd and Graham's *Oxford Handbook of Presocratic Philosophy* (2008, OUP), as well as Giannis Stamatellos's *Introduction to Presocratics: A Thematic Approach to Early Greek Philosophy*. (2012, Wiley), and John Palmer's monographs: *Parmenides and Presocratic Philosophy*. (2009, OUP) and *Plato's Reception of Parmenides*. (1999, OUP) for recent previous studies that deal with the influence of Presocratic ideas in later classical thinkers.

INTRODUCTION

3

motion and activity, materiality, form or soul, causation, medicine, dreams and wakefulness, and existence itself. Inquiries into these concepts assume, whether it is explicitly articulated or not, a theory of nature itself. Thus, the art of understanding some of the complexity of even investigating this reception is to consider that the term or concept, "nature" meant different things over the course of the time period of interest to us in this volume.

What is the meaning of "nature" in Presocratic and in later classical inquiries? In the early Greek literary tradition, talking of something's nature (*phusis*) is generally a way to describe the outward characteristics of a thing.[7] But, notably, it has been suggested that there was a unity in the long inquiry known to us today as Presocratic natural philosophy, namely, that when taken as a cohesive body of inquiry and work, the Presocratics used *phusis* as a term to mean something intrinsic about a thing—that which things really are.[8] Likewise, it has been argued that *phusis* means "origin" only occasionally and that there is no unifying interpretation of the use of the term across extant texts and authors.[9]

Part of the question in this debate is whether nature means the nature of all things, or whether it means the nature of a particular thing. For example, according to Beardslee's early twentieth century study of the development of the term and concept over time, the Milesians, or earliest of the first wave thinkers, "... focused their attention not on a particular example of the phenomenon, but on earthquakes or lightning-flashes in general. Their inquiries were directed towards classes of natural phenomena, and they exhibit this feature of science, that it investigates the universal and the essential, not the particular and the accidental." Beardslee then provides a history of the term's use in early Greek thought: "particular" in the Hippocratic thinkers, "character of things in general" in the Pythagoreans, "universal nature" in Plato's Lysis, "particular nature" in fourth century colloquial usage[10]. Beardslee concludes that: "Until the close of the fifth century there is no direct proof that *phusis* was used for Nature in general."[11]

Even in what we consider later classical thought, the meaning of "nature" continues to lack consistency. When authors were indeed thinking about similar problems to those of one or more Presocratic philosopher, a shift in method and focus means that these comparisons are not always easily drawn. A key example of this is found in Aristotle, who redefined "nature" as an *archē*, an

---

7 John Walter Beardslee, Jr. 1918. *The Use of* Physis *in Fifth-Century Greek Literature*. Chicago: The University of Chicago Press, 8–9.

8 Lovejoy 1909, 376/ op. cit. Beardslee 1918, 11 fn. 3.

9 Cf. Beardslee 1918, 12 and 59.

10 Beardslee, 58– 61.

11 Beardslee, 63.

inner principle, of motion (*kinêsis*) and rest (*stasis*) in his most general work on nature philosophy, the *Physics* (192b13-22) Despite the fact that he is in dialogue with the Presocratic Ionian thinkers, the Pythagoreans, Parmenides, and Plato, his complex and self-contained treatment of nature might seem a world apart from the first wave thinkers' styles of inquiry and conclusions. Yet, Aristotle's interest in natural objects is part of his interest in explaining change, and the idea that nature comes from and exists as a single underlying material element, or principle of change and rest, recalls rather than supplants the Presocratic inquiries.

Plato's philosophy of nature, on the other hand, is less certain, told in the *Timaeus* as only a likely tale (38c). For Plato, the notion of material change, as opposed to the steadfast form or Idea (*eidos*) inherent in nature, called into question the possibility for veracity at all in an account of nature. Thus, at the heart of Plato's physics is something rather immaterial. Instead of studying the nature of natural beings, it provides an hypothesis about the entire picture. His theory of nature, then, is not a study of individual bodies subject to change; rather, it gives an account of the whole. As aforementioned, Plato talks about nature in other ways outside of his philosophy of nature. In these instances, we see nature means the *nature of,* x, or a particular kind of thing. This approach to thinking of nature is employed throughout Plato's Socratic dialogues, as interlocutors seek truth about the essence of ideas. So too, Plato and Plato's Socrates's interest in *human nature* marks a turn from talking about the natural world to talking specifically about human psychology and community. But, just as we recognize the mark of Presocratic natural philosophy in Aristotle's philosophy of nature, we see here too an echo of a turn in Presocratic philosophy—from the inquiry into the nature of phenomena in the Ionian thinkers to the interest in humanity and community in Heraclitus and others.

In the spirit that fits well with the plurality of views on nature proffered by Plato, Aristotle, the Hippocratics, and indeed the Presocratics themselves, the contributors to the present volume have each brought their individual understanding of the nature and challenges of the idea of reception to bear. The resulting work highlights a familiar disparity of views regarding the major interpretive issues in Presocratic studies but also in conceptions of this idea of reception itself. This is to say that this volume does not purport to offer an interpretive or methodological solution to understanding the reception of Presocratic natural philosophy. The editors aim, rather, to highlight the complexity, relative opacity, and yet the obvious importance, of scrupulous scholarship on the reception of Presocratic natural philosophy in Plato and Aristotle. To this end, this volume brings together a global array of voices in Presocratic studies

INTRODUCTION

that include the perspectives of rising scholars in the field along with those of established voices.

The contributions have been organized according to a division among thematic, topical, and methodological lines. While some chapters address broad methodology and continue the conversation about aforementioned concepts present both in Presocratic and later classical authors, other chapters address either misinterpretations and misattributions of specific Presocratic ideas in later classical authors, or work to uncover an overlooked or "hidden" influence of the former in the latter.

1 Reception: Methodology and Grounding Concepts

The first four chapters each take up in depth and overarching discussions regarding the meanings of the concepts, *nature, reception, principles/causes/ elements*, and the *beginning of science*, for studies on the reception of Presocratic natural philosophy. These chapters likewise each consider multiple Presocratic figures in their approach to saying something about the reception of Presocratic natural philosophy in Plato and Aristotle. Because of their relatively global approach, these chapters are intended to scaffold, as much as possible, the studies undertaken in the subsequent eleven chapters. Readers will also find cross-references among the first three of these chapters.

Gottfried Heinemann's chapter continues the discussion about the ancient Greek concept of nature introduced here. Specifically, he establishes this foundation on the philosophical project of the Presocratics as he explores the root of the study of nature in ancient Greek thought, beginning with the Presocratic nature philosophers before turning to Plato, and then to Aristotle. In the end, Heinemann shows Aristotle's own work on nature to be a sophisticated result of a complex conversation both with the earliest Greek philosophers and with Plato. Aristotle's works mark a return to a philosophical focus on the natural, but they likewise entail a new way to define nature, in terms of regularity and necessity.

Andrew Gregory takes up the question of Plato's reception of Presocratic natural philosophy generally, ultimately arguing for a nuanced reading of certain passages in the Platonic corpus, including the famous *Phaedo* passage (96a ff), where Socrates details his original interest in and then subsequent disenchantment with Presocratic natural philosophy.

Justin Habash proposes that we reconceive our understanding of the chain of conceptions of nature that runs from the Presocratics through the so-called Sophists to later classical thinkers like Plato and Aristotle. Habash argues that despite their variations, conceptions of nature among the *physiologoi* almost invariably contain purposive strains that serve as precursors to Aristotle's more fully developed conception of a teleological nature.

Daniel Graham discusses the beginning of science in Presocratic philosophy, arguing that Parmenides and Anaxagoras are the authors of the "revolution that launched scientific astronomy," specifically through theories of the source of lunar light and the explanation of eclipses. Their new scientific conceptions replaced all other accounts of these phenomena and have held sway through the present time. Other scholars point to the problems of specific barriers within the reception of certain ideas.

2 Hidden Reception: Exploring Sources and Developing Themes

Misinterpretations, unacknowledged influences, and misattributions of Presocratic ideas in later classical thought frequently occurred because of a hidden or obscured intermediary, or due to unrecognized sources. Scholars writing on what we here call "hidden reception," identify and examine unrecognized links in the chains of specific ideas and concepts as they develop through ancient Greek thought. These chapters provide new ways to understand not only individual thinkers, but also the broader tapestry of ancient Greek philosophy itself.

Oliver Primavesi presents a special case of reception, in that his very project calls into question the meanings of categories like "Presocratic" and "later classical thinkers." Namely, he investigates a case of Presocratic influence in later classical thought within the Presocratic period. Using relatively recent evidence and deft philological analysis, he offers a convincing argument for the influence of the Pythagorean numerical ratios in the Empedoclean cosmic cycle.

In his chapter engaging the Pythagoreans, Owen Goldin points to specific forms of methodological influence of Presocratic protologic on later classical thought when he argues that Aristotle's theory of demonstration integrates Platonic ideas of definition with later Pythagorean distinctions between causally basic realities and their derivatives.

Omar Álvarez Salas traces references to Pythagoras in Aristotle's extant and lost works, arguing that despite never naming Pythagoras in his texts, Aristotle nevertheless implicitly refers to him as often as he does other relevant early Greek thinkers, in the context of the other "so-called" Pythagoreans. This conclusion provides an alternative position to the more standard reading by scholars that Aristotle was not as engaged with Pythagoras' doctrines as he was with

INTRODUCTION

other previous thinkers or that Aristotle was hesitant to include Pythagoras as a member of the Pythagoreans.

Christopher Kurfess provides compelling support from Simplicius's commentary on Aristotle's *Physics* to suggest that views on Eleatic *archai* presented by Aristotle in the opening books of the *Physics*, *Metaphysics*, and *De Anima* were first articulated by Theophrastus in a work Simplicius called, *Natural History*. Kurfess's research and analysis makes possible a reconsideration not only of the relationship between Theophrastus and Aristotle, but also of the reception of certain Eleatic formulations, as we have come to know them by way of Aristotle.

Dirk Couprie illuminates the spherical earth bias present in Presocratic reception after Aristotle, occasioned, as he argues, by Aristotle's polemical treatment of the flat earth cosmology. The spherical earth bias, which Couprie finds not only in the doxography but also in modern interpreters, has led to a general lack of understanding about the characteristics and distinctive features of the flat earth cosmology. His article provides a careful treatment of these features.

Tiberiu Popa and Timothy Crowley investigate the so-called elements of nature. Popa shows us the role elemental varieties, including quasi-elementary simple bodies, play as explanatory devices both in cosmological and ontological accounts among Diogenes of Apollonia, Anaximenes, early Hippocratic works, Plato, Aristotle, and Theophrastus. While Popa is cautious in discussing the specific reception of such a role, he provides convincing evidence that simple stuffs helped early cosmological and ontological theory move from basic Ionian material monism to material dualism, as Popa calls the Hippocratic prescriptive emphasis on fire and water, to the more complex theories of simple bodies, elements, and their properties found in later classical thinkers. With a focus on Empedocles and Aristotle, Crowley examines the reception of Empedocles' four element hypothesis. Taking as a starting point Aristotle's remark at *Metaphysics* Alpha, that Empedocles was the first to talk of four material elements, Crowley discloses part of the historically significant and long-standing reception of a theory that was still being discussed in 17th century science. Crowley finds a fundamental difference between Empedocles' four element hypothesis and a four element hypothesis otherwise.

Iakovos Vasiliou and Lilliana Carolina Sánchez Castro focus on reception as it relates to questions of the soul. Vasiliou argues that Plato relies heavily on Anaxagorean concepts of *nous*, separation, and mixture in establishing a teleological framework that explains the relationship of body and soul in the *Phaedo*, focusing on the role of the philosopher's way of life on Plato's theory of body-soul separation. Sanchez Castro tackles Aristotle's engagement with the Heraclitean notion of the soul in *De Anima*, arguing that despite barely a passing mention of the Ephesian's views on *psuche*, Aristotle deliberately includes Heraclitus' view as a way to illustrate the soul as a cognitive principle.

Both Barbara Sattler and Rosemary Wright focus on Plato's careful adaptation of the ideas of earlier thinkers. Sattler first sketches different forms of philosophical reception in the Presocratics, Plato, and Aristotle before turning to a specific focus on the way Plato receives and modifies atomistic theory. Sattler argues that Plato's conscientious construction of atomist thought in the *Timaeus* is a deliberate attempt to be explicit about key points of disagreement while incorporating the ways in which Plato agrees with atomic theory. Ultimately, Sattler offers a new way to understand why, despite atomic influence on his work, Plato does not name or directly refer to the atomists in his corpus. Wright, on the other hand, offers an analysis of the intersection between Presocratic cosmogonical and cosmological conclusions and Plato's use of myths in the *Gorgias, Phaedo, Republic*, and *Phaedrus*. Delivering an expert summary of a wide swath of Presocratic views, Wright argues that despite that Plato takes Presocratic cosmology as subjects of myth, or likely stories, they serve as a basis for his views about immortality. In an appendix to her chapter she lays out the evidence for understanding the *Timaeus* to follow closely on the conversation in the *Republic*, thus connecting the ideas of nature in these two key dialogues.

2.1   *On Reading This Volume*

Due to the indirect, complicated, and sometimes wily nature of addressing Presocratic reception—especially given that "Presocratic" is such a broad and deep category of thinkers and topics itself—the volume allows for multiple ways of entry to read, compare, contrast, and digest the rich contributions contained within.

The first way of entry is linear and straightforward. It takes the first four chapters as a unit constituting a theoretical propaedeutic to the subsequent eleven chapters. Readers can study them first, and use them as a guide to beginning more specific studies on the figures and themes discussed in later chapters.

These first four chapters reveal themselves to be a less straightforward trailhead, however, when one realizes that the aforementioned concepts weave into each other, and that the unit is at times inconsistent: overlapping, converging, but also diverging in complementary, at times challenging, ways. Nevertheless, the muddiness they reveal helps to put the subsequent eleven studies into their proper context and alerts readers to the real interpretive issues with which any study of Presocratic reception must contend.

INTRODUCTION

The next points of entry take just one of the four initial chapters and then looks to between one and four more specific studies in subsequent chapters, which can be identified as thematically and/or stylistically resonant. On this approach, some possible pathways include: "nature, principles, and elements": read chapter one, followed by chapters five, eight, ten, and eleven; "reception, nature, and soul": read chapter two, followed by chapters twelve, thirteen, and fifteen; "purpose, nature, Plato, and Aristotle": chapter three, followed by chapters thirteen, fourteen, and fifteen; "scientific inquiry, nature, cosmos, and reception": read chapter four, followed by chapters six, seven, and nine. This list, however, is far from exhaustive; the engaged reader will discover many more such theme-based adventures in the pages of this volume.

A final suggestion for beginning an exploration of the pages that follow eschews the scaffolding provided by the first four chapters and uses the following topical guide to begin reading more narrowly about one or more Presocratic thinker(s), theme(s) in nature philosophy, passage(s), or later classical thinker(s): **Aristotle:** ch. 1, ch. 3, ch. 6, ch. 7, ch. 8, ch. 9, ch. 11, ch. 12; **Plato:** ch. 13, ch. 14, ch. 15, ch. 2, ch. 3; **Empedocles:** ch. 1, ch. 5, ch. 10, ch. 11, ch. 15; **Cosmology:** ch. 4, ch. 5, ch. 9, ch. 13, ch. 14, ch. 15; **Heraclitus:** ch. 3, ch. 12, ch. 15; **Eleatic:** ch. 7, ch. 1, ch. 3, ch. 10; **Pythagorean:** ch. 7, ch. 5, ch. 6, ch. 15; **Milesians:** ch. 1, ch. 3, ch. 8, ch. 10, ch. 15; **Atomism:** ch. 2, ch. 3, ch. 13, ch. 14, ch. 15; **Phaedo 96a ff:** ch. 1, ch. 2, **Soul:** ch. 2, ch. 12, ch. 13; **Timaeus:** ch. 1, ch. 2, ch. 3, ch. 13, ch. 14, ch. 15, ch. 1; **Theophrastus:** ch. 8, ch. 10.

∵

How did the most famous classical philosophers benefit from the inquiries and findings of these Presocratics? How exactly was Presocratic natural philosophy received in early Greek philosophy and in later classical times? To what extent does the history of science owe a debt to the explorations and conclusions of the earliest Greek philosophers? With this volume, we strive to address these questions.

> Chelsea C. Harry
> Berlin
> July 2019

PART 1

Reception: Methodology and Grounding Concepts

∴

CHAPTER 1

Peri Phuseôs: Physics, Physicists, and *Phusis* in Aristotle

Gottfried Heinemann

1 Introduction: What Is It to Inquire *peri phuseôs*?

There is some truth in Charles Kahn's claim that *phusis* is a "catchword" for early Greek philosophy.[1] But *peri phuseôs* ("on nature", i.e. the formula later used as its uniform book title) is primarily the catchword for its 4th century reception. In Aristotle, *peri phuseôs* is a topic he shares with, and inherits from, Plato. Plato's *Timaeus* is an extended lecture *peri phuseôs*.[2] Passages in the *Phaedo* and especially in *Laws* x present Plato's criticism of contemporary teachings *peri phuseôs*;[3] in other dialogues, the topic is only touched in passing. Of the *Corpus Aristotelicum*, 40 per cent are devoted to *peri phuseôs epistêmê* ("science of nature").[4] The relevant field of study derives from the Milesians: Thales is commonly received as its founder, and Anaximander was (probably) the first to have contributed to the corresponding genre in writing. From when the formula *peri phuseôs* was used to refer to that topic is disputed. As a matter of fact, there is no relevant evidence in the fragments of early Greek philosophy.[5] But the formula is common usage in the 4th century. In the present paper, my concern is what the formula means when it is applied in the 4th century reception of early Greek philosophy.

---

1 Kahn 1960, 201 (see below penultimate paragraph in section 2.2).
2 The topic of the lecture is termed περὶ φύσεως τοῦ παντός (*Ti.* 27a4: "on the nature of the universe"; similarly 47a7). Its scope is "from the origination (γένεσις) of the cosmos to the nature of man" (27a5-6). The formula also occurs without limiting genitive (57d6), which is evidently shorthand for περὶ φύσεως τοῦ παντός. In other cases, περὶ φύσεως goes with a limiting genitive to indicate the special topic at issue.
3 In *Phd.* 96a ff., Anaxagoras serves as example of a general failure of provide teleological explanations; in *Laws* x, 888e ff., the target is a general assumption that the elements are prior to soul (891c2-4, see below section 3.1). – For a fuller treatment of Plato see Andrew Gregory's contribution to this volume. Two minor quibbles will be addressed in n. 49 and 65.
4 That is, pp. 184–789 in Bekker's edition. The discipline is termed περὶ φύσεως ἐπιστήμη at the very beginning (*Ph.* 1 1, 184a15). Its scope is described intermediately (*Mete.* 1 1, 338a20-339a9).
5 See below section 2.1

© KONINKLIJKE BRILL NV, LEIDEN, 2021 | DOI:10.1163/9789004443358_003

Phusikê ("physics") is Aristotle's shorthand for such phrases as *peri phuseôs epistêmê/historia/theôria/*or *methodos* ("science/research/contemplation/branch of investigation concerning nature").[6] Correspondingly, *phusikos* ("physicist") refers to the practitioner of *phusikê*, and *phusika* to the relevant writings. This is especially so in Aristotle's own cross-references and reflections: to ask whether it belongs to the *phusikos* to treat a topic is to ask whether that topic belongs to *phusikê*.[7] By contrast, *phusiologos* ("he who gives an account of nature") is regularly applied to Aristotle's earlier predecessors only. Whereas *phusiologos* does not occur in extant pre-Aristotelian literature, there are three occurrences of *physikos*,[8] one of which (in the Derveni papyrus) has been unconvincingly claimed to anticipate Aristotelian usage.[9]

---

6   Occurrences of περὶ φύσεως ἐπιστήμη in Aristotle include: *Ph.* I 1, 184a15 and *Cael.* I 1, 268a1-4; of περὶ φύσεως (or: φύσιν) ἱστορία: *Cael.* III 1, 298b2 and *Part. an.* I 1, 639a12; of περὶ φύσεως θεωρία: *Ph.* VIII 1, 251a6; of περὶ φύσεως μέθοδος: *Part. an.* I 4, 644b16 (for μέθοδος see also *Ph.* I 1, 184a11; *Ph.* III 1, 200b13; *Mete.* I 1, 338a25). I found no occurrence of περὶ φύσεως φιλοσοφία in Aristotle, but see *Ph.* III 4, 202b30-203a4 where that phrase may be inferred from τὸν περὶ φύσεως πραγματευόμενον (b35) and ἧφθαι τῆς τοιαύτης φιλοσοφίας (a2).

   Note that φυσική is adjective, but functions as a noun, as do ἰατρική (sc. τέχνη: "medicine"), ἀνδριαντοποιική (sc. τέχνη: "sculpture") etc. For φυσική ἐπιστήμη in Aristotle, see e.g. *Part. an.* I 1, 640a1; for φυσικὴ μέθοδος: *IA* 2, 704b13; for φυσικὴ φιλοσοφία: *Metaph.* VI 1, 1026a18; *Part. an.* II 7, 653a9; *De longaev.* 1, 464b33. Probably, φυσικὴ ἱστορία at *Part. an.* II 3, 650a32 and *IA* 1, 704b10 must be taken in a narrower sense, referring to Aristotle's *Hist. an.*

   None of the terms mentioned are easy to translate. "Science" or "(branch of) scientific knowledge" for ἐπιστήμη, "inquiry" for ἱστορία, "contemplation" for θεωρία, and "discipline" or "(branch of) investigation" for μέθοδος are just placeholder translations, and will do no harm when taken as such. Other placeholder translations used in the sequel are "nature" for φύσις, "physics" or "natural science" for φυσική, "art" or "craftsmanship" for τέχνη, etc.

7   See, e.g., *Ph.* II 2; 194a16; *Ph.* III 4, 204a1; *Part. an.* I 1, 639b8; *Metaph.* VI 1, 1026a5.

8   To the single pre-Aristotelian occurrence of φυσικός mentioned in LSJ (Xenophon, *Mem.* III 9,1: "inborn") and by Bernabé (2017, 43–45), add [Hippocrates], *Steril.* 18, 10 (= *Mul.* III 230, Littré VIII 442.28: "responsive to natural constraints") and Pap. Derveni, fr. F14 (first line, see below). Both in Xenophon and in the medical text, φυσικός is used as an adjective. In the Derveni papyrus, the term is commonly assumed to function as a noun (but see below). – The inscription in Velia (*SEG* 38, #1020) describing Parmenides as φυσικός is much later (1 c. BCE or CE) and must be dismissed as evidence for pre-Aristotelian language (contra Bernabé 2017, 44).

9   On the occurrence in the Derveni papyrus see KPT p. 115; Janko 2008, 43 f.; Ferrari 2014, 58 f.; Piano 2016a, 90; Janko 2016, 11 f. and 17; Kotwick 2017, 68 (§4) – the text in Kotwick being essentially Janko's, see Janko 2016, 7. The papyrus has].περ φυσ..[according to KPT, but Piano, Janko, and Kotwick unambiguously read φυσικ[, supplements to].περ include οἷ]απερ or καθ]άπερ (KPT) and ὥ]σπερ (Janko 2008, Ferrari, Piano, and Kotwick).

The terms mentioned – both *phusiologos* and the trias *phusikê/-kos/-ka* – are probably 4th century, if not Aristotelian, neologisms. And more importantly, none of them is self-explanatory: each derives its meaning from the meaning of *peri phuseôs*.

Is the formula *peri phuseôs* self-explanatory? A straightforward explanation would derive the meaning of *peri phuseôs* from the meaning of *phusis*, following a scheme such as:

(SE)   To ask what *peri phuseôs* means is to ask what *phusis* means.

I will argue that this is the way in which both the author of *On ancient medicine*, in his reaction to Empedocles-type *philosophiê*,[10] and Aristotle understand the formula. But Aristotle's approach along this line will turn out to be far more sophisticated than might be expected. It is straightforward with respect to the meaning of *peri phuseôs*. But the burden of the question – What is it to inquire *peri phuseôs*? – is transferred to the definition of *phusis*. I will argue that this explains some awkward moves in Aristotle's discussion of the concept in *Physics* II 1.

Ferrari claims that Democritus is the target; Parmenides is suggested by Janko (2016, 17). KPT consider the possibility "that the Derveni author refers to Orpheus as a μυθόλογος who is in fact a φυσικός." But μυθόλογος does not occur in their reading of the papyrus; by contrast, Janko (2008, 48) had [μυθο]λόγωι in Col. IV.6. Other reconstructions of Col. IV.6 include [ἱερο]λόγωι (Sider 1997, Bernabé 2007), [ἱερῶι] λόγωι (LM vol. 6, p. 382 = Piano 2016b; Janko in Kotwick 2017, 72 §12) and [ἀστρο]λόγωι (KPT); [φυσιο]λόγωι was once considered possible by Parássoglou and Tsantsanoglou (1988, quoted after Janko 2002, 8), but seems to have been abandoned since.

Both Ferrari ("physicist") and Janko (2016, 17: "natural scientist") assume that in the Derveni papyrus, the meaning of φυσικός is just the same as in Aristotle. By contrast, Kotwick (2017, 108 f.) retains an earlier suggestion by Janko (2001, 3, referring to Most 1987) that a φυσικός may be an "allegorist," that is, someone who gives natural explanations to religious phenomena; for this meaning of φυσικός and for (post-Aristotelian) parallels see Most 1987, 7–9. In addition, Piano (2016a, 90) rightly points to the context with prayer and with sacrifice or divination in which φυσικός seems to occur.

It should be also noted that whereas φυσικ[is certain, the supplement φυσικ[ός is not; φυσικ[ῶς (adv.) may be an alternative (I am grateful to Valeria Piano who pointed this out to me in personal communication).

In conclusion, Ferrari's and Janko's (2016) assumption is far from evident. The possibilities that in the Derveni papyrus, the term φυσικός is used as a noun but has a different meaning, or is not used as a noun at all, cannot be ruled out.

10   [Hippocrates], *VM* 20,1. See below sect. 2.2.

2 *Peri phuseôs* before Aristotle: Scope of Inquiry and Approach

2.1 *Explanations of* peri phuseôs *in Terms of Reference (Burnet, Naddaf)*

As a preliminary, I will discuss an influential variant of SE, straightforward explanation by reference. Assuming that the meaning of *phusis* reduces to reference, all questions pertaining to the meaning of *peri phuseôs* would reduce to triviality. The scheme is this:

(SER)   To ask what *peri phuseôs* means is to ask what *phusis* is. For whatever thing the term *phusis* refers to is the very thing into which to inquire is to inquire, and about which to write is to write, *peri phuseôs*.

As I said, a tacit presupposition in SER is that the meaning of *phusis* is to be explained in terms of reference.[11] As a consequence, something is presupposed to exist to which, in the formula *peri phuseôs*, the term *phusis* refers. In short, the question as to what *phusis means* reduces to the question as to what *phusis is*. Scholars who – in their interpretation of early Greek philosophy – take this for granted include John Burnet and, as it appears, Gerard Naddaf.

According to Burnet, (i) Ionian science was concerned with "the primary substance" or "stuff,"[12] (ii) that substance was referred to by *phusis*,[13] and (iii) *peri phuseôs historia* was "the name originally given to science."[14] Burnet rightly claims that, given (i) and (ii), the (alleged) fact that "the Ionians called science Περὶ φύσεως ἱστορίη" can be understood "at once."[15] Substitute *phusis* for "the primary substance": what you get from (i) is that Ionian science was concerned with *phusis*, which straightforwardly explains (iii).

In a similar vein, Naddaf claims that (i) "the pre-Socratics [...] were interested [...] in a history of the universe; in an explanation of its origin [...], of the stages of its evolution [...], and finally, of its result, the *kosmos* as we know it [...]"; and that (ii) "the term *phusis*, in the expression *peri phuseōs* or *historia peri phuseōs*, refers, at a minimum (sic!), to the origin and the growth of the universe, from the beginning to end."[16] Again, what you get from (i) by

---

11   I have argued elsewhere that this is misleading. See Heinemann 2001, ch. 1–4; Heinemann 2006a, sect. 3.1 and passim.

12   Burnet 1930, 12 and passim ("stuff": ibid. 10).

13   Burnet 1930, 10 with reference to Euripides fr. 910 N.

14   Burnet 1930, 10n2 with reference to Plato, *Phd.* 96a7.

15   Burnet 1930, 11. Of course, Περὶ φύσεως (sic!) ἱστορίη is Burnet's partial (re?)translation of Plato's περὶ φύσεως ἱστορία into Ionian.

16   Naddaf 2005, 20.

PERI PHUSEÔS: PHYSICS, PHYSICISTS, AND PHUSIS IN ARISTOTLE

substituting *phusis* for "history ..." is that the "pre-Socratics" sought an explanation of *phusis*,[17] which easily explains the (alleged) fact that (iii) they employed "the expression *historia peri phuseōs*" to describe their enterprise.[18]

Both Burnet and Naddaf offer unified accounts of the scope and thematic concern of early Greek philosophy, and are able to adduce evidence in support of their respective accounts. To a large extent, the books of both are devoted to this. Both accounts are disputed, and are arguably overstated, to say the least. More importantly (for my present concern), the link between the issues mentioned – (i) scope of early Greek philosophy, (ii) meaning of *phusis*, and (iii) meaning of *peri phuseôs* – does not work the way suggested in either account.

The only occurrence of *peri phuseôs* Burnet adduces is the mentioning of "that branch of expertise which is called *peri phuseôs historia*" in Plato's *Phaedo*.[19] Neither Philolaus (fr. 6) nor *On ancient medicine* (c. 20) are cited; nor does Burnet rely on such speculations as Guthrie's about bipartite book titles allegedly testified for Gorgias and Melissus by Sextus and Simplicius, respectively, taken as evidence that *peri phuseôs* was a book title in the mid-5th century.[20] Rather, the passage in the *Phaedo* is claimed by Burnet to be "the oldest and most trustworthy statement as to the name originally given to science," and is deemed sufficient to substantiate his assumption that "the Ionians called science Περὶ φύσεως ἱστορίη."[21]

But the passage in the *Phaedo* is no case in which straightforward explanation by reference (SER) works. Rather, the meaning of *peri phuseôs* is to be inferred from the catalogue of questions attached: "to know the causes of each

---

17   Naddaf adds: "*phusis* as absolute *archê*," as "process of growth,"and as "result" (Naddaf 2005, 20 – to be properly inserted in (i)).

18   Note that (iii) is not even unequivocally claimed, but is taken for granted throughout Naddaf 2005. My quotation is from p. 28. Concerning p. 16, see below n. 36.

19   Plato, *Phd.* 96a7-8; Burnet 1930, 10 – "branch of expertise": σοφία (my tr.).

20   Guthrie, 1962, 73 (similarly KRS, p. 102n1; Mouraviev 1997, 38; Sedley 1998, 22; Rossetti 2006, 117 f.; Palmer 2009, 205n25; Harriman 2015, 19 f.; Nethercut 2017); contra Schmalzriedt 1970, 128; Mansfeld 2016, 96 ff.; Zhmud 2018, 56. – The titles mentioned are Περὶ τοῦ μὴ ὄντος ἢ Περὶ φύσεως for Gorgias (Sextus Empiricus, *Adv. math.* 7,65 = DK 82 B 3) and Περὶ φύσεως ἢ περὶ τοῦ ὄντος for Melissus (Simplicius, *In Ph.* 70,16 and *In De caelo* 557,10 = DK 30 A 4). The argument runs as follows: The bipartite title in Gorgias is a parody of that in Melissus. Hence both must be genuine. The bipartite title in Melissus presupposes familiarity with the plain title Περὶ φύσεως. Hence, the latter must have been used in the mid-5th century. The argument is a non-starter since in both cases the probability that no bipartite but alternative titles are referred to must be taken into account: it would run as well with περὶ τοῦ ὄντος only (concerning alternative titles indicated by ἢ see Mansfeld 2016, 97; Buchheim 1989, 182 f.; Primavesi 2007, 189; differently, Newinger 1973, 1n3).

21   Burnet 1930, 10n2 and 11.

(kind of) thing(s), etc."[22] Evidently, this suggests that the formula *peri phuseôs* must be tacitly completed with a limiting genitive such as *tôn hapantôn* ("of everything") or *tôn pragmatôn* ("of things"), referring to the realm of things under investigation and anchoring *hekaston* ("each thing" or "each kind of things") in the sequel. If so, the *phusis* of things is what accounts for the coming into being, perishing, and existence of things, both in general and for each kind separately. Explanations in terms of reference are blocked by the limiting genitive; in particular, *phusis* (at *Phd.* 96a8) does not refer to "primary substance" or "stuff." As a consequence, SER does not work. In sum, Burnet presents no occurrence of the formula *peri phuseôs* to which his explanation applies.

As regards the meaning of *phusis*, Burnet's favourite evidence is the Euripidean praise of the practitioner of "inquiry" (*historia*), described as "inspecting the ageless order (*kosmos*) of immortal nature (*phusis*)."[23] Burnet takes this as "clear evidence that, in the fifth century B.C., the name *phusis* was given to the everlasting something of which the world was made" – on which he would "almost be willing to rest his case."[24] I agree that in the Euripidean fragment, "immortal nature" refers to the subject of the ordering mentioned, not to its result.[25] But I would deny that *phusis* does so refer. Rather, *athanatos phusis* ("immortal nature") appears to be a periphrasis, meaning "what by its nature is immortal" and thus referring to the heavenly bodies.[26]

Leaving the Euripidean fragment aside, Burnet's account of the meaning of *phusis* is just a 4th century affair. Insofar as his interpretation of the evidence he adduces is sound, Burnet relies on Plato's observation in *Laws* X that materialist doctrines go with calling the elements 'the *phusis*.'[27] Quite the same usage

---

22 Plato, *Phd.* 96a9. See below sect. 2.2. – I am using "thing" in a generic sense so as to include, e.g., humans.

23 Euripides fr. 910.5 f. N.: ἀθανάτου καθορῶν φύσεως κόσμον ἀγήρων. – But note that Burnet (1930, 10) reads ἀγήρω (gen.) rather than ἀγήρων (acc.), and translates "the ordering of immortal ageless φύσις" (ibid. 10n2).

24 Burnet 1930, 10; ibid. 363.

25 Naddaf (2005, 29) has nothing to say about the way φύσις is related to κόσμος in the fragment. Similarly Schmalzriedt (1970, 92 f.) who, like Heinimann (1945, 105 f.), assumes that φύσις refers to nature as a totality.

26 Thus, ἀθάνατος φύσις contrasts with θνητὴ φύσις ("mortal nature," that is, what by its nature is mortal), mentioned in Sophocles (fr. 590), Democritus (DK 68 B 297) and Plato (*Symp.* 207d1 and *Tht.* 176a7-8). See Heinemann 2019.

27 Plato, *Leg.* 891c2-4 (cf. Burnet 1930, 363): πῦρ καὶ ὕδωρ καὶ γῆν καὶ ἀέρα πρῶτα ἡγεῖσθαι τῶν πάντων εἶναι, καὶ τὴν φύσιν ὀνομάζειν ταῦτα αὐτά, ψυχὴν δὲ ἐκ τούτων ὕστερον. In the sequel, Plato adds that this – the reversion of priorities mentioned at 891c2-4 (and discussed in more detail at 891e5 ff.) – accounts for "the unreasonable opinion of whatever humans have ever devoted themselves to the investigations on nature" (*Leg.* 891c7-9: ...

PERI PHUSEÔS: PHYSICS, PHYSICISTS, AND PHUSIS IN ARISTOTLE

is described by Aristotle in *Metaph.* V 4,[28] and is alluded to in *Physics* VIII 9, with the atoms thus named.[29] Burnet mentions the latter passage in passing,[30] but seems to ignore the former. Still, the evidence he adduces would support the claim that in the language of the 4th century materialists cited by Plato, the term *phusis* was employed to refer to the elements, to the atoms or, more generally, to the primary stuff they postulated. Assuming that those materialists used the formula *peri phuseôs* to refer to their field of study, application of SER would yield a meaning of that formula such as "on the primary stuff." But nothing would follow concerning other contexts – and especially concerning early Greek philosophy.[31]

Differently from Burnet, Naddaf mentions (and even quotes) the passage in *On ancient medicine* (c. 20) where medical expertise is distinguished from Empedocles-type *philosophiê*, and the formula *peri phusios* is used to refer to a genre in writing.[32] But Naddaf fails to comment on that passage,[33] and especially does not adduce it in support of his claim that the formula *peri phuseôs* was regularly employed to indicate the subject matter of early Greek philosophy.[34]

ἀνοήτου δόξης ... ἀνθρώπων ὁπόσοι πώποτε τῶν περὶ φύσεως ἐφήψαντο ζητημάτων). See below section 3.1.

28   Aristotle, *Metaph.* V 4 1014b32-5: καὶ τῶν φύσει ὄντων τὰ στοιχεῖά φασιν εἶναι φύσιν, οἱ μὲν πῦρ οἱ δὲ γῆν οἱ δ' ἀέρα οἱ δ' ὕδωρ οἱ δ' ἄλλο τι τοιοῦτον λέγοντες, οἱ δ' ἔνια τούτων οἱ δὲ πάντα ταῦτα.

29   Aristotle, *Ph.* VIII 9, 265b25 = DK 68 A 58 (vol. II, p. 99.7): καὶ γὰρ οὗτοι τὴν κατὰ τόπον κίνησιν κινεῖσθαι τὴν φύσιν λέγουσιν. Simplicius (*in Ph.* 1318.33 ff. = DK 68 B 168, quoted Burnet 1930, 337n1) adds that in the language of the atomists cited, φύσις refers to the atoms. But I see no evidence that this language may be ascribed to Democritus (as DK suggests).

30   Burnet 1930, 337n1.

31   Burnet tries to evade this conclusion by misrepresenting Plato as "expressly" attributing the language described to all investigators into nature; see Burnet 1930, 364 referring to *Leg.* 891c7-9 (cf. my footnote above). Burnet mistakes the reference in that passage as being to the use of φύσις described at 891c3. But the reference is to the reversion of priorities mentioned at 891c2-4. Note that in Burnet's quotation of 891c2-3 (at p. 363), the crucial passage (c3-4: ψυχὴν δὲ ἐκ τούτων ὕστερον) is missing.

32   Naddaf 2005, 22 f., quoting *VM* 20,1 and part of 20,2. – On that genre, and its development from Anaximander to Democritus and Plato, see also Naddaf 1997 and Rossetti 2006.

33   In the French version, *VM* 20 is described as the earliest occurrence of the formula in extant Greek literature (Naddaf 1992, 17 f.). But again, no interpretation of the passage is offered. – I am not sure about the chronology. Philolaus may be earlier than *VM*. But I am also not sure about the meaning of περὶ δὲ φύσιος καὶ ἁρμονίας ὧδε ἔχει in Philolaus (DK 44 B 6). It is far from evident that περὶ φύσιος functions as a grammatical component of περὶ ... φύσιος καὶ ἁρμονίας. The latter phrase may well be taken to indicate just one topic (the relation to each other of φύσις and ἁρμονία) rather than two (φύσις and ἁρμονία).

34   Rather, *VM* 20 provides Naddaf with a cue for mentioning the theory of civilization in *VM* 3, which he claims to be "an integral part of the third stage of an investigation of the *peri phuseôs* type" (Naddaf 2005, 173 = 23n51; cf. Naddaf 1992, 54 = 28n59).

Indeed, Naddaf is far from eager to substantiate that claim.[35] Rather, he seems to rest his case on the observation that "the vast majority of commentators, both ancient and modern, concur that the primary goal of the written works of the pre-Socratics was to provide a *historia peri phuseōs*."[36] But note that this is ambiguous. The statement quoted can be either taken to suggest that "commentators" (one may add: starting with the author of *On ancient medicine*) employed the formula *peri phuseôs* to describe the "pre-Socratic" enterprise, or that "the pre-Socratics" themselves did so. In the former case, the statement would be consistent with the view that the language described is (mostly) a 4th century (and later) affair, and does not belong to early Greek philosophy but to its reception.[37] In the latter case, one cannot help concluding that Naddaf fails to adduce any evidence in support of his claim.

As regards meanings, Naddaf's primary concern is with the meaning of *peri phuseôs* rather than *phusis*. His approach appears to be this: to explain that formula in terms of extension and then to assume that *phusis* – especially "in the expression *peri phuseōs* or *historia peri phuseōs*,"[38] but also in other contexts where the scope of inquiry is at issue – refers to that extension, viz. "from beginning to end."[39] But this may be misleading. Taken at its face value,

---

35   Of course, there is no relevant evidence in [Hippocrates] *De victu*, c. 2 – which Naddaf (2005, 23) represents as claiming that "the principles of medicine are subject to an investigation of nature in general (*peri phuseōs historia*)". But the formula περὶ φύσιος occurs neither in *De victu* nor in *Airs Waters Places* (*Aer.*) to which Naddaf (2005, 173 = 22n49) refers for the environmental factors mentioned in *De victu* 2. Note that in *Aer.* 2, the relevant topics are termed μετεωρολόγα, which corresponds to late 5th century usage. What is more, the transition from *Aer.* 15 to 16 – περὶ μὲν τῆς φύσιος τῆς διαφορῆς καὶ τῆς μορφῆς τῶν ἐν τῇ Ἀσίῃ καὶ τῇ Εὐρώπῃ οὕτως ἔχει (Littré ΙΙ 62.11-12: "so much for the difference, in nature and in shape, between the inhabitants of Asia and the inhabitants of Europe," tr. Jones) – addresses a readership unfamiliar with the formula περὶ φύσεως, and so may Philolaus, DK 44 B 6 (see above).

36   Naddaf 2005, 16. Naddaf offers no reference for *"historia peri phuseōs,"* and I cannot either. In particular, that phrase does not occur in Plato. Probably, the reference is to *Phd.* 96a7, with the word order tacitly changed (same change in Schmalzriedt 1970, 89 and passim).

37   So does especially the incipit ΗΡΑΚΛΕΙΤΟΥ ΠΕΡΙ ΦΥΣΕΩΣ which Naddaf (1992, 18 and 2005,16) claims to be attributed to Heraclitus by West (1971, 9), but which West dates "after the 5th century" (ibid.). I could not, however, verify West's claim (ibid.) that the incipit quoted is attested to Heraclitus by Aristotle.

38   Naddaf 2005, 22.

39   Naddaf 2005, 21, quoting [Hippocrates], *De natura pueri*, c. 27. In his interpretation of that passage and of the author's summary (in c. 29), Naddaf assumes that φύσις means "growth" here, and that "from beginning to end" (c. 27: ἐξ ἀρχῆς ἐς τέλος, c. 29: μέχρις ἐς τέλος; Littré VII 528.22-27; 530.7-9) qualifies that growth rather than the author's account (c. 27: τὰ ῥηθέντα, c. 29: πᾶσαν ... ὅκως μοι ἐν τοῖσι λόγοισιν ἀποπέφανται). Naddaf's conclusion that "(w)hen it comes to enquiring into the *phusis* of something, it is the whole

Naddaf's "from beginning to end" describes the extension of a concept (i.e. *phusis*). But that phrase may rather describe the extensiveness of a development (which Naddaf would claim is referred to by *phusis*). Taken in this way, Naddaf's account of the meaning of *peri phuseôs* may be even consistent with the general rule, stated by Aristotle, that "*phusis* is always the *phusis* of something."[40] His remark that in Xenophon (*Mem.* I 1), *peri phuseôs* "is found ... with its natural genitive: *tōn pantōn*"[41] may be taken as acknowledging the fact that in early Greek philosophy, the realm of things investigated is typically referred to as "everything" (*panta*),[42] which means that the formula *peri phuseôs* must not be mistaken to indicate that realm. But Naddaf is far from explicit in this.

2.2 *Explanations of* peri phuseôs *in Terms of Approach: Genetic and Dispositional Characteristics of Things*

Phusis, to repeat, is always the *phusis* of something – which is usually indicated by a limiting genitive or left to be inferred from the context. When the context fails to provide the information required, it is quite a safe guess that a general statement – universal or existential – is made.[43] There are rare exceptions from this rule. In particular, such adverbial phrases as *phusei* ("by nature") or *kata phusin* ("according to nature") are occasionally used in such a way that it is pointless to ask: "nature of what?"[44] That is to say, *phusis* is used absolutely.

---

process from beginning to end which is understood" (ibid.) suggests that the scope of inquiry is indicated, and is described as a process comprising a totality of stages, by φύσις. None of this is evident, nor does the passage quoted evidently reflect the language of early Greek philosophy (which question Naddaf does not seem to address).

40 Aristotle, *Ph.* II 1, 192b34: ὑποκείμενον γάρ τι (which I take to have existential force: "there is a subject"; differently Ross 1936, 501 ad loc.). – Similarly Naddaf 2005, 31 (commenting on Xenophon, *Mem.* I 1,11-15): "there is always *phusis* of something" (that is, not only of the universe).

41 Naddaf 2005, 31.

42 See Long 1999,10 f. (independently, Heinemann 2000, 20n25). For details, see below section 2.2.

43 For instance, the Heraclitean saying that "nature tends to hide" (DK 22 B 123: φύσις κρύπτε-σθαι φιλεῖ) is a universal statement, meaning that whatever things are investigated, their nature is probably hidden. By contrast, the claim in the *Corpus Hippocraticum* that no disease "comes about without a nature" (*Aer.* 22, Littré II 78.2: οὐδὲν ἄνευ φύσιος γίγνεται) amounts to an existential statement, meaning that there is always something the nature of which accounts for the disease.

44 Democritus, DK 68 B 267: φύσει τὸ ἄρχειν οἰκήιον τῶι κρέσσονι ("by nature, ruling belongs to the stronger"). The question whether φύσει refers to the nature of the stronger or to the nature of the weaker is evidently not to the point.

This is especially so when *phusis* is paired with *anagkê* ("necessity").[45] Necessity is usually supposed to reside in the "natures" of particular things. But necessity may also be supposed to reside in the "nature" of things in general. In a more traditional language, the necessity which governs human affairs is equated with the rule of Zeus. That's why *anagkê phuseôs* ("natural necessity") may be even considered as a name of the highest god.[46]

I agree with Naddaf that *peri phuseôs* has *tôn (ha)pantôn* ("of everything") as "its natural genitive." This is the regular way the formula is used.[47] A possible variant is *tôn pragmatôn* ("of things");[48] another variant, preferred by Plato, which suggests a unity formed of all things is *tou pantos* (sing.: "of the universe") or equivalently *tou holou*.[49] In the complete formula, the genitive clause indicates the subject matter of inquiry; the meaning of *peri phuseôs* may be indicated by a catalogue of questions such as

(1) "how the so called ... *kosmos* is (*echei* – or "... came into existence": *ephy*), and by what necessities each of the heavenly phenomena is generated;"[50]

(2) "the causes of each (kind of) thing(s), on what account each (kind of) thing(s) comes into being, on what account it perishes, and on what account it exists;"[51]

---

45 Cf. Euripides, fr. 757 N, where κατὰ φύσιν (v. 8) = ἀναγκαίως (v. 5). See also Thucydides, V 105,2 where ὑπὸ φύσεως ἀναγκαίας ("due to necessary nature") attributes the rule of the stronger to a universal law. Again, there is no such question as: "nature of what?".

46 Euripides, *Troad.* 886. I agree with Heinimann and Schmalzriedt that φύσις is used absolutely here. But no "Allphysis" (Schmalzriedt 1970, 117; cf. Heinimann 1945, 105: "Idee einer alles umfassenden und beherrschenden, unsterblichen φύσις") or "sum-total of reality" (Guthrie 1965, 351; cf. Graeser 1989, 13: "Inbegriff von Realität") is referred to. Rather, the meaning of φύσις at *Troad.* 886 derives from the meaning of the adverbial phrases mentioned above (see Heinemann 2005, 35 f.).

47 *Dissoi Logoi* (DK 90), c. 8,1; Xenophon, *Mem.* I 1,11 (see above, end of sect. 2.1).

48 Philolaus, DK 44 B 6 – cf. Huffman 1993, 96 ff. (but see also n. 33 above).

49 For τοῦ παντός, see *Ti.* 27a4. For τοῦ ὅλου, cf. *Phdr.* 270c where it is asked whether medical knowledge περὶ φύσεως (c9) manages ἄνευ τῆς τοῦ ὅλου φύσεως (c2: "without the nature of the universe"), with ὅλον echoing μετεωρολογία (a1), see Heinemann 2000, 39n85. Gregory (this volume) suggests that, rather, "the nature of the whole man" is referred to. The issue is disputed and hard to settle.

50 Xenophon, *Mem.* I 1,11: ὅπως ὁ καλούμενος ... κόσμος ἔχει καὶ τίσιν ἀνάγκαις ἕκαστα γίγνεται τῶν οὐρανίων. – Instead of ἔχει, Naddaf (1992, 39 and 2005, 30) reads ἔφυ, which is not in the mss. (see Bandini's apparatus criticus, Bandini and Dorion 2000, 5) but is mentioned by Dindorf (1862, 6) as a then popular emendation which gains some support from an imitation in Lucianus (*Icaromenippus* 4: ἐγένετο). Both Breitenbach/Mücke (1889, 44) and Smith (1903, 8) read and comment on ἔφυ without even mentioning ἔχει. But I was unable to trace Naddaf's fuller version of the Greek, viz. "*hopōs kosmos ephu*" (loc. cit.).

51 Plato, *Phd.* 96a9-10: εἰδέναι τὰς αἰτίας ἑκάστου, διὰ τί γίγνεται ἕκαστον καὶ διὰ τί ἀπόλλυται καὶ διὰ τί ἔστι. Reference to kinds is suggested by the examples to follow (*Phd.* 96b ff.).

(3) "from the beginning, what the human being is and how it originally came to be and from what things it was compounded;"[52]

(4) "what the human being is in relation to foods and drinks, and what it is in relation to other practices, and what will be the effect of each thing on each individual."[53]

Since the subject matter – "each of the heavenly phenomena," "each kind of thing," "the human being" – appears in the catalogue, its specification by a limiting genitive is redundant. General clauses such as *tôn (ha)pantôn* ("of everything") or *tôn pragmatôn* ("of things") are just forms to be filled in when the catalogue is composed. That's why *peri phuseôs* does also without "its natural genitive" – and does so in the last three passages quoted.[54] The omission does no harm but still is an omission: without "its natural genitive," *peri phuseôs* is elliptical.[55]

The conclusion suggests itself that *phusis*, in the formula *peri phuseôs*, does not indicate the subject matter of inquiry but its approach. That is, *phusis* indicates a kind of questions to be asked about the subject matter of inquiry. So far, however, this conclusion does not directly pertain to early Greek philosophy but to its late 5th and early 4th century reception. In a way, this is unavoidable since it is far from evident that the formula *peri phuseôs* belongs to early Greek philosophy. Rather, the formula belongs to its late 5th and 4th century reception.

But the conclusion stated above is also true of early Greek philosophy. In the extant fragments, the subject matter of inquiry is either explicitly specified or summarily referred to by *panta*, "everything."[56] The meaning of *phusis*

---

52   [Hippocrates], *VM* 20,1 (Littré I 620.11-12): ἐξ ἀρχῆς ὅ τί ἐστιν ἄνθρωπος καὶ ὅπως ἐγένετο πρῶτον καὶ ὁπόθεν συνεπάγη (tr. Schiefsky).

53   Ibid. 20,3 (Littré I 622.7–9): ὅ τι τέ ἐστιν ἄνθρωπος πρὸς τὰ ἐσθιόμενά τε καὶ πινόμενα καὶ ὅ τι πρὸς τὰ ἄλλα ἐπιτηδεύματα καὶ ὅ τι ἀφ' ἑκάστου ἑκάστῳ ξυμβήσεται (tr. Schiefsky).

54   Limiting genitives are also avoided when the subject matter is indicated paratactically. Examples in Plato include: περὶ φύσεώς τε καὶ τοῦ ὅλου (*Lysis* 214b5: "on nature and the universe"); περὶ φύσεώς τε καὶ τῶν μετεώρων (*Prt.* 315c5: "on nature and things in the sky"); and ἀδολεσχία καὶ μετεωρολογία φύσεως πέρι (*Phdr.* 270a1: "sophistication and account of things in the sky concerning nature").

55   I disagree with Schmalzriedt, who claims that where such extensions as τῶν ἁπάντων etc. are lacking, the formula περὶ φύσεως is used absolutely (1970, 95: "absoluter Gebrauch"), so as to indicate that nature as a totality is at issue (ibid. 117: "die Vorstellung einer die Dinge übergreifenden Allphysis"). Similarly with Schmalzriedt: Heinimann 1945, 106.

56   Opening passages which highlight πάντα include: Heraclitus, DK 22 B 1; Parmenides, DK 28 B 1.31 f. and B 8.60 f.; Empedocles, DK 31 B 6.1; Anaxagoras, DK 59 B 1; Diogenes of Apollonia, DK 64 B 2. To Democritus, περὶ τῶν ξυμπάντων is attested as an *incipit* by Cicero and Sextus (DK 68 B 165). In Xenophanes, the same formula may underlie the phrase ἀμφὶ θεῶν τε καὶ ἄσσα λέγω περὶ πάντων (DK 21 B 34.2) which is rendered "about the gods, and

corresponds to the kind of questions asked about the things under consideration. There are two such kinds of questions, one pertaining to the origin of a thing and to the way it is by virtue of that origin, and the other pertaining to the way it is and behaves irrespectively of its origin. Correspondingly, there is also a dualism of meanings inherent in the concept.

(a)   On the *genesis* account, *phusis* refers (a1) to the origin of a thing, (a2) to the way it derives from that origin, or (a3) to the way it is, and is disposed to behave, by virtue of its derivation from that origin, correspondingly to the conjugated forms *phuô* (to bring forth), *phuomai* (to become or grow), and *pephuka* (to have become or grown). Taken in this way, the *phusis* of a thing is the profile of its genetic characteristics (in short: its genetic profile).

(b)   On the *dunamis* account, *phusis* is just the way a thing is, and is reliably disposed to behave, regardless of its origin and of its way of becoming. That is to say, the *phusis* of a thing is the profile of its dispositional characteristics (in short: its dispositional profile).[57]

This distinction is clearly brought out by the catalogues of questions in *On ancient medicine* (c. 20) quoted above. Catalogue (3) corresponds to the genetic profile which the author claims is sought by *philosophiê*. Catalogue (4) corresponds to the dispositional profile which the author claims must be sought by *iêtrikê* ("medicine").

In short, *phusis* may suggest becoming or being. There has been much dispute about which of the two is primary, or to which the other can be reduced.[58]

---

such things as I say concerning all things" by Lesher (1999, 229; similarly Fränkel 1969, 382; Long 1999, 10; Tor 2017, 130), but may be also translated "about the gods and about everything I speak of" (KRS, #186). See also below n. 93. As far as I can see, Habash's "purposive nature" (this volume) is addressed in presocratic language by πάντα (+ steering agency, see below) rather than φύσις. Diogenes of Apollonia who equates the steering agency with a stuff which is also the common φύσις of things may be an exception.

57   The terminology thus introduced corresponds to the distinction between "genetic" and "dynamic constitution" in my earlier publications (Heinemann 2000, 31 ff.; Heinemann 2005, 30 ff.; etc.). – According to Naddaf, the formula περὶ φύσεως presupposes a γένεσις account of φύσις. A δύναμις account of φύσις was famously attributed Herodotus by Vlastos (1975, 19) as follows: "In his prose, the *physis* of any given thing is that cluster of stable characteristics by which we can recognize that thing and can anticipate the limits within which it can act upon other things or can be acted upon by them."

58   Proponents of becoming (γένεσις account of φύσις) include Heidel (1910, 96 f.), Thimme (1935), Diller (1939, 242 f.), Patzer (1939, 220 ff.), Heinimann (1945, 89 ff.), Kahn (1960, 201 f.), Solmsen (1960, 96), and Naddaf (1992 and 2005, passim); of being (and hence, more or less explicitly, of δύναμις accounts of φύσις): Lovejoy (1909, 376), Holwerda (1955, 7), Guthrie (1962, 82), Kirk (1962, 228 ff.), Vlastos (1975, 19), und Kerferd (1981, 111). Burnet's

PERI PHUSEÔS: PHYSICS, PHYSICISTS, AND *PHUSIS* IN ARISTOTLE   25

The dispute is unsettled. Arguably, there is nothing to settle since the dualism is primitive.[59] But if so, weights are still distributed differently as contexts differ. 5th century contexts in which genetic conceptions of *phusis* prevail include early Greek philosophy and traditionalist accounts of human values. Dispositional conceptions of *phusis* prevail in professional languages and in prudential and anthropological discourse.

At part of the occurrences in the fragments of early Greek philosophy,[60] *phusis* is clearly the genetic profile of the thing(s) under consideration. In another part, the meaning of *phusis* is easily derived from that.[61] In the remaining part, that genetic profile is pertinent does not positively suggest itself, but *phusis* makes good sense on this assumption.[62] That's why I consider the testimony in *On ancient medicine* (c. 20) as trustworthy. I agree with Heinimann and Kahn that in early Greek philosophy, *phusis* is the "catchword" for "a view which takes the true essence of things to be something grown,"[63] and for a philosophy which, as a consequence, seeks the "essential character" of a thing "by discovering *from what source* and *in what way* it has come to be what it is."[64] In particular, the *phusis* of things accounts for their generation, interactions, and perishing. But it should be noted that the *phusis* of things does not account for their combination into a universal order (*kosmos*), of which divine steering or creationist accounts may be offered instead.[65]

"primary substance" may be taken in both ways but is most easily integrated as a kind of origin into the γένεσις account.

59   Similarly, Beardslee (1918, 2 und passim), Mannsperger (1969, 39 ff.), Bremer (1989, 255), and Buchheim (1999, 22 ff.).

60   Notably, in Parmenides, DK 28 B 10, and Empedocles, DK 31 B 8.4. See Heinemann 2005, 24–27.

61   This is especially the case when the φύσις of some thing is its composition from primary stuff (e.g. in Parmenides, DK 28 B 16.3; Empedocles, DK 31 B 63 and B 110.5 (?); Diogenes of Apollonia, DK 64 B 2), or derivatively the primary stuff of which it is composed (for the 4th century evidence adduced by Burnet, see above sect. 2.1).

62   Notably, in Heraclitus (DK 22 B 1, B 112, B 123; pap. Derveni col. IV 7) and Philolaus (DK 44 B 1 and B 6).

63   Heinimann 1945, 94: "eine Anschauung, die das wahre Wesen der Dinge für etwas Gewordenes hält".

64   Kahn 1960, 202 (italics his – "catchword": ibid.; "essential character": ibid. 201). I also agree with Naddaf (passim, see above section 2.1) that this requires to account for the relevant development "from beginning to end."

65   As to divine steering, see the use of κυβερνάω in Anaximander (DK 12 A 15), Heraclitus (DK 22 B 41), Parmenides (DK 28 B 12), and Diogenes of Apollonia (DK 64 B 5); cf. Heinemann 2002, 54 ff. Gregory (this volume) rightly adds [Hippocrates], *De victu* 10 (Littré VI, 486.10). In Heraclitus, the steering authority (i.e. the λόγος in Habash's interpretation, this volume) is assisted by an executive agency (lightning) who handles the rudder (DK 22 B 64: οἰακίζει). The distinction of governing authority from executive agency in Heraclitus

A similar language is employed by such traditionalist devotees of noble values as Pindar and some Sophoclean characters to express their conviction that there is no excellence except by virtue of being "born for excellence,"[66] and that noble birth must prove itself by noble conduct.[67] The abandonment of that language does not only reflect a devaluation of noble excellences. It reflects a change of approach to human affairs. In the 2nd half of the 5th century, *phusis* becomes the catchword for a view which takes achievement to be a matter of capacity,[68] and for a methodology in such professions as medicine (*iatrikê*), higher education (*sophistikê*), and rhetoric, which seeks standards of correctness by inquiring into the dispositional profile of things.[69]

---

is confirmed by fr. 3+94 (Pap. Derveni, col. IV 7–9) where Erinyes act as "ministers of Justice," so as to impose "natural" limits on the sun ("natural": κόσ]μου κατὰ φύσιν, line 7, text: LM=Piano=Kotwick). A creationist account of cosmic order is offered by Anaxagoras; Empedocles gives, at least, room to a creationist interpretation (Sedley 2007, 52 ff.).

As Gregory (ibid.) observes, 'to prevail' (κρατεῖν) is another term used to describe the steering agency. But there is a difference. The establishment and maintenance of order is not just a matter of stable force ratios but of the character (rational or at least divine) of the agency who prevails. Divine steering, as in Heraclitus and others, is something different from the rule of the stronger, as described in the Melian dialogue (Thucydides V 105, 2: ... οὗ ἂν κρατῇ, ἄρχειν).

66   My "by virtue of being 'born for excellence' " (quoting Pindar, *Ol.* 10.20: φύντ' ἀρετᾷ) paraphrases Pindar's φυᾷ (at *Ol.* 2.86 and 9.100, *Pyth.* 8.44, *Nem.* 1.25 and 7.54). As often, adverbial clauses provide the clue to the meaning of the φύσις words here. In general, φύσις is a "cluster of ... characteristics" that belong to a thing (Vlastos 1975, 19). Adverbial phrases like φύσιν or φυᾷ (or equivalently, the use of πέφυκα as copula) indicate that a characteristic is an item in that cluster.

67   Sophocles, *Ant.* 37–8: καὶ δείξεις τάχα εἴτ' εὐγενὴς πέφυκας εἴτ' ἐσθλῶν κακή ("you will soon prove whether you are born noble or from the best bad"). Noble conduct would verify Ismene's noble birth. Failure would give rise to the paradox that Ismene is born both noble (ἐσθλῶν [sc. πεφυκυῖα]) and bad ([sc. πέφυκας] κακή). Similarly Sophocles, *Aj.* 471–2. *Phil.* 1310–3.

68   The δύναμις account of φύσις attributed to Herodotus by Vlastos (see above n. 57) applies also to medical language (von Staden 1998, 269; Heinemann 2005, 37 ff.), and to the use of φύσις as a term for talents, characters and all kinds of (e.g. professional) capacities (Heinemann 2006b, 44 ff.).

69   [Hippocrates], *De arte* 5,6 makes it explicit that availability of criteria for correctness and incorrectness counts as the mark of τέχνη, that is, of professional excellence insofar as it is a matter of expertise (cf. Heinimann 1976, 163 f.). Plato's *Cratylus* (387a ff.) adds to this that only the φύσις of the things involved provides the criteria required. The pairing of "nature" and "correctness" in a Euripidean fragment (206 N. – a piece of advice concerning rhetoric, larded with methodological language) suggests that this is a late 5th century commonplace. That φύσις means dispositional profile is explicit in *VM* 20,3, but is more or less tacitly presupposed at a host of occurrences (see sect. 3.4 ff. in Heinemann 2006b).

Interestingly, the denial of φύσις implied in the Protagorean homo mensura doctrine (on which see Habash, this volume) undermines his own professional expertise in higher

3 Natures and Natural Things in Plato and Aristotle

3.1 *Plato: Nature and Craftsmanship*

On ancient medicine offers the most explicit discussion of the meaning of *phusis* in extant pre-Aristotelian literature. There is nothing similar in Plato.[70] Plato's use of *phusis* and its cognates exhibits no systematic unity but follows a variety of pre-Platonic patterns, thus revealing Plato's reactions to, and his more or less innovative uses of, pre-Platonic conceptions. In general, dispositional profile is the core meaning of *phusis*, which explains Plato's use of the term. For instance, in the middle books of the *Republic*, *philosophos phusis* is the kind of character and talent required by the philosophical curriculum.[71] This corresponds to the Protagorean scheme according to which "instruction requires both nature (i.e. talent) and exercise."[72] To be sure, insofar as nature precedes nurture in time, *philosophos phusis* is something inborn, and is a matter of breeding in Plato's *Kallipolis*. But it is consistently described by Plato in terms of just capacity and disposition.

Forms are another example. There are passages where a form is the paradigmatic bearer of a property *F*, and is referred to by description as "what in (or: by) its nature is *F*."[73] More often, however, self-predication is avoided by equating the form with its nature.[74] As a rule, the nature a form *is* is the nature it *has*. Since forms are natures, "nature" (*phusis*), in three of the rare passages where the term is used absolutely, is the realm of forms.[75] It goes without saying that there is nothing in extant pre-Platonic literature on which such language is modelled. Rather, the pairing of nature with form derives its plausibility from the argument of Plato's *Cratylus*. On the one hand, natures are required to provide dialectic with criteria for correctness and incorrectness in

---

  education (σοφιστική) which involves the assessment of "natures" (i.e. talents, cf. DK 80 B 3: φύσεως καὶ ἀσκήσεως διδασκαλία δεῖται); for a parody of that assessment, see v. 487 in Aristophanes' *Clouds*.

70 A remote echo of *VM* 20.1–3 may be perceived in *Phdr.* 269e-270d, with ἀδολεσχίας καὶ μετεωρολογίας φύσεως πέρι (270a1) corresponding to φιλοσοφίη (20,1) and Ἱπποκράτης τε καὶ ὁ ἀληθὴς λόγος (270c9-10) corresponding to ἰητρική (20,2); see Heinemann 2000, 39n85. At *Resp.* V 454b ff., female φύσις, involving gendered capacities for procreation and non-gendered capacities for political rule, is subject to disambiguation.

71 For details, see Heinemann 2007, 66–71.

72 Protagoras, DK 80 B 3 (see above n. 69).

73 *Symp.* 210e5-6: τι ... τὴν φύσιν καλόν; *Resp.* VI 501b2: τὸ φύσει δίκαιον καὶ καλὸν καὶ σῶφρον.

74 See, e.g., *Resp.* V 476b where αὐτοῦ δὲ τοῦ καλοῦ ... τὴν φύσιν ἰδεῖν (b6-7) = ἐπ' αὐτὸ τὸ καλὸν ... ἰέναι τε καὶ ὁρᾶν καθ' αὐτὸ (b10-11), and *Soph.* 255de where ἢ θατέρου φύσις (d9) = ἢ ἰδέα ἢ θατέρου (e5-6).

75 *Phd.* 103b5, *Resp.* X 597b ff., *Prm.* 132d2.

the use of words as "tool(s) ... for dividing being."[76] On the other hand, the criteria in question are provided by the forms which serve as models to which philosophers are able to refer.[77] Hence, the natures required may be equated with forms. But it should be noted that Plato is nowhere explicit about this.[78]

Similarly, there is no question in Plato's *Timaeus* about whether the "producer" (*dêmiourgos*) of the universe refers to a "model" (*paradeigma*) or not. The question is, to what model, eternal or one which has come into being. The answer is that, since the product is fine and the producer is good, the model to which he refers must be eternal.[79] Plato's use of *phusis* and its cognates exhibits the same variety of patterns in the *Timaeus* as in other dialogues. But two distinctions are noticeable. There are, on the one hand, two kinds of natures the producer of the universe finds: (a) forms belonging to the model, and (b) necessities belonging to the receptacle which provides the conditions for forms to be instantiated. And there are, on the other hand, (c) natures of more or less ordinary things the producer of the universe composes thereof.

To the latter things, the claim in Plato's *Sophist* seems to apply that "the so-called natural things (*ta phusei legomena*) are made by divine craftsmanship."[80] But that statement is not so aimed. My translation is misleading in that it suggests that "natural" (*phusei*) corresponds to a commonplace classification of things.[81] Rather, a "popular theory" is reported according to which "nature

---

76   "Natures": cf. *Cra.* 387c1-2: ᾗ πέφυκε τὰ πράγματα λέγειν τε καὶ λέγεσθαι καὶ ᾧ; "dialectic": cf. 390cd: διαλεκτικός; "tools ...": cf. 388b13-c1: ὄργανον ... διακριτικὸν τῆς οὐσίας (tr. Reeve).

77   "Model": παράδειγμα. For forms as "models," see, e.g. *Euthphr.* 6e5, *Resp.* VI 484c8, 501e3, *Resp.* VII 540a9, *Prm.* 132d2 – Needless to say, this is not the whole story about Platonic forms. It is a minimal account explaining why forms are required by dialectic (*Prm.* 135bc), and why inspection of forms is required by the establishment and supervision of evaluative usages (*Resp.* VI 484d2: νόμιμα καλῶν τε πέρι καὶ δικαίων καὶ ἀγαθῶν).

78   Plato's *Cratylus* is an inquiry into the "natural" correctness of names. The dialogue ends when it comes to inquire into the "natural" capacity of things to be named (387d4-5: ᾗ πέφυκε τὰ πράγματα ... ὀνομάζεσθαι). Alternatives – stability vs. flux – are only adumbrated (439c ff., cf. 397bc and 411c); forms are just mentioned (439c8).

79   *Ti.* 29a. Note that ὁ ... δημιουργός (sc. ἐστιν) ἀγαθός (29a2-3) is far from tautology. At the first pertinent occurrence in the *Timaeus* (28a6), the meaning of δημιουργός is just "producer," that is, (a person who acts as) efficient cause (αἴτιον, *ibid.* a4) of a becoming. But the question about good and bad (29a2-4) also suggests a professional framework (which, of course, is taken for granted for δημιουργοί at 24a5-7). Within this framework, the distinction between good and bad δημιουργοί (cf. [Hippocrates] *VM* 1,2) corresponds to the distinction between correctness and incorrectness which is constitutive of τέχνη.

80   *Soph.* 265e3: τὰ ... φύσει λεγόμενα ποιεῖσθαι θείᾳ τέχνῃ.

81   I know of no pre-Aristotelian evidence for a commonplace classification of things into natural and, say, artificial. Questions raised in such domains as medicine (or similarly, education), whether some outcome is due to nature or art, are quite another issue and, in particular, do not result in classifications of things.

PERI PHUSEÔS: PHYSICS, PHYSICISTS, AND PHUSIS IN ARISTOTLE

begets" animals, plants, and minerals "as a result of some spontaneous cause that generates without thought:"[82] *ta phusei legomena* are the things which this theory classifies as "natural." In *Laws* x, unnamed opponents are said to hold a similar view, claiming "that all things which come, came, or will come into being are partly by nature, partly by craftsmanship, and partly due to chance."[83] But this classification turns out to be bipartite rather than tripartite. The "greatest and finest" things are made by "nature and chance;" subsequently "smaller" things are added by craftsmanship.[84] The list of things belonging to the former class is an expansion of the list of natural things in the *Sophist*; additions are the elements, the stuffs of which heavenly bodies are made, the heaven and the heavenly bodies themselves.[85]

From the standpoint advocated in the *Laws*, this view – and similarly the views of all previous investigators into nature[86] – involves a reversal of priorities: body (viz. the elements) is falsely considered prior to soul, and nature to art.[87] Plato's point is that (i) the universe (*to pan*) is an orderly whole (*kosmos*), and that (ii) both the establishment of order (in the *Timaeus*) and its maintenance (in the *Laws*) are the business of reason (*nous*) which, in turn, is ineffective without (iii) the mediating operation of soul (*psuchê*).[88] That's why divine craftsmanship accounts for that order and, hence, for the existence of the so-called natural things.

---

82   *Soph.* 265c7-8: τὴν φύσιν αὐτὰ γεννᾶν ἀπό τινος αἰτίας αὐτομάτης καὶ ἄνευ διανοίας φυούσης (tr. Cornford, modified). For the list of things, see ibid. c1-3; "popular theory": cf. c5: τῶν πολλῶν δόγμα καὶ ῥῆμα.

83   *Leg.* x, 888e4-6: Λέγουσί πού τινες ὡς πάντα ἐστὶ τὰ πράγματα γιγνόμενα καὶ γενόμενα καὶ γενησόμενα τὰ μὲν φύσει, τὰ δὲ τέχνῃ, τὰ δὲ διὰ τύχην.

84   *Leg.* x, 889a4-5: τὰ μὲν μέγιστα αὐτῶν καὶ κάλλιστα ἀπεργάζεσθαι φύσιν καὶ τύχην, τὰ δὲ σμικρότερα τέχνην. The pairing of nature and chance is quite consistent with the theory mentioned in the *Sophist*.

85   *Leg.* x, 889b1-c6. According to a remark in the sequel, it is a consequence of the view described that the elements are regarded as "first of all things," and are named "the φύσις" (ibid. 891c2-3 – see above n. 27). Plato does not explicitly attribute this to anybody. But there is independent evidence for the usage described (see above n. 28 f.).

86   *Leg.* x, 891c7-9 (see above n. 27).

87   *Leg.* x, 891c2-4 (elements prior to soul) and 889a4-8 (nature prior to art); cf. *ibid.* 891e ff. and passim.

88   For (i), see *Ti.* 29a5 and *Leg.* x 897c-898c. For (ii), see *Ti.* 29a6-7: the appropriate model is λόγῳ καὶ φρονήσει περιληπτόν ("to be grasped by reasoning and thought"); that is to say, it is νοητόν ("falling into the province of νοῦς," ibid. 30c7 and passim, tr. LSJ). According to *Leg.* 897b1-4, the governing soul functions properly if and only if "it takes in reason" (νοῦν ... προσλαβοῦσα). For (iii), see *Ti.* 30b3: νοῦν δ' αὖ χωρὶς ψυχῆς ἀδύνατον παραγενέσθαι τῳ ("nothing can have reason without soul"); similarly *Soph.* 249a4-8.

3.2 *Aristotle: Natures and Natural Things*

Aristotle agrees with the account of craftsmanship tacitly presupposed in Plato's *Timaeus*. In short, craftsmanship (*technê*) is mental representation of form (*eidos*) transferred by practical syllogism into efficient causation so as to get that form instantiated.[89] But he agrees with Plato's opponents on the non-consideration of divine craftsmanship and also offers no divine steering account of universal order.[90] In particular, Aristotle finds no fault with the classifications reported in Plato's *Sophist* and *Laws*. Rather, he adopts variants of the latter as the starting points in his own accounts of the meaning of *phusis* (*Physics* II 1) and of the preservation of form in becoming (*Metaph.* VII 7–9).

Aristotle, of course, repudiates the pairing of nature with chance, which informs the cosmologies Plato attributes to his opponents. But he also rejects Plato's proposal in response to pair nature (*phusis* in the sense of "primordial becoming") with soul and, hence, with reason (*nous*),[91] which would amount to conflating nature with divine craftsmanship and is no option for Aristotle. Rather, the explanatory role of divine craftsmanship is assigned by Aristotle to the dispositional profiles of things. That form (*eidos*) is "nature" (*phusis*), is a locution Aristotle borrows from Plato. But Aristotle links this locution back to pre-Platonic conceptions, according to which *phusis* is always the *phusis* of something and accounts for the genetic or dispositional profile of the thing or things of which it is the *phusis*. Accordingly, Aristotle insists against Plato that forms are never separate, but exist by virtue of being instantiated by things. In short, nature (*phusis*) is instantiated form transferred into efficient causation.[92]

But Aristotle also allows that form exists by virtue of being represented by the human mind. There is, therefore, an analogy between nature (*phusis*) and

---

89 *Metaph.* VII 7, 1032a32-b2, b5-b14. "Mental representation of form": cf. b13 where each τέχνη is equated with the relevant εἶδος, which, however, can exist in two ways, represented by the mind of the producer (ἐν τῇ ψυχῇ, b1) or instantiated by his product (in this latter sense, τέχνη at *Ph.* II 1, 193a31). The definition in *Eth. Nic.* VI 4 (τέχνη = ἕξις μετὰ λόγου ἀληθοῦς ποιητική, 1140a10) adds to this that τέχνη is a disposition (ἕξις) which, taken as a power (*Metaph.* IX 2, 1046b3: δύναμις) may be distinguished from its manifestation to which the passage in *Metaph.* VII 7 refers.

90 In particular, *Metaph.* XII 10, 1075a11-25 offers no such account, see Heinemann 2016a, 48 ff.; Heinemann 2016b, 276 ff.

91 *Leg.* X, 892c, "primordial becoming": γένεσις ... περὶ τὰ πρῶτα (c2-3).

92 This is, of course, not the whole story. Both matter and form may function as "nature," since the dispositional profiles of materials contribute to the dispositional profile of hylomorphic compounds (see, e.g., Lennox 1997). But it should be noted that the dispositional profiles of materials are subject to the requirements of hypothetical necessity which, of course, are determined by form.

PERI PHUSEÔS: PHYSICS, PHYSICISTS, AND PHUSIS IN ARISTOTLE   31

craftsmanship (*technê*): both provide ways in which form (instantiated or represented) is transferred into efficient causation. The analogy is asymmetrical in that nature is prior to, and is "imitated" by craftsmanship. Divine craftsmanship would reverse priorities. But for this, the divine mind would be required to represent forms and to engage in efficient causation, which he does not according to Aristotle.

Evidently, that nature is explanatory in the way described does not hold of all kinds of things. It does not hold of artificial things since in this case represented rather than instantiated form is explanatory. Nor does it hold of abstract or separable entities with respect to which efficient causation has no role to play. Hence, Aristotle denies that "natural science" (*phusikê*) is "about everything" (*peri pantôn*).[93] It is about "natural things" (*phusei onta*) – that is, I will argue, about the things for which the approach described works.

That "natural science" is about "natural things" is just a catchy slogan which, however, is serviceable as a guide through the preliminaries in Aristotle's *Physics*. The hypothesis in *Physics* I 2, "that natural things are some or all of them in motion,"[94] derives its significance from that slogan. And so do the conclusions in *Physics* I 5 and I 7, that "the things which come into being naturally all are or are out of contraries," and that "substratum (*hupokeimenon*) and form (*morphê*)" are "the causes and principles of natural things out of which they are and have come into being primarily."[95] One would ask, why care about natural things? The answer is that not just natural things are at issue but the subject matter of natural science.

At the beginning of *Physics* II 1, the classification of "things" (*onta*) into "natural" (*phusei*) and "due to other causes"[96] is just taken for granted. So are the examples of natural and artificial things listed in the sequel;[97] and so is

---

93   Cf. *Part. an.* I 1, 641a36-b1: "Ὥστε περὶ πάντων ἡ φυσικὴ γνῶσις ἂν εἴη, which is meant to refute the assumption that all soul (including mind) belongs to the subject matter of natural science. Aristotle's premise that natural science is not "about everything" marks a break with the self-description of early Greek philosophy. Aristotle is evidently aware of this when he describes early Greek philosophers as "giving natural accounts," or as "lisping," περὶ πάντων (*Metaph.* I 8, 988b27; 10, 993a15 f.). On "lisping," see Cooper 2012, 340 ff. But Cooper seems to take περὶ πάντων as qualifying ἔοικεν (993a15) rather than indicating the topic on which early philosophy appears as lisping.

94   *Ph.* I 2, 185a13: τὰ φύσει ἢ πάντα ἢ ἔνια κινούμενα εἶναι (tr. Charlton, modified) – "hypothesis": *ibid.* a12-13: ὑποκείσθω.

95   *Ph.* I 5, 188b26-27: ὥστε πάντ' ἂν εἴη τὰ φύσει γιγνόμενα ἢ ἐναντία ἢ ἐξ ἐναντίων (tr. Charlton, modified); *Ph.* 7, 190b17-20: εἴπερ εἰσὶν αἰτίαι καὶ ἀρχαὶ τῶν φύσει ὄντων, ἐξ ὧν πρώτων εἰσὶ καὶ γεγόνασι ..., ὅτι γίγνεται πᾶν ἔκ τε τοῦ ὑποκειμένου καὶ τῆς μορφῆς (see below n. 119) for the omission.

96   *Ph.* II 1, 192b8-9: Τῶν ὄντων τὰ μέν ἐστι φύσει, τὰ δὲ δι' ἄλλας αἰτίας.

97   Examples of natural things: *Ph.* II 1, 192b9-11; of artificial things: b16.

especially Aristotle's claim that only natural things have an internal *archê* of motion and rest.[98] In view of the discussion in Plato's *Sophist* and *Laws*, both classification and lists ought not to be taken as commonplace. Rather, Aristotle seems to join Plato's opponents to which a similar classification and similar examples are attributed in *Laws* x.[99]

But in one important respect, the parallel with Plato is misleading: In *Laws* x, the way things come into being is at issue; things are therefore classified by origin. In *Physics* II 1, no account of different ways in which natural and artificial things come into being is presupposed. There is no such account in the *Physics*. And what is more, the account Aristotle offers in *Metaph.* VII 7–9 does not apply to the elements, but elements are nevertheless adduced as examples of natural things in *Physics* II 1.[100] Parts of animals are another troubling item in Aristotle's list of examples, since the definition of *phusis* offered in the sequel does not apply.[101] So what to do with that list?

Aristotle's list is a variant of the list in Plato's *Laws* x. Animal parts are added; non-elemental stuffs, heavenly bodies, etc. are subsumed under "and things like that."[102] The list in Plato's *Laws* is the summary of a naturalist cosmogony. Aristotle's may be read as a sketchy plan of natural science in terms of

---

98   *Ph.* II 1, 192b12-20.

99   Aristotle's "we say" (*Ph.* II 1, 192b12: φαμέν) echoes Plato's "some people say" (*Leg.* X, 888e4: λέγουσί ... τινες; see above n. 83).

100   *Ph.* II 1, 192b10-11: καὶ τὰ ἁπλᾶ τῶν σωμάτων, οἷον γῆ καὶ πῦρ καὶ ἀὴρ καὶ ὕδωρ ("and the simple bodies, viz. earth, fire, air, and water"). Aristotle's account in *Metaph.* VII 7 requires that natural things are generated by a formal nature of the same species (ὑφ' οὗ ἡ κατὰ τὸ εἶδος λεγομένη φύσις ἡ ὁμοειδής, 1032a24; see below). But this is not true of the elements. According to *Gen. corr.* I 5, 320b17-21 (text: Buchheim 2010, 35) elements may be generated by something of the same genus or species (e.g. fire by fire, b20) or just by an actuality (ὑπ' ἐντελεχείας, b21), e.g. fire by friction in thunderstorms (*Mete.* II 9, 369b4-7; III 1, 370b4-7 etc.); the claim that thunderclouds already contain the fire which appears as lightning is unfounded according to Aristotle (*Mete.* II 9. 369b11-370a10).

101   By that definition, the φύσις of x is an ἀρχή of motion and rest, which belongs to x both immediately and essentially (*Ph.* II 1, 192b20-23 – "immediately": πρώτως, "essentially": καθ' αὑτὸ καὶ μὴ κατὰ συμβεβηκός; see Stavrianeas 2015, 49). But if x is my hand, the ἀρχή which controls its motion and rest resides in a part of my soul which Aristotle locates in the heart (*De motu an.* 8, 702a21 ff. and passim, cf. Nussbaum 1985, 153). The φύσις of an animal part is always the φύσις of the whole animal, and belongs only derivatively to the part. For an animal part, motion and rest are episodes in its functioning as an instrument to the activities that make up animal life (βίος, on which see Kosman 1987, 376 f.; Lennox 2010) – that is, in its contribution to the functioning of the animal body as an instrument of the soul which is the φύσις of that animal (for the soul as "nature," see *Part. an.* I 1, 641b9-10 and, particularly, *Gen. an.* II 4, 740b36-741a3). – In addition, note that elements and animal parts are just potentialities according to *Metaph.* VII 16, 1040b5-8.

102   *Ph.* II 1, 192b11: καὶ τὰ τοιαῦτα.

PERI PHUSEÔS: PHYSICS, PHYSICISTS, AND *PHUSIS* IN ARISTOTLE

its subject matter (to which parts of animals undoubtedly belong).[103] The list marks the field of interest Aristotle is setting out to traverse. His account of *phusis* indicates the unified approach he is going to follow thereby.[104]

The procedure is described in the *Metaphysics*. Aristotle's *phusikê* is a "special science."[105] Its starting point is to answer the canonical questions as to "Is it?" and "What is it?,"[106] just by "marking off some particular being, some genus" as its subject matter,[107] and by either grasping the what-is-it by observation or taking it as an hypothesis.[108]

Accordingly, Aristotle's next step in *Physics* II 1 is to exhibit an observed difference between the things listed as natural and the things which "are not constituted by nature."[109] Each of the former has an internal *archê* of motion and rest, but the latter do not. That is to say, such things as beds and shirts do have an "innate impulse to change" but only by virtue of their being made of such-and-such stuffs, not *qua* bed or *qua* shirt.[110] Aristotle adds that this is so

---

103   Plants are also listed in *Mete.* I 1 (339a7). However poorly it is represented in the extant *Corpus Aristotelicum* (but see Herzhoff 2016, 174 ff.), botany is nevertheless an integral part of Aristotelian natural science.

104   Aristotle's catchword for this is μέθοδος (*Ph.* I 1, 184a11; *Ph.* III 1, 200b13; *Mete.* I 1, 338a25 *Part. an.* I 4, 644b16; *IA* 2, 704b13 etc.) which, on the one hand, suggests "method" and, on the other hand, refers to the scope of inquiry to which the method applies (see Lennox 2015). That scope may be narrower, but at the occurrences mentioned it is just the scope of natural science (περὶ φύσεως ἐπιστήμη or φυσική). To such cases, my paraphrase "field of interest traversed, with a unified approach thereby followed" applies.

105   *Metaph.* IV 1, 1003a22-23: ἐν μέρει λεγομένη (sc. ἐπιστήμη).

106   *An. post.* II 1, 89b24-5: εἰ ἔστι, τί ἐστιν. Note that these are also the leading questions in *Ph.* III–IV (see Heinemann 2016c, 43 f.). In *Ph.* III 1, only the second question is asked: the first question is superfluous since it was already answered in *Ph.* I 2 and II 1 (185a12-14; 193a3-9).

107   *Metaph.* VI 1, 1025b8-9: περὶ ὄν τι καὶ γένος τι περιγραψάμενοι περὶ τούτου πραγματεύονται (tr. *ROT*, modified). The claim in *Metaph.* IV 3, that "nature is one particulatr genus of being" (ἐν γάρ τι γένος τοῦ ὄντος ἡ φύσις, 1005a34) equates φύσις with the γένος that belongs to φυσική. This is one of the rare cases where φύσις is used absolutely by Aristotle.

108   *Metaph.* VI 1, 1025b11-12: αἱ μὲν αἰσθήσει ποιήσασαι αὐτὸ δῆλον αἱ δ' ὑπόθεσιν λαβοῦσαι τὸ τί ἐστιν.

109   *Ph.* II 1, 192b12-13: τὰ μὴ φύσει συνεστῶτα "observed difference": φαίνεται διαφέροντα (b12), "things listed as natural": πάντα ... ταῦτα (b12).

110   *Ph.* II 1, 192b13-20. I am rendering μεταβολή by "change" and κίνησις (that is, change in place, quality or magnitude) by "motion". But I leave ἀρχή untranslated. The term refers to something which, on the one hand, determines a "beginning" but, on the other hand, is also a "governing" agency (see Fritsche 2010). None of the two specifications is evidently off the point here. But far more context would be required for determining the way they are related to each other. As Fritsche (2010, 11) rightly notes, "the variety of the meanings of the expression [viz, 'principle of motion', *GH*] depends on the variety of the determinations of motions."

(A) "on the assumption that *phusis* is a certain principle, in the sense of a cause, of the thing to be moved and at rest in which it [i.e. the principle] is present primarily as such and not by coincidence."[111]

The formula contained in (A), viz.

(D) "*Phusis* is a certain principle, in the sense of a cause, of the thing to be moved and at rest in which it [i.e. the principle] is present primarily as such and not by coincidence,"

will subsequently be adopted by Aristotle as a definition of *phusis*.[112] By contrast, (A) states no definition but an assumption which underlies the preceding discussion – and in the light of which that discussion must be reread.[113] In (A), *phusis* is not a definiendum but has a meaning which corresponds to the preceding use of the term. That is to say, *phusis* is just the *phusis* by virtue of which things are *phusei onta*. In addition, it is tacitly presupposed that:

(P) The *phusis* by virtue of which things are *phusei onta* is the *phusis* they have.

Thus, (A) boils down to the claim that the difference observed between the things listed as natural on the one hand and beds and shirts on the other is a mark to distinguish natural things.

Importantly, the latter claim is not derived from the observation recorded earlier. Granted that bees have an internal *archê* of motion and rest whereas beds have not, and that this is an observable fact, there is still a question of generalisability. That the difference thus observed is a mark to distinguish natural things does not follow. The generalisation required is part of the hypothesis by which the what-is-it of the subject matter of *phusikê* is taken for granted.

What it is in *Phys* II 1 to be "by nature" (*phusei*) is not easy to spell out. In his first summary, Aristotle claims to have explained the meaning of "by nature and according to nature."[114] He does not indicate a distinction between the two

---

111 *Ph.* II 1, 192b20-23: ὡς οὔσης τῆς φύσεως ἀρχῆς τινὸς καὶ αἰτίας τοῦ κινεῖσθαι καὶ ἠρεμεῖν ἐν ᾧ ὑπάρχει πρώτως καθ' αὑτὸ καὶ μὴ κατὰ συμβεβηκός. For the grammar, see Fritsche 2010, 25: κινεῖσθαι etc. is accusative with infinitive, depending on τοῦ, and with the relative clause ἐν ᾧ etc. as subject.

112 *Ph.* II 1, 192b32: "φύσις is what was said (τὸ ῥηθέν)."

113 The sentence does not begin with ὥστε but with ὡς, followed by genitivus absolutus. On the meaning of this see LSJ, lemma ὡς, C I 3; and Kühner/Gerth 1898–1904, II 93 f. According to Wardy (1993, 27; on *Ph.* II 2, 194a34), "ὡς plus participle is the ideal Greek construction for *not* making a commitment" (emphasis his). But Aristotle is surely committed to the definition of φύσις involved.

114 *Ph.* II 1, 193a2: τί τὸ φύσει καὶ κατὰ φύσιν. Note that the scope of the definite article (which may be read as a substitute for inverted commas here) comprises not just φύσει but φύσει καὶ κατὰ φύσιν.

PERI PHUSEÔS: PHYSICS, PHYSICISTS, AND *PHUSIS* IN ARISTOTLE

phrases and, as a matter of fact, explains only the latter. "According to nature" (*kata phusin*) are (i) things which have a nature and (ii) their essential attributes.[115] The latter, he adds, "have no nature but are by nature and according to nature."[116] In sum, I agree with Ross that "... here and elsewhere, Aristotle seems to intend no distinction" between *phusei* and *kata phusin*.[117] Hence, the things classified as *phusei* at the beginning of *Physics* II 1 are just the things which have a *phusis*, and are therefore referred to in the sequel by such phrases as "things that have an internal *archê* of motion and change."[118]

Aristotle has already established in *Physics* I 7 that matter and form are the principles out of which natural things "are and have come into being primarily and not by coincidence, but each thing as it is referred to according to its *ousia*."[119] Hence, both matter and form meet the corresponding requirement mentioned in (D). But it goes without saying that this – to belong "primarily" to the thing in question – is just an additional requirement. The basic requirement is to be a principle of motion and rest. Hence, the matter of which a thing consists and the form by virtue of which it is a specimen of its kind are just candidates for being the *phusis* of that thing.

Surprisingly, the subsequent discussion concerning matter and form does without that basic requirement. A kind of substitute is Antiphon's heritability test.[120] *Phusis* is heritable. Assuming that a wooden bed is buried and sprouts, the product will be wood, not a bed. Hence, to be constituted of wood belongs to the *phusis* of the bed, but to exhibit such artificial features as are customary for beds does not. Aristotle takes this to argue that in general, matter is the *phusis* and *ousia* of natural things,[121] and (if matter is reduced to elements)

---

115   *Ph.* II 1, 192b35-36 – "things which have a nature": ταῦτα (b35), referring back to ὅσα τοιαύ-την ἔχει ἀρχήν (b33).

116   *Ph.* II 1, 193a1: ... οὐδ' ἔχει φύσιν, φύσει δὲ καὶ κατὰ φύσιν ἐστίν.

117   Ross 1936, 501 (on 192a36-193a1).

118   In particular, τῶν φύσει ὄντων (*Ph.* II 1, 193a10; *Metaph.* V 4, 1014b19 and passim) is equivalent with τῶν ἐχόντων ἐν αὐτοῖς ἀρχὴν κινήσεως καὶ μεταβολῆς (*Ph.* II 1, 193a29-30) or τῶν ἐχόντων ἀρχὴν κινήσεως ἐν αὐτοῖς ᾗ αὐτά (*Metaph.* V4, 1015a14-15), respectively.

119   *Ph.* I 7, 190b17-20 (see above n. 95) – "not by coincidence ...": μὴ κατὰ συμβεβηκὸς ἀλλ' ἕκαστον ὃ λέγεται κατὰ τὴν οὐσίαν.

120   *Ph.* II 1, 193a12-17. It is difficult to extract any information concerning Antiphon from Aristotle's report. The thought experiment is probably Antiphon's; κλίνης φύσις τὸ ξύλον (a11) is probably Aristotle's shorthand for something in Antiphon; of course, κατὰ νόμον sounds like Antiphon (cf. DK 87 B 44, passim): Antiphon's conclusion may have contained something like φύσει ξύλον, νόμῳ κλίνη. By contrast, οὐσία ("substance") is probably Aristotle's catchword for the materialist theories he finds supported by Antiphon's thought experiment. Kelsey who attributes the focus on substance to Antiphon (2015, 34) seems to miss the point in Aristotle's subscription to the heritability test (ibid. 35n4).

121   *Ph.* II 1, 193a9-11.

that "the whole *ousia*" is elements, and the rest is just transitory facts about elements.[122] In the sequel, Aristotle seems to subscribe to the heritability test. Forms of natural things are heritable. His slogan that "from human, human comes into being" is a paradigm case analogous to Antiphon's claim that from wood, wood comes into being. Granted that matter passes the heritability test and hence counts as nature, this will therefore also apply to form.[123]

The heritability claim quoted is just a variant of the stronger principle that "human begets human" presupposed in the *Metaphysics* account of natural becoming.[124] Only the latter version attributes causal efficacy to form. That is to say, two different functions are attributed to form. Becoming is by something and of something.[125] On the one hand, natural becoming is the becoming of some y with a certain form F which is the *phusis* of y.[126] On the other hand, the becoming is effected by this same form F insofar as it is also the *phusis* of some x different from y.[127] In a sense, this is just a restatement of the claim in *Physics* II 7 that form, mover, and end often coincide.[128] But the *Metaphysics* is more explicit about one crucial point: that the mover is F, the form, rather than x, the thing which instantiates F.[129]

In outline, Aristotle's answer to Plato is this: human begets human. Hence, divine craftsmanship has no business in the generation of natural things. Nor has divine reason (*nous*) in the preservation of universal order. Forms are natures. In Plato, for a form (*eidos*) to be a nature (*phusis*) is to provide a standard

---

122 *Ph.* II 1, 193a17-28. This, of course, is the materialistic theory of Plato's opponents in *Laws* X.

123 *Ph.* II 1, 193b8-12, "from human, human": γίγνεται γὰρ ἐξ ἀνθρώπου ἄνθρωπος (b12; similarly b8).

124 *Metaph.* VII 7, 1032a25: ἄνθρωπος γὰρ ἄνθρωπον γεννᾷ; "natural becoming": cf. ibid. a16: γενέσεις ... φυσικαί.

125 *Metaph.* VII 7, 1032a13-14: ὑπό ... τινος, τί. I am skipping ἔκ τινος (a14), which refers to matter here but in Aristotle's formula for heritability may refer to the antecedent both qua matter and form (see above on *Ph.* II 1, 193b8-12: wood from wood and human from human).

126 *Metaph.* VII 7, 1032a23: τὸ γὰρ γιγνόμενον ἔχει φύσιν, οἷον φυτὸν ἢ ζῷον.

127 *Metaph.* VII 7, 1032a24-25: ὑφ᾽ οὗ ἡ κατὰ τὸ εἶδος λεγομένη φύσις ἡ ὁμοειδής (αὕτη δὲ ἐν ἄλλῳ). Note that the cause is equated with F rather than x.

128 *Ph.* II 7, 198a24-27 ("mover" is my shorthand for τὸ ὅθεν ἡ κίνησις πρῶτον, a26). Here, too, Aristotle adduces the the stronger principle that "human begets human" (a25-26).

129 According to *Ph.* II 7, the mover is "equal in form" (τῷ εἴδει ταὐτό, 198a26) with the what-is-it (τὸ τί ἐστι, i.e. form) and the what-for (τὸ οὗ ἕνεκα, i.e. end). This leaves much open but should probably be read against the background of the rule stated at *Ph.* II 3, 195b21-25 which privileges the most specific cause (τὸ αἴτιον ἑκάστου τὸ ἀκρότατον, b22), which is either x qua instantiating F, or F qua being instantiated by, and being the φύσις of, x. The alternative depends (modulo "art imitates nature") on whether τοῦτο, b24, refers to ἄνθρωπος qua οἰκοδόμος κατὰ τὴν οἰκοδομικήν or to οἰκοδομική.

of correctness either in craftsmanship (*technê*) or in other activities which Plato conceives on that model. According to Aristotle, for a form to be a nature is to be so instantiated in things as to function as both mover and end. Hence, Aristotle's inquiry into nature (*peri phuseôs*) is an inquiry into the way form functions as mover and end. The straightforward interpretation of this worn out formula is just to the point.[130]

So far, this is still a program for Aristotelian natural science.[131] Its execution is beyond the scope of this paper. But one remark is in order. As Kelsey has convincingly argued, the point in *Physics* II 7 is "that form is a principle of movement, primarily by being an end."[132] Hence, forms are unmoved movers.[133] So the question as to how form functions as mover and end may boil down to a question about the functioning of unmoved movers, of which the origin of animal motion in a thermic reaction to the representation of a desirable object is just one case.[134] The example is telling: one has to engage with the details of Aristotelian science in order to understand what it is for a form to be a nature according to Aristotle.

I have interpreted Aristotle's account of nature as a reaction to Plato, who in turn reacted to early Greek philosophy and especially to its 4th century reception. What Aristotle offers is both a rejection and a variant of Plato's criticism. It is a rejection in one respect which may appear as a mere matter of rhetoric but betrays a commitment. Inquirers into nature are "them" for Plato, but "us" for Aristotle.[135] And Aristotle means it. On the one hand, when it comes to ask whether it belongs to the *phusikos* to treat a topic, the *phusikoi* provide the examples he follows.[136] On the other hand, his criticism usually presupposes a shared point of view. This is even the case when Aristotle comments that Empedocles, in his account of the formation of bone, "says nothing about nature."[137] Aristotle's criticism is that Empedocles does not explain the regularity

---

130   See above section 1.

131   I agree with Fritsche (2010, 29) that Aristotle's account of φύσις in *Ph.* II 1 "just formulates a research project".

132   Kelsey 2015, 41.

133   See *Ph.* II 7, 198b1-4. The what-is-it (τὸ τί ἐστιν) and the form (μορφή) function as end (τέλος) and what-for (οὗ ἕνεκα) and, hence, are something which "moves without being in motion" (κινεῖ μὴ κινούμενον). Note that divinity (τὸ ... παντελῶς ἀκίνητον καὶ πάντων πρῶτον, b2-3) is not at all Aristotle's paradigm case of an unmoved mover.

134   *De motu an.* 8, 701b33-35. The representation is an unmoved mover: οὐ κινούμενον κινεῖ (*De motu an.* 6, 700b35; cf. *De an.* III 10, 433b11-12).

135   "Them": Λέγουσί πού τινες (*Leg.* X, 888e4); "us": φαμέν (*Ph.* II 1, 192b12). See above.

136   See, e.g., the discussion in *Ph.* III 4, 202b36-203b4.

137   *Gen. corr.* II 6, 333b18: οὐδὲν ... περὶ φύσεως λέγει. Note that the allusion is not just to a book title but to the fact that Empedocles ranked as a paradigmatic writer on that topic.

in the formation of bone, that is (on Empedoclean premises), of the maintenance of a certain proportion (*logos*) in the mixture of elements. Aristotle's account of natural becoming would therefore apply. Regularity must be explained in terms of *ousia* and *phusis*, "about which he says nothing."[138] There is no point in asking whether Aristotle's criticism does justice to Empedocles. Aristotle's agenda is different, and rightly so. His reaction to the shortcomings he finds in his predecessors is at the same time his way to bring out, and to secure, the continuity of Aristotelian science with early Greek philosophy.

Bibliography

Aristoteles Graece, rec. I. Bekker . 1831. (= *Aristotelis opera*, ed. Academia Regia Borussia, vol. I, II), Berlin.

Bandini, Michele/Dorion, Louis-André. 2000. *Xénophon: Mémorables*, tome 1, Paris: Les belles lettres.

Beardslee, J.W., Jr. 1918. *The Use of* physis *in Fifth-Century Greek Literature*, Diss. Chicago.

Bernabé, Alberto. 2007. "Papyrus Derveni", in: *Poetae Epici Graeci. Testimonia et Fragmenta*, pars II, fasc. 3, ed. Albertus Bernabé, (Bibliotheca Teubneriana), Berlin-New York: De Gruyter, p. 169–269, 315–328.

Bernabé, Alberto. 2017. "En torno a la φύσις ¿Que entendian los griegos por φυσικός?", *Archai* nº 21, sep.-dec. 2017, 39–78, https://doi.org/10.14195/1984-249X_21_2.

Breitenbach, Ludwig. 1889. *Xenophons Memorabilien*, 6. Aufl. bearbeitet von R. Mücke, Berlin: Weidmann.

Bremer, Dieter. 1989. "Von der Physis zur Natur. Eine griechische Konzeption und ihr Schicksal", *Z. philos. Forschung* 43, 241–264.

Buchheim, Thomas. 1989. *Gorgias von Leontinoi. Reden, Fragmente und Testimonien*, Hamburg.

Buchheim, Thomas. 1999. "Vergängliches Werden und sich bildende Form. Überlegungen zum frühgriechischen Naturbegriff", *Archiv für Begriffsgeschichte* 41, 7–34.

Buchheim, Thomas. 2010. *Aristoteles. Über Werden und Vergehen*, übers. und erl. (Aristoteles. Werke in deutscher Übersetzung, begr. von E. Grumach, fortges. von H. Flashar, hg. von Chr. Rapp, Bd. 12, Teil IV), Berlin: Akademie Verlag – Darmstadt: wbg.

Burnet, John. 1930. *Early Greek Philosophy*, 4th ed. London.

---

138   *Gen. corr.* II 6, 333b4-18 (quotation of b18: περὶ ἧς οὐδὲν λέγει, b18). Aristotle's reference is probably DK 31 B 96 (of which he quotes lines 1–3 at *De an.* I 5, 410a4-6). Note that "bone" is a kind of stuff here.

Cooper, John M. 2012. "Conclusion – and Retrospect: *Metaphysics* A 10", in: *Aristotle's Metaphysics Alpha. Symposium Aristotelicum*, ed. by C. Steel, with a new edition of the Greek text by O. Primavesi, Oxford etc.: OUP.

Diller, Hans. 1939. "Der griechische Naturbegriff", *Neue Jahrbücher für antike und deutsche Bildung* 2 (=114) 241–257.

Dindorf, Ludwig. 1862. *Xenophontis Memorabilia Socratis* accedit *Anonymi Apologia Socratis*, Oxford.

DK = Diels, Hermann und Kranz, Walter [DK]. 1956. *Die Fragmente der Vorsokratiker*, 8. Aufl. hg. von W. Kranz, Berlin.

Ferrari, Franco. 2014. "Democritus, Heraclitus, and the Dead Souls: Reconstructing Columns I–VI of the Derveni Papyrus", in: *Poetry as Initiation. The Center for Hellenic Studies Symposium on the Derveni Papyrus*, edited by Ioanna Papadopoulou and Leonard Muellner, Washington, DC: Center for Hellenic Studies, Distributed by Harvard University Press, Cambridge, Massachusetts, and London, England, 53–66.

Fränkel, Hermann. 1969. *Dichtung und Philosophie des frühen Griechentums*, 3. durchges. Aufl., repr. München 1976.

Frede, Michael und Patzig, Günther. 1988. *Aristoteles, Metaphysik Zeta*, 2 Bde., München.

Fritsche, Johannes. 2010. "Aristotle's usage of ἀρχὴ κινήσεως ('principle of motion') and the two definitions of nature in *Physics* II, 1", *Arch. Begriffsgeschichte* 52, 7–31.

Graeser, Andreas. 1989. "Die Vorsokratiker", in: *Klassiker der Naturphilosophie*, hg. von G. Böhme, München: Beck 1989, 13–28.

Guthrie, W.K.C. 1962, repr. 1988. *A History of Greek Philosophy*, vol. 1, *The earlier Presocratics and the Pythagoreans*, Cambridge.

Guthrie, W.K.C. 1965, repr. 1990. *A History of Greek Philosophy*, vol. 2, *The Presocratic tradition from Parmenides to Democritus*, Cambridge.

Harriman, Benjamin. 2015. "The Beginning of Melissus' *On Nature or on What-Is*: A Reconstruction", *Journal of Hellenic Studies* 135, 19–34.

Heidel, W.A. 1910. *Peri physeos*. A Study of the Conception of Nature Among the Pre-Socratics, *Proc. Amer. Acad. Arts and Sciences*, Vol. 45, no. 4.

Heinemann, Gottfried. 2000. "Natural Knowledge in the Hippocratic Treatise *On Ancient Medicine*", in: *Antike Naturwissenschaft und ihre Rezeption*, Bd. 10, hg. von J. Althoff et al., Trier, 13–41.

Heinemann, Gottfried. 2001. *Studien zum griechischen Naturbegriff*, Teil I: *Philosophische Grundlegung: Der Naturbegriff und die "Natur"*, Trier.

Heinemann, Gottfried. 2002. " 'Naturen' und 'Naturgesetze' ", in: *Antike Naturwissenschaft und ihre Rezeption*, Bd. 12, hg. von J. Althoff et al., Trier, 45–67.

Heinemann, Gottfried. 2005. "Die Entwicklung des Begriffs *physis* bis Aristoteles", in: *Physik-Mechanik*, hg. von A. Schürmann (*Geschichte der Mathematik und der Naturwissenschaften in der Antike*, hg. von G. Wöhrle, Bd. 3), Stuttgart: Steiner, 2005, 16–60.

Heinemann, Gottfried. 2006a. "Aristoteles und die Unverfügbarkeit der 'Natur'", in: *Umwelt-Handeln. Zum Zusammenhang von Naturphilosophie und Umweltethik*, hg. von K. Köchy und M. Norwig (*Lebenswissenschaft im Dialog*, Bd. 2), Freiburg-München: Alber, 167–205.

Heinemann, Gottfried. 2006b. "Natur und Regularität. Anmerkungen zum voraristotelischen Naturbegriff", in: *Naturgesetze. Historisch-systematische Analysen eines wissenschaftlichen Grundbegriffs*, hg. von K. Hartbecke und Chr. Schütte, Paderborn: mentis 2006, 37–53.

Heinemann, Gottfried. 2007. "*Physis* in *Republic* V, 471c – VII, 541c", in: *The Ascent to the Good* (Proc. Conf. Madrid-Getafe, Apr. 2003), ed. by F. Lisi, St. Augustin: Academia Verlag, 65–78.

Heinemann, Gottfried. 2016a. "Vom Wert der Vielheit in pluralistischen Kosmologien. Notizen zu Aristoteles (mit Fußnoten zu Thomas von Aquin und Whitehead)", in: *Wünschenswerte Vielheit. Diversität als Kategorie, Befund und Norm*, hg. von Th. Kirchhoff und K. Köchy (*Lebenswissenschaft im Dialog*, Bd. 21), Freiburg-München: Alber, 23–58.

Heinemann, Gottfried. 2016b. " 'Besser ... nach Maßgabe der Substanz des jeweiligen Gegenstandes' (*Phys.* 198b8-9). Innere und äußere Finalität bei Aristoteles", in: *Aristoteles und die moderne Biologie*, hg. von R. Timme und G. Heinemann, Freiburg-München: Alber, 225–278.

Heinemann, Gottfried. 2016c. "Time as 'measure'. Aristotle's non-metrical account of time in *Physics* IV", in: *Le temps chez Aristote*, cinquième rencontre aristotélicienne (Thessalonique, 12–15 Mai 2012), textes réunies et publiés par D. Sfendoni-Mentzou, Paris: Vrin – Bruxelles: Ousia 2016, 39–68.

Heinemann, Gottfried. 2019. "Sterbliche und unsterbliche Natur: Kontexte eines vielzitierten Euripides-Fragments", in: *Grenzen des Menschseins – Sterblichkeit und Unsterblichkeit im frühgriechischen Denken*, hg. von V. Bachmann und R. Heimann, Wiesbaden: Springer vs, 13–37.

Heinimann, Felix. 1945. *Nomos und Physis*, repr. Darmstadt 1980.

Heinimann, Felix. 1976. "Eine vorplatonische Theorie der *techne*" (1961), in: *Sophistik*, hg. von C.J. Classen, Darmstadt 1976, 127–169.

Herzhoff, B. 2016. "Wer war der Peripatetiker Nikolaos, der Verfasser des Kompendiums der Philosophie des Aristoteles und Bearbeiter seiner Schrift über die Pflanzen?", in: Althoff, J./Föllinger, S./Wöhrle, G. (Hg.): *Antike Naturwissenschaft und ihre Rezeption*, Bd. 26, Trier, 135–187.

Holwerda, Douwe. 1955. *Commentatio de vocis quae est PHYSIS vi atque usu praesertim in Graecitate Aristotele anteriore*, Diss. Groningen.

Huffman, Carl A. 1993. *Philolaus of Croton: Pythagorean and Presocratic*, a commentary on the fragments and testimonia with interpretive essays. Cambridge.

Janko, Richard. 2001. "The Derveni Papyrus (Diagoras of Melos, *Apopirgizontes logoi?*): A New Translation", *Classical Philology* 96, 1–30.

Janko, Richard. 2002. "The Derveni Papyrus: an Interim Text", *ZPE* 141, 1–62.

Janko, Richard. 2008. "Reconstructing (Again) the Opening of the Derveni Papyrus", *ZPE* 166, 37–51.

Janko, Richard. 2016. "Parmenides in the Derveni Papyrus: New Images for a New Edition", *ZPE* 200, 3–23.

Jouanna, Jacques. 1988. *Hippocrate, Des vents, De l'art*, Texte établi et traduit par J. Jouanna, Paris.

Jouanna, Jacques. 1990. *Hippocrate. De l'ancienne médecine*, Texte établi et traduit, Paris.

Kahn, Charles H. 1960. *Anaximander and the Origins of Greek Cosmology*, New York.

Kelsey, Sean. 2015. "Aristotle on interpreting nature", in: *Aristotle's Physics. A Critical Guide*, ed. by M. Leunissen, CUP, 31–45.

Kerferd, G.B. 1981. *The Sophistic Movement*, Cambridge.

Kirk, G.S. 1962. *Heraclitus. The Cosmic Fragments*, 2nd. ed. Cambridge.

Kosman, L.A. 1987. "Animals and other beings in Aristotle", in: *Philosophical issues in Aristotle's biology*. Ed. by A. Gotthelf and J.G. Lennox. Cambridge, New York: Cambridge University Press 1987, 360–391.

Kotwick, Mirjam E. 2017. *Der Papyrus von Derveni*, gr./dt., eingeleitet, übersetzt und kommentiert, basierend auf einem griechischen Text von Richard Janko, Berlin/Boston: De Gruyter.

KPT = Kouremenos, Theokritos/Parassoglou, George M./Tsantsanoglou, Kyriakos. 2006. *The Derveni Papyrus*, ed. with introd. and comm., Firenze: Olschki.

KRS = Kirk, G. et. al. 1983. *The Presocratic Philosophers*, 2nd. ed. Cambridge.

Kühner, Raphael and Gerth, Bernhard. 1898–1904, repr. 2015. *Ausführliche Grammatik der griechischen Sprache*, 3. Aufl., Zweiter Teil: *Satzlehre*, 2 Bde. Darmstadt: wbg.

Lennox, James G. 1997. "Material and Formal Natures in Aristotle's *De partibus animalium*", in: *Aristotelische Biologie*, hg. von W. Kullmann und S. Föllinger (Philosophie der Antike, Bd. 6), Stuttgart 1997, 163–181.

Lennox, James G. 2010.: "*Bios* and Explanatory Unity in Aristotle's Biology", in: *Definition in Ancient Philosophy*, ed. by D. Charles, OUP, 329–355.

Lennox, James G. 2015. "How to study natural bodies: Aristotle's *methodos*", in: *Aristotle's Physics. A Critical Guide*, ed. by M. Leunissen, CUP, 10–30.

Lesher, J.H. 1999. "Early Interest in Knowledge", in: *The Cambridge Companion to Early Greek Philosophy*, ed. by A.A. Long, CUP, 225–249.

Littrè, Émile. 1839–1861. *Oeuvres complètes d'Hippocrate: Traduction nouvelle avec le texte grec*, 10 vols., Paris.

LM = Laks, André/Most, Glenn. 2016. *Early Greek Philosophy*, 9 vols. (Loeb Classical Library 524–532), Cambridge, Mass. – London: Harvard U. Pr.

Long, A.A. 1999. "The Scope of Early Greek Philosophy", in: *The Cambridge Companion to Early Greek Philosophy*, ed. by A.A. Long, CUP, 1–21.

Lovejoy, A.O. 1909. "The Meaning of Φύσις in the Greek Physiologers", *The Philosophical Review* 18, 369–383.

LSJ = Liddell, Henry G. und Scott, Robert. 1968, repr. 1989. *A Greek-English Lexicon*, rev. by H.S. Jones et al., with a Supplement, Oxford.

Mannsperger, Dietrich. 1969. *Physis bei Platon*, Berlin.

Mansfeld, Jaap. 2016. "Melissus between Miletus and Elea", in: Jaap Mansfeld et al, *Melissus between Miletus and Elea* (*Eleatica* 2012), a cura di Massimo Pulpito, St. Augustin: Academia.

Most, Glenn W. 1987. "Alcman's 'Cosmogonic' Fragment (Fr. 5 Page, 81 Calame)", *CQ* 37.1,. 1–19.

Mouraviev, Serge. 1997. "Titres, sous-titres et articulations du livre d'Héraclite d'Éphese", in: *Titres et articulations du texte dans les oeuvres antiques*. Actes du Colloque International de Chantilly 13–15 decembre 1994, éd. par J.-C. Fredouille et al., Paris: Institut d'Études Augustiniennes – Turnhout: Brepols, 35–53.

Naddaf, Gerard. 1992. *L'origine et l'evolution du concept grec de physis*, Lewiston, NY etc.

Naddaf, Gerard. 1997. "Plato and the Περὶ φύσεως tradition", in: *Interpreting the* Timaeus – Critias, Proc. IV Symposium Platonicum, ed. by T. Calvo and L. Brisson, Sankt Augustin: Academia 1997, 27–36.

Naddaf, Gerard. 2005. *The Greek Concept of Nature*, Albany: SUNY Pr.

Nethercut, Jason S. 2017. "Empedocles' 'Roots' in Lucretius' *De rerum natura*", *American Journal of Philology* 138, 85–105.

Newiger, Hans-Joachim. 1973. Untersuchungen zu Gorgias' Schrift Über das Nichtseiende, Berlin – New York: De Gruyter.

Nussbaum, Martha C. 1985. *Aristotle's De motu animalium* (1978), pbk repr., with corr., Princeton: U. Pr.

Palmer, John. 2009. *Parmenides and Presocratic Philosophy*, Oxford: OUP.

Patzer, Harald. 1939/93. Physis. Grundlegung zu einer Geschichte des Wortes (Habilitationsschrift Marburg 1939), Stuttgart 1993.

Piano, Valeria. 2016a. *Il papiro di Derveni tra religione e filosofia* (*STCPF – Studi e testi per il Corpus dei papiri filosofici greci e latini*, 18) Firenze: Leo S. Olschki.

Piano, Valeria. 2016b. "P.Derveni III-VI: una riconsiderazione del testo", *ZPE* 197, 5–16.

Primavesi, Oliver. 2007. "Zur Überlieferung und Bedeutung des Empedokleischen Titels 'Katharmoi' ", in: Katharsiskonzeptionen vor Aristoteles. Zum kulturellen Hintergrund des Tragödiensatzes, hg. von M. Vöhler und B. Seidensticker, 2007. Berlin – New York: De Gruyter, 183–225.

Ross, W.D. 1936. Aristotle's Physics. A revised text with introduction and commentary by W.D. Ross, Oxford: Clarendon, repr. 1998 (Sandpiper Books).

Rossetti, Livio. 2006. "Caratteristiche tipologiche dei trattati Περι φύσεως nei secoli VI-V a.C.", *Noua tellus* 24.2, 111–146.

ROT = *The Complete Works of Aristotle. The Revised Oxford Translation (ROT)*. 1984. ed. by J. Barnes, Princeton.

Schmalzriedt, Egidius. 1970. ΠΕΡΙ ΦΥΣΕΩΣ. Zur Frühgeschichte der Buchtitel, München.

Sedley, David. 1998. (pbk. ed. 2003) *Lucretius and the Transformation of Greek Wisdom*, CUP.

Sedley, David. 2007. *Creationism and Its Critics in Antiquity*, Berkeley etc.: U. of California Pr.

Sider, David. 1997. "Heraclitus in the Derveni Papyrus", in: *Studies on the Derveni Papyrus*, ed. by A. Laks and G. Most, Oxford, 129–148.

Smith, Josiah R. 1903. *Xenophon: Memorabilia*, Boston etc.: Ginn.

Solmsen, Friedrich. 1960. *Aristotle's* System of the Physical World. A Comparison with His Predecessors, Ithaca, N.Y.

Stavrianeas, Stasinos. 2015. "Nature as a principle of change", in: *Aristotle's Physics. A Critical Guide*, ed. by M. Leunissen, CUP, 46–65.

Thimme, Otto. 1935. *physis, tropos, êthos. Semasiologische Untersuchung über die Auffassung des menschlichen Wesens (Charakters) in der älteren griechischen Literatur*, Diss. Göttingen.

Tor, Shaul. 2017. *Mortal and Divine in Early Greek Epistemology: A Study of Hesiod, Xenophanes and Parmenides (Cambridge Classical Studies)* Cambridge.

Vlastos, Gregory. 1975. *Plato's* Universe, Oxford.

von Staden, Heinrich. 1998. "Dynamis: the Hippocatics and Plato", in: *Philosophy and Medicine*, ed. by K.J. Boudouris, vol. II, Athens, 262–279.

Wardy, Robert. 1993. "Aristotelian Rainfall or the Lore of Averages", *Phronesis* 38.1, 18–30.

West, M.L. 1971. *Early Greek Philosophy and the Orient*, Oxford: Clarendon.

Zhmud, Leonid. 2018. "*Physis* in the Pythagorean Tradition", *Philologia Classica* 13.1, 50–68.

CHAPTER 2

Plato's Reception of Presocratic Natural Philosophy

Andrew D. Gregory

It is commonly thought that the *locus classicus* and most evident place to start for Plato's reception of presocratic natural philosophy (PSNP) is the passage known as Socrates' autobiography *Phaedo* 96a ff. Here Socrates talks of his early interest in *peri phuseôs historian*, the "enquiry concerning nature," followed by his subsequent disenchantment with this type of enquiry.[1] He is then excited by the possibility of explanation in terms of *nous* in the works of Anaxagoras, but is disappointed with the results and so takes up his *deuteros plous*, the "second sailing." Undeniably this is important evidence, but in what follows I wish to press two points. Firstly, I would caution against a too stereotypical interpretation of the *Phaedo* passage, such that it is seen as a blanket condemnation of all PSNP. Secondly, the *Phaedo* passage is far from being our only source of information on Plato's attitude to PSNP, or indeed the most interesting or most important source. Subsequent to these points, I will argue that Plato is not uniformly critical of all PSNP either in the *Phaedo* or elsewhere. I will also argue that Plato has more than one critique of PSNP and importantly Plato has more than one taxonomy for PSNP. These critiques and taxonomies are related to those of the *Phaedo*, (note the plurals here) but they are not identical and have some subtle and interesting differences which allow us a much richer account of Plato's reception of PSNP. Plato's reactions to PSNP also point to some interesting facts about PSNP.

1 Caution

I will begin with some words of caution. Plato was not, and indeed made no claim to be a historian of PSNP or presocratic philosophy more generally. As with Aristotle, there are issues concerning how we should treat what Plato tells us about the presocratics and how we should understand his attitude to them.[2]

---

1 How the autobiography of Plato's character Socrates relates to that of the historical Socrates is open to question, cf. Aristophanes *Clouds* 230 ff., Plato *Apology* 19b-d and 26d.

2 On Aristotle, see H. Cherniss 1935 *Aristotle's Criticism of Presocratic Philosophy*. Baltimore: John Hopkins Press, and the debate that has followed, on Plato see M.M. McCabe. *Plato and His Predecessors*. Cambridge U.P., 2000.

© KONINKLIJKE BRILL NV, LEIDEN, 2021 | DOI:10.1163/9789004443358_004

At least in part this is tied up with the issues of what Plato was attempting to do with his dialogues and the arguments he gave to his interlocutors, issues which we can hardly settle here. Did Plato faithfully record the views of the presocratics as he understood them? Even here, the "as he understood them" may be problematic, as with Aristotle.[3] Or did Plato caricature some presocratic views into more extreme positions for his interlocutors, for his own dialectical/ philosophical/dramatic purposes? Was the presocratic person or the presocratic idea the main focus for Plato?[4] This issue is made more problematic by the fragmentary and contested state of the evidence on PSNP (and the fact that sometimes Plato's works are part of that evidence) such that in places it is difficult to give a definitive answer.[5] This is exacerbated by that fact that Plato rarely named presocratic thinkers.[6] Plato may well have alluded to some or indeed many of them, but evidence of allusion is notoriously difficult to deal with.[7] We do not have, and indeed there may not be clear cut criteria for deciding on whether a passage alludes to a previous thinker or not. A further consideration here is whether it is possible for us, nearly 2,500 years distant from Plato's milieu, to pick up all the resonances and nuances of allusions. I will also add a word of caution in that views on Plato's own natural philosophy vary widely. Those who believe that Plato had no interest in generating a serious natural philosophy of his own are likely to find the view that Plato dismissed PSNP as a whole a conducive one. So beware that I take the view that Plato did take the possibility of giving his own account of nature seriously and in line with that I find the idea that he had a varied and sophisticated reception of PSNP attractive.[8] While the "no interest" view is rare in its extreme form now, there is

---

3 The standard complaint about Aristotle is that he saw the presocratics very much in the terms of his own philosophical structures and categories.

4 One might argue that this is complex as at least the dramatic portrayal of persons is related to their philosophical ideas in Plato, e.g. the appearance/disappearance of Protagoras' head in the *Theaetetus*.

5 In relation to the *Phaedo* at least, there is clear reference to the Pythagoreans and Sedley, D. Platonic Causes, *Phronesis* 43, 1998, pp. 114–132, J. Bryan. *Likeness and Likelihood in the Presocratics and Plato*. Cambridge UP, 2015, G. S. Betegh. *Greek Philosophy and Religion*. A companion to ancient philosophy/edited by Mary Louise Gill and Pierre Pellegrin. London: Blackwell 2016, have all made cases for other interesting precursors.

6 See Rosemary Wright's chapter in this volume. There are further questions here. What reason did Plato have for naming some previous thinkers and not others? What reason did Plato have for naming them in some passages but not others where it can be argued that they are clearly alluded to?

7 E.g., is Empedocles alluded to/critiqued in the myth of the reversing cosmos in the *Politicus*?

8 See A. D. Gregory. *Plato's Philosophy of Science*. London: Duckworth, 2000. *Ancient Greek Cosmogony*. London: Duckworth, 2007.

a wide spectrum of views on how interested Plato was in giving an account of the natural world and what sort of status such an account had for him.[9]

1.1   Peri Phuseôs Historian

It is of critical importance for our understanding of Plato's reception of PSNP that we are clear about the meaning of this phrase at *Phaedo* 96a8. *Historian* is relatively unproblematic, though I prefer "enquiry" to "investigation" as giving a looser, less methodologically rigid and more philosophical sense to the project which I believe to be appropriate.[10] Burnet's "natural history" has too many resonances with the nineteenth century discipline and overly restricts the sense of *historia*.[11] The real issue here though is the Greek term *phusis*, literally "nature," with the cognate terms *phusikoi* and *phusiologoi*, literally "naturalists" and "those who talk about nature." It is highly misleading here to translate *phusis* as "physics" or something similar, or to translate *phusikoi* or *phusiologoi* as "physicists."[12] PSNP was much broader than any modern conception of physics, including e.g. zoogony and meteorology. This should be clear from any cursory inspection of PSNP and what is included in works titled "*Peri Phuseôs.*"[13] It should also be clear from Plato at *Phaedo* 96a5 where the questions Socrates first mentions in relation to *peri phuseôs historian* are to do with coming to be, existing and perishing, zoogony, psychology, epistemology and cosmology. Physics/physicist also has connotations of physicalism or materialism, that is someone who believes the world to consist of physical or material entities only. Again, for many thinkers who would ordinarily be counted within the canon of PSNP, that is not so. Anaxagoras and *nous* would be a key example here, not least because Plato recognised Anaxagoras and *nous* as part of PSNP. So too physics/physicist carries methodological connotations (that the work is, e.g. empirical or experimental) which are inappropriate for PSNP.

---

9   Some would say the simple fact that Plato wrote the *Timaeus* attests to his interest in natural philosophy, others on the contrary that the 'likely tale' or *muthos logos* status of the account is problematic and/or that the account is largely taken from Pythagorean sources.

10   I would avoid the idea that there was a unitary investigation of nature rather than methodological diversity among the presocratics and 'investigation' may imply a more empirical approach than was actually the case.

11   There is not much to be gleaned from Plato's other uses of *historia* and its cognates (*Phaedrus* 244c9, *Cratylus* 437b1, *Sophist* 267e2) other than he is generally positive about it. Whether *peri phuseôs historian* is Plato's own phrase or a term he has picked up from some other source is unknown.

12   Cf. Gottfried Heinemann's chapter in this volume.

13   The '*Peri Phuseôs*' title may have been given to at least some presocratic works later. However, *phusis* is clearly an important topic in those works, Plato clearly sees there is a *peri phuseôs* tradition and explicitly attributes a study of *phusis* to the Hippocratics.

The term *phusis* also has connotations which are not fully captured by the translation "nature." Firstly, it has a sense of giving the origins, development and current constitution of something, as LSJ have it "*origin … the natural form or constitution* of a person or thing *as the result of growth.*" Secondly, *phusis* derives from *phuein*, "to grow" and so can carry a strong organic sense to it. Thirdly, as Mourelatos has recently argued, *phuein* can have a sense of dynamic being, of coming into being where, *esti* expresses a more static sense of being.[14] All of this can be seen in the *Phaedo* 96a ff., where Plato clearly thinks *peri phuseôs historian* encompasses more than what we would understand by physics and is particularly interested in why each thing comes to be, exists, and perishes. That Plato treats *phusis* in a dynamic manner can also be seen from how he treats these topics and also from how he treats the more abstract questions (still part of *peri phuseôs historian*) of why one person becomes taller than another or why one number is greater than another. So too we can see this in the *Timaeus* where Plato gives his account of *phusis*, giving the origins, development and current constitution of the cosmos and living things. The cosmos itself is a living thing and there is of course great emphasis on coming into being. In the *Timaeus* Plato also makes significant use of the phrase *kata phusin*, "according to nature."[15]

So *peri phuseôs historian* is the enquiry concerning nature, with nature being understood in the early Greek sense of "nature." As much as I admire PSNP, it was not physics being conducted by physicists, or even wholly materialist. Examined in this manner, that may seem relatively evident, but it is alarming how often terms such as physics, physicist and materialist are used in this context even in relatively modern work.[16]

On a related issue, I generally translate *aitia* and its cognates as "reason" or "explanation" in Plato rather than "cause."[17] There are very good grounds for a similar approach to Aristotle, translating his four *aitiai* as "four reasons" or "four explanations" or four "becauses."[18] Much of this also applies to Plato and it is also important to avoid overly modern, physical, or mechanical connotations of "cause" in places. I am also reluctant to give Aristotelian names to

---

14 A.P.D. Mourelatos. Reviews of Laks and Most, Early Greek Philosophy, *Bryn Mawr Classical Review*, 2018.

15 *Timaeus* 47c is an important example here.

16 See e.g. S. Menn. On Socrates' First Objection to the Physicists. *Oxford Studies in Ancient Philosophy* 2010, pp. 37–63.

17 See Vlastos, G.L. Reasons and Causes in the Phaedo. Reprinted with revisions in *Platonic Studies*, 2nd edition, Princeton U.P, 1981, pp. 76–110, cf. D. Sedley. Platonic Causes, *Phronesis* 43, 1998, pp. 114–132.

18 See M. Hocutt. 'Aristotle's Four Becauses', *Philosophy* 189, 1974, pp. 385–399.

Plato's *aitiai* (material, formal, efficient or teleological) as again this can introduce significant distortions and anachronisms. We may ultimately decide that some of Plato's *aitiai* might reasonably in some sense be called causes, though that requires considerable discussion.

2   *Phusis* and the Presocratics

Having taken care to consider the meaning of *phusis* in Plato's *Phaedo*, we also ought to take care in considering the meaning of *phusis* in the presocratics, especially as the transmitted title of many of their works is simply *Peri Phuseôs*, "Concerning Nature." Again, *phusis* here is nature not physics! There is a temptation here, born out of generosity to the presocratics to try to interpret their natural philosophy as physically or mechanically as possible. The goal here is to try to find greater affinities with modern science such that we can then have a higher opinion of PSNP. There are serious historiographical objections to such an approach, which will tend to highlight the supposed affinities between ancient and modern thought while excluding the differences. It is also important to recognise that on an objective analysis of the evidence, many of the presocratics were not physical or mechanical thinkers.[19] It is equally important to recognise that this is Plato's perception of a significant portion of PSNP as well. So in the *Philebus* Plato has Socrates say:

> Well, Protarchus, should we say that the whole universe is ruled by unreason, irregularity and chance, or on the contrary, just as some of those

---

19   Some examples of this mechanisation of the presocratics: Anaximander has been consistently contested, as Conche (1991) pp. 139 ff. has put it, we can have an 'interprétation mécaniste' or an 'interprétation vitaliste', cf. Babut (1972) p. 2, that Anaximander 'Substitue un processus de séparation purement mécanique des éléments constitutifs du monde à la generation.' Parallel attempts to attribute vortices and a mechanical separation have been made with Anaximenes. Lonie (1981) has argued for the Hippocratics having had mechanical views of some physiological processes. Betegh (2004) p. 355 has argued for mechanistic explanation in the Derveni Papyrus. Attempts have been made to downplay the role of *nous* in Anaxagoras to make his vortex more mechanical and Love and Strife in Empedocles have been seen as mechanical forces. There have even been attempts to 'mechanise' Homer, with suggestions that the self-mobile entities of Hephaestus' workshop (*Iliad* XVIII, esp. 414 ff.) and the self-steering ships of the Phaeacians (*Odyssey* VIII, 555 ff.) were in fact mechanical devices (see Gregory 2021, Ch. 2). Leucippus and Democritus are widely, though in my view incorrectly accepted as mechanists (see Gregory 2021 Ch. 7).

PLATO'S RECEPTION OF PRESOCRATIC NATURAL PHILOSOPHY

who came before us said (*hoi prosthen hêmôn elegon*), say that *nous* and a marvellous organising intelligence steer (*diakubernan*) it.[20]

Plato then recognized that there were people before him who believe that an intelligence steered the whole universe. Cosmology in this sense is clearly part of *peri phuseôs historian* for Plato. A little later we also get: "This supports those of old who believed that *nous* always rules the universe."[21] Fowler in the Loeb attributes this view to: "Anaxagoras and probably some now unknown precursors."[22] It is interesting that Fowler chose to comment here (and not at 28d) and in this manner. I believe this is indicative of two things, a tight focus on Anaxagoras and *nous* generated by the idea that the *Phaedo* defines Plato's attitude to PSNP and a failure to recognise that there were interesting presocratic uses of *kubernan*, to steer or govern. Plato may be referring to Anaxagoras here but we can be rather more positive about the supposedly "unknown precursors."

There was a tradition in PSNP of using the verb *kubernan* in important cosmological contexts and we can find its use in Anaximander, where the *apeiron* "surrounds all and steers all" (*periechein hapanta kai panta kubernan*), the Hippocratics and Heraclitus where "all is steered through all,"[23] Parmenides where a goddess sits in the middle and steers all,[24] and Diogenes of Apollonia who says that:

> In my view that which has intelligence is called air by men, and all men are steered (*kubernasthia*) by this and it has a control (*kratein*) over all

---

20   Plato, *Philebus* 28d. So disagreeing with Gottfried Heinemann in this volume, that Plato always refers to the practitioners of PSNP as 'them'—where Plato criticises it is 'them', when he agrees it is 'us'. See also *Phaedrus* 270d and possibly *Phaedo* 108e (see below for both).

21   Plato, *Philebus* 30d.

22   H.N. Fowler and W.R.M. Lamb, *Plato: Statesman, Philebus, Ion.* Loeb Classical Library, 1925, p. 269 note 1.

23   Heraclitus DKB41. All things are steered (*ekubernêse*) through all. Cf. Heraclitus DKB64, The thunderbolt steers (*oiakizei*) all things. For the Hippocratics, *On Regimen*, 1/10 tells us that: "In a word, everything was arranged (*diakosmêsato*) in the body by fire, in a manner suitable to itself ... The hottest and strongest fire, which controls (*epikrateitai*) all things, manages everything according to nature (*kata phusin*), it is imperceptible to sight or touch. In this are soul, mind, understanding, growth, change, diminution, separation, sleep, waking. This steers all things though all (*panta dia pantos kuberna*) both here and there and is never still."

24   Parmenides Fr. 12. The narrower rings are full of unmixed fire, those close by are full of night but with some measure of flame. In the middle of this there is a goddess, who steers (*kubernai*) all things, ruling the hateful birth and mixture of all things, sending female to have sex with male, and conversely male with female.

things. This seems to be a God to me and to have permeated everywhere, to arrange all things and to be in all things.[25]

Diogenes is worth quoting here for two reasons. Firstly, he uses both *kubernan* and *kratein* (to control or have power over) together and there are further presocratic thinkers who use *kratein* or its cognates in a similar manner or on its own.[26] This broadens our group of presocratics. Secondly, it should be clear from this that steering, at least for Diogenes is thoroughgoing and ongoing. By that I mean that it affects all parts of the cosmos and does so at all times, not just for cosmogony.[27] Where the steering principle has been recognised there has been a tendency to play down its role, suggesting it applies only to some part of the cosmos or only for a specific period. It is worth noting that in both Plato and Aristotle the role of steering is thoroughgoing and ongoing.[28] The role of *kubernan* and *kratein* in PSNP then is not easily dismissed even if it has been downplayed in many accounts. It is important to recognise here that a taxonomy of teleology/non-teleology for the presocratics does not result in an empty set for teleology and that Plato is quite aware of this.[29]

3   Demarcating PSNP

One objection to what I have been arguing so far might be to say that what Plato understood by *peri phuseôs historian* was different from how the presocratics understood PSNP. I doubt that there is any significant dissonance here though. Consider this first from an ancient point of view. We might look at who Aristotle includes when he talks of *phusikoi* and *phusiologoi* which will give us a reasonably standard canon of presocratic philosophers and PSNP.[30] We might also simply ask who among the presocratics entitled

---

25   Diogenes of Apollonia Fr. 5.

26   The Hippocratic *On Regimen* I/10 uses *kubernein* and *kratein* as well, Anaximenes uses *kratein* (as our soul, being air, holds us in order (*sungkratei*), so wind and air envelop the whole *kosmos* DK13B2), The Derveni Papyrus too (col. 19, 3 air controls (*epikratei*) all), and Anaxagoras (DKB12 *pantôn nous kratein*, 'nous controls all', DKB12 *kai tês perichôrêsios tês sumpasês nous ekratêsen* 'and nous controlled the whole revolution').

27   Uses of *kubernein* Heraclitus DKB41 and Hippocratic author, *On Regimen* I/10 would also suggest that steering is ongoing and thoroughgoing.

28   See e.g. Plato *Politicus* 272d ff., Aristotle *Meteorology* I/2.

29   See also Justin Habash's chapter in this volume on purposiveness among the presocratics.

30   One might also compare here those whom Aristotle considered to be *muthologoi* and *theologoi*.

their work "*Peri Phuseôs*" or something similar, which will give us pretty much the same results. More critically and possibly more contentiously we might then ask who and what Plato considered to be part of PSNP. If we then work through Socrates' autobiography and the *Phaedo* more generally looking at the ideas/people named and alluded to we will get similar results, as indeed we will if we work our way in similar fashion through Plato's other works and the *Timaeus* in particular. In both the *Phaedo* and the *Timaeus* Plato appears to be remarkably knowledgeable about PSNP in both breadth and depth.[31]

A different line of approach would be to look at the question of demarcation for PSNP from a modern perspective. What does and what does not count as PSNP? Clearly we must have some criteria as not all of presocratic thought is on natural philosophy. One way to do this would be to say if the presocratic in question is a physical/mechanical thinker then they are part of PSNP and everyone else is excluded.[32] That would exclude Homer, Hesiod and the Orphics. Whether that would exclude anyone from the standard canon of PSNP would depend on how physically and mechanically it is possible to interpret their work. The point of such an approach would be that now Plato's critique in the *Phaedo* would be of the whole of PSNP so construed. Alternatively, one might characterise PSNP in terms of material causation.

Of course one can easily produce other demarcation criteria. One might argue that PSNP was characterised by invariance, loosely that given the same circumstances the same things happen, in contrast to the capricious interventions of the gods in Homer and Hesiod. So too one might use parsimony as a criterion, contrasting the ontological profligacy of myth, or the use of natural explanations, or the use of argument and observation against the authority of an account being derived from the gods or the muses. A combination of these criteria would again produce a reasonably standard canon of PSNP.

The term "mechanical" is used far too freely for the presocratics. It should be clear that explanations based around *kubernein* and *kratein* are not mechanical but are important for many presocratics. Anaximander also used many biological metaphors in explanation, the *gonimos*, "seed" and the bark similes in cosmogony, the use of *ekkrinein* "to secrete" in separation from the *apeiron*.

---

31   One might argue that the *Timaeus* is a running commentary on PSNP. In the *Phaedo*, Socrates exhibits very good knowledge of the people and ideas he criticizes, so too in the myth, see Sedley *ibid.*

32   Cf. Laks (2018) and Laks and Louguet (2002).

Many other presocratics used biological rather than mechanical metaphors. Anaxagoras did not always fail to make use of *nous* in explanation (*nous*) originates motion and controls (*kratein*) the separating off (B12, B13) and even when Anaxagoras fails to make use of *nous* the explanations are not mechanical as again he relies on biological metaphors. More radically, and I only have space to state rather than argue here, there is a case that Leucippus and Democritus did not use mechanical explanations as despite their sparse materialist ontology the dominant explanatory metaphors for how like to like sorting occurs are biological (birds flocking together), agricultural (whirled sieve sorting like seeds), and maritime (beach pebbles).[33]

3.1 *Peri Phuseôs Skopein*

While the *Phaedo* phrase *peri phuseôs historian* is well known, at *Phaedrus* 270cd, Socrates says: "So consider what Hippocrates and true reason (*ho alêthês logos*) say concerning nature (*peri phuseôs skopei*)." It is significant Plato and Hippocrates had a dynamic conception of *phusis*, as at *Phaedrus* 270d we ought to investigate its power to act (*skopein tēn dunamin autou*). With the multiple uses of *skopein* in this passage, we could just as easily use *peri phuseōs skopein* as we could *peri phuseōs historian*. Here *skopein* means "to consider/examine/observe."[34] In the next line we have "it is necessary to take in mind the nature of anything" (*dei dianoeisthai peri hotououn phuseôs*). Here *dianoeisthai* standardly means to have in mind or to intend. It is highly interesting that here it is possible for there to be *ho alêthês logos*, about the enquiry/examination concerning nature. Whether *ho logos* is reason or account, it is clearly *alêthês* 'true'. There is also much here that is reminiscent of the *Phaedo*. Socrates says that we should not trust the authority of Hippocrates, but see if what he says agrees (*sumphônei*) with our investigation of the matter, echoing the famous use of *sumphônein* in relation to hypotheses at *Phaedo* 100a5. As with *Phaedo* 99de, at *Phaedrus* 270de there is an association of the wrong method with blindness. What is this method? First it must be considered whether what we are investigating is simple or multiform (*haploun hê*

---

33 Like to Like in Leucippus and Democritus is not a force, but a principle of sorting which occurs only within a vortex. See A. Gregory Leucippus and Democritus on Like to Like and ou mallon. *Apeiron: a Journal for Ancient Philosophy*, 46, 446–468, 2013. See Sextus Empiricus *Against the Mathematicians* VII 116–118 for the biological metaphors, also note that what surrounds each cosmos and gives it integrity for Leucippus and Democritus is a *humen*, a biological membrane, Diogenes Laertius IX, 31.

34 The verb *skopein* is common in Plato, interlocutors often beginning speeches with *skopei*, 'consider'.

PLATO'S RECEPTION OF PRESOCRATIC NATURAL PHILOSOPHY 53

polueides), then if it is simple we must consider what ability it has to act or be acted upon, and if it is diverse then we must number its forms and then proceed for each as with something simple. This discussion of method is prompted by Socrates' question of whether it is possible to gain any worthwhile knowledge of the nature of the soul (*psuchês oun phusin*, 270c1) without the nature of the whole man (*tês tou holou phuseôs*, 270c2). Phaedrus replies that if Hippocrates is to be trusted, we cannot know the body either except by this means of pursuing the enquiry (*Phaedrus* 270c). This may not tell us a great deal methodologically, but what is important here is that Plato clearly thinks that there is a proper method for conducting *peri phuseôs skopein* and this is at least part of it. One indication that we undervalue this *Phaedrus* passage is that PSNP is often referred to as *peri phuseôs historian*. It is indeed proper to try to find a Greek term for PSNP which does not import modern conceptions of physical science. However PSNP could equally be referred to as *peri phuseôs skopein*.[35] Should we be quite so fixated by Socrates' autobiography as a source for Plato's reception of PSNP? The *Phaedrus* passage is good evidence against too stereotypical a reading of the *Phaedo* giving a blanket rejection or condemnation of PSNP.

4 Presocratic Medical Writers

The *Phaedrus* passage raises another question. Should the Hippocratic and other early medical writers be considered to be part of PSNP? Although usually excluded from the canon of presocratic philosophy, we should at least consider whether they form part of PSNP.[36] The Hippocratic *On Regimen* would have a strong case, with a strong Heraclitean influence and in particular I/10 on the origins and nature of the cosmos deals with many PSNP themes. So too the Hippocratic *On the Sacred Disease*, which argues that the sacred disease (epilepsy) and indeed all other diseases have a *phusis* would be a strong contender. In relation to *Phaedrus* 270cd, it would seem that Plato certainly considered Hippocrates to be part PSNP. Hippocrates is concerned with the *phusis* of the body and its component parts (270c 3–5) and clearly has important things to say about the proper method for *peri phuseôs skopein*. We might also look at

---

35 Aristotle also talks of *peri phuseôs epistêmê/historia/theôria/or methodos*, see Gottfried Heinemann in this volume, note 6.

36 So, e.g. G.S. Kirk, J.E. Raven, and M. Schofield, *The Presocratic Philosophers*. 2nd edition, Cambridge U.P 1983 and J. Barnes. *The Presocratic Philosophers*. 2nd edition. Routledge and Kegan Paul: London and New York 1982 omit them as do many others.

Gorgias 501a, where we find that: "Medicine has examined (*eskeptai*) the nature (*phusin*) of what it looks after and the explanation (*aitian*) of what it does and can give an account (*logon ... dounai*) of each." So again we have *skopein* and *phusis*, and it is clear that medicine can give an explanation of its practice (Cf. *Phaedo* and its treatment of *aitiai*) and can give an account of both (Cf. Plato *passim* on giving accounts).

There are several reasons why this is important. If we are asking what the Greeks thought was PSNP, or more specifically what someone who followed directly after PSNP though was PSNP, here we have good evidence that medical writers were included for Plato. We ought to be very suspicious of any modern definition of PSNP which ignores this fact. There is also a broader aspect to accepting Hippocrates and other early medical writers as part of PSNP. This is that Plato clearly gives some of their thought a positive reception. As we have seen Hippocrates is endorsed on method and it is well known that Plato's replenishment theory of pleasure and pain is influenced by earlier medical work. The later part of the *Timaeus* is also fruitful ground here as Plato discusses the nature of the body, the nature of disease and how to treat disease in a manner which clearly reflects earlier medical work as much as the earlier astronomy, cosmology and theory of matter treats presocratic thought in these areas.[37] It is significant here that in his treatise on natural philosophy, Plato includes the nature of the body, disease, and treatment and again sees these as part of PSNP. That he does should be no surprise. Plato clearly buys into the conception of *phusis* as origins, development, and current state and wants to give an account of the entire cosmos and its contents. He also buys into the idea of the macrocosm-microcosm analogy (seen in presocratics such as Anaximander, Hippocratic *On Regimen*, etc.) so here we have the account of the microcosm to match the earlier account of the macrocosm. I am also inclined to agree with Levin's recent work that Plato saw the medical tradition as a rival, both in terms of giving an account of *phusis* and in prescribing how we should lead a good life.[38] As with the physical cosmos and the presocratics, Plato in the *Timaeus* took over the focal points of the debates in medicine, critiqued some views, and took over and transformed others in order to generate his own account.

---

37 The main sources for Plato here are generally thought to be Philolaus and Philistion (see e.g. G.E.R. Lloyd. *In the Grip of Disease*. Cambridge U.P., 2013 p. 153) though Plato addresses a wide number of debates/issues here, not least minimal intervention self-healing versus radical intervention.

38 S.B. Levin. *Plato's Rivalry with Medicine: A Struggle and Its Dissolution*. Oxford UP, 2014.

5 *Phusis, Peri Phuseôs* and Enquiry

I entirely agree with Gottfried Heinemann in this volume that *phusis* is always *phusis* of something. That may be a particular thing, all particular things taken individually, or everything collectively, as in the nature of the cosmos.[39] I also agree with Heinemann that we cannot derive the meaning of *peri phuseôs* directly from determining the meaning or extension of *phusis*. I would go a step further and say that *historia* and *skopein* are also critical for understanding the presocratic project. Consider *Odyssey* x, 303 where Hermes gives Odysseus the Moly plant and says he will tell him its *phusis*, the earliest recorded use of *phusis*. Does he give information *peri phuseôs* for the Moly?[40] He does, so should this be considered part of the presocratic enquiry into nature? Typically for Homer this is information imparted by a god to a human.[41] It is not a human investigation of nature and it is noteworthy that the terms *historia* and *skopein* do not occur in Homer.[42] How much one wants to build in to this contrast between Homer and the presocratics would be too much to discuss here, though a rejection of capricious gods both as part of the explanation of a *phusis* and as the source of any explanation would both be involved.[43] To conduct *peri phuseōs historian* or *peri phuseôs skopein* is for humans to investigate the nature of something in a certain way. Plato objected not to the investigation of nature, but the way that some, though not all presocratics conducted that investigation.

6 Is There Approval of some PSNP in the *Phaedo*?

Does Plato approve of some PSNP in the *Phaedo*? An interesting passage here is *Phaedo* 108e-109a7, where Socrates says that:

---

39 So I take *Phaedo* 96a8 ff. to be about each and every individual thing, while the *Phaedrus* passage is about the whole human and the *Timaeus* (27a4, 47a7) iwill talk of the nature of the whole or the nature of the cosmos.

40 See Gregory (2021) Ch. 2 on how much information is involved here, and whether the coming Odysseus/Circe confrontation is hero vs. minor goddess or man vs. witch, cf. Naddaf (2005).

41 Note also that 'Moly' is the plant's name in the divine language that humans have no access to except via the gods. On the reliability of information given by gods to humans in Homer, see Gregory (2021) Ch. 3.

42 Nor do they occur in Hesiod.

43 Invariance, parsimony, generality and depth of explanation are some of the epistemological merits one might claim for the presocratics contra Homer and Hesiod. See also Gregory (2021) Ch. 2 on the lack of contraries for *phusis* and the lack of phrases such as *kata phusin* in Homer and Hesiod, and their relevant use of *moira* and related terms.

> I am now persuaded that, firstly, if (the earth) is *peripherês* and in the centre of the heavens, then it requires neither air to prevent it falling nor any other necessitation of this sort, but the uniformity of the heaven itself in every way and the equipoise of the earth itself is sufficient to restrain it. For something which is equipoised and is placed in the middle of something homogenous cannot yield to being moved aside in any way, but in like manner will remain steadfast.

If this is a report of a presocratic view (which Socrates is persuaded by) then the problem of the shape of the earth in the *Phaedo* is easily resolved. I have left the contested word *peripherês* here untranslated. Most naturally it would mean flat and round but that seems to clash with other passages which would suggest a spherical earth. If Plato did mean a spherical earth here, it is odd that he does not use *strongulos* (round, 97e1) or *sphairos* (spherical, 110b7) as he does in other passages in the *Phaedo*. The conditional is then important. If the earth is *peripherês*, it stays in position and implicitly a spherical earth would do so as well on this reasoning, *a fortiori*. The key thing here is the positive reception of a piece of PSNP but I would also note the way in which Plato transforms the received view from a flat round earth to a spherical one for his own purposes. The most likely candidate for reference here is Anaximander, who did indeed hold that the earth is flat and round and that it stays in place. One might compare here the more critical line taken on theories of the earth's immobility at *Phaedo* 99b6-8: "This is why one man surrounds the earth with a vortex, making the earth remain still because of the heavens, while another supports it on a base of air, as though it were a broad kneading trough."[44] Possible allusions here are Anaxagoras, Leucippus, and Democritus for the vortex theory and Anaximenes for the supported by air theory. Here again we see good knowledge of PSNP.

A second candidate for a presocratic theory which receives a positive welcome in the *Phaedo* is the like to like principle, though again we need to exercise caution. Like to like was actually a family of relationships, depending on what is thought to be like and how that likeness is mediated. The first recorded instance of like to like is Homer, "God always leads like to like,"[45] which Plato quotes at *Lysis* 214a6. In the *Phaedo*, Plato relies on the principles that like is

---

44   Is καρδόπῳ, which usually means "kneading trough," the right text? A more plausible alternative in the context of something broad being supported by air is καρδοπίῳ, the lid of a kneading trough as. Aristotle specifically mentions a lid in this sort of context, *De Caelo* 294b13-30.

45   Homer, *Odyssey* XVII, 218.

PLATO'S RECEPTION OF PRESOCRATIC NATURAL PHILOSOPHY 57

known by like and like perceives like for the relation of the soul to the forms (*Phaedo* 79c ff.).[46] Both of these principles can be found in Empedocles (by earth we see earth, by water, water etc.),[47] and Aristotle *Metaphysics* 1000b makes clear that both perception and knowledge are involved here.[48] If we go later in Plato, then Sextus Empiricus tells us that:

> There is an old view which, as I said previously, has long been prevalent among the *phusikoi*, that like recognises like. Democritus confirmed of this opinion and Plato spoke of it in his *Timaeus*. Democritus founds his argument on both animate and inanimate things. For animals, he says, flock with animals of the same kind—doves with doves, cranes with cranes, and so with the other irrational animals. Similarly in the case of inanimate things, as can be seen from seeds that are being winnowed and from pebbles on the sea-shore. For in the one case the whirl of the sieve separately arranges lentils with lentils, barley with barley, wheat with wheat; and in the other case, by the motion of the waves, oval pebbles are pushed into the same place as oval pebbles, and round pebbles as round as pebbles, as though the similarity in things has some sort of ability for leading things together.[49]

In the *Timaeus* Plato accepts that like is sorted with like, but disagrees with Democritus on whether like to like sorting is sufficient for cosmos formation. In relation to these passages, it is important that we recognise that at *Phaedo* 99b, Plato has Socrates be critical of those who are: "Unable to distinguish between the real reason (*aition*) for something and that without which the reason (*aition*) could ever be a reason (*aition*)." Socrates then rejects physical explanations as inadequate in general and specifically in cosmology rejects explanations in terms of some physical support for the earth (a vortex, or air supporting the earth) in favour of explanations which state why it is good for the earth to be where it is and be stable. However, at *Timaeus* 46de we find that:

---

46   Arguably elsewhere in the *Phaedo* as well—81d according to Woolf, R. G. (2004) The practice of a philosopher. Oxford Studies in Ancient Philosophy 26:97–129 and possibly 64a and 84b.

47   Empedocles, DKA17.

48   Cf. Sextus Empiricus, *Adversus Mathematicos*, 1. 302–3. Arguably one can find like to like in many other places among the presocratics as well, certainly in the Derveni Papyrus, Col. 25 7-9 and possibly in Parmenides Fr. 8, 25.

49   Democritus Fr. 164, Sextus Empiricus *Against the Mathematicians* VII 116–118.

All of these are *sunaitiai* (auxiliary explanations), which the god uses as tools to instantiate the form of the good. However, they are thought by most men to be not the *sunaitiai* but the *aitiai* of all things, cooling and heating, packing together and dispersing and all such actions ... we must speak of both types of *aitiai*, but keep separate those which with the aid of mind generate that which is beautiful and good, from those which are devoid of understanding and in each case produce chance, unordered results.

A change, or at least a refinement from the *Phaedo*? Or, given that Plato does accept some ideas from PSNP in the *Phaedo*, and the passages we have seen from the *Timaeus*, *Phaedrus*, and the *Gorgias*, do we sometimes frame Socrates' critique of PSNP in the *Phaedo* too harshly or too stereotypically? I read Iakovos Vasiliou's chapter in this volume with great interest. I am sympathetic to his view that:

Plato is already employing Anaxagorean ideas in the *Phaedo*, suitably modified of course, with respect to the *mikrokosmos*: the compound of body and soul that is the individual human being.

If that is so, here is more PSNP which Plato accepted or modified.[50]

7   **Anaxagoras and Taxonomies**

Plato in the *Phaedo* clearly had an objection to Anaxagoras' natural philosophy. According to Socrates, Anaxagoras' book made the claim that: "Nous orders and is the reason for everything."[51] Socrates then expected an explanation of everything in terms of the best, as intelligence would surely choose the best ordering in each case. However, he then says: "I found a man making no use of *nous* nor ascribing to it any reason for the ordering of things, employing instead air, aether, water, and many other absurdities."[52] Socrates is critical of those who "cannot discriminate between different things, the real reason and that without which the reason could ever be a reason."[53] It is important here

---

50   See too Gottfried Heinemann's chapter in this volume on how the presocratics and Plato treat the term *phusis*.

51   Plato, *Phaedo* 97b. Cf. Anaxagoras DKB12.

52   Plato, *Phaedo* 98b.

53   Plato, *Phaedo* 99b.

to recognise that Plato did not object to the project of explaining the natural world. He expected a certain type of explanation of the shape and position of the earth and of the motions of the sun, moon and stars but did not get what he hoped for. As we have seen, he returns in the *Phaedo* to give his own account of the shape and position of the earth and the *Timaeus* will give a full account of the nature and motions of the heavens. This critique can then be used to generate a taxonomy for PSNP, those who employ *nous*, or perhaps those who employ teleology, and those who do not.

The status of this critique is a matter of debate, as Plato also has criticism of PSNP in terms of forms, which he thinks are required to solve the puzzles outlined at 96d ff. This is further complicated by the fact that at *Phaedo* 99c Socrates says:

> They do not truly believe that it is the good (*agathos*) and proper which binds and holds everything together. I would most gladly become any-one's student concerning such a reason and how it prevails; but since I was deprived (*esterêthên*) of this, neither able to find it myself nor to learn it from any other, would you like, Cebes, for me to demonstrate how I worked out and created for myself a second voyage (*deuteros plous*) in search of explanation?

The nature of this *deuteros plous* has been the subject of considerable debate. Is it a second best way? If so, what is it second best to, and how can it be second best if it involves the method of hypothesis and the postulation of forms? Does Socrates abandon teleology entirely here? The debate is too large to address fully here, but I would counsel against taking a too rigid and stereotypical view of the *deuteros plous* as simply a second best. One sense of *deuteros plous* is taking to the oars when there is no wind, that is we must do things for our-selves, do something active. This is interesting relative to *Phaedo* 96b and some of the questions that Socrates asked himself in his youth:

> Is it blood with which we think, or air, or fire, or is it none of these? Is it the brain (*ho engkephalos*) which grants the sensations of hearing, sight and smell, are memory and opinion produced from these, and is it from memory and opinion acquiring stability that knowledge is produced?[54]

---

54 The views of Empedocles, Diogenes of Apollonia/Anaximenes, Heraclitus and Alcmaeon. Plato as ever is remarkably well informed on PSNP!

Note the use of *ho engkephalos*, brain, rather than Plato's usual *he psuche*, mind/soul here, and the external and causal explanation of the acquisition of knowledge. The second voyage requires the soul to hypothesize and to work for itself. So the phrase *deuteros plous* may be ironic, but complex in its irony, with the first voyage easier and simpler in its ontology and its demands on the human mind with the second voyage harder but richer and more rewarding.

On the issue of teleology, I side with those who believe that teleology is still part of the *deuteros plous*. One of the first things that Socrates does when setting out on this second voyage at *Phaedo* 100b is "hypothesise there to be something beautiful itself by itself and similarly a good (*agathos*) and a large and all the others." I would also agree with Sedley that the explanation of the earth's stability at *Phaedo* 108e involves teleology,[55] and would argue that at *Phaedo* 99c8 *esterêthên*, "I was deprived (of learning about teleology)" is an aorist, where a sense of being deprived for all time would require a perfect tense. Plato's character Socrates does indeed go on to learn about such teoelogy in the *Timaeus*.[56] All this is by way of saying that the *Phaedo* reception of PSNP is not simple. Plato clearly approves of some PSNP in the *Phaedo* and he has more than one critique of PSNP. What I want to press next is that Plato had interesting further critiques of PSNP outside of the *Phaedo* and that he had other taxonomies for PSNP as well.

8   Cosmogony, Plausibility and Chance

Laws 889b is an important passage for Plato's cosmogony and his criticism of PSNP:

> Let me put it more clearly. Fire, water, earth and air all exist due to nature and chance (*phusei ... kai tuchê*) they say, and none to skill, and the bodies which come after these, earth, sun, moon and stars, came into being because of these entirely soulless entities. Each being moved by chance, according to the power each has, they somehow fell together in a fitting

---

55 Sedley *ibid* p. 370. Cf. J.G. Lennox. Plato's Unnatural Teleology. In D.J. O'Meara (ed.) *Platonic Investigations*, Washington D.C U.P, 1985, pp. 195–218, G. Fine. Knowledge and Belief in Republic v-vii. Companions To Ancient Thought 1, *Epistemology*, ed. S. Everson, Cambridge U.P. 1990, pp. 85–115. I agree with Sedley that "To understand the *Phaedo's* teleological programme we must distinguish Plato's own authorial voice from the voice of his character Socrates."

56 Agreeing with Sedley *ibid* p. 7.

PLATO'S RECEPTION OF PRESOCRATIC NATURAL PHILOSOPHY

and harmonious manner, hot with cold or dry with moist or hard with soft, all of the forced blendings happening by the mixing of opposites according to chance. In this way and by these means the heavens and all that pertains to them have come into being and all of the animals and plants, all of the seasons having been created from these things, not by intelligence, they say, nor by some god nor some skill, as we say, but through nature and chance (*phusei kai tuchê*).[57]

Key to Plato's conception of the cosmos is that it is a "fitting and harmonious" ordering of its components. As we saw earlier, Plato accepts like to like sorting as a phenomenon but does not believe it to be adequate to explain cosmos formation. Here we see why. Like to like sorting will not give a "fitting and harmonious" blend of opposites. That can only happen by chance acting against the tendency of like to like sorting, which is utterly implausible for Plato. The phrase "nature and chance" (*phusei kai tuchê*) is interesting here. A more subtle point concerns what are taken to be the elements of earth, water, air, and fire. Does their nature come about by chance? According to Plato in the *Timaeus*, no. These elements decompose into component parts and the component parts are chosen by the demiurge (with intelligence and executed with skill) as they are the best. This criticism of some PSNP is related to the *Phaedo* criticism concerning *nous* and explanation, but is by no means the same as it. It will generate a different taxonomy for PSNP based on "nature and chance."

9   Zoogony and Plausibility

The following passage from *Timaeus* 44e concerning the human head is also interesting in relation to PSNP:

> In order that it should not roll around on the ground, with its heights and depths of every kind, and be at a loss in scaling these things and climbing out of them, they gave it body as a means of support for ease of travel.

Now think of Empedocles' account of anthropogony, with the separate body parts moving around until they join up to form the first humans.[58] Those

---

57   Cf. *Timaeus* 35a6-8 where blending sameness, difference and being is difficult and not something that would occur by chance.

58   Empedocles DKB57: On the earth there burst forth many faces without necks, arms wandered bare bereft of shoulders, and eyes wandered needing foreheads. DKB61: Many

which cannot move themselves (heads, and indeed many other parts) will get stuck in ruts adding a layer of improbability and implausibility to the account. What follows in the passage beginning at *Timaeus* 45a ff. adds further layers to this critique. Not only do we need the right parts, but there is a necessary order to these parts (head, neck, chest, abdomen, etc.) and the parts must also be in the correct orientation (face, throat, breasts, genitalia, etc. to the front) or we do not have properly formed humans. This strategy of adding layers of implausibility to accounts of how things might come about by chance is applied to cosmogony and stoichogony (the origin of the elements) as well, as we have seen. It is of great importance to consider these ideas in context. In the modern world our ideas of cosmogony, zoogony, and stoichogony are founded on highly complex models which have taken many years to develop. This makes these ideas plausible to many, even if there is still disagreement, some arguing that belief in evolution is akin to believing that a whirlwind sweeping through a junk yard could assemble a jumbo jet.[59] This debate was still going strong in late antiquity and an interesting comparison is Lucretius, *De Rerum Natura*, 5, 186–194, who argued that infinite time/atoms/space will generate our cosmos by chance and Cicero, *On the Nature of the Gods* II, XXXVII, who argued that if we had a bag full of innumerable letters and threw them on the ground we would not get the Annals of Ennius, not even a single verse.

10   Multiplicities

Some presocratics postulated unlimited multiplicities, whether they were worlds (co-existent or successive), shapes and sizes of atoms or non-viable biological forms. The following passage from the *Philebus*, while it is in the specific context of the analysis of limited and unlimited, might equally well apply to Leucippus and Democritus, or Empedocles:

> The indefinite plurality of things and in things makes you in each case indefinite of thought and someone of neither status nor account, since you have never yet examined the number in anything.[60]

---

sprang up two faced and two breasted, man faced ox progeny, and conversely ox headed man progeny.

59   F. Hoyle, *The Intelligent Universe*. Michael Joseph, 1983, p. 19.

60   Plato, *Philebus* 17e5, cf. *Philebus* 64e and *Theaetetus* 183b. Is this one reason why Plato does not name some of his predecessors?

PLATO'S RECEPTION OF PRESOCRATIC NATURAL PHILOSOPHY 63

There are several word plays in the Greek here which associate allowing indefinite plurality in the world with being indefinite in thought and suggest that if you cannot give an account in either words or numbers then you are a person of no account. Plato's account of the world is determinate. For Plato there is a single, unique cosmos, there are a small and definite number of mathematically specific shapes for the ultimate building blocks of matter, and there are unitary, well designed species. All of these entities are designed or chosen by the demiurge as the best available. Similar sentiments to the *Philebus* passage can be found in the *Timaeus*. The following passage at directly after the *Timaeus'* description of how the two basic types of triangles combine to form the complex plane triangles and squares and these then form the three dimensional elements:

> If in considering all this someone should raise the quite proper question of whether the number of *kosmoi* should be said to be unlimited or limited, he will suppose that the view that they are infinite is that of someone who is indefinite (*apeirou*) on a matter on which he should be definite.[61]

Again we have the play on indefinite in the world and of thought, though here it could be rendered "inexperienced on a matter in which he should be experienced."[62] Related to the objection to indeterminate multiplicities is an implicit objection to some *ou mallon* explanations. Here *ou mallon* means "not rather" and is in effect an expression of indifference. Simplicius tells us that:

> Leucippus supposed there to be an infinite number of atoms that are always in motion and have an infinite number of shapes on the grounds that nothing is such rather than such (*dia to mêden mallon toiouton ê toiouton einai*).[63]

---

61   Plato, *Timaeus* 55c. This passage goes on to question whether there is one or five *kosmoi*. If we take the uses of *kosmoi* here as "worlds," then it is hard to see why Plato should even begin to consider this. However Plato has just had Timaeus describe the organization of the elements out of their component parts. Each element has *summetria* and *taxis* and so might be considered a *kosmos* in itself, using *kosmeo* and its cognates to describe the process of ordering the elements. The passage can then be read as an objection to the idea that there are unlimited shapes and sizes of atoms rather than unlimited worlds, something that Plato has had Timaeus object to previously at 31a ff.

62   *Emmelôs* at *Timaeus* 55c7 is also interesting as a contrast to the *plêmmelôs* (discordant) behaviour prior to the ordering of the *kosmos* in the critical passage on the ordering of the *kosmos* at *Timaeus* 30a.

63   Simplicius *Physics* 28, 8. Cf. Simplicius *Physics* 28, 24, Simplicius *De Caelo* 295, 7, Aristotle *Physics* 203a21, Aristotle *On Generation and Corruption* 314a22.

It is notable in the *Timaeus* that the demiurge has a reason for all that he does and specifically he chooses the best types of triangles as the foundational entities. So again we have a slightly different line of criticism of some PSNP which could again be used to generate different taxonomies for PSNP, those who posit multiplicities, and those who use *ou mallon* explanations. We might also look at the way Plato treats flux and stability in the early part of the *Theaetetus* as that can also generate a related but different taxonomy for presocratic philosophy, as will the gods and giants passage of the *Sophist*.

11   Eudoxus and Astronomy

Let me turn now to two specific instances of Plato's reception of PSNP. The astronomy of the *Timaeus* is committed to the idea that all of the motions of the heavens are either regular circular motions (RCM) as in the case of the stars, or are combinations of two RCM s, as in the case of the sun, moon, and five planets.[64] The system of Eudoxus (c390-c337) makes the same assumptions but is more complex, with three RCM s for the sun and moon and four for the planets. It is commonly assumed that Eudoxus influenced Plato, but there is a little evidence for this other than the suspect assumption that Plato was previously disinterested in astronomy and so must have been influenced by someone in producing the *Timaeus* model.[65] Certainly there is a written first record in the *Timaeus* and if Plato was first with a prototype of an RCM system then we can see Eudoxus' more complex system as a refinement of it. This accords with the evidence of Simplicius, who says that:

> Plato assigned circular, regular, and ordered motions to the heavens, and offered this problem to the mathematicians, which hypotheses of regular, circular and ordered motion are capable of saving the phenomena of the planets, and first Eudoxus of Knidos produced the hypothesis of the so-called unrolling spheres.[66]

---

64   The objection that Plato would not have been able to account for all the celestial phenomena he was aware of with RCM can be met simply by citing the fact that Eudoxus' model could not account for all known phenomena either: "The unrolling spheres of Eudoxus' school do not save the phenomena, not only those that were found later, but also those known before and recognised by them." Simplicius *in De Caelo* 504.17 ff.

65   See Gregory (2000) Ch. 2 on the interpretation of the infamous Republic VII passage on astronomy, which is not as problematic as if often assumed.

66   Simplicius *in De Caelo* 492.31 ff., cf. 488.18 ff.

PLATO'S RECEPTION OF PRESOCRATIC NATURAL PHILOSOPHY   65

However we resolve that priority question, there are important influences here that can be traced back into presocratic thinking. Circular motion can be traced back to Anaximander and the idea of regular circular motion can be traced to the Pythagoreans as Geminus tells us:

> The Pythagoreans, who were the first to apply themselves to investigations of this kind, assumed the movements of the Sun, the Moon and the five planets to be circular and uniform. They would not admit, with reference to things divine and eternal, any disorder such as would make them move at one time more swiftly, at one time more slowly, and at another time stand still.[67]

The ideas of a central spherical earth, stable without physical support, with the stars orbiting it and the division of the heavens into fixed and wandering stars can all be traced back to the presocratics. *Timaeus* 40c is also interesting in the amount of practical, empirical knowledge it conveys:

> The dances of these stars and their juxtapositions with one another (1), the circling backs and advances of their own cycles (2), which of the gods come into contact with each other and which into opposition (3), which cover each other relative to us (4), and for what periods they each disappear and again re-appear (5).

When planets pass each other in the zodiac, they can be close to one another (1), be so close that they appear to merger into one large object (3), or occlude one another (4). Planets can undergo retrograde motion (2) and Mercury and Venus disappear as they become close to the sun then reappear on the other side of the sun (5), a phenomenon much studied by the Babylonians. Either Plato was more of an observer than is generally accepted, or he gleaned a great deal of astronomical information from the PSNP tradition. A more global consideration for the *Timaeus* is that it is very self-conscious in producing an account of the cosmos which gives origins, development, and current constitution, very much in line with the presocratic *peri phuseôs* tradition.

---

67   Geminus, *Isagoge* I, 19–21.

12   The Pythagorean Question

Was Plato a Pythagorean and what was his attitude to Pythagorean Natural Philosophy? Whether Plato was a Pythagorean or not is too large a question to address fully here. We are in need of criteria for what it would mean to say that Plato was a Pythagorean post-Burkert and the shift to treating the evidence of Plato and Aristotle on Pythagoras and the early Pythagoreans as primary.[68] Does it make any more sense to call Plato a Pythagorean than it would to call him a Parmenidean or a Heraclitean, especially if Plato transformed Pythagorean natural philosophy for his own purposes, as he did with other presocratics? An interesting example here is how the demiurge constructs the orbits of the sun, moon and five planets is the *Timaeus*. That Plato uses a musical scale that derives from Philolaus is well known and indeed the general idea of a harmony of the heavens may well be Pythagorean. The ratios for one octave of this scale are: $1 - 9/8 - 81/64 - 4/3 - 3/2 - 27/16 - 243/128 - 2$. Although these ratios may look arbitrary, in fact they are generated from the powers of 2 and 3. So $9/8$ is $3^2/2^3$, $81/64$ is $3^4/2^6$, etc. The Pythagorean justification of the series $1 - 2 - 3 - 4$, the *tetraktys*, for the production of a musical scale was that $1 + 2 + 3 + 4 = 10$, the Pythagorean perfect number.[69] The Pythagorean justification for there being 10 celestial bodies (earth, sun, moon, five planets, central fire and counter-earth), some of which could not be observed, was that this too was in accord with the perfect number. Plato's approach is the reverse of this. He accepts that there are the sun, moon, and five naked eye planets and develops the Philolaus scale as far as to generate ratios for the orbits of these entities.[70] His final number, 27, has no significance in itself.[71] Secondly, in the *Timaeus* and subsequent works there is no mention of any audible harmony of the heavenly bodies. There is a harmony to the structure of the world soul, but no sound. This, of course, differs from the Pythagoreans, and also differs from the myth

---

68   See Burkert (1972).

69   See Aristotle *Metaphysics* 986a8 on the significance of 10.

70   See Aristotle *Metaphysics* 986a and *De Caelo* 293a25. Also cf. Simplicius' report of Plato's challenge to 'save the phenomena' (see below) and Aristotle *De Caelo* 293a on the Pythagoreans 'doing violence to' the phenomena in order to bring them into line with their theory.

71   Plato's alleged ban of observation from astronomy at *Republic* 530b6-c1 might be thought to run contrary to this approach. I have argued there is no such ban A. D. Gregory. *Plato's Philosophy of Science*. London: Duckworth, 2000, (Ch. 2), but a contrast between how one does astronomy and how it ought to be used in the education of the guardians. The *Timaeus* certainly does not recognise any such ban. As Vlastos comments (1975) p. 50, it is saturated in the language of observational astronomy, and see in particular Timaeus 47a ff. on eyesight and astronomy.

PLATO'S RECEPTION OF PRESOCRATIC NATURAL PHILOSOPHY

of Er at *Republic* 617bc. As we saw in the last section, the idea of combinations of RCM is new and builds on earlier, possibly Pythagorean ideas of singular RCM. Plato's cosmology is also quite different from that of Philolaus, which had a central fire, surrounded by sun, moon, earth, counter-earth, five planets, and the stars.[72]

A second important consideration in the *Timaeus* is the relation between number and matter. According to Aristotle, for the Pythagorean's sensible substances were constituted from number.[73] In the *Timaeus* though, matter is constituted from shape not number and the approach is geometrical rather than arithmetical. The basic units in the *Timaeus* are 1, 1, $\sqrt{2}$ and the 1, $\sqrt{3}$, 2 triangles, which combine to form the three dimensional shapes for earth, water, air, and fire. These triangles cannot be broken down any further, as Aristotle's criticism makes clear. Here Plato takes over the presocratic scheme of the elements as earth, water, air, and fire and transforms it to his own ends. None of these elements are primary (contrary to Thales on water, Anaximenes on air, and Heraclitus on fire) and indeed none are elements in the sense that they cannot be decomposed into parts.[74] It may well be that the Pythagoreans were the first to emphasize the importance of number in the investigation of the natural world, but Plato takes on that insight and transforms its application in important ways. It is important to reject the idea of a homogenous, unitary Pythagorean/Platonic "number mysticism" and to be able to discern the differences in their approaches.[75]

13 Conclusion

Plato's reception of PSNP is complex and points to some interesting facts about PSNP. We need to look beyond Socrates' autobiography in the *Phaedo* in order to grasp its full breadth and to understand it fully. Aristophanes may have forced a stereotyped dichotomy for PSNP and its critics in *The Clouds* for comic effect but there is no need to follow him in thinking about Plato's reception of

---

72 Cf. Rosemary Wright's chapter in this volume, section v.

73 Aristotle, *Metaphysics* XIII/6, 1080b16-22.

74 Here is a further criticism of some PSNP (are elements properly elements?) and a possible further taxonomy fro PSNP based on it.

75 It is arguable that numerology was not part of original Pythagoreanism but was read in by later commentators (L. Zhmud. Plato as Architect of Science, *Phronesis* 43, 1999, pp. 211–244). If that is true, there is still a need to distinguish Plato's views in the Timaeus from that sort of numerology, especially as Aristotle perceives such numerology at least in Philolaus.

PSNP.[76] One important lesson we should learn from Plato's reception of PSNP is that we should not construe PSNP in too narrow a fashion. It was not just natural philosophy done by "the presocratic philosophers" (at least some medical writings should be considered) and that natural philosophy encompassed a very broad range of questions and approaches, not just materialist of mechanist views. It is important to recognise that there was a significant PSNP tradition based on the idea of *kubernan* and *kratein*. PSNP has been termed *peri phuseôs historian* but could equally well be termed *peri phuseôs skopein*. Plato clearly had multiple criticisms of PSNP and had multiple ways of generating taxonomies of PSNP. This too may indicate that PSNP was actually rather more diverse than some modern accounts allow. Those criticisms were in many ways interesting, sophisticated, and show a good knowledge of PSNP.

Plato's reception of PSNP may also be rather more positive than some accounts allow. The *Phaedrus* passage shows approval of some PSNP methodology and the *Phaedo* clearly approves of some PSNP ideas. That Plato criticizes the *physiologoi* should be taken as a sign of his interest, rather than his disinterest in natural philosophy. It is not the investigation or explanation of nature *per se* that worries him, but the methods and explanations that the *physiologoi* employ. The *Phaedo* does not argue that tallness, Socrates in prison, or the shape and position of the earth are matters of no interest, rather that some PSNP explanations of these phenomena are not adequate. When it comes to his own natural philosophy, Plato accepted some PSNP ideas and transformed others to his own ends.

It is critical that we do not treat Socrates' autobiography too stereotypically or use it as the single source for Plato's reception of PSNP. There is important material in Plato which gives us a much richer and more interesting account of Plato's reception of PSNP and also gives us important evidence on the nature of PSNP.[77]

Bibliography

Babut, D. 1972. 'Le divin et les dieux dans la pensée d'Anaximandre'. *Revue des Étude Grecques* 85, 1–32.

---

76 Plato's 'Gods and Giants' passage at *Sophist* 245e ff. might be the closest to such stereotyping, but Plato has reasons for this.

77 My thanks to Jon Griffiths, Ondrej Krasa, Hugh MacKenzie and an anonymous reader and for their comments.

Barnes, J. 1982. *The Presocratic Philosophers*. 2nd edition. Routledge and Kegan Paul: London and New York.

Betegh, G. S. 2004. *The Derveni Papyrus*. Cambridge: Cambridge University Press.

Betegh, G.S. 2016a. *Greek Philosophy and Religion*. A companion to ancient philosophy/ edited by Mary Louise Gill and Pierre Pellegrin. London: Blackwell.

Betegh, G.S. 2016b. Archelaus on Cosmogony and the Origins of Social Institutions. *Oxford Studies in Ancient Philosophy*.

Bryan, J. 2015. *Likeness and Likelihood in the Presocratics and Plato*. Cambridge UP.

Burkert, W. 1972. *Lore and Science in Ancient Pythagoreanism*. Cambridge MA, Harvard University Press.

Cherniss, H. 1935. *Aristotle's Criticism of Presocratic Philosophy*. Baltimore: John Hopkins Press.

Conche, M. 1991. *Anaximandre. Fragments et Témoignages*. Paris: Presses Universitaires de France.

Fine,G. 1990. Knowledge and Belief in Republic V-VII. Companions To Ancient Thought 1, *Epistemology*, ed. S. Everson, Cambridge U.P.

Fowler, H.N. and Lamb, W.R.M. 1925. *Plato: Statesman, Philebus, Ion*. Loeb Classical Library.

Gregory, A.D. 2000. *Plato's Philosophy of Science*. London: Duckworth.

Gregory, A.D. 2007. *Ancient Greek Cosmogony*. London: Duckworth.

Gregory, A.D. 2013. Leucippus and Democritus on Like to Like and ou mallon. *Apeiron: a Journal for Ancient Philosophy*, 46: 446–468.

Gregory, A.D. 2021. *Early Greek Philosophies of Nature*. London: Bloomsbury.

Hocutt, M. 1974. 'Aristotle's Four Becauses', *Philosophy* 189, 1974, pp. 385–399.

Hoyle, F. 1983. *The Intelligent Universe*. Michael Joseph.

Kirk, G.S., J.E. Raven, and M. Schofield. 1983. *The Presocratic Philosophers*. 2nd edition, Cambridge U.P.

Laks, A. 2018. *The Concept of Presocratic Philosophy*. G. Most (trans). Princeton, NJ: Princeton University Press.

Laks, A. and Louguet, C. 2002. *Qu'est-ce que la philosophie présocratique?* Villeneuve d'Ascq: Presses universitaires du septentrion.

Lennox, J.G. 1985. Plato's Unnatural Teleology. In D.J. O'Meara (ed.) *Platonic Investigations*, Washington D.C U.P.

Levin, S.B. 2014. *Plato's Rivalry with Medicine: A Struggle and Its Dissolution*. Oxford UP.

Lloyd, G.E.R. 2013. *In the Grip of Disease*. Cambridge U.P.

Lonie, I.M. 1981. 'Hippocrates the Iatromechanist'. *Medical History* 25, 113–50.

McCabe, M.M. 2000. *Plato and His Predecessors*. Cambridge U.P.

Menn, S. 2010. On Socrates' First Objection to the Physicists. *Oxford Studies in Ancient Philosophy* pp. 37–63.

Mourelatos, A.P.D. 2018. Reviews of Laks and Most, Early Greek Philosophy, *Bryn Mawr Classical Review*.

Naddaf, G. 2005. The Greek Concept of Nature. SUNY.

Sedley, D. 1998. Platonic Causes, *Phronesis* 43: 114–132.

Vlastos, G.L. 1981. Reasons and Causes in the Phaedo. Reprinted with revisions in *Platonic Studies*, 2nd edition, Princeton U.P, 76–110.

Vlastos, G.L. 1975. *Plato's Universe*. Clarendon, Oxford.

Zhmud, L. 1999. "Plato as Architect of Science," *Phronesis* 43: 211–244.

Zhmud, L. 2012. *Pythagoras and the Early Pythagoreans*. Cambridge: Cambridge U.P.

CHAPTER 3

Presocratic Echoes: The Reception of Purposive Nature in Classical Greek Thought

Justin Habash

One cannot make much headway into understanding the ancient Greeks without talking about the idea of nature. Contrary to the view held by some scholars, however, no single, universally agreed-upon idea of nature exists among the Greeks.[1] If there is such a thing as a "Greek concept of nature," it is an evolving idea fluidly composed of multiple voices across several centuries of thought in ancient Greece. Nature as an idea that describes and shapes the world around us and the things in it must first be *discovered* since the precise features are not intuitive. As early philosophical thinkers wrestle with the nature (φύσις) of things around them, however, the way the concept of nature operates changes. In other words, the story of the Greek idea of nature cannot be told without the idea of reception.

A complete account of the story of nature in the ancient Greek world would include (at a minimum) a discussion of Hesiod, Homer, the poets, historians, and Hippocratics, in addition to the Presocratics, the "later classical" thinkers, and Hellenistic philosophers,[2] but there is obviously not space enough for this entire story here. I hope instead that I can frame a small but vital part of that larger narrative in this chapter by focusing on the way in which the idea of nature is conceived and modified in key thinkers from the Presocratics to the Sophists to Plato and Aristotle. This account, perhaps itself just a "likely story" given the nature of the evidence that has come down to us, is to some extent at odds with the traditional account that portrays Aristotle's notion of nature as a final cause as the first real attempt to think of nature as purposive. Instead, I argue that important features of the idea of nature as purposive and prescriptive emerge in the earliest Greek philosophers, is then challenged and modified by some of the thinkers known as 'Sophists', and recovered and expanded by Plato and Aristotle.

---

1   Naddaf 2005. For an effective critique of key elements of Naddaf's thesis, see Heinemann, this volume.

2   For various accounts of the Greek idea of nature, treated as a "figure" or "concept," see Sallis 2016 and Naddaf 2005.

© KONINKLIJKE BRILL NV, LEIDEN, 2021 | DOI:10.1163/9789004443358_005

My reading begins with an examination of the various ways in which the ideas of nature put forward by the Greek *physiologoi* (many of whom are Presocratics) can be understood to contain purposive features. I turn next to an account of the way the idea of nature is used quite differently by various so-called Sophists of the 5th century. While the receptive link of a concept between thinkers of different periods is never straightforward, I argue that select Sophists aim to use the idea of nature to further political ends. It is in some sense these ends, and the features of the resulting idea of nature, that reject or radically alter key Presocratic facets of the idea of nature and in so doing serve as a catalyst for Plato and Aristotle. In the final section of the chapter, then, I turn to making the argument that part of the impetus in the later classical thought of Plato and Aristotle for a more robust, fully teleological understanding of nature arises as a defense of nature as a real principle with purposive and prescriptive force. Plato, and to a larger extent Aristotle, can be read in this light as at least in part aiming to "correct the record" and establish the way the idea of purposive nature plays a role in political life and, even more broadly for Aristotle, the value of inquiry into the nature of things through the lens of final causality.

1 Presocratic Conceptions of Purposive Nature

Through two centuries of thought and argument, those thinkers known as the Presocratic philosophers took a general idea on the periphery of Greek thought, and transformed it into a philosophical concept robust enough to explain a remarkable array of phenomena. The concept of nature is central to the Greeks understanding of themselves and their place in the cosmos. As Heinneman so keenly reminds us earlier in this volume, drawing from Aristotle, "*physis* is always the *physis* of something." As with other similar developments, one discovery spawned many more, and the "nature" of things began to be used to supply answers to all manner of new questions. Further, the development of a more sophisticated and diverse conceptual framework among the Presocratics also opened up the ability of early Greek thinkers to pursue such answers through argumentation and dispute.[3] The main thrust of my argument in this section is crucial but controversial for it is here that I make the case that while early Greek thinkers understood the idea of

---

3   This section is a short version of a more complete account of the development of the idea of purposive nature among early Greek thinkers in Habash 2016a.

PRESOCRATIC ECHOES

nature differently, they almost invariably understood it to possess *purposive* features.[4]

Despite the lack of a single, associated term like *physis* in any surviving fragments, it is clear the Milesian thinkers were debating how things came to be through conversations about what things are. The earliest conceptions of nature gave the Milesian thinkers a way to unite all phenomena under a universal concept; that is, every thing had a "nature," and was connected to the origin of the cosmos. The link between the origin and what something is was nothing particularly new: ancient Greek myths are full of such connections. Giving a *natural* description of the potential connection between origin and the current state of things was innovative, however. The first recorded *physiologos*, Thales, boldly asserted that everything was water, and by providing all things with a common nature, initiated the possibility of conceiving of nature as a series of transformations rather than births.[5]

Although Thales emphasized the idea of nature as a unifying source, his fellow Milesians, Anaximander and Anaximenes, emphasized the process element of nature to a much greater extent. For Anaximander, the entities in nature exhibited fundamental relationships to one another, in particular an innate opposition that dictated specific kinds of behavior.

Of those who say the source is one and in motion and boundless, Anaximander, the son of Praxiades of Miletus, the successor and student of Thales, said the source and element of existing things was the boundless (ἄπειρον), being the first one to apply this term to the source (ἀρχή). And he says it is neither water nor any other of the so-called elements, but some other boundless nature (φύσιν ἄπειρον), from which come to be all the heavens and the world-orders in them:

> From what things existing objects come to be, into them too does their destruction take place, according to what must be: for they give recompense and pay restitution to each other for their injustice according to the ordering of time, expressing it in these rather poetic terms (B1).

The cosmos was, in effect, *steered* by these natural relationships, more or less guided by a process of natural reciprocity for Anaximander. In what is perhaps the first instance of reception in natural philosophy that incorporates then expands upon ideas from previous thinkers, Anaximenes sought to combine

---

4   Ibid.
5   Panchenko 1993, 392.

Thales' idea of material source as nature with Anaximander's emphasis on process into a *single material constituent* imbued with a *specific process of alteration*.

> Anaximenes ... like Anaximander, declares that the underlying nature is one and unlimited but not indeterminate, as Anaximander held, but definite, saying that it is air. It differs in rarity and density according to the substance ⟨it becomes⟩. Becoming finer it comes to be fire; being condensed it comes to be wind, then cloud, and when still further condensed it becomes water, then earth, then stones, and the rest come to be from these. He too makes motion eternal and says that change also comes to be through it (A5).[6]

Air, for Anaximenes, is the source of all things, even the gods, and it becomes all things through the alternating processes of condensation and rarefaction. Although they think about nature in significantly different ways, the earliest philosophical conceptions of nature all assume a unified cosmos that is *guided* by means of natural processes.

But the idea of nature does not begin to *classify* different entities within the world until Xenophanes uses it in this way, and he does so, at least to our knowledge, without using the specific term *physis*, at least in the fragments we possess. The wandering poet from Colophon diversifies the universal quality of nature by frequent use in connection with "all things," that is, nature begins to apply to specific *groups* of entities, marking them out from others:

> We all come into being from earth and water (πάντες γὰρ γαίης τε καὶ ὕδατος ἐκγενόμεσθα, B33).
>
> for all things (πάντα) are from the earth and to the earth all things (πάντα) come in the end (ἐκ γαίης γὰρ πάντα καὶ εἰς γῆν πάντα τελευτᾷ, B27).

Although he uses the idea of nature to classify natural things by the fact that they "come into being and grow," his use of nature as a method of clarification is most readily apparent in his fragments on the divine. There he goes to considerable lengths to distinguish the features of divine nature from human nature. Broadly speaking, Xenophanes uses the idea of nature dynamically, sometimes aligning the nature of the thing with what it *does*, other times more simply with what it *actually* is (as opposed to what it only seems to be). Although

---

6 Translation from McKirahan 2010, 48.

PRESOCRATIC ECHOES

Xenophanes does not use the term *physis* in the fragments we possess, we may take his fragments as prime examples of what Heinemann labels the "dualism of meanings inherent in the concept," (of physis). While his fragments on natural things fit the "genetic profile" by their focus on origin and growth, the fragments on the divine fit the "dispositional profile" of *physis* approaches when inquiring into the nature of something by the way it is or the way it behaves.[7] Eschewing the Homeric tendency of blurring the lines by describing certain mortals as "godlike" and certain gods as behaving as humans do, Xenophanes holds that divine nature must be different from mortal nature because their *activities* are so different. In effect, *what something is* relates directly to *what it does* or *what it is capable of doing*:

> Homer and Hesiod have attributed to the gods all sorts of things which are matters of reproach and censure among men: theft, adultery, and mutual deceit (πάντα θεοῖς ἀνέθηκαν Ὅμηρός θ' Ἡσίοδός τε, ὅσσα παρ' ἀνθρώποισιν ὀνείδεα καὶ ψόγος ἐστίν. κλέπτειν μοιχεύειν τε καὶ ἀλλήλους ἀπατεύειν, B11).
>
> But mortals suppose that gods are born, wear their own clothes, and have a voice and a body (ἀλλ' οἱ βροτοὶ δοκέουσι γεννᾶσθαι θεοὺς τὴν σφετέρην ἐσθῆτα ἔχειν φωνήν τε δέμας τε, B14).
>
> But if horses or oxen or lions had hands
> Or could draw with their hands and accomplish such works as men
> Horses would draw the figures of the gods as similar to horses and the oxen as similar to the oxen,
> And they would make the bodies
> Of the sort which each of them had. (B15)
> Ethiopians say that their gods are snub-nosed and black;
> Thracians that theirs are blue-eyed and red-haired. (B16)

The essential "theological" fragments can be strung together in the following way to form a cogent picture of the whole of Xenophanes' thought on the nature of the divine:

> "One god is greatest among gods and men, not at all like mortals in body or in thought" (B23) and as such "whole he sees, whole he thinks, and whole he hears" (B24), "but completely without toil he shakes all things by the thought of his mind" (B25), and "always he abides in the same

---

7 See Heinemann's discussion of genetic and dispositional profiles, this volume.

place, not moving at all, nor is it seemly for him to travel to different places at different times" (B26).[8]

The divine knows all and shakes all things by the thought of his mind, while man is constrained by the necessary processes of learning and discovery. Yet Xenophanes suggests hope for humanity, potential for a kind of progress toward greater understanding and the application of this knowledge to improve human life: "Indeed not from the beginning did gods intimate all things to mortals but as they search in time they discover better" (οὔτοι ἀπ' ἀρχῆς πάντα θεοὶ θνητοῖσ' ὑπέδειξαν, ἀλλὰ χρόνωι ζητοῦντες ἐφευρίσκουσιν ἄμεινον, B18). Xenophanes uses the idea of nature to craft a theory of everything that weaves together natural philosophy, social commentary, theological questions, and epistemological considerations, and that assigns a particular place to mankind but holds out the promise ofgrowth. In this way, 'what something is' or its nature, is the key to human discovery of broader knowledge.

Heraclitus, though no fan of Xenophanes' polymathy, develops his own version of a theory of everything through a strong connection between the *physis* of things and his famous *logos* that "steers all things."[9]

> Although this account holds forever, men ever fail to comprehend both before hearing it and once they have heard. Although all things come to pass in accordance with this account, men are like the untried when they try such words and works as I set forth, distinguishing each according to its nature and telling how it is. But other men are oblivious of what they do awake, just as they are forgetful of what they do asleep. (B1)

For Heraclitus, φύσις is a riddle that "loves to hide" and requires a new approach that embraces paradox, subtlety, and dogged investigation of what lies beneath the surface. Instead of a simple means of classification of natural things, Heraclitus develops a notion of φύσις as a ἁρμονίη of fundamental opposites. This unity manifests itself in different ways:

---

8 While there is no evidence that Xenophanes laced the ideas in these fragments together in this particular order, any attempt to interpret the ideas of the earliest Presocratic philosophers necessarily imposes a framework and a largely arbitrary order upon them. This particular order has the advantage that it arranges Xenophanes' ideas on the divine from the broadest, most general description to more specific facets of divine nature.

9 For an extended account of this reading, see Habash 2019.

PRESOCRATIC ECHOES

Beginning is together with end [on a circle] (ξυνὸν γὰρ ἀρχὴ καὶ πέρας ἐπὶ κύκλου [περιφερείας], B103).

A road up and down is one and the same (ὁδὸς ἄνω κάτω μία καὶ ὡυτή, B60).

The sea is the purest and foulest water: for fish drinkable and life-sustaining; for men undrinkable and deadly (θάλασσα ὕδωρ καθαρώτατον καὶ μιαρώτατον ἰχθύσι μὲν πότιμον καὶ σωτήριον, ἀνθρώποις δὲ ἄποτον καὶ ὀλέθριον, B61).

Ubiquitous throughout his fragments, φύσις as ἁρμονίη is what gives each individual thing its particular identity while also serving as a pattern that runs throughout the cosmos. Recognized only by those few who have taught themselves how to "listen" to the riddle and see beyond the obvious conflict of opposites, φύσις as ἁρμονίη is the basic pattern underlying the λόγος, that divine plan by which the cosmos is steered. Thus it is that humans gain access to the divine through the idea of nature.

But nature as a principle of unity of opposites fails to really describe *what something is*, or so we can easily imagine Parmenides saying in response to Heraclitus. To reveal the connection between truth and reality in the cosmos, nature as a concept must "show forth" what-is. It must get to the heart of what is *real* not by guesswork or observation but through reason. Parmenides thus reconceives of the starting point of the study of nature from the entities in the world, as his predecessors suppose, to the basic metaphysical criteria for anything that exists.[10] Only those things that possess these attributes have natures, properly speaking, and only these are "real." Although some scholars interpret Parmenides as seeking to "purify" the idea of nature by removing its dynamic components, thus relegating φύσις to "mere opinion," a better understanding is that Parmenides creates a division between the "being" and "becoming," or the identity (τὸ ἔον) and activity (φύσις), facets of nature. Using the idea of limits and the recurring analogy of paths, Parmenides establishes a firmer foundation for cosmological inquiry by first establishing the metaphysical and epistemological criteria for what exists. Conceiving of nature and inquiry in terms of limits and paths illustrates the fundamental purposiveness in Parmenides' theory.

A fairly typical reading of the Presocratic period is that the pluralists that follow him are, in various ways, responding to Parmenides, but with respect to the idea of nature, this happens in an unusual, underappreciated way. In

---

10   My view is heavily indebted to Patricia Curd's. See Curd 2004 and 2006.

separating what is "real" from what "becomes," Parmenides creates a divide in the idea of nature that bears itself out in a similar fashion in the different pluralist theories of subsequent thinkers. The structural aspects of real identity are separate from, but connected with, the motive forces that shape the growth of entities. This basic bifurcation is replicated alternatively by Empedocles as roots and Love and Strife, by Anaxagoras as homeomerous ingredients and *Nous*, and by Philolaus as limiters, unlimiteds, and ἁρμονίη. In such theories, the latent purposiveness in earlier conceptions of nature is replaced by much more explicit discussions of the role of these forces in shaping the nature of things.

Finally, Democritus sits at the crossroads as both *physiologos* and humanist. Famous for advancing the physical theory of atomism, Democritus provides the most elaborate account of the physical structure of reality, largely consistent with the Parmenidean principles of the real. The true nature of reality is atoms and void and all events are subject only to necessity, but this "reality" (ἐτεή) is both contrasted with custom and inherently opaque to human beings:

> "By convention sweet and by convention bitter, by convention hot, by convention cold, by convention colour; but in reality atoms and void" (νόμῳ γλυκὺ καὶ νόμῳ πικρόν, νόμῳ θερμόν, νόμῳ ψυχρόν, νόμῳ χροιή· ἐτεῇ δὲ ἄτομα καὶ κενόν, B125).
>
> "That in reality we do not know what kind of thing each thing is or is not has been shown many times" (ἐτεῇ μέν νυν ὅτι οἷον ἕκαστον ἔστιν ἢ οὐκ ἔστιν οὐ συνίεμεν, πολλαχῇ δεδήλωται, B10).

And yet, whereas in many ways the earliest Greek philosophers understood man and cosmos to operate through the same principles, a new idea of nature as related to a specifically *human nature* comes upon the scene in the fifth century. Democritus, if he is not at the forefront of this new way of thinking, is at least swept along by it in certain characterizations he offers that depart significantly from conceiving of nature as utterly reducible to atoms, void, and necessity. For Democritus, atoms and void are ἐτεή, a "reality" that is set apart from mankind, while φύσις is instead reserved by Democritus for descriptions of nature with recognizably purposive features, as when he says in the ethical fragments:

> More people become good by practice than by nature (πλέονες ἐξ ἀσκήσιος ἀγαθοὶ γίνονται ἢ ἀπὸ φύσιος, B242).
>
> Nature and teaching are similar. For teaching reshapes the man, and in reshaping makes his nature (ἡ φύσις καὶ ἡ διδαχὴ παραπλήσιόν

ἐστι. καὶ γὰρ ἡ διδαχὴ μεταρυθμίζει τὸν ἄνθρωπον, μεταρυθμοῦσα δὲ φυσιοποιεῖ, B33).

Rather than conceiving of these facets of nature as linked, Democritus separates the reality (ἐτεή) of atoms and void that satisfy Parmenides' metaphysical criteria from the nature (φύσις) that is not "set apart from us" but is rather a recognizable force in the shaping of the human experience. In keeping these largely distinct, Democritus holds two entirely different ways to think about the nature of things.

At a minimum this account illustrates that the idea of nature is far from a monolithic construction that is universally agreed upon by the earliest Greek philosophers. Instead, these thinkers embrace a wide range of conceptions of what nature means and the implications for physical and metaphysical knowledge. Yet each conception bears the hallmarks of purposiveness, and it is this teleological undercurrent in the earliest strands of philosophy that helps give rise to the prescriptive concept of φύσις that plays such a dominant role in subsequent philosophical debates in ancient Greek philosophy. The conceptions of nature among the Sophists are in some ways just as diverse as those among the *physiologoi*, leading, in part, to the struggle of modern commentators to articulate what unifies these disparate thinkers in a cogent way.[11] The void left by the lack of consensus among the Presocratics leads to the problematic, and possibly corrupted views of nature found in the sophistic movement. Nature may be interpreted in various directions that represent significant departures from the conceptions of nature offered by the *physiologoi* that center on notions of harmony or other various imminent ends in nature. Further still, the theories offered by the *physiologoi* lack a kind of tangible reality, perhaps leading the sophists to grasp at more tangible sources and definitions of nature. Easily identifiable aspects of the human experience like advantages and desires would have seemed far more real than elusive notions of natural ends. The route to understanding purpose in nature may have seemed much closer to home. As a result, many of the thinkers of the sophistic movement continue the trend of innovation by exploring the implications of the idea of nature in new ways. In Protagoras' case, this amounts to an attack on previous notions but in others it is simply an expansion of the concept of nature in ways that are perhaps both more relevant and more readily identifiable. In the following section, I explore the notions of nature offered by several early thinkers of the sophistical movement.

---

11   See Barney 2006, 79.

2 Hidden Catalyst: The Sophistic "Corruption" of *Physis*

Defining the Sophists according to anything like consistent beliefs is equally as problematic as doing so for the Presocratics. In fact, for a variety of reasons, defining the Sophists is even more challenging.[12] Much like the problems with grouping the earliest *physiologoi* based on shared beliefs, the term sophists lacks cohesive power.[13] What seems beyond dispute, however, is that some among the earliest Sophists demonstrated a substantially different conception of nature than their *physiologoi* predecessors and contemporaries. Arguably Plato's largest complaint against the Sophists is the professionalization that occurs through charging fees, but perhaps more problematic than their being the "merchants of learning" is that the Sophists invariably become the merchants of political power. As theoretical speculation gives way to practical concerns, knowledge becomes a tool for political and social advantage. That is to say, when the knowledge of what things are is not for the sake of knowledge itself, but rather a means to legal or political advantage, or wealth, as it might be when deployed in a persuasive public speech, for example, it is easy to think of that knowledge as "corrupted" by the end it serves.

The earliest member of the sophistical movement is Protagoras, a student of Democritus. Protagoras famously claims: "Of all things the measure is man, of things that are that they are, of things that are not that they are not" (πάντων χρημάτων εἶναι μέτρον τὸν ἄνθρωπον, τῶν μὲν ὄντων ὡς ἔστιν, τῶν δὲ οὐκ ὄντων ὡς οὐκ ἔστιν, A14).[14] In the *Theaetetus,* Socrates clarifies this view by saying: "he means something like this: that as each thing appears to me, so it is to me" (152a). In the *Cratylus,* the relativism is expanded to include others in an obvious way: "as they seem to be to me, so they are to me; as they seem to you, so they are to you" (385e). Reduced to mere appearance, the nature of any given thing is entirely relative to the perceiver. As a result, nature lacks the universal, prescriptive power attributed to it by most other early Greek thinkers. By rendering the concept of nature powerless and meaningless, Protagoras effectively calls into question the entire project of

---

12 Notomi 2014 highlights specific problems of a tradition of Sophists that "repeated their predecessors' words with little care and often from memory, most fragments have been transmitted without their original contexts, and we often find the testimonies unreliable in general. Many anecdotes appear as free and often malicious fictions. Accordingly, their reliability as historical sources differs enormously. These features make any attempt at reconstruction of the Sophists' thoughts extremely difficult," 95.

13 Ibid, 96.

14 All translations from the Sophist thinkers come from Graham 2010.

PRESOCRATIC ECHOES

early Greek philosophy. Seeking the "real" outside of ourselves, as something apart from the perceiver, is a waste of time.[15] Such conclusions were derived from familiarity with the ideas of the early Greek *physiologoi* whose "contradictory speculations" neglected "the one thing that mattered, how to take care of one's own affairs and the business of the state."[16] The natural philosophers "claim[ed] to possess the secret of the universe" but in reality were only "chasing chimeras" and "pitting one opinion against another, each more incredible than the last."[17]

Beyond the diversity in conceptions of nature, however, the lack of a clear, determinate reality in the conceptions of nature offered by the *physiologoi* also likely contributed to this hostile reaction by the "practical men." The portrayal by Empedocles and Anaxagoras of the nature of something as a shifting mixture of roots or homeomerous stuffs may have led Protagoras to draw the inference that things lacked a fixed and enduring nature. In a similar fashion, Protagoras may have been simply extending his teacher Democritus' skepticism relative to the nature of things to its logical conclusion.[18] If we cannot *know* the true nature of things, perhaps this is because no enduring nature in fact exists; the supposed division between the "real" and the perceptible collapses in on itself. Protagoras' approach thus consists of "abandoning physiologia" and as a result he "knocks down the physical scaffolding of truth."[19] Richard McKirahan offers a different interpretation of Protagoras' thought, based primarily on the myth in Plato's *Protagoras*. He suggests that it is "possible that Protagoras intends *aidōs and dikē* [which Zeus has given to humans] as part of human nature and that if human nature lacked these moral qualities life as we know it would not be possible."[20] On this view, man is still the measure of all things, and "the *nomoi* of a community have some basis in human nature, that is, in (distinctively human) *phusis*."[21] Even if McKirahan's tentatively offered thesis is correct, however, Protagoras is clearly rejecting the more substantial role Democritus suggests for φύσις in human affairs, in favor of an emphasis on law as the primary source of proper action and justice. At best, on McKirahan's

---

15   Guthrie 1971 contends that Protagoras' ideas constitute "a denial of the very meaning of *physis*," 186. For a view that contrasts Protagoras with Democritus, see Vlastos 1945, 591–592.

16   Guthrie 1971, 186.

17   Ibid, 186–187.

18   See especially 68B7 and 68B10.

19   Vlastos 1945, 591.

20   McKirahan 2010 419.

21   Ibid.

reading, φύσις means a few generic traits that historically separated humans from other beasts, but offers little in the way of an ethical guide for current individual or communal decisions. In short, even if φύσις does "exist" for Protagoras, it is a relic of a previous age, an outmoded means of interpreting being and knowing. In establishing man as the "measure of all things" in fundamental opposition to the supposition by the Presocratics of natural principles which govern all things, Protagoras thereby sharpens the divide between justice "by nature" and justice "by law."

The relationship between the concepts of nature and justice becomes far more central as the sophistical movement flourishes, and prominent Sophists offer different accounts of which idea of justice is superior based upon different accounts of nature. While Protagoras dismisses the idea of φύσις, Antiphon staunchly defends nature in his stark presentation of the contrast between nature and law. Aristotle reports that Antiphon argues for the idea that the nature of physical things is their primary component (*Physics* 193a9-17). Of course, a primary component is more difficult to identify when it comes to human nature, but Antiphon defends the idea of human nature by using biological and behavioral commonalities that affect all members, stretching across communities: "For we all breathe the same air through our mouth and our nose, and we laugh when we are happy and cry when we are sad" (γὰρ εἰς τὸν ἀέρ[α] ἅπαντες κατὰ τὸ στόμ[α] [κ]αὶ κατ[α] τὰς ῥῖνας κ[αὶ γελῶμε]ν χ[αίροντες καὶ] δακρύομε[ν] λυπούμενοι, B44). Referring to the common traits of human nature, Antiphon claims that we are able to "learn from these things"; law and custom, on the other hand, are relative to location and community such that "[the laws and customs of those who live nearby] we know and respect; those of people dwelling far away we neither know nor respect" ([τοὺς νόμους τῶν ἐγγυτέ]ρων ἐπ[ιστάμε]θα τε κ[αὶ σέβομεν], τοὺς δὲ [τῶν τῆ]λοῦ οἰκ[ουν]των οὔτε ἐπι[στ]άμεθα οὔτε σεβόμεν, B44). Placing too much value on custom leads us to "become barbarians to one another," when instead humans ought to realize that "in all ways we are all equally fitted by nature, at least, to be both barbarians and Greeks" (ἐν τ[ο]ύτωι οὖν πρὸς ἀλλήλους βεβαρβρώμεθα, ἐπεὶ φύσει γε πάντα πάντες ὁμοίως πεφύκ[α]μεν καὶ βάρβαροι καὶ Ἕλλην[εσ] εἶναι, B44).

Expanding on this idea, Antiphon suggests an essential difference between nature and law with respect to justice when he says, "Thus a man would use justice in a way most advantageous to himself if, in the presence of witnesses, he held the laws in esteem, whereas when he was alone, he valued the works of nature" (χρῶιτ᾽ ἂν οὗ ἄνθρωπος μάλιστα ἑαυτῶι ξυμφ[ε]ρόντως δικαιο[σ]ύνηι, εἰ μετὰ μὲν μαρτύρων τοὺς νόμους μεγάλους ἄγοι, μονούμενος δὲ μαρτύρων τὰ τῆς φύσεως, B44). Juxtaposing the "factitious" laws with the "necessary" works of

PRESOCRATIC ECHOES

nature, Antiphon develops an idea of nature associated especially with the notion of advantages and disadvantages for human beings. While laws are to be observed, one only need to do so in order to avoid conflict with "those who agreed on them." Any violations of the prescriptions of φύσις, on the other hand, will have adverse consequences since "even if he eludes all men, the evil that results is no less; even if all observe, it is no more" (ἐάν τε πάντας ἀνθρώπους λάθηι, οὐδὲν ἔλαττον τὸ κακόν, ἐάν τε πάντες ἴδωσιν, οὐδεν μεῖζον, B44). In the final analysis, he who violates the laws of nature "is harmed, not because of opinion, but in truth" (οὐ γὰρ διὰ δόξαν βλάπτεται, ἀλλὰ δι᾽ ἀλήθειαν, B44). Jonathan Barnes argues that "Antiphon means to urge the claims of *phusis* above those of *nomos*" but denies that the sophist is doing more than simply asserting a "statement of fact."[22] There is, Barnes suggests, no indication of an "injunction or recommendation" on Antiphon's part; he does not say, "follow nature when you can get away with it," nor does he establish this as a view that he is "concerned to refute."[23] Alternatively, G.B. Kerferd believes Antiphon asserts a normative claim, though not one so simple as to suggest that φύσις is a better guide in all situations. The normative claim instead comes about since "it is what advantages man and his nature that is viewed as good"; as a result, since "laws and the norms of society" are instead "fetters and bonds imposed on [nature]" that fail to "contribute to what is required," φύσις rather than νόμος provides the key to the best life.[24] The "natural indicators" for what should be considered advantageous are pleasure and pain, thus Antiphon can be considered "the earliest advocate of hedonism in Greek philosophy."[25] Nature guides our choices by pleasure and pain, steering us toward what is advantageous and away from what is disadvantageous.

The essential link that Antiphon uncovers between φύσις and the advantageous is expanded by key Sophists in some of Plato's dialogues, particularly as they relate to political questions. Plato's characterization of the Sophists is remarkably varied, but could hardly be described as charitable. In the *Sophist*, he presents them as masters of a question and answer approach, while more characteristically in the *Protagoras* as dedicated speech-makers.[26] But it is in the *Gorgias* and the *Republic* that Plato frames the Sophists by their views rather than their methods. The two chief antagonists in those dialogues, Callicles and Thrasymachus, offer substantially different accounts of justice grounded in

---

22   Barnes 1979, 211–212.
23   Ibid.
24   Kerferd 1981, 116.
25   McKirahan 2010, 410–411.
26   Barney 2006, 78.

particular conceptions of φύσις and its relation to νόμος and δίκη. While Antiphon had suggested the basic hedonistic connection between nature and pleasure based on the idea of pleasure as advantageous, in the *Gorgias*, Callicles unabashedly expands the pleonectic component of human nature. In short, human nature necessitates that we "strive to have more (*pleon echein*) of the good, understood as wealth and power and the pleasures they can provide."[27] Collapsing the distinction between custom and nature, Callicles speaks of this striving as *nomos physeos*, the law of nature, in a way that invariably governs the behavior of all men.[28] Some men are strong by nature and able to take more of what they want, others are unable to do so. Nevertheless, in seeking to ensure they at least have an equal amount of wealth and power, the weak inevitably resort to laws. The inescapable pursuit of advantage over others necessitates that the weak use νόμος as a tool in order to subjugate the strong and mitigate the advantage they enjoy by nature. Thus, human nature as an endless striving for more, for the satisfaction of particular desires, emerges in the story of philosophy.[29] Living well for humans means fulfilling *physis* as desires, and the resulting view is that what is just *by nature*, that is, taking as much as one can for himself, is declared unjust by law.

Thrasymachus, the representative Sophist in the *Republic*, presents a more intricate position that extends the sophistical views of Antiphon and Callicles to their logical conclusion. In so doing Thrasymachus challenges the value of philosophy. Taking up the now familiar idea that "the ultimate standard ... is one's own advantage," Thrasymachus confidently asserts that "justice is nothing other than the advantage of the stronger" (*Republic* 338c).[30] Pressured by Socrates for clarity, Thrasymachus retreats under the barrage of Socratic questions and departs from Callicles' stated view when he revises his position to suggest that it is actually *injustice* that is "to one's own profit and advantage"

---

27   Ibid., 83.

28   *Gorgias* 483e3; see especially Kerferd 1981, 112, and McKirahan 2010, 408.

29   Although *physis* is generally understood to be universal and necessary, occasionally thinkers maintained the opposite characterization. This view is perhaps best articulated in an account from Pseudo-Demosthenes in the fourth century B.C., who claims that "*phusis* is without order and private to each individual but the *nomoi* are common, in order, and the same for all," McKirahan 2010, 422. On such a view, there is no such thing as "human" nature; nature as a theoretical concept that determines identity and actions applies only to individuals. While Pseudo-Demosthenes does not elaborate in any real detail, it seems that the facets of individual nature are nevertheless primarily affiliated with and recognized by the presence of particular desires, such that "*phusis*, if it is wicked, often has low desires," as cited in McKirahan 2010, 422.

30   McKirahan 2010, 413.

while justice bids us do what is better for others (*Republic* 343b-344c). Thrasymachus draws the obvious implication: "Injustice, if it is on a large enough scale, is stronger, freer, and more masterly than justice" (344c). Nature, in a way, sanctions injustice and men delude and weaken themselves if they seek justice or spend much time at all contemplating it. Presenting a more "general" depiction of human nature than the pleonectic version offered by Callicles, Thrasymachus avoids limiting advantages to satisfaction of desires and thus "cannot be refuted just by attacking hedonism."[31] Although explicitly challenging Socrates with showing that justice has greater value than injustice, Thrasymachus also issues an implicit challenge as his argument "calls for an answer to the question of what our interests and advantages really are."[32] This, I take it, is one of the reasons that φύσις plays such a prominent if underappreciated role in the *Republic*.

3 Plato and Aristotle: Defending and Expanding *Physis*[33]

Plato's treatment of the Sophists has been a subject of continued debate,[34] but one way to read Plato, in light of the foregoing account, is to understand certain dialogues, and arguments contained therein, as an attempt to safeguard philosophy, from relativistic impulses that make the pursuit of wisdom a useless or childish endeavor. Such a defense, however, hinges on the expression of a strong sense of φύσις, such that "justice and laws should derive from and be based on nature."[35] In response to Thrasymachus' challenge in the *Republic* that injustice is superior to justice, Socrates grounds the idea of justice on an idea of purposive nature that goes beyond individual advantages. In doing so, he fashions an understanding of φύσις by expanding certain purposive features of the various concepts of nature among the *physiologoi*. The "best interests" for human beings extend beyond personal advantage with nature prescribing what is the "best" or just for all. Thus philosophy as the pursuit of wisdom in connection with what nature prescribes is more than worthwhile: it is vital to living the good life.

---

31 Ibid.

32 Ibid.

33 Select portions of this section appeared first in Habash 2016b, reprinted here with permission from American Catholic Philosophical Association.

34 See Corey 2015, Tell 2010.

35 Notomi 2014, 107.

Plato's attempt to defend and define φύσις thus pulls specific facets from both the Sophists and the *physiologoi*. The idea that nature establishes advantageous norms is not a conception taken from the *physiologoi*; the source for this appears to be the Sophists. In the *Phaedo*, however, Plato recounts Socrates' description of his initial encounter with the ideas of Anaxagoras. Presenting himself as a kind of self-confessed *physiologos*, fascinated by Anaxagoras' suggestion that all things are arranged by *Nous* for the best, Socrates is inevitably disappointed when Anaxagoras does not follow through in providing accounts of how this is so. Instead of discussing salient features of the cosmos and clarifying why they are such instead of possible alternatives, and in particular elaborating on how this is "for the better," Anaxagoras lapses into explanations that resort to minute physical causes. Socrates then describes the turn he made, suggesting a "second sailing" in which he abandons the study of the natural world through the use of his senses and turns instead to discussion and the investigation of truth through arguments (*Phaedo* 99d-e). In short, the *aim* of the project of the early Greek philosophers is right; it is the method that is flawed. While Plato's *Timaeus* may deal with purposive features in the construction of the cosmos, the practical effect of a purposive φύσις that can serve as a model for human society is found in the *Republic*. In laying out the just city in the early part of that dialogue, Plato returns time and again to what is best *by nature*. Oftentimes, in alarming fashion for his interlocutors, what is best by nature is in stark contrast to human desires. Plato seems to understand φύσις as it applies to humans, more in terms of capacity; that is, closely, but not exclusively, connected with desires and emotions. One striking example, and a likely application of Heraclitus' notion of φύσις, is the discussion of the nature of the best soldiers in *Republic* II.

The discovery of justice in Plato's *Republic* hinges on the determination of roles in the just city according to the idea of nature. Given the importance of the guardians' role, Socrates contends, these soldiers should be free from other kinds of labor and possess "the greatest skill and devotion" (374e). Equally important, however, is that this kind of work "also requires a person whose nature is suited to that way of life" (374e). Comparing the guardian with a dog, Socrates makes the case that these guardians need an "invincible and unbeatable spirit" in addition to keen senses, notable speed, and superior strength. Such natures, however, may be far too savage toward the soldier's own citizens. What is necessary, it seems, is to find a nature that is "both gentle and high-spirited at the same time" (375c). Laying out the problem, Socrates says that "a gentle nature is the opposite of a spirited one" and that since these natures cannot coexist in a single individual, it seems there can be no such thing as a good guardian. Socrates is not stalled long, however, referring back to the analogy of

PRESOCRATIC ECHOES

good soldiers with well-trained dogs, as he points out that seemingly paradoxical natures do exist "in which these opposites are indeed combined" (375d). The well-trained dog is "gentle as can be to those he is used to and knows, but the opposite to those he does not know" (375e). Thus, Socrates adds a philosophical component to the guardian's nature because it guides the individual in judging well and distinguishing based on knowledge. Helpfully, Plato specifies the nature of a "fine and good guardian" for us: it contains the attributes of philosophy, spirit, speed, and strength (376c).

There is no conception of nature as the unification of opposites before Plato except in Heraclitus; the Ephesian sage is the source for this idea.[36] Socrates here plays the role of a Heraclitean sage who is able to recognize the unity in opposites, that is, the existence of an underlying "fitting-together" (ἁρμονίη) of opposite traits. Broadly speaking, the mark of the philosopher as a leader is the ability to recognize the *logos* that nature has laid out for a just society, but more specifically through the crucial ability to, in Heraclitus' words, "distinguish each according to its nature and tell how it is" (22B1). Recognizing such natures and establishing an accompanying system of task assignment is essential to the establishment of a just society for Plato. Not only does nature operate in recognizable patterns, but these serve as prescriptive models for the best society. Not only can the idea of nature be used to answer political questions, but it is essential if we are ever to have a universally discoverable truth upon which political institutions and practices can be grounded.

Aristotle's approach to defining and understanding φύσις is decidedly more systematic than Plato's, beginning with the *Physics*. But Aristotle's approach may be less about defending philosophy against corrupting influences by purifying central philosophical concepts like φύσις. Instead, Aristotle seeks to develop an appropriate philosophical method that can redefine philosophy as a way of life while achieving a more comprehensive understanding of the nature of things.[37] Rather than broad theorizing or *a priori* generalizations in his attempt to give a comprehensive account, Aristotle derives his method from

---

36   One may attempt, as Seth Benardete has done, to tease such an idea out of the single use of *physis* regarding the Moly flower in the Homer's *Odyssey* since the flower is white while the root is black and "to dig up the Moly is to expose to the light its flower and its root; they belong together regardless of the contrariety in their colors," Benardete 1997, 86. Benardete contends that it is this knowledge of nature as opposites specifically applied to the link between "the mind of man together with his build" that ultimately saves Odysseus from Circe.

37   Lennox 2015.

the careful study of natural beings.[38] Philosophy as such becomes the study of natures since these are the "sources of change in natural things."[39] Aristotle's understanding of the different "parts" of his "unitary project of investigation" is thus "strongly dependent upon a specific conception of the natural world."[40] Derived from close and careful observation of all manner of natural beings, Aristotle's specific conception of the natural world is fundamentally defined by the teleological quality found in all things. Purposiveness is found not only in the large-scale construction of the cosmos, and the prescribed advantages, or what is "best" in human affairs, but within every natural being as final cause. Aristotle's objection to the ideas of purposive nature offered by his predecessors center on their supposed poor understanding of the precise nature of final causes: "That for the sake of which actions and changes and movements take place, they assert to be a cause in a way, but not in this way, i.e. not in the way in which it is its *nature* to be a cause" (*Metaphysics* 988b6-8).[41] Referring to Anaxagoras and Empedocles without naming them, he says, "For those who speak of reason or friendship class these causes as goods; they do not speak, however, as if anything that exists either existed or came into being for the sake of these, but as if the movements started from these" (986b8-10). As Aristotle makes clear, his conception of the natural world is framed in terms of causes. The error of his Presocratic predecessors is that they had not adequately conceived of, and clearly articulated, the precise idea of nature as a cause "for the sake of which." As final causes, that is, as a truly teleological nature in Aristotle's view, not only natures but their ends themselves become objects of study. Aristotle's defense of φύσις and the pursuit of wisdom is in some ways a secondary effect of his quest for precision and clarity in explanations and understanding of the natural world. Reorienting φύσις to be understood more clearly through the lens of causality, and all that entails, provides a more comprehensive and reliable account of all things. How far one might extend the parallels is certainly debatable, as the relationship between Aristotle's different works remains one of the more disputed points in recent scholarship, but his specific conception of nature and natural beings may shed light beyond the biological works to provide better answers to the role of nature in political and ethical questions.

Although they cannot be considered fully teleological, the multivocal ideas of nature we find in early Greek accounts contain purposive undercurrents. It

---

38 See Harry 2015. Harry notes that "Aristotle explicitly distances himself from Platonic-style natural philosophy," citing *Physics* 203a16 and *Metaphysics* 1001a12, p. 2. n5.

39 Lennox 2015, 16.

40 Falcon 2005, 1.

41 Emphasis in the translation by W.D. Ross.

is these undercurrents, and their implications, that those thinkers known as Sophists reject and attempt to purge from the idea of nature, so as to relegate nature to the sidelines as a potential guide for human choice. But it is these same undercurrents, I argue, that Plato and Aristotle seek to rehabilitate and expand upon in order to shore up the idea that nature (*physis*) is a viable philosophical idea.[42]

Bibliography

Benardete, Seth. 1997. The Bow and the Lyre: A Platonic Reading of the Odyssey. Lanham: Rowman & Littlefield.

Barnes, Jonathan. 1979. The Presocratic Philosophers, 2 volumes. London: Routledge and Kegan Paul.

Barney, Rachel. 2006. "The Sophistic Movement." In A Companion to Ancient Philosophy, edited by Mary Louise Gill and Pierre Pellegrin. Malden, M.A.: Blackwell Publishing.

Curd, Patricia. 2004. The Legacy of Parmenides: Eleatic Monism and Later Presocratic Thought. Las Vegas: Parmenides.

Curd, Patricia. 2006. "Parmenides and After: Unity and Plurality." In A Companion to Ancient Philosophy, edited by Mary Louise Gill and Pierre Pellegrin. Malden: M.A.: Blackwell.

Corey, David. D. 2015. *The Sophists in Plato's Dialogues*. Albany: SUNY Press.

Falcon, Andrea. 2005, *Aristotle and the Science of Nature: Unity without Uniformity*. Cambridge: Cambridge University Press.

Graham, Daniel. 2010. *The Texts of Early Greek Philosophy: The Complete Fragments and Selected Testimonies of the Major Presocratics*, 2 vols. Cambridge: Cambridge University Press.

Grote, George. 1884. A History of Greece; from the earliest period to the close of the generation contemporary with Alexander the Great, a new edition in twelve volumes, London: John Murray.

Guthrie, W.K.C. 1971. The Sophists: A History of Greek Philosophy, volume 3. Cambridge: Cambridge University Press.

Habash, Justin. 2016a. Early Greek Philosophy and the Discovery of Nature. PhD Dissertation, Duquesne University.

---

42   I would like to thank Ron Polansky, Michael Harrington, and Tim Quinn for their helpful comments. Select portions of this chapter also formed part of my argument in a previous paper on Plato's reception of Presocratic ideas and are reprinted here with full permission from the American Catholic Philosophical Association.

Habash, Justin. 2016b. Plato's Debt: Justice and Nature in Early Greek Philosophy. *Proceedings of the American Catholic Philosophical Association* 90: 97–108.

Habash, Justin. 2019. Heraclitus and the Riddle of Nature. *Epoché* 23: 275–286.

Hadot, Pierre. 2006. *Veil of Isis: An Essay on the History of the Idea of Nature*, Cambridge, M.A.: Harvard University Press.

Harry, Chelsea. 2015. *Chronos in Aristotle's Physics: On the Nature of Time*, Cham: Springer.

Kerferd, G.B. 1981. The Sophistic Movement. Cambridge: Cambridge University Press.

Lennox, James, G and Robert Bolton, ed. 2010. *Being, Nature, And Life In Aristotle: Essays in Honor of Allan Gotthelf*. Cambridge: Cambridge University Press.

Lennox, James G. 2015. "How to study natural bodies: Aristotle's μέθοδος." In *A Critical Guide to the Physics*, ed. Mariska Leunissen, Cambridge: Cambridge University Press.

McKirahan, Richard, D. 2010. *Philosophy Before Socrates: An Introduction with Texts and Commentary*, 2nd ed. Indianapolis: Hackett.

Naddaf, Gerard. 2005. *The Greek Concept of Nature*. Albany: SUNY Press.

Notomi, Noburu. 2014. "The Sophists." In The Routledge Companion to Ancient Philosophy, ed. Frisbee Sheffield and James Warren. New York: Routledge.

Panchenko, Dimitri. 1993. "Thales and the Origin of Theoretical Reasoning," *Configurations* 1.3: 387–414.

Tell, Hakan. 2010. *Plato's Counterfeit Sophists*. Washington, D.C: Center for Hellenic Studies.

Sallis, John. 2016. *The Figure of Nature: On Greek Origins*. Bloomington: Indiana University.

Sedley, David. 2010. "Teleology, Aristotelian and Platonic." In *Being, Nature, And Life In Aristotle: Essays in Honor of Allan Gotthelf*. Cambridge: Cambridge University Press.

Vlastos, Gregory. 1945. "Ethics and Physics in Democritus (part I)," *Philosophical Review* 54: 578–592.

CHAPTER 4

The Reception of Early Greek Astronomy

Daniel W. Graham

The story of the reception of ancient works has a great deal to teach us. The works and words and ideas of the past become fodder for later ages, offering inspiration, models of style and content, or targets for criticism. The works of the past are sometimes disdained, neglected and lost, sometimes rediscovered, revived and idolized, sometimes adopted, transformed and appropriated. By studying reception, we find that conceptions of the past are no more permanent than the certainties of the present. One discipline, however, seems to display a more stable connection between its past and its present: natural science. Science seems to offer a reliable method for turning research into knowledge; its history can boast a string of successes leading to a better grasp of natural processes, often measured by an improved ability to manipulate those processes for beneficial ends. This brings us to a question about ancient Greek science. Did it achieve anything like the status of modern science, and if so, when and how?

Most historians of science do not recognize anything like a practice of scientific method in Greece before the late fourth century BC at the earliest—and some would put the practice centuries after that.[1] I have argued that the successful practice of science begins in the times of the Presocratics, specifically in the early fifth century BC, in the field of astronomy.[2] This thesis raises all kinds of questions, including a number that revolve around the reception of Presocratic ideas. If the Presocratics made rapid breakthroughs in science, why do we not see this in the early histories and doxographies of early philosophy? Further, even if some sources missed the importance of the new ideas, is there any evidence in the records of later times that can indicate that scientific inquiry was progressing in a significant way? These questions may, however, seem simplistic or misguided. There have been important voices pointing out the fact that science, even or especially in its modern incarnation, does not proceed in a linear fashion, but sometimes goes on wild goose chases, and sometimes reinvents itself in scientific revolutions that seem to be driven more by

---

1 On the Presocratics, Lloyd 1970, 49; Dicks 1970, 60; Vlastos 1975, 87; Grant 2007, 18. On astronomy, Goldstein and Bowen 1983, 330–332, 340.
2 Graham 2013.

© KONINKLIJKE BRILL NV, LEIDEN, 2021 | DOI:10.1163/9789004443358_006

ideological fervor (as in a political revolution) than by reason and method.[3] I shall have to say something about the new historiography of science. But suffice it to say for now that even proponents of the revolutionary model recognize periods of "normal science" in which progress within a shared framework or paradigm is definitive of the practice.[4] In this chapter I shall (1) lay out the historical evidence for an early scientific revolution in astronomy; (2) examine responses to the new astronomy from the fifth and fourth centuries BC; (3) follow the further development of astronomical conception into the Hellenistic and early Roman Empire periods; and (4) consider whether the beneficiaries of the new approach to astronomy were aware of their benefactors.

1

As students of early philosophy have long recognized—at least since the time of Plato and Aristotle—the earliest philosophers were above all natural philosophers—Aristotle called them *phusikoi* or *phusiologikoi*—propounding theories of the cosmos, typically with stories of how the world arose from a primeval state of disorder, and how it acquired its present shape with an earth surrounded by heavenly bodies dancing around it and populated by plants, animals, and human beings.[5] What we see when we study the early philosophers is a proliferation of naturalistic theories to explain the phenomena of nature, including portentous phenomena such as earthquakes, thunder and lightning, eclipses, and tornadoes—phenomena traditionally explained by activities of the gods.[6] The natural philosophers' theories are innovative and original. But the theorists offer no reliable way to test the theories. As the sixth century goes on theories multiply, but no way is found to discriminate between theories so as to determine which is true and which false. Indeed, early critics point out the inaccessibility of the phenomena explained and the unavailability of any method to test the truth of the theories proposed.[7]

In the early fifth century BC all of this changes in one important domain, or so I claim. The turning point comes, ironically, with the one philosopher who seems most hostile to naturalistic explanations: Parmenides. After

---

3   Kuhn 1996.

4   Kuhn 1996, 10–42; for a discussion of recent methodological developments in the history of science, see Graham 2013, 19–40.

5   Arist. *Metaph.* 983b6 ff.

6   Vlastos 1975, 3–22; Graham 2006.

7   Xen. *Hell.* 1.1.11-15; Hippoc. *VM* 1, *Nat. hom.* 1.

THE RECEPTION OF EARLY GREEK ASTRONOMY

demonstrating the futility of the whole project of natural philosophy, he offers his own cosmology as one that cannot be surpassed, in the *Doxa*, or Opinion, part of his poem. He goes on in his cosmology to offer a remarkable observation: the moon is ever gazing at the rays of the sun (B15) as it wanders around the earth with borrowed light (ἀλλότριον φῶς) (B14). In other words, the moon is itself a dark planet, illuminated only by the light of the sun. Its shining surface always faces the sun. This latter fact accounts then for the phases of the moon: the side of the moon facing the sun is illuminated. All of this is pretty routine astronomy today, but no ancient source in any culture we know of had ever made a *causal* connection between the moon's light and the sun's position. And indeed, once an observer makes the connection, he can see that the phase of the moon correlates perfectly with the angular distance of the moon from the sun. When the new moon first appears, it is a crescent above and to the left of the setting sun, which it is near. Each night it moves farther to the left as the illuminated portion grows larger, until as the sun is setting in the west the full moon is rising in the east. Then the luminous portion shrinks as the moon nears the rising sun in the east. Parmenides' insight allows one to *predict* the phase of the moon each night.

Parmenides also makes two other remarkable observations: the Morning Star is the Evening star (later called the planet Venus), and the earth is spherical.[8] The former observation had already been known for a thousand years in Babylonia, but was apparently unknown to any Greek philosopher before Parmenides.[9] The latter is remarkable at a time when all Greek cosmological models posited a flat earth. Why Parmenides advanced it we do not know. It is possible that recognizing the unity of the Morning and Evening Stars helped Parmenides see that the position of heavenly bodies relative to the sun was important. And he further recognized that the moon would go through the observed phases only if it were a spherical body, which might inductively suggest the sphericity of all heavenly bodies.[10] But this much remains speculation.

What makes Parmenides' insight important is that it initiated a new approach to the heavens that bore immediate fruit. Anaxagoras seems to have grasped the significance of making the sun the source of the moon's light—the doctrine of heliophotism. If that is so, then (1) the moon is opaque, or it would always be visible at night; (2) it orbits below the sun, or it would always be visible at night; (3) it is spherical, to account for the shape of the shadows in its phases; (4) both the sun and the moon are permanent bodies rather than

---

8   Aët. 2.15.7 = DK 28a40a.

9   See Hunger and Pingree 1999, 57, 73–75; Graham 2013, 94.

10   See Graham 2013, 103; Popper 1998, 133–135; Arist. *Cael.* II.11.

being, as some theories said, "new every day," for even when the sun has set in the middle of the lunar month, it is lighting the moon; (5) the moon is massy because it is spherical and opaque, and presumably earthlike; (6) the paths of the sun and moon go under the earth (see point (4)). All the these points are acknowledged by Anaxagoras in his astronomical opinions.[11] But Anaxagoras also used the implications of Parmenides' insight to solve a so-far intractable problem: how to explain eclipses.

If the moon is a permanent opaque body orbiting below the sun, at the end of the lunar month when it becomes invisible, it is lurking in the vicinity of the sun. We do not see it because it is in conjunction with the sun: the back side of the moon is illuminated and the front side (toward the earth) is in shadow. But since the moon is about the same size as the sun as viewed from earth, if the moon happened to pass directly between earth and the sun, it would occult the sun and block its light: a solar eclipse. Furthermore, if the moon were in opposition to the sun and the moon entered into the shadow of the earth, the moon would be darkened: a lunar eclipse. Thus the model suggested by Parmenides offered a new explanation of both solar and lunar eclipses: they resulted from the blocking (*antiphraxis* in Aristotle's vocabulary)[12] of the sun's light to the earth or to the moon, respectively. If this new implication—let us call it a hypothesis—were correct, solar eclipses could happen only at the time of the new moon, lunar eclipses only at the time of the full moon. Anaxagoras proposed these new explanations for the first time.[13]

The hypothesis of heliophotism had important implications for the relationship of the sun and the moon, and suggested a new geometry of the heavens. Most strikingly, it led to the antiphraxis hypothesis as an explanation of eclipses with further predictive implications. Anaxagoras makes one further intriguing claim about the sizes of the moon and the sun: the moon is about the size of the Peloponnesus, the sun larger.[14] This claim strikes the modern reader as bizarre and arbitrary. But it has a possible explanation. On February 17, 478 BC, an annular solar eclipse passed over southern Greece, almost completely obscuring the Peloponnesus in its umbra. On the supposition that the moon is much closer to the earth than the sun, Anaxagoras could have seen the moon's shadow as approximating the diameter of the moon, and hence judged the moon as being about the size of the peninsula it darkened. On one ancient account, Anaxagoras was in Athens at the time, where he would have

---

11   Hippol. *Haer.* 18.6-10 = DK 59A42.

12   E.g. Arist. *An. post.* 90a16.

13   See Graham 2013, esp. 137–176.

14   Plut. *De fac.* = *Mor.* 932a; Hippol. *Haer.* 1.8.8 = 59A4; Diog. Laert. 2.8 = 59A1.

THE RECEPTION OF EARLY GREEK ASTRONOMY 95

witnessed the eclipse and could have questioned travelers from the nearby Peloponnesus.[15]

Heliophotism gives the true explanation of lunar light, and the antiphraxis theory of eclipses is true. A fortuitous eclipse may have confirmed the hypotheses for the young philosopher Anaxagoras. The two theories that emerge from this story offer the first scientific breakthrough in astronomy. But how was it received? Already by the time of Anaxagoras there had been a plethora of proposed explanations of lunar light and of eclipses. What was lacking was any kind of consensus. Would the intellectual community accept the new theories as the major advances they were, or merely file them away as more unfounded speculations? Today we take it for granted that science has a powerful method that can test its claims and vindicate some theories while refuting others. Early Greek philosophers offered naturalistic explanations much like those of modern scientists, but without a well-developed methodology for testing theories and without the institutional infrastructure of modern science. In some sense modern science is defined in part by the open reception of its products. How would intellectuals receive the new astronomical theories?

2

Almost immediately Anaxagoras' contemporary Empedocles accepted heliophotism. He speaks of "the sun's ray, having hit the broad circle of the moon" (DK 31B43), and observes that the moon "gazes into the bright circle of her lord's face" (B47). The moon "spins around the earth, a circular borrowed light" (B45). Empedocles' poetic lines, his B47 recalling Parmenides' B15, and his B45 actually quoting περὶ γαῖαν ... ἀλλότριον φῶς of Parmenides' B14, reveal that Empedocles has read his Parmenides and also picked up on his theory of lunar light. Furthermore, he also seems to share Anaxagoras' theory of eclipses: the moon "did away with his [the sun's] rays/to the earth from above, and it obscured the earth/as much as was the width of the bright-eyed moon" (B42). It is possible indeed that Empedocles independently grasped the importance of Parmenides' insight and developed its consequences. Or he may have come to the theory first so that Anaxagoras learned the theory of eclipses from Empedocles. Yet Anaxagoras was in a unique position to study the solar eclipse of 478, as Empedocles was not, for the latter's native city of Acragas on Sicily was outside the umbra of the eclipse. And Anaxagoras seems to have been only

---

15   Graham and Hintz 2007.

twenty-two years old at the time, while Empedocles was seventeen or younger, and hence still under the tutelage of his elders. So it seems most likely that Anaxagoras was the first thinker to interpret eclipses as the blocking of the sun's light.[16]

In the later fifth century it appears that Philolaus, who held that the earth is a planet orbiting around a central fire with the sun, the moon, and the five known planets, also accepted the antiphraxis theory. In his innovative cosmos, not only the earth and the moon, but also the counter-earth, which he posited as an additional heavenly body, caused eclipses by screening light.[17] We are not well informed about Democritus' astronomy, but he seems to have accepted heliophotism as well.[18]

We get one interesting perspective from the historian Thucydides. Probably writing in the early fourth century BC about events from the late fifth century, he records a solar eclipse on August 3, 431 BC. He mentions the fact that the eclipse occurred during the new moon, "which seems to be the only time when this can happen" (2.28.1). He records a partial solar eclipse occurring at the new moon in 424 (4.52.1). Finally, he records the lunar eclipse of August 27, 413, which caused the superstitious general Nicias to postpone his retreat from Syracuse, with disastrous consequences. He notes that "the moon happened to be full" (7.50.4). Although he never expressly acknowledges it, the historian seems to be aware of the one new theory that predicts that solar eclipses occur in the dark of the moon, while lunar eclipses occur at the time of the full moon. Perhaps with this science in mind, he judges that Nicias "was too devoted to divination" (7.50.4). From Thucydides we get a glimpse of how an educated non-philosopher might draw on the new astronomical theories to understand and evaluate historical events.

Plato, the great philosopher of the mid-fourth century BC, has little to say about lunar light and eclipses. But he does adopt for his cosmology a spherical earth introduced by Parmenides (*Phd.* 109–110, esp. 109a). As a sphere in the middle of the cosmos, the earth has no need of any force to keep it in place. Evidently it keeps its position by the principle of indifference advocated by Anaximander (for his disk-shaped earth). The earth has irregular surface features, but overall it is a perfect sphere. In his more detailed and scientific *Timaeus,* Plato posits a spherical cosmos, but has little to say about the shape of the earth itself. Yet in any case, the choice of a spherical earth brings up the

---

16   See Graham 2013, 137–176.

17   See Graham 2015.

18   Plut. *De fac.* 929c = DK 68A89a; Graham 2013, 198–201.

possibility of radial symmetry for the cosmos and a new kind of explanation in which heavenly orbits are regular and perfect.[19]

Plato's student Aristotle provides detailed arguments for a spherical earth, which include two scientifically correct arguments: in effect he proves the sphericity of the earth. The observer's view of the stars varies with latitude, which would happen only on a spherical surface. And the shadows of the earth projected onto the moon during the initial and final stages of a lunar eclipse show that the earth is spherical (*Cael.* 11.14). The latter proof also assumes the antiphraxis theory of eclipses, which Aristotle embraces, and indeed cites as a paradigm of scientific explanation (*An. Post.* 11.2, 8). By Aristotle's time the insights of Parmenides have begun to serve as principles of cosmological and astronomical reasoning. Aristotle notes by the way that mathematicians have estimated the circumference of the earth to be 400,000 stades (*Cael.* 11.14, 298b15-17). What methods were used he does not say. But he reports perhaps the first of a series of increasingly accurate measurements of the earth. Clearly the shape of the earth has become a matter of "normal science" to be measured and incorporated in astronomical observations and geographical plots. Aristotle accepts without demur a theory of lunar light that fits poorly with his own metaphysics of the superlunary spheres, in which everything is eternal and changeless (except for circular motion).

3

While earlier philosophers reflect on or react to their predecessors from time to time, Aristotle for the first time institutes something like a modern tendency to search the literature of the topics he addresses, assembling opinions (*doxai*) or authoritative opinions (*endoxa*) in his quest to survey theories and arrive at the right explanation.[20] This tendency is carried on by Aristotle's colleague and student Theophrastus in a tradition that has come to be known as doxography. Eventually the information was pared down to lists of opinions on standardized topics, with the author or authors of a given opinion named. Unfortunately, virtually all context for the opinions is omitted, so that the reader cannot in general reconstruct the theories behind the opinions, at least not from the doxographic notices themselves. Furthermore, the opinions are arranged not in

---

19   See Furley 1987, 53–57, who traces the origins of the picture to Parmenides.
20   Arist. *Eth. Nic.* 1145b1-7, with Owen 1961; Nussbaum 1982.

chronological or historical order, but in some sort of logical ordering of types of opinions.[21]

For our purposes, however, what is interesting about astronomical advances can be extracted from the doxography. By checking the dates of the authors of the various opinions on the moon's light and on the causes of eclipses, we can ascertain that after Anaxagoras there are no new theories on these subjects—with one exception. A Babylonian astrologer named Berosus offers a theory according to which the moon has a luminous side and a dark side, with the luminous side always facing the sun.[22] The resulting theory makes no predictions other than those of the heliophotism theory, while losing the causal connection. In a certain sense, then, it is a spin-off of heliophotism without offering any advantages. In any case, no Greek theorist offered new theories of lunar light or of eclipses after Anaxagoras. This suggests that theoretical consensus was reached soon after the theories in question were proposed. One caveat must be noted: Epicurus and his followers regarded cosmological and astronomical theories as unprovable in practice; they were satisfied if they could find hypotheses that in principle sufficed to explain the phenomena.[23] Their accounts of lunar light and eclipses include the generally accepted ones, but the Epicureans refused to endorse any particular explanations.[24]

On the shape of the earth, the doxographies are not helpful. They say that Thales and the Stoics make the earth spherical, while Anaximander, Anaximenes, Leucippus, and Democritus make it flat (Aët. *Plac.* 3.10.1-5). Thales, however, as Aristotle reports, views the earth as like a raft floating on a primeval sea. What we can say is that Plato, Aristotle, the Stoics, and everyone else with serious scientific interests (excluding, that is, the Epicureans) come to see the earth as spherical, from the fourth century BC on. For the Stoics we have the following report:

> [The Stoics] believe that both the heavenly bodies and the earth (which is motionless) are spherical. The moon does not have its own light but takes it from the sun's illumination. The sun is eclipsed when the moon occults the part facing us, as Zeno illustrates in *On the Whole*. For it is visible passing under and concealing the sun and then moving on. ... The moon is eclipsed when it enters into the shadow of the earth. Hence it is eclipsed only at the time of the full moon.
>
> DIOG. LAERT. 7.145–146 = *SVF* I.119, II.650

---

21 See Mansfeld and Runia 2009 for the structure of doxographic collections.

22 See Toulmin 1967.

23 Epicurus *Ep.Pyth.* 85–7; *Ep. Hdt.* 79–80.

24 Lucr. 5.753–57; Epicurus *Ep. Pyth.* 96.

THE RECEPTION OF EARLY GREEK ASTRONOMY

Here we get the spherical earth, heliophotism, and antiphraxis all in a single account of heavenly phenomena. There is nothing new or original about this astronomical account, but we do see something absent from early Greek natural philosophy: the perpetuation of a single authoritative theory from theorist to theorist, and now from school to school, as the only viable theory of celestial motion and of its more prominent phenomena.

We have been focusing on philosophers. But in the Hellenistic period we meet a group of highly skilled mathematicians who are also astronomers and cosmologists. How do they respond to the new astronomical theories? Aristarchus of Samos, who flourished around 280 BC, developed the first heliocentric theory, making the earth orbit the sun instead of vice versa. His one extant treatise is *On the Sizes and Distances of the Sun and Moon*. There he starts from six hypotheses, of which three are significant for the present study:

Hypotheses
1. That the moon receives its light from the sun.

    ...

3. That, when the moon appears to us halved, the great circle which divides the dark and bright portions of the moon is in the direction of our eye.

    ...

5. That the breadth of the (earth's) shadow is (that) of two moons. (trans. Heath from Heath 1913)

The study that results seems to be more a mathematical exercise than a scientific study, for the author provides values for inputs that he knew were not accurate—for instance, he gives the angular size of the sun as 2° (hypothesis 6), when he knew it was ½. What is important, however, is that heliophotism plays a vital role in the argument, for establishing the angles, sizes, and distances of the three heavenly bodies he studies in the treatise. The sun's illumination of the moon and the earth's blocking of that illumination provide the starting point for determining the geometry of the heavens. If the calculation were an exercise for Aristarchus, it could provide the template for an accurate measurement of the positions of the bodies, when accurate values were substituted for arbitrary or oversimplified ones.

One important offspring of fifth-century BC astronomical theories is the work of Eratosthenes of Cyrene, who worked in Alexandria, Egypt from about 245 BC for about fifty years. An all-around scientist and scholar, he made a famous measurement of the earth. Hypothesizing that the sun was at an infinite distance from the earth, so that its rays were parallel in all place on the earth, that Alexandria was (in round numbers) 5000 stades north of Syene, with both cities lying on the same meridian, that at noon of the summer solstice the sun was directly overhead at Syene (for Syene was on the Tropic of Cancer), and that at the same time the sun was 1/50th of a meridian circle below the zenith in Alexandria, he used geometry to calculate the circumference of the earth as 250,000 stades. The calculation makes use of approximations and simplifications (for instance, the two cities are not on the same meridian, and there was no precise way of determining the distance between the two cities). Furthermore, the exact length of the stade (600 Greek feet) is controversial, given that several standards were in use. Depending on the length of his stades, Eratosthenes' estimate varies from about 44,000 to 46,000 km, whereas the correct value is about 40,000 km.[25] Given the means at Eratosthenes' disposal, his estimate was remarkably good. At this point the speculations of Presocratic philosophers were turning into creditable science, providing an estimate that would stand for centuries as the best approximation of the earth's size.[26]

We cannot follow in detail the influence on later Hellenistic astronomers for lack of extant texts. But we can say that heliophotism and antiphraxis became staples of ancient Greek astronomy, to the point of becoming textbook materials. In his first century BC *Introduction to the Phenomena*, Geminus says:

> Eclipses of the sun arise from the moon's occultation of the sun. For as the sun travels higher through the sky with the moon below it, whenever the sun and the moon come to be in the same position, the moon as it passes under blocks (ἀντιφράττει) the rays of the sun traveling toward us. This is why these phenomena should properly be called not "eclipses" but "occultations": for the sun will never give out (ἐκλείψει) even in part, but it becomes invisible to us because of its occultation by the moon ... The main evidence that the sun is eclipsed by interposition of the moon is (1) the fact that it does not happen on any other day than the 30th [of the lunar month], when the moon is in conjunction with the sun, and (2) the fact of the magnitude of the eclipse is proportionate to the viewer's proximity to the path of the eclipse. (10.1–2, 6)

Geminus goes on to explain lunar eclipses:

> Eclipses of the moon arise from the moon's entering into the shadow of the earth. For just as other bodies illuminated by the sun cast a shadow,

---

25   Cleomedes *Caelestia* 1.7.64-120.

26   Posidonius arrives at a similar (and slightly better) estimate of 240,000 stades about a century later, using a different method; Cleomedes *Caelestia* 1.7.8-47.

so also the earth, which is illuminated by the sun, casts a shadow ... In each case as part of [the moon] enters the shadow of the earth it loses its light from the sun because of the interposition of the earth. For at that time the sun, the earth, the earth's shadow, and the moon are aligned along a straight line. The reason that eclipses do not happen on any other day than the full moon is that only then are the sun and the moon in opposition. (11.1, 3–4)

Here the proposed explanation of solar and lunar eclipses, based on antiphraxis, has become textbook science, to be learned by students at the outset of their study of the science. The predictions of when solar and lunar eclipses could happen in the lunar month have been confirmed repeatedly, and have thus become evidence that proves the theory.

In the mid-second century AD, Claudius Ptolemy, who would write the most influential ancient treatise on astronomy, was still using Presocratic insights as astronomical principles. In explaining solar eclipses he says,

This [namely parallax] is the reason why in the case of solar eclipses, which are caused by the moon passing below and blocking [the sun] ... [in contrast to lunar eclipses] the same [solar] eclipse does not appear identical, either in size or in duration, in all places [on earth where it is visible].

Alm. 4.1, trans. TOOMER

The theory of lunar light, eclipses, and a spherical earth are now part of the fabric of ancient astronomy, making possible a faithful rendering of celestial phenomena. Yet one thing that drops out of the scientific presentation is any concern for the history of the subject. In some sense heliophotism, antiphraxis, and the spherical earth were now commonplaces of the science of the heavens, the common property of every astronomer. Who had originated the ideas, when, and why, were questions that did not arise in the practice of the science.

4

We can, then, ask another question of the reception of early Greek astronomical ideas: who knew the originators of the ideas? In fact it is unusually difficult to discover the identity of the scientific innovators discussed here. My narrative to this point makes it seem self-evident who the innovators were and how their ideas were transmitted. But the line of ancient transmission made it difficult to see who discovered what. So there is a story here about obfuscation as well as clarification of the discovery of new scientific ideas. One might go so far as to say that the historiography of early Greek astronomy reveals one of the most confused and confusing chapters in the history of science.

The doxographic tradition collected and catalogued the opinions of thinkers on important topics, as we have seen. Here is the version of Aetius, compiled around the first century AD, on the topic of the moon's light:

1. Anaximander, Xenophanes, and Berosus (declare that) the moon has its own light.
2. Aristotle (declares that it has) its own (light), but it is dimmer somehow.
3. The Stoics (declare that its light) is murky in appearance, for it is airlike.
   ...
5. Thales was the first to say that it is illuminated by the sun.
6. Pythagoras, Parmenides, Empedocles, Anaxagoras, and Metrodorus (declare) likewise. ... (2.28, trans. Mansfeld and Runia)

On this view, Thales, the very first philosopher, got the theory of the moon's light correct from the very beginning. Pythagoras also understood it and only later Parmenides and Anaxagoras. Meanwhile, neither Aristotle nor the Stoics appreciated the advance made by Thales.

As to the theory of solar eclipses, we get the following:

1. Thales was the first to say that the sun undergoes an eclipse when the moon with its earthy nature courses perpendicularly in between (it and the earth) ...
2. The Pythagoreans and Empedocles hold a similar view. (2.24, trans. Mansfeld and Runia)

There follow a series of other theories of mostly pre-Parmenidean figures.

On the theory of lunar eclipses we are told:

1. Anaximander (declares that the moon is eclipsed) when the mouth on the wheel (of fire) is obstructed.
   ...
7. Thales, Anaxagoras, Plato, Aristotle, the Stoics, and the [mathematical] astronomers agree in unison that it (the moon) produces monthly concealments by travelling together with the sun and being

THE RECEPTION OF EARLY GREEK ASTRONOMY

illuminated by it, whereas it produces eclipses by descending into the shadow of the earth which interposes itself between two heavenly bodies, or rather when the moon is obstructed (by the earth). ... (2.29, trans. MANSFELD and RUNIA)

In this version, Anaxagoras is just one of many thinkers holding the view originated by Thales.

According to the doxographers, two figures discovered heliophotism and antiphraxis in the sixth century BC, up to a century before Parmenides and Anaxagoras: Thales of Miletus and Pythagoras of Samos. If this is so, then the foundations of scientific astronomy were laid from the very beginnings of Greek philosophy, and the great figures of the sixth century left only minor details to be worked out. Yet there are serious problems for the claim that Thales and Pythagoras understood the heavenly phenomena. In the first place, neither Thales nor Pythagoras seems to have left a written record of his speculations. The former lived in a time when writing was just beginning to be used for serious communication soon after the invention of the Greek alphabet; the latter allegedly did not wish to commit his secret religious lore to writing, but passed it on orally within the circle of the brotherhood he founded. Although there are some titles of works attributed to Thales in antiquity, Aristotle himself, one of our earliest and best sources of early philosophy, seems to have had no writings of Thales at his disposal. Rather, he speaks of the Milesians works only by hearsay from others.[27] What Aristotle reports does not comport well with the view of Thales as a great astronomer. According to Aristotle, Thales saw the earth as like a raft floating on a primeval sea.[28] If that were the case, the heavenly bodies could not pass under the earth so as to produce eclipses.

There are, however, a number of notices, some very early, that attribute to Thales the feat of predicting an eclipse, most likely the solar eclipse of 585 BC.[29] Certainly Thales became known as an astronomer with miraculous abilities. Some scholars have used the notices to infer that Thales had gained access to Babylonian astrological records, which recorded centuries of heavenly observations, including sightings of eclipses, and were used to identify recurring patterns from which future eclipses could be predicted.[30] Unfortunately, Mesopotamian predictions were not developed as early as Thales, and

---

27   E.g., Arist. *Metaph.* 984a2-3, *Cael.* 294a28-30.

28   Arist. *Cael.* 294a28-33.

29   Hdt. 1.74.2 = 11A5; Plin. *HN* 2.53; Diog. Laert. 1.23; see Stephenson and Fatoohi 1997.

30   Blanche 1968; Hartner 1969.

furthermore, observations from Babylon or perhaps Ninevah would not be valid for predicting solar eclipses at another site with a different latitude and longitude. Consequently, there is no way he could have made a quasi-scientific prediction of an eclipse.[31] Now it is possible he used some more empirical rule-of-thumb method—for instance based on the intervals between lunar and solar eclipses—to make his prediction.[32] In that case he may have made a prediction that worked out in one year, though he did not use a generally reliable indicator. In any case, we get no early corroboration that Thales used a geometrical and physical model to understand eclipses, however he may have arrived at his prediction. And Aristotle's description of his earth as floating on a sea positively precludes the motion of heavenly bodies as passing under the earth as they would have to, to allow for antiphraxis.

Another major challenge for the claim that Thales discovered heliophotism and antiphraxis comes from the reaction to his theory. Thales' successors in Miletus, Anaximander, followed by Anaximenes, with the former being reportedly Thales' student, the latter, Anaximander's student, show no signs of having learned anything about heliophotism or antiphraxis. For Anaximander, the heavenly bodies are circular tubes of fire surrounded by air, which renders them invisible except at an opening where the fire shines out. Thus what we identify as the sun is just the opening of a large wheel that occupies the whole orbit of the body. The moon has a similar structure, though its orbit is closer to the earth and its fire is less intense. Eclipses are caused by the blocking of the opening; presumably the phases of the moon are likewise slow blockings of the moon's opening. On this theory, there is no correlation between the relative positions of earth, sun, and moon and eclipses, and no correlation between the moon's light and the sun. Did Anaximander miss the great scientific breakthrough of his master? Did he not realize that the moon's phases depend on its angular distance from the sun?

Anaximenes offers his own, perhaps more conventional, theory, with the moon and sun as two-dimensional bodies like leaves blown by a jetstream. They move around above the surface of a flat, round earth, being obscured by high mountains in the earth but never dipping below the earth's surface. The moon has its own source of light. We are not told of a theory of eclipses, but one anonymous notice may give his theory, namely that eclipses are caused by clouds blocking the light of the sun or moon. Here again there is

---

31   See Hunger and Pingree 1999, 183–84; Rochberg 2004, 139; cf. Kahn 1970, 115, Lloyd 1991, 293–294.

32   Van der Waerden 1954, 87; Sambursky 1956, 11–12; Hartner 1969; O'Grady 2002, 140, 142; Couprie 2011, 55–62.

THE RECEPTION OF EARLY GREEK ASTRONOMY 105

no recognition of any dependence of the moon on the sun for its light, or any correlation between the relative position of heavenly bodies and eclipses. Similarly, Xenophanes and Heraclitus assign to the moon its own light and recognize no causal connection between the sun, the moon, and the earth as far as illumination or eclipses. Thus if Thales made a scientific or conceptual breakthrough, no one seems to have noticed the advantages of his theory. It is, of course, possible that Thales understood lunar light and eclipses and failed to communicate his views to his followers.[33] But given the lack of any follow-up to his alleged theories, and in light of evidence that he viewed the world as a flat sea with an earth floating on it—which would preclude the possibility of a freely moving sun and moon, and an earth that could block the sun's light—it seems more likely that he did not make the leap to understanding lunar light or eclipses.

How then did Thales get the reputation for inventing the heliophotism and antiphraxis theories? Aristarchus of Samos attributes the view to him.[34] We can probably trace the reputation to the work of Aristotle's student Eudemus, who wrote a study of astronomy. He seems to have reasoned that since Thales predicted an eclipse, he understood the science of eclipses.[35] If so, he already knew what Eudemus knew, namely that the moon gets its light from the sun and the screening of the sun's light by the earth causes lunar eclipses, while the screening of the sun's light by the moon causes solar eclipses. The report that Thales predicted an eclipse thus becomes the evidence for reconstructing his theory, based on the understanding of the fourth century, not the sixth century, BC. But, as we have seen, Thales could not have predicted an eclipse, at least not scientifically, so that his lucky guess led to an anachronistic assessment of his abilities.

The other possible hero of the story is Pythagoras, whose scientific prowess included astronomical knowledge. According to Aetius, as we have seen, Pythagoras understood lunar light, and the Pythagoreans, more generally, accepted the antiphraxis theory of solar eclipses. Here the evidence is even more obscure than in the case of Thales. For there are no early accounts that attribute advanced astronomical views to Pythagoras. But we do find a close similarity in some remarks of Aristotle. He speaks of unnamed Pythagoreans holding that fire lies at the center of the cosmos, with the planets and even the

---

33 As claimed by Hartner 1969, 69–70; criticized by Mosshammer 1981, 147.

34 *P Oxy.* vol. 53, no. 3710, col. ii, fr. c, lines 36–43.

35 Dercyllides from Theon astr. 198, 14 = 11A17; Kirk, Raven, and Schofield 1983, 82; Guthrie 1962, 49; see Bowen 2002, 311–15 (who thinks we should be careful about deriving the account of the theory from the fact of the prediction).

earth circling around it (*Cael.* II. 13, 293a17-27). Along with the earth there is a counter-earth, also circling the central fire. Both the earth and the counter-earth can block the sun's light to the moon, which helps to explain why lunar eclipses are more frequent than solar eclipses (*ibid.* b18-25). In this Pythagorean system, lunar eclipses are caused by antiphraxis, and there are at least two bodies that can cause such an eclipse, the earth and the counter-earth.

This theory is the one and only Pythagorean system that offers explanations of eclipses and other heavenly phenomena. We can, in fact, name the author: Philolaus of Croton, who wrote in the late fifth century and came to live in Thebes. What is important here is that Philolaus is writing not before, but after Anaxagoras. The Pythagorean is clearly aware of the latest developments in astronomy, and while he offers unique features—most notably making the earth a planet orbiting a central fire with other heavenly bodies—he is also a beneficiary of earlier science. Aristotle seems to know only Philolaus as offering a Pythagorean astronomy, and Philolaus comes a half century or so after Anaxagoras.[36] One can, of course, maintain that he has inherited his theory from early Pythagoreans or even from Pythagoras himself, but only by indulging in unfounded speculations. Since Walter Burkert's pioneering work on Pythagoras, scholars have increasingly seen that the founder of the movement was a religious guru rather than a systematic philosopher.[37] Indeed, we may have orally-transmitted evidence of his rather primitive astrological lore.[38]

Once the scientific theory of lunar light and eclipses by antiphraxis became known, it was relatively easy to look for early proponents of the theory, based either on their alleged success in predicting eclipses or on the theories of their later followers. But the only historically plausible sequence of events leads from Parmenides to Anaxagoras and Empedocles. A history of the reception shows that once Anaxagoras propounded the theory, there were no further efforts to develop a new explanation. All his successors assented to the new theory, down to Aristotle, Zeno of Citium, Aristarchus, Eratosthenes, Geminus, and Claudius Ptolemy—and after them to Copernicus, Galileo, Kepler and modern astronomers. Indeed, the same theory survived different cosmic hypotheses: the geocentric, hestiocentric, and heliocentric models which made the center of the cosmos the earth, the central fire, or the sun, respectively. Some theories saw the heavenly bodies moving on nested spheres, some had epicycles moving on deferents, some had ellipses, but all accepted heliophotism and antiphraxis. The reception of these theories demonstrates a strong

---

36   See Huffman 1993, 231–288 and esp. 241; Graham 2015.
37   Burkert 1972.
38   Huffman 2013.

THE RECEPTION OF EARLY GREEK ASTRONOMY

and long-lasting consensus, one consistent with the recognition of a scientific advance.

One historical question remains: did later thinkers recognize who were the first discoverers of the theories in question? Aristotle may well have known, though he is more non-committal than usual about the authors of these discoveries, even if he accepted them whole-heartedly. But after him we get revisionary histories like that of Eudemus, which make Thales or Pythagoras the authors of heliophotism and antiphraxis.

There is one learned man of the Roman imperial period who made an effort to understand the theories in question and their origins: Plutarch of Chaeronea. He recognizes the importance of Anaxagoras in the transmission of heliophotism:

> Anaxagoras was the first to put down in writing in the clearest and boldest terms of all a theory concerning the illumination and shadow of the moon. This theory, which was not old or generally accepted, at this time went about whispered in secret with caution rather than confidence, among a few men. For the people did not put up with natural philosophers or what were called star-gazers, who attributed divine events to irrational agencies, indifferent powers, and necessary effects.
>
> *Nic.* 23.2–3

Here Plutarch gives credit to Anaxagoras for stating the theory clearly and authoritatively. (It is dubious, however, that the theory was a target of suspicion in the early fifth century; the prosecutions Plutarch goes on to mention occurred in the latter fifth century BC.) By contrast Plato, in a playful passage of the *Cratylus,* uses a speculative etymology of σελήνη (moon) to suggest that Anaxagoras' theory of the moon's light was already known to the ancients who named the moon (409a7-b8). Plutarch's interpretation is consistent with the fact that Parmenides had already recognized the sun as the source of the moon's light, but in a poetic context that precluded a scientific exposition of the theory. Indeed, Plutarch observes that the theory was a new one that had not previously gained much acceptance.

Plutarch studies lunar phenomena at length in his treatise, or rather a rambling dialogue, *The Face on the Moon.* There he shows that he is aware of some of the latest astronomical theories, as well as ancient lore and contemporary controversies, about the moon. In that work he cites Parmenides B15 (929b) and alludes to his B14 (the moon has a "borrowed light" 929a),[39] and goes on

---

39   Plutarch is the source of our one citation of B14, in *Adv. Col.* 1116a.

to cite Anaxagoras B18: "The sun imparts to the moon his brightness" (929b). Plutarch goes on to cite Empedocles B42, which poetically describes a lunar eclipse as a blocking of the sun's light (929c). After refuting competing theories, he concludes that "There remains then the theory of Empedocles that the moonlight which we see comes from the moon's reflection of the sun" (929e, tr. Cherniss and Hembold). While Plutarch never quite commits himself to any one author of the theory of heliophotism, he ascribes the view to Parmenides, Anaxagoras, and Empedocles. Since both Parmenides and Empedocles use poetic discourse to introduce the theory, we can concur with Plutarch that only Anaxagoras actually expounds it in a scientific way.[40] The theory of the moon's light is closely bound up with the theory of eclipses. "When the three bodies, earth and sun and moon, get into a straight line, eclipses take place because the earth deprives [ἀφαιρεῖται] the moon, or the moon, on the other hand, deprives the earth of the sun [i.e., the sun's light]" (932d-e, tr. Cherniss and Hembold). At this point Plutarch gets away from the original theorists and can help us no more. But it is clear that he recognizes the three philosophers who first grasped the source of lunar light, and whose understanding of this phenomenon led to the explanation of eclipses. In his work of antiquarianism, scientific popularization, literate discussion, and genteel scholarship, he correctly identified the authors of the revolution that launched scientific astronomy.

A study of the reception of early astronomical theories shows that one set of interconnected theories was accepted immediately and widely among natural philosophers and disseminated to intellectuals like Thucydides. So successful was the new scientific conception that it effectively put an end to further speculation on the subject. It went on to provide the foundation for developments in mathematical astronomy that increasingly mapped out the geometry of the heavens, and eventually was embodied into introductory textbooks of the subject. In time the very success of the theory may have tended to focus attention on its applications rather than its origins. So obvious had it become that retrospective historical or doxographical accounts projected the theory back to thinkers who lived a century before the actual inventors of the theory. Yet one learned scholar-essayist, Plutarch, managed to identify the inventors, even if he could not follow the exact sequence of events that led to the theory. In some

---

40   It is not that a poet is not capable of arguing: Parmenides argues extensively in his B8, for instance. But we see no clear-cut argument and only allusions to evidence supporting the astronomical insights of Parmenides and Empedocles in the fragments themselves (the moon always gazes on her lord's shining face—get the point? Parm. B15, Emp. B47).

THE RECEPTION OF EARLY GREEK ASTRONOMY

important way, science had outstripped history much as happened again in modern times, and history had to rediscover the roots of a science that to its practitioners seemed timeless and self-evident.

Bibliography

Blanche, Lenis. 1968. "L'éclipse de Thalès et ses problèmes." *Revue Philosophique de la France et de l'Étranger* 158: 153–99.

Bowen, Alan C. 2002. "Eudemus' History of Early Greek Astronomy: Two Hypotheses." In *Eudemus of Rhodes*, edited by William W. Fortenbaugh, 307–22. New Brunswick, N.J.: Transaction Publishers.

Burkert, Walter. 1972. 1962. *Lore and Science in Ancient Pythagoreanism.* Trans. Edwin L. Minar, Jr. Cambridge, Mass.: Harvard University Press.

Couprie, Dirk L. 2011. *Heaven and Earth in Ancient Greek Cosmology: From Thales to Heraclides Ponticus.* New York: Springer.

Dicks, D. R. 1970. *Early Greek Astronomy to Aristotle.* Ithaca: Cornell University Press.

Furley, David. 1987. *The Greek Cosmologists, vol. 1: The Formation of the Atomic Theory and Its Earliest Critics.* Cambridge: Cambridge University Press.

Goldstein, Bernard R., and Alan C. Bowen. 1983. "A New View of Early Greek Astronomy." *Isis* 74: 330–40.

Graham, Daniel W. 2006. *Explaining the Cosmos: The Ionian Tradition of Scientific Philosophy.* Princeton: Princeton University Press.

Graham, Daniel W. 2015. "On Philolaus' Astronomy." *Archive for History of Exact Sciences* 69: 217–30.

Graham, Daniel W. 2013. *Science before Socrates: Parmenides, Anaxagoras, and the New Astronomy.* Oxford: Oxford University Press.

Graham, Daniel W., and Eric Hintz. 2007. "Anaxagoras and the Solar Eclipse of 478 B.C." *Apeiron* 40: 319–44.

Grant, Edward. 2007. *A History of Natural Philosophy: From the Ancient World to the Nineteenth Century.* Cambridge: Cambridge University Press.

Guthrie, W. K. C. 1962. *History of Greek Philosophy.* Vol. 1. Cambridge: Cambridge University Press.

Hartner, Willy. 1969. "Eclipse Periods and Thales' Prediction of a Solar Eclipse: Historic Truth and Modern Myth." *Centaurus* 14: 60–71.

Heath, Sir Thomas. 1913. *Aristarchus of Samos: The Ancient Copernicus.* Oxford: Clarendon Press.

Huffman, Carl A. 1993. *Philolaus of Croton: Pythagorean and Presocratic.* Cambridge: Cambridge University Press.

Huffman, Carl A. 2013. "Reason and Myth in Early Pythagorean Cosmology." In *Early Greek Philosophy: The Presocratics and the Emergence of Reason*, edited by Joe McCoy, 55–76. Washington, DC: The Catholic University of America Press.

Hunger, Hermann, and David Pingree. 1999. *Astral Sciences in Mesopotamia*. Leiden: Brill.

Kahn, Charles H. 1970. "On Early Greek Astronomy." *Journal of Hellenic Studies* 90: 99–116.

Kirk, G. S., J. E. Raven, and M. Schofield. 1983. 1957. *The Presocratic Philosophers*. 2nd edn. Cambridge: Cambridge University Press.

Kuhn, Thomas S. 1996. *The Structure of Scientific Revolutions*. 3rd edn. Chicago: University of Chicago Press.

Lloyd, G. E. R. 1991. "The Debt of Greek Philosophy and Science to the Ancient near East." In *Methods and Problems in Greek Science*, 278–98. Cambridge: Cambridge University Press.

Lloyd, G. E. R. 1970. *Early Greek Science: Thales to Aristotle*. New York: W. W. Norton.

Mansfeld, Jaap, and David T. Runia. 2009. *Aëtiana: The Method and Intellectual Context of a Doxographer*. Vol. 2: *Compendium*. Leiden: E. J. Brill.

Mosshammer, Alden A. 1981. "Thales' Eclipse." *Transactions of the American Philological Association* 11: 145–55.

Nussbaum, Martha C. 1982. "Saving Aristotle's Appearances." In *Language and Logos: Studies in Ancient Philosophy Presented to G. E. L. Owen*, edited by Malcolm Schofield and Martha Craven Nussbaum, 267–93. Cambridge: Cambridge University Press.

O'Grady, Patricia F. 2002. *Thales of Miletus: The Beginnings of Western Science and Philosophy*. Aldershot: Ashgate.

Owen, G. E. L. 1961. "*Tithenai ta phainomena*." In *Aristote et les problèmes de méthode*, edited by Suzanne Mansion, 83–103. Louvain: Publications Universitaires de Louvain.

Popper, Karl R., and Jørgen Mejer. 1998. In *The World of Parmenides: Essays on the Presocratic Enlightenment*, edited by Arne F. Petersen. London: Routledge.

Rochberg, Francesca. 2004. *The Heavenly Writing: Divination, Horoscopy, and Astronomy in Mesopotamian Culture*. Cambridge: Cambridge University Press.

Sambursky, Shmuel. 1956. *The Physical World of the Greeks*. London: Routledge & Kegan Paul.

Stephenson, F. Richard, and Louay J. Fatoohi. 1997. "Thales' Prediction of a Solar Eclipse." *Journal for the History of Astronomy* 28: 279–82.

Toulmin, Stephen. 1967. "The Astrophysics of Berossos the Chaldean." *Isis* 58: 65–76.

van der Waerden, B. L. 1954. *Science Awakening* Groningen: P. Noordhoff.

Vlastos, Gregory. 1975. *Plato's Universe*. Seattle: University of Washington Press.

PART 2

Hidden Reception: Exploring Sources and Developing Themes

∴

CHAPTER 5

Pythagorean Ratios in Empedocles' Physics

Oliver Primavesi

ὁ ἄναξ οὗ τὸ μαντεῖόν ἐστι τὸ ἐν Δελφοῖς
οὔτε λέγει οὔτε κρύπτει ἀλλὰ σημαίνει.

The Lord whose is the oracle in Delphi
neither speaks out nor conceals, but gives a sign.
HERACLITUS fr. 14 MARCOVICH

∴

1 Pythagoreanism in Empedocles?[1]

Historians of Greek culture regard the second Persian invasion in 480 BC as
the watershed between the archaic and the classical periods. In the historiography of Greek philosophy, by contrast, the 6th and 5th century thinkers are
grouped together as the 'Presocratics' or the 'Early Greek thinkers', whereas a
new epoch is assumed to begin only towards the end of the 5th century, with
the philosophy of Socrates and Plato. It follows that an important part of the
'reception of Presocratic natural philosophy in later classical thought' takes
place *within* the Presocratic period. A well-known case in point is the reception of Eleatic ontology in later Presocratic thought,[2] whereas the impact of

---

1 The present chapter 5 was made possible by the textual discoveries of Marwan Rashed (2001b
   and 2014). It owes much to the participants of a seminar on Empedocles held in the *Munich
   School of Ancient Philosophy* in Winter 2019/20, and in particular to a series of written comments offered by Lara Trivellizzi. In compiling the bibliography and related matters, the author was kindly supported by his research assistant Michael Neidhart. Dr Michael McOsker
   (Ohio Wesleyan University) not only translated a preliminary version (Primavesi 2017b) into
   English, but also checked the English of the present version and adapted the format of references and bibliography to the style of the present volume. Thanks are also due to Joulia
   Strauss who provided the five diagrams for sections 3.3 and 4.1–2, to Ute Primavesi who once
   more proved herself a valiant huntress of typographical errors, and, last but not least, to an
   anonymous reader whose remarks were perceptive and helpful.
2 See the comprehensive study of Curd 1998.

© KONINKLIJKE BRILL NV, LEIDEN, 2021 | DOI:10.1163/9789004443358_002

Pythagoreanism on the philosophy of the 5th century BC is more difficult to pin down: in order to do so, one has to delineate, as far as possible, a dividing line between 5th century Pythagoreanism[3] and the influential Platonizing *reinterpretation* of Pythagoreanism that was inaugurated in the mid-fourth century BC, by Plato's pupils Speusippus and Xenocrates.[4] The present chapter is devoted to the reception of Pythagorean number philosophy by Empedocles of Agrigentum (c. 484–424 BC),[5] the premier philosopher-poet of Classical Greek literature. In particular, we will discuss fresh evidence for Empedocles' physics which has gradually come to light during the last twenty years, and we will argue that this evidence yields insights into the Pythagorean numerical ratios that structure the time-table of Empedocles' cosmic cycle.[6]

1.1 *A Strong Claim in Simplicius*

Empedocles was 'an emulator (*zelotes*) and *a personal pupil (plesiastes)* of Parmenides—*but even more so of the Pythagoreans*'—so he is first introduced in the massive commentary on Aristotle's *Physics* which we owe to the learned

---

3 As illustrated, in particular, by the authentic fragments of Philolaus (on which see the fundamental commentary by Huffman 1993) and by the fragments of Aristotle's lost monograph on the Pythagoreans (on which see, e.g., Primavesi 2014).

4 The basic analysis of the difference between authentic 5th century Pythagoreanism and the Platonic reinterpretation was provided by Burkert 1972 ('Lore and Science'). Zhmud 2012 offers a kind of 'anti-Burkert': Under the influence of Alexander Zajcev's theory according to which it was all of a sudden that Greek civilization rose to its top level (on this *'Greek Miracle'* see Zajcev 1993), Zhmud aims to replace Burkert's evolutionary account of Pythagoreanism ('From Lore to Science', as it were) with the reverse account: he claims that the first Pythagoreans did 'Science' right from the start, whereas the prominence of 'Lore' in our evidence is due to Hellenistic decadence (cf. Zajcev 1996). While Burkert's picture is generally more convincing, his attempt at establishing a link between the Pythagorean *tetraktys* and animal sacrifice is a case where his search for 'Lore' in early Pythagoreanism has lead him astray (see below 1.3.4).

5 In the present chapter, Empedocles will be quoted from Mansfeld and Primavesi (New Edition, revised and enlarged, 2021, hereafter MP), 392–563. References to Diels/Kranz [6]1951 (= DK) will be added in brackets where possible. The English translations of Fragments from Empedocles' poems and of indirect sources on Empedoclean thought will in general be based on Wright 1981, Inwood 1992, and Laks/Most 2016.

6 For a first sketch of this hypothesis, see Primavesi 2016, 12–27. For an account of its gradual development, see Primavesi 2017a. A great part of the evidence needed for proving the hypothesis was first assembled in Primavesi 2017b. In the present chapter, the whole argument has been restructured, polemics has been cut down to a minimum and some central topics like the concept of *tetraktys* and the Pythagorean *Oath* have received a more thorough treatment.

Neo-Platonist Simplicius (1st half of the 6th century AD).[7] The first part of this characterization is fully supported by the crucial influence of both main parts of Parmenides' poem (i.e., *Aletheia* and *Doxa*) on Empedocles' theory of principles, as attested by the extant fragments of his work.[8] All the more surprising is the second claim, the one about Empedocles' Pythagoreanism. Few will doubt that in the more exoteric parts of Empedocles' work there are references to Pythagorean tales about metempsychosis in general, or to the legend according to which Pythagoras was an incarnation of the Hyperborean Apollo in particular. But it is not immediately clear how one could justify the much stronger claim that Empedocles' affiliation to the Pythagoreans was *even more* important than the one to Parmenides. The first question we should ask when faced with late antique claims about early Greek philosophy concerns authorship: has Simplicius copied his characterization of Empedocles as a whole from an earlier source or is he relying, wholly or in part, on his own first-hand knowledge of Empedocles' work?

1.2   *Authorship of the Claim*

Hermann Usener (1834–1905) counted the reference to Parmenides and its larger context in Simplicius among Simplicius' excerpts from Theophrastus' lost work *On Physical Doctrines*,[9] which was of considerable importance for the later doxographical tradition.[10] Usener's source criticism is quite convincing here, since the characterization of Empedocles as an emulator (*zelotes*) of Parmenides is quoted and explicitly ascribed to Theophrastus by Diogenes Laertius.[11] Yet the passage in Diogenes does *not* feature the additional qualification of

---

7   Simp. *in Phys.* A 2; Diels 1882, 25.19–21: οἱ δὲ τέτταρας (scil. τὰς ἀρχὰς λέγουσιν), ὡς Ἐμπεδοκλῆς ὁ Ἀκραγαντῖνος, οὐ πολὺ κατόπιν τοῦ Ἀναξαγόρου γεγονώς, Παρμενίδου δὲ ζηλωτὴς καὶ πλησιαστὴς καὶ ἔτι μᾶλλον τῶν Πυθαγορείων, cf. Emp. fr. 1 MP (A 7 DK) = Thphr. fr. 227A Fortenbaugh et al. (1992, 412), lines 6–8.

8   Reinhardt 1916, 208–9, O'Brien 1981, 30–1, Curd 1998, 155–71, and Palmer 2009, 260–317 and 324–336.

9   Usener 1858, 32.9–12 (*Theophrasti de physicorum opinionibus reliquiae* fr. 3): οἱ δὲ τέσσαρας ὡς Ἐμπεδοκλῆς ὁ Ἀκραγαντῖνος, οὐ πολὺ κατόπιν τοῦ Ἀναξαγόρου γεγονώς, Παρμενίδου δὲ πλησιαστὴς καὶ ζηλωτής [μᾶλλον δὲ Πυθαγορείων]. The title of Theophrastus' work was either Φυσικῶν δόξαι or Φυσικαὶ δόξαι; on this, and for a defence of Φυσικαὶ δόξαι, see Mansfeld 1992b. On Usener's 1858 dissertation and its seminal importance for the ground-breaking work of his pupil Hermann Diels on the doxographical tradition, see Mansfeld and Runia 1997, 6–8.

10   For a comparative assessment of Aristotle's and Theophrastus' contributions to the doxography of ancient natural philosophy, see Mansfeld and Primavesi 2021, 28–35.

11   D.L. 8.55; Dorandi 2013, 632, lines 52–54 (= Thphr. fr. 227B; Fortenbaugh et al. 1992, 412, lines 6–8): ὁ δὲ Θεόφραστος Παρμενίδου φησὶ ζηλωτὴν αὐτὸν γενέσθαι καὶ μιμητὴν ἐν τοῖς ποιήμασι· καὶ γὰρ ἐκεῖνον ἐν ἔπεσι τὸν Περὶ φύσεως ἐξενεγκεῖν λόγον.

116 PRIMAVESI

Empedocles as a *personal pupil* (*plesiastes*) of Parmenides, let alone the second half of the characterization, which concerns his affiliation to the Pythagorean School. Accordingly, Usener regarded the latter as an addition by Simplicius.[12] Hermann Diels went even further and had the secondary expansion of Theophrastus' note begin with the qualification of Empedocles as a personal pupil of Parmenides;[13] he felt entitled to do so both by the manuscript tradition—which strongly suggests a word order that favours that analysis more than the minority reading adopted by Usener[14]—and by the parallel passage in Diogenes Laertius.[15] In support of Diels' position, Joseph Bidez concluded from the passage in Diogenes that Theophrastus, while recognizing the indebtedness of Empedocles' philosophical poetry to both the poetic form and the philosophical contents of Parmenides' poem, did *not* transform this intertextual evidence into a biographical hypothesis of personal acquaintance between Empedocles and Pythagoras. Accordingly, Bidez adopted Diels' analysis of the passage in Simplicius and regarded not only the reference to the Pythagorean School but also the second part of the reference to Parmenides as later additions to Theophrastus' short characterization.[16] Finally, Walter Burkert, while not going into the details of the reference to Parmenides, followed the lead of Usener, Diels and Bidez in that he ascribed to Simplicius the claim that Empedocles was

---

12 Usener 1858, 32, app. crit. to line 11: 'μᾶλλον δὲ Πυθ. de suo adiecit Simplicius'.

13 Diels 1879, 477.17–8 (*Theophrasti Physicorum opiniones* fr. 3), where Diels has marked, with wider letter spacing, what he thinks to be the Theophrastean portion of the text (cf. Diels 1879, 473: 'Diductis litteris Theophrastea a citantium vel explicantium scriptorum verbis distinxi'): οἱ δὲ τέτταρας ὡς Ἐμπεδοκλῆς ὁ Ἀκραγαντῖνος, οὐ πολὺ κατόπιν τοῦ Ἀναξαγόρου γεγονώς, Παρμενίδου δὲ ζηλωτὴς καὶ πλησιαστὴς καὶ ἔτι μᾶλλον τῶν Πυθαγορείων. In the apparatus to line 18, Diels adds: '*narratio de Pythagoreorum disciplina a Theophrasto aut aliena est aut certe immutata redditur a Simplicio*'.

14 Παρμενίδου δὲ πλησιαστὴς καὶ ζηλωτής, μᾶλλον δὲ Πυθαγορείων F (Usener 1858) : Παρμενίδου δὲ ζηλωτὴς καὶ πλησιαστὴς καὶ ἔτι μᾶλλον τῶν Πυθαγορείων DE (Diels 1879). Accordingly, the possibility of treating καὶ πλησιαστὴς as part of the later addition was much more obvious to Diels than it had been to Usener.

15 Diels ³1912, 200, *app. crit.* to A 7, line 13 (= Diels and Kranz ⁶1951, 283, app. to line 28): 'καὶ ... Πυθαγορείων wohl nicht aus Theophrast vgl. Diog. § 54', which in the light of the typographical demarcation in Diels 1879, 477.17–8 surely means that he identifies the later expansion with the *seven* words καὶ πλησιαστὴς καὶ ἔτι μᾶλλον τῶν Πυθαγορείων, not just with the *five* words καὶ ἔτι μᾶλλον τῶν Πυθαγορείων.

16 Bidez 1894, 125: 'Les mots : πλησιαστὴς καὶ ἔτι μᾶλλον τῶν Πυθαγορείων sont-ils de Théophraste? C'est très douteux. L'extrait, tel qu'il est rapporté dans Diogène, ferait croire que Théophraste n'avait pas transformé en rapports personnels ce qu'il présente comme une ressemblance dans la forme de l'exposé. Empédocle imite Parménide : tous deux, en effet, ils formulent leur physique en vers, et, dans l'introduction des φυσικά, Empédocle a fait à son devancier des emprunts très considérables'.

PYTHAGOREAN RATIOS IN EMPEDOCLES' PHYSICS

predominantly influenced by his affiliation to the Pythagorean School.[17] We will refrain, then, from tracing this remarkable claim back to Theophrastus; rather, we must regard it as an assertion added to Theophrastus' characterization of Empedocles by Simplicius himself. But what was Simplicius' evidence for his claim?

1.3   Simplicius' Possible Evidence

1.3.1   Simplicius' Knowledge of Empedoclean and Parmenidean Texts
Though only writing in the first half of the 6th century AD, Simplicius offers, in his commentaries on Aristotle, by far the most quotations from Empedocles (c. 155 lines), even more than Aristotle (c. 89 lines) and Plutarch (c. 81 lines), let alone Sextus Empiricus (c. 44 lines), Clement of Alexandria (c. 43 lines), and Hippolytus of Rome (c. 43 lines)—to mention just the five authors who, in this respect, come next in importance after Simplicius. Furthermore, a large number of Simplicius' Empedoclean quotations (c. 118 lines) are not found in any earlier author.[18] Last not least, Simplicius moves forwards and backwards in the text of Empedocles with perfect ease, as his indications of book numbers and of the relative locations of his quotations clearly show;[19] in other words, he is thoroughly acquainted with a copy of an original text. In the case of Parmenides, the importance of Simplicius is even greater:[20]

> The latest author known to have used a manuscript of the whole work is Simplicius, who quoted extensively from the most significant part of it on account of its rarity (διὰ τὴν σπάνιν τοῦ Παρμενίδου συγγράμματος, t. 213). In all, Simplicius cites two thirds of our surviving hundred and fifty lines; for nearly three quarters of these, or half of all that survives, he is our sole authority.

In addition to that, Simplicius, in his commentary on Aristotle's *De caelo*, also displays a detailed knowledge of Aristotle's (now lost) monograph *On the Pythagoreans*,[21] arguably the most authoritative source on early Pythagoreanism.

---

17   Burkert 1972, 289–90 n. 59: 'Theophrastus mentioned only his relation to Parmenides, but Simplicius added καὶ ἔτι μᾶλλον τῶν Πυθαγορείων (ζηλωτής) ...'.

18   For the statistics see Primavesi 2002, 184–191.

19   See Martin and Primavesi 1999, 103–111.

20   Coxon 1986, 1, with a quotation of Simp. *in Phys.* 144.28 Diels.

21   Rose 1886, fr. 200: Simp. *in Cael.* 386.9–23 Heiberg (ἐν τῆι τῶν Πυθαγορείοις ἀρεσκόντων συναγωγῆι), Rose 1886, fr. 204: *in Cael.* 511.25–512.1 + 512.12–14 H. (ἐν τῶι περὶ τῶν Πυθαγορικῶν and ἐν τοῖς Πυθαγορικοῖς), and Rose 1886, fr. 205.1: *in Cael.* 392.16–32 H. (ἐν τῶι δευτέρωι τῆς συναγωγῆς τῶν Πυθαγορικῶν and ἐν τῆι τῶν Πυθαγορικῶν συναγωγῆι).

We may assume, then, that Simplicius is likely to know what he is talking about. But in order to subject this assumption to closer examination, we have to decide first whether the extant fragments of Empedoclean poetry come from *two different poems*, 'Purifications' and 'On Nature'. If we must distinguish two poems, it will be necessary to identify the Pythagorean components of either poem separately and then to examine whether Simplicius is likely to be referring to both poems or only to one of them, and if so, which.

1.3.2 Empedocles' Two Poems[22]

While all extant papyrus fragments and quotations of Empedoclean poetry are invariably cast in epic hexameters, it is nevertheless possible, on entirely formal grounds, to divide them up into two quite distinct groups that differ (i) by the medium of communication assumed in the text, (ii) by the *persona* ('poetic I'), and (iii) by the addressee(s).

One set of fragments belongs to an open farewell letter in which a god in exile (*daimon*), who is about to return to the table of the blessed ones, addresses his mortal friends in the city of Acragas.[23] This exoteric farewell letter features both the exposition of a mythical law in observance of which the divine *persona* had to go through a series of mortal incarnations, and a number of moral precepts for his mortal friends whom he is going to leave on earth. The other set of fragments, by contrast, belongs to an oral discourse: a mortal *persona* who, being mortal, has to rely on the Muse, is secretly instructing a single pupil, Pausanias. This esoteric oral discourse features a physical theory based on the assumption of six fundamental principles. These are the four *elements* fire, water, earth, and air,[24] whose total mass never increases or decreases,[25] as well

---

22 The traditional distinction between 'Purifications' (*Katharmoi*) and 'On Nature' (*Peri Physeos/Physika*) was doubted by Osborne 1987 and by Inwood 1992, and convincingly defended by Kingsley 1995, 363–366 and Kingsley 1996. See further Primavesi 2007 and Primavesi 2013, 685–88.

23 One should not conflate the *persona* of the 'Purifications' with the historical Empedocles, as e.g. Burkert 1972, 153–4 does: '... how could he have called himself a god, if he was not able actually to perform, or at least to pretend to perform, extraordinary and amazing feats?' In particular, the undeniable difference between this divine *persona* and the human *persona* of 'On Nature' should prevent us from doing so.

24 Emp. fr. 66b.249 MP (DK 31 B 17.18): πῦρ καὶ ὕδωρ καὶ γαῖα καὶ αἰθέρος ἄπλετον ὕψος.

25 Emp. fr. 66b.261–264 MP (DK 31 B 17.30–33): καὶ πρὸς τοῖς οὔτ' ἄρ τι ἐπιγίγνεται οὐδ' ἀπολήγει· / εἴ τε γὰρ ἐφθείροντο διαμπερές, οὐκ ἂν ἔτ' ἦσαν· / τοῦτο δ' ἐπαυξήσειε τὸ πᾶν τί κε; καὶ πόθεν ἐλθόν; / πῆι δέ κε κἀξαπόλοιτο, ἐπεὶ τῶνδ' οὐδὲν ἐρῆμον.

PYTHAGOREAN RATIOS IN EMPEDOCLES' PHYSICS

119

as the two *forces* Love and Strife.[26] The complex interaction of these six entities can be described as a system of three *functions*:

(i) The function of Love is to combine *different* elements, or portions of different elements, into organic compounds ('living beings').

(ii) The function of Strife is to dissolve combinations of different elements.

(iii) As soon as the elements are set free by Strife, their *own* function becomes apparent. It consists in enacting the attraction of *like to like* which is inherent in them:[27] Unless prevented from doing so by Love, the four elements form, by themselves, four homogeneous concentric masses, each being located at the natural place of the element in question.

The theory describes the course of the world as a *cosmic cycle*, i.e., a periodic alternation between the global unification of the four elements, gradually brought about by Love—from four pure, divine elemental masses into divine unity ('*Sphairos*')—and their global separation, gradually brought about by Strife—from divine unity ('*Sphairos*') to four pure, divine elemental masses.

Now it seems rather unlikely that an exoteric letter written by a god and an esoteric oral discourse of a mortal teacher would have coexisted within one and the same 5th century BC epic poem. This impression is confirmed by the fact that the coexistence of two *personae* corresponds with the coexistence of two different book titles, as two Empedoclean quotations in Diogenes Laertius clearly show. The proem of the divine letter is quoted under the title 'Purifications' (*Katharmoi*),[28] which perfectly suits both the account of the God's purification by a series of incarnations and the rules for a pure life which the God imposes on his mortal friends—and on mankind in general—on occasion of his final departure. On the other hand, the dedication of the human teacher's oral instruction to Pausanias is quoted under the generic title 'On Nature' (*Peri Physeos*)[29] which is obviously equivalent to the title *Physica* under which related Empedoclean fragments are quoted by other authors. Both variants of

---

26 Emp. fr. 57 MP (DK 31 B 16): ἦ γὰρ καὶ πάρος ἦν τε καὶ ἔσσεται, οὐδέ ποτ', οἴω, / τούτων ἀμφοτέρων κενεώσεται ἄσπετος αἰών. Emp. fr. 66b.250–257 MP: Νεῖκός τ' οὐλόμενον δίχα τῶν, ἀτάλαντον ἀπάντηι, / καὶ Φιλότης ἐν τοῖσιν, ἴση μῆκός τε πλάτος τε· / τὴν σὺ νόωι δέρκευ, μηδ' ὄμμασιν ἧσο τεθηπώς· / ἥτις καὶ θνητοῖσι νομίζεται ἔμφυτος ἄρθροις, / τῆι τε φίλα φρονέουσι καὶ ἄρθμια ἔργα τελοῦσι, / Γηθοσύνην καλέοντες ἐπώνυμον ἠδ' Ἀφροδίτην· / τὴν οὔ τις μετὰ τοῖσιν ἑλισσομένην δεδάηκε / θνητὸς ἀνήρ· σὺ δ' ἄκουε λόγου στόλον οὐκ ἀπατηλόν.

27 Emp. frs 58.1–3 MP (DK 31 B 22.1–3), fragments 59–61 MP, and Müller (1965), pp. 27–65.

28 D.L. 8.54.

29 D.L. 8.60.

this title (*Peri Physeos/Physica*) quite adequately indicate that the oral instruction by Empedocles' human teacher is an exposition of a system of Natural Philosophy. While the two titles (*Katharmoi* and *Peri Physeos/Physica*) may not be authentic, their coexistence speaks strongly in favour of distinguishing the two poems, since these titles are never confused with each other or presented as synonyms, and since both titles were used already in the 4th century BC: Aristotle himself quotes the title *Physica*,[30] while his pupil Dicaearchus of Messana reports that the 'Purifications' were recited at the Olympic Games.[31] More specific evidence can perhaps be gathered from the Hellenistic biographer Lobon of Argos, who compiled a list of Empedocles' works.[32] Although lost, it can be reconstructed from Diogenes Laertius[33] and the *Suda*.[34] According to the most plausible reconstruction of that list, the poem 'On Nature' differed in book number and line number (3 books in 3000 lines) from the 'Purifications' (2 books in 2000 lines).[35] It is true that the *line* numbers (1000 lines per book) look a trifle schematic, but the *book* numbers are in tune with those mentioned in the extant quotations from Empedocles' poems. So we will assume, in the light of this evidence, the existence of two separate poems and we will therefore have to examine the Pythagorean character of each poem separately.[36]

1.3.3   Pythagoreanism in the 'Purifications' and in 'On Nature'

In the fragments of Empedocles' 'Purifications', reference to the oldest form of Pythagoreanism, or, for that matter, to the 'Pythagorean variant of Orphism', is unmistakable throughout.[37] In the first book of the poem,[38] the divine persona discloses a mythical law on the incarnations of guilty gods that is strikingly similar to the old Pythagorean legend, reported already in Aristotle's monograph on the Pythagoreans,[39] according to which Pythagoras was the final incarnation of Hyperborean Apollo:[40] in both cases, the God has to take on an earthly existence for

---

30   Arist. *Mete.* 4, 382ª1.

31   Dicaearch. fr. 85 Mirhady (2001, 86–89; Emp. fr. 3 MP).

32   Lobon of Argos, *On Poets*, fr. 12 Garulli (2004, 183; Emp. fr. 4 MP).

33   D.L. 8.77 *sub fin.*

34   *Suda* ε 1002; Adler 1935, 258.19–21.

35   Zuntz 1965, Primavesi 2006b, Primavesi 2007.

36   On the assignment of fragments to either work, see Primavesi 2013, 688–94.

37   Burkert 1972, 133: 'It is the Pythagorean variant of Orphism that is manifest in Pindar, Empedocles, Herodotus, and Plato'.

38   Emp. frs 8–24 MP (B 115, 158, 117–9, 121–3, 116, 125, 124, 120, 142, 127, 146–7, 126, 148, 153a DK).

39   Arist. fr. 191 Rose (1886, 153–56).

40   Rose 1886, 154 quotes, in particular, Ael. *VH* 2, 26 (Ἀριστοτέλης λέγει ὑπὸ τῶν Κροτωνιατῶν τὸν Πυθαγόραν Ἀπόλλωνα Ὑπερβόρειον προσαγορεύεσθαι), D.L. 8.11, lines 117–118 Dorandi (αὐτοῦ οἱ μαθηταὶ δόξαν εἶχον περὶ αὐτοῦ ὡς εἴη Ἀπόλλων ἐξ Ὑπερβορέων ἀφιγμένος), Iamb.

PYTHAGOREAN RATIOS IN EMPEDOCLES' PHYSICS

a certain time by being involved in the general cycle of *metempsychosis*, until he is allowed to return to the immortal gods in the end.[41] Furthermore, the commandments for a pure life contained in the second book of the 'Purifications', such as the bans on eating beans[42] and on killing animals,[43] seem to be adopted from the Pythagorean *acusmata* as transmitted by Aristotle.[44] All in all, then, there is considerable common ground between the 'Purifications' and the Pythagorean legend: the story of a god in exile who at the end of his mortal incarnations provides the defiled human race with commandments for leading a pure life.

In 'On Nature', by contrast, the role of Pythagoreanism seems to be fairly limited. On first glance, the fragments of that poem yield just two pieces of evidence. (i) Empedocles has the mortal teacher ask his pupil Pausanias *to hide inside of his voiceless breast*[45] the teachings about physics—thereby following *Pythagorean* habits, as Plutarch observed:[46] the strictly confidential speech situation presupposed in 'On Nature' mirrors the Pythagorean commandment of keeping the divine master's teachings secret.[47] (ii) In the physical theory, Empedocles specifies the mixture-ratios by means of which the four elements make up the homoeomerous components of living organisms. In the extant

---

VP 28 (140), p. 79.13–14 Deubner (καὶ ἓν τοῦτο τῶν ἀκουσμάτων ἐστι· 'τίς εἶ, Πυθαγόρα;' φασὶ γὰρ εἶναι Ἀπόλλωνα Ὑπερβόρεον). According to Heraclides Ponticus, who had studied with Aristotle in Plato's Academy, the series of Apollo's incarnations began with Euphorbus (a Trojan mentioned in *Iliad* 16.808 and 850) and culminated with Pythagoras, who remembered all previous incarnations (Heraclid.Pont. fr. 86 Schütrumpf et al. 2008, 166–169, with Kerényi 1937, 22–4 [= 19–21]).

41 Burkert 1972, 216: 'But the solemn, pompous mien which Pythagoras and Empedocles have in common is precisely the manner of the shaman—Empedocles the "deathless god" and Pythagoras the "Hyperborean Apollo"'.

42 Emp. fr. 37 MP (B 141 DK).

43 Emp. frs 30–4 MP (B 135–138 DK).

44 Arist. frs 194–6 Rose (fr. 197 should be removed) with Burkert 1972, 166–92. Also relevant are Iamb. *VP* 109; Deubner 1937, 62.23–63.11, and *ibid.* 82–86; Deubner 1937, 47.4–50.17, with Burkert 1972, 167–70, as well as Iamblichus' report on the separation of the Pythagoreans into '*acusmatici*' and '*mathematici*' (Iamb. *Comm.Math.* 25; 76.16–77.24 + 78.6–8 Festa, with Burkert 1972, 193–7) which might go back to Aristotle.

45 Fr. 45 MP (B 5 DK): στεγάσαι φρενὸς ἔλλοπος εἴσω. This fragment was transmitted in a very corrupt form, but was convincingly restored by Wyttenbach 1797 and Diels 1901 (στεγάσαι Diels : στέγουσαι ms. ‖ ἔλλοπος Wyttenbach : ἀλλ' ὅπερ ms. ‖ εἴσω Diels : ἐλάσσω ms). See also fr. 43 MP (B 3 DK), lines 6–8, where the mortal teacher addresses his pupil in the following terms: 'And the flowers of glorious honour shall not force you to accept these from mortals on condition that you say more than is sanctioned, in audacity, and then to sit on the peaks of wisdom!' (μηδέ σέ γ' εὐδόξοιο βιήσεται ἄνθεα τιμῆς / πρὸς θνητῶν ἀνελέσθαι, ἐφ' ὧι θ' ὁσίης πλέον εἰπεῖν / θάρσεϊ, καὶ τότε δὴ σοφίης ἐπ' ἄκροισι θοάζειν).

46 Plu. *Quaest. conv.* 728 E (IV 286.18–20 Hubert 1938).

47 On Pythagorean silence and secrecy see Burkert 1972, 178–179.

fragments of 'On Nature', such ratios are preserved for blood and muscles (1 part earth, 1 part fire, 1 part water, 1 part air),[48] as well as for bones (2 parts earth, 2 parts water, 4 parts fire),[49] and for tendons (1 part fire, 1 part earth, 2 parts water).[50] Now these mixture-ratios seem to betray Pythagorean influence since, according to Aristotle, the distinctive contribution of the early Pythagorean School to Greek philosophy consists in attempting a mathematical account of natural phenomena—applied mathematics, as it were.[51] But even so, our two pieces of evidence, though not negligible, do not by themselves justify ascribing to 'On Nature' a *predominantly* Pythagorean character: Pythagoreanism, while being absolutely central in the 'Purifications', seems to be rather marginal in 'On Nature'—at least as far as the evidence collected by Diels/Kranz goes.[52]

1.3.4   The Holy *Tetraktys* of the Pythagoreans

Hermann Diels tried to uncover yet another, much more fundamental Pythagorean element in Empedocles' physics. According to him, Empedocles' motive for introducing a set of *four* elements was his 'Pythagorean predilection for the holy *tetraktys*'[53]—i.e., primarily, for the set of the first four integers and their sum.[54] This hypothesis, however, is rather shaky, as we will see. There is,

---

48   Emp. fr. 98 MP (B 98 DK).

49   Emp. fr. 100 and fr. 97 MP (B 96 and A 78 DK).

50   Emp. fr. 97 MP (A 78 DK).

51   See Arist. *Metaph.* A 5, 985^{b}23–26: ἐν δὲ τούτοις καὶ πρὸ τούτων οἱ καλούμενοι Πυθαγόρειοι τῶν μαθημάτων ἁψάμενοι πρῶτοι ταῦτα προήγον, καὶ ἐντραφέντες ἐν αὐτοῖς τὰς τούτων ἀρχὰς τῶν ὄντων ἀρχὰς ᾠήθησαν εἶναι πάντων, and the reconstruction of the argument by Primavesi 2014.

52   Zeller/Nestle 1920, 1024: 'Der Einfluß des Pythagoreismus tritt nur in dem mystischen Teil seiner Lehre, in den Aussprüchen über die Seelenwanderung und die Dämonen, und in den hiermit zusammenhängenden Lebensvorschriften entschieden hervor; in der Physik dagegen macht er sich teils gar nicht, teils nur an einzelnen untergeordneten Punkten geltend'.

53   Diels 1899, 15: 'Empedokles selbst hat zwar die Vierzahl der Elemente, der pythagoreischen Vorliebe für die heilige Tetraktys folgend, zuerst aufgestellt und, was wichtiger ist, die eleatische Forderung des ewigen, unveränderlichen Prinzips (zwischen den unendlichen Atomen Leukipps und dem starren Eins des Parmenides vermittelnd) in seinen vier 'Wurzeln' des Seins zum Ausdruck gebracht und damit den herrschenden Begriff des Elementes geschaffen, aber er kennt den später dafür gewöhnlichen Namen στοιχεῖα noch nicht'. The same equation of *tetraktys* and *tetrad* ('Vierzahl') underlies the otherwise cautious remark in Zeller and Nestle 1920, 951: 'Die pythagoreische Wertschätzung der Vierzahl ist bekannt; doch möchte ich den Einfluß dieser Bestimmung auf Empedokles nicht zu hoch anschlagen, da er sonst in der Physik vom Pythagoreismus nur wenig aufgenommen hat'.

54   On the Pythagorean *tetraktys* see Delatte 1915 and Kucharski 1952.

PYTHAGOREAN RATIOS IN EMPEDOCLES' PHYSICS

to be sure, no reason to doubt the 'holy' character of the *tetraktys*, since it was regarded by Pythagoreans, according to one of their *acusmata*, as the most precious legacy of Pythagoras/Apollo to the school, on a par with Apollo's sanctuary in Delphi.[55] Yet if the veneration of the Pythagorean *tetraktys* were responsible for Empedocles' fundamental decision to choose a set of *four* elements, we should assume that *tetraktys* designated simply 'a set of four items', so that the terms *tetrad* and *tetraktys* could be used interchangeably.[56] It is true that the wide meaning of *tetraktys* as presupposed by Diels would be in tune with the manifold uses of the term that we find in the later Platonic tradition. Theon of Smyrna (c. AD 100), for instance, lists no less than 11 different *tetractyes*; and the feature common to all of them is precisely that they are sets of four items:[57]

(i) The sum of the first four integers: 1 + 2 + 3 + 4 = 10. (ii) The two tetrads produced by multiplying the monad by two: 1 / 2 / 4 / 8, and by three: 1 / 3 / 9 / 27. (iii) The four mathematical dimensions: Point, Line, Plane, and Solid. (iv) The four simple bodies: fire, air, water, and earth. (v) Those four among the five geometrical solids that correspond to the four elements: *pyramid* (fire), *octahedron* (air), *icosahedron* (water), and *cube* (earth). (vi) The first four numbers and the four dimensions as mirrored by the growth of living beings: The semen corresponds to the monad and the geometrical point, the growth in length to the dyad and the line, the growth in width to the triad and the plane, and the growth in volume to the tetrad and the solid. (vii) Four levels of social organization: Individual, household, village, city-state. (viii) The correspondence between the four critical faculties of the soul and the first four numbers: intellect corresponds to the monad, knowledge to the dyad, opinion to the triad, and sense perception to the tetrad. (ix) The three parts of the soul, reason, spirit, and appetite, together with the body. (x) The four seasons: spring,

---

55 Iamb. *VP* 82; p. 47.15–16 Deubner (= Ch. 3, Πυθαγόρας καὶ οἱ ἀπ' αὐτοῦ, fr. 106 MP): τί ἐστι τὸ ἐν Δελφοῖς μαντεῖον; τετρακτύς· ὅπερ ἐστὶν ἡ ἁρμονία, ἐν ᾗ αἱ Σειρῆνες. The reference to the sirens implies that the *tetraktys* is also underlying the harmony of the spheres; see Pl. *R.* 10, 617b 6–8 (Slings): ἐπὶ δὲ τῶν κύκλων αὐτοῦ (scil. τοῦ ἀτράκτου) ἄνωθεν ἐφ' ἑκάστου βεβηκέναι Σειρῆνα συμπεριφερομένην, φωνὴν μίαν ἱεῖσαν, ἕνα τόνον· ἐκ πασῶν δὲ ὀκτὼ οὐσῶν μίαν ἁρμονίαν συμφωνεῖν, with Delatte 1915: 259–261 and Kucharski 1952: 75–77 (Appendice III). Delatte 1915: 261 aptly remarks: 'La plus grande révélation qu'Apollon-Pythagore a faite aux hommes est celle de l'harmonie des sphères ...'.

56 Kucharski 1952, 18 n. 2: 'Nous employons ici les termes *tétractys* et *tétrade* équivalemment, c'est-à-dire en prenant ce dernier terme au sens de quatre premiers nombres et, plus généralement, dans celui d'une série ou d'un ensemble de quatre choses'.

57 Theo Sm. 93.17–99.23 Hiller; cf. Delatte 1915, 255, and Kucharski 1952, 31–36.

124   PRIMAVESI

summer, autumn, and winter. (xi) The four ages in life: child, teenager, adult, elderly person.

It is far from certain, however, that the very general meaning of *tetraktys* implied by Theon's list represents a pre-Empedoclean use of the term,[58] since virtually all of Theon's more specific examples presuppose philosophical innovations by Plato or Aristotle.[59] Liddell/Scott/Jones seem to accept just the first two of Theon's eleven *tetraktyes*, since their entry on *tetraktys* offers just the following examples:

(i)   The sum of the first four numbers $(1 + 2 + 3 + 4 = 10)$;[60]
(ii) The sum of the first four even numbers $(2 + 4 + 6 + 8 = 20)$ *plus* the sum of the first four odd numbers $(1 + 3 + 5 + 7 = 16)$, i.e. 36;[61]

---

58   A 5th century BC *terminus ante quem* for the word is suggested by the fact that the Pythagorean philosopher Philolaus of Croton (DK 44 A 11) is reported to have defined the *tetraktys* as the 'origin of health'. See Huffman 1993, 355–6, who, *pace* Zhmud 2012, 302 n. 56, concludes that there is *no* valid objection to the authenticity of A 11. By contrast, the Lysis testimonium about the *tetraktys* (DK 46, 4, from Athenagoras) is deemed inauthentic by Burkert 1972, 461 with n. 71.

59   (iii) On the derivation of line, plane, and solid in the Academy see, e.g., Arist. *Metaph.* A 9, 992ᵃ10–13. (iv) The term simple bodies (ἁπλᾶ σώματα) for the four elements was coined by Aristotle, see e.g. *Cael.* A 1, 268ᵇ27–29. (v) The theory of the regular geometrical solids and their correspondence with the four elements was introduced by Pl. *Ti.* 53c–55c. (vi) According to Aristotle, *An.* A 2, 404ᵇ18–21, the composition of the Animal-itself of the One and length and width and thickness was described in *On Philosophy*; the concept of an 'Animal-itself' presupposes the theory of forms. (viii) According to Aristotle, *An.* A 2, 404ᵇ21–27, the correspondence between the four critical faculties of the soul and the first four numbers was linked to the theory that ideas are numbers; on the possible reference to Xenocrates or to Plato's unwritten doctrines see Burkert 1972, 25–26 with n. 49. (ix) The theory of three parts of the soul, reason (λογιστικόν), spirit (θυμικὸν), and appetite (ἐπιθυμητικόν), was developed by Pl, *R.* 4, 439d–441a.

60   LSJ 1996, 1781 s.v. τετρακτύς I, quote Theo Sm. 93.19–20 Hiller: τὴν μὲν γὰρ τετρακτὺν συνέστησεν ἡ δεκάς. ἓν γὰρ καὶ β΄ καὶ γ΄ καὶ δ΄ ι΄. See further Delatte 1915, 247–68, especially 256: 'Cependant la somme de quatre nombres ordinairement identifiée avec la tétractys est 10, formé par l'addition des quatre premiers nombres : 1, 2, 3 et 4', and Kucharski 1952, 32: 'Cette tétrade était capitale pour les Pythagoriciens, qui lui assignaient, comme nous le dit bien Théon de Smyrne [94.3–4 Hiller], le premier rang, reconnaissant « qu'elle semble renfermer toute la nature de l'univers (δοκεῖ τὴν τῶν ὅλων φύσιν συνέχειν) ... »'.

61   LSJ 1996, 1781 s.v. τετρακτύς II, quote Plu. *De Iside et Osiride* 381F–382A: ἡ δὲ καλουμένη τετρακτύς, τὰ ἓξ καὶ τριάκοντα, μέγιστος ἦν ὅρκος, ὡς τεθρύληται, καὶ κόσμος ὠνόμασται, τεσσάρων μὲν ἀρτίων τῶν πρώτων, τεσσάρων δὲ τῶν περισσῶν εἰς ταὐτὸ συντιθεμένων, ἀποτελούμενος. In contrast to the usual Greek view according to which the one is not a number, but the unit of all numbers (cf. Arist. *Metaph.* N 1, 1088ᵃ6–8), Plutarch's double *tetraktys* presupposes the classification of the one as *first odd number*. The latter classification, however, is clearly implied in the exposition of Pythagorean numbers by Speus. Fr. 4,

PYTHAGOREAN RATIOS IN EMPEDOCLES' PHYSICS

(iii) The series of ratios between four numbers that correspond to the four chief musical intervals (6 : 8 : 9 : 12).[62] This *tetraktys* is constructed by multiplying the three ratios corresponding to the three perfect intervals of music (*fourth* ≈ 3 : 4, *fifth* ≈ 2 : 3, *octave* ≈ 1 : 2) by 2, 3, and 6, respectively (*fourth* ≈ 6 : 8, *fifth* ≈ 6 : 9, *octave* ≈ 6 : 12), so that the whole series (6 : 8 : 9 : 12) includes the tone (*major second* ≈ 8 : 9) as well.

The evidence selected by Liddell/Scott/Jones suggests that the core meaning of *tetraktys*, as opposed to metaphorical extensions, is restricted to sets of four numbers that are subject to an arithmetical operation, like summing them up or establishing ratios between them. So with regard to a possible 5th century BC meaning of *tetraktys* we must, if possible, choose between the general meaning suggested, for instance, by Theon of Smyrna and presupposed by Diels, and the specific meaning as recognized by Liddell/Scott/Jones.

Now given that *tetraktys* seems to have been consciously coined by the Pythagoreans as a technical term,[63] its original technical meaning is probably to be gathered from its *word formation*. Eduard Schwyzer tried to support the interpretation of *tetraktys* as 'tetrad, set of four items' by assuming that the word was formed on the model of *triktys*, a word that had been conjectured in a fragment of a dialogue of Sophron of Syracuse (5th century BC)[64] and to which Schwyzer ascribed the meaning 'triad'.[65] Walter Burkert went even further in that direction: he assumed that *triktys* designates the 'triad of different sacrificial animals' and concluded, on that basis, that *tetraktys* not only designates a 'tetrad' made up of four unequal members, but that it was meant to characterize the 'tetrad' in question as a 'higher, bloodless secret' as compared with the sacrifice of three different animals.[66] But in fact, *triktys* is altogether

---

      lines 22–27 Lang (= Isnardi Parente 1980, fr. 122, p. 114.21–26 = F 28, lines 18–22 Tarán), as Cherniss 1944, 303 n. 202 pointed out.

62   LSJ 1996, 1781 s.v. τετρακτύς II (with the correction noted in LSJ 1996, Supplement, 293 s.v. τετρακτύς II) quote *Excerpta ex Nicomacho* c. 7; p. 279.8–12 Jan: κἀντεῦθεν ἡ πρώτη τετρακτὺς τὴν τῶν συμφωνιῶν πηγὴν ἔχουσα ἀναφαινομένην τῶν ς η θ ιβ, ὑπάτης τε καὶ μέσης καὶ νήτης καὶ παραμέσης ἔχουσα λόγον καὶ τὸν ἐπόγδοον περιλαμβάνουσα.

63   Delatte 1915, 249: 'Ce mot mystérieux dont l'origine et l'emploi sont exclusivement pythagoriciens [...]'.

64   Sophr. fr. 3 Kassel and Austin (2001, 193) = Ath. 9.480b (III.A 301.5 Olson), where Schweighäuser 1804, 161–162 suggested replacing, on the basis of Hsch. τ 1391, the transmitted form τρικτοι' (defended by LSJ 1996, 1824 s.v. τριττύα) by τρικτύς.

65   Schwyzer 1939, 597: 'τετρακτύς ,Zahl 4' Pythag. wohl erst nach τρικτύς Sophr'.

66   Burkert 1972, 187: 'The τετρακτύς, a 'tetrad' made up of unequal members, is a cryptic formula, only comprehensible to the initiated. The word inevitably reminds of τρικτύς, the 'triad' of different sacrificial animals. Is the sacrificial art of the seer, involving the shedding of blood, superseded by a 'higher', bloodless secret?'.

126   PRIMAVESI

unsuitable as a model for the formation of *tetraktys* if the latter is supposed to mean 'tetrad, set of four items'. For *triktys* means, as its Attic equivalent *trittys*, 'a third of a *phyle*', i.e., of a larger administration unit,[67] whereas the noun that means 'triad of different sacrificial animals' is certainly not *triktys*, as assumed by Schwyzer and Burkert, but the feminine *first* declension noun *triktya*.[68] So if *tetraktys* had indeed been formed on the model of *triktys*, the original meaning of *tetraktys* would have to be 'the fourth part (of a *phyle*)', which is completely out of the question. We conclude that the attribution of the general meaning 'tetrad, set of four items' to the technical term *tetraktys* rests on (i) the secondary expansion of its use in later Platonism and (ii) a wrong analysis of its word-formation.

A far more plausible analysis of the word-formation of *tetraktys* was published by Johannes Lohmann in 1959. He suggested analysing *tetraktys* as a verbal noun formed from *tetrazomai* ('operate with the tetrad') and ending in *-tys*.[69] It is true that there are two homonymous verbs spelt *tetrazō* in Greek: whereas the one is indeed derived from *tetras* ('tetrad') and means 'to deal with a tetrad',[70] the other is derived from *tetrax* ('Guinea-fowl')[71] and means 'to cackle

---

67   The only attested occurrence of τρικτύς is the plural nom. in Hesychius τ 1392 (IV.74 Hansen and Cunningham): τρικτῦς (Salmasius, M. L. West: τρικτῆς ms.)· μέρη φυλῆς ('parts of a *phyle*'). The more precise meaning 'a third of a *phyle*' is confirmed by the use of the verb τρικτυαρχέω as an equivalent of the Attic τριττυαρχέω in Delian inscriptions of the 3rd und 2nd centuries BC, for which see LSJ 1996 s.v. τριττυαρχέω.

68   Hesychius τ 1391 (IV.73 Hansen and Cunningham): τρικτύα· τριάδα. ἔνιοι θυσία κάπρου, κριοῦ, ταύρου ('*triktya*: triad; according to some: sacrifice of a boar, a ram, and a bull') has to be interpreted in the light of Photius τ 482; III.498 Theodoridis, where Hesychius' second meaning is attributed to the equivalent first declension noun *trittya*: τριττύαν θυσίαν. Καλλίμαχος μὲν (fr. 578 Pfeiffer) τὴν ἐκ κριοῦ, ταύρου καὶ κάπρου κτλ. Accordingly, in Hsch. τ 1391 the explanation in the *nominative* ('sacrifice of a boar, a ram, and a bull'), which implies the interpretation of the lemma τρικτύα as a nom., must be the authentic one, whereas the prepended *accusative* τριάδα ('triad'), which implies the interpretation of τρικτύα as a heteroclitic acc. of τρικτύς (for parallels see Choerob. *In Theod.* 234.1–3 and 332.4–5 Hilgard), instead of the regular acc. τρικτύν, is a misguided secondary addition (cf. Schmidt 1862, 174). It follows that the original (pre-Hesychian?) form of Hsch. τ 1391 must be restored as follows: τρικτύα· { τριάδα. ἔνιοι} θυσία κάπρου, κριοῦ, ταύρου, so that the only support for τρικτύς meaning 'triad' (and for Schweighäuser's conjecture in Sophron fr. 3 K.-A.) has disappeared.

69   Lohmann 1959, 283 (= 1970, 74) n. 1: 'Etymologisch ist τετρακτύς ein *Verbal*-Substantiv zu τετράζομαι „mit der Tetrade *operieren*", was bisher nicht bemerkt worden ist'. For the suffix see Kühner and Blass 1892: 272 (§ 329/28): 'Fem. auf τύ-ς, G. τύ-ος, Abstrakta zur Bezeichnung der Handlung des Verbums, entsprechend den lateinischen Wörtern auf tus, ūs, doch im Genus verschieden'.

70   Philostratus, *Gymnasticus* 47 uses *tetrazo* in the meaning 'observe a four day cycle in physical exercise', which implies its derivation from τετράς ('tetrad', with τετράζω < *tetrád-j-ō*).

71   For the meaning of τέτραξ see Thompson 1936, 282–283.

PYTHAGOREAN RATIOS IN EMPEDOCLES' PHYSICS

like a Guinea-fowl';[72] and it is also true that in Ionian and Attic Greek, *tetraktys* could only be derived from the latter, ornithological *tetrazō*.[73] Yet in the morphology and word formation of *Doric*, i.e. of the dialect in which Pythagorean and Ps.Pythagorean writings are invariably cast, the stems of all verbs ending in *-zō* (as, for instance, *tetrazō*) are treated as *guttural* stems, regardless of etymology.[74] It follows that in Doric the substantive derived from *tetrazō* and ending in *-tys* will always be *tetraktys*, no matter whether the underlying verb *tetrazō* is regarded as being derived from the dental stem *tetrad-* or from the guttural stem *tetrag-*. Thus, Lohmann's analysis of the word-formation of the Pythagorean term *tetraktys* is morphologically impeccable. As to the original meaning of *tetraktys*, Lohmann concludes that the word was *not* formed in order to designate 'tetrad, set of four items' but rather '*operating* with a tetrad, i.e. with a set of four numbers'—which is precisely the core meaning suggested by Liddell/Scott/Jones s.v. *tetraktys*, as we have seen—and he correctly points out that this meaning perfectly matches the one and only scientific discovery of the Pythagoreans that is reliably attested for pre-Empedoclean times. The early 5th century BC Pythagorean Hippasus of Metapontum was able to demonstrate that the ratios of the first four natural numbers correspond to the perfect intervals in music: 4 : 3 produces the fourth, 3 : 2 the fifth, 2 : 1 the octave, 4 : 1 the double octave.[75] In other words, it is by 'operating with the set of the first

---

72   The eminent ornithologist Alexander the Myndian (fr. 21 Wellmann 1891, 552 = Ath. 9.398d; III.A 128.12–13 Olson) uses *tetrazo* in the meaning 'cackle like the τέτραξ, on laying an egg' (ὅταν ᾠοτοκῇ δὲ—scil. ὁ τέτραξ—, τετράζει τῇ φωνῇ) which implies its derivation from τέτραξ (with τετράζω < *tetrág-j-ō). It must be said, however, that Aristophanes treats the bird name τέτραξ as being formed from a *k*-stem (*Birds* 883/4: τέτραχι), so that the classical Attic form of the affiliated verb would have to be *τετράττω rather than τετράζω.

73   In Ionian and Attic Greek only the verbal noun formed from *tetrág-j-ō/*tetrák-j-ō (< *tétrax* 'Guinea-fowl') would be τετραχ-τύς, after the model of the Homeric noun ῥυστακ-τύς ('*dragging about, rough handling*', from ῥυστάζω), whereas the verbal noun formed from *tetrád-j-ō (< *tetrás* 'tetrad') would have to be *τετρασ-τύς, after the model of the Homeric noun ὀαρισ-τύς ('*familiar converse, fond discourse*', from ὀαρίζω).

74   Buck 1955, 115–116 (§ 142): 'ξ in the future and aorist of verbs in -ζω. The extension of ξ, which is regular in the case of guttural stems, to other verbs in -ζω, which regularly have σσ, σ (δικάσω, ἐδίκασα), is seen in some isolated examples even in Homer (πολεμίξομεν, as, conversely ἥρπασε beside ἥρπαξε) and Hesiod (φημίξωσι). But as a general phenomenon it is characteristic of the West Greek dialects'; cf. Schwyzer 1939, 737–738; Risch ²1974, 296 (§ 109a).

75   Lohmann 1970, 107: '... die berühmte τετρακτύς (die übrigens—was man vielfach vergißt—nicht einfach „Tetrade", sondern vielmehr das „Operieren mit der Tetrade" bedeutet, so in der Musiktheorie die „Oktave" als 1 : 2, die „Quint" als 2 : 3, und die „Quart" als 3 : 4)'. See Theo Sm. 93.21–4 Hiller, with Delatte 1915, 257–8, Kucharski 1952, 32, Burkert 1972, 369–78, and Barker 2014: 186 and 202. The historicity of the experiment undertaken

128 PRIMAVESI

four integers', i.e. by performing a Pythagorean *tetraktys*, that Hippasus laid the foundation of musical theory.

With regard to the Pythagoreanism of Empedoclean physics, the preceding analysis yields a negative conclusion and a positive one: Diels was wrong to claim that the mere introduction of a set of four elements by Empedocles can count as an application of the Pythagorean *tetraktys*. On the other hand, the Pythagorean influence which we suspected behind the mixture ratios by which Empedocles tried to account for the composition of blood, muscles, bones, and tendons[76] has been confirmed, at least up to a certain point: All numbers which we found employed in the few examples of such mixture-ratios still extant (1, 2, and 4) are chosen from the series of the first four integers, so that, *if* the same held for *all* of Empedocles' mixture-ratios and *if* in some of them also the number 3 was used, it is by 'operating with the set of the first four integers', i.e., by performing a *tetraktys*, that Empedocles established his mixture ratios. We conclude that the holy *tetraktys* of the Pythagoreans may well have formed part of the conceptual framework of Empedocles 'On Nature'. Even if this is true, however, the field of its application is still too small to justify Simplicius' claim.

1.3.5 'On Nature' as Simplicius' Principal Source

Notwithstanding the centrality of Pythagoreanism in the 'Purifications', the assumption that Simplicius' characterization of Empedocles is based on that poem is unconvincing. Strictly speaking, his claim that Empedocles' affiliation to the Pythagoreans was even more important than his affiliation to Parmenides presupposes a *common point of reference*, yet Parmenides' influence clearly concerns only Empedocles' poem 'On Nature'. Furthermore, the Empedoclean quotations in Simplicius, notwithstanding their unparalleled abundance, are restricted almost exclusively to 'On Nature': he has 77 quotations from that poem[77] and just *one* short quotation from the

---

by Hippasus is accepted by Burkert 1972, 375–8, Zhmud 2012, 309–10, and Barker 2014, 186 (with n. 3) and 202.

76 According to Emp. fr. 98, fr. 100 and fr. 97 MP (B 98, 96, and A 78 DK, all quoted above, section 1.3.3), blood and muscles consist of 1 part earth, 1 part fire, 1 part water, 1 part air; bones of 2 parts earth, 2 parts water, 4 parts fire; and tendons of 1 part fire, 1 part earth, 2 parts water.

77 Emp. A 7 DK: *in Phys.* 25.19–21 Diels.— A 28(ii): *Phys.* 25.21–26,4.— A 52(ii): *in Cael.* 293.18–23 Heiberg.— A 52(iii): *in Cael.* 305.21–25.— B 8.3: *Phys.* 161.19; 180.30; 235.23; *in Cael.* 306.5.— B 17.1–8+10–35: *Phys.* 158.1–159.4.— B 17.1–2: *in Phys.* 161.16.— B 17.7–8+10–13: *in Cael.* 141.1–6; 293.25–294.3.— B 17.7–8: *Phys.* 25.29–30; 1318.25–26; *in Cael.* 530.14–15.— B 17.17^b–20: *in Phys.* 26.1–4.— B 17.21: *in Phys.* 188.26.— B 17.29: *in Phys.* 1184.7.— P.Strasb. a(ii) 30: *in Phys.* 161.20.— B 20.1–7: *in Phys.* 1124.12–18.— B 21.1–14: *in Phys.* 159.13–26.— B

PYTHAGOREAN RATIOS IN EMPEDOCLES' PHYSICS

'Purifications',[78] which he may well owe to an intermediate source.[79] It follows that Simplicius is rather unlikely to have characterized Empedocles in a way that was not justified by the poem 'On Nature' in the first place. In the *extant* fragments of 'On Nature', however, Pythagorean secrecy and the possible application of the Pythagorean *tetraktys* seem too marginal to justify Simplicius' characterization of Empedocles, as we have seen. On the other hand, of the c. 480 extant lines of Empedoclean verse, c. 390 lines (including the Strasburg papyrus) come from the three books of 'On Nature', which is a very rich documentation in comparison with other Presocratic works, but which represents, even on the most optimistic count,[80] far less than one-third of the original text. So we may form the working hypothesis that 'On Nature' contained Pythagorizing elements that provided sufficient evidence in support of Simplicius' claim, but are not or not completely preserved in our fragmentary tradition.

1.4 *Two Possible Objections*

One might object that two other explanations of Simplicius' claim are also plausible: Simplicius might depend either on the Empedoclean biographical tradition or on a Platonizing *reinterpretation* of 'On Nature' that was sometimes combined with a reference to Empedocles' Pythagoreanism.

21.3–12: *in Phys.* 33.8–17.— B 22.1–9: *in Phys.* 160.28–161.7.— B 23.1–11: *in Phys.* 160.1–11.— B 26.1–12: *in Phys.* 33.19–34.3.— B 26.1–2: *in Phys.* 160.16–17.— B 26.1: *in Phys.* 1184.7; 1185.19.— B 26.10: *in Phys.* 1124.23.— B 26.11–12: *in Phys.* 160.20–21; 1125.1–2.— B 27.1: *in Phys.* 1183.30.— B 27.3–4: *in Phys.* 1183.32–1184.1.— B 27.4: *in Cael.* 591.5.— B 29.3: *in Phys.* 1124.2.— B 30.1–3: *in Phys.* 1184.14–16.— B 31.1: *in Phys.* 1184.4.— B 35.1–15: *in Cael.* 529.1–15.— B 35.3–15, 16–17: *in Phys.* 32.13–33.2.— B 35.5: *in Cael.* 587.11.— B 35.10–13: *in Cael.* 587.14–17.— B 53: *in Phys.* 327.18; 330.35; 358.11; 1318.28.— B 57.1: *in Cat.* 337.2–3; *in Cael.* 586.12; *in An.* 250.23 Hayduck.— B 57.2–3: *in Cael.* 587.1–2.— B 58: *in Cael.* 587.18–19.— B 59.1: *in Cael.* 587.20.— B 59.2: *in Phys.* 327.20; *in Phys.* 331.2.— B 59.2–3: *in Cael.* 587.22–23.— B 61.2: *in Phys.* 372.1.— B 61.2: *in Phys.* 380.20; 381.3–4; 381.7; 381.13–14; 383.4–5.— B 62.1–8: *in Phys.* 381.31–382.3.— B 71.1–4: *in Cael.* 530.1–4.— B 73.1–2: *in Cael.* 530.6–7.— B 75.1–2: *in Cael.* 530.9–10.— B 75.2: *in Phys.* 331.9.— B 85: *in Phys.* 331.7.— B 86: *in Cael.* 529.23.— B 87: *in Cael.* 529.25.— B 95: *in Cael.* 529.27.— B 96.1–4: *in Phys.* 300.21–25.— B 98.1–5: *in Phys.* 32.6–10.— B 98.1: *in Phys.* 331,5.— B 103: *in Phys.* 331.12.— B 104: *in Phys.* 331.14.— B 105.3: *in Phys.* 392.24–25.27; *in An.* 21.31.— B 108.2: *in An.* 202.30f.— The commentary on *An.*, however, has been attributed to Priscianus Lydus; see Steel 1997, 105–140.

78   Emp. B 115.1–2: *Phys.* 1184.9–10.

79   O'Brien 1981, 88–90.

80   That is to say, if we discard Lobon's claim that the five books of Empedoclean poetry (i.e., the two books of the 'Purifications' and the three books of 'On Nature') contained 1000 lines each, and assume instead, with Wright 1981, 21, that 'on the Homeric model', these five books 'could average five to six hundred lines each'.

1.4.1 The Biographical Tradition on Empedocles

Simplicius was not the first to regard Empedocles as a Pythagorean; his claim looks back to a nine-century long tradition. That Empedocles was affiliated with the Pythagoreans was first asserted by authors of the fourth century BC (e.g. Alcidamas the rhetor and Neanthes of Cyzicus the elder) and thus became part of the biographical tradition that was synthesized, in the late 2nd century AD, by Diogenes Laertius.[81] According to this tradition, Empedocles would at first have been a personal pupil of Pythagoras himself,[82] or of early Pythagoreans (Hippasus and Brotinus),[83] or else of 'Telauges', allegedly the son and successor of Pythagoras.[84] Later, or so the story goes, Empedocles was expelled from the school on the ground that he had committed the crime of publishing Pythagorean secrets under his own name (*logoklopia*).[85] On the basis of that biographical tradition, Diogenes Laertius not only places the biography of Empedocles in the Pythagorean section of his *Lives of the Philosophers*,[86] but he

---

81 D.L. 8.51–77. The basic analysis of Diogenes' sources for this section was provided by Bidez 1894.

82 Alcidamas the Rhetor (4th century BC) claims that Empedocles took over the qualities of solemnity and pretention in his life-style and behaviour from Pythagoras (D.L. 8.56, Dorandi 2013, 632–33.57–63 = Alcidamas fr. 8, Avezzù 1982, 52), which presupposes a personal acquaintance (Burkert 1972, 215–6 with n. 29; Schorn 2007, 130 n. 91). The historian Timaeus of Tauromenium (c. 350–260 BC) also explicitly names Empedocles as a student of Pythagoras (D.L. 8.54; Dorandi 2013, 632.37–9 = FGrHist 566 F 14 Jacoby; cf. Burkert 1972, 111 with n. 7).

83 Neanthes of Cyzicus the elder (4th century BC; cf. Burkert 2000) cites a spurious letter written by a certain Telauges (D.L. 8.55 Dorandi 2013, 632.48–52 = FGrHist 84 F 27 = Thesleff 1965, 189: *Ep. ad Philol.*) and addressed to Philolaus (D.L. 8.53, Dorandi 2013, 631.30–1), in which Hippasus and Brotinus rather than Pythagoras are named as Empedocles' Pythagorean teachers.

84 The biographer Hippobotus (1st half of 2nd century BC; cf. Engels 2007, 176) quotes a (spurious) hexameter (DK 31 B 155) in which the *persona* addresses Telauges as the son of Pythagoras and Theano (apud D.L. 8.43, Dorandi 2013, 624–5.484–9 = Hippobotus fr. 14, Gigante 1983, 186). According to D.L., this address to Telauges (who in Neanthes still figured only as the alleged author of the spurious letter to Philolaus) is meant to suggest that Telauges was the *teacher* of Empedocles. D.L. may owe to Hippobotus not only the quotation but also its interpretation (Engels 2007: 187).

85 Neanth. FGrHist 84 F 26 Jacoby 1926 (= D.L. 8.55; 632.44–51 Dorandi) and Timae. FGrHist 566 F 14 Jacoby 1950 (= D.L. 8.54; 632.37–9 Dorandi); cf. Burkert 1972, 454 with n. 37 and 220 with n. 12 *sub fin.*, as well as Zhmud 2012, 160–161. It has been suggested to relate this charge to the 'Purifications'; cf. Burkert 1972, 220 with n. 12 (building on a suggestion made by Kahn 1960): 'In this case the *Katharmoi* would actually contain, in different form, the ἱερὸς λόγος, i.e., the secret doctrine of Pythagoras'. It must be said, however, that the esoteric Poem 'On Nature' would seem to be a far more plausible candidate for the disclosure of real secrets than the exoteric 'Purifications'.

86 D.L. 8.

PYTHAGOREAN RATIOS IN EMPEDOCLES' PHYSICS

even presents him as a Pythagorean *par excellence* by setting him directly after his life of Pythagoras,[87] i.e. *before* Epicharmus, Archytas, Alcmaeon, Hippasus, and Philolaus.[88] Yet with regard to Simplicus' perfect acquaintance with both Parmenides' poem and Empedocles' 'On Nature', it seems very improbable that he should have relied on the biographical tradition for his own assessment of the relative importance of Empedocles' Parmenidean and Pythagorean affiliations. It would be strangely unbalanced to characterize Empedocles by *subordinating* one feature that is obviously of prime importance for his philosophy (i.e., Parmenides' influence) to another feature, i.e. the Pythagorean affiliation, if the evidence for the latter had been confined to the biographical tradition.[89]

1.4.2   The Platonizing Reinterpretation of Empedocles

Apart from the biographical tradition, the evidence on which an ascription of Pythagoreanism to Empedocles could be based may have taken quite different forms:

(i)   Empedocles may have built on or referred to a doctrine that is indeed attested for Pythagoras or his school.

(ii)   An authentic Empedoclean text may have been later ascribed to Pythagoras or his school.

(iii) A doctrine which was in fact held neither by the Pythagoreans nor by Empedocles may have been ascribed to both, thereby creating a fictitious common denominator.

All of these possibilities were already well established around AD 200, i.e., three centuries before Simplicius, since all three of them are employed by Hippolytus of Rome:[90]

(i)   Hippolytus says that Empedocles, as a follower of Pythagoras, taught the transmigration of souls,[91] i.e., a doctrine which was already ascribed to

---

87   D.L. 8.1–50. The basic commentary on that section was provided by Delatte 1922.

88   D.L. 8.50; 629.579–581 Dorandi: λεκτέον δὲ νῦν περὶ Ἐμπεδοκλέους πρῶτον· κατὰ γάρ τινας Πυθαγόρου διήκουσεν.

89   This is not to deny that the general conclusion reached by Mary Lefkowitz in her important book *The Lives of the Greek Poets* will hold for Empedocles as well (Lefkowitz 1981: viii): '... virtually all the material in all the lives is fiction, and ... ancient biographers took most of the information on ancient poets from the poets' own works'. This approach was applied to the legends on Empedocles' death by Ava Chitwood 1986, cf. also Chitwood 2004: 12–58.

90   Hippol. *Haer.* VII.29–31, with Mansfeld 1992a, 208–231.

91   Hippol. *Haer.* VI.26.2: εἶναι γὰρ οὗτοι (i.e., Pythagoras and Plato) τῶν ψυχῶν μετενσωμάτωσιν νομίζουσιν, ὡς καὶ Ἐμπεδοκλῆς πυθαγορίζων λέγει.

132   PRIMAVESI

Pythagoras by his contemporaries[92] and which was indeed put to poetical use by Empedocles in his 'Purifications'.[93]

(ii) Authentic lines from Empedocles' 'On Nature' are quoted by Hippolytus as *Pythagorean* in order to supply evidence for the Pythagoreans' assumption of an eternal cosmos.[94]

(iii) The so called 'Two Worlds Theory', i.e. the Platonizing concept of an 'intelligible world' (*kosmos noetos*) as opposed to the visible or sensible one (*kosmos horatos* or *aisthetos*)—though in fact first attested only in Philo of Alexandria[95]—is ascribed by Hippolytus *both* to Pythagoras[96] and to Empedocles.[97]

The last point is not only the most dubious one from a historical perspective, but also of particular importance *for* our present purpose, since it involves a Platonizing reinterpretation of Empedocles' cosmic cycle that is adopted, with individual variations, not only by other Neo-Platonic commentators like Syrianus, Proclus, Asclepius, and Philoponus, but also by Simplicius, as has been shown by Denis O'Brien and Jaap Mansfeld.[98] These Neo-Platonists claim that the *temporal* alternation between One and Many within Empedocles' cosmic cycle is not to be taken literally, as Aristotle had done, but rather to be seen as a concealed, allegorical reference to the *ontological* difference between the

---

92   Xenoph. fr. 43 MP (DK 21 B 7).

93   Emp. fr. 10 MP (DK 31 B 117).

94   Hippol. *Haer.* 6.25.1 introduces a quotation of Emp. fr. 57 MP (B 16 DK) as follows: τοιγαροῦν καὶ περὶ τῆς διαμονῆς τοῦ κόσμου ἀποφαίνονται τοιοῦτόν τινα τρόπον οἱ Πυθαγόρειοι. Later (*Haer.* 7.29.10) he quotes the same lines as Empedoclean.

95   Ph. *De opificio* 16, I 5 Cohn and Wendland: (scil. ὁ θεός) βουληθεὶς τὸν ὁρατὸν κόσμον τουτονὶ δημιουργῆσαι προεξετύπου τὸν νοητόν (scil. κόσμον). See further Runia 2001, 136 ad loc. and especially the fundamental contribution of Runia 1999. Along the same lines, Fine 2016 has cogently argued that Plato's *Phaedo* is not only not committed to the Two Worlds Theory, but even rejects it.

96   Hippol. *Haer.* 6.24.1: δύο οὖν κατὰ Πυθαγόραν εἰσὶ κόσμοι· εἷς μὲν νοητός, ὃς ἔχει τὴν μονάδα ἀρχήν, εἷς δὲ αἰσθητός.

97   Hippol. *Haer.* 7.31.3: κόσμον γάρ φησιν εἶναι ὁ Ἐμπεδοκλῆς ⟨τοῦτον⟩, τὸν ὑπὸ τοῦ νείκους διοικούμενον τοῦ πονηροῦ, καὶ ἕτερον νοητόν, τὸν ὑπὸ τῆς φιλίας, καὶ εἶναι ταύτας τὰς διαφερούσας ἀρχὰς δύο, ἀγαθοῦ καὶ κακοῦ. See also *Haer.* 7.29.17, where Hippolytus claims, with regard to Emp. fr. 8b.5 MP (= B 115.6 DK: τρίς μιν μυρίας ὥρας ἀπὸ μακάρων ἀλάλησθαι), that the 'blessed ones' (μάκαρες) have been brought by Love into the Unity of the Intelligible Cosmos (μάκαρας καλῶν τοὺς συνηγμένους ὑπὸ τῆς φιλίας ἀπὸ τῶν πολλῶν εἰς τὴν ἑνότητα τοῦ κόσμου τοῦ νοητοῦ). On Hippolytus' interpretation of Empedocles (*Haer.* 7.29–31) in general see Mansfeld 1992a, 208–231.

98   O'Brien 1981, 73–90 and 101–107; Mansfeld 1992a, 245–262. See also Primavesi 2013, 725–726 with further references.

PYTHAGOREAN RATIOS IN EMPEDOCLES' PHYSICS 133

Intelligible and the Sensible. In particular, the Empedoclean *Sphairos*—i.e., the divine state of cosmic unity regularly brought about by Love and later destroyed by Strife—is 'decoded' as the timeless intelligible world (*kosmos noetos*) of the Platonizing 'Two Worlds Theory', a reading that obviously requires explaining away or neutralizing the temporally finite nature of the *Sphairos*. This condition, in turn, is met by transferring the attribute of temporal finiteness from the cosmic One to the duration of the *souls' dwelling in the intelligible world*. This surprising move was made possible by invoking Empedocles' other poem, the 'Purifications', as reinterpreted by Plutarch who had taken the myth of the guilty god's purification by a series of incarnations as an allegory on the punishment of defiled souls *in general*.[99] So Hippolytus and later Platonists detemporalized the cosmic cycle expounded in 'On Nature' by reinterpreting it as a mere allegory of the story about the souls' fall and return that they had extracted from the 'Purifications' in the first place.[100]

Now some of the later commentators think, with Hippolytus, that Empedocles owes the Platonizing views, which they anachronistically ascribe to him, to *Pythagoras*. Syrianus, for instance, asserts that Empedocles, *just like his fellow-Pythagoreans*, distinguished between intelligible substances and sensible substances.[101] If this historical construction were also shared by Simplicius, as Loredana Cardullo has suggested,[102] we would, perhaps, not have to look anywhere else for the evidence behind Simplicius' claim on the overwhelming importance of Empedocles' Pythagorean affiliation: The claim might simply be based on the Platonizing views ascribed since Hippolytus to both Empedocles and Pythagoras.

It is certainly true that Simplicius upholds one version of the Platonizing reinterpretation of Empedocles: he asserts, for instance, that Empedocles'

---

99 Plu. *De esu carnium* 1 7, 996b: ἀλληγορεῖ γὰρ ἐνταῦθα τὰς ψυχάς, ὅτι φόνων καὶ βρώσεως σαρκῶν καὶ ἀλληλοφαγίας δίκην τίνουσαι σώμασι θνητοῖς ἐνδέδενται.

100 See, for instance, Proclus *In Hes. erg.* 48–62 Fr. *LVI,19–24 Marzillo (= Emp. fr. 8c MP): δόγμα γάρ ἐστιν Ἐμπεδόκλειον, ὃ βούλεται τὰς πάσας τῶν ἀνθρώπων ψυχὰς εἶναι καὶ προϋφεστάναι παρὰ τῶι δημιουργῶι καὶ τῆι προνοίαι καὶ προκόπτειν ἐκεῖ καὶ ἀναβαίνειν εἰς τελεωτέρους βαθμούς· ἐπειδὰν δὲ πρὸς τὰ γήϊνα ταυτὶ καὶ φθαρτὰ τὴν ὁρμὴν μετατρέψαιεν, εὐθὺς αὐτὸ τοῦτο λαμβάνουσιν ἐπιτίμιον, τὸ ἐκεῖθεν μεταπεσεῖν ἐπὶ τὰ σώματα καὶ τὴν μετὰ τούτων διαγωγήν.

101 Syrian. *in Metaph.* 43.6–9 Kroll: ἀλλ' οὔτε πάντα φθείρειν φήσομεν Ἐμπεδοκλέα (οὐ γὰρ δεῖται τῆς τοιαύτης πρὸς ἑαυτὸν συμφωνίας), ἀλλ' ὥσπερ τοὺς ἄλλους Πυθαγορείους οὕτω καὶ αὐτὸν εἰδέναι τὰς μὲν νοητὰς οὐσίας τὰς δὲ αἰσθητάς.

102 Cardullo 2011, 819: 'A partire da Porfirio e fino a Simplicio, i principali rappresentanti delle diverse scuole neoplatoniche ... crearano una sorta di "aurea catena" che diacronicamente univa, come in un'unica tradizione dalle radici antichissime, sapienti di epoche diverse: orfici, pitagorici, fisiologi come Parmenide ed Empedocle, Platone, persino Aristotele a volte'.

description of a temporal alternation of Love's rule and Strife's rule is to be explained as featuring a poet's 'more mythical way' of expressing himself.[103] In a similar vein, he characterizes as *enigmatic* Empedocles' description of Love as *producing* the intelligible world by way of unification, and of Strife as *producing* the sensible world by way of separation (since in fact they do not come to exist in time at all).[104] But contrary to Cardullo's specific claim about Simplicius,[105] the *Pythagorean* features Simplicius ascribes to Empedocles in such contexts have nothing to do with Platonizing theorems: Cardullo's evidence consists of one passage where Simplicius *compares* two of six Empedoclean principles (Love/Strife) with a Pythagorean pair of opposites which had already been listed by Aristotle (odd/even),[106] and of another passage where Simplicius ascribes to Empedocles an *enigmatic way of expressing himself* that was also employed by the Pythagoreans.[107] These comparatively marginal remarks fall short of what is needed to explain Simplicius' radical claim on Empedocles' Pythagoreanism, since they do not even begin to trace any element of the Platonizing reinterpretation of Empedocles back to Pythagoras.

So our working hypothesis as presented at the end of the preceding section (1.3) is still unrefuted: we submit that the lost parts of the poem 'On Nature' are likely to have contained Pythagorizing elements that provided sufficient evidence to justify Simplicius' strong claim. Moreover, there seems to be a witness in support of that claim that has not yet been recognized as such and that clearly antedates the Platonizing allegorization of the Cycle. To this witness we will now turn.

---

103 Simp. *in Cael.* 530.12–13 Heiberg introduces a quotation of fr. 66b.239–240 MP (B17.7–8 DK) as follows: τοῦ Ἐμπεδοκλέους ὡς ποιητοῦ μυθικώτερον παρὰ μέρος τὴν ἐπικράτειαν αὐτῶν λέγοντος [...].

104 Simp. *in Cael.* p. 140.25–30 Heiberg: ὁμοίως δὲ καὶ Ἐμπεδοκλῆς τόν τε ὑπὸ τῆς Φιλίας ἐνούμενον νοητὸν κόσμον παραδιδοὺς αἰνιγματωδῶς, ὡς ἔθος ἦν τοῖς Πυθαγορείοις, καὶ τὸν ὑπὸ τοῦ Νείκους ἀπ' ἐκείνου διακρινόμενον αἰσθητὸν οὔτε γινόμενα οὔτε φθειρόμενα ἐν χρόνῳ φησίν, ἀλλὰ τὸν μὲν νοητὸν κόσμον κατὰ τὸ ὂν ἑστάναι, τὸν δὲ αἰσθητὸν κατὰ τὸ γινόμενον καὶ τοῦτον τῇ διαδοχῇ φησιν ἀιδίως ἀνακυκλεῖσθαι.

105 Cardullo 2011, 836: 'Sebbene i contesti [*scil.* in Simplicio] nei quali l'agrigentino viene definito pitagorico o, in generale, seguace dei pitagorici siano soltanto un paio, è tuttavia possibile ritrovare in Simplicio la medesima interpretazione neoplatonica, già vista in Siriano, Asclepio e Filopono, per la quale la lettura pitagorizzante dell'opera di Empedocle era funzionale'.

106 Simp. *in Phys.* 189.2–3 Diels: τὸ δὲ περιττὸν καὶ ἄρτιον ἀρχὰς οἱ Πυθαγόρειοι τίθενται, ὥσπερ τὸ νεῖκος καὶ τὴν φιλίαν μετὰ τῶν τεττάρων στοιχείων Ἐμπεδοκλῆς.

107 Simp. *in Cael.* 140.25–27 Heiberg: [...] Ἐμπεδοκλῆς τόν τε ὑπὸ τῆς Φιλίας ἐνούμενον νοητὸν κόσμον παραδιδοὺς αἰνιγματωδῶς, ὡς ἔθος ἦν τοῖς Πυθαγορείοις [...].

PYTHAGOREAN RATIOS IN EMPEDOCLES' PHYSICS

2   The Pythagorean *Oath* and Empedocles' Cosmic Time-Table

2.1   *Introduction*

In the following section, we will argue that evidence for a Pythagorizing structure of Empedocles' cosmic cycle is provided by one of the Pseudo-Pythagorean texts of the Hellenistic period, namely, by the so-called *Oath* of the Pythagoreans that seems to be alluded to by Posidonius (1st half of the 1st century BC)[108] and is first quoted in full, as far as our knowledge goes, in the first century AD:[109]

οὐ μὰ τὸν ἀμετέραι γενεᾶι παραδόντα τ ε τ ρ α κ τ ύ ν ,
π ᾱ γ ὰ ν ἀενάου φύσεως ῥ ι ζ ώ μ α τ ' ἔχουσαν.

---

1 οὐ] ναὶ Hippol. *Haer.* VI.23.4, *Carm.Aur.* 47 ‖ γενεᾶι Porph. *V.P.*
20, Iamb. *VP* 162 : κεφαλᾶι Sext. *M* 7.94; Hippol. l.c.; Stob. I.10.12;
v.l. ap. Theo Sm. 94 Hiller : ψυχᾶι Ps.-Plu. *Plac.* 877A; Sext. *M* 4.2;
Theo Sm. l.c.

No, by him who handed over the tetraktys *to our race, the* pāgā *('source'?) of ever-flowing nature that holds the* rhizōmata *('root-systems'?).*

These two lines purport to be the vow by which the ancient Pythagoreans had to promise not to make public the teachings of the school.[110] In the first line, Pythagoras/Apollo himself is both invoked as a divine witness to the oath and praised for having given to mankind the great gift of the *tetraktys*. In the second line, the *tetraktys* is characterized as the *pāgā* ('source'?)[111] of nature that

---

108   The expression ἀέναος φύσις from the second line of the *Oath* is quoted in Posidonius (c. 135 BC–c. 51 BC), as Kidd 1988, 833 pointed out: 'Posidonius was possibly playing on the famous Pythagorean oath, πηγὴν ἀενάου φύσεως ῥιζώματ' ἔχουσαν'. Cf. Posidon. fr. 239 Edelstein and Kidd (²1989, 211), lines 7–9: καθόλου δ' ἂν εἶπε, φησίν, ἰδών τις τοὺς τόπους, θησαυροὺς εἶναι φύσεως ἀενάου ἢ ταμιεῖον ἡγεμονίας ἀνέκλειπτον, and the translation by Kidd 1999, 309: 'And in general, says he [Posidonius], anyone looking at the area [Turdetania, rich in ores, i.e., modern Andalusia] would have said that it was a treasure house *of everlasting nature* or an unfailing treasury of an empire'.

109   Pythag. *Iusiur.*, Thesleff 1965, 170.15–16 = DK 58 B 15 = Pythagoras, ältere Pythagoreer fr. 29 MP. See further Delatte 1915, 249–53 (transmission: 249–50 n. 1), Zeller and Nestle 1920, 1025 n. 2, Burkert 1972, 186–8, and Zhmud 2012, 300–3. Our earliest witness to the full text is 'Aëtius' (1st c. AD), Diels 1879, 282a8–11 (Ps.-Plutarch) and 282b3–6 (Stobaeus).

110   The negative form (≈ 'not to make public') is better attested than the positive form (≈ 'to keep secret'), as our little *apparatus criticus* shows.

111   According to LSJ 1996 s.v. πηγή, the singular of this word (or of its doric equivalent πᾱγά) normally means 'fount, source'; and occasionally 'stream'. We will come back to the meaning of πηγή below.

contains 'root-systems' (*rhizōmata*, a word known as the technical term for Empedocles' four elements).[112] That is quite remarkable since there is no other text in the whole of classical Greek literature that makes a connection between *pēgē* and *rhizōmata*—except Empedocles' 'On Nature'.[113] In that poem, *rhizōmata* and *pēgē* signify two closely interrelated key concepts of the physical system, as we will presently see.

The unique terminological agreement between the Pythagorean *Oath* and Empedocles' 'On Nature' will not be due to chance, as Walther Kranz and Walter Burkert correctly observed. But whereas Kranz thought that Empedocles depends on the *Oath* here,[114] Burkert pointed out that the second line of the *Oath* also contains the expression *aenaos physis* ('ever-flowing nature') in which the word *physis* is clearly not used in its original meaning, 'individual result of growth, individual form',[115] but in its secondary meaning, 'totality of beings, totality of nature'. In this meaning, however, *physis* alone, i.e. without a modifier like 'of all things' (τῶν ὅλων) or 'of everything' (τοῦ παντός), is not attested earlier than the mid-fifth century BC;[116] therefore, it is very unlikely to occur in this meaning in a text antedating Empedocles' 'On Nature'.[117] We conclude with Burkert that the second line of the *Oath* is alluding to Empedocles' 'On Nature', not the other way round. More specifically, the *Oath* suggests that Empedoclean physics is heavily *indebted* to Pythagoras/Apollo.

The nature of that alleged indebtedness depends, in the first place, on the meaning which the term *tetraktys* has in the *Oath*: As we have seen in section 1.3.4, the original meaning of *tetraktys* as implied by Liddell/Scott/Jones and spelt out by Lohmann 1959 ('operating with a set of four numbers') was later

---

112   According to LSJ 1996 s.v. ῥίζωμα I, the basic meaning of that botanical term is *'the mass of roots* of a tree'—that is to say: 'a root-system'. We will come back to the meaning of ῥίζωμα below.

113   Emp. fr. 49b.1 MP (B 6.1 DK): ῥιζώματα; fr. 67b.10 (B 23.10 DK): πηγήν.

114   Kranz 1938, 438: '... Jene ersten vier Zahlen aber ergaben die heilige τετρακτύς, die heißt παγὰν ἀενάου φύσεως ῥίζωμά τ' ἔχουσαν. Kein Zweifel, daß Empedokles den alten Eid, der sie enthält, gekannt hat, sonst hätte er nicht von der πηγὴ θνητῶν, ὅσσα γε δῆλα γεγάκασιν gesprochen, nicht die Elemente ῥιζώματα πάντων genannt ...'.

115   The word φύ-σις is obviously derived from φύ-ομαι ('to grow'); accordingly, it was originally used to designate the result of growth, i.e., the physical form of individual plants (φυ-τά), animals, and human beings, or else the physical form of *species* of such organisms. See further Patzer 1993, 247–77 (= 37–67).

116   Burkert 1972, 186 n. 155: 'the general idea of φύσις is scarcely likely to have existed before the second half of the 5th century'. According to Patzer 1993, 276 (= 66), Philol. DK 44 B 1 provides the earliest evidence for the use of φύσις in the sense of 'Gesamtheit all dessen [...], was als Gewordenes (φύεσθαι im erweiterten Sinne) da ist'.

117   Zhmud 2012, 301–3, in his discussion of the *Oath*, has not noticed that its second line brims with Empedoclean terminology.

PYTHAGOREAN RATIOS IN EMPEDOCLES' PHYSICS

trivialized to the secondary meaning 'a set of four items'. On a reading of the *Oath* that is based on this later meaning of *tetraktys*, the divine gift of Pythagoras/Apollo to mankind would be identified with the number four as exemplified by the *rhizomata*, i.e., by Empedocles' four elements, which in turn would be described as a source of nature. Yet the interesting question is whether the *Oath* lends itself also, or perhaps even better, to a reading that presupposes the original meaning of *tetraktys*: Can a *pāgā* of nature that holds the *rhizōmata* be considered as an 'operating with a set of four numbers' or as a result thereof?

We will answer this question in the affirmative and we will expound our argument for doing so in two steps: we will first decode the second line ('*the* pāgā *of ever-flowing nature that holds the* rhizōmata') by identifying it as a circumlocution for 'Empedocles' cosmic cycle', and we will then show that its use as a description of the Pythagorean *tetraktys* makes sense as soon as we take the *tetraktys* in its original meaning. On that reading, the *time-table* of Empedocles' cosmic cycle is here assumed to be structured according to the ratios of the *tetraktys* (1 : 2 : 3 : 4). The first step requires clarifying the precise meaning and function of *rhizōmata* and *pēgē* in Empedocles' physical system—and accomplishing this neglected task will by no means be straightforward.

2.2 Rhizōmata *and* Pēgē *in the Pythagorean* Oath *and in Empedocles'* 'On Nature'

2.2.1 *Rhizōmata* = 'elemental networks'

The human teacher of 'On Nature' enigmatically characterizes the four elements of the physical system—fire and earth, air and water—as *rhizōmata* ('root-systems'). He then designates each of the four elements by the name of a God in order to emphasize its divinity:[118]

> τέσσαρα γὰρ πάντων ῥ ι ζ ώ μ α τ α πρῶτον ἄκουε·
> Ζ ε ὺ ς ἀργὴς "Η ρ η τε φερέσβιος ἠδ᾽ Ἀ ϊ δ ω ν ε ύ ς
> Ν ῆ σ τ ί ς θ᾽, ἣ δακρύοις τέγγει κρούνωμα βρότειον.

---

2 ἀργὴς Stob., alii : αἰθὴρ Ps.-Plu. (mss. & versio araba) : Ἀρὴς Ps.-Plu. apud Eus.

Hear first of all the four rhizomata *('root-systems') of all things: Radiant Zeus, life-bringing Hera, and Aïdoneus, and Nēstis who moistens with tears the human spring.*

---

118   Emp. fr. 49b MP (B 6 DK).

138   PRIMAVESI

For our purposes it is vital to find out in what sense exactly the elements are called *rhizomata* here: does this expression refer to the elements as such or to the state in which the elements are during specific phases of the cosmic cycle? In order to answer this question, we will have to examine the four divine names and their epithets first.

Zeus and Hera evidently form a couple, so that it is highly probable that Aï-doneus (whose name is an epic equivalent of 'Hades') and Nēstis ('the fasting one') also form a couple. Therefore, Christian Gottlob Heyne (1729–1812) plausibly identified Empedocles' Nēstis with the consort of Hades, Persephone.[119] Since Nēstis is attested as a Sicilian Goddess,[120] 'Nēstis' may well be a Sicilian cult-name for Persephone[121] and thus be familiar to Empedocles.

As to the *physical counterparts* of the divine names, Empedocles provided three of the divine names with epithets or an adjectival clause which indicate how to decode the names in question. Zeus' epithet *argēs* (ἀργής, gen. ἀργῆτος 'radiant') strongly suggests his equation with *fire*: since *argēs* is the Homeric epithet of Zeus' lightning bolts,[122] the connection of that epithet with Zeus himself clearly characterizes the latter as *master* of those radiant lightning bolts (*Zeus argi-keraunos*),[123] which in turn would seem to put his identity with fire beyond reasonable doubt.[124] Similarly, the elemental aspect of Hera seems to be hinted at by her epithet *pheresbios* (φερέσβιος 'life-bringing'). Since this epithet is exclusively used in connection with *Earth* or her crops by poets from Hesiod onwards,[125] its use as an epithet of Hera strongly suggests the equation of that Goddess with Earth[126]—the *hieros gamos* of Zeus and

---

119   Heyne 1776 p. IX (note); cf. Kingsley 1995, 351–352.

120   Alexis fr. 323; Kassel and Austin 1991, 191.

121   The Sicilian version of Persephone's mythical abduction by Hades, on which see Richardson 1974, 75–77, was certainly known to the 4th century BC tragedian Carcinus the younger (TrGF 1, 70 Carcinus F 5; Snell and Kannicht 1986, 213–214) but it is probably implied already by Pindar *Nemean* 1.13–15.

122   Cf. e.g. Il. 8.131–133: καί νύ κε σήκασθεν κατὰ Ἴλιον ἠΰτε ἄρνες, / εἰ μὴ ἄρ' ὀξὺ νόησε πατὴρ ἀνδρῶν τε θεῶν τε· (= Zeus) / βροντήσας δ' ἄρα δεινὸν ἀφῆκ' ἀργῆτα κεραυνόν and Od. 5.128: Ζεύς, ὅς μιν κατέπεφνε βαλὼν ἀργῆτι κεραυνῶι.

123   Cf. e.g. Il.19.121: Ζεῦ πάτερ ἀργικέραυνε.

124   Kingsley 1995, 46–48 suggested identifying Hades with *Fire*. This suggestion is not unrelated to his larger project of showing that subterranean fire matters in Empedocles and of thereby providing the legend of his suicidal jump into a fiery volcano (Mt. Etna) with a conceptual grounding in his philosophical poetry.

125   Hes. *Th.* 693: γαῖα φερέσβιος, *h. Ap.* 341: γαῖα φερέσβιος, *h. Dem.* 450: φερέσβιον οὖθαρ ἀρούρης, *h. Hom.* XXX.9: ἄρουρα φερέσβιος, and *TrGF* 3, A. F 300.6–7 Radt: Αἴγυπτος ἁγνοῦ νάματος πληρουμένη / φερέσβιον Δήμητρος ἀντέλλει στάχυν.

126   Snell 1944, 159: 'So wie Zeus durch das homerische Adjektiv ἀργής, das bei Homer dem Blitz zukommt, als Feuer-Aether bestimmt ist, so kann φερέσβιος nur Beiwort der Erde

Hera being actualized, as it were, whenever a fiery lightning bolt strikes the earth. That Nēstis stands for the element of *water*, is made clear by the adjectival clause which explicitly associates her with *tears* and with the *spring of mortals*. Out of the four Empedoclean elements, then, only *aër* will be left for the consort of Nēstis/Persephone, i.e., for Aïdoneus/Hades. Now if we keep in mind that the epic meaning of *aër* is '*fog*',[127] which was only generalized to '*air*' in post-Homeric Greek, the equation of Aïdoneus/Hades and *aër* is entirely plausible: (i) Homer uses the epithet *ēeroeis* (ἠερόεις 'foggy'), i.e., a clear derivative of *aër* (ἀήρ), in order to characterize the province of darkness (*zophos*) that *Hades* holds from time immemorial.[128] (ii) The equation of Aïdoneus/Hades with '*fog, air*' indicates that this God is invisible himself and makes the dead invisible, and this in turn is in tune with the popular derivation of 'Hades' (Ἅιδης) from the Greek adjective *a-idēs* (ἀϊδής 'invisible'), attested by Plato.[129]

Thus, Empedocles suggests the following equations in his presentation of the four *rhizomata*: 'Zeus = Fire', 'Hera = Earth', 'Aïdoneus = Air', 'Nēstis = Water'. These equations are confirmed by almost all extant ancient interpretations of our fragment,[130] and, in particular, by the (lost) doxographical handbook of 'Aëtius'. Of our two main sources for 'Aëtius', Stobaeus and Ps.-Plutarch's *Placita philosophorum*, Stobaeus shares the above interpretation of Empedocles'

---

  sein, denn es ist eine, allerdings auf einem Mißverständnis beruhende Umwandlung des homerischen Beiworts φυσίζοος, ähnlich wie von Sophokles das homerische ζείδωρος zu βιόδωρος umgewandelt ist: beidemal verstand man nicht mehr die eigentliche Bedeutung 'Spelt hervorbringend', sondern deutete das unbekannt gewordene homerische Wort als 'Leben schaffend', und so heißt es schon Hes. Theog. 693 und Hom. hy. Ap. 341 γαῖα φερέσβιος'.

127 Cf. LfgrE 1979, col. 188–191.

128 Il. 15.191: Ἀΐδης δ' ἔλαχε ζόφον ἠερόεντα.

129 See Pl. *Grg.* 493b, *Phd.* 81c, and *Cra.* 403a, with Enache's aptly titled 2008 paper 'Der unsichtbare Totengott'.

130 Heraclit. *All.* 24.6, p. 30 Bouffartigue: Ζῆνα μὲν εἶπε τὸν αἰθέρα, γῆν δὲ τὴν Ἥραν, Ἀιδωνέα δὲ τὸν ἀέρα, τὸ δὲ δακρύοις τεγγόμενον κρούνωμα βρότειον τὸ ὕδωρ, Athenag. *Legatio* 22.1, p. 68,6–8 Marcovich: εἰ τοίνυν Ζεὺς μὲν τὸ πῦρ, Ἥρα δὲ ἡ γῆ, καὶ ὁ ἀὴρ Ἀϊδωνεύς, καὶ τὸ ὕδωρ Νῆστις, στοιχεῖα δὲ ταῦτα (τὸ πῦρ, ἡ γῆ, τὸ ὕδωρ ὁ ἀήρ), οὐδεὶς αὐτῶν θεὸς ἔσται, οὔτε Ζεύς, οὔτε Ἥρα, οὔτε Ἀϊδωνεύς, D.L. 8.76, lines 283–4 Dorandi: Δία μὲν τὸ πῦρ λέγων, Ἥρην δὲ τὴν γῆν, Ἀιδωνέα δὲ τὸν ἀέρα, Νῆστιν δὲ τὸ ὕδωρ, Ach.Tat. *Isagoga* 3, 31.15–16 Maass: καὶ τὸ μὲν πῦρ Δία λέγει καὶ αἰθέρα, τὴν δὲ γῆν Ἥραν, τὸν δὲ ἀέρα Ἀιδωνέα, τὸ δὲ ὕδωρ Νῆστιν, and Ps.-Probus *in Verg. Buc.* 6.31; *Appendix Serviana* 333–334 Hagen: [...] *ut accipiamus* Zeὺς ἀργής *ignem, qui sit* ζέων *et candens, quod ignis est proprium,* [...] Ἥρη *autem* φερέσβιος *terram tradit, quae victum firmet, de qua Homerus* ζείδωρος ἄρουρα. [...] Ἠδ' Ἀϊδωνεύς: *Ditem quidem patrem glossa significat, sed accipere debemus aera* [...] Νῆστις *aquam significat, quae scilicet sincero habitu cuncta confirmet.*

140   PRIMAVESI

divine names,[131] whereas the Greek tradition of Ps.-Plutarch (the mediaeval Greek mss. and Eusebius), while agreeing with 'Zeus = Fire' and 'Nēstis = Water', offers the alternative equations 'Hera = Air' and 'Aïdoneus = Earth',[132] but further evidence for these is virtually non-existent.[133] Diels assumed that in this case only Ps.-Plutarch goes back to 'Aëtius', whereas Stobaeus would be depending on another source here.[134] It is true that Stobaeus has *displaced* the paragraph on Empedocles' divine names[135] and attached it to the beginning of an Empedoclean paragraph taken from another source (*De Homero*),[136] and that he has appended a further clause from *De Homero* to his explanation of 'Aïdoneus'.[137] But in spite of these typically Stobaean modifications,[138] he *shares* with the Greek tradition of Ps.-Plutarch's *Placita* the two highly idiosyncratic formulae for fire and water: both authors assign the name of Zeus to 'the boiling and the ether' (τὴν ζέσιν καὶ τὸν αἰθέρα) and the name of Nēstis to 'the semen and the water' (τὸ σπέρμα καὶ τὸ ὕδωρ), whereas these formulae are not attested in any relevant source other than Stobaeus and Ps. Plutarch's

---

131   Stob. 1.10.11[b], I 121.16–20 Wachsmuth: Δία μὲν λέγει τὴν ζέσιν καὶ τὸν αἰθέρα, Ἥραν δὲ φερέσβιον τὴν γῆν, ἀέρα δὲ τὸν Ἀιδωνέα, (ἐπειδὴ φῶς οἰκεῖον οὐκ ἔχει ἀλλ' ὑπὸ ἡλίου καὶ σελήνης καὶ ἄστρων καταλάμπεται). Νῆστιν δὲ καὶ κρούνωμα βρότειον τὸ σπέρμα καὶ τὸ ὕδωρ.

132   Ps.-Plu. *Plac.* 1.3, 878 A, p. 59.4–6 Mau 1971: Δία μὲν γὰρ λέγει τὴν ζέσιν καὶ τὸν αἰθέρα, Ἥρην τε φερέσβιον τὸν ἀέρα, τὴν δὲ γῆν τὸν Ἀιδωνέα. Νῆστιν δὲ καὶ κρούνωμα βρότειον οἰονεὶ τὸ σπέρμα καὶ τὸ ὕδωρ and Eus. *PE* xiv.6, II.296.7–10 Mras: Δία μὲν γὰρ λέγει τὴν ζέσιν καὶ τὸν αἰθέρα, Ἥρην τε φερέσβιον τὸν ἀέρα, τὴν γῆν τὸν Ἀιδωνέα. Νῆστιν δὲ καὶ κρούνωμα βρότειον οἰονεὶ τὸ σπέρμα καὶ τὸ ὕδωρ.

133   Cf., however, the section on the so-called scientific hymns in Men.Rh. 337.1–4 Spengel; here quoted after Russell and Wilson 1981, 12 + 14: εἰσὶ δὲ (scil. οἱ φυσικοὶ ὕμνοι) τοιοῦτοι, ὅταν Ἀπόλλωνος ὕμνον λέγοντες ἥλιον αὐτὸν εἶναι φάσκωμεν, καὶ περὶ τοῦ ἡλίου τῆς φύσεως διαλεγώμεθα, καὶ περὶ Ἥρας ὅτι ἀήρ, καὶ Ζεὺς τὸ θερμόν. But this isolated counterexample does certainly not justify the claim that 'the opinion that Empedocles identified Hera with ἀήρ (rather than with earth) and Zeus with fire, whether true or not, was very generally held in antiquity' (Russell and Wilson 1981, 236 *ad loc.*).

134   Diels 1879, 88–90 and 286–7.

135   If Stobaeus had kept the original Aëtian arrangement as preserved in an abridged form by Ps.-Plutarch he would have placed the quotation of Emp. fr. 49b MP (B 6 DK) and its interpretation in 1.10.16[a] between Ecphantus and Plato, i.e., immediately after 1.127.18 Wachsmuth. In fact, he has inserted the interpretation in an expanded form much earlier, immediately after 1.10.11[a]; 1.121.16 W.

136   Ps.-Plu. *Vit.Hom.* ch. 99–100, Kindstrand 1990, 47–8.

137   Ps.-Plu. *Vit.Hom.* ch. 97 *sub fin.*; Kindstrand 1990, 47.1017–8: ἐπειδὴ φῶς οἰκεῖον οὐκ ἔχει ἀλλ' ὑπὸ ἡλίου καὶ σελήνης καὶ τῶν ἄλλων ἄστρων καταλάμπεται.

138   See Mansfeld and Runia 1997, 218–231 on the two techniques, *connecting up* and *coalescing*, that are used by Stobaeus 'to combine material from different chapters of Aëtius' (p. 218) and to 'interpose other doxographic material' (p. 225).

Placita,[139] i.e. they are specifically Aëtian. This fact, which seems to have been overlooked in previous treatments of the matter, proves that the explanation of the divine names in Stobaeus goes back to the same source as the one in Ps.-Plutarch, i.e. from 'Aëtius', notwithstanding Stobaeus' modifications.[140] Furthermore, thanks to the first edition of Qusṭā ibn Lūqā's *Arabic translation* of Ps.-Plutarch's *Placita* (1980)[141] we know that the Arabic Ps.-Plutarch shares with Stobaeus the equation of Hera with Earth and of Aïdoneus with Air. Now, the Arabic translation of Ps.-Plutarch's *Placita* is the only source to offer the correct reading of Ps.-Plutarch in some passages,[142] so its authority matches that of the Greek transmission of Ps.-Plutarch. Therefore, the agreement of the Arabic Ps.-Plutarch and Stobaeus in our passage proves that Stobaeus has faithfully *preserved* the Aëtian equations:[143] These equations were also in the original text of Ps.-Plutarch as correctly rendered by the Arabic translation, and it is the Greek transmission of Ps.-Plutarch that has gone astray.[144]

---

139 Apart from our Aëtian passage in Ps.-Plutarch and Stobaeus, the expression τὸ σπέρμα καὶ τὸ ὕδωρ occurs only in Ammon. *in Int.* 36,19 Busse, and the expression τὴν ζέσιν καὶ τὸν αἰθέρα occurs nowhere else at all.

140 All in all, Stob. 1.10.11ᵇ (1 121.16–122.10 Wachsmuth) contains the following: a) the authentic Aëtian explanation of the name 'Zeus', and explanations of 'Hera' and 'Aïdoneus'; b) insertion of a phrase from Ps.-Plu. *Vit.Hom.* ch. 97 *sub fin.*, c) the authentic Aëtian explanation of the name 'Nēstis'; d) Ps.-Plu. *Vit.Hom.* ch. 99–100. The synopsis in Diels 1879, 88–89 remains useful even though his conclusions are outdated.

141 Daiber 1980. This indispensable edition, a masterpiece of Graeco-Arabic scholarship, features three marginal, but potentially misleading infelicities, as Mansfeld and Runia 1997, 154 and 160–1 have pointed out: (i) Daiber's book-title is 'Aetius Arabus' whereas what Daiber has in fact edited is a 'Ps.-Plutarchus Arabus'. (ii) The subtitle is 'Die Vorsokratiker in arabischer Überlieferung', whereas what the book in fact offers is 'Die Vorsokratiker *und Nachsokratiker* in arabischer Überlieferung'. (iii) The stemma on p. 325 presents Stob. as a direct descendant of Ps.-Plu. *Plac.* (= β) and the Arabic translation as a direct descendant of Aëtius (= α), whereas in fact the Arabic translation is a direct descendant of Ps.-Plu. *Plac.* (= β) and Stob. a direct descendant of Aëtius (= α). See the stemma offered by Mansfeld and Runia 1997, 328.

142 For examples see Mansfeld and Runia 1997, 158–161.

143 See Daiber 1980, 104–105 (Arabic text/German translation) and 341–342 (app. crit. and commentary). Kingsley 1994, 246 with n. 46 was bound to miss the stemmatic impact of that piece of evidence altogether, since he believed that 'the Arabic version of Aëtius has followed Stobaeus in this particular section—not pseudo-Plutarch'. On the contrary: It is precisely the fact that Qusṭā is here, as always, translating Ps.-Plutarch—a fact put beyond doubt here by the conjunctive error Ζεὺς αἰθὴρ instead of Stobaeus' correct Ζεὺς ἀργής, as Mansfeld 1995, 110 (= 334) pointed out—that makes the agreement between Qusṭā and Stobaeus so important since it clears the way for a reconstruction of the present passage in Aëtius.

144 We have briefly summarized the result of the preceding argument in tabular form in Emp. fr. 49c MP, where the left hand column contains the Aëtian interpretation preserved by

We conclude that the term *rhizomata* refers to the four elements with regard to their powerful presence *in our world of coming-to-be and passing-away*: Zeus who throws lightning bolts at the earth, Hera who ensures our survival by offering crops, Aïdoneus/Hades into whose foggy realm[145] we will disappear after our death, and his consort, Nēstis/Persephone, who feeds our tears when we mourn our kin—and therefore fast (*Nēstis* 'the fasting one').[146]

Accordingly, we should try to make sense of the term *rhizōmata* itself in a way that accounts for the presence of these elements in our world—especially since the *rhizōmata* are explicitly related, through the possessive genitive 'of all things' (πάντων), to all the transient compounds made from them. In order to do so, we must take into account that according to Empedocles the elements are present in our world at *two* levels. On one hand, they form divine homogeneous masses: the sun, the atmosphere, the sea, the earth. On the other hand, considerable portions of the four elements have been and are being absorbed by Love into organic compounds.[147] The *interaction* between the two levels follows the principle of 'like to like', for it is assumed that each of those large elemental masses is in sympathy and contact with all its cognate particles that are bound in organic compounds:[148]

> For all of these: sun and earth and sky and sea, are in alliance with those parts of themselves that have been struck off and have grown in mortal beings.

Stob. and by the Arabic version of ps.-Plu. *Plac.* (*Zeus = Fire; Hera = Earth; Aïdoneus = Air; Nestis = Water*), whereas the right hand column contains the heterodox interpretation reported by the extant Greek mss. of Ps.-Plu. *Plac.* and by Eus. (*Zeus = Fire; Hera = Air; Aïdoneus = Earth; Nestis = Water*).

145 Cf. Il.15.191: Ἀΐδης δ' ἔλαχε ζόφον ἠερόεντα, already quoted above n.128.

146 Heyne 1776 p. IX (note): 'Als Proserpina benetzt sie das Auge der Sterblichen (den sterblichen Quell, versteht sich, der Thränen,) mit Thränen; indem sie auf die Menschen das harte Schicksal des Todes eindringen läßt'.

147 In this context, it is interesting to notice that the elements count as *daimones*, i.e., as Gods of diminished status, when portions of them are being drawn into compounds under rising Love; see Emp. fr. 155 MP (B 59 DK): αὐτὰρ ἐπεί (φησί) κατὰ μεῖζον ἐμίσγετο δαίμονι δαίμων, (ὅτε τοῦ Νείχους ἐπεκράτει λοιπὸν ἡ Φιλότης), / ταῦτά τε συμπίπτεσχον, ὅπηι συνέχυρσεν ἔκαστα, / ἄλλα τε πρὸς τοῖς πολλὰ διηνεχῆ ἐξεγένοντο.

148 Emp. fr. 58 MP (B 22 DK), lines 1–3: ἄρθμια μὲν γὰρ ταῦτα ἑαυτῶν πάντα μέρεσσιν, / ἠλέκτωρ τε χθών τε καὶ οὐρανὸς ἠδὲ θάλασσα, / ὅσσα φιν ἐν θνητοῖσιν ἀποπλαγχθέντα πέφυκεν.

PYTHAGOREAN RATIOS IN EMPEDOCLES' PHYSICS

In a similar vein, the human teacher warns his pupil Pausanias that the elemental parts which have been functioning as bearers of his thought so far will leave him as soon as he lets himself be distracted. In this case, each of them will rush off in order to join its own elemental mass:[149]

> But if your own appetite should turn to different things, such as the innumerable vulgar distractions that offer themselves to men and dull their minds, those (elemental thoughts) will leave you straightaway in the course of time, yearning to reach their own cognate race.

The two quotations show that in our world each of the four elements has taken the form of a *network* which links the respective elemental mass with all its cognate particles in exile.[150] On the other hand, the noun *rhizōma* ('root-system') is perfectly suited to designate such a network. We conclude that *rhizōmata* is *not* just an equivalent of *rhizai*, and that we must free ourselves from the widespread undertranslation of *rhizōmata* as 'roots'. In particular, the term *rhizōmata* does *not* designate the elements *qua* 'roots', i.e., starting points, of the cosmic cycle; in other words: the term does not characterize the four elements during the state of total separation when they have formed four concentric, chemically pure spheres. Rather, the technical meaning of *rhizōma* in Empedocles is 'e l e m e n t a l n e t w o r k'. By forming four elemental networks, the divine elements maintain their individual unity, albeit in a diminished form, during the transitional phases of the cosmic cycle, i.e. the transitions from radical fourfold separation to complete unity and from complete unity to radical fourfold separation. The fragment in question should be translated as follows:[151]

> Hear first of all the four e l e m e n t a l n e t w o r k s of everything: Gleaming Zeus, life-bringing Hera, and Aïdoneus, and Nēstis, who moistens with tears the human spring.

---

149 Emp. fr. 125 MP (B 110 DK), lines 6–9: εἰ δὲ σύ γ' ἀλλοίων ἐπορέξεαι, οἷα κατ' ἄνδρας / μυρία δειλὰ πέλονται ἅ τ' ἀμβλύνουσι μερίμνας, / ἦ σ' ἄφαρ ἐκλείψουσι, περιπλομένοιο χρόνοιο / σφῶν αὐτῶν ποθέοντα φίλην ἐπὶ γένναν ἱκέσθαι.

150 Cf. the definition of 'network' offered by the *Cambridge International Dictionary of English* (1995), page 950: 'a large system consisting of many similar parts that are connected together to allow movement or communication between or along the parts or between the parts and a control centre'.

151 Emp. fr. 49b MP (B 6 DK).

144 PRIMAVESI

2.2.2 *Pēgē* = 'stream of life'

Pēgē, the second of the two Empedoclean terms employed in the Pythagorean *Oath*, occurs in a fragment from Empedocles' 'On Nature', the first eight lines of which are devoted to a simile: Painters, though using a limited number of colours, are nevertheless able to paint, on votive panels (*anathēmata*), a huge variety of beings: plants, men and women, animals, and Gods:[152]

> *As when painters embellish votive panels, two men being quite competent in art thanks to their skill, who, having grasped pigments of many colours in their hands, and having fitted them—more of some and less of others— in close combination, produce, out of these, shapes resembling all things, creating trees, men and women, wild beasts, birds, water-dwelling fish, and long-lived gods, too, highest in honour ...*

From this simile, the teacher concludes in the following two lines of the same fragment that Pausanias must not let himself be deceived into thinking that the *pēgē* of living beings comes *from elsewhere* ('*állothen*'):[153]

> οὕτω μή σ' ἀπάτη φρένα καινύτω ἄλλοθεν εἶναι
> θνητῶν, ὅσσα γε δῆλα γεγάκασιν ἄσπετα, πηγήν.

> *So do you not let prevail in your mind the error that the* pēgē *of all mortal beings that have appeared in countless numbers, comes from elsewhere!*

What does *pēgē* mean in this passage? The word has always been translated as 'source' here, and at first sight this seems reasonable enough since 'source' is indeed the normal meaning of *pēgē* in the singular. It is true that in early epic poetry, where only the plural *pēgai* is attested, *pēgai* can designate not just *a plurality of sources*[154] but also *the waters of a*

---

152 Emp. fr. 67b MP (B 23 DK), lines 1–8: ὡς δ' ὁπόταν γραφέης ἀναθήματα ποικίλλωσιν / ἀνέρες ἀμφὶ τέχνης ὑπὸ μήτιος εὖ δεδαῶτε, / οἵτ' ἐπεὶ οὖν μάρψωσι πολύχροα φάρμακα χερσίν, / ἁρμονίηι μείξαντε τὰ μὲν πλέω, ἄλλα δ' ἐλάσσω, / ἐκ τῶν εἴδεα πᾶσιν ἀλίγκια πορσύνουσι, / δένδρεά τε κτίζοντε καὶ ἀνέρας ἠδὲ γυναῖκας / θῆράς τ' οἰωνούς τε καὶ ὑδατοθρέμμονας ἰχθῦς / καί τε θεοὺς δολιχαίωνας τιμῆισι φερίστους.

153 Emp. fr. 67b MP (B 23 DK), lines 9–10.

154 LSJ 1996, Supp. s.v. πηγή II.1, quote two Homeric examples: Il. 21.311–2 (ἀλλ' ἐπάμυνε τάχιστα, καὶ ἐμπίμπληθι ῥέεθρα / ὕδατος ἐκ πηγέων, which is to say that the waters of the Simois come from *many springs* or *sources*) and Il. 22.147–8 (κρουνὼ δ' ἵκανον καλλιρρόω· ἔνθα τε πηγαί / δοιαὶ ἀναΐσσουσι Σκαμάνδρου δινήεντος, i.e., the Scamander is fed by *two springs* or *sources*).

PYTHAGOREAN RATIOS IN EMPEDOCLES' PHYSICS

river.[155] It is also true that the latter use of the plural remains common in 5th century and later poetry,[156] but of course, this fact in itself does not speak against translating the *singular* as 'source'. Yet in our passage, that received translation is unsatisfactory: if 'source' were correct, then the expression '*pēgē* of all mortal beings' (θνητῶν ... πηγή) could scarcely designate 'the source which *consists of* all mortal beings': what could such an all-embracing source still be a source of? Rather, the expression would have to designate 'the source *from which* all mortal beings come'.[157] But this option is not convincing either, for two reasons: (i) in the context of Empedocles' physical system, the starting points from which all mortal beings come are certainly the four elements. Why should one characterize these, in the singular, as *one single source*? (ii) If we admitted, just for argument's sake, that there *is* such a single four-element-source, then lines 9–10 of our fragment would insist that this four-element-source does *not come from elsewhere*. This would be unobjectionable as far as it goes; the point could be, for instance, that the four elements are true *first causes*, that there are no 'elements of the elements'. But this point could by no means be presented as a conclusion from the preceding simile, which illustrates the fact that combining a limited number of materials can yield a great variety of products, but it is certainly not concerned with the 'prehistory' of those materials. On the contrary, it is quite irrelevant for the point of the simile whether the pigments used by the two painters were themselves made out of other

---

155   See Hes. *Th.* 282–3: Ὠκεανοῦ παρὰ πηγὰς / γένθ', with the commentary by West 1966: 247 'πηγὰς: 'waters', the usual sense of πηγαί in the plural'. Oceanus, as an earth-encircling river, cannot have any springs, as Diggle 1970, 103 observed: 'The commentators' 'springs, sources of Ocean' do not exist'. Wilamowitz ²1895, 94 (commentary to E. *HF* 390) urged that πηγαί be translated as 'waters' also in Il. 23.148: 'Ψ 148 will der Phthiote Achilleus dem Spercheios opfern ἐς πηγάς, ὅτι τοι τέμενος βωμός τε θυήεις: natürlich in Phthia, am unteren laufe des flusses'. Richardson 1993, 185 (*ad loc.*) ventures to disagree: 'But the springs seem the most suitable place for an altar and precinct'.

156   The Hesiodic use of πηγαί Ὠκεανοῦ is adopted by Pi. fr. 39.2 Maehler (1989, 10): Ὠκεανοῦ παρὰ παγᾶν, E. *Phaëth.* TrGF 5.2, fr. 773.33 Kannicht (2004, 806): παγαῖς τ' ἐπ' Ὠκεανῶ, and Call. *Lav.Pall.* 10–11: παγαῖς ἔκλυσεν Ὠκεανῶ / ἱδρῶ καὶ ῥαθάμιγγας. For more ordinary rivers see A. *Pers.* 311 πηγαῖς τε Νείλου γειτονῶν Αἰγυπτίου, with Wilamowitz ²1895, 94: 'so bezeichnet Aisch. Pers. 311 ... die persische provinz Aegypten, nicht etwa die Nilquellen'; E. *HF* 390–2: Ἀναύρου παρὰ παγὰς / Κύκνον ξεινοδαΐκταν / τόξοις ὤλεσεν, with Wilamowitz ²1895, 94: 'πηγαί im plural bedeutet gewässer [...], nicht quelle. Kyknos wohnt an der küste'; E. *HF* 1295–7: φωνὴν γὰρ ἥσει χθὼν ἀπεννέπουσά με / μὴ θιγγάνειν γῆς καὶ θάλασσα μὴ περᾶν / πηγαί τε ποταμῶν, where Heracles is more likely to be prevented from crossing the *waters* of rivers than from crossing their *springs*: why should one be bothered to cross a *spring*?

157   In other words, the genitive θνητῶν would not indicate what the source consists of (*genetivus materiae*), but whom the source belongs to (*genetivus possessivus*).

146 PRIMAVESI

materials or whether they grew naturally or, for that matter, whether they have always been in existence.

Now if *pēgē* cannot be translated as 'source' in our passage after all, we should remind ourselves that in 5th century BC poets the singular *pēgē* was occasionally also used in the meaning 'stream, river'. This usage is attested not only in Aeschylus, but also in another fragment of Empedocles' 'On Nature'. As far as Aeschylus is concerned, Liddell/Scott/Jones[158] quote a passage from the *Persians* in which Queen Atossa reports to the chorus how she dipped her hands in a river before presenting a sacrifice, in order to become ritually pure again after a nightmare:[159]

> *I claim to have beheld these things at night. But when I had risen and dipped my hands in the clear-flowing river* (pēgē)*, then, with incense in my hand, I approached an altar ...*

With regard to the pace and syntactical structure of Atossa's narrative and to her eagerness to bring the sacrifice, it is rather implausible that she should have travelled, in the time *between* nightmare and sacrifice, to the *spring* of the river, up in the mountains, to touch the headwaters. Therefore, Liddell/Scott/Jones seem to be quite right in presupposing that Atossa purified herself from her nightmare by touching a *river* that was flowing by Susa, the residence of the Achaemenid kings.[160] This interpretation is confirmed by two close parallel passages from Greek drama: in Aristophanes' *Frogs* the

---

158 LSJ 1996 s.v. πηγή I. 1. *sub finem.*

159 A. *Pers.* 200–3: καὶ ταῦτα μὲν δὴ νυκτὸς εἰσιδεῖν λέγω. / ἐπεὶ δ᾽ ἀνέστην καὶ χεροῖν καλλιρ-ρόου / ἔψαυσα πηγῆς, ξὺν θυηπόλωι χερί / βωμὸν προσέστην ... On purification rituals after nightmares see Immisch 1897, 129: 'Die Träume verlangen entweder das ἡλίῳ λέγειν oder Lustration ... oder Opfer und Gebet', and Eitrem 1915, 96–97: 'Sowohl vom Schlafe und einem bösen ... oder bedeutsamen Traume ... wie von einem bösen Worte ... von einem unliebsamen ... Kusse (sc. reinigt man) sich durch Wasser'. On the purificatory use of water in general, see Rohde ²1898, II.405: 'Zur religiösen Reinigung ist *Wasser aus fliessen-den Quellen oder Flüssen* oder aus dem Meere erforderlich', and on washing one's hands before presenting a sacrifice see Eitrem 1915, 93: 'Besonders wird aber den Griechen und Römern immer und immer wieder eingeschärft, daß man »mit reinen *Händen*« opfere'.

160 One might think of the modern river Šahur, cf. Asheri et al. 2007, 487: 'The city (sc. of Susa) was situated on the site of the modern Šuš, on the river Šahur, a tributary of the Choaspes'. But for determining the river that Aeschylus meant, we must take into consideration that Hdt. 1.188.1 still names, in connection with Susa, only the famous Choaspes itself, which lies somewhat further west, and from which King Cyrus' drinking water was brought—even when he was on military expeditions.

PYTHAGOREAN RATIOS IN EMPEDOCLES' PHYSICS

purification from an unlucky dream is achieved through the water of a *river* (*ek potamōn*),[161] and in a papyrus fragment from an unknown tragedy purification from a nightmare is sought at the clear-flowing current of river Alpheius.[162]

Now this use of singular *pēgē* in the meaning '*stream, river*' was adopted in Empedocles' 'On Nature' as well, as is clear from the only other extant Empedoclean occurrence of *pēgē*:[163]

ἀλλὰ θεοὶ τῶν μὲν μανίην ἀποτρέψατε γλώσσης,
ἐκ δ' ὁσίων στομάτων καθαρὴν ὀχετεύσατε πηγήν.

But, Gods, turn aside from my tongue their madness and from my pious lips conduct the stream (pēgē) so that it stays pure!

In the second line, the mortal teacher asks the gods to perform an activity which he designates as *ocheteúein* (ὀχετεύειν), a verb that means '*conduct* water *by a conduit* or *canal*'.[164] In the present passage, the water to be conducted is designated as *pēgē* and it stands for the teacher's oral discourse. The *pēgē* in question *comes from* the teacher's pious lips, i.e. *from* the source, so that *pēgē* itself cannot be translated as 'source' in the strict sense of a starting point. And it would be equally implausible to translate *pēgē* as 'headwaters' here, since the divine guidance that the teacher asks for is certainly expected to benefit his discourse as a whole, not just, say, the proem. Whereas the teacher can take for granted the purity of the source, i.e., of his pious lips, he asks the gods to conduct the *whole stream* of his discourse in a way which ensures that its initial purity is maintained throughout. It should be obvious that *pēgē* is to be translated as 'stream' here, not as 'source': on the latter translation, the teacher's prayer would lose much of its force.

---

161 Ar. *Ra.* 1338–40: ἀλλά μοι, ἀμφίπολοι, λύχνον ἅψατε / κάλπισί τ' ἐκ ποταμῶν δρόσον ἄρατε, / θέρμετε δ' ὕδωρ, / ὡς ἂν θεῖον ὄνειρον ἀποκλύσω.

162 TrGF 2 (Adespota) F 626 d lines 37–39 Kannicht and Snell (1980, 183): φόβος τις αὐτὴν δεῖμά τ' ἔννυχον πλανᾶι / [... ... .] ... εν τῶιδε κοινωνεῖ τάδε / [... ... ... καλ]λίρουν ἐπ' Ἀλφειοῦ πόρον. See further Groeneboom 1930, 114 (*ad* 201–204), who quotes, among other parallels, A.R. IV.662–4: Ἔνθα δὲ Κίρκην / εὖρον ἁλὸς νοτίδεσσι κάρη ἐπιφαιδρύνουσαν· / τοῖον γὰρ νυχίοισιν ὀνείρασιν ἐπτοίητο.

163 Emp. fr. 43 MP (B 3 DK), lines 1–2.

164 LSJ 1996 s.v. ὀχετεύω 1.

We conclude that *pēgē* means 'stream' not only in Aeschylus' *Persians* but also in Empedocles fr. 43 MP (B 3 DK). It follows that we are free to translate *pēgē* as 'stream' in Empedocles fr. 67b MP (B 23 DK) as well:[165]

> *So do you not let prevail in your mind the error that the stream* (pēgē) *of all mortal beings that have appeared in countless numbers, comes from elsewhere!*

The great advantage of this translation is that it provides the obvious solution to the problem discussed earlier in the present section: the meaning of the two lines just quoted is that Empedocles' 'stream of live' originates from nowhere else than from the four elemental masses.

2.3 *Making Sense of the Pythagorean* Oath

2.3.1   The Cosmic Cycle and the *Tetraktys*

In the preceding section, we have established the original meaning of the two Empedoclean terms (*pēgē* and *rhizōmata*) employed in the Pythagorean *Oath*: in Empedocles, *pēgē* signifies the 'stream of living beings' or the 'stream of a philosophical discourse', and *rhizōmata* signifies the four 'elemental networks' that emerge during the transitional periods of the cosmic cycle. It remains to be seen whether the two Empedoclean terms have *kept* their Empedoclean meanings in the Pythagorean *Oath*. If so, the *Oath* will have to be translated as follows:

> οὐ μὰ τὸν ἁμετέρᾱι γενεᾶι παραδόντα τ ε τ ρ α κ τ ύ ν ,
> π ᾱ γ ὰ ν ἀενάου φύσεως ῥ ι ζ ώ μ α τ ' ἔχουσαν.

> *No, by him who handed over the* tetraktys *to our race, the* stream *of ever-flowing nature that governs the* elemental networks!

As soon as the *pāgā* (*pēgē*) mentioned here is translated—according to its specifically Empedoclean usage—as 'stream' (instead of 'source') and as soon as we realize that this 'stream of ever-flowing nature' is said here to *govern* Empedocles' elemental networks (*rhizomata*),[166]—the identification of the

---

165   Emp. fr. 67b MP (B 23 DK), lines 9–10. Empedocles uses a similar image when he describes the wonderful variety of different types of beings created through Love's unificatory work as *pouring forth* (fr. 69b MP [= DK 31 B 35], lines 16–7): τῶν δέ τε μισγομένων χεῖτ᾽ ἔθνεα μυρία θνητῶν, παντοίαις ἰδέηισιν ἀρηρότα, θαῦμα ἰδέσθαι.

166   For ἔχειν meaning 'to govern, to carry' see Arist. *Metaph.* Δ 23, 1023ᵃ8–11: Τὸ ἔχειν λέγεται πολλαχῶς, ἕνα μὲν (scil. τρόπον) τὸ ἄγειν κατὰ τὴν αὐτοῦ φύσιν ἢ κατὰ τὴν αὐτοῦ ὁρμήν, διὸ λέγεται πυρετός τε ἔχειν τὸν ἄνθρωπον καὶ οἱ τύραννοι τὰς πόλεις καὶ τὴν ἐσθῆτα οἱ ἀμπεχόμενοι.

PYTHAGOREAN RATIOS IN EMPEDOCLES' PHYSICS

pāgā with Empedocles' cosmic cycle seems to be rather obvious. This result, in turn, makes it possible to understand in what sense the formula 'stream of ever-flowing nature that holds the *rhizōmata*' can be used as an appositional characterization of the Pythagorean *tetraktys* in its original, mathematical sense. Empedocles' cosmic cycle, i.e., each of its revolutions, is a process evolving over time, and it seems to be subdivided into phases of fixed duration. The traditional evidence for ascribing such a cosmic *time-table* to Empedocles' poem 'On Nature' is the following:[167]

(i) The duration of the state of divine unity, i.e.the lifespan of the *Sphairos* which comes to an end when Strife's invasion begins, is explicitly said to be *fixed* by an oath:[168]

αὐτὰρ ἐπεὶ μέγα Νεῖκος ἐνὶμμελέεσσιν ἐθρέφθη
ἐς τιμάς τ' ἀνόρουσε τελειομένοιο χρόνοιο,
ὅς σφιν ἀμοιβαῖος πλατέος παρ' ἐλήλαται ὅρκου ...

But when Strife had grown in his limbs, and rushed upon his honours, as the time was coming to an end, the time to be given in exchange that was delineated by them in a broad oath ...

(ii) Aristotle notes that Love's expansion and Strife's invasion take 'equal times'.[169] Although Aristotle does not specify the evidence for this observation, the fixed lifespan of the *Sphairos* strongly suggests that the durations of Love's expansion and Strife's invasion, too, were not only equal, but fixed.

---

167 O'Brien 1969, 85–92 tried to elicit the duration of the cosmic cycle as described in 'On Nature' from the passage of the 'Purifications' according to which the guilty god's exile lasts 'thrice *myrioi* seasons' (Emp. fr. 8b.5 MP = B 115.6 DK: τρίς μιν μυριὰς ὥρας ἀπὸ μακάρων ἀλάλησθαι). But whereas the mythical law disclosed in the first book of 'Purifications' mirrors, in an allegorical way, the general structure of the cosmic cycle as expounded in 'On Nature' (see Primavesi 2013, 717–9), it is quite unwarranted to transplant specific details from one context into the other. Furthermore, we have no means of telling whether, in the line just quoted, the adjective *myrioi* bears the meaning '*ten thousand*' (LSJ 1996 s.v. μύριος II) or its Homeric meaning '*numberless, countless, infinite*' (LSJ 1996 s.v. μύριος I). This ambiguity will not have come by accident: it seems that the myth of the 'Purifications' is meant both to allude to and to mask the esoteric cosmic time-table of 'On Nature' rather than to spell it out.

168 Emp. fr. 77 MP (B 30 DK).

169 Emp. fr. 93a MP (Arist. *Ph.* Θ 1, 252ᵃ31–32): τὸ δὲ καὶ δι' ἴσων χρόνων (scil. κρατεῖν καὶ κινεῖν ἐν μέρει τὴν φιλίαν καὶ τὸ νεῖκος) δεῖται λόγου τινός.

(iii) Aristotle's byzantine expositor George Pachymeres refers to a fixed number of 'time units' (*chronoi*) during which the production of the *Sphairos* by Love and of a cosmos by Strife takes place.[170]

Given that the appositive clause 'the stream of ever-flowing nature that governs the elemental networks' refers to a cosmic cycle regulated by a time-table, the elucidation of the *tetraktys* by means of that appositive clause begins to make sense: a time-table can, in principle, be structured by performing a mathematical *tetraktys*, i.e. by making use of the numerical ratios between four numbers.

Furthermore, the semantic choices that we have to make in interpreting the *Oath* seem to be *interdependent*. Taking *tetraktys* in its original, mathematical meaning ('operating with a set of four numbers' or the result of such operation) does not make sense unless we interpret the '*pāgā* that holds the *rhizomata*' according to its specifically Empedoclean meaning ('the cosmic cycle'), since on the unspecific meaning ('the source that holds the elements') the *pāgā* can not be introduced as an apposition to the mathematical *tetraktys* in any meaningful way. And vice versa: taking the '*pāgā* that holds the *rhizomata*' in its specifically Empedoclean meaning ('the cosmic cycle') does not make sense unless we interpret the *tetraktys* according to its original, mathematical meaning ('operating with a set of four numbers' or the result of such an operation), since 'the cosmic cycle' can not be introduced as an apposition to *tetraktys* in its trivial later meaning ('a set of four items') in any meaningful way.

This interdependence is quite remarkable. We may perhaps grant the theoretical possibility that the author of the *Oath* just combined the later meaning of *tetraktys* ('a set of four items') with an unspecific reading of 'the *pāgā* of ever-flowing nature that holds the *rhizomata*' ('the source that holds the elements').[171] But why on earth should a combination thus produced suit the original meaning of the Pythagorean *tetraktys* ('operating with a set of four numbers') and the specifically Empedoclean meaning of 'the *pāgā* of ever-flowing nature that governs the *rhizomata*' ('the cosmic cycle') even better? We conclude that in the *Oath* the mathematical *tetraktys* is, rightly or wrongly, described as structuring the time-table of Empedocles' cosmic cycle.

---

170   Emp. fr. 91b MP (Georgios Pachymeres *in Phys.*, Cod. Laur. 87.5, fol. 6ᵛ): ὁ δ' Ἐμπεδοκλῆς (scil. ἔλεγε) κατὰ περίοδον χρόνων τοσῶνδέ ποτε μὲν τὸν Σφαῖρον ἐκ τῆς φιλίας γίνεσθαι, ποτὲ δὲ κόσμον ἐκ τοῦ νείκους.

171   It would be slightly odd, however, to equate a *set* of four items with a *source* holding these items.

PYTHAGOREAN RATIOS IN EMPEDOCLES' PHYSICS

2.3.2 The *Oath* as a Pseudo-Pythagorean Text

On our reading, the *Oath* ascribes to Pythagoras/Apollo the theory of an *Empedoclean cosmic cycle structured by the mathematical tetraktys*, so that, in fact, the *Oath* intertwines *two* claims:

(i) The time-table of Empedocles' cosmic cycle is structured in accordance with the numerical ratios of the mathematical *tetraktys* (e.g., 1 : 2 : 3 : 4).

(ii) Not only the mathematical *tetraktys* but also its cosmological application, *i.e.*, the supposedly Empedoclean theory of the cosmic cycle, are the gift of Pythagoras to the human race.

The historical truth of claim (ii) can be safely ruled out: today, no historian of Greek philosophy would consider the possibility that Empedocles owes his post-Parmenidean natural philosophy to Pythagoras. Claim (i), by contrast, deserves serious consideration.

Unlike claim (ii), which is about authorship and provenance, claim (i) is a claim about *contents* which could be easily checked by readers who had access to Empedocles 'On Nature', which was accessible at least until the 6th century AD, as the many quotations in Simplicius clearly show.[172] So it was easy to check whether the time-table of Empedocles' cosmic cycle is in fact structured in accordance with the numerical ratios of the *tetraktys* or not. We may add that claim (i) has also inspired the biographical tradition, already mentioned, according to which Empedocles was taught by 'Telauges', a (fictitious) son of Pythagoras.[173] The late-antique handbook of the lives and works of pagan Greek authors,[174] which forms the basis of the Byzantine *Suda*, ascribes a monograph in four books on the *tetraktys* to 'Telauges',[175] thereby suggesting that Empedocles owes the knowledge of the *tetraktys* which he betrays in his work directly to a member of Pythagoras' family.

The *Oath* has been identified as 'a typical specimen of pseudo-Pythagorica' of the Hellenistic period.[176] The purpose of these writings consists in

---

172 See above sections 1.3.1 and 1.3.5.

173 According to Hippobotus fr. 14 Gigante 1983, 186 (= D.L. 8.43, lines 484–9 Dorandi) the (spurious) hexameter DK 31 B 155 in which 'Empedocles' addresses 'Telauges' as the son of Pythagoras and Theano is meant to suggest that 'Telauges' was the *teacher* of Empedocles.

174 Hsch.Mil. (6th century AD), Ὀνοματολόγος ἢ Πίναξ τῶν ἐν παιδείᾳ ὀνομαστῶν.

175 Suda τ 481; IV 538.23–5 Adler = TELAUGES *De Tetract.*; Thesleff 1965, 189.10–1: Τηλαύγης Σάμιος, Πυθαγόρου τοῦ πάνυ υἱὸς καὶ μαθητής, φιλόσοφος, διδάσκαλος Ἐμπεδοκλέους. ἔγραψε περὶ τῆς τετρακτύος βιβλία δ' ('Telauges of Samos, son and student of the great Pythagoras, philosopher, teacher of Empedocles. He wrote a work *On the tetraktys* in four books').

176 Zhmud 2012, 302.

emphasizing the importance of Pythagoreanism for Greek philosophy as a whole by producing evidence for the claim that some of the most famous philosophical works of the Classical period were in fact plagiarizing the supposedly corresponding works and doctrines of early Pythagoreans.[177] In order to create that impression, Doric versions of Plato's *Timaeus*, Aristotle's *Categories*, and the Peripatetic doctrine of the eternity of the universe were produced in the Hellenistic period and then ascribed to early Pythagoreans (real or fictional), like 'Timaeus of Locri',[178] 'Archytas of Tarentum',[179] or 'Ocellus Lucanus'.[180] In order to fulfil their function, however, these Pseudo-Pythagorean writings had to employ a specific mixture of truth and falsehood. The fake dialect and the fake ascription had to be combined with more or less recognizable doctrines of philosophers of the classical period: the doctrine could be adapted, the style of argument could be simplified, objections raised against the original version could be taken into account, but the doctrine in question had to remain identifiable as such lest the evidence for plagiarism and for the decisive Pythagorean influence on later thought be undermined.

In the case of the *Oath*, the fake elements are, as usual, the Doric dialect and the claim that a member of the Pythagorean school (in this case, Pythagoras himself) is the true author. On the other hand, the doctrine *for which* Pythagoras' authorship is maintained by claim (ii) is the Empedoclean theory of the cosmic cycle—in so far as this theory is, according to claim (i), a cosmological application of the mathematical *tetraktys*. Now if claim (i) were unfounded, i.e., if the time-table of Empedocles' cosmic cycle were *not* structured by the numerical ratios of the mathematical *tetraktys*, then the object for which Pythagorean authorship is claimed in (ii), i.e., the cosmological application of the *tetraktys*, would be non-existent. Considered against the background of other Pseudo-Pythagorean texts, this scenario seems very implausible indeed: the noble cause of Pythagoreanism would have been ill-served by claiming Pythagorean authorship for clearly non-existent theories.

---

177 On the Hellenistic Pseudo-Pythagorica in general, see now Centrone 2014. Among earlier contributions, the paper by Burkert 1961, the introduction by Thesleff 1961 (with the review by Burkert 1962), and the collection of texts in Thesleff 1965 (with the review by Burkert 1967) remain fundamental. For 'Timaeus of Locri', 'Ps.-Archytas', and 'Ocellus Lucanus' however, one should consult the critical editions mentioned in the following notes.

178 A critical edition and a German translation of Ti.Locr. was provided by Walter Marg (1972); a commentary by Matthias Baltes (1972).

179 A critical edition of Ps.-Archyt., with translation and commentary, was provided by Thomas Alexander Szlezák 1972.

180 A critical edition of Ocell., with commentary, was provided by Richard Harder (1926).

PYTHAGOREAN RATIOS IN EMPEDOCLES' PHYSICS

2.4 Conclusion

We are now in the position to state our working hypothesis more precisely: to make sense both of Simplicius' claim about Empedocles' Pythagoreanism and of the Pythagorean *Oath*, we surmise that the time-table of Empedocles' cosmic cycle is indeed structured in accordance with the numerical ratios of the Pythagorean *tetraktys* (e.g., 1 : 2 : 3 : 4). In order to test that hypothesis, we will do well to forget the *tetraktys* for a while and to analyse the structure of the cosmic cycle in purely qualitative terms first.

3 The Structure of Empedocles' Cosmic Cycle[181]

According to Empedocles, the world's course is determined by a regular alternation of a period of increasing Love which leads towards *complete mixture* of the four elements, and a period of increasing Strife which leads towards *complete separation* of the four elements.[182] Throughout the cycle, Love is consistently depicted as inside, whereas Strife is consistently depicted as outside. What changes in the relationship between Love and Strife is merely the way the cosmos, which is filled with the four elements and is more or less spherical in shape,[183] is *divided up* between the two agents. In the phase of increasing mixture, Love starts out from the centre and occupies a larger and larger portion of the cosmos in a process of centrifugal expansion, forcing Strife further and further toward the periphery.[184] Conversely, in the phase of increasing separation Strife starts out from the periphery and in a process of centripetal invasion penetrates further and further into the cosmos from all sides, compressing Love back into the centre. Each process—increasing

---

181 The basic insights on the structure of Empedocles' cosmic cycle are due to Panzerbieter 1844, Dümmler 1889, Bignone 1916, and O'Brien 1969. See further Primavesi 2013, 694–704 and 707–713.

182 Emp. fr. 66b MP, lines 232–3: διπλ' ἐρέω· τοτὲ μὲν γὰρ ἓν ηὐξήθη μόνον εἶναι / ἐκ πλεόνων, τοτὲ δ' αὖ διέφυ πλέον' ἐξ ἑνὸς εἶναι.

183 Emp. fr. 127 MP (A 50 DK = Aëtius II.31): Ἐμπεδοκλῆς τοῦ ὕψους τοῦ ἀπὸ τῆς γῆς εἰς τὸν οὐρανόν, ἥτις ἐστὶν ἀφ' ἡμῶν ἀνάτασις, πλείονα εἶναι τὴν κατὰ τὸ πλάτος διάστασιν. κατὰ τοῦτο τοῦ οὐρανοῦ μᾶλλον ἀναπεπταμένου διὰ τὸ ᾠῷ παραπλησίως τὸν κόσμον κεῖσθαι.

184 Emp. fr. 69b MP (B 35 DK), lines 7–17: τῶν δέ τε μισγομένων χεῖτ' ἔθνεα μυρία θνητῶν· / πολλὰ δ' ἄμειχθ' ἕστηκε κεραιομένοισιν ἐναλλάξ, / ὅσσ' ἔτι Νεῖκος ἔρυκε μετάρσιον· οὐ γὰρ ἀμεμφέως / τῶν πᾶν ἐξέστηκεν ἐπ' ἔσχατα τέρματα κύκλου, / ἀλλὰ τὰ μέν τ' ἐνέμιμνε μελέων τὰ δέ τ' ἐξεβεβήκει. / ὅσσον δ' αἰὲν ὑπεκπροθέοι, τόσον αἰὲν ἐπήιει / ἠπιόφρων Φιλότητος ἀμεμφέος ἄμβροτος ὁρμή· / αἶψα δὲ θνήτ' ἐφύοντο, τὰ πρὶν μάθον ἀθάνατ' εἶναι, / ζωρά τε τὰ πρὶν ἄκρητα διαλλάξαντα κελεύθους. / τῶν δέ τε μισγομένων χεῖτ' ἔθνεα μυρία θνητῶν, / παντοίαις ἰδέηισιν ἀρηρότα, θαῦμα ἰδέσθαι.

154

mixture and increasing separation—has a cosmic state of *divine* perfection as its goal. The process of mixture brought about by Love's expansion leads to a state of *cosmic rest* in which the four elements are completely mixed and combined into a spherical god, the *Sphairos*;[185] the latter is probably also referred to as Apollo.[186] Strife's centripetal invasion, by contrast, leads to a state in which the four elements have assembled themselves, by the inherent attraction of like to like, in four concentric masses that rotate around each other. At the centre, there is a sphere of earth, surrounded by the spherical shells of water, air, and fire. The moment in which Strife's centripetal invasion is accomplished is also the starting-point of Love's centrifugal expansion, so that the existence of the four pure masses falls in the first phase of increasing Love. Like the *Sphairos* (Apollo), these four perfect masses are regarded as fully divine, whereas in the remaining parts of the cycle their individual divinity is compromised and diminished. This holds for the two transitional phases during which they form elemental networks (*rhizomata*), i.e. the phase of increasing mixture and that of increasing separation. It is no accident that in these phases the elements are referred to merely as *daimones* (δαίμονες) rather than *theoi* (θεοί).[187]

3.1 Two Zoogonies

More specifically, the cosmic cycle is characterized by a 'twofold arising and a twofold passing away of mortal beings':[188] one arising-and-passing-away taking place during the universal process of fusion, while the other arising-and-passing-away accompanies the universal process of separation.[189] By 'mortal beings' (θνητά) Empedocles means only the short-lived heterogeneous combinations

---

185   See Emp. frs 72–76 MP.

186   Emp. fr. 192b MP (Ammon. *in Int.* p. 249.1–10 Busse 1897); the text of the embedded Empedoclean quotation (B 134 DK) is here corrected after Olymp. *in Grg.* 4.3, Cod. Marc. Gr. Z. 196 (= 743) *in margine*: διὰ ταῦτα δὲ καὶ ὁ Ἀκραγαντῖνος σοφὸς ἐπιρραπίσας τοὺς περὶ θεῶν ὡς ἀνθρωποειδῶν ὄντων παρὰ τοῖς ποιηταῖς λεγομένους μύθους, ἐπήγαγε—προηγουμένως μὲν περὶ Ἀπόλλωνος, περὶ οὗ ἦν αὐτῷ προσεχῶς ὁ λόγος, κατὰ δὲ τὸν αὐτὸν τρόπον καὶ περὶ τοῦ θείου παντὸς ἁπλῶς ἀποφαινόμενος—· οὔτε γὰρ ἀνδρομέη(ι) κεφαλῇ(ι) κατὰ γυῖα κέκασται, / οὐ χέρες, οὐ θοὰ γοῦν', οὐ μήδεα λαχνήεντα, / ἀλλὰ φρὴν ἱερὴ καὶ ἀθέσφατος ἔπλετο μοῦνον, / φροντίσι κόσμον ἅπαντα καταΐσσουσα θοῇσιν. On this passage, see further Primavesi 2006c.

187   Emp. fr. 155 MP (B 59 DK): αὐτὰρ ἐπεὶ (φησί) κατὰ μεῖζον ἐμίσγετο δαίμονι δαίμων, / ὅτε τοῦ Νείκους ἐπεκράτει λοιπὸν ἡ Φιλότης / ταυτά τε συμπίπτεσκον, ὅπηι συνέκυρσεν ἕκαστα, / ἄλλα τε πρὸς τοῖς πολλὰ διηνεκῆ ἐξεγένοντο.

188   Emp. fr. 66b MP, line 234: δοιὴ δὲ θνητῶν γένεσις, δοιὴ δ' ἀπόλειψις.

189   Emp. fr. 66b MP, lines 235–6: τὴν μὲν γὰρ πάντων ξύνοδος τίκτει τ' ὀλέκει τε, / ἡ δὲ πάλιν διαφυομένων θρεφθεῖσα διέπτη.

of elements, in explicit contrast to the *long-lived gods (theoi dolichaiōnes)* of his physics[190] as for instance the divine *Sphairos*. Thus Empedocles' allusion to the twofold arising and twofold passing away of mortal beings implies that a production and a dissolution of short-lived combinations take place in each of the two transitional phases of the cosmic cycle—not only during the transition from the four masses to the *Sphairos* (Love's centrifugal expansion) but also during the transition from the *Sphairos* to the four masses (Strife's centripetal invasion). On either side of the cycle, Love *produces* the combinations, and Strife *destroys* them: Empedocles' basic assumption is that Love forms particular combinations of the elements both in the phase of increasing fusion, as it gradually gains strength, as well as in that of increasing separation, as it weakens.

The two transitional phases of the cosmic cycle are subdivided into single stages, four of which, the *zoogonic* stages, are attested by ps.-Plutarch:[191]

Ἐμπεδοκλῆς (i) τὰς πρώτας γενέσεις τῶν ζῴων καὶ φυτῶν μηδαμῶς ὁλοκλήρους γενέσθαι, ἀσυμφυέσι δὲ τοῖς μορίοις διεζευγμένας, (ii) τὰς δὲ δευτέρας συμφυομένων τῶν μερῶν εἰδωλοφανεῖς, (iii) τὰς δὲ τρίτας τῶν ὁλοφυῶν, (iv) τὰς δὲ τετάρτας οὐκέτι ἐκ τῶν στοιχείων, οἷον ἐκ γῆς καὶ ὕδατος, ἀλλὰ δι' ἀλλήλων ἤδη, τοῖς μὲν πυκνωθείσης ⟨τῆς⟩ τροφῆς, τοῖς δὲ καὶ τῆς εὐμορφίας τῶν γυναικῶν ἐπερεθισμὸν τοῦ σπερματικοῦ κινήματος ἐμποιησάσης.

(iii) ὁλοφυῶν Karsten cl. fr. 164 MP (B 62 DK), line 4 (οὐλοφυεῖς) : ἀλληλοφυῶν mss.

Empedocles says (i) that the first generations of animals and plants were not at all born as complete entities, but were disconnected, with parts that had not grown together; (ii) the second generations, when the parts had grown together, had the appearance of phantasms; (iii) the third generations were those of the whole-natured beings; (iv) the fourth ones no longer came from homoeomerous materials like earth and water, but at this stage were produced by each other, because of the condensation of their food for some, and for others also because women's beauty caused an excitation of the spermatic movement.

---

190 Emp. fr. 66b MP, lines 272 and 320: καί τε θεοὶ δολιχαίωνες τιμῆισι φέριστοι.

191 Emp. fr. 151 MP (A 72 DK = Aëtius v.19.5a). The fact that the Aëtian lemma covers just the four *zoogonical* stages does not imply, of course, that there were no *non*-zoogonical stages in Empedocles' cosmic cycle, this fact is rather due to the question to which the respective chapter in Aëtius is devoted: Περὶ ζῴων γενέσεως, πῶς ἐγένοντο ζῷα καὶ εἰ φθαρτά.

As we will presently see, the first two zoogonic stages take place during Love's expansion, whereas the third and the fourth zoogonic stages occur during Strife's invasion.[192]

3.1.1 The Zoogony During Love's Expansion

In the first stage, isolated body parts arise and wander about unconnected: temples without a neck, arms without shoulders, eyes without brows.[193] In the second, Love's strength has increased to the point where it is capable of combining the individual limbs of the first stage to form more or less monstrous combinations,[194] the composition of which is dictated entirely by chance.[195] The *direction* indicated by the transition from the first to the second stage clearly shows that both stages fall in the phase of increasing mixture, i.e. of Love's expansion, that leads from the four separate masses to the *Sphairos*.

3.1.2 The Zoogony During Strife's Invasion

The third zoogonic stage takes place, or so we will argue in the present section, after the destruction of the *Sphairos*, in the first phase of Strife's invasion. Fire quickly rises up from the earth,[196] and deposits uniform, unarticulated, mute, ungendered living beings on the earth's surface.[197] This stage is followed by the fourth, which corresponds to our present situation: life now reproduces itself by passing through living beings of the same kind. Every living thing, or its seed,

---

192   Dümmler 1889, 216–247, Bignone 1916, 584, O'Brien 1969, 196–236, and Primavesi 2013, 711–713.

193   Emp. fr. 153b MP (B 57 DK): ἧι πολλαὶ μὲν κόρσαι ἀναύχενες ἐβλάστησαν, / γυμνοὶ δ᾽ ἐπλάζοντο βραχίονες εὔνιδες ὤμων, / ὄμματά τ᾽ οἶ᾽ ἐπλανᾶτο πενητεύοντα μετώπων. Fr. 154 MP (B 58 DK = Simp. *in Cael.* p. 587,18–19 + 24–26 Heiberg 1894): ἐν ταύτῃ οὖν τῇ καταστάσει ᾽μουνομελῆ᾽ ἔτι τὰ ᾽γυῖα᾽ ἀπὸ τῆς τοῦ Νείκους διακρίσεως ὄντα ᾽ἐπλανᾶτο᾽ τῆς πρὸς ἄλληλα μίξεως ἐφιέμενα ... ἐπὶ τῆς Φιλότητος οὖν ὁ Ἐμπεδοκλῆς ἐκεῖνα εἶπεν, οὐχ ὡς ἐπικρατούσης ἤδη τῆς Φιλότητος, ἀλλ᾽ ὡς μελλούσης ἐπικρατεῖν, ἔτι δὲ τὰ ἄμικτα καὶ μονόγυια δηλούσης.

194   Emp. fr. 156 MP (B 60 DK = Plu. *Adv. Col.* 1123B): εἰλίποδ᾽ ἀκριτόχειρα ...; fr. 157a MP (B 61 DK): πολλὰ μὲν ἀμφιπρόσωπα καὶ ἀμφίστερνα φύεσθαι, / βουγενῆ ἀνδρόπρωιρα· τὰ δ᾽ ἔμπαλιν ἐξανατέλλειν / ἀνδροφυῆ βούκρανα, μεμειγμένα, τῆι μὲν ἀπ᾽ ἀνδρῶν / τῆι δὲ γυναικοφυῆ σκιεροῖς ἠσκημένα γυίοις.

195   Emp. fr. 155 MP (B 59 DK): αὐτὰρ ἐπεὶ (φησί) κατὰ μεῖζον ἐμίσγετο δαίμονι δαίμων, / ὅτε τοῦ Νείκους ἐπεκράτει λοιπὸν ἡ Φιλότης / ταῦτά τε συμπίπτεσκον, ὅπηι συνέκυρσεν ἕκαστα, / ἄλλα τε πρὸς τοῖς πολλὰ διηνεκῆ ἐξεγένοντο.

196   Emp. fr. 86 MP (B 51 DK): Ἐμπεδοκλῆς ᾽καρπαλίμως δ᾽ ἀνόπαιον᾽, ἐπὶ τοῦ πυρός.

197   Emp. fr. 164 MP (B 62 DK): νῦν δ᾽ ἄγ᾽, ὅπως ἀνδρῶν τε πολυκλαύτων τε γυναικῶν / ἐννυχίους ὅρπηκας ἀνήγαγε κρινόμενον πῦρ, / τῶνδε κλύ᾽· οὐ γὰρ μῦθος ἀπόσκοπος οὐδ᾽ ἀδαήμων. / οὐλοφυεῖς μὲν πρῶτα τύποι χθονὸς ἐξανέτελλον, / ἀμφοτέρων ὕδατός τε καὶ εἴδεος αἶσαν ἔχοντες· / τοὺς μὲν πῦρ ἀνέπεμπε θέλον πρὸς ὁμοῖον ἱκέσθαι, / οὔτε τί πω μελέων ἐρατὸν δέμας ἐμφαίνοντας / οὔτ᾽ ἐνοπὴν οἶόν τ᾽ ἐπιχώριον ἀνδράσι γυῖον.

PYTHAGOREAN RATIOS IN EMPEDOCLES' PHYSICS   157

comes from another individual of the same species: mammals bear young, birds lay eggs, trees produce fruit.[198] The most spectacular ruse by which Love tries to oppose the invasion of Strife is the *sexual reproduction* of ephemeral combinations, that is, mortal beings,[199] a process in which the offspring's genetic inheritance comes in equal parts from the father and the mother.[200]

It is again the *direction* indicated by the transition from one zoogonic stage to the other which will enable us to clarify the position of the third and the fourth stage within the cosmic cycle. By a lucky coincidence, a comprehensive description of the relevant transition was brought to light in the original wording by the Strasburg papyrus. We now know that the transition is triggered by Strife during the separation of the elements at the point when fire, in its ascent, reaches the periphery of the cosmos. At this moment, Strife demonstrates its increasing strength by violently splitting the uniform, unarticulated beings of the third stage into halves, male and female. So when the sun rises for the first time, the living beings, which have been mute up to this point, produce their first sound, the cry of pain with which they react to their division,[201] and from now on they carry within themselves the desire for sexual (re)union.[202] Thus the transition from the third to the fourth stage is brought about by splitting the whole-natured beings of the third stage into halves, and both stages are caused by a continuous *centrifugal* movement of fire. Both features, taken together, leave no doubt that the sequence of these two stages forms part of the

---

198   See Emp. fr. 167 MP (B 79 DK = Arist. *GA* A 23, 731ᵃ1–5): ἐν δὲ τοῖς φυτοῖς ... οὐ κεχώρισται τὸ θῆλυ τοῦ ἄρρενος, διὸ καὶ γεννᾷ αὐτὰ ἐξ αὑτῶν, καὶ προΐεται οὐ γονήν, ἀλλὰ κύημα τὰ καλούμενα σπέρματα. καὶ τοῦτο καλῶς λέγει Ἐμπεδοκλῆς ποιήσας· οὕτω δ᾽ ᾠοτοκεῖ μακρὰ δένδρεα πρῶτον ἐλαίης.

199   Emp. fr. 66b MP, lines 253–255: ἥτις καὶ θνητοῖσι νομίζεται ἔμφυτος ἄρθροις, / τῇ τε φίλα φρονέουσι καὶ ἄρθμια ἔργα τελοῦσι, / Γηθοσύνην καλέοντες ἐπώνυμον ἠδ᾽ Ἀφροδίτην, and *ibid.* lines 302–304: τοῦτο μὲν ἂν βροτέων μελέων ἀριδείκετον ὄγκον· / ἄλλοτε μὲν Φιλότητι συνερχόμεθ᾽ εἰς ἓν ἅπαντα / γυῖα τὰ σῶμα λέλογχε, βίου θηλοῦντος ἐν ἀκμῆι.

200   Emp. fr. 169 MP (B 63 DK =Arist. *GA* A 18, 722ᵇ8–13): διὸ καὶ Ἐμπεδοκλῆς ἔοικεν, εἴπερ οὕτω λεκτέον, μάλιστα λέγειν ὁμολογούμενα τούτῳ τῷ λόγῳ ... φησ3): διὸ καὶ Ἐμπεδοκλῆς ἔοικεν, εἴπερ οὕτω λεκτέον, μάλιστα λέγειν ὁμολογούμενα τούτῳ ἀλλὰ διέσπασται μελέων φύσις· ἡ μὲν ἐν ἀνδρός ... .

201   Emp. fr. 87 MP, lines 11–17: [... ὁππότ]ε δὴ συνετύγχανε φ[λογ]μὸς ἀτειρής / [θνητῶν ἡνεκέ]ως ἀνάγων π[ο]λυπήμ[ον]α κρᾶσιν, / [δὴ τότε πολλὰ ζώι]α φυτάλμια τεκνώθ[η]σαν / [οὐλομελῆ, τῶν ν]ῦν ἔτι λείψανα δέρκεται Ἠώς. / ὅππουτ[ε δ᾽ ἠλέκτωρ ἀρθ]εὶς τόπον ἐσχάτιο[ν β]ῆ / δὴ τό[θ᾽ ἕκαστα διετμήθη κλαγ]γῆι καὶ ἀὐτῆι / θεσπε[σίηι. The point of lines 15–17 was first perceived by Marwan Rashed. See further Emp. fr. 168 MP.

202   Emp. fr. 172 MP (B 64 DK = Plu. *Quaest. nat.* 917C): τὸ συντρέφεσθαι καὶ συναγελάζεσθαι τὰ θήλεα τοῖς ἄρρεσιν ἀνάμνησιν ποιεῖ τῶν ἀφροδισίων καὶ συνεκκαλεῖται τὴν ὄρεξιν, ὡς ἐπ᾽ ἀνθρώπων Ἐμπεδοκλῆς ἐποίησε· τῶι δ᾽ ἐπὶ καὶ πόθος εἶσι δι᾽ ὄψιος ἀμμιμνήισκων. Both the splitting in halves and its erotic consequences were famously employed by Pl. *Smp.* 190D–191A.

158 PRIMAVESI

process of increasing separation which leads from the *Sphairos* back to the four separate masses.

It seems clear by now that both the period of Love's expansion and the period of Strife's invasion include a zoogony and that both zoogonies consists of *two* zoogonic stages each. There is no need to resuscitate the suggestion, once made by Denis O'Brien, of postulating two further zoogonic stages in addition to the four attested ones.[203]

3.2 The Two Abiotic Stages After and Before the Turning Point

The combined evidence of the Strasburg papyrus and of the indirect tradition shows that both Love's expansion and Strife's invasion involve, in addition to their respective zoogonic stages as summarized by Aëtius, one *abiotic* stage each, during which Love is not yet, or no longer, capable of producing individual organic compounds. The two abiotic stages in question immediately follow and precede the turning point of the cosmic cycle, i.e. the transition from Strife's invasion to Love's expansion.

Strife's invasion comes to a natural end when Strife, closing in from all sides, has compressed Love into a single point, the 'centre of the whirlwind',[204] that is, the centre of the earth. At this moment, the complete separation of the four elements is achieved: thanks to the innate attraction of like to like, the elements have now formed four pure, concentric masses that rotate around each other at maximum speed.[205] At the same moment, Love's expansion begins.[206] We are explicitly told, however, that Love's expansion does *not immediately*

203　O'Brien 1969, 218–227.

204　Emp. fr. 66b MP, lines 288–289: [Ἀλλ' ὅτ]ε δὴ Νεῖκός [τ' ἀνυ]πέρβατα βέν[θε' ἵκηται] / δ[ίνη]ς, ἐν δὲ μέσ[ηι] Φ[ιλ]ότης στροφά[λιγγι γένηται,] …; Emp. fr. 69b MP (B 35 DK), lines 3–4: … ἐπεὶ Νεῖκος μὲν ἐνέρτατα βένθε' ἵκηται / δίνης, ἐν δὲ μέσηι Φιλότης στροφάλιγγι γένηται … .

205　Emp. fr. 88 MP (Plu. *De facie* 926D–927A = fr. 26a Bignone): ὥσθ' ὅρα καὶ σκόπει, δαιμόνιε, μὴ μεθιστὰς καὶ ἀπάγων ἕκαστον, ὅπου πέφυκεν εἶναι, διάλυσίν τινα κόσμου φιλοσοφῇς καὶ τὸ νεῖκος ἐπάγῃς τὸ Ἐμπεδοκλέους τοῖς πράγμασι, μᾶλλον δὲ τοὺς παλαιοὺς κινῇς Τιτᾶνας ἐπὶ τὴν φύσιν καὶ Γίγαντας καὶ τὴν μυθικὴν ἐκείνην καὶ φοβερὰν ἀκοσμίαν καὶ πλημμέλειαν ἐπιδεῖν ποθῇς, χωρὶς τὸ βαρὺ πᾶν καὶ χωρὶς … τὸ κοῦφον· ἔνθ' οὔτ' ἠελίοιο δεδίσκεται ἀγλαὸν εἶδος, / οὐδὲ μὲν οὐδ' αἴης λάσιον δέμας, οὐδὲ θάλασσα, ὥς φησιν Ἐμπεδοκλῆς, οὐ γῆ θερμότητος μετεῖχεν, οὐχ ὕδωρ πνεύματος, οὐκ ἄνω τι τῶν βαρέων, οὐ κάτω τι τῶν κούφων· ἀλλ' ἄκρατοι καὶ ἄστοργοι καὶ μονάδες αἱ τῶν ὅλων ἀρχαί, μὴ προσιέμεναι σύγκρισιν ἑτέρου πρὸς ἕτερον μηδὲ κοινωνίαν, ἀλλὰ φεύγουσαι καὶ ἀποστρεφόμεναι καὶ φερόμεναι φορὰς ἰδίας καὶ αὐθάδεις οὕτως εἶχον ὡς ἔχει πᾶν οὗ θεὸς ἄπεστι κατὰ Πλάτωνα (*Timaeus* 53B), τουτέστιν, ὡς ἔχει τὰ σώματα νοῦ καὶ ψυχῆς ἀπολιπούσης, ἄχρις οὗ τὸ ἱμερτὸν ἧκεν ἐπὶ τὴν φύσιν ἐκ προνοίας, Φιλότητος ἐγγενομένης καὶ Ἀφροδίτης καὶ Ἔρωτος, ὡς Ἐμπεδοκλῆς λέγει καὶ Παρμενίδης καὶ Ἡσίοδος … .

206　Emp. fr. 66b MP, line 290 and fr. 69b MP (B 35 DK), line 5: ἐν τῆι δὴ τάδε πάντα συνέρχεται ἓν μόνον εἶναι.

PYTHAGOREAN RATIOS IN EMPEDOCLES' PHYSICS

bring about new organic compounds of different elements: Love needs some time in order to make the elements willing to form compounds with each other,[207] for instance by gradually reducing the speed of their rotation and by assimilating them to each other.[208] But *when* Love has regained sufficient power, it forms the elements into organic compounds, which means, by Empedoclean standards, that they become mortal again, whereas before they *had learnt to be immortal* (ἀθάνατα).[209] This previous experience of 'learning to be immortal' cannot just have been based on the eternal existence of the elements as such, since *that* feature remains unaffected by the fact that the elements must now form living compounds again, so that there would be no contrast. Instead, the reference must be to the four divine pure masses which have come to be at the turning point of the cycle and which are 'immortal' in the sense of being free of mixture and dissolution. But even this qualified use of the term 'immortal' implies that the elements must have existed in the form of four pure masses at least for *some time*. If the total separation were 'not a condition that can endure', as O'Brien maintained,[210] it could scarcely count as a state of immortality, and a merely instantaneous freedom of mixture and dissolution is not a very meaningful concept, nor is it a state which the elements can have *learned* to be in. We conclude that the *first* stage of Love's expansion is the life-time of the four divine pure masses, and that these divine masses are, like the *Sphairos*, to be reckoned among the long-lived gods (*theoi dolichaiōnes*) of Empedoclean physics.[211]

A second abiotic stage will occur towards the end of Strife's invasion, immediately *before* the turning point of the cycle. This abiotic stage, previously known only from Plutarch's vivid description of the 'dissolution of the world-order' (*dialysis kosmou*),[212] has been illustrated by the Strasburg papyrus in a detailed way. At the end of the present fourth zoogonic stage all living beings still extant will be torn apiece by the agents of Strife (the *Harpies*); and their limbs will be subject to putrefaction (*sēpsis*).[213] The portions of elements set

---

207 Emp. fr. 69b MP (B 35 DK), line 6: οὐκ ἄφαρ, ἀλλὰ θελημὰ συνιστάμεν᾽ ἄλλοθεν ἄλλα.

208 Emp. fr. 58 MP (B 22 DK), lines 4–5: ὡς δ᾽ αὔτως ὅσα κρῆσιν ἐπαρκέα μᾶλλον ἔασιν, / ἀλλήλοις ἔστερκται ὁμοιωθέντ᾽ Ἀφροδίτηι.

209 Emp. fr. 69b MP (B 35 DK), lines 14–15: αἶψα δὲ θνήτ᾽ ἐφύοντο, τὰ πρὶν μάθον ἀθάνατ᾽ εἶναι, / ζωρά τε τὰ πρὶν ἄκρητα διαλλάξαντα κελεύθους.

210 O'Brien 1969, 78.

211 Emp. fr. 66b MP, lines 272 and 320: καί τε θεοὶ δολιχαίωνες τιμῆισι φέριστοι.

212 Emp. fr. 88 MP (Plu. *De facie* 926D–927A = fr. 26a Bignone), already quoted above n. 205.

213 Emp. fr. 87 MP, lines 1–3: [ἄν]διχ᾽ ἀπ᾽ ἀλλήλω[ν] πεσέ[ει]ν καὶ π[ότ]μον ἐπισπεῖν / [πό]λλ᾽ ἀεκαζομέν[ο]ισιν ἀ[να]γκα[ίης ὕ]πο λυγρῆς / [ση]πομένοις. Φιλίην δ᾽ ἐ[ρατ]ὴν [ἡμῖ]ν νυν ἔχουσιν / [Ἅρ]πυιαι θανάτοιο πάλοις [ἤδη παρέσ]ονται.

free by the *sēpsis* of the limbs will join their respective cosmic masses, while the speed at which these masses rotate around each other still increases until the end of Strife's invasion.[214] We conclude that the *third* and final stage of Strife's invasion is the *sēpsis* of the limbs and the movement of the remaining portions of single elements towards the completion of the four masses. This final stage of the cycle was probably characterized as the 'great whirlwind' (*Dīnos*).[215]

3.3   *Conclusion: The Seven Phases of the Cosmic Cycle*

All in all, then, the cosmic cycle seems to be subdivided into the following seven phases:

Love's expansion	1. Four pure divine masses	(Initial abiotic phase)
	2. Single limbs	(1st zoogonic stage)
	3. Chance combinations	(2nd zoogonic stage)
Cosmic Rest	4. The divine *Sphairos*	
Strife's invasion	5. Whole-natured beings	(3rd zoogonic stage)
	6. Sexual reproduction	(4th zoogonic stage)
	7. Cosmic Dissolution (*Dīnos*)	(Final abiotic phase)

The cyclical arrangement of these seven phases is illustrated by Figure 5.1.

It remains to be seen whether the structure of the cosmic cycle is compatible with what we have shown to be the message of the Pythagorean *Oath*, i.e., with the claim that the durations of the single phases of Empedocles' cycle are regulated by the numerical ratios of the Pythagorean *tetraktys*. Fortunately, there is no need for us to speculate about how this might possibly work, since important information on that point has recently and unexpectedly been provided by a set of Florentine Scholia on the time-table of the cosmic cycle, to which we now turn.

---

214   Emp. fr. 66b MP, lines 273–287: [ἐ]ν τῆι δ᾽ ἀΐσσοντα [διαμπ]ερὲς οὐδ[αμὰ λήγει] / [π]υκνῆισιν δίνηισ[ιν] ... / 275 [ν]ωλεμές, οὐδέ πο[τ᾽ ... / [παῦρ]οι δ᾽ αἰῶνες πρότερ]οι / [πρὶν] τούτων μεταβῆνα]ι ... / [πά]ντηι δ᾽ ἀΐσσον[τ]α διαμ[περὲς οὐδαμὰ λήγει·] / [οὔ]τε γὰρ ἠέλιος Τ[ιτ]ὴν ο[ὔτ᾽ ἄπλετος αἰθήρ] / 280 [ὀρ]μῆ⟨ι⟩ τῆιδε γέμον]τε ... / [οὔ]τε τι τῶν ἄλλων ... / [ἀλ]λὰ μεταλλάσσον[τ᾽ ἀΐσσ]ει κύκλωι [ἅπαντα.] / [ἄλλο]τε μὲν γὰρ γαῖ᾽ [ἀβ]άτη θέει ἠελ[ίου τε] / [σφαῖρα,] τόσην δὴ κα[ὶ ν]υν ἐπ᾽ ἀνδράσι τ[ιέμεν ἐστίν·] / 285 [ὣς δ᾽ α]ὕτως τάδ[ε π]άντα δι᾽ ἀλλήλων [γε δραμόντα,] / [κἄλλο]υς τ᾽ ἄλλ᾽ [ἔσχη]κε τόπους πλαγ[χθέντ᾽ ἰδίους τε·] / [οὐ δή πω] μεσάτους τ[ι ἐσε]ρχόμεθ᾽ ἐν μ[όνον εἶναι].

215   Emp. fr. 87.8–10a MP: [ἐξικ]νούμε[θα γὰ]ρ πολυβενθ[έα Δῖνον], ὀΐω, / [μυρία τ(ε) οὐκ] ἐθέλουσι παρέσσε[ται ἄλγ]εα θυμῶι / [ἀνθρώποις]. The supplement πολυβενθ[έα Δῖνον] is based on the analogy σφαῖρα : Σφαῖρος = δίνη : Δῖνος in conjunction with the two Empedoclean occurrences of βένθεα ... δίνης (frs 66b.288–9 and 69b.3–4 MP); cf. Martin/Primavesi 1999, 304–306.

PYTHAGOREAN RATIOS IN EMPEDOCLES' PHYSICS

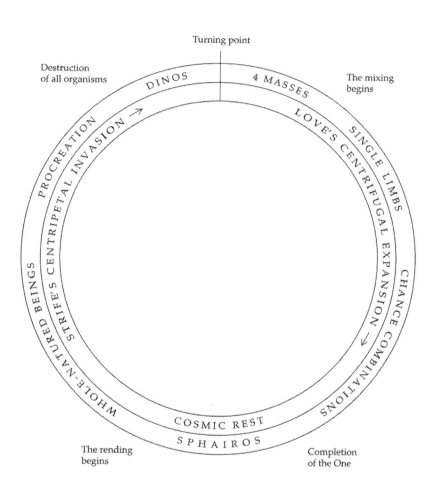

FIGURE 5.1 The seven phases of the cosmic cycle

4 The Time-Table of the Cosmic Cycle

4.1 *The Basic Structure of the Time-Table According to the Florentine Scholia*

The Florentine manuscript Laur. 87.7 forms part of the first extant manuscript edition of the complete works of Aristotle; this edition was manufactured in the 12th century in the so called *scriptorium* of Ioannikios.[216] The manuscript in question covers Aristotle's *Physics, De caelo, De generatione et corruptione* and the *Meteorologica*.[217] From the sections containing the *Physics* (folia 1r–120r) and the *De generatione and corruptione* (folia 199v–246r), Marwan Rashed has brought to light a set of Byzantine scholia that both help to elucidate Aristotle's remarks about Empedocles' cosmic cycle and add some further details to them.[218] It goes without saying that the scholia must be treated in close connection with the Aristotelian passages to which they refer. Through some of these scholia the basic tripartite structure of a *time-table* of the cosmic cycle became known; that tripartite structure has been convincingly reconstructed by Rashed 2014. In what follows, we offer an overview of the relevant passages of Aristotle along with their scholia.

4.1.1 Arist. *Ph.* Θ 1, 250ᵇ26–9 with Scholium B

According to Aristotle, Empedocles has the world be in motion in both transitional periods, i.e., when Love makes One out of Many and when Strife makes Many out of One. In the intermediate times, by contrast, there is a period of cosmic rest:[219]

---

216   The modern research on Ioannikios was inaugurated by Wilson 1983, who believed (p. 168) 'that the most likely date for Ioannikios is the last third or quarter of the twelfth century'. An even earlier date was made probable by Vuillemin-Diem and Rashed 1997, 178: 'le travail de Ioannikios remonte probablement aux alentours des années 1135–1140'. Degni 2008 provided a comprehensive description of all manuscripts then known to have been written by Ioannikios and his colleagues; yet an important manuscript containing Aristotle's *Nicomachean Ethics* and *Poetics*, the *Codex Riccardianus* 46, was added to the list by Baldi 2011, 20: 'Gli aspetti sopra evidenziati inducono a ritenere il Riccardiano un manufatto realizzato nel *milieu* costantinopolitano nel quale operava anche il noto copista Ioannikios'.

217   For a codicological description of the Florentine manuscript by Jürgen Wiesner see Moraux et al. 1976, 296–298.

218   Rashed 2001a, 141–5 published two relevant scholia on the *Physics*; Rashed 2001b brought an increase in the available material to a total of seven scholia on the *Physics* and *Gen. corr.*, which Primavesi 2006a re-edited on the basis of a collation *in situ*; this article also contains photographs of the seven scholia in question. For further important addenda see Rashed 2014.

219   Arist. *Ph.* Θ 1, 250ᵇ26–9 (= Emp. fr. 92/Ia MP).

PYTHAGOREAN RATIOS IN EMPEDOCLES' PHYSICS

... ἢ ὡς Ἐμπεδοκλῆς ἐν μέρει κινεῖσθαι καὶ πάλιν ἠρεμεῖν, κινεῖσθαι μὲν ὅταν ἡ φιλία ἐκ πολλῶν ποιῇ τὸ ἓν ἢ τὸ νεῖκος πολλὰ ἐξ ἑνός, ἠρεμεῖν δ᾽ ἐν τοῖς μεταξὺ χρόνοις.

... or else as Empedocles says, viz. that there is motion and rest in turns, motion when Love makes the One out of the Many or Strife the Many out of the One, and rest in the intermediate times.

The plural 'intermediate times' (*metaxy chronoi*) does, of course, not indicate that there is more than one intermediate time per cycle, but rather that there are infinitely many revolutions of the cycle, so that the intermediate times in question occur regularly. Now scholium B informs us that these intermediate times begin when Love comes to rest 'after 60 time units', and that during the intermediate times Strife too is at rest and does not immediately begin its work of dissolution:[220]

παυομένης γὰρ καὶ τῆς φιλίας μετὰ τοὺς ξ χρόνους, οὐκ εὐθὺς ἤρξατο ποιεῖν ἀπόσπασιν τὸ νεῖκος, ἀλλ᾽ ἠρέμει.

For when Love, too, came to rest after the sixty time units, Strife did not immediately start rending, but stayed at rest.

The 60 time units (*chronoi*)[221] mentioned here define the duration of Love's centrifugal expansion. At the end of these 60 units of time, Love can pause since it has completed the construction of the *Sphairos*, whereas the 'intermediate time', which subsequently lasts until the beginning of Strife's invasion, designates the lifespan of the *Sphairos*. It is important to notice that the lifespan of the *Sphairos* is not considered to belong to the time of Love's activity, but rather as a time in which both Strife and Love are at rest.

4.1.2   Arist. *Ph.* Θ 1, 252ᵃ7–10 with Scholium C

Aristotle describes the Empedoclean cycle as a tripartite structure: Love's rule—common rest—Strife's rule:[222]

---

220   Scholium B Rashed (Cod. Laur. F, fol. 91r, line 6) on 250ᵇ29 (= Emp. fr. 92/Ic MP).

221   For the plural χρόνοι meaning 'periods of time', cf. LSJ 1996 s.v. χρόνος I.2.a: 'pl. of points or periods of time' with reference to Pl. *Lg.* Z, 798a8–b1. In discussions of musical rhythm, χρόνος indicates 'a unit of time' cf. LSJ 1996 s.v. v.3: 'in Rhythmic and Music *time* ... *time unit*'.

222   Arist. *Ph.* Θ 1, 252ᵃ7–10 (= Emp. fr. 92/IIa MP; DK 31 A 38).

... ὅπερ ἔοικεν Ἐμπεδοκλῆς ἂν εἰπεῖν, ὡς τὸ κρατεῖν καὶ κινεῖν ἐν μέρει τὴν φιλίαν καὶ τὸ νεῖκος ὑπάρχει τοῖς πράγμασιν ἐξ ἀνάγκης, ἠρεμεῖν δὲ τὸν μεταξὺ χρόνον.

... which is what Empedocles seems to say: it happens by necessity for things that Love and Strife are in power, i.e., cause motion, alternately, while they are at rest during the intermediate time.

This description of the tripartite structure of the cycle corresponds to the passage in Aristotle just cited above under (i); in particular, the singular 'intermediate time' (*ton metaxy chronon*) confirms that there is only one intermediate time of common rest per cycle. But this time, Aristotle explicitly equates *causing motion* with *being in power*. It follows that during the intermediate time of rest neither Love nor Strife is considered to be in power.

This interpretation is confirmed by scholium C, which designates the 60 time units of Love's activity (already mentioned in scholium B) as the time of Love's *being in power*:[223]

καὶ ⟨οὐκ⟩ εὐθὺς μετὰ τὴν παρέλευσιν τῶν ξ χρόνων ἐν οἷς ἐκράτησεν ἡ φιλία γενέσθαι διάσπασιν.

And that the rending begins ⟨not⟩ immediately after the passing of the sixty time units during which Love was in power.

4.1.3 Arist. *Ph.* Θ 1, 252ª27–8 + 31–2 with Scholium E

Aristotle complains that Empedocles does not provide a proper argument for his assumption that Love and Strife are in power alternately and for equal times:[224]

εἰ δὲ προσοριεῖται τὸ ἐν μέρει, λεκτέον ἐφ᾿ ὧν οὕτως, [...]· τὸ δὲ καὶ δι᾿ ἴσων χρόνων δεῖται λόγου τινός.

If he is going to add that it (viz. their rule) occurs alternately, he should first adduce cases where such a state of things exists [...]; and the additional assumption of equal times stands also in need of an argument.

Scholium E clarifies that Aristotle's 'equal times' refer to the duration *of Love's rule* and *Strife's rule*, respectively:[225]

---

223   Scholium C Rashed (Cod. Laur. F, fol. 93r, line 9) on 252ª9–10 (= Emp. fr. 92/IIb MP), with Rashed's emendation of the initial καὶ to καὶ ⟨οὐκ⟩.

224   Arist. *Ph.* Θ 1, 252ª27–8 + 31–2 (= Emp. fr. 93a MP).

225   Scholium E Rashed (Cod. Laur. F, fol. 93v, line 20) on 252ª31 (= Emp. fr. 93b MP).

PYTHAGOREAN RATIOS IN EMPEDOCLES' PHYSICS

κρατεῖν τὸ νεῖκος καὶ τὴν φιλίαν (scil. δι' ἴσων χρόνων).

Strife and Love are ruling (viz. for equal times).

The combined evidence of scholia B, C, and E yields the conclusion that both Love and Strife are in power, and cause movement, for 60 time units each.

4.1.4 Arist. *GC* B 6, 334^{a}5–9 with Scholium J

Aristotle reports that Empedocles described the present period, i.e. the period of Strife's rule, as similar to the earlier period of Love's rule, inasmuch as both periods are characterized by a common feature, i.e. motion. According to Aristotle this similarity implies that the motion common to both periods should be put down to a common cause, whereas Empedocles regards Love as the cause of motion in one period and Strife as cause of motion in the other. But if, on the other hand, we assumed for both periods a *single* cause of motion, which would then evidently have to be different from both Love and Strife, that other cause of motion would be entitled to the status of a principle, whereas Love and Strife would lose that status:[226]

> ἅμα δὲ καὶ τὸν κόσμον ὁμοίως ἔχειν φησὶν ἐπί τε τοῦ νείκους νῦν καὶ πρότερον ἐπὶ τῆς φιλίας. τί οὖν ἐστὶ τὸ κινοῦν πρῶτον καὶ αἴτιον τῆς κινήσεως; οὐ γὰρ δὴ ἡ φιλία καὶ τὸ νεῖκος. ἀλλὰ τίνος κινήσεως ταῦτα αἴτια, εἰ ἔστιν ἐκεῖνο ἀρχή;

> *At the same time he says that the universe is in the same state now under the rule of Strife as it was earlier under the rule of Love. What, then, is the first mover and the first cause of movement? It cannot, evidently, be Love and Strife: rather these are the causes of particular movements only, if that other is the principle.*[227]

Scholium J illustrates Aristotle's criticism by making explicit, and justifying, an important premiss which Aristotle had taken for granted: if we admit, for argument's sake, that Strife has managed, even just once, to operate as a true principle of motion up until the end of the 60 time units of its being in power, then evidently it cannot continue to be the principle of motion for the ensuing period of Love's power. In other words, neither Strife nor Love can be

---

226 Arist. *GC* B 6, 334^{a}5–9 (= Emp. fr. 95a MP; DK 31 A 42 [ii]).
227 Translation after Williams 1982, 48–49 (with slight modifications). See also the helpful note *ad loc.* in Williams 1982, 172–173.

166 PRIMAVESI

the required principle of motion *common* to both transitional periods of the cosmic cycle:[228]

ἀλλ᾽ ἐπεί ποτε καὶ ἅπαξ ἐκινήθησαν ὑπὸ τοῦ νείκους ἕως εἰς τοὺς ξ χρόνους, τί τὸ αἴτιον τῆς κινήσεως;

But after they have been moved even a single time[229] by Strife up until the end of his 60 chronoi, what will then be the cause of motion?

The scholium confirms that the period during which Strife is in power and causes movement lasts 60 time units, too, and that it is *immediately* followed by Love's 60 time units.

4.1.5 Arist. *GC* A 1, 315ᵃ4–8 with Scholium G

According to Aristotle, Empedocles maintains that the elements are ungenerated, but at the same time, though everything is united in the *Sphairos*, he claims that each of the four elements comes-to-be anew out of the *Sphairos*:[230]

ἅμα μὲν γὰρ οὔ φησιν ἕτερον ἐξ ἑτέρου γίνεσθαι τῶν στοιχείων οὐδέν, ἀλλὰ τἆλλα πάντα ἐκ τούτων, ἅμα δ᾽ ὅταν εἰς ἓν συναγάγῃ τὴν ἅπασαν φύσιν πλὴν τοῦ νείκους, ἐκ τοῦ ἑνὸς γίγνεσθαι πάλιν ἕκαστον.

For he denies that any one of his elements comes-to-be out of any other, insisting on the contrary that they are the things out of which everything else comes-to-be; and yet (having brought the entirety of existing things, except Strife, together into one) he maintains, simultaneously with that denial, that each element once more comes-to-be out of the One.

Scholium G provides four valuable pieces of information: (i) What Aristotle misleadingly calls 'the coming-to-be of each of the four elements' is in fact

---

228 Scholium J Rashed (Cod. Laur. F fol. 236v, line 2) on 334ᵃ6–7 (= Emp. fr. 95b MP).

229 The unusual phrase ποτὲ καὶ ἅπαξ seems to be first attested in a letter by the Byzantine diplomat Leo Magister Choerosphactes (*Ep.* 10 lines 11–5, p. 52 + 54 Strano; on the author, see Kazhdan 1991), written in AD 896 to the Bulgarian ruler Symeon. This suggests that the excerpts preserved by the Florentine scholia may well have been taken during the 'first Byzantine humanism', i.e., between AD 850 and AD 950.

230 Arist. *GC* A 1, 315ᵃ4–8 (= Emp. fr. 94a MP).

PYTHAGOREAN RATIOS IN EMPEDOCLES' PHYSICS

brought about just by way of *separation* (διακρίσει). (ii) The 'coming-to-be' of each of the four elements is accomplished 'after 100 time units' (μετὰ ρ χρόνους), that is to say, 100 time units after the entirety of existing things, except Strife, was brought together into the One.[231] (iii) The 'coming-to-be' of each of the four elements is accomplished 'just when Strife's rule has come to an end' (νείκους ἐπικρατήσαντος),[232] i.e., after the sixty time units of Strife's rule. (iv) The 'coming-to-be' of each of the four elements refers to the restoration of each element 'in its entirety' (σύμπαν),[233] i.e., to the restoration of the *four pure masses*:[234]

διακρίσει μετὰ ρ χρόνους / νείκους ἐπικρατήσαντος / σύμπ(αν)

By dissolution, after 100 chronoi / at the end of Strife's rule / each element as a whole.

Now if the restoration of the four pure masses, i.e. the period of Strife's rule, is accomplished 100 units of time after the completion of the *Sphairos*, and if the period of Strife's rule begins with the destruction of the *Sphairos* and lasts for sixty time units, then Strife's rule begins 40 time units after the completion of the *Sphairos*, so that the intermediate time which falls between the end of Love's rule and the beginning of Strife's rule, i.e. the lifespan of the *Sphairos*, lasts 40 time units. All in all, then, the Florentine scholia have yielded the following basic time-table of the cosmic cycle:[235]

Rule of Love:	60 time units
Sphairos:	40 time units
Rule of Strife:	60 time units

The cyclical arrangement of the three periods attested by the Florentine time-table is illustrated by Figure 5.2.

---

231   The point of reference is supplied by the Aristotelian phrase commented upon here, see Primavesi 2008, 18 n. 50.

232   On the aorist expressing the completed action here see Primavesi 2008, 18 n. 49.

233   Rashed 2014, 322, convincingly suggested connecting σύμπαν with the Aristotelian ἕκαστον.

234   Scholium G Rashed (Col. Laur. F, fol. 201v, line 1) on 315ᵃ7–8 (= Emp. fr. 94c MP).

235   This was first pointed out by Rashed 2014.

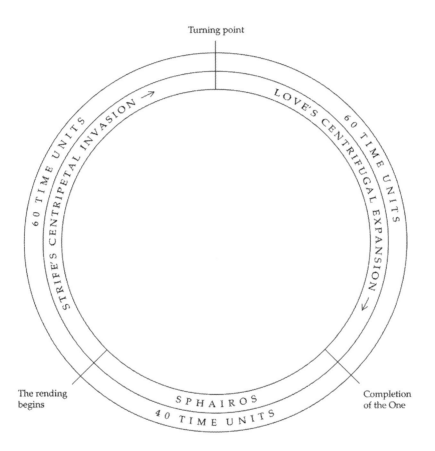

FIGURE 5.2 The basic structure of the cosmic time-table as deduced from the Florentine scholia by Rashed 2014

4.2 *The Florentine Time-Table and the* Tetraktys

4.2.1 A Pythagorean Subdivision of the Florentine Time-Table

At first sight, the figures 60—40—60 look fairly arbitrary. The natural starting point for any attempt at making sense of them is the well-known fact that within pre-Platonic thought the analysis of natural phenomena by means of numbers or numerical ratios is the specific contribution of the *Pythagorean School.*[236] If, then, a key for decoding the time-table preserved by the Florentine scholia is available, it is likely to come from a source in which the cosmic cycle of Empedoclean physics is linked with Pythagorean number-philosophy. Now above in part two, we saw that the ps.-Pythagorean *Oath* strongly suggests a reading of Empedocles' cosmic cycle according to which its time-table is structured by the numerical ratios of the Pythagorean *tetraktys* (i.e., 1 : 2 : 3 : 4). This result can, and should, now be applied to the cosmic time-table as transmitted by the Florentine scholia. For its sequence of 60 time units (Love's expansion) + 40 time units (*Sphairos*) + 60 time units (Strife's invasion) can be decoded as an abridged version of a time-table consisting of *two tetraktyes* that have the 40 time units of the *Sphairos* in common: one for Love and one for Strife, one increasing (Love's Rule + *Sphairos*) and one decreasing (*Sphairos* + Strife's Rule), just as Plutarch attests a double *tetraktys* in which one *tetraktys* has been added to another one (as we have seen in section 1.3.4).[237] On this reading, the first period of 60 time units (Love's centrifugal expansion) consists of 10 + 20 + 30 times, and the second period of 60 time units (Strife's centripetal invasion) consists of 30 + 20 + 10 times:

LOVE'S *TETRAKTYS*

$\overline{10 : 20 : 30 : \mathbf{40}}$

$\underline{\mathbf{40} : 30 : 20 : 10}$

STRIFE'S *TETRAKTYS*

The fact that on our reconstruction of the Pythagorean subdivision of the Florentine time-table, the lifespan of the *Sphairos* belongs to both Love's

---

236   Arist. *Metaph.* A 5, 985[b]23–26, already quoted above n. 51.

237   Plu. *De Iside et Osiride* 381F–382A; Sieveking 1928, 74–5: ἡ δὲ καλουμένη τετρακτύς, τὰ ἓξ καὶ τριάκοντα, μέγιστος ἦν ὅρκος, ὡς τεθρύληται, καὶ κόσμος ὠνόμασται, τεσσάρων μὲν ἀρτίων τῶν πρώτων, τεσσάρων δὲ τῶν περισσῶν εἰς ταὐτὸ συντιθεμένων, ἀποτελούμενος.

170 PRIMAVESI

tetraktys and Strife's *tetraktys* corresponds exactly to the treatment of this 'intermediate time' in scholia B and C: it is a time of ceasefire and rest for *both* Love and Strife.

All in all, the Pythagorean subdivision of the Florentine time-table yields *seven phases* the cyclical arrangement of which is illustrated by Figure 5.3.

4.2.2   'Time units' = *aiōnes*

It is true that in this time-table the numbers of the standard tetraktys have been multiplied by ten.[238] This fact does, of course, not affect the basic numerical ratios (1 : 2 : 3 : 4), and we have already seen, in section 1.3.4, that a tetraktys could also be constructed by multiplying the three ratios corresponding to the three perfect intervals of music (3 : 4, 2 : 3, and 1 : 2) by 2, 3, and 6, respectively, so that the whole series (6 : 8 : 9 : 12) includes the tone (8 : 9) as well.[239] Yet in the present case, one would still like to understand the reason for the multiplication. One the one hand, the factor 10 in the ratio 10 : 20 : 30 : 40 may be seen as a way to include also the *sum* of the *tetraktys* (1 + 2 + 3 + 4) in the mathematical structure of the time-table.[240] On the other hand, the abstract term 'time unit' (= chronos) is quite unlikely to have served as a time unit already in the ultimate source of the scholia, which will have referred rather to a specific time unit. Empedoclean usage clearly suggests identifying the original time unit in question with an *aiōn*, i.e. with the maximum lifespan of a human being,[241] since Empedocles does not use any other sufficiently extended time unit. In connection with this time unit, however, the numbers of the basic tetraktys, 1, 2, 3, and 4, would have been altogether unsuitable for constructing a time-table of the history of the universe: Strife's expansion, for instance, which includes the whole of human history, must certainly take more than just six human lifetimes.

---

238   Cf. Emp. fr. 93b MP (scholium D Rashed, on Arist. *Ph.* Θ 1, 252ᵃ31 τὸ δὲ καὶ δι' ἴσων χρόνων): πρὸς ῑ. This might refer to the multiplication by ten.

239   Nicom. *Exc.* ch. 7; v. Jan 1895, 279.8–12: κἀντεῦθεν ἡ πρώτη τετρακτὺς τὴν τῶν συμφωνιῶν πηγὴν ἔχουσα ἀναφαινομένην τῶν ϛ η θ ιβ, ὑπάτης τε καὶ μέσης καὶ νήτης καὶ παραμέσης ἔχουσα λόγον καὶ τὸν ἐπόγδοον περιλαμβάνουσα.

240   This point was made by the anonymous reader of the penultimate version of the present chapter.

241   See Emp. fr. 90 MP (B 129 DK), lines 5–6: ῥεῖ' ὅ γε τῶν ὄντων πάντων λεύσσεσκεν ἕκαστα / καί τε δέκ' ἀνθρώπων καί τ' εἴκοσιν αἰώνεσσιν (where the original ἕκαστα has been restored instead of the minority reading ἕκαστον); fr. 66b MP, lines 276–7: [παῦρ]οι δ' αἰῶνες πρότεροι ... / [πρὶν] τούτων μεταβῆναι ... .

PYTHAGOREAN RATIOS IN EMPEDOCLES' PHYSICS

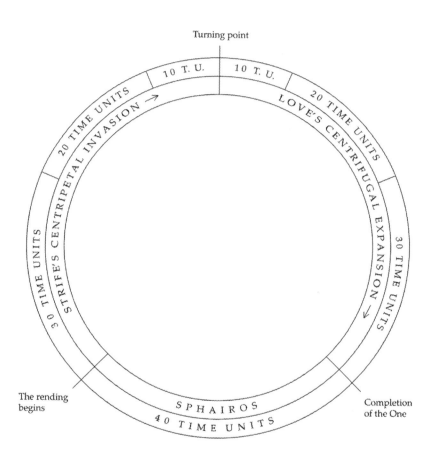

FIGURE 5.3 The subdivision of the cosmic time-table in accordance with the proportions of the double *tetraktys*

172   PRIMAVESI

The assumption that the abstract *chronoi* (as mentioned in the scholia) have replaced original *aiōnes* also yields a possible *reason* for that replacement. In scholium A the *Sphairos* is called 'thinkable world-order' (διανοητὸς διάκοσμος).[242] While this term clearly alludes to the Platonizing reinterpretation of the Empedoclean *Sphairos* as an 'intelligible world' (νοητὸς κόσμος) which we have mentioned in part one of this chapter, it modifies this reinterpretation in a way that suits the logic of a cosmic *time*-table: on a literal reading of 'On Nature', the divine *Sphairos* comes to be and passes away at fixed points of time,[243] so that it cannot possibly be identified as the timeless intelligible world, yet it remains true that he can be cognized only by his own *thought*,[244] not by anybody's sense perceptions. So it seems that the immediate source of the scholia is building on and intelligently modifying a Platonic source. In a Platonizing context, however, the employment of *aiōn* as a specific time unit would have seemed to be precluded by Plato's basic contrast between *aiōn* (eternity abiding in the One) and *chronos* (an image of eternity, moving according to number).[245] Even a proven expert like Simplicius is capable of misinterpreting an occurrence of *aiōn* (in the sense of 'individual livespan') as meaning 'timeless eternity' in Empedocles.[246] We may conclude that if, in Platonic circles, the Empedoclean time unit *aiōn* was correctly understood at all, it was liable to be replaced, for clarity's sake, by the abstract term *chronos*.

4.2.3   The Seven Phases of the Cosmic Cycle and the Double *Tetraktys*
In part three of this chapter, we showed that the purely qualitative analysis of the extant fragments of and testimonia on the poem 'On Nature' yields a cosmic cycle of seven qualitatively different phases. These can now be matched with the seven durations produced by the subdivision of the Florentine timetable according to the ratios of the double *tetraktys*:

---

242   Emp. fr. 92/Ib MP (= scholium A Rashed, Cod. Laurentianus F, fol. 91ʳ, line 5), on Arist. *Ph.* Θ 1, 250ᵇ28 (ὅταν ἡ φιλία ἐκ πολλῶν ποιῇ τὸ ἕν): τὸν σφαῖρον τὸν διανοητὸν διάκοσμον.

243   Emp. fr. 77 MP (B 30 DK): αὐτὰρ ἐπεὶ μέγα Νεῖκος ἐνὶμμελέεσσιν ἐθρέφθη / ἐς τιμάς τ' ἀνόρουσε (scil. τὸ Νεῖκος) τελειομένοιο χρόνοιο, / ὅς σφιν ἀμοιβαῖος πλατέος παρ' ἐλήλαται ὅρκου ... .

244   According to Simp. *in Phys.* 475.23–24 Diels mathematical objects are διανοητά, i.e. neither intelligible nor sensible but something in between: thinkable. On the *Sphairos* thinking himself see Emp. B 134 DK as quoted in Olymp. *in Grg.* 4.3, Cod. Marc. Gr. Z. 196 (= 743) *in margine*: οὔτε γὰρ ἀνδρομέη(ι) κεφαλῆ(ι) κατὰ γυῖα κέκασται, / οὐ χέρες, οὐ θοὰ γοῦν᾽, οὐ μήδεα λαχνήεντα, / ἀλλὰ φρὴν ἱερὴ καὶ ἀθέσφατος ἔπλετο μοῦνον, / φροντίσι κόσμον ἅπαντα καταΐσσουσα θοῆισιν. For the vulgate version see fr. 192b MP (Ammon. *in Int.* 249.1–10 Busse).

245   Pl. *Ti.* 37D 5–7: εἰκὼ δ' ἐπενόει κινητόν τινα αἰῶνος ποιῆσαι, καὶ διακοσμῶν ἅμα οὐρανὸν ποιεῖ μένοντος αἰῶνος ἐν ἑνὶ κατ' ἀριθμὸν ἰοῦσαν αἰώνιον εἰκόνα, τοῦτον ὃν δὴ χρόνον ὠνομάκαμεν.

246   Simp. *in Cael.* 141.7–9 Heiberg, commenting on Emp. fr. 66b MP, line 242 (= B 17.11 DK): ὥστε τὰ ἀπὸ τοῦ νοητοῦ κόσμου διὰ τοῦ Νείκους διακριθέντα ἀντὶ τοῦ αἰωνίως εἶναι γίνονται μὲν καὶ 'οὔ σφισιν ἔμπεδος αἰών', ἀιδίως δὲ ἀνακυκλοῦνται.

PYTHAGOREAN RATIOS IN EMPEDOCLES' PHYSICS

Love's expansion	1. Four pure divine masses	10 time units
	2. Single limbs	20 time units
	3. Chance combinations	30 time units
Cosmic rest	4. The divine *Sphairos*	40 time units
Strife's invasion	5. Whole-natured beings	30 time units
	6. Sexual reproduction	20 time units
	7. Cosmic dissolution (*Dīnos*)	10 time units

But why should the three phases of Love's expansion should become continually *longer* (10–20–30 *chronoi*), and why should the three phases of Strife's invasion become continually *shorter* (30–20–10 *chronoi*)? We suggest that the *increasing duration* of the phases of Love's *tetraktys* corresponds to the *decreasing speed* of cosmic movement during Love's expansion, from the rotation of the four masses at maximum speed to the immobility of the *Sphairos*, whereas the decreasing duration of the phases of Strife's *tetraktys* corresponds to the increasing speed of the cosmic movement during Strife's invasion, from the immobility of the *Sphairos* to the rotation of the four masses at maximum speed.[247] For instance, the movement of the cosmos accelerated considerably under the rule of Strife up to the present day:[248]

|907 E 9| Ἐμπεδοκλῆς· ὅτε ἐγεννᾶτο τὸ τῶν ἀνθρώπων γένος ἐκ |E 10| τῆς γῆς, τοσαύτην γενέσθαι τῷ μήκει τοῦ χρόνου διὰ τὸ βραδυ-|F 1|πορεῖν τὸν ἥλιον τὴν ἡμέραν, ὁπόση νῦν ἐστιν ἡ δεκάμηνος· |F 2| προϊόντος δὲ τοῦ χρόνου τοσαύτην γενέσθαι τὴν ἡμέραν, ὁπόση νῦν ἐστιν ἡ ἑπτάμηνος· διὰ τοῦτο καὶ τὰ δεκάμηνα γόνιμα καὶ |F 3| τὰ ἑπτάμηνα, τῆς φύσεως τοῦ κόσμου οὕτω μεμελετηκυίας αὔξεσθαι ἐν μιᾷ ἡμέρᾳ (ἣ τότε) καὶ νυκτὶ τὸ βρέφος.

F 3 ἣ τότε καὶ dedimus (τῇ τότε καὶ iam Reiske) : ἣ τίθεται *mss.* : τε καὶ Qusṭā ibn Lūqā Daiber 1980, 501

Empedocles : When the race of human beings was born from the earth, the day lasted for as long a time as ten months last now because the sun moved slowly, but as time went on the day came to last as long as seven months do now. This is why both ten-month embryos and seven-month ones are viable, since in this way, the nature of the world has ensured that the embryo grows in a single day (as it lasted then) and night.

---

247 In assuming these changes of speed during the cosmic cycle, we follow O'Brien 1969, 46–54.
248 Emp. fr. 165 MP (Ps.-Plu. *Plac.* 907 E9–F3 [line numbering after the 1599 Frankfurt edition of Plutarch's *Moralia*] = Aëtius V.18.1 [Dox. 427ª17–28 Diels] = A 75 DK).

The time when human beings were 'born from the earth' falls in the third zoo-gonical stage ('whole-natured beings'), so that the acceleration of solar motion described here covers the third and fourth zoogonical stages, i.e., the present rule of Strife which is bringing about a transition from the *Sphairos* to the four masses. Conversely, the transition from the four masses to the *Sphairos* under Love's rule will have been accompanied by a deceleration of solar motion. These gradual changes in speed over the course of the cycle seem to be reflected in the different durations of the individual phases of the cycle: the slower the cosmic motion, the longer the respective phases of the cycle; the faster the motion, the shorter the phases. The cyclical arrangement of these seven phases in accordance with the proportions of the double *tetraktys* is illustrated by Figure 5.4.

4.2.4   Proof of the Pudding: The Time to Be Given in Exchange

Although the folia of cod. Laur. 87.7 which contain the scholia attesting the durations of the cosmic time-table are quite distant from each other (91r–93v, 201v, 236v), all the durations indicated are internally coherent. Furthermore, these durations are compatible with the other evidence (Simplicius' claim, the Pythagorean *Oath*, the Aristotelian testimonia on the 'equal times'). Even so, we may still feel that these are necessary conditions of authenticity, but not sufficient ones.[249] It is true that the hypothesis that we are dealing with a high-class forgery here is unconvincing, since in this case the forger would have made it very difficult to decode the underlying Pythagorean scheme: the scholia do not offer the full scheme of the two *tetractyes*, but only an outline of it, and they do not employ the basic Pythagorean numbers, but multiples by ten of the *sums* involved (60 time units for the rule of Love, 60 time units for the rule of Strife, 100 time units for the lifespan of the Sphairos plus Strife's rule). In addition to that, the Pythagorean *Oath* presupposes a Pythagorean time-table for Empedocles' Cycle, as we have seen, but it is even more improbable that the Florentine scholia and the *Oath* go back to a single complex forgery. By contrast, the assumption that the mathematical *tetraktys* was indeed a key element in Empedocles' Pythagoreanism is remarkably well in tune with his cultural and intellectual background. The most notable cultural achievement of his hometown Agrigentum in the second half of the fifth century BC was a splendid series of six peripteral temples, in the so called *Valle dei Templi*, and the characteristic feature of these temples is their architectural Pythagoreanism: an increasingly sophisticated application of simple numerical ratios to all proportions of the building.[250]

---

249   Rashed 2014, 314.

250   For this claim and for the evidence on which it is based see Mertens 2006, 381–99: 'Die Bauschule von Agrigent – Konzeption und Entwurf hochklassischer Tempel'. Accordingly,

PYTHAGOREAN RATIOS IN EMPEDOCLES' PHYSICS

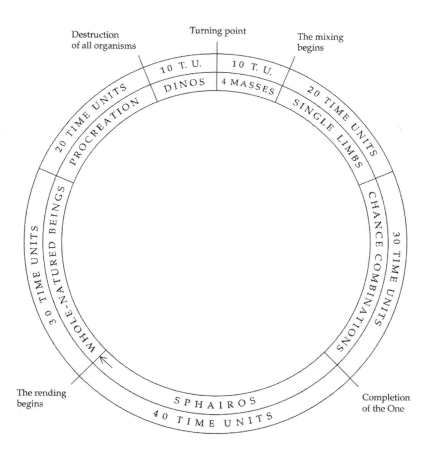

FIGURE 5.4 The seven phases of the cosmic cycle in accordance with the proportions of the double *tetraktys*

Yet we will not be content with pointing out that the hypothesis of authenticity is on balance more plausible than the hypothesis of a forgery. Rather, we will try to argue that the assumption that the cosmic cycle is structured by two overlapping *tetractyes* is even *indispensable* for decoding the one extant fragment in which Empedocles mentions the duration of the *Sphairos* and the oath by which it is regulated.

After the formation of the *Sphairos* and for the duration of its lifespan, there is an intermediate time of cosmic rest that comes to an end when Strife, whose strength has been restored during the period of rest, invades the *Sphairos* from without and destroys it.[251] The period of rest, i.e. the lifespan of the *Sphairos*, is characterized as a time 'to be given in exchange' (*amoibaios*); its duration is delineated by an oath sworn by Love and Strife:[252]

αὐτὰρ ἐπεὶ μέγα Νεῖκος ἐνιμμελέεσσιν ἐθρέφθη
ἐς τιμάς τ' ἀνόρουσε (scil. τὸ Νεῖκος) τελειομένοιο χρόνοιο,
ὅς σφιν ἀ μ ο ι β α ῖ ο ς πλατέος παρ' ἐλήλαται ὅρκου ...

But when Strife had grown in his limbs, and rushed upon his honours, as the time was coming to an end, the time to be given in exchange that was delineated by them in a broad oath ...

If the lifespan of the *Sphairos* is a time meant to be given in exchange, the obvious question is 'in exchange for what?' One expects that the two gifts exchanged by Love and Strife should be of equal value.[253] Yet it is quite implausible that Strife should have granted the *Sphairos* to Love in return for the remainder of the cosmic cycle (so that the duration of the *Sphairos* would match the duration of all other periods of the cycle), as suggested by O'Brien 1969.[254] For this would imply, as O'Brien himself admits, that not only Strife's

---

there might be a kernel of historical truth in the tendentious anecdote (D.L. 8.63, lines 126–7 Dorandi) according to which Empedocles described his fellow-Agrigentines as 'feasting as if they were to die tomorrow and building houses as if they were to live forever' (Ἀκραγαντῖνοι τρυφῶσι μὲν ὡς αὔριον ἀποθανούμενοι, οἰκίας δὲ κατασκευάζονται ὡς πάντα τὸν χρόνον βιωσόμενοι). Wilamowitz 1929, 630 n. 1 proposed a conjectural emendation of D.L. 8.63 (line 126 Dorandi) which includes the attribution of the anecdote to the historian Timaeus; alternatively, one might also think of restoring a reference to Ps.-Aristipp. Περὶ παλαιᾶς τρυφῆς fr. 8 (Dorandi 2007, 170) who is introduced as a source on Empedocles in D.L. 8.60, lines 103–4 Dorandi.

251 Emp. fr. 78 MP (B 31 DK): πάντα γὰρ ἐξείης πελεμίζετο γυῖα θεοῖο ... .
252 Emp. fr. 77 MP (B 30 DK).
253 O'Brien 1969, 83.
254 O'Brien 1969, 83.

PYTHAGOREAN RATIOS IN EMPEDOCLES' PHYSICS   177

invasion (i.e., Strife's rule), but also Love's expansion (i.e., Love's rule), belongs, 'in a sense', to Strife.[255] And it would also imply that the lifespan of the divine *Sphairos* belongs to Love. Yet according to Aristotle, the lifespan of the *Sphairos* does *not* belong to the period of Love's rule (nor, for that matter, to the period of Strife's rule), since for both Love and Strife, ruling means causing motion,[256] and during the lifespan of the *Sphairos* there is no motion. It would be very strange indeed if Love received from Strife a time in which neither Love nor Strife rules in exchange for a time in which both Love and Strife rule alternately.

It is hard to see how we could resolve that impasse unless we assume the cosmic cycle to be structured according to the double *tetraktys*. For on this assumption, both the *tetraktys* of Love and the *tetraktys* of Strife include the 40 time units of the *Sphairos* (as illustrated by Figure 5.5).

That is to say that the lifespan of the *Sphairos* belongs to both Love and Strife, not as a period of common rule but as a period of common ceasefire and rest:[257] Both have sworn each other to observe faithfully the forty time units of rest implied in their respective *tetraktys*.[258] A ceasefire presupposes that it is respected by both combatants *at the same time*. Therefore, it is entirely natural that the forty time units of rest that Love grants to Strife and the forty time units that Strife grants to Love are temporally coextensive. That is the reason why the only time meant to be given in exchange is the lifespan of the *Sphairos*: it is meant to be given in exchange by either party to the other one. We submit that the Pythagorizing time-table of the cosmic cycle suggested by the Florentine scholia allows a straightforward interpretation of the otherwise incomprehensible lines in which Empedocles addresses the duration of the cosmic rest.

---

255   O'Brien 1969, 80: 'The purpose of the present analysis is to explain how movement dominated by Love *as well as* movement dominated by Strife *both* in a sense 'belong' to Strife, as the author of movement and plurality'. See also O'Brien 1969, 77: 'Any separation and any movement will have 'belonged' to Strife in the way that the Sphere 'belongs' to Love'.

256   Arist. *Ph.* Θ 1, 252ᵃ7–8 τὸ κρατεῖν καὶ κινεῖν ἐν μέρει τὴν φιλίαν καὶ τὸ νεῖκος.

257   Scholium B Rashed (already quoted above, section 4.1 (i)): παυομένης γὰρ καὶ τῆς φιλίας μετὰ τοὺς ξ χρόνους, οὐκ εὐθὺς ἤρξατο ποιεῖν ἀπόσπασιν τὸ νεῖκος, ἀλλ᾽ ἠρέμει ('For when Love, too, *came to rest* after the sixty time units, Strife did not immediately start rending, but *stayed at rest*').

258   Even the Pythagorean link between oath and *tetraktys* seems to be inspired by Empedocles, although the *function* of the Pythagorean *Oath* is, of course, totally different from that of the divine oath in Empedocles.

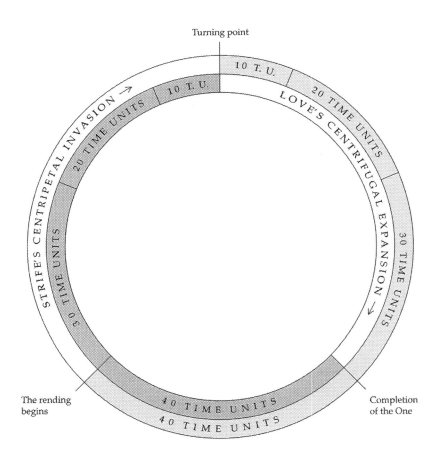

FIGURE 5.5 The 40 time units of the *Sphairos* as embedded both in the *tetraktys* of Love and in that of Strife

PYTHAGOREAN RATIOS IN EMPEDOCLES' PHYSICS   179

4.2.5 Hinting at the Divine *Orthos Logos*

The result of the preceding section leaves little doubt that the time-table of Empedocles' cosmic cycle was indeed structured in accordance with a Pythagorizing double *tetraktys*. But if this is true—in which way could the time-table have been expounded in the poem 'On Nature'? And why was so remarkable a feature of the poem never *quoted* in Empedocles' original wording, at least as far our evidence goes? In order to answer these questions, we have to complete our picture of the strictly confidential speech situation presupposed in 'On Nature'[259]—a confidentiality that was traced back by Plutarch to Empedocles' obedience to the Pythagorean commandment of keeping the teachings of Pythagoras/Apollo secret, as we have seen.[260] To this picture, we must now add a fragment from the proem of 'On Nature' that is quoted by Sextus Empiricus and according to which the mortal teacher's lecture, apart from being secret, is also characterized as being subject to a *restriction of its contents*: the teacher begs his muse to disclose just those words that it is right for ephemeral mortals to hear.[261] In other words, there seems to be a certain risk of going too far and of unveiling more than is permitted by *Themis*, i.e. by divine law.

More information on the dividing line between communicable and incommunicable principles of Empedoclean philosophy is offered by Sextus Empiricus in the immediate context of his quotation of the fragment last mentioned.[262] He distinguishes between a simple *one-level interpretation* of Empedocles—according to which the Empedoclean criteria of truth are just the well-known six principles (Love and Strife and the four elements)—and a more complex *two-level interpretation* of Empedocles the defenders of which claim that the Empedoclean critera of truth are not the sense perceptions corresponding to the six principles, but rather the 'correct proportion' (*orthos logos*), and that there are two kinds of correct proportion, the 'human correct

---

259   Cf. Emp. fr. 41 MP (B 2 DK), lines 8–9: σὺ δ' οὖν, ἐπεὶ ὧδ' ἐλιάσθης, / πεύσεαι· οὐ πλέον ἠὲ βροτείη μῆτις ὄρωρεν ('But you, since you have *withdrawn* here, / you will learn no more than what is within the reach of human intelligence'). Emp. fr. 42 MP (B 111 DK), lines 1–2: φάρμακα δ' ὅσσα γεγᾶσι κακῶν καὶ γήραος ἄλκαρ / πεύσηι, ἐπεὶ μούνωι σοὶ ἐγὼ κρανέω τάδε πάντα ('As many as are the remedies for ills, and protection against old age, / you will learn them, since *for you alone* I shall accomplish all these things').

260   Plu. *Quaest. conv.* 728 E (IV 286.18–20 Hubert 1938), quoting, and commenting upon, Emp. fr. 45 MP (B 5 DK): στεγάσαι φρενὸς ἔλλοπος εἴσω.

261   Emp. fr. 43 MP (B 3 DK, quoted by S.E. *M* 7.125, II.30–31 Mutschmann), lines 3–5: καὶ σέ, πολυμνήστη λευκώλενε παρθένε Μοῦσα, / ἄντομαι· ὧν θέμις ἐστὶν ἐφημερίοισιν ἀκούειν, / πέμπε παρ' Εὐσεβίης ἐλάουσ' εὐήνιον ἅρμα ('And you, much-remembering muse, white-armed maiden, I beseech you: *the words that it is right for ephemeral beings to hear* send to me, driving your well-reined chariot from the halls of piety').

262   The author thanks Marwan Rashed for pointing out to him the importance of S.E. *M* 7.122 (= Emp. B 2 DK [Introduction] = CTXT-8 Inwood) and its larger context for the present problem.

180   PRIMAVESI

proportion' which may be freely shared with others, and the 'divine correct proportion' which must not be disclosed in so many words:[263]

> (§ 115) Empedocles of Acragas, according to those who seem to interpret him in a rather simple manner, transmits six criteria of truth. For having laid down two efficient principles of all things, Love and Strife, and having at the same time designated as material principles the four—earth and water and air and fire,—he declared that all these are criteria. [...] (§ 122) But there have been others who have asserted that according to Empedocles the criterion of truth is not the sense perceptions, but correct proportion, and of correct proportion one kind is divine, the other human. And of these the divine must remain unexpressed, whereas the human may be expressed.

We may safely assume that the human correct proportion is to be identified with the mixture-ratios by means of which the four elements make up the homoeomerous components of living organisms (see above, section 1.3.3). As to the divine correct proportion, by contrast, the passage in Sextus yields a threefold conclusion: Sextus knows an interpretation of Empedocles according to which (i) the correct proportion that can be expressed is supplemented by a correct proportion that must remain unexpressed; (ii) the knowledge of this additional correct proportion comes from a divine source; (iii) Empedocles has expressly avoided to *spell out* the divine correct proportion.

In the light of the preceding sections of the present chapter the one candidate that can possibly meet the first two conditions is the holy *tetraktys*, since it is both a correct proportion underlying Empedocles' cosmic cycle and the legacy of Pythagoras/Apollo to the Pythagorean school.[264] We will assume, then, that the additional principle which according to Empedocles' prayer to his muse should not be disclosed (B 3 DK) has to be identified with the holy *tetraktys*.

---

263 S.E. *M* 7.115+122; II.28+30 Mutschmann, English translation after Bury 1935, 63 + 67 (with modifications): (115) Ἐμπεδοκλῆς δὲ ὁ Ἀκραγαντῖνος κατὰ μὲν τοὺς ἁπλούστερον δοκοῦντας αὐτὸν ἐξηγεῖσθαι ἓξ κριτήρια τῆς ἀληθείας παραδίδωσιν. δύο γὰρ δραστηρίους τῶν ὅλων ἀρχὰς ὑποθέμενος, φιλίαν καὶ νεῖκος, ἅμα τε τῶν τεσσάρων μνησθεὶς ὡς ὑλικῶν, γῆς τε καὶ ὕδατος καὶ ἀέρος καὶ πυρός, πάσας ταύτας ἔφη κριτήρια τυγχάνειν. [...] (122) ἄλλοι δὲ ἦσαν οἱ λέγοντες κατὰ τὸν Ἐμπεδοκλέα κριτήριον εἶναι τῆς ἀληθείας οὐ τὰς αἰσθήσεις ἀλλὰ τὸν ὀρθὸν λόγον, τοῦ δὲ ὀρθοῦ λόγου τὸν μέν τινα θεῖον ὑπάρχειν τὸν δὲ ἀνθρώπινον, ὧν τὸν μὲν θεῖον ἀνέξοιστον εἶναι τὸν δὲ ἀνθρώπινον ἐξοιστόν. The two halves of this report are separated from each other by a lengthy excursus (116–121) on the well known principle of perceiving like by like.

264 Cf. the *acusma* transmitted by Iamb. *VP* 82; p. 47.15–16 Deubner (τί ἐστι τὸ ἐν Δελφοῖς μαντεῖον; τετρακτύς· ὅπερ ἐστὶν ἡ ἁρμονία, ἐν ᾗ αἱ Σειρῆνες) and Pythag. *Iusiur.*, Thesleff 1965, 170.15–16 (οὐ μὰ τὸν ἁμετέραι γενεᾶι παραδόντα τετρακτύν, / πᾱγὰν ἀενάου φύσεως ῥιζώματ' ἔχουσαν), both already quoted.

PYTHAGOREAN RATIOS IN EMPEDOCLES' PHYSICS

By consequence, the scheme of the double *tetraktys* underlying the Pythagorean time-table of Empedocles' cosmic cycle is most unlikely to have been expounded in one comprehensive passage (now lost) of the poem 'On Nature'. On the contrary, it seems far more in tune both with the respect for the divine *orthos logos* and with Empedocles' poetical technique to assume that in the course of the increasingly detailed descriptions of the cosmic cycle[265] the treatment of individual phases was enriched, here and there, by unobtrusive indications of their respective duration. Two such discrete hints at a certain number of time units (i.e., of *aiōnes*)[266] that define the individual phases of the cosmic cycle even seem to be extant.

Lines 276–8 of 'On Nature' I, preserved by the Strasburg Papyrus, describe the few final 'time units' (*aiōnes*) of chaotic dissolution towards the end of Strife's rule:[267]

[παῦρ]οι δ' αἰῶνες πρότερ[οι ⏑⏑–⏑⏑–×]
[πρὶν] τούτων μεταβῆνα[ι ⏑–⏑⏑–⏑⏑–×]
[πά]ντηι δ' ἀΐσσον[τ]α διαμ[περὲς οὐδαμὰ λήγει·]

It will still take a few time units ...
before they (the elements) pass over from these ...
and they never cease from continuously shooting in all directions.

And among the quotations from 'On Nature', there is the following description of Pythagoras' mental power:[268]

ὁππότε γὰρ πάσηισιν ὀρέξαιτο πραπίδεσσιν,
ῥεῖ' ὅ γε τῶν ὄντων πάντων λεύσσεσκεν ἕκαστα
καί τε δέκ' ἀνθρώπων καί τ' εἴκοσιν αἰώνεσσιν.

_____

ἕκαστα Iamb. cod. Laur. F et Porph. : ἕκαστον Iamb. cod. Cizensis C (saec. XVI.)

For whenever he reached out with all his thinking organs, he easily saw all
the experiences of all beings in ten and in twenty human aiōnes.

---

265   On repetition combined with expansion as a key feature of Empedocles' poetical technique see Reinhardt 1916, 51–56.

266   On the interpretation of the 'time units' mentioned in the scholia as Empedoclean *aiōnes* see above, section 4.2.2.

267   Emp. fr. 66b MP, lines 276–8.

268   Emp. fr. 90 MP (B 129 DK), lines 4–6. That Empedocles is referring to Pythagoras here was first stated by Timaeus of Tauromenium and only occasionally doubted. See further Zhmud 2012, 39 n. 48.

At first glance, one might think of the myth of the Hyperborean Apollo here and of the series of his incarnations culminating in Pythagoras. On that reading of the lines, which underlies their traditional ascription to the 'Purifications', they would describe the range of past events remembered by Pythagoras as a result of the previous transmigrations of his soul, or rather, of the previous incarnations of Apollo. But Günther Zuntz correctly pointed out that the lines contain neither a specific reference to Pythagoras' previous reincarnations nor any indication that Pythagoras' extraordinary knowledge was restricted to *past* events, i.e., to *memory*; the point is, rather, to acknowledge Pythagoras' intellectual power which penetrated future and past alike.[269] Accordingly, the assignment of the fragment to the 'Purifications' was doubted by Leonid Zhmud,[270] and rightly so: the poem 'On Nature' featured, as we have argued, a Pythagorizing time-table according to which we are now living near the end of the twenty *aiōnes* of sexual reproduction during Strife's invasion, and approaching the final ten *aiōnes* of cosmic dissolution. Therefore, the reference to ten and twenty *aiōnes* speaks strongly in favour of assigning the fragment under review to that poem: The point seems to be that Pythagoras foresaw the impending ten *aiōnes* of cosmic dissolution and looked back to the twenty *aiōnes* of sexual reproduction. At the same time, however, Empedocles implicitly acknowledges, by associating Pythagoras with 'twenty and ten *aiōnes*', that it was Pythagoras who disclosed to the inner circle of his pupils the general scheme of the *tetraktys* which has now been applied to the cosmic cycle by Empedocles.

4.3   *Conclusion: A Pythagorizing Answer to Parmenides*

The philosophical problem Empedocles had to face was the need to reconcile what Parmenides had only juxtaposed by having the *aletheia*-part of his poem be followed by the *doxa*-part: an ontology emphasizing the ungenerated and imperishable nature of being and its indivisibility and unchangeability on the one hand, and a physics accounting for coming-to-be and passing-away and for change in general on the other. Empedocles seems to provide a deeper answer to the Parmenidean problem than hitherto assumed. He does not

---

269   Zuntz 1971, 209, commenting upon the last line of our quotation: '... this verse does not by itself refer to Pythagoras' ('ten or twenty'!) reincarnations—how could this reference possibly have been combined with the preceding clause 'whenever he strained with all his mind' [...]—but defines the range of his mental power: Pythagoras 'saw what happened in ten or twenty lives of men'; he was thus comparable to the seer who ἤιδει τά τ' ἐόντα τά τ'ἐσσόμενα πρό τ' ἐόντα (*Il.* 1.70)'.

270   Zhmud 2012, 40: 'there is, however, no certainty that B 129 does in fact belong to the *Purifications*; it could equally well be placed in the poem *On Nature*'.

PYTHAGOREAN RATIOS IN EMPEDOCLES' PHYSICS

content himself with ascribing the apparent coming-to-be and passing-away to the interaction of ungenerated and imperishable elements and powers and with mitigating the apparent divisibility of the elements by the original concept of elemental networks (*rhizōmata*). Rather, he emphasizes the pivotal role of simple numerical ratios on the cosmological as well as on the physiological level. It is this feature of his system which fully justifies Simplicius' claim about the importance of Pythagoreanism in Empedocles's physics. Not only the mixture of homoeomerous components in short-lived organisms but also the duration of the phases of the cosmic cycle, are based on numerical ratios involving the first four integers or their multiples. While his solution to the Parmenidean problem of course does not include the allegorical reading of the *Sphairos* as a timeless intelligible world that was suggested by later Platonists, Empedocles has subordinated the temporal durations of *all seven stages* of the cosmic cycle to the timeless mathematical structure of the Pythagorean *tetraktys*. In this sense he can even maintain that the four elements always subsist 'unmoved in accordance with the cycle':[271]

ταύτηι δ᾽ αἰὲν ἔασιν ἀκίνητοι κατὰ κύκλον.

Bibliography

Adler, Ada. 1935. *Suidae Lexicon* Pars IV: Π–Ψ. Leipzig: Teubner.

Asheri, David, Allan Lloyd, Aldo Corcella. 2007. *A Commentary on Herodotus. Books I–IV*. Edited by Oswyn Murray and Alfonso Moreno, Oxford: Oxford University Press.

Avezzù, Guido. 1982. *Alcidamante, Orazioni e frammenti*. Rome: "L'Erma" di Bretschneider.

Baldi, Davide. 2011. 'Nuova luce sul Riccardiano 46', in *Medioevo greco. Rivista di storia e filologia bizantina* 11, 13–22.

Baltes, Matthias. 1972. Timaios Lokros, *Über die Natur des Kosmos und der Seele*. Leiden: Brill.

Barker, Andrew. 2014. 'Pythagorean harmonics', in *A History of Pythagoreanism*, edited by Carl A. Huffman, 185–203. Cambridge: Cambridge University Press.

Bernays, Jacob. 1866. *Theophrastos' Schrift über Frömmigkeit: Ein Beitrag zur Religionsgeschichte mit kritischen und erklärenden Bemerkungen zu Porphyrios' Schrift über Enthaltsamkeit*. Berlin: Wilhelm Hertz.

Bidez, Joseph. 1894. *La biographie d'Empédocle*. Ghent: Clemm (Engelcke).

---

271   fr. 66b MP, line 244 (B 17 DK, line 13) = fr. 68b MP (B 26 DK), line 12.

Bignone, Ettore. 1916. *I poeti filosofi della Grecia. Empedocle: Studio critico, traduzione e commento delle testimonianze e dei frammenti.* Turin: Fratelli Bocca.

Buck, Carl Darling. 1955. *The Greek Dialects: Grammar, Selected Inscriptions, Glossary.* Chicago: University of Chicago Press.

Burkert, Walter. 1961. 'Hellenistische Pseudopythagorica', *Philologus* 105, 16–43 and 226–246.

Burkert, Walter. 1962. Review of Thesleff 1961, *Gnomon* 34, 763–768.

Burkert, Walter. 1967. Review of Thesleff 1965, *Gnomon* 39, 548–556.

Burkert, Walter. 1972. *Lore and Science in Ancient Pythagoreanism.* Translated by Edwin L. Minar, Jr. Cambridge, MA: Harvard University Press. (German original: 1962. *Weisheit und Wissenschaft: Studien zu Pythagoras, Philolaos und Platon*, Nuremberg: Hans Carl.)

Burkert, Walter. 2000. 'Neanthes von Kyzikos über Platon. Ein Hinweis aus Herculaneum', *MH* 57, 76–80.

Bury, Robert Gregg. 1935. *Sextus Empiricus: Against the Logicians*, with an English Translation. Loeb Classical Library, 291. Cambridge MA and London: Harvard University Press.

Busse, Adolf. 1897. *Ammonius: In Aristotelis De interpretatione commentarius.* Berlin: Georg Reimer.

Cambridge International Dictionary of English. 1995. Cambridge: Cambridge University Press.

Cardullo, Rosa Loredana. 2011. 'Empedocle πυθαγορικός. Un invenzione neoplatonica?', *λόγον διδόναι. La filosofia come esercizio del render ragione: Studi in onore di Giovanni Casertano*, edited by Lidia Palumbo, 817–839. Naples: Loffredo.

Centrone, Bruno. 2014. 'The pseudo-Pythagorean writings', in *A History of Pythagoreanism*, edited by Carl Augustus Huffman, 315–340. Cambridge: Cambridge University Press.

Cherniss, Harold. 1944. *Aristotle's Criticism of Plato and the Academy.* Volume I, Baltimore: The Johns Hopkins Press.

Chitwood, Ava. 1986. 'The Death of Empedocles', *AJP* 107, 175–191.

Chitwood, Ava. 2004. *Death by Philosophy: The Biographical Tradition in the Life and Death of the Archaic Philosophers Empedocles, Heraclitus, and Democritus.* Ann Arbor: University of Michigan Press.

Coxon, Allan Hartley. 1986. *The Fragments of Parmenides.* Assen/Maastricht: Van Gorcum.

Curd, Patricia. 1998. *The legacy of Parmenides: Eleatic monism and later presocratic thought.* Princeton: Princeton University Press.

Daiber, Hans. 1980. *Aetius Arabus. Die Vorsokratiker in arabischer Überlieferung.* Wiesbaden: Franz Steiner.

Degni, Paola. 2008. 'I manoscritti dello 'scriptorium' di Gioannicio', in *Segno e testo 6*, 179–248.

PYTHAGOREAN RATIOS IN EMPEDOCLES' PHYSICS 185

Delatte, Armand. 1915. 'La tétractys Pythagoricienne', in *Études sur la littérature Pythagoricienne*, edited by A. Delatte, 249–68. Paris: Honoré Champion.

Delatte, Armand. 1922. *La Vie de Pythagore de Diogène Laërce*. Brussels: Lamertin.

Deubner, Ludwig. 1937. *Iamblichi de vita pythagorica liber*. Leipzig: Teubner; (Second edition edited by Ulrich Klein. 1975. Stuttgart: Teubner.)

Diels, Hermann. 1879. *Doxographi Graeci*. Berlin: Georg Reimer.

Diels, Hermann. 1882. *Simplicii in Aristotelis physicorum libros quattuor priores commentaria*. Berlin: Georg Reimer.

Diels, Hermann. 1899. *Elementum: Eine Vorarbeit zum griechischen und lateinischen Thesaurus*. Leipzig: Teubner.

Diels, Hermann. 1901. *Poetarum philosophorum fragmenta*. Berlin: Weidmann.

Diels, Hermann. 1903. *Die Fragmente der Vorsokratiker: Griechisch und deutsch*. Berlin: Weidmann, ³1912.

Diels, Hermann and Walther Kranz. 1951. *Die Fragmente der Vorsokratiker: Griechisch und deutsch*. Sixth edition, Vol. 1. Berlin.

Diggle, James. 1970. *Euripides Phaethon*. Cambridge: Cambridge University Press.

Dorandi, Tiziano. 2007. 'Il Περὶ παλαιᾶς τρυφῆς attributo a Aristippo nella storia della biografia antica', in *Die griechische Biographie in hellenistischer Zeit*, edited by Michael Erler und Stefan Schorn, 157–72. Berlin and New York: De Gruyter.

Dorandi, Tiziano. 2013. *Diogenes Laertius Lives of Eminent Philosophers*. Cambridge: Cambridge University Press.

Dümmler, Ferdinand. 1889. *Akademika: Beiträge zur Litteraturgeschichte der Sokratischen Schulen*. Gießen: J. Ricker'sche Buchhandlung.

Edelstein, Ludwig and Ian Gray Kidd. 1989. *Posidonius I: The Fragments*. Second edition. Cambridge: Cambridge University Press.

Eitrem, Samson. 1915. *Opferritus und Voropfer der Griechen und Römer*. Kristiania: Jacob Dybwad.

Enache, Cătălin. 2008. 'Der unsichtbare Totengott', *RhM* N. S. 151, 61–82.

Engels, Johannes. 2007. 'Philosophen in Reihen: Die Φιλοσόφων ἀναγραφή des Hippobotos', in *Die griechische Biographie in hellenistischer Zeit*, edited by Michael Erler and Stefan Schorn, 173–94. Berlin and New York: De Gruyter.

Festa, Nicola. 1891. *Iamblichi De communi mathematica scientia liber*. Leipzig: Teubner. (Second edition edited by Ulrich Klein. 1975. Stuttgart: Teubner.)

Fine, Gail, 2016. 'The 'Two Worlds' Theory in the *Phaedo*', in *The British Journal for the History of Philosophy* 24/4, 557–573.

Fortenbaugh, William Wall, Pamela Margaret Huby, Robert William Sharples, and Dimitri Gutas. 1992. *Theophrastus of Eresus. Sources for his Life, Writings, Thought and Influence*. Part One: *Life, Writings, Various Reports, Logic, Physics, Metaphysics, Theology, Mathematics*. Leiden: Brill.

Garulli, Valentina. 2004. *Il Περὶ ποιητῶν di Lobone di Argo*. Bologna: Patròn.

Gigante, Marcello. 1983. 'Frammenti di Ippoboto. Contributo alla storia della storiografia filosofica', in *Omaggio a Piero Treves*, edited by Attilio Mastrocinque, 152–93. Padua: Antenore.

Groeneboom, Pieter. 1930. *Aeschylus' Persae*. Groningen and Den Haag: J.B. Wolters.

Hansen, Peter Allan and Ian Campbell Cunningham. 2009. *Hesychii Alexandrini Lexicon. Volumen IV: T–Ω*, Berlin and New York: De Gruyter.

Harder, Richard. 1926. *'Ocellus Lucanus': Text und Kommentar*, Berlin: Weidmann.

Heiberg, Johan Ludvig. 1894. *Simplicii In Aristotelis De caelo commentaria*. Berlin: Georg Reimer.

Heyne, Christan Gottlob. 1776. 'Vorrede', in *System der stoischen Philosophie*, Erster Theyl, edited by Dieterich Tiedemann, III–XVIII. Leipzig: Weidmanns Erben und Reich.

Hilgard, Alfred. 1889. 'Georgii Choerobosci diaconi et oecumenici magistri prolegomena et scholia in Theodosii Alexandrini canones isagogicos de flexione nominum subscriptis discrepantiis scripturae codicum', in *Theodosii Alexandrini canones, scholia, Sophronii Patriarchae Alexandrini excerpta*. Volumen prius: *Theodosii Canones et Choerobosci Scholia in Canones nominales continens*, edited by Alfred Hilgard, 101–417. Leipzig: Teubner.

Hiller, Eduard. 1878. *Theonis Smyrnaei Philosophi Platonici Expositio rerum mathematicarum ad legendum Platonem utilium*. Leipzig: Teubner.

Hubert, Kurt. 1938. *Plutarchi moralia, Vol. IV*. Leizpig: Teubner.

Huffman, Carl Augustus. 1993. *Philolaus of Croton: Pythagorean and Presocratic: A Commentary on the Fragmenta and Testimonia with Interpretive Essays*. Cambridge: Cambridge University Press.

Huffman, Carl Augustus. 2005. *Archytas of Tarentum. Pythagorean, Philosopher and Mathematician King*, Cambridge: Cambridge University Press.

Huffman, Carl Augustus. (ed.) 2014. *A History of Pythagoreanism*. Cambridge: Cambridge University Press.

Immisch, Otto. 1897. 'Char. XVI—Δεισιδαιμονίας ις′, in *Theophrasts Charaktere*, edited by Die Philologische Gesellschaft zu Leipzig, 120–34. Leipzig: Teubner.

Inwood, Brad. 1992. (Revised edition 2001). *The Poem of Empedocles: A Text and Translation with an Introduction*. Toronto, Buffalo and London: University of Toronto Press.

Isnardi Parente, Margherita. 1980. *Speusippo. Frammenti.* Edizione, traduzione e commento. Precedono testimonianze sull'Academia scelte e ordinate di Marcello Gigante, (= La Scuola di Platone, volume primo), Napoli: Bibliopolis.

Jacoby, Felix. 1926. *Die Fragmente der griechischen Historiker. Zweiter Teil: Zeitgeschichte, A: Universalgeschichte und Hellenika, Nr. 64–261*. Berlin: Weidmann.

Jacoby, Felix. 1950. *Die Fragmente der griechischen Historiker. Dritter Teil: Geschichte von Staedten und Voelkern, B: Autoren ueber einzelne Staedte (Laender), Nr. 297–607*. Leiden: Brill.

v. Jan, Karl. 1895. *Musici scriptores Graeci*. Leipzig: Teubner.

Kahn, Charles Henry. 1960. 'Religion and Natural Philosophy in Empedocles' Doctrine of the Soul', in *Archiv für Geschichte der Philosophie* 42, 3–35.

Kannicht, Richard and Bruno Snell. 1986. *Tragicorum Graecorum Fragmenta*. Vol. 1: *Didascaliae tragicae, Catalogi tragicorum et tragoediarum, Testimonia et fragmenta tragicorum minorum*. Editio correctior et addendis aucta. Göttingen: Vandenhoeck und Ruprecht.

Kannicht, Richard and Bruno Snell. 1980. *Tragicorum Graecorum Fragmenta*. Vol. 2: *Fragmenta adespota, testimonia volumini 1 addenda, indices ad volumina 1 et 2*. Göttingen: Vandenhoeck und Ruprecht.

Kannicht, Richard. 2004. *Tragicorum Graecorum Fragmenta*. Vol. 5: *Euripides*. Two volumes. Göttingen: Vandenhoeck und Ruprecht.

Kassel, Rudolf and Colin Austin. 1991. *Poetae Comici Graeci*. Vol. 2: *Agathenor—Aristonymus*. Berlin and New York: De Gruyter.

Kazhdan, Alexander Petrovich. 1991. 'Choirosphaktes, Leo', in *The Oxford Dictionary of Byzantium*, edited by A. Kazhdan, I, 425–6. Oxford: Oxford University Press.

Kerényi, Karl. 1937. 'Pythagoras und Orpheus', in *Aufsätze zur Geschichte der Antike und des Christentums*, edited by F. Altheim et al., 16–49. Berlin: Die Runde, 1937. (Reprinted 1996 in *Humanistische Seelenforschung*, 14–41. Stuttgart: Klett-Cotta.)

Kidd, Ian Gray. 1988. *Posidonius II. The Commentary: (ii) Fragments 150–293*. Cambridge: Cambridge University Press.

Kidd, Ian Gray. 1999. *Posidonius III. The Translation of the Fragments*. Cambridge: Cambridge University Press.

Kindstrand, Jan Fredrik. 1990. *[Plutarchi] De Homero*. Leipzig: Teubner.

Kingsley, Peter. 1994. 'Empedocles and his Interpreters: The Four-Element Doxography', in *Phronesis* 39/3, 235–254.

Kingsley, Peter. 1995. *Ancient philosophy, mystery, and magic: Empedocles and Pythagorean tradition*. Oxford: Oxford University Press.

Kingsley, Peter. 1996. 'Empedocles' Two Poems', *Hermes* 124/1, 108–111.

Kranz, Walther. 1938. 'Kosmos als philosophischer Begriff frühgriechischer Zeit', *Philologus* 93, 430–448.

Kucharski, Paul. 1952. *Étude sur la doctrine Pythagoricienne de la tétrade*. Paris: Les Belles Lettres.

Kühner, Raphael and Friedrich Blass. 1890–92. *Ausführliche Grammatik der Griechischen Sprache*, Erster Teil: Elementar- und Formenlehre. Third Edition. Two Volumes. Hannover: Hahnsche Buchhandlung.

Laks, André and Glenn Most. 2016. *Early Greek Philosophy. Volume V. Western Greek Thinkers Part 2*, Loeb Classical Library, 528. Cambridge MA and London: Harvard University Press.

Lang, Paul. 1911. *De Speusippi Academici Scriptis. Accedunt Fragmenta*. Dissertatio Inauguralis, Bonn: Carl Georgi.

Lefkowitz, Mary. 1981. *The Lives of the Greek Poets*. Baltimore MD: Johns Hopkins University Press.

LfgrE 1979: *Lexikon des frühgriechischen Epos* (LfgrE). Begründet von Bruno Snell, Band 1 (A), Göttingen.

Lohmann, Johannes. 1959. 'Der Ursprung der Musik', *Archiv für Musikwissenschaft* 16, 148–173, 261–291, and 400–403.

Lohmann, Johannes. 1970. *Musiké und Logos*: Aufsätze zur griechischen Philosophie und Musiktheorie. Edited by Anastasios Giannarás. Stuttgart: Musikwissenschaftliche Verlags-Gesellschaft.

LSJ 1996: *A Greek-English Lexicon*, compiled by Henry George Liddell and Robert Scott, revised and augmented throughout by Sir Henry Stuart Jones, with a revised supplement 1996, Oxford: Oxford University Press.

Maehler, Herwig. 1989. *Pindarus*. Pars II: *Fragmenta, Indices*. Leipzig: De Gruyter.

Mansfeld, Jaap. 1992a. *Heresiography in Context: Hippolytus' Elenchos as a Source for Greek Philosophy*. Leiden: Brill.

Mansfeld, Jaap. 1992b. '*Physikai doxai* and *problêmata physika from Aristotle to Aëtius* (and *Beyond*)', in *Theophrastus: His Psychological, Doxographical and Scientific Writings*, edited by William Wall Fortenbaugh and Dimitri Gutas, 63–111. New Brunswick NJ and London: Rutgers University Press. (Reprinted with additions in: Mansfeld/Runia 2010, 33–97.)

Mansfeld, Jaap. 1995. 'Critical Note: Empedocles and his Interpreters', *Phronesis* 40, 109–115 (Reprinted in: Mansfeld/Runia 2010, 333–40).

Mansfeld, Jaap and Oliver Primavesi. 2021. *Die Vorsokratiker*. Überarbeitete und erweiterte Neuausgabe. Stuttgart: Reclam.

Mansfeld, Jaap and David Theunis Runia. 1997. *Aëtiana: The Method and Intellectual Context of a Doxographer*. Volume One: *The Sources*, Leiden: Brill.

Mansfeld, Jaap and David Theunis Runia. 2010. *Aëtiana. The Method and Intellectual Context of a Doxographer*. Volume Three: *Studies in the Doxographcial Traditions of Ancient Philosophy*, Leiden: Brill.

Marcovich, Miroslav. 1986. *Hippolytus: Refutatio omnium haeresium*. Berlin and New York: De Gruyter.

Marcovich, Miroslav. 1990. *Athenagoras: Legatio pro Christianis*. Berlin and New York: De Gruyter.

Marg, Walter. 1972. *Timaeus Locrus, De natura mundi et animae*. Leiden: Brill.

Martin, Alain and Oliver Primavesi. 1999. *L' Empédocle de Strasbourg* (P. Strasb. gr. *Inv. 1665–1666), Introduction, edition et commentaire*. Berlin and New York: De Gruyter.

Mau, Jürgen. 1971. *Plutarchi Moralia*. Vol. V, Fasc. 2, Pars 1. Leipzig: Teubner.

Mertens, Dieter. 2006. *Städte und Bauten der Westgriechen. Von der Kolonisationszeit bis zur Krise um 400 vor Christus*. Munich: Hirmer.

Mirhady, David C. 2001. 'Dicaearchus of Messana: The sources, text and translation', in *Dicaearchus of Messana: Text, translation, and discussion*, edited by William Wall

Fortenbaugh and Eckart Schütrumpf, 1–142. New Brunswick and London: Rutgers University Press.

Moraux, Paul and Dieter Harlfinger, Dieter Reinsch, and Jürgen Wiesner. 1976. *Aristoteles Graecus: Die griechischen Manuskripte des Aristoteles*. Erster Band: Alexandrien–London. Berlin and New York: De Gruyter.

Müller, Carl Werner. 1965. *Gleiches zu Gleichem. Ein Prinzip frühgriechischen Denkens*. Wiesbaden: Harrassowitz.

O'Brien, Denis. 1969. *Empedocles' Cosmic Cycle. A Reconstruction from the Fragments and Secondary Sources*. Cambridge: Cambridge University Press.

O'Brien, Denis. 1981. *Pour interpréter Empédocle*, Paris and Leiden: Les Belles Lettres.

O'Meara, Dominic John. 2014. 'Iamblichus' *On the Pythagorean Life* in context', in *A History of Pythagoreanism*, edited by Carl Augustus Huffman, 399–415. Cambridge: Cambridge University Press.

Osborne, Catherine. 1987. 'Empedocles Recycled', *CQ* 37, 24–50.

Palmer, John. 2009. *Parmenides and Presocratic Philosophy*. Oxford: Oxford University Press.

Panzerbieter, Friedrich. 1844. 'Beiträge zur Kritik und Erklärung des Empedokles', in *Einladungs-Programm des Gymnasium Bernhardinum in Meiningen zu der öffentlichen Prüfung, welche am 26. und 27. März und zu der Schulfeierlichkeit, welche am 30. März zum Schluß des Schuljahrs im grossen Auditorium stattfinden wird*, 1–35. Meiningen: Hildburghausen, gedruckt bei Friedrich Wilhelm Gadow & Sohn.

Patzer, Harald. 1993. *PHYSIS. Grundlegung zu einer Geschichte des Wortes*. Stuttgart: Franz Steiner.

Primavesi, Oliver. 2002. 'Lecteurs antiques et byzantins d'Empédocle: De Zénon a Tzétzès', in *Qu'est-ce que la Philosophie Présocratique?*, edited by A. Laks and C. Louguet, 183–204. Villeneuve d'Ascq (Nord): Presses universitaires du Septentrion.

Primavesi, Oliver. 2006a. 'Empedokles in Florentiner Aristoteles-Scholien', *ZPE* 157, 27–40.

Primavesi, Oliver. 2006b. 'Die Suda über die Werke des Empedokles', *ZPE* 158, 61–75.

Primavesi, Oliver. 2006c. 'Apollo and Other Gods in Empedocles', in *La costruzione del discorso filosofico nell'età dei Presocratici/The Construction of Philosophical Discourse in the Age of the Presocratics*, edited by Maria Michela Sassi, 51–77. Pisa: Edizioni della Normale.

Primavesi, Oliver. 2007. 'Zur Überlieferung und Bedeutung des Empedokleischen Titels Καθαρμοί', in *Katharsiskonzeptionen vor Aristoteles*, edited by Martin Vöhler and Bernd Seidensticker, 183–225. Berlin and New York: De Gruyter.

Primavesi, Oliver. 2008. *Empedokles* Physika I. Berlin and New York: De Gruyter.

Primavesi, Oliver. 2013. '§13: Empedokles', in *Grundriss der Geschichte der Philosophie, Die Philosophie der Antike. Band 1: Frühgriechische Philosophie*, edited by Hellmut Flashar, Dieter Bremer und Georg Rechenauer, 667–739. Basel: Schwabe.

Primavesi, Oliver. 2014. 'Aristotle on the "so-called Pythagoreans": from lore to principles', in *A History of Pythagoreanism*, edited by Carl Augustus Huffman, 227–49. Cambridge: Cambridge University Press.

Primavesi, Oliver. 2016. 'Empedocles' Cosmic Cycle and the Pythagorean Tetractys', *Rhizomata* 4, 5–29.

Primavesi, Oliver. 2017a. 'Zur Genese der Tetraktys-Hypothese', in *Götter und Schriften rund ums Mittelmeer*, edited by Friedrich Kittler, Peter Berz, Joulia Strauss, and Peter Weibel, 83–103. Paderborn: Wilhelm Fink.

Primavesi, Oliver. 2017b. 'Tetraktys und Göttereid bei Empedokles: Der pythagoreische Zeitplan des kosmischen Zyklus', in *Götter und Schriften rund ums Mittelmeer*, edited by Friedrich Kittler, Peter Berz, Joulia Strauss, and Peter Weibel, 229–316. Paderborn: Wilhelm Fink.

Rashed, Marwan. 2001a. *Die Überlieferungsgeschichte der aristotelischen Schrift* De generatione et corruptione. Wiesbaden: Reichert.

Rashed, Marwan. 2001b. 'La chronographie du système d' Empédocle: documents byzantins', *Aevum antiquum* NS 1, 237–262.

Rashed, Marwan. 2014. 'La chronographie du système d' Empédocle: addenda et corrigenda', *Les Études philosophiques*, n° 3, 315–342.

Reinhardt, Karl. 1916. *Parmenides und die Geschichte der griechischen Philosophie*. Bonn: Friedrich Cohen.

Richardson, Nicholas James. 1974. *The Homeric Hymn to Demeter*. Oxford: Oxford University Press.

Richardson, Nicholas James. 1993. *The Iliad: A Commentary: Books 21–24*. Cambridge: Cambridge University Press.

Risch, Ernst. 1974. *Wortbildung der homerischen Sprache*. Second Edition. Berlin: De Gruyter.

Rohde, Erwin. 1898. *Psyche: Seelenkult und Unsterblichkeitsglaube der Griechen*. Second Edition. Two Volumes. Freiburg i.B., Leipzig, and Tübingen: J.C.B. Mohr (Paul Siebeck).

Rose, Valentin. 1886. *Aristotelis qui ferebantur librorum fragmenta*. Leipzig: Teubner.

Runia, David Theunis. 1999. 'A Brief History of the Term Kosmos Noétos from Plato to Plotinus', in *Traditions of Platonism: Essays in Honour of John Dillon*, edited by John J. Cleary, 151–72. Aldershot: Ashgate.

Runia, David Theunis. 2001. *Philo of Alexandria: On the Creation of the Cosmos according to Moses. Introduction, Translation and Commentary*. Leiden, Boston and Cologne: Brill.

Russell, Donald Andrew and Nigel Guy Wilson. 1981. *Menander Rhetor*. Oxford: Oxford University Press.

Schmidt, Moritz. 1862. *ΗΣΥΧΙΟΣ. Hesychii Alexandrini Lexicon:* Volumen Quartum: *Σ— Ω, Pars 1.* Jena: Friedrich Mauke.

Schorn, Stefan. 2004. *Satyros aus Kallatis: Sammlung der Fragmente mit Kommentar.* Basel: Schwabe.

Schorn, Stefan. 2007. ' "Periegetische Biographie"—"Historische Biographie" ': Neanthes von Kyzikos (FgrHist 84) als Biograph', in *Die griechische Biographie in hellenistischer Zeit,* edited by Michael Erler und Stefan Schorn, 115–56. Berlin and New York: De Gruyter.

Schorn, Stefan. 2014. 'Pythagoras in the historical tradition: from Herodotus to Diodorus Siculus', in *A History of Pythagoreanism,* edited by C.A. Huffman, 296–314. Cambridge: Cambridge University Press.

Schütrumpf, Eckart, Peter Stork, Jan van Ophuijsen, and Susan Prince. 2008. *Heraclides of Pontus. Texts and translation.* New Brunswick and London: Rutgers University Press.

Schweighäuser, Johann. 1804. *Animadversiones in Athenaei Deipnosophistas, Tomus Sextus. Animadvers. in lib. XI. et XII.* Strasburg: Typographia Societatis Bipontinae, Anno XII.

Schwyzer, Eduard. 1939. *Griechische Grammatik,* Erster Band: Allgemeiner Teil. Lautlehre. *Wortbildung. Flexion.* Munich: C.H. Beck.

Sieveking, Wilhelm. 1928. *Plutarchi Moralia Vol. II.3. De Iside et Osiride.* Leipzig: Teubner.

Snell, Bruno. 1944. 'Hera als Erdgöttin', *Philologus* 96, 159–160.

Steel, Carlos. 1997. *Priscian* On Theophrastus on Sense-Perception *with 'Simplicius'* On Aristotle On the Soul 2.5–12. Translated by Pamela Huby and Carlos Steel, in collaboration with J.O. Urmson, notes by Peter Lautner. London: Duckworth.

Strano, Gioacchino. 2008. *Leone Choirosphaktes: Corrispondenza. Introduzione, testo critico, traduzione e note di commento.* Catania: Centro studi sull'antico cristianesimo.

Szlezák, Thomas Alexander. 1972. *Pseudo-Archytas Über die Kategorien.* Berlin and New York: De Gruyter.

Tarán, Leonardo. 1981. *Speusippus of Athens: A Critical Study with a Collection of the Related Texts and Commentary,* Leiden: Brill.

Thesleff, Holger. 1961. *An Introduction to the Pythagorean Writings of the Hellenistic Period.* Åbo: Åbo Akademi.

Thesleff, Holger. 1965. *The Pythagorean Texts of the Hellenistic Period.* Åbo: Åbo Akademi.

Thompson, D'Arcy Wentworth. 1936. *A Glossary of Greek Birds.* Second Edition. Oxford: Oxford University Press.

Usener, Hermann. 1858. *Analecta Theophrastea.* Diss. Bonn.

Vuillemin-Diem, Gudrun and Marwan Rashed. 1997. „Burgundio de Pise et ses manuscrits grecs d'Aristote: Laur. 87.7 et Laur. 81.18", in *Recherches de Théologie et Philosophie médiévales* 64, 136–198.

Wellmann, Max. 1891. 'Alexander von Myndos', *Hermes* 26, 481–566.

West, Martin Litchfield. 1966. *Hesiod, Theogony.* Oxford: Oxford University Press.

v. Wilamowitz-Moellendorf, Ulrich. 1895. *Euripides Herakles. Zweite Bearbeitung.* Vol. II. Berlin: Weidmannsche Buchhandlung.

v. Wilamowitz-Moellendorf, Ulrich. 1929. 'Die Καθαρμοί des Empedokles', *Sitzungsberichte der Preußischen Akademie der Wissenschaften, phil.-hist. Klasse*, 1929, (XXVII), 626–61. Berlin: Verlag der Akademie der Wissenschaften.

Williams, Christopher John Fardo. 1982. *Aristotle's* De Generatione et Corruptione Oxford: Oxford University Press.

Wilson, Nigel Guy. 1983. "A mysterious Byzantine scriptorium: Ioannikios and his colleagues", *Scittura e civiltà* 7, 161–176.

Wright, Maureen Rosemary. 1981. *Empedocles: The Extant Fragments.* New Haven and London: Hackett.

Wyttenbach, Daniel. 1797. *Πλουτάρχου τοῦ Χαιρωνέως τὰ ἠθικά.* Plutarchi Chæronensis moralia, id est, opera, exceptis vitis, reliqua. Eight Volumes. Oxford: Oxford University Press.

Zajcev, Alexander. 1993. *Das griechische Wunder: Die Entstehung der griechischen Zivilisation.* Konstanz: Universitätsverlag Konstanz.

Zajcev, Alexander. 1996. 'Das „griechische Wunder" und sein Ende im Hellenismus', in *Hellenismus: Beiträge zur Erforschung von Akkulturation und politischer Ordnung in den Staaten des Hellenistischen Zeitalters,* edited by Bernd Funck, 693–700. Tübingen: J.C.B. Mohr (Paul Siebeck).

Zeller, Eduard and Wilhelm Nestle. 1920. *Die Philosophie der Griechen in ihrer geschichtlichen Entwicklung,* Erster Teil: *Allgemeine Einleitung. Vorsokratische Philosophie.* Zweite Hälfte. Sixth edition. Leipzig: O. R. Reisland.

Zhmud, Leonid. 2012. *Pythagoras and the Early Pythagoreans.* Oxford: Oxford University Press.

Zuntz, Günther. 1965. 'De Empedoclis librorum numero coniectura', *Mnemosyne*, Ser. IV, 18/4, 365.

Zuntz, Günther. 1971. *Persephone. Three Essays on Religion and Thought in Magna Graecia.* Oxford: Oxford University Press.

CHAPTER 6

Pythagoreanism and the History of Demonstration

Owen Goldin

According to Aristotle, to have scientific knowledge is to be able to offer a systematic body of demonstrations (*apodeixeis*), accounts which explain necessary and recurrent features of the world by showing how they follow from certain causally basic facts, which do not themselves demand explanation. The details of his account of scientific knowledge, laid out primarily in the *Posterior Analytics*, are, like many other aspects of Aristotle's thought, best understood as refutations and developments of the responses to certain philosophical puzzles that faced Aristotle's predecessors. Most notable among these is of course Plato, and recent work on the *Posterior Analytics* has concentrated on understanding the work as a response to, and development of, Platonic themes. Thus, Ferejohn has clarified how Aristotle fully works through the Socratic enterprise of showing how the answer to a "what is it" question grounds the answer to a "why is it" question.[1] Bronstein has shown how the *Posterior Analytics* can be understood as a series of nested solutions to the learner's paradox of Plato's *Meno*.[2] Both have explored how Aristotle adopts and adapts Plato's method of division as a crucial aspect of his own scientific methodology. But Aristotle has a number of additional philosophical predecessors, some of whom can be called "Presocratic," others of whom are contemporaries of Socrates or Plato. Aristotle's philosophical responses to what these other predecessors had to say in the fields of physics and metaphysics are well recognized: this is not so much the case with regard to issues in epistemology and the philosophy of science worked through in the *Posterior Analytics*. Perhaps this is because scholars have presumed that, although Presocratic and Pythagorean philosophers were engaged in doing science, they did not reflect on what theoretical or scientific knowledge is. The recognized exception here is Parmenides, as the first part of his poem concerns the "way of inquiry." Here, a goddess tells Parmenides that inquiry seeks an account of the form "it is," and this insight is of central importance to the nature of definition as developed by Plato and Aristotle. But no matter how one interprets Parmenides' poem, it offers little

---

1 Ferejohn 2013.
2 Bronstein 2016.

© KONINKLIJKE BRILL NV, LEIDEN, 2021 | DOI:10.1163/9789004443358_008

precedent for Aristotle's account of demonstration, which, goes beyond statements of the form "it is" insofar as it links such statements together to form a kind of deduction that reveals causal and conceptual relations.[3]

Nonetheless, Aristotle's theory of demonstration has significant precedent outside of the writings of Plato. This is to be found within the Pythagorean tradition. As Aristotle is aware, certain Pythagoreans thought that understanding, in the strict sense, demanded proofs and explanations. Aristotle himself provides evidence concerning the structure of the earliest such accounts, which appealed to a "table of opposites." The presence of one feature was inferred and explained on the basis of the presence of another feature with which the table associates it. Aristotle respects the table as a source of *endoxa*, the generally held beliefs that provide a starting point for dialectical inquiry,[4] but rejects the accounts based on them as not truly explanatory, on the grounds that they do not distinguish cause and effect. In this paper I argue that the later Pythagoreans Philolaus and Archytas did recognize that it is crucial to distinguish the principles, which are basic, and items that are derivative, which are made sense of as resultant from the principles. Even in its early stages, Greek mathematics provided examples of this. Aristotle's theory of demonstration can be understood as a way of integrating these Pythagorean and mathematical insights with the Socratic/Platonic account of definition.

In order to trace how Aristotle's theory of demonstration builds on and responds to the thought of his predecessors, we must first lay out the main lines of this theory, which, like Solmsen and Barnes,[5] I take to be independent of the theory of syllogism which is grafted onto it.

---

3   Granted, within Parmenides' poem the goddess does present an *argument* for her conclusion that the way of inquiry is that of "it is," and she does refer to her argument as an "elenchus" (DK B 7.5-6). As Lloyd writes: "The method, then, no less than the content, of the Way of Truth is revolutionary. ... He is the first thinker to set up a fundamental opposition between the senses and abstract argument or reason, and to express an unequivocal judgement on the relative trustworthiness of each," Lloyd 1979, 70–1. Nonetheless it is hard to see how the goddess could maintain that inquiry itself must proceed through a deduction. On a standard interpretation of Parmenides, according to which Parmenides is a "numerical monist," arguing that there is only one thing that can exist or be said, this would be impossible. Inquiry could not result in an elenchus insofar as any argument involves multiplicity of parts (unless the argument is a kind of ladder to be dispensed with). On the "numerical monist" interpretation, and for an argument against it, see Curd 1998.

4   See for example: *Ph.* 3.2 201b24-7, *Metaph.* Γ 2 1004b27-1005a5.

5   Solmsen 1928; Barnes 1981, 17–59. Ferejohn does not go so far as to posit a demonstrative theory that had been worked out prior to the development of the syllogistic, but suggests that the term *apodeixis* in *An. post.* 1.2 is being used in a preliminary sense that does not presuppose syllogistic theory. "I interpret the noun *apodeixis* and its derivatives in these early chapters to

PYTHAGOREANISM AND THE HISTORY OF DEMONSTRATION

1) Many regular, necessary features of the world are learned only by virtue of a certain kind of discursive logos, which reveals the relationships that hold among certain features of the world. This logos is called a demonstration (*apodeixis*) (*An. post.* 1 2 71b17-9).

2) Demonstration must rest on insights that do not demand demonstration. Aristotle calls these principles (*arkhai*) (*APo.* 1 2 71b20-4).

3) A demonstration explains by showing how the derivative features of the world can be inferred from the principles, which are causally basic. For this reason, a demonstration distinguishes causally basic realities from those that are derivative (*APo.* 1 2 71b29-33).

4) An adequate demonstration fully works through all of the relevant relations. A demonstration can make no appeal to any demonstrable feature of the world that is not itself demonstrated on the basis of indemonstrables (*APo.* 1 2 72a6-8).

Even independent of the application of syllogistic theory, there is of course much more to Aristotle's theory of demonstration than this. He has much to say on the various kinds of principles, and the method by which one should inquire into what the principles are and what demonstrations are to be based on them. But it is the above four characteristics of demonstration that are anticipated in Pythagorean thought.I take up each of these points in turn.

1 Demonstration

A passage from Iamblicus' *On the General Mathematical Science*, generally accepted as having been derived from Aristotle's lost writings on the Pythagoreans,[6] distinguishes between the *mathematikoi* and the *akousmatikoi*. The *mathematikoi* take the distinction between the varieties of Pythagoreanism to derive from different ways that Pythagoras himself conveyed his teachings.

> Pythagoras came from Ionia, more precisely from Samos, at the time of the tyranny of Polycrates, when Italy was at its height, and the first men of the city-states became his associates. The older of these [men] he addressed in a simple style, since they, who had little leisure on account of their being occupied in political affairs, had trouble when he conversed with them in terms of learning (*mathēmata*) and demonstrations

---

the generic notion of epistemic justification and not specifically to the syllogistic theory of justification developed later in the treatise." Ferejohn 2013, 75, n. 27.

6 See Burkert 1972, 195–200; Huffman 2015, Horky 2013, 16–7.

(*apodeixeis*). He thought that they would fare no worse if they knew what to do, even if they lacked the reason (*aitia*) for it, just as people under medical care fare no worse when they do not additionally hear the reason why they are to do each thing in their treatment. The younger of these [men], however, who had the ability to endure the education, he conversed with in terms of demonstrations and learning. So, then, these men [i.e. the mathematicians] are descended from the latter group, as are the others [i.e. the akousmatics] from the former group

IAMBLICHUS, *On the General Mathematical Science* 77.4–8[7]

The Pythagoreans were a kind of brotherhood, bound by a lifestyle of ritual prohibitions and prescriptions. Most of the elements of this lifestyle, as expressed in the *akousmata*,[8] seem arbitrary to us, and no doubt were so considered by the Pythagoreans'contemporaries. What reasons could there be behind these rules? Why not eat beans? Why not pick up food that fell on the floor (Diogenes Laertius, *Lives of the Philosophers* 8.34)? For each rule, there are three alternatives: it is indeed arbitrary, it is a means to some end (unknown to us), or following it is an intrinsic good (although we cannot recognize that). The Pythagoreans surely did not accept these rules as arbitrary. Aristotle reports that there were causes (*aitiai*) behind them which were sometimes made explicit and sometimes not,[9] but not everyone was capable of grasping these causes. The behaviors are prescribed for extrinsic purposes (when they are for the sake of something that results from the behaviors) or for intrinsic purposes (when the behaviors are themselves good, regardless of their result).[10] It is not hard to imagine a defense of religious or cultural taboos as habituating one in self-control, a disposition which is a good external to the acts in question.[11] But we see no evidence among the Pythagoreans for such a justification.[12] We can

---

7   Horky 2013, 15–6.

8   On the *akousmata* see especially Burkert 1972, 166–92. Many are collected in DK A 58C, Boehm 1905 and Dumont 1988.

9   See Iamblichus *VP* 86, also derived from Aristotle: "In some cases an account is appended concerning why this must be done (ἐπιλέγεται τί δεῖ), for example, one must bear offspring in order to leave another in one's place, to serve the gods, but for others there is no additional account."

10   Cf. Plato, *Resp.* 2 357b-d, Aristotle, *Eth. Nic.* 1 1 1094a3-5.

11   On this see Maimonides, *Guide for the Perplexed* Book 3, chapter 33.

12   Granted, DL 8.1.34, quoting Iamblichus, in turn quoting Aristotle, does relate that the prohibition against picking up food that has fallen on the floor might be for the sake of habituating oneself against gluttony, but the suggestion that the prescription is for the sake of habituation was tentatively put forward by Aristotle, for whom habituation is key in ethical training, and he does suggest another possibility: the crumbs are "on the side of

PYTHAGOREANISM AND THE HISTORY OF DEMONSTRATION

infer that the elements of the Pythagorean lifestyle were themselves taken to be good, either for the individual or the community. Nonetheless, the fragment from Aristotle tells us that there was some reasoning behind them, which, except for the most straightforward cases (like the obligation to have children) only the intellectual elite were in a position to learn. What form do these *logoi* take? Aristotle, if not the Pythagoreans themselves, called the accounts that revealed their purpose "demonstrations." So two major questions arise. First, what light is shed on them from the fact that they were called "demonstrations"? Surely Aristotle does not think that they constitute demonstrations in his strict sense. We are led to consider how the term "demonstration" (*apodeixis*) was used prior to Aristotle, especially in theoretical contexts. Second, to what extent can we reconstruct the form that these demonstrations take?

We begin with the term *apodeixis*. The verb *apodeiknunai* has the basic sense of "showing forth." Its earliest uses were in regard to cases in which one, via a speech, revealed something that would have been otherwise concealed or in dispute. It is distinguished from an *epideixis*, which, according one of the senses of the term,[13] is a showing off of the speaker, in order to reveal his or her abilities; rhetoricians would customarily give an *epideixis* to an audience of prospective students, in order to display the speaker's rhetorical abilities. An *apodeixis*, in contrast, shows something about the world, not the speaker; it shows that something is the case.[14] Especially illustrative here is the use of *apodeixis* in the proemium of Herodotus' *Histories*:

> This is the display of the inquiry (ἱστορίης ἀπόδεξις) of Herodotus of Halicarnassus, so that things done by man not be forgotten in time, and that great and marvelous deeds, some displayed by the Hellenes, some by the barbarians, not lose their glory, including among others what was the cause (δι᾽ ἣν αἰτίην) of their waging war on each other.

As events recede into the past, it is up to Herodotus to inquire what happened and why. The *apodeixis* that Herodotus offers is an account not only of what happened, but also of why it happened. It reveals the cause (*aitia*) of the war, the deeds that were responsible for it.[15]

---

someone's death" (ἐπὶ τελευτῇ τινος). I am not sure what this means but the preposition ἐπί suggests a tabular association with death, instead of life.

13   See Plato, *Grg.* 447a–c.

14   On this see Huffman 2005 and Thomas 2000, 221–8.

15   On this see especially Nagy 1994, 215–29.

The Hippocratic writings also employ *apodeixis*. Sometimes the term is used not to refer to a kind of logos, but to a state or process that results in a perceptible result or symptom, referred to as the object of ἀποδεικνύναι.[16] So in this case the demonstrator is the cause; what is demonstrated is an effect. But the writings also use the term in the sense familiar from Herodotus, as referring to a spoken or written exposition,[17] sometimes to such an exposition that justifies its conclusions on the basis of argument, especially a discourse that reveals the causes of things.[18] In this case what is demonstrated is the existence of an underlying condition, which is the cause of the symptoms. (In both cases the usage differs from that of Aristotle, according to which, the object of ἀποδεικνύναι is the effect whose cause is revealed in the demonstration.) As Lloyd has emphasized,[19] these medical writings are not so different in form from legal speeches in regard to rhetorical strategy. The medical author, like the orators in the law courts, is offering an account in a forum in which that account competes with others. As in the courtroom, the account given is intended to reveal what happened and why it happened. Insofar as a demonstration shows something, there is something that is shown. Because what becomes manifest through a demonstration is not illusory, a demonstration has a true conclusion, for which reason the term is often rendered as "proof."[20] Thus, the author of *On the Nature of Man* repeatedly indicates that his goal is to prove or demonstrate (ἀποδεικνύναι) what the constituents of the human body are, why their interactions have certain results, and that the conclusions drawn follow of necessity from his account.[21] There is an emphasis on the necessity of what is said to be demonstrated, suggesting that one mark of demonstration is the necessity of the conclusion drawn, but as Lloyd points out, it is unclear what this necessity is: (The necessity of the inference to the conclusion? The necessity of the fact in question, itself? Something else?). It is accordingly unclear exactly what it means to call an account a demonstration.[22]

---

16   Examples include *VM* 19.41; *Fract.* 19, 10,12; 31.31; *Prorrh.* 2 15,3.

17   *De Arte*, 3.3, 9.

18   *Nat. Hom*, 2.23; 5.26.

19   Lloyd 1987, 83–108.

20   See for example the Loeb translations of the passages cited in n. 18 above in Jones 1931. As Thomas 2000, 222 points out, "proof" in such contexts is "nearer to the sense of 'show[ing] decisively' than formal proof."

21   See Lloyd 1987, 114–23.

22   Lloyd 1987, 120: "Clearly, logical and physical, conceptual and causal, necessity are not here differentiated. Many instances represent a conflation of one or more ideas that we might distinguish. Often the underlying idea seems merely to be the claim that something is always or usually the case. At the limit, the addition of the term *necessarily* appears to reflect little more than the writer's desire to assert his point with emphasis."

The term *apodeixis* is however sometimes used to refer to purported proofs or arguments based on probabilities (of which the conclusion is that something is the case, not that something is probably the case). For example, at *Phaedo* 92d and *Theaetetus* 162e, Plato uses the term to refer to a variety of argument that encompasses proofs based on probabilities, of which the conclusions lack certainty, and for that reason might be false. Similarly, within the *Rhetoric* Aristotle considers enthymeme a variety of demonstration, understood as an inferential variety of *pistis* (a means employed by a speaker to persuade a listener to do something or endorse a view).[23] "Enthymeme" here does not have the sense that it does in later rhetorical theory (a syllogism with a missing premise); rather, the term refers to any speech that derives its appeal from its argumentative structure.[24] A conclusion is inferred on the basis of at least one agreed-upon premise, and in this way the conclusion is shown to be the case. Since Aristotle recognizes that successful rhetorical speeches need not argue for a true conclusion, when he says that an enthymeme is an *apodeixis*, he is not using *apodeixis* in the strict sense of the *Posterior Analytics*, or even in the somewhat looser sense of the *Topics* (1.1 100a26-7) according to which demonstration is marked by having principles that are primary in justification but not, as in *Posterior Analytics*, primary in explanation. The term *apodeixis* as applied to an enthymeme is equivocal, like the term "eye" when applied to a formerly living eye that is no longer able to see,[25] or to the image of an eye;[26] perhaps in English scare quotes would be employed.

The term *apodeixis* can be used to refer to an argument with a false conclusion. Because there is no evidence that Aristotle himself accepted the prohibitions and prescriptions, the validity of which was "demonstrated" by the *mathematikoi*, we can conclude that in the passage from Iamblichus in question he is using the term in this derivative sense, to refer to purported

---

23   Aristotle, *Rh.* 1.1 1355a4-8: ἐπεὶ δὲ φανερόν ἐστιν ὅτι ἡ μὲν ἔντεχνος μέθοδος περὶ τὰς πίστεις ἐστίν, ἡ δὲ πίστις ἀπόδειξίς τις (τότε γὰρ πιστεύομεν μάλιστα ὅταν ἀποδεδεῖχθαι ὑπολάβωμεν), ἔστι δ' ἀπόδειξις ῥητορικὴ ἐνθύμημα, καὶ ἔστι τοῦτο ὡς εἰπεῖν ἁπλῶς κυριώτατον τῶν πίστεων, τὸ δ' ἐνθύμημα συλλογισμός τις, "Since it is clear that the inquiry fitting for a *tekhnē* concerns ways of inducing conviction, and a way of inducing conviction is a kind of *apodeixis* (for we have the highest degree of conviction when we take something to have been subject to an *apodeixis*, and since an enthymeme is a rhetorical demonstration, and this is, so to speak, the most important mode of persuasion, and an enthymeme is a kind of deduction ...".

24   On this see Burnyeat 2016, 3–56.

25   Aristotle, *De an.* 2.1 412b20-1.

26   See Aristotle *Cat.* 1 1a2-3.

proofs that this or the other obligation is binding, by showing how the obligations follow from certain reasons (*aitiai*).

Aristotle is contrasting the *akousmatikoi* and the *mathematikoi* on the grounds that the former accepted certain doctrines and strictures simply because they were asserted. They would be the ones who, purportedly, backed up certain views simply by saying "*ipse dixit*": "that's what he said."[27] The *mathematikoi*, in contrast, gave more: an account by which the point at issue is inferred. This signals a significant juncture in the history of epistemology. The early Pythagoreans are the first Greek thinkers to show an explicit awareness of the distinction between two kinds of nonempirical belief: that accepted on the basis of testimony, and that accepted on the basis of some sort of reasoning. The latter is signaled as preferable. The Pythagoreans have taken a step towards the teaching of the *Theaetetus* that knowledge (*epistēmē*) is a belief plus something else, a *logos*, a direct antecedent to the common though much disputed definition of knowledge as justified true belief.

2   Inference

The second key feature of a demonstration, as Aristotle accounts for it, is that it is inferential. To what extent is this anticipated in the Pythagorean tradition?

We need to be careful here, as Aristotle himself is the first to articulate the notion of inference, when he defines a *sullogismos* as "a *logos* in which, from certain things being posited, something different from what was posited necessarily follows, from their being the case" (*An. pr.* 1.1 24b18-20). As has been often noted, this definition encompasses far more than the notion of syllogism, as Aristotle analyzes it within the *Prior Analytics*, for which reason it is often translated as "deduction." Any argument offered as a proof or demonstration would meet this definition, but nothing is thereby said about the form the argument must take, or of how exactly the conclusion is thought to follow from the premises. The notion of deduction implicit in earlier conceptions of demonstration is inchoate and nontechnical. Further, there is no evidence of anyone prior to Aristotle holding the view that a deduction proper involves more than one premise. But even if drawing a conclusion from a single premise (as in the conversion of a predication) is to count as a deduction, surely a deduction, demonstrative or otherwise, cannot consist in a monadic indication of some being (like the Parmenidean ἔστι). Nor could it be something said

---

27   DL 8.1.46.

PYTHAGOREANISM AND THE HISTORY OF DEMONSTRATION   201

that leads the mind from one being to another in a single jump – how would such a jump be rational? How would the second feature be "shown"? We need a notion of logical form, some sort of structure or rule that determines how one can infer the existence of one sort of thing from the existence of another, supplemented by the indication of that first kind of thing. We see precisely this sort of logic in Aristotle's report concerning the early Pythagoreans.

In earlier work I have argued that the "table of opposites" attributed to "the Pythagoreans" in Aristotle's *Metaphysics* A 5 986a23-4 is an authentic Pythagorean representation of the relationships thought to hold among associated characteristics.[28] On the basis of both textual and anthropological evidence I argued that the table is a diagram expressing a world view shared by many prescientific peoples: all features of reality can be classified as having either positive or negative value. The table of opposites can be used to show why certain features of the world, found in the same column, are found together. It can also show why such features of the world ought to go together.[29] The relationship between two items in the same column is apparently symmetrical; there is no indication that one is more causally basic than the other.[30]

It is likely that the conceptual correlations found in the table is the source not only of a number of accounts making sense of a number of features of the world, but also of many of the prescriptions, prohibitions, and ritual practices that constituted the Pythagorean lifestyle. For example, the version of the table that Aristotle preserves for us has the good, and the right, on the right-hand column. This means that the right is good, the good is right. Such an association is the source not only of the widespread European belief that righthandedness is the norm, not only in the sense that most people are right

---

28   Goldin 2014, 171–193.

29   A common way of expressing the view that one item A ought to be with another item, B, is to say that A ἁρμόττει B (in the dative). *Harmonia* is of course a crucial notion in later Pythagorean thought. Although we do not have direct evidence for this, it is not inconceivable that earlier Pythagoreans would have employed this term in regards to items in the same column of the Table of Opposites. The first clear reference to the notion of *harmonia* among the presocratics is in the fragments of Philolaus, for whom features of the world are to be explained on the basis of the fitting together of opposites, classified as limits and unlimited (DK B 6). This is an advance over the kind of dualism found in the Doxa section of Parmenides' poem, which I take to be a simplification of the ontological scheme implicit in the table of opposites, according to which opposed opposites and their associated features exclude each other. But Pythagorean interest in musical scales and their mathematical basis predated Philolaus, and it is not inconceivable that the general strategy of explaining order and structures through the appropriate fitting together of disparate aspects of the world did so as well.

30   On this see Goldin 2014.

handed, but also in the sense that right-handedness is normative – that people should be right-handed–a belief which results in the once widespread practice of forcing children to write with their right hands, contrary to their inclinations.[31] I propose that the sort of account that would justify this (the right hand is κρεῖττον, which means both "stronger" and "better") would underlie the Pythagorean prescription that one ought to enter a temple with the right foot, Iamblichus (*VP* 156, 5–9.) Rightness and goodness correspond; entering with the left foot would show that one does not recognize either the special characteristics of where one was going, or the special characteristics of the right side. Similarly, one ought not to injure the good, and, since white is ranked with the good, one ought not to slaughter a white rooster.[32] This sort of account, I propose, would be of the sort of proof (*apodeixis*) that, according to the above passage, the *mathematikoi* possessed, and the *akousmatikoi* did not, by which some sense was made of the Pythagorean way of life. That the Pythagoreans employed their table in this way is confirmed by means of Aristotle's occasional citations of how it was employed in Plato's Academy. To pick a familiar example, within the *Nicomachean Ethics* Aristotle appeals to how the unlimited and the bad were in the same column (2.6 1106b28-35). He does so to indicate that what deviates from limit is bad, and that bad states of character deviate from limit. Aristotle appeals to the Pythagorean table in dialectical support of his own account of why actions without limit are bad: a mean is a kind of a limit, and it is the action in accordance with that limit that is rational and accordingly partially constitutive of the human good, happiness. Although for Aristotle, *limit* is the cause of goodness, and not vice versa, this is not the case for the Pythagoreans of the table of opposites. As noted above, in the Pythagorean table, the relationship between two items in the same column is symmetrical; there is no priority.[33] The good and the limit, or the good and the right, have equal status as being present on the same column of the table of opposites.

Given both a feature that is listed on the table, and the table, one can infer, as it were, the presence of another feature listed in the same column. We see here a kind of protologic making possible a kind of deduction, which Aristotle

---

31   On this see Lloyd 1962, 56–66; repr. with additional material in 1991, 27–48.

32   The logic here is explicitly given in DL 8.34.10. A number of other *akousmata*, such as "do not urinate turning toward the sun" (Iamblichus, *Protrep.* 115.19–20) are open to such interpretations.

33   It seems to have been Speusippus who understood one of the columns as that of the good, and the other column that of the bad, prioritizing good and bad as the chief items in the right and left columns, accordingly. See Goldin 2015, n. 3, 7, and 41.

PYTHAGOREANISM AND THE HISTORY OF DEMONSTRATION

would have regarded as a "demonstration," that reveals the reasons behind Pythagorean commands and prohibitions.

3 Causation

As we have seen, the protologic of the Pythagorean table of opposites allows the mind to move from the existence of one feature of the world to the other, but neither one column of the table nor the other is taken to be causally basic. Consider how "right" and "male" are both in the same column. From "right" one can infer "male" and vice versa. This obviously cannot be intended to hold in all cases: even if someone's father had been to the right, and one's mother to the left, the correlation will be disproven as soon as one's point of view pivots 180 degrees. (That is not of course to deny that the correlation might be understood as having normative force, according to which the man should be on the right from some determinate point of view.) But it does suggest that there will be certain key situations in which the correlation will be observed. Suggestive here is the assertion of Parmenides, whom ancient historiographers associated with the Pythagoreans (DL 9.3.21), that males develop on the right side of the uterus; females on the left (DK B 17). The issue is not even broached as to whether the side of the uterus determines gender or whether a baby of a certain gender moves to one side of the uterus; the two simply go together, just as throughout Parmenides' account of the way of seeming, certain characteristics are identified with light and others with darkness.[34]

Although the table likely predates Pythagorean mathematical researches, it is interesting to note that there is mutual entailment in many mathematical contexts as well. So, in geometry, if one can often infer a conclusion from a premise, one can often infer a premise from a conclusion. For example, one can infer that two lines on a plane are parallel on the basis of the fact that a line that intersects both results in opposite interior angles, and one can infer that the intersecting line results in opposite interior angles on the basis of the initial lines being parallel. Aristotle points out that this is what makes geometrical analysis possible (*An. post.* 1.12 78a6-13). But Aristotle also recognizes causal hierarchy. This is why he insists that the upward and the downward paths of inference must be sharply distinguished (*Eth. Nic.* 1.4 1095a31-b1): in a proper demonstration in geometry or any other science, the premises express the

---

34   In DK B 9, Parmenides goes so far as to say that all things have been named light and darkness, and thereby identifies (or says that mortals identify) all correlative characteristics, an uncompromising dualism that is alien to earlier Pythagorean thought.

cause by which one can explain why the conclusion holds (*An. post.* 1.2 71b20-2). Those propositions that express the basic truths, on the basis of which one can explain derivative truths, are principles (*archai*) (*Metaph.* Δ 1 1013a14-6).

As we have already noted, this distinction between principles and derivative truths is absent from the early Pythagorean scheme represented in the table of opposites. If the "demonstrations" of the validity of Pythagorean precepts did indeed employ the table, Aristotle's report that the *mathematikoi* offered demonstrations that revealed their causes must be interpreted as quasi-inferential (with the table, and the presence of one opposite as "posited," and a correlative opposite as quasi-deduced) but falling short of his notion of demonstration insofar as it does not reveal an *aitia* that stands in an asymmetrical relation with what is demonstrated. According to a world view that "explains" by means of symmetrical associations and linkages, neither of the associated items are the cause of each other.

At what point does an asymmetric notion of causation become clear in Greek philosophy? All human beings, of course, make appeal to some things being responsible for other things in contexts where this is not reversible. The most obvious case is that of the responsibility of human beings for their actions. (It is no accident that the primary sense of *aitia* is responsibility or blame, especially in a legal context.) The question before us however is the point at which people become explicitly aware of the asymmetric character of causation. Plato is clearly aware of the asymmetry of cause and effect, even if the varieties of causation are not distinguished in as clear and clean a matter as they are in Aristotle. Forms are responsible for certain features of the things that participate in them, while the participants are not responsible for the character of the Forms. Soul, regarded by Plato as a self-mover, is responsible for motion of moved things but the moved is not responsible for the motion of soul. Plato's argument for the necessity of a self-mover at *Phaedrus* 245c-e would make no sense without this asymmetry.

But does the recognition of the asymmetry of cause and effect date from before Plato? The fragmentary state of the evidence, and the fact that most of it is testimony, freely employing later vocabulary, makes this hard to say. If, as Aristotle indicates,[35] the Milesians did indeed employ the term *arkhē*, it was in the manner of mythological accounts like that of Hesiod, referring to the origin or source from which things come to be.[36] Every origin is indeed asymmetric with that which originates from it, but, although Aristotle takes the term *arkhē*

---

35   *Metaph.* A 5 983b6ff.

36   On this see Graham 2016, 58.

PYTHAGOREANISM AND THE HISTORY OF DEMONSTRATION   205

to be synonymous with *aition* (as both cause and explanation, see *Metaph.* Δ 1 1013a16-17) it is not clear what relation the notion of as origin, as employed by early Greek philosophers, might have to that of a cause, that is, that which is responsible or is indicated as the answer to a "why" question.[37]

There is evidence that this realization has a source within the Pythagorean tradition itself, in the thought of Philolaus. We begin with another passage from Iamblichus, also generally agreed to have been largely derived from Aristotle:

> The Pythagoreans devoted themselves to mathematics. They both admired the accuracy of its reasonings, because it alone among things that humans practice contains demonstrations, and they saw that general agreement is given in equal measure to theorems concerning attunement (τὰ περὶ τὴν ἁρμονίαν), because[38] they are [established] through numbers, and to mathematical studies that deal with vision, because they are [established] through diagrams. This led them to think that these things and their principles are quite generally the causes of existing things. Consequently, these are what anyone who wishes to comprehend things in existence – how they are – should turn their attention to, namely numbers and geometrical forms of existing things and proportions, because everything is made clear through them. So, then, by attaching the powers of each thing to the causes and primaries – only things that were less opportune or less honorable than them – they defined other things too in nearly the same manner. Therefore, their education in numbers and the objects of mathematics seemed to come through these subjects and in this general sketch. Such was also the method of demonstrations among them, which both began from such principles and thus attained fidelity and security in their arguments.[39]

Here we are told that the *logoi* of the *mathematikoi*, identified at *VP* 77.9–10 as demonstrations, gain their "fidelity and security" by virtue of identifying

---

37   Significantly, another source reports that Hipparchus employed the notion of a *arkhē* to refer to a geometrical premise, albeit not an ultimate one. On this see Huffman 2006, 83–4: "What is important about this is that it indicates that in the latter part of the fifth century mathematics had advanced far enough to distinguish between more and less fundamental propositions and was concerned to try to determine a set of first principles." Hipparchus may well have taken a geometrical principle to not only be that out of which a proof arises, but a kind of epistemological cause, that which, when appropriately grasped, in the context of a proof, is the cause of one's cognitive grasp of the proven proposition.

38   Retaining ὅτι.

39   Iamblichus, *On the General Mathematical Science* 78.8-26, tr. Horky 2013, 31.

necessary relationships that hold among certain "powers." Pythagorean demonstration restricts itself to working through the relationships that hold among the characteristics (or "powers") that in turn are "attached to" those primaries that are their ontological ground. Insofar as we are not told what the primary entities or powers are, we might suspect that we have an appeal to the Pythagorean table of opposites as a universal explanatory scheme. What is new here is the assertion that these *mathematikoi* were mathematicians in our sense. They dealt with numbers, which allowed them to account for the fittingness (*harmonia*) of things,[40] and with geometrical features of things, which ground accounts of optics. The Pythagorean table of opposites, as it is reported by Aristotle, included odd and even, which are likely what is referred to here as principles of number. But the table included much more. Odd and even did not have a privileged role. Aristotle is here talking about a different group of Pythagoreans, who do give number a special role.

The question of when certain Pythagoreans took special interest in, and did original research in mathematics is highly contested. But it is clear that Philolaus plays an important role in the development of Pythagorean mathematics, and that it was due to his thought that Pythagoreanism came to be closely associated with the study, not just of mathematics in general, but the study of *number*.

Again, much of the evidence derives from Aristotle, who says that some Pythagoreans, identified only as different from the ones who posited the table of opposites, took the principles of all things to be numbers, which are said to be causes in the sense of the *matter* out of which other things are constituted (*Metaph.* A 5 985b23-986a21). Following Burkert, most scholars agree Aristotle has in mind Philolaus, or Pythagoreans closely associated with him.[41] Philolaus' Fr.4 survives as partial collaboration: "And indeed all things that are known have number. For it is not possible that anything whatsoever be understood or known without this."[42] It is a difficult and complex issue as to whether Aristotle is right to interpret Philolaus as ascribing to number the key ontological role as that out of which things are composed, or whether, as Huffman has argued (on the basis of a minimalistic reading of this fragment), Philolaus grants to number only an epistemological role (insofar as all things are known through number).[43] On the more expansive reading, Philolaus can be credited

---

40 There is here a possible reference to the sort of numerical fittingness responsible for musical modes.

41 Burkert 1972, 218–38.

42 Trans. Huffman 2016.

43 Huffman 2006, 172–6.

with the insight that the principles of explanation and intelligibility are also causal principles of reality. I am sympathetic to this traditional interpretation; after all, Parmenides had already declared that "the same thing is for being and thinking (*noein*)" (fr. 3), and his influence was already pervasive at the time of Philolaus' writing. The matter is however uncertain, and even if we accept Huffman's more conservative account of Philolaus, we can see the latter playing a crucial role in the development of the theory of demonstration.

Historians of science are agreed that even if the numerical basis of the musical scale was not known to Pythagoras, it was to Philolaus, and is presumably a paramount example of what is known by number. The octave, for example, is known by the numerical ratio of 2 to 1. Is the "demonstration" that a musical octave corresponds to this ratio a demonstration in a stricter sense than that we have been able to attribute to the earlier *mathematikoi*, according to which the demonstration makes some feature of the world intelligible by showing how it belongs to a kind of thing that accompanies another thing? Does the demonstration isolate the ratio as the cause of the octave? That is not clear. If in fact Aristotle is right and these Pythagoreans took number to be the basic entities and other things to be derivative entities, the latter would be caused by the former, and the demonstrations at issue would, like Aristotelian demonstrations, explain an effect as arising necessarily from a cause. But Fr. 4 alone does not enable us to draw this conclusion, especially if interpreted minimalistically, as Huffman does. For inferences on the basis of the association between numbers and qualitative features can go in both directions. Cut a monochord string in half; one knows one will get an octave. Play an octave interval on a monochord; one knows one has reached the half-way point. If this is as far as Philolaus' demonstrations go, he would have been oblivious to the question of *why* certain ratios rations are or are not concordant.

In his recent *Plato and Pythagoreanism*,[44] Horky points out that this is precisely the criticism that Socrates levels against Pythagorean acoustics, in the *Republic*: "They don't investigate, for example, which numbers are consonant and which aren't or what the explanation is of each (διὰ τί ἑκάτεροι)" (531c).[45] Certain physical ratios result in sounds with a certain pleasing phenomenological character, and whenever certain sounds when sounded together have this character, certain ratios are to be found. Left unexplored is which is responsible for which, and what it is about the concordant ratios, or sounds, that lies behind them having the character by which they are grouped together. Horky

---

44   Horky 2013.
45   Tr. Grube and Reeve, 1992.

associates this with Socrates' dissatisfaction with the "mystic secrecy" of the *akousmata*,[46] and offers as evidence of Plato's dissatisfaction with Philolaus' more exoteric accounts a passage in the *Phaedo* in which Cebes relates to Socrates that in the *logoi* of Philolaus and his associates he heard "nothing clear" (σαφὲς οὐδὲν) (61d-e). Horky writes that, "by this he seems to mean that Philolaus' arguments were not *demonstrated precisely* in accordance with a rigorous philosophical methodology."[47]

Perhaps Philolaus did not work through lines of causal dependence with as much perspicuity as Plato did, in identifying Forms as explanatory of various phenomena, or as Aristotle thought that demonstrations in the sciences do. But that is not to say that Philolaus, and, by implication, other *mathematikoi* who followed him, were oblivious to the relation of causal and explanatory priority. They took note of this, and they recognized that the sort of accounts by which we make the world intelligible must distinguish what is causally prior from that which is caused – even if there is no clear evidence that they used the term *apodeixis* (demonstration) to refer to such accounts. In order to show this, I begin by briefly considering the generally accepted lines of interpretation of Philolaus' philosophy as developed by Huffman: Philolaus is a natural philosopher in the tradition of the Milesians. He aims at rationalistic accounts of the origin of familiar, experienced features of the world. While each of the Milesians identified one or more kinds as *arkhai*, principles from which other things emerged, Philolaus refrains from identifying any particular kind of stuff as an *arkhē*, because he thinks that there is no such stuff. Rather, there is a plurality of kinds of stuff, unlimiteds, that are such as to take on determinate characteristics, by which there arise things, and characteristics of things.[48] He accordingly identifies as principles "unlimiteds" in general, supplementing them with "limiters," principles of determination. The two alone do not suffice; there is also required a *harmonia*, a fitting together, of the limiter and the unlimited. This harmony is not itself called a principle; it is what arises when a limiter actually limits an unlimited. This harmony leads to, or, perhaps is,[49] the being of the explanandum. Both a limiter and an unlimited are principles, as starting points, those items that must preexist that for which they are principles. But, as Huffman has argued, "principle" must have another sense here too, one familiar from the Hippocratic corpus.[50] The limiter and unlimited are principles,

---

46   Horky 2013, 173.

47   *Ibid.*, 171.

48   See Barnes 1983, 387ff.

49   This is the suggestion of Horky 2013, 146.

50   Huffman 2006, 78–92.

as causes. They are not simply necessary conditions for what emerges; they are themselves responsible for the characteristics of that which emerges.

The knowledge of the arithmetical foundation of the musical scale exhibited by Fragment 6a indicates that among Pythagoreans, Philolaus, at the very least, took number as an example of such limiter, at least in the context of sound. According to Aristotle, what Philolaus elsewhere identifies as the principles of number, even and odd, are to be understood as principles of unlimited and limiter, respectively (*Metaph.* A 5 986a23-4); numbers when harmonized (as when musical notes are arranged in a scale) will also be a being of some sort. So, we have a hierarchy. Regardless of the ontological status of these principles, odd and even are principles of number, number is a principle of harmony, and harmony is in turn a principle of musical structures. We have progressed far from accounts that simply identify the symmetrical relationships between items in the same column of opposites. The relationship between principle and that of which it is a principle is asymmetric. The derivative entity is understood only as resultant from its principles, but not vice versa. Like Aristotelian demonstrations, Philolaus' accounts do more than justify their conclusions, they explain them. If Horky is right, and Plato condemns Philolaus' accounts on the grounds that they are "not clear," it is not because the fundamental distinction between causal principle and explanandum has not been made. In distinguishing between principle and derivative entity, Philolaus is signaling a recognition of the distinction between the sort of the thing that is a cause and the sort of thing that is an effect.

Who first employed the term *aitia*, or a variant, in a way that recognized the asymmetrical distinction? We are not sure, but it may well have been another thinker associated with the Pythagorean tradition, Plato's friend Archytas.[51] The story, again, begins with the Pythagorean table of opposites.

In his *Physics* commentary, Simplicius comments on Aristotle's refutation of unnamed predecessors who identified motion with items belonging to the "second column": difference, inequality and non-being. Simplicius tells us that this is a reference to the second column of the Pythagorean table of opposites. He reports that Alexander faults Plato with having made this same mistake. Simplicius proceeds to clear Plato of this charge by showing how Plato himself takes the motion of the elements to result from their disequilibrium, not the other way around. Accordingly, Plato did not identify motion and inequality. According to Simplicius, Plato's realization that inequality stands in an asymmetrical causal relationship with motion follows Archtyas. In support, he cites

---

51   Plato, *Seventh Letter*, 350a.

testimony from Eudemus, who, although mistaken in taking Plato to identify motion and its cause, reports that Archytas did make the appropriate distinction. According to Eudemus,

> Plato says that motion is the great and the small and not-being and the uneven and as many things as have the same force as these (ὅσα τού- τοις ἐπὶ ταὐτὸ φέρει). But it seems paradoxical to say that motion is just this. For, when motion is present, that in which it is present seems to be moved, but, when something is unequal or uneven, it is ridiculous to require in addition that it is moved. It is better to say that these are causes [of motion] just as Archytas does. (431.4-12)[52]

As Huffman has argued against Burkert,[53] Eudemus is distinguishing between Archytas and those Pythagoreans who posited the table of opposites. Although Archytas recognizes that inequality is associated with motion, he is said to differ from these Pythagoreans insofar he recognizes it is unequal distribution that is the origin of motion, and not vice versa. The evidence from Eudemus via Simplicius shows us that Archytas explicitly indicates that the table of opposites is deficient as a theoretical account of the sorts of regular associations found in the world; even if the opposites that the table identifies are principles of a sort, the table fails to distinguish which of these are more causally basic than others.

4 Unmediated Steps in Demonstration

The fourth feature of Aristotle's account demonstration that can be traced to Pythagorean thought is the need for demonstration to be made up of atomic inferential steps: No step in a demonstration should be such that it is itself subject to demonstration. Again, the evidence is less certain than one would hope, but in my view it indicates that it is likely that the source of this insight is again, the Pythagorean Archytas.

The first extent instances of the term *apodeixis* being used in an epistemological or metatheoretical context, in which the author does not simply refer to proof but reflects on their epistemological force, are found in passages by Plato and Archytas. The two were friends and contemporaries, and the dating of the

---

52 The translation is from Huffman 2005, 508.

53 Huffman 2005, 509–12, responding to Burkert 1972, 47, n. 106.

PYTHAGOREANISM AND THE HISTORY OF DEMONSTRATION

respective texts is uncertain. It is Plato, however, who apparently employs the term in a less rigorous fashion. As noted above, he sometimes employed it in regard to a nonprobative argument. DK B4 4 of Archytas, in contrast, employs the term as a way of pointing to the clarity, completeness, and revelatory nature of inferential mathematical lines of thought. Archytas offers important clues concerning thoughts on what features a demonstration must have to accomplish its cognitive goals. DK B4 4 reads

καὶ δοκεῖ ἁ λογιστικὰ ποτὶ τὰν σοφίαν τῶν μὲν ἀλλᾶν τεχνῶν καὶ πολὺ διαφέρειν, ἀτὰρ καὶ τᾶς γεωμετρικᾶς ἐναργεστέρω πραγματεύεσθαι ἃ θέλει. *** καὶ ἃ ἐκλείπει αὖ ἁ γεωμετρία, καὶ ἀποδείξιας ἁ λογιστικὰ ἐπιτελεῖ καὶ ὁμῶς, εἰ μὲν εἰδέων τεὰ πραγματεία, καὶ τὰ περὶ τοῖς εἴδεσιν

I offer a provisional translation:

And it seems that logistic is indeed far superior to the other crafts in regard to wisdom, and deals with it intends to deal with in a clearer manner than does even geometry ... And again, in those respects in which geometry is deficient, logistic completely works through demonstrations, and likewise, if there is something that deals with shapes, (logistic completely works through) matters dealing with shapes, as well.

Much is unclear here. First, we have a reference to mathematical demonstrations. There is an explicit reference to the demonstrations of "logistic," which is said to give more adequate accounts than does geometry. The implication is that geometry gives demonstrations too, but that those of logistic are superior. What these demonstrations of logistic are is a contentious issue; as we shall see, there is still unclarity concerning exactly what logistic is. There is a bit more evidence concerning the history of geometry, but the evidence is indirect and incomplete. The earliest geometrical proof may have simply consisted in diagrams that show certain relations.[54] We are however on sure ground in attributing inferential proofs to geometers contemporary with Archytas, for they were aware of the incommensurability of the side of a square with its diagonal, and there is no way for this to have been determined except through a one of a number of possible proofs that this must be so.[55] Further, we are on sure ground in attributing some of the first steps of the axiomatization of geometry

---

54   For a speculative reconstruction of the sorts of proof (δεῖξις) that the Pythagoreans may have employed prior to the first stages of the axiomatization of geometry, see McKirahan 2013, 180–2. Units, when arrayed in certain ways, show (δεικνύναι) certain regular relationships; one can "see" that these relationships can be generalized.

55   On the first proofs of the incommensurability of the diagonal, see Mueller 2006, 703–4.

to Archytas' contemporary Hippocrates of Chios, who is reported to be the first geometer to compile an *Elements* (Proclus, *in Eucl.* 66.7). There is however no evidence that geometers at the time of Archytas would have attempted to ground such proofs on a determinate set of basic premises that were not themselves subject to proof.

The next question to face in interpreting this fragment concerns craft *logistikē*. Two interpretations have emerged in the literature. The first, championed by Neubager, identifies *logistikē* with the techniques of Babylonian algebra which, on the basis of how closely much of Book 2 of Euclid's *Elements* parallels Babylonian modes of calculation, must have been taken over by the Greeks at an early period. Neugebauer explicitly cites Archytas' fragment in this regard. On his view, Archytas' meaning is that the sort of algebraic techniques that had been borrowed from the Babylonians are able to solve problems that purely geometrical techniques cannot.[56] As Rowe explains, "His point was that rigorous axiomatic reasoning in the style of Euclid arose rather late, and that Archytas, a contemporary of Plato, was bearing witness to the primacy of algebraic content over the geometrical form in which the Greeks dressed their mathematics."[57] The second, developed by Klein, on the basis of an analysis of Plato's *Gorgias*, which contrasts *logistikē* and *arithmetikē*, takes *logistikē* to be the study of numbers in relation to one another, as opposed to the study of the internal character of a countable assemblage.[58] As such, it would encompass most of what is now referred to as "arithmetic," as well as ratio theory. Neubager's account has the advantage of having some basis in the evidence, such as it is, concerning how the ancient Greeks actually figured out mathematical problems. But its direct support is tenuous at best, and the view that any inferential structure was incidental to the nature of Greek geometrical thinking is gainsaid by Aristotle's *Posterior Analytics* (written only a generation after Archytas), the first book of which takes geometry to be paradigmatic for the inferential structure of science. That geometrical proofs existed and were recognized as such shows that it would have been a commonplace that geometry is not a matter of the application of recognized tricks in the determination of relationships, but is rather based on inferences from accepted premises. For this reason, I, following Huffman,[59] accept Klein's view that *logistikē* here refers to the study of numbers in relation to one another, and is here being contrasted with the study of magnitudes as arrayed in space, in relation to one another.

---

56   Neugebauer 1936, 245–259.
57   Rowe 2010, 133.
58   Klein 1068, 17–25.
59   Huffman 2005, 240–4.

PYTHAGOREANISM AND THE HISTORY OF DEMONSTRATION 213

This science is not a mere technique that allows a certain answer to be generated; it is, as Plato puts it, a study of realities, as is geometry. Although we do not have definitive support for it, the most natural reading of Archytas Fr. 4 is to take *logistikē* to be an inferential variety of mathematical geometry, since, as we have seen, demonstrations in the contexts of rhetoric and medicine were understood as inferential proofs. Archytas is surely not making the point that a non-inferential mode of mathematics is superior than an inferential mode. He is rather saying that the demonstrations of *logistikē* are more adequate than those of geometry. In what sense?

There are two major possibilities of interpretation. According to the first, the proofs of *logistikē* are more complete or perfect on formal grounds. According to the second, Archytas' remarks have nothing to do with formal consideration; his point is that the proofs of *logistikē* are deficient in some other respect.

The first line of interpretation is the traditional one, although scholars have been at a loss in saying what exactly Archytas thought was structurally lacking in the proofs of geometry. It has recently been argued against by Huffman. According to Huffman, Archytas' point is that numerical calculation accomplishes more than geometry in regard to the practical enterprises faced by human beings. On this account, when Archytas unpacks his claim that the demonstrations of *logistikē* are more fully carried out than those of geometry on the basis that they are more clear or evident (ἐναργής) the point is not that it is the conclusion that is more evident or clearly shown, but that it deals with its objects in a more vivid or concrete way. It brings the matter home, as it were.

Huffman's argument, like all arguments for a certain interpretation of Archytas, is circumstantial. He offers the following as evidence for his interpretation. First, in DK B 3, Archytas praises *logistikē* for its use in matters of equity. "Once calculation was discovered. It stopped discord and increased concord. For people do not want more than their share, and equality exists, once this has come into being. For by means of calculation we will seek reconciliation in our dealings with others ..."[60] Archytas goes on to explain how those with a command of *logistikē* will be able to detect the injustices of others, and the awareness on the part of the unjust of their knowledge will act as a deterrent against unjust deeds.[61] This understanding of the value of *logistikē* is consonant with Huffman's interpretation of DK B 3. But it certainly does not clinch the case.

---

60   Huffman 2005, 183.
61   *Ibid*, 235–6.

Stronger evidence is found in Huffman's survey of the use of the term ἐπι-τελεῖν, which most commonly means "carry out'" or "to put into effect" something that exists only "in thought or in word."[62] Examples are the carrying out of commands, the fulfilling of oracles, the fulfilling of a promise, or the putting into effect of a design. Interpreting the fragment along these lines, it tells us that the proofs of *logistikē* are put into effect in a manner different from, or to a lesser extent than, geometrical proofs.[63] It is not beyond the bounds of semantic possibility for Archytas' meaning to be that what *logistikē* reveals is only truly revealed when put into effect. After all, a good example is sometimes what is needed in order to bring a general point home; after hearing that example one might say "now I see what you mean." But if this were Archytas' meaning, he would be making two separate points in regard to *logistikē*. The first is that it finds its completion in attaining its intended use within practical human affairs, and second, that it has maximal cognitive value when seen as applied to human affairs. Presumably on this interpretation Archytas supports each of these points in other passages.

One problem with this argument is that in all of the cases cited by Huffman, in which the verb ἐπιτελεῖν means "to put into effect" the putting into effect in question is part of the semantic content of the object of the verb. A command is the sort of thing that is uttered with the intention of its being followed. An oracle is the sort of thing that is uttered with the intention of having it be seen to be fulfilled. A promise is meant to be kept—or is at least understood as having that intention behind its utterance. A design is a paradigm that is intended to be followed in making something. This is not so in regard to *apodeixis*, the core meaning of which is a showing forth. Following the cues of the other uses of the verb, to ἐπιτελεῖν a demonstration is to *really* show something, to have its being manifest really, fully accomplished. The accomplishment in question is cognitive, not practical.

Within the *Prior Analytics* Aristotle talks of what it takes to ἐπιτελεῖν a deduction (*sullogismos*). It is not to apply it in everyday affairs; it is to *fully* deduce, which means to express the deduction in question via a "perfect" syllogism, or a sequence of them (*An. pr.* 1 24 26b29-30). The term "perfect" is τέλειος, which shares the root of ἐπιτελεῖν. Aristotle specifies a perfect syllogism by virtue of its being cast in a certain logical form, one according to which one "needs no external term in order to show the necessary result" (24b23–24). Scholars disagree about what it is about a perfect syllogism, as specified by Aristotle,

---

62   Ibid. 237–8.

63   *Ibid*, 249–50.

that he thinks allows it to satisfy this criterion, but the important point for our purposes is that a deduction is perfect on account of its having two features. First, its structure is such that it fully reveals why the conclusion follows as a necessary result from its premises. Second, no relevant premise is left out; in terms of Aristotelian syllogistic, no middle term is missing. Although neither the terms τέλειος nor ἐπιτελεῖν are employed in the *Posterior Analytics*, which is specifically concerned with the formal and epistemological character of those deductions that qualify as demonstrations, within that work the idea of perfect deductions is present and is fully worked through. Not only are demonstrations to be cast as first figure syllogisms (which are perfect deductions), their premises are to be unmediated. That is to say that no premises are implicit. In order for a demonstration to *really* show that its conclusion holds, and to show why it holds, it must be fully worked through.

I suggest that Archytas too is making the same point. To say that a demonstration is ἐναργής is to say that it is an account that *really* makes things manifest and shows things as they are. The demonstrations of geometry do not reveal geometrical truths with as much clarity as is desired because they have not been worked through as fully as they could have been. Steps are missing; the form of the exposition is somewhat obscure.

This interpretation has two main advantages. While on Huffman's reading Archytas is making two independent points, on the present, more traditional interpretation, his first point directly supports the second. Further, this line of interpretation is in accordance with Aristotle's usage of the term ἐπιτελεῖν when an inference (such as a demonstration) is its object.

But what could Archytas mean by saying that *logistikē*, unlike geometry, fully carries out its demonstrations? In order to answer this, I turn to the thought of predecessor and fellow Pythagorean Philolaus, and surviving Greek geometrical texts.

Recall Philolaus DK B 4: "And indeed all things that are known have number. For it is not possible that anything whatsoever be understood or known without this." As noted above, this fragment has traditionally been given a metaphysical reading, on the basis of Aristotle's declaration that the Pythagoreans took number to be the principles of things, that, ultimately, all things are number.[64] Huffman has recently argued for a more minimalistic interpretation, limiting itself to what is said in what can be reliably identified as Philolaus' words. On his account, Philolaus' point is epistemological. Things are known by virtue of their numerical relations. Restricting ourselves to this more conservative

---

64   Examples can be found in Guthrie 1979, 181–305; Barnes 1983, 378–83.

reading, Philolaus' point would be that those aspects of a thing that are intelligible to us are the ones that are grasped through the study of numbers. As we have seen, those studies are arithmetic and *logistikē*. The spatial aspects of things, studied by number, are missing–unless it is the case that those spatial aspects are at bottom numerical aspects. The only reason we might have to attribute to Philolaus this possibility is the metaphysical reading of DK B 4: if all things are number, the spatial aspect of reality, too, is to be understood on the basis of number, and nothing besides number (as there is no such thing). In this case, there is a gap between the kind of accounts that arithmetic and *logistikē* give us and what it is that we aim to know. On the more restrictive reading of Philolaus, if we take Archytas to be building on Philolaus, he would be saying the geometry tries to discuss aspects of the world, such as spatiality, that ultimately cannot be fully understood. The demonstrations of geometry are necessarily incomplete as they try to understand what is not numerical, and accordingly cannot be understood. If we take Archytas to be building on Philolaus, understood in the metaphysical sense, his point would be that in principle the spatial aspects of things can be understood through the sciences of number. But, as they are, they do not do so. The only aspects of number that they do fully make intelligible are their internal character (as odd, even, prime and the like) and the relationships that they have to one another, as made clear through addition, subtraction, multiplication, division, and theory of ratios. Once one's study of spatial figures goes beyond these attributes, one's demonstrations will have gaps.

Archytas likely did not specify the respects in which he thought geometrical demonstrations fall short, for we have no evidence of what he thought was required to *really show* a mathematical proposition, that is, what it takes for there to be a mathematical demonstration. Insofar as he worked at a time in which the incommensurability of the diagonal would have been common knowledge, he would have been aware of what we now recognize as genuine mathematical proofs, and there is evidence that he himself demonstrated how to duplicate a cube.[65] It fell to Aristotle to lay out with precision the

---

65   DK A 14 and 15, on which see Huffman 2005, 342–401. The evidence is uncertain here. Eratosthenes reports that Archytas offered a demonstration, but that this was not a sufficient answer to the architectural challenge posed by the Delian oracle that his account was meant to address: to come up with a practical way of building a cubical space of double the volume of another cube. On the other hand, Plutarch tells us that Archytas was able to solve the practical problem, but that his solution was deficient insofar as it lacked the theoretical rigor of a demonstrative proof, suggesting that Plato had Archytas in his sights at *Resp.* 7 527c-528b when he suggests that Pythagorean mathematicians had an undue focus on practical application and neglected theorization concerning intelligibles.

PYTHAGOREANISM AND THE HISTORY OF DEMONSTRATION

conditions that must be met for the proposition in question to be shown in a strong sense, that is, proven, but that is not to say that such an account is required for one to argue that a certain argument does not in fact constitute a proof. Jurors and attorneys with no training in logic often are able to make apt criticisms of the arguments of others, declaring that the case is not proven. Typically, such an objection takes the form of challenging a stated or implicit premise: "how do you know that such and such might not be the case"? As Aristotle sees in *An. post.* 1.3, such objections are forestalled only if all premises are either such that this sort of question simply cannot arise (that is to say, they are principle), or follow of necessity from that sort of premise. Archytas' point, I suggest, is that premises concerning spatial relations give rise to "how do you know that?" sorts of objections, in a way that premises concerning numbers do not, at least for those who have mastered the arts of arithmetic and calculation.

In making such an observation, Archytas would have been anticipating the sorts of objections made against antiquity's most famous fully worked out body of proof, Euclid's *Elements*. Bertrand Russell famously condemned the book for its inferential gaps;[66] it took Hilbert to more adequately work through the ultimate premises of geometry so that its demonstrations were in fact fully completed, to the point where there are no gaps. Mueller has given a partial defense of the *Elements* by arguing that the diagrams Euclid appeals to play a crucial role; the proofs are incomplete without appeal to what intuition reveals, when one makes use of diagrams.[67] If fully worked through mathematical proofs fulfill their function of cognitively revealing quantitative relations, even for those not in possession of logical theory, it stands to reason that one can be aware that there has not been maximal cognitive revelation, even in the absence of such a theory. Archytas, I suggest, was aware that this is the case in regard to geometrical proofs, in a manner, or to an extent, that is not the case in regard to demonstrations concerning numbers. But the account of

---

Huffman speculates that the two reports can be reconciled by the thesis that Archytas did indeed offer a legitimate mathematical demonstration, but that it was motivated by practical concerns; it was not part of a body of proof that would constitute a science of solid geometry. This interpretation is in accordance with Huffman's interpretation of DK B 4: for Archytas, science is primarily oriented towards making sense of the particulars before one. I omit consideration of these texts in my account of Archytas' role in the history of demonstration, on account of the unclear conflicting evidence they offer, but they do offer some collaborating testimony that Archytas was aware of the sort of geometrical account that later philosophers recognized as demonstrative.

66   Russell 1902, 165–167.
67   Mueller 1969, 289–309.

demonstration that would allow for a more precise account of what exactly is missing waits for Plato and Aristotle.[68]

Three key elements of Aristotle's theory of demonstration have Pythagorean antecedents. Demonstration is a revelatory discourse that is 1) inferential, 2) explicitly based on premises that are not themselves demonstrated on the basis of more basic premises, and 3) explanatory, insofar as the premises express those basic facts that are explanatory of the conclusion. Missing is the requirements that inferential steps be explicit and complete, and an account of the sorts of premises that ground demonstration; according to Aristotle, the primary role is played by definition. The centrality of definition to explanation is an insight that derives not from the Pythagoreans but from Plato.[69]

As in other aspects of his philosophical thinking, the great achievement of Aristotle is a systematic synthesis of the insights of his predecessors, of such richness and complexity that it opens up new philosophical puzzles and problems that these predecessors could never have pondered.[70]

---

68   As far as we know, Plato was the first to explicitly indicate that demonstrative proofs must rest on undemonstrated casual principles. We see this in the Divided Line passage of the *Republic*, in which we are told that mathematical reasoning rests on starting points or principles that are "hypotheses," to be distinguished from the beings or truths that are deduced on their basis, and that mathematicians err in taking their starting points to be such hypotheses (*Resp.* 6 510b-511d). Plato presumes that we are familiar with "hypothesis" as a term that the mathematicians themselves used. The hypotheses of the mathematicians are said to be opposed to the unhypothetical first principle attained by dialectic. This unhypothetical principle is usually identified with the Form of the Good, which is said to be the cause of the being of things. The difficulties of this passage are many, but it is clear that Plato has here anticipated the third and fourth aspects of Aristotle's theory of demonstration–mathematical accounts, in order to be fully adequate, are inferences on the basis of determinate causal and epistemological starting points. (What Plato did not recognize, according to Aristotle, was that different sciences, concerned with different genera, must have different starting points.) Likewise, in the *Theaetetus*, we are told that a science involves belief (doxa) in the context of a certain logos, which must be grounded on direct apprehension (αἴσθησις) of elements (στοιχεῖα) (202b); in at least one example of how this works,that in which the elements are the material constituents of a things, as the wheels and so forth are in respect to a wagon, (207a-c), these elements are in some sense responsible for the object known (even if Plato does not here use the word "cause" to refer to them). Plato is again discussing themes present in the epistemology of Pythagoreans prior to or contemporary to him, although the chronology and matter of who influenced whom cannot be determined.

69   On this see especially Ferejohn 2013, 2013.

70   I am grateful for editorial help provided by Jeffrey Smeland, Jacob Terneus, and Kevin McKevitt, and, especially, to correspondence with Carl Huffman.

PYTHAGOREANISM AND THE HISTORY OF DEMONSTRATION

Bibliography

Barnes, Jonathan. 1981. "Proof and the Syllogism." In *Aristotle on Science: the 'Posterior Analytics': Proceedings of the 8th Symposium Aristotelicum Held in Padua from September 7 to 15, 1978*, edited by Enrico Berti. 1–59. Roma, Italy: Editrice Antenore.

Barnes, Jonathan. 1983. *The Presocratic Philosophers*. London: Routledge.

Boehm, Fritz. "De symbolis Pythagoreis." Doctoral diss. Berlin, 1905. https://archive.org/details/bub_gb_vUH_e5zKAgC.

Bronstein, David. 2016. *Aristotle on Knowledge and Learning: The Posterior Analytics*. Oxford: Oxford University Press.

Burkert, Walter. 1972. *Lore and Science in Ancient Pythagoreanism*. Translated by Edwin L. Minar, Jr. Cambridge, MA: Harvard University Press.

Burnyeat, Myles F. 2015. "Enthymeme: Aristotle on the Logic of Persuasion." In *Aristotle's Rhetoric: Philosophical Essays*, edited by David J. Furley and Alexander Nehamas. Princeton: Princeton University Press.

Curd, Patricia. 1998. *The Legacy of Parmenides*. Princeton: Princeton University Press, 1998. Reprint Las Vegas: Parmenides Publishing, 2004.

Dumont, Jean-Paul, ed. 1988. *Les Présocratiques*. Paris: Gallimard.

Ferejohn, Michael T. 2013. *Formal Causes: Definition, Explanation, and Primacy in Socratic and Aristotelian Thought*. Oxford: Oxford University Press.

Goldin, Owen. 2014. "The Pythagorean Table of Opposites, Symbolic Classification, and Aristotle." *Science in Context* 28.2: 171–193.

Graham, Daniel. 2006. *Explaining the Cosmos: The Ionian Tradition of Scientific Philosophy*. Princeton: Princeton University Press.

Grube, G. M. A. and C. D. C. Reeve trans. 1992. *Plato: Republic*. Indianapolis: Hackett.

Guthrie, W. K. C. 1979. *A History of Greek Philosophy: Volume 1, The Earlier Presocratics and the Pythagoreans*, rev. ed. Cambridge: Cambridge University Press.

Horky, Phillip. 2013. *Plato and Pythagoreanism*. New York City: Oxford University Press.

Huffman, Carl. 2005. *Archytas of Tarentum: Pythagorean, Philosopher and Mathematician King*. Cambridge: Cambridge University Press.

Huffman, Carl. 2016. *Philolaus of Croton: Pythagorean and Presocratic*. Cambridge: Cambridge University Press, 2006.

Huffman, Carl. 2015. "Pythagoreanism." *The Stanford Encyclopedia of Philosophy*, edited by Edward N. Zalta. http://plato.stanford.edu/archives/spr2015/entries/pythagoreanism/.

Huffman, Carl. 2016. "Philolaus." *The Stanford Encyclopedia of Philosophy*, edited by Edward N. Zalta. https://plato.stanford.edu/archives/sum2016/entries/philolaus/.

Jones, William H. S. trans. 1931. *Hippocrates, Volume IV: Nature of Man*. Cambridge: Harvard University Press.

Klein, Jacob. 1968. *Greek Mathematical Thought and the Origin of Algebra*. trans. Eva Brann. Cambridge: MIT Press.

Lloyd, G. E. R. 1962. "Right and Left in Greek Philosophy." *The Journal of Hellenic Studies*, 82, 56–66.

Lloyd, G. E. R. 1979. *Magic, Reason, and Experience*. Cambridge: Cambridge University Press.

Lloyd, G. E. R. 1987. *The Revolutions of Wisdom: Studies in the Claims and Practice of Ancient Greek Science*. Berkeley: University of California Press.

Lloyd, G. E. R. 1991. *Methods and Problems in Greek Science: Selected Papers*. Cambridge: Cambridge University Press, 1991.

McKirahan, Richard. 2013. "Philolaus on Number" In *On Pythagoreanism,* ed., Gabriele Cornelli, Richard McKirahan, Constantinos Macris. Berlin: De Gruyter.

Mueller, Ian. 1969. "Euclid's Elements and the Axiomatic Method." *The British Journal for the Philosophy of Science*, 20.4: 289–309.

Mueller, Ian. 2006. "Greek Mathematics to the Time of Euclid." In *A Companion to Ancient Philosophy,* edited by Mary Louise Gill and Pierre Pellegrin. Malden: Blackwell.

Nagy, Gregory. 1994. *Pindar's Homer: The Lyric Possession of an Epic Past*. Baltimore: Johns Hopkins University Press.

Neugebauer, Otto. 1936. "Zur geometrischen Algebra." *Quellen und Studien zur Geschichte der Mathematik, Astronomie und Physik B: Studien* 3: 245–259.

Rowe, David. 2010. "Otto Neugebauer's Vision for Rewriting the History of Ancient Mathematics." In *Historiography of Mathematics in the 19th and 20th Centuries,* ed. Volker Remmert, Martina Schneider, Henrik Sørensen. 123–41. Cham: Birkhäuser Basel.

Russell, Bertrand. 1902. "The Teaching of Euclid." *The Mathematical Gazette* 2.33:165–167.

Solmsen, Friedrich. 1928. *Die Entwicklung der aristotelischen Logik und Rhetorik.* ed. W. Jaeger, Neuephilologische Untersuchungen, Heft 4. Berlin: Weidmann.

Thomas, Rosalind. 2000. *Herodotus in Context: Ethnography, Science and the Art of Persuasion*. Cambridge: Cambridge University Press.

CHAPTER 7

Aristotle's Outlook on Pythagoras and the (So-Called) Pythagoreans

Omar D. Álvarez Salas

1

Our knowledge of early Pythagoreanism, as every scholar may be aware of, is severely hindered by the lack of an adequate number of dependable sources, in particular regarding the achievements of Pythagoras himself and of the earliest circle of Pythagoreans.[1] Significant though they may be, the scant explicit references to Pythagoras by his contemporaries do not allow for a clear and easy judgment as to whether he founded a philosophical school or instead a kind of religious brotherhood. Moreover, the issue cannot be solved by resorting to the few references to Pythagoras in works written by authors of the Classical period, since they allow for a variety of interpretations. Plato himself, for all the reverence he may have had for such an impressive man,[2] fails to provide us with further details regarding any definite set of doctrines held by Pythagoras himself. Whether this was due to an effort of not making explicit his debt towards a thinker who might have exercised a major influence on the shaping of his own thought, be it through the means of Socrates or of other people, or to a respectful treatment of a man to whom he may refer elsewhere in an oblique or veiled manner,[3] we cannot definitely say. In the face of Plato's literary way of dealing with particular themes in the form of a narrated dialogue in which some characters (mostly the namesakes of real people) are

---

1 For the testimonies about Pythagoras reference is made to *Die Fragmente der Vorsokratiker*, ed. Hermann Diels and Walther Kranz (Berlin: Weidmann, 1951[6]), henceforth DK; a much narrower selection of the Pythagorean material is found in *Early Greek Philosophy*, 9 vols. ed. André Laks and Glenn Most (Harvard: Loeb Classical Library, 2016), Vol. IV. Western Greek Thinkers. Part 1, chapters 10–18 (henceforth LM).

2 At *Resp.* x 600a-b Plato depicts Pythagoras as worshipped by his followers to the extent of naming after him the way of life that he instituted for them.

3 Consider, for instance, Plato's allusion to "certain Prometheus" who brought to mankind a "path" of discovery as a gift at *Phlb.* 16c5-d4; on this point, see John Palmer, "The Pythagoreans and Plato," in *A History of Pythagoreanism*, ed. Carl Huffman (Cambridge: Cambridge University Press, 2014), 219 ff.

© KONINKLIJKE BRILL NV, LEIDEN, 2021 | DOI:10.1163/9789004443358_009

engaged, Aristotle's extant works represent the oldest surviving textual corpus of systematical character in the history of Western philosophy, since almost all previous such production was superseded at some point in the Late Antiquity (or the Middle Ages) textual transmission by Aristotle's own πραγματεῖαι and, hence, did not reach us. Therefore, Aristotle's treatment of the main thinkers that, according to his own view, preceded him in the research of the fourfold causality (as well as of the problems connected with it), which he identified as the foundation of his own system of thought, undoubtedly was and remains to this date the most valuable source of information regarding the earliest Greek philosophy.[4]

For the time being, even if mainly in the last three decades the idea followed by scholars like Zeller and even Guthrie that doxography proper started only with Aristotle (or with Plato, at the earliest) has been challenged and importantly corrected, it is generally thought (and sometimes stated and acknowledged in the relevant scholarship) that, notwithstanding the fact that no whole work of truly historiographical character by Aristotle has come down to us, the ultimate *source* for our knowledge of all pre-Platonic philosophy—with the exception of those doctrines that were not committed to writing, such as that of Socrates, on which Plato himself is our main witness—is represented by the extant works of the Stagirite himself, as well as by the excerpts, epitomes, paraphrases and, when traceable, literal quotations from his lost works in later authors, all this mainly filtered through the means of the commentaries produced in the Late Antiquity and the Middle Ages. Now, in view also of Theophrastus' well-known dependence on Aristotle for the elaboration of his own highly praised Φυσικαὶ δόξαι (rather than Φυσικῶν δόξαι), which were viewed by Diels as the ultimate origin of all later doxographical accounts regarding the earliest Greek thinkers, then Aristotle's critical judgment, through his associate's influential work, cast an inescapable shadow over all later compilations dealing with the origins of Greek philosophical thought.

In the case of Presocratic philosophy in general, besides our being seriously limited and even prevented from approaching it directly, all the more so as

---

4   Aristotle's most complete overview of previous philosophical thought is contained in the chapters 3–10 of *Metaphysics* A, of which there is a new critical edition along with a series of essays on each of its chapters in *Aristotle's* Metaphysics *Alpha*, ed. Carlos Steel and Oliver Primavesi (Oxford: Oxford University Press, 2012); a similar but shorter doxographical passage is found at Arist. *Phys.* I 2–4, on which see Jaap Mansfeld, "Aristotle, Plato, and the Preplatonic Doxography and Chronography," in *Storiografia e dossografia nella filosofia antica*, ed. Giuseppe Cambiano (Turin: Tirrenia, 1986), 1 ff.

ARISTOTLE'S OUTLOOK ON PYTHAGORAS AND THE PYTHAGOREANS

we do not even possess a single complete work of any of its representatives, it has been rightly underlined by Harold Cherniss that the scanty fragments, which have come down to us were quoted—and this not just by Aristotle—for purposes other than the objective illustration of Presocratic thought itself. As has been repeatedly observed by scholars around the world since Cherniss's groundbreaking intervention—in spite of Guthrie's early objections and of Aristotle's rehabilitation by Burkert and Philip as a star witness for the Pythagorean doctrines—, Aristotle had no intention to write a history of philosophy nor shows any awareness of a real historical scruple in recording the doctrinal creeds of his predecessors.[5] Aristotle's reports on the doctrines held by previous thinkers have been found to contain a big number of mistakes or, rather, misinterpretations, probably due to an effort to make them fit into the patterns of his own thought, and to a lesser degree to his ungenerous attitude towards a way of research that he himself qualified as a chanceful hitting of an unforeseen target or as a "stammering" expression of a "primitive" thinking, which appears fully compatible with Plato's ungenerous castigation of Presocratic cosmological theories as a groping around in the dark for a true insight.[6] As a consequence of this, conversely, his extant works may not be viewed as unquestionable 'sources' for the reconstruction of earlier systems of thought, in spite of their undeniable value as testimonies, often unique in kind and number.

More recent assessments of Aristotle's method of work have led to a sensibly more modulated appraisal of his critical intervention at least on issues of historical import. In fact, the researches carried out by a number of scholars initially led by Snell and Classen (and then by Patzer, who followed in their footsteps), who first drew the attention of scholars to a series of doxographical patterns common to Plato and Aristotle and similar to those found in other authors from the Classical period, have suggested that shaping of intellectual pedigrees anticipating doxography proper already took place at a relatively early stage. i.e., among the Sophists, developing to full maturity mainly at the hands of Hippias. Later on, the study of the proto-historiographical techniques was greatly improved and refined by the huge work done in the field of doxography during the last few decades, which has definitely shown Aristotle's

---

5   For examples of this see Harold F. Cherniss, *Aristotle's Criticism of Presocratic Philosophy* (Baltimore, MD: The John Hopkins University Press, 1935), 339–346 (Chapter VI); for a recent and well-balanced appraisal of the role played by Aristotle as a "historian" of earlier philosophical thought, see Michael Frede, "Aristotle's Account of the Origins of Philosophy," *Rhizai* 1 (2004), 9 ff.

6   Arist. *Metaph.* 985a 5–17; Pl. *Phd.* 99b 4–8.

(and Plato's) reliance on what has been termed "Preplatonic doxography." As a result of the work done on the intellectual background of Aristotle as a 'historian' of previous thought, nowadays there can be no doubt that he must have borrowed from his predecessors, *i.e.* Plato and even earlier thinkers, not just a host of topics or problems. He also 'inherited' from them an already established method for organizing the views held by a series of previous thinkers, which are combined in the shape of thematic clusters around each one of the subjects or problems at issue. It has been shown, for instance, that Gorgias put forth a classification of ontological doctrines from a systematical point of view, being the earliest surviving one such procedure, of which there seems to be a reflection in Aristotle (*Phys.* A 184 b 15–25)—as well as in Plato (*Soph.* 242c)—, where they are arranged according to the number and the nature of the principles postulated in them: the principles assumed could be one or many, and, if the former, they could be moved or unmoved and, if the latter, they could be ranged from two to infinite.[7] For his part, Hippias put together the oldest surviving "inventory of related ideas," which he collected from a wide variety of authors and literary genres, as he himself explicitly states in a famous passage—perhaps from the proem of the Συναγωγή—describing his modus operandi.

In this connection, some attention has also been paid to a widely spread doxographical technique, which consists in a classificatory device whereby an intellectual category is created by applying a (more or less appropriate) linguistic label either to the members of a real, definite school or to a collectivity of more or less unrelated thinkers that are envisaged as if they constituted in fact such a coherent entity.[8] An instance of this—which will be dealt with at length in the following pages—may be seen in the thoroughgoing use, in the accounts of the Pythagorean scientific theories afforded by Aristotle in his extant treatises, of the collective designation οἱ Πυθαγόρειοι (i.e. 'the Pythagoreans'), instead of the names of individual thinkers, purportedly to the exclusion of Pythagoras himself, as is usually held by most scholars and as we shall discuss hereafter.

---

7   For an overview of the doxographical issues mentioned above, see Mansfeld, "Preplatonic Doxography," 1 ff.

8   G. Cambiano, "Tecniche dossografiche in Platone," in *Storiografia e dossografia*, 61 ff.; the instance of the imaginary 'Heracliteans' that are named in Plato's *Theaetetus* (179e) has been recently explored in Omar Álvarez Salas, "Cratylus and the reception of Heraclitus' doctrine in Athens," in *El libro de Heráclito 2500 años después*, ed. Omar Álvarez and Enrique Hülsz (Mexico: UNAM, 2015), 239–268.

2

As is widely known, in the particular instance of Pythagoras and the other Pythagoreans of the 6th to early 5th centuries B.C., things are often said to stand even worse than with the other Presocratics (which were already poorly dealt with by the later tradition), because, in addition to the problems posed by the disastrous textual transmission of Greek archaic literature as a whole and, more specifically, by the loss of virtually all Presocratic written products, there is the huge obstacle constituted by the common belief that, in the case of Pythagoras, we are solely dealing with the founder of a 'sect' that was governed by non-written religious injunctions and superstitious behavioral prescriptions.[9] Moreover, it has been stressed that his followers attributed their full body of doctrine and all of their own new discoveries to the Master himself, in spite of their stemming not just from his immediate entourage, but also from those Pythagoreans known to have lived several generations after him. In particular, this tradition is usually brought emphatically to mind by those scholars who endeavor to account for the fact that, in Aristotle's extant works, Pythagoras' own name is seldom used, if anytime at all, while talking is usually made of doctrines (mostly, but not exclusively, of a scientific character) that are assigned to a vaguely construed and loosely named—as well as chronologically indefinite—group of anonymous 'Pythagoreans'.

Such a skeptical position in regard to Pythagoras' own participation in the Pythagorean doctrinal corpus was inaugurated by Eduard Zeller who emphasized the basically religious character of the community founded in Croton by the Samian philosopher, and it was taken to the extreme by Erich Frank, who squarely rejected any contribution to science from any actual Pythagorean and whimsically claimed instead that "all the discoveries attributed to Pythagoras himself or to his disciples by later writers were really the achievement of certain South Italian mathematicians of Plato's time," which were in no way related to the "genuine Pythagoreans who are attested ... since the sixth century as a religious sect similar to the Orphics."[10] After that, a more balanced judgment, but still pointing in the direction of distrust, was reached by the outstanding study on Pythagoras and the ancient Pythagoreanism produced by Walter Burkert. In

---

9 See, for instance, Carl Huffman, "Pythagoras," in *The Stanford Encyclopedia of Philosophy* (Winter 2018 Edition), ed. Edward N. Zalta, https://plato.stanford.edu/archives/win2018/entries/pythagoras/.

10 Frank, *Plato*, vi, as quoted and translated into English by Charles H. Kahn, *Pythagoras and the Pythagoreans. A Brief History* (Indianapolis/Cambridge: Hackett Publishing Company, Inc., 2001), 2.

226 ÁLVAREZ SALAS

fact, Burkert managed to trace back to Philolaus (around the middle of the 5th century B.C.) the Pythagorean cosmology and number-philosophy reported by Aristotle, thereby excluding in his view any connection to Pythagoras himself, who was just left with a pre-rational explanation of the cosmos and a shaman-like performance as a charismatic religious and political leader.[11]

As for Burkert's interpretation of the Aristotelian evidence, which remains to this date on the whole the unchallenged *communis opinio*—except for the partial rectifications brought about by the rightful criticisms of Kahn, Zhmud, and Riedweg, to name just the top few—we may sum it up in the following points: a) the main concern of the Stagirite was to bring out the common background to the Platonic theory of ideas and to the Pythagorean cosmology based on elemental number units, the former being his "real target"; b) the further detailed reports contained in the *Physics* (at 202b30 ff., on the *apeiron*) and in the *On the Heavens* (at 293a17-b30, on the cosmic system with its Earth revolving around the central hearth and the so-called harmony of the spheres) are primarily concerned with Philolaus' theories and world picture, whereas at *Metaphysics* 985b 23–986a 21 a detailed account of Philolaus' theory of principles is given, along with an allusion to the counter-Earth included as tenth celestial body in his planetary system; c) there is a consistent and intentional avoidance of Pythagoras' name in Aristotle's reports on Pythagorean (scientific) doctrines, which according to Burkert must be interpreted as indicative of a cautious reservation in regard to the elusive figure of a man, whom Aristotle would have seen as no more than a religious prophet and a wonder-working sage, but who did not take part at all in the advancement of scientific knowledge that was solely due to Pythagoreans later than him, starting with Philolaus; d) the adjectival participle καλούμενοι ("so-called") sometimes associated with the collective expression "the Pythagoreans," with which he refers most of the time in an anonymous way to this group of thinkers, even if it may not *per se* give proof of a deliberate reservation vis-à-vis the attribution of the said doctrines to such an evanescent society, might be seen nonetheless as conveying a nuance similar to that of our modern "quotation marks."

While point a) is to be considered virtually beyond discussion and point b), having been established on solid ground by Burkert and discussed at length in a now classical monograph,[12] should remain outside my present concern for

---

11   Walter Burkert, *Lore and Science in Ancient Pythagoreanism*, English transl. by Edwin L. Minar (Harvard: Harvard University Press, 1972), 217; 298; 426 f.

12   Carl Huffman, *Philolaus of Croton: Pythagorean and Presocratic* (Cambridge: Cambridge University Press, 1993), 231 ff., 240 ff.; while Huffman (on pp. 57–64) came to partly disagree with Burkert's appraisal of Pythagorean cosmology in Aristotle, Philolaus is rehabilitated

economy reasons, I will address here mainly, as suggested in this contribution's title, the point c) with more than passing references to point d), insofar as it can throw some light on the former.

3

In Aristotle's extant textual corpus, the name of Pythagoras himself, according to mainstream scholarship, is found only twice, if we are to leave out the chronological connection to Alcmaeon established at *Metaph.* 986a 29 f.: καὶ γὰρ ἐγένετο τὴν ἡλικίαν Ἀλκμαίων ⟨νέος⟩ ἐπὶ γέροντι Πυθαγόρᾳ.[13] In fact, Zeller—followed in this by Ross and Jaeger—did quickly away with it arguing that it was an interpolation of a marginal gloss, on the ground that it was apparently yet unknown to Alexander of Aphrodisias (*in Metaph.* 42.3–4)—who may nonetheless have simply passed over it in his compendious summary of the passage at issue—but was already commented upon by Asclepius (*in Metaph.* 39.21–27), and whose presumable source Burkert identified in a list of 'hearers' of Pythagoras already in his old age drawn up at Iambl. *VP* 104. There, Alcmaeon appears as a disciple of an elderly Pythagoras among actual Pythagoreans like Philolaus, Eurytus and Archytas, but, at the same time, alongside complete outsiders like Epimenides, Leucippus and even the legendary Thracian Zalmoxis, with absolute disregard for any chronological and doctrinal coherence, as is the case also at other points of Iamblichus' account of Pythagoreanism. However, on the assumption that it was not Aristotle himself who (in conformity with a practice notably attested in some instances from Plato's works) pointed to the relative chronology of Pythagoras and Alcmaeon in a context where the close resemblance between the latter and the Pythagoreans regarding the opposites as principles is brought up (*Metaph.* 986a 22 ff.), it would not be improper to wonder how a scholiast came up with the idea to fetch the chronological indication about Pythagoras and Alcmaeon from the list of the former's purported disciples displayed at Iambl. *VP* 104, rather than to use

---

as the latter's ultimate reference in Malcolm Schofield, "Pythagoreanism: emerging from the Presocratic fog (Metaphysics A 5)," in *Aristotle's Metaphysics* Alpha, ed. Steel and Primavesi, 142 f., 147 ff.

13 In Oliver Primavesi's recent edition of book Alpha the passage was printed as quoted above, but with the portions of text omitted in the β manuscript branch bracketed—καὶ γὰρ [ἐγένετο τὴν ἡλικίαν] Ἀλκμαίων [⟨νέος⟩ ἐπὶ γέροντι Πυθαγόρᾳ]. Diels (Alcm. 24 A 3 DK) had restored ⟨νέος⟩ for the sake of stylistic smoothness while referring to Pl. *Tht.* 183e and Pl. *Soph.* 217c; to these passages, I would add here Pl. *Parm.* 127a and Diog. Laert. IX 41 (= Democr. 68 B 5 DK).

228   ÁLVAREZ SALAS

the source wherefrom this piece of information had been extracted, which some evidences will allow us to pinpoint in the Peripatetic Aristoxenus.

From this prominent philosopher and music theorist native to Tarentum, where he grew up in a Pythagorean milieu and who was fond of counting as Pythagorean every intellectual active in South Italy—including Alcmaeon himself, who is featured among the Pythagoreans from Croton in the famous "Catalogue of Pythagoreans" laid out at Iambl. *VP* 267, which is likely to go back to Aristoxenus himself—,[14] Iamblichus has been found to draw either directly or through Nicomachus, even if he handled the information somewhat freely in accordance with the treatment of the topic at issue. In the process, he could eventually abridge or else modify—deliberately or accidentally—the information he was excerpting from an earlier source. This may be the case also for the passage under discussion (Iambl. *VP* 104), which rather than originally authored by Iamblichus himself (as is usually held to be the case) might have been concocted by him based on at least one recognizable source, which might ultimately turn out to be again Aristoxenus. The main clue for identifying this thinker as the origin of the onomastic portion of text embedded there by Iamblichus in the larger frame of his own discussion of the Pythagorean σύμβολα (Iambl. *VP* 103–105) lies in the recurrence of the former's well-known theme of the admission to the Pythagorean society of enthusiastic newcomers, not only from the surrounding barbarian peoples—Lucanians, Messapians, Peucetians and Romans are explicitly named by him elsewhere[15]— but also especially the legendary lawgivers Charondas from Catane and Zaleucus from Locri,[16] who

---

14   Burkert, *Lore and Science*, 105 n. 40; for a critical take on Aristoxenus' probable authorship of the catalogue of Pythagoreans, see Carl Huffman, "Two Problems in Pythagoreanism," in *The Oxford Handbook of Presocratic Philosophy*, ed. Patricia Curd and Daniel W. Graham (Oxford: Oxford University Press, 2005), 297–299.

15   For the references, see following note. Pythagoras' success with the barbarians inhabiting South Italy is also famously evoked at Porph. *VP* 19: γενομένων δὲ τούτων μεγάλη περὶ αὐτοῦ ηὐξήθη δόξα, καὶ πολλοὺς μὲν ἔλαβεν ἐξ αὐτῆς τῆς πόλεως ὁμιλητὰς [...] πολλοὺς δ' ἀπὸ τῆς σύνεγγυς βαρβάρου χώρας βασιλεῖς τε καὶ δυνάστας, which is a famous passage widely held to be an excerpt from a work by his fellow Peripatetic Dicaearchus (Pyth. 14 A 8a DK = Dicaearch. Fr. 40 Mirhady = Pyth. 10a. P25 + 10c. D5 LM, over against Dicaearch. Fr. 33 Wehrli, where just Porph. *VP* 18 is printed), who came from Messina, Sicily.

16   On the purported Pythagorean affiliation of Charondas and Zaleucus, who are mentioned in a passage going back to Aristoxenus, where he also comes to speak about Lucanians, Messapians, Peucetians and Romans approaching Pythagoras, see Porph. *VP* 21–22 (= Aristox. Fr. 17 Wehrli = Pyth. 14 A 12 DK = Pyth. 10b. T24 LM); further mentions of Charondas and Zaleucus as Pythagoreans can be read at Iambl. *VP.* 33; 130; 172; the barbarian peoples to which Aristoxenus refers in the passage quoted above turn up as well at Diog. Laert. VIII 14 (= Pyth. 10a. P26 LM), which thus may be seen as (partly) based on him, all the more so as Aristoxenus appears as source of the immediately following paragraphs (Diog. Laert.

ARISTOTLE'S OUTLOOK ON PYTHAGORAS AND THE PYTHAGOREANS   229

are set in the midst of several other names of real or purported Pythagorean thinkers probably drawn likewise from Aristoxenus' catalogue mentioned
above (Iambl. *VP* 267),[17] where Alcmaeon shows up among the Pythagorean
ranks from Croton. The complete absence of such kind of information in the
parallel passage at Iambl. *Protr.* 105–106 Pistelli—in which large fragments
also found at Iambl. *VP* 103–105 are reproduced *verbatim*, but where the adjective πρεσβύτῃ following Πυθαγόρᾳ is dropped and Pythagoras' students are
altogether skipped—reminds us that, in composing his summa *On Pythagoreanism*, Iamblichus was demonstrably resorting to a host of earlier works on
this subject, which he searched for excerpts he made fit into each particular
context by fleshing them out or cutting them down,[18] which entailed a high
risk of repetitions, incongruities and gross mistakes.

As an upshot of the above discussion, it can be ascertained that the debatable connection between Alcmaeon and Pythagoras at *Metaph.* 986a 29 f. need
not be regarded as a late insertion by an unknown scholiast, but may be seen
instead as a valuable piece of information on their relative chronology probably stemming from Aristotle himself.[19]

VIII 15–16 = Aristox. Fr. 43 Wehrli), where Charondas and Zaleucus are also mentioned;
one may infer therefrom that similar passages containing either the names of the two
lawgivers or of the four Italic peoples above mentioned derive likewise from Aristoxenus
(cf. Iambl. *VP.* 241); for a contrary view on this point see Huffman, "Two Problems in
Pythagoreanism," 298. Doubts about the ascription to Aristoxenus of the entirety of the
two passages quoted above that are ascribed to him by Wehrli are raised in Huffman, "The
Peripatetics on the Pythagoreans," in *A History of Pythagoreanism*, ed. Huffman, 292 n. 25.

17   Exception should be made for the Pythagoreans Aristaeus (whose notable absence from
the catalogue as preserved in Iamblichus has been remarked by some scholars) and
Bryson (whose name might be a 'normalization' of the somewhat rarer Bryas, which is
mentioned twice in the catalogue, as from Croton and as from Tarentum), and for the
non-Pythagoreans Zalmoxis and Epimenides, who may have been included here either by
Iamblichus or by his intermediate source because of their being linked with Pythagoras in
some well-known traditions regarding a joint *katabasis* or descent into an underground
cavity (on Zalmoxis, see Hdt. IV 95 f. = Pyth. 14 A 2 DK = Pyth. 10a. P30 LM; on Epimenides,
see Diog. Laert. VIII 3); inserting here Leucippus seems just a gratuitous touch of solidar-
ity with an elusive personage hard to classify.

18   On Iamblichus' rhetorical skills to compose a praise for Pythagoras from a wide range of
materials, see Dominic O'Meara, *Pythagoras Revived: Mathematics and Philosophy in Late
Antiquity* (Oxford: Oxford University Press, 1990), 36: "Iamblichus follows all of those prescriptions [*i.e.* those pertaining to the rhetorical praise] marshalling the various source-
materials available to him so as to fit them into the required compositional structure."

19   For Aristotle's probable authorship of the accurate chronological remark about
Alcmaeon and Pythagoras, see Leonid Zhmud, *Pythagoras and the Early Pythagoreans*
(Oxford: Oxford University Press, 2012), 122 n. 74; 123 n. 79; Schofield, "Pythagoreanism,"
156 n. 33, also concurs with this view. An overview of the problem with the main

Notwithstanding, even on the widely accepted hypothesis of its being an incorporated marginal gloss (awkwardly comprising the two separate wings [ἐγένετο τὴν ἡλικίαν] and [ἐπὶ γέροντι Πυθαγόρᾳ] on each side of Ἀλκμαίων, according to the modern editors of the *Metaphysics*), it may ultimately be traced back to a 4th century B.C. doxographical tradition of Pythagoreanism such as that arguably represented by the so-called "Catalogue of Pythagoreans," whose most obvious candidate for authorship would be Aristoxenus, a one-time associate of Aristotle at the Lyceum and, on account of his first-hand knowledge and personal Pythagorean background, maybe one of the latter's main informants on Pythagorean matters.[20]

Now, once argued for vindicating the likelihood of Pythagoras' cameo in the *Metaphysics*, the two remaining canonical occurrences of this thinker's own name in the *Corpus Aristotelicum* as we know it are found at *Rhet.* 1398b9-15 and at *Mag. mor.* 1182a 11 ff., the first being a 'harmless' statement taken from Alkidamas—which is quoted by Aristotle along with other instances of induction being used as a rhetorical device by the orators—on the honors received by wise men abroad, namely those the Greeks from Italy granted to the Samian incomer Pythagoras, where the reference to Pythagoras is purposefully set between that to Chilon, whom the Lacedaemonians admitted in their γερουσία, notwithstanding their not being fond of learning, and that to the ongoing honors paid by the people of Lampsacus to Anaxagoras, whom they buried in their land, even if he was a foreigner there.[21] This context might suggest that motivations similar to those prevailing in the cases of Chilon and Anaxagoras led the Italiote Greeks to homage the sage Pythagoras of Samos,[22] being reportedly acclaimed as an outstanding personage and even invited to address a

---

supporters of the α manuscript branch reading at *Metaph.* 986a 29 f. or of its rejection can be found in Constantinos Macris, "Pythagore," in *Dictionnaire des philosophes antiques*, Vol. VII: D'Ulpien à Zoticus, ed. Richard Goulet (Paris: CNRS Éditions, 2018), 719.

20 Aristoxenus' father (or grandfather) was the Pythagorean Spintharos, a close friend of Archytas and a contemporary of the last Pythagoreans, whom Aristoxenus himself still got to know, according to Diog. Laert. VIII 46 (= Aristox. Fr. 19 Wehrli); on Aristoxenus' deep acquaintance with Pythagoreanism, see Leonid Zhmud, "Aristoxenus and the Pythagoreans," in *Aristoxenus of Tarentum. Texts and Discussion*, ed. Carl Huffman (New Brunswick, N.J.: Transaction Publishers, 2012), 223–250.

21 Arist. *Rhet.* 1398b9-15 (= Pyth. 14 A 5 DK = Pyth. 10a. P45 LM): καὶ ὡς Ἀλκιδάμας, ὅτι πάντες τοὺς σοφοὺς τιμῶσιν· "Πάριοι γοῦν Ἀρχίλοχον καίπερ βλάσφημον ὄντα τετιμήκασι [...] καὶ Λακεδαιμόνιοι Χίλωνα καὶ τῶν γερόντων ἐποίησαν ἥκιστα φιλόλογοι ὄντες, καὶ Ἰταλιῶται Πυθαγόραν, καὶ Λαμψακηνοὶ Ἀναξαγόραν ξένον ὄντα ἔθαψαν καὶ τιμῶσι ἔτι καὶ νῦν, κτλ."

22 For a similar take on this passage, see Macris, "Pythagore," 707; Zhmud, *Pythagoras and the Early Pythagoreans*, 43 f.

ARISTOTLE'S OUTLOOK ON PYTHAGORAS AND THE PYTHAGOREANS

series of public speeches to different age and sex groups of Crotoniate citizens forthwith upon arrival in their city.[23]

This type of reference is in line with other biographical information about the Samian thinker that has been retrieved elsewhere by Aristotle, who included it in several of his works, extant or lost. As a matter of fact, there is a striking pendant to Aristotle's notice cited above on honors paid to Pythagoras by the Greeks of South Italy in a quotation that records some instances of rivalry against big personalities, with Socrates being subject to the Lemnian Antilochus' and the seer Antiphon's antagonism and Pythagoras being vied by Cylon and Onatas,[24] among other similar cases, which our witness Diogenes Laërtius (II 46) says to come from the now lost third book of Aristotle's *Poetics*,[25] but that is suspected to be instead an excerpt from the likewise lost work *On Poets*.[26]

As for the passage from the *Magna Moralia*,[27] which identifies Pythagoras as the first Greek thinker who undertook to treat about 'excellence' (ἀρετή), albeit in connection with an arithmological speculation that, according to Aristotle, is not fitting to the subject matter, namely the ἀρεταί, some attempts at explaining it away have been carried out. Among these there is first of all Burkert's own, who championed the 20th century crusade to erase Pythagoras' name from the history of philosophical thought, and who relied here heavily on the assumption that the *Magna Moralia* was not a genuine work by Aristotle. However, several outstanding scholars have argued that it may well be an early writing of this philosopher, dating to his years in Athens as a young man, which

---

23 Porph. *VP* 18 (Pyth. 14 A 8a DK = Pyth. 10a. P25 LM = Dicaearch. Fr. 40 Mirhady = Dicaearch. Fr. 33 Wehrli); take note, however, that the earliest extant testimony on Pythagoras' speeches delivered at Croton is Antisthenes as quoted by Porphyr. *schol. ad Od.* I, 1 (= Antisth. v A 187 Giannantoni = Antisth. Fr. 51 Decleva Caizzi = Pyth. 10b. T14 LM).

24 Here I follow the unanimous manuscript reading καὶ Ὀνάτας (καὶ ὀνάτας P¹Φ: καιονατάς B: καὶ ὀνάτης FPˣ) with Diels (Pyth. 14 A 15 DK), Marcovich (Diogenes Laertius. *Vitae Philosophorum*, ed. Miroslav Marcovich, Stuttgart-Leipzig: Teubner, 1999) and Dorandi (Diogenes Laertius. *Lives of Eminent Philosophers*, ed. Tiziano Dorandi, Cambridge: Cambridge University Press, 2013) instead of Menage's (now deprecated) correction Κροτωνιάτης accepted by Long (*Diogenis Laertii vitae philosophorum*, ed. Herbert S. Long, Oxford: Clarendon Press, 1964).

25 There is an echo of this same passage from Aristotle at Diog. Laert. VIII 49, where the source is not indicated, yet.

26 Diog. Laert. II 46 (= Arist. Περὶ ποιητῶν, fr. 75 Rose): τούτῳ (sc. τῷ Σωκράτει) τίς, καθά φησιν Ἀριστοτέλης ἐν τρίτῳ Περὶ ποιητικῆς, ἐφιλονείκει Ἀντίλοχος Λήμνιος καὶ Ἀντιφῶν ὁ τερατοσκόπος, ὡς Πυθαγόρᾳ Κύλων καὶ Ὀνάτας· κτλ.

27 Arist. *Mag. mor.* 1182a 11 ff. (I 1, 6 Susemihl): πρῶτος μὲν οὖν ἐνεχείρησεν Πυθαγόρας περὶ ἀρετῆς εἰπεῖν, οὐκ ὀρθῶς δέ· τὰς γὰρ ἀρετὰς εἰς τοὺς ἀριθμοὺς ἀνάγων οὐκ οἰκείαν τῶν ἀρετῶν τὴν θεωρίαν ἐποιεῖτο· οὐ γάρ ἐστιν ἡ δικαιοσύνη ἀριθμὸς ἰσάκις ἴσος.

is in full agreement with the *constat* that virtually all of his production on Pythagorean subjects was written during his stay at the Academy.[28] At any rate, even if most scholars that accept this work as Aristotle's own and, therefore, validate its reference to Pythagoras, lean towards taking this occurrence as a sign of his conformance to the tendency typical among his early colleagues—i.e. the Old Academy members—to attribute to Pythagoras every kind of doctrine regardless of its having been proposed by a later Pythagorean,[29] there is not a hint of such a procedure in this particular instance. In fact, stating that "justice is a number equal times equal," *i.e.*, a square number, is by all accounts just as primitive and naïve a doctrine as any other Pythagorean arithmological lore that has been found likely to trace as far back as the 6th century B.C., such as the well-known speculations about the *tetraktys* or 'fourness',[30] a symbolic equilateral triangle composed out of unit-points (represented by rows of pebbles or dots) standing for the four first whole numbers, *i.e.*, the positive integers, which are involved in the expression of the three musical ratios (2:1, 3:2, and 4:3) and which added together would produce the most perfect number, i.e. ten or decad ($1 + 2 + 3 + 4 = 10$).[31] Unsurprisingly enough, Aristotle himself, in a well-known passage where he discusses the forerunners of Socrates' endeavor to arrive at universal definitions,[32] takes issue with a Pythagorean previous

---

28   On this point see Zhmud, *Pythagoras and the Early Pythagoreans*, 57 nn. 112–114.

29   This view is held, among others, by Zhmud, *Pythagoras and the Early Pythagoreans*, 57 f. n. 118, who follows here in the footsteps of Burkert, *Lore and Science*, 79 f., 81.

30   For a discussion of the multi-level significance of the *tetraktys* pattern in ancient Pythagoreanism and for its inclusion in the earliest core of doctrine that may be reasonably attributed to Pythagoras himself, see Kahn, *Pythagoras and the Pythagoreans*, 31 ff.; this is contested by Zhmud, *Pythagoras and the Early Pythagoreans*, 300 f., 303 n. 61, 408 n. 81, 425 f., who holds the *tetraktys* and the doctrine of the decad to be a projection by Speusippus of Platonic teachings onto Pythagoras or, for that matter, onto the Pythagoreans.

31   Even if the authenticity of the formerly held as the most ancient testimony on the paramount importance of the number 10 seems now doubtful (Stob. *ecl. I prooem. cor.* 3 [p. 16, 20 W] = Philol. 44 B 11 DK, which was taken by Diels to be a literal quotation from Philolaus' Περὶ φύσιος, as opposed to Huffman, *Philolaus of Croton*, 347), the doctrine itself finds a strong confirmation in Aristotle's own discussion of the Pythagorean number cosmology at *Metaph.* 985b23 ff. (= Anon. Pyth. 58 B 4 DK = Pyths. Anon. 17 D1 LM), where he works in some comments about the significance of the decad for the Pythagoreans (at *Metaph.* 986a8-12); for an explicit definition of the number 10 or decad as the potency of number 4 with regard to the Pythagorean doctrine, see Aët. I 3, 8 Diels ([Plut.] *epit.* I 3 = Stob. *ecl. phys.* I c. 10, 12), where also the Pythagorean oath by the *tetraktys* is quoted, which might go back likewise "to the earliest stratum of Pythagorean tradition," according to Kahn, *Pythagoras and the Pythagoreans*, 35 (*contra* see Zhmud, *Pythagoras and the Early Pythagoreans*, 300 f.).

32   Arist. *Metaph.* 1078b21-23 (= Anon. Pyth. 58 B 4 DK = Pyths. Anon. 17 D20a LM).

attempt to establish definitions for a handful of concepts by relating them to numbers, which he dates to a time prior to Democritus—τῶν μὲν γὰρ φυσικῶν ἐπὶ μικρὸν Δημόκριτος ἥψατο ... οἱ δὲ Πυθαγόρειοι πρότερον κτλ.—, thus meaning it to be a doctrine likely to belong to the core teachings originally stemming from Pythagoras himself or arisen very close to this philosopher's time.[33] In fact, on the assumption of a virtual synchronicity between Philolaus and Democritus (Diog. Laert. IX 38), whom Apollodorus turns into Socrates' younger contemporary by dating his birth to the 80th Olympiad (460–457 b.C.),[34] then the paramount significance of the decad such as was featured presumably in the former's treatise Περὶ φύσιος,[35] and perhaps even its potential being in the *tetraktys* or 'fourness'—along with other similar number speculations—may safely be attributed on Aristotle's own authority either to Pythagoras himself or to his immediate entourage.[36]

Now, among the notions reportedly defined through the numerological procedure called forth at *Metaph.* 1078b21-23, Aristotle explicitly names the right moment (καιρός), justice (τὸ δίκαιον) and marriage (γάμος), being this a partial reprise of the point made at *Metaph.* 985b26 ff., where also δικαιοσύνη and καιρός occur among other similar instances of Pythagorean number speculation,[37]

---

33   Such an inference is supported by the commentary of Alex. Aphr. *in Metaph.* 37, 7–12 Hayd. (to Arist. *Metaph.* 1078b23): ἢ [...] οὐ περὶ Δημοκρίτου τε καὶ Λευκίππου μόνον λέγει, ἀλλὰ περὶ πάντων τῶν φυσικῶν τῶν προειρημένων· τῶν μὲν γὰρ ἦσαν πρεσβύτεροι, τοῖς δὲ συνήκμασαν. ἢ μᾶλλον ὅτι αὐτὸς μὲν Πυθαγόρας πρὸ Δημοκρίτου τε καὶ Λευκίππου ὀλίγον ἐγένετο, πολλοὶ δὲ τῶν Πυθαγόρου ἀκουσάντων συνήκμασαν τούτοις. On the speculations about the decad as a Pythagorean doctrine of long standing, see Kahn, *Pythagoras and the Pythagoreans*, 34; for a recent assessment of Aristotle's treatment of Pythagorean number symbolism as a true reflection of a very ancient teaching, see Schofield, "Pythagoreanism: emerging from the Presocratic fog (Metaphysics A 5)," 143 ff. (especially 148 n. 14).

34   Diog. Laert. IX 41, where however Thrasyllus' dating of Democritus' birth to the third year of the 77th Ol. [470/469 b.C.] is set over against Apollodorus' own estimate; both dates would ultimately be compatible with Democritus' statement at that same passage of his being young in Anaxagoras' old age.

35   For some testimonies of Philolaus' special interest in the decad—setting aside Theo. Smyrn. 106, 10 = Philol. 44 B 11 DK, where also Philolaus' purported quotation at Stob. *ecl. I prooem. cor.* 3 is included (= Pyths. R. 18 R48 LM)—, see Luc. *Laps.* 5 (= Philol. 44 A 11 DK = Philol. 12 D 29 LM) and *Theolog. Arithm.* p. 82, 10 de Falco (= Philol. 44 A 13 DK).

36   A further reference to the numerological speculations which the Pythagoreans heaped upon the perfection of number 'ten' is found at [*Pr.*] 910b23-39, regardless of its legitimate attribution to Aristotle.

37   Arist. *Metaph.* 985b26-31: ἐπεὶ δὲ τούτων οἱ ἀριθμοὶ φύσει πρῶτοι, ἐν δὲ τούτοις ἐδόκουν θεωρεῖν ὁμοιώματα πολλὰ τοῖς οὖσι καὶ γιγνομένοις, μᾶλλον ἢ ἐν πυρὶ καὶ γῇ καὶ ὕδατι, ὅτι τὸ μὲν τοιονδὶ τῶν ἀριθμῶν πάθος δικαιοσύνη τὸ δὲ τοιονδὶ ψυχή τε καὶ νοῦς ἕτερον δὲ καιρὸς καὶ τῶν ἄλλων ὡς εἰπεῖν ἕκαστον ὁμοίως, κτλ.

234 ÁLVAREZ SALAS

which Alexander of Aphrodisias in his commentary explains to have been attached by the Pythagoreans to certain definite numbers, inasmuch as their properties were equated with those concepts.[38] Justice in particular was thus conceived at Arist. *Mag. mor.* 1182a 11 ff. as "the product of the first number taken an equal number of times" (ἀριθμὸς ἰσάκις ἴσος),[39] and, according to the symbolic Pythagorean saying of unmistakably acousmatic ring quoted elsewhere by Aristotle himself, this was apparently also tantamount to "justice is the requital (or retaliation) for another thing,"[40] just as is suggested by the reciprocal correspondence between the factors generating the first square number (*i.e.* 2 x 2 = 4) that we saw above associated with that same notion.

Therefore, once reconstructed the whole frame of reference within which the attribution to Pythagoras himself of such an undeniably archaic definition of justice may be made, one indeed that proceeds from a type of number speculation also attested for other pieces of Pythagorean teaching arguably going back to the earliest—*i.e.*, 6th century B.C.—core of doctrines, then we may confidently associate it with its very founder and be assured of Aristotle's knowledgeable handing down of the related ancient tradition. Hence, the subsistence of the reference to Pythagoras himself found at Arist. *Mag.*

---

38 Alex. Aphr. *in Metaph.* 37, 17–39, 12 Hayd.: τῆς μὲν γὰρ δικαιοσύνης ἴδιον ὑπολαμβάνοντες εἶναι τὸ ἀντιπεπονθός τε καὶ ἴσον, ἐν τοῖς ἀριθμοῖς τοῦτο εὑρίσκοντες ὄν, διὰ τοῦτο καὶ τὸν ἰσάκις ἴσον ἀριθμὸν πρῶτον ἔλεγον εἶναι δικαιοσύνην· τὸ γὰρ πρῶτον ἐν ἑκάστῳ τῶν τὸν αὐτὸν λόγον ἐχόντων μάλιστα εἶναι τοῦτο ὃ λέγεται. τοῦτον δὲ οἱ μὲν τὸν τέσσαρα ἔλεγον, ἐπεὶ πρῶτος ὢν τετράγωνος εἰς ἴσα διαιρεῖται καὶ ἔστιν ἴσος (δὶς γὰρ δύο) [...] καιρὸν δὲ πάλιν ἔλεγον τὸν ἑπτά· δοκεῖ γὰρ τὰ φυσικὰ τοὺς τελείους καιροὺς ἴσχειν καὶ γενέσεως καὶ τελειώσεως κατὰ ἑβδομάδας, ὡς ἐπ' ἀνθρώπου. [...] γάμον δὲ ἔλεγον τὸν πέντε, ὅτι ὁ μὲν γάμος σύνοδος ἄρρενός ἐστι καὶ θήλεος, ἔστι δὲ κατ' αὐτοὺς ἄρρεν μὲν τὸ περιττὸν θῆλυ δὲ τὸ ἄρτιον, πρῶτος δὲ οὗτος ἐξ ἀρτίου τοῦ δύο πρώτου καὶ πρώτου τοῦ τρία περιττοῦ τὴν γένεσιν ἔχει.

39 As Aristotle's expression is translated by Kahn, *Pythagoras and the Pythagoreans*, 34, whereby number 2 is meant, *i.e.* the first plural number, over against 1, which in the Pythagorean view of arithmetic is both even and odd and does not count as really a number—on this see Arist. *Metaph.* 986a17-21.

40 Arist. *Eth. Nic.* 1132b21-23 (= Anon. Pyth. 58 B4 DK = Pyths. Anon. 17 D4 LM): δοκεῖ δέ τισι καὶ τὸ ἀντιπεπονθὸς εἶναι ἁπλῶς δίκαιον, ὥσπερ οἱ Πυθαγόρειοι ἔφασαν· ὡρίζοντο γὰρ ἁπλῶς τὸ δίκαιον τὸ ἀντιπεπονθὸς ἄλλῳ (likewise Arist. *Mag. mor.* 1194a 29-b 2). The translation "suffering in return with someone else" given by Laks-Most for the last sentence— where I find ἄλλῳ to be more naturally felt as a neuter on account of its following τὸ ἀντιπεπονθός—seems hardly tenable or intelligible (any more than the non-equivalent "ce qui est subi en retour par autrui" printed in the French edition of their collection), since the mathematical backdrop against which this definition is unfolded perfectly matches the numerological definition of justice given at Arist. *Mag. mor.* 1182a 11 ff., as well as the explanation given in Alexander of Aphrodisias' commentary quoted above (n. 56), thus making plain that the technical sense of reciprocal proportionality (cf. Euc. 6 Def. 2 and 6.14) is also here by far the more probable reading of τὸ ἀντιπεπονθός.

mor. 1182a 11 ff. cannot simply be dismissed either on the ground of a suspicion about this work's inauthenticity, or on account of the contrasting appearance of the Pythagoreans instead of their Master at the other passages of the *Corpus Aristotelicum* where that same definition of justice comes up (*Metaph.* 985b29, *Metaph.* 1078b21-23, *Eth. Nic.* 1132b21-23 and *Mag. mor.* 1194a 29-b 2). In fact, it will be shown in the following pages how Pythagoras' name was used in the monographs that Aristotle wrote on Pythagorean subjects in his early years spent at the Academy and, being connected there both with scientific or religious doctrines and with the legendary traits surrounding the Samian philosopher,[41] subsequently made way in the next stage of written production of the Stagirite for the collective designation οἱ Πυθαγόρειοι, which proved to be a more powerful doxographical tool for his later works of synthesis.

4

At this point, account must be taken of the fact that Aristotle, besides making frequent allusions to Pythagorean scientific doctrines—which he very seldom connects with individual names, even though he sometimes does and often taking issue with them in an important number of passages in his extant works of philosophical and scientific character— devoted likewise two special monographs to set out and critically address the Pythagorean scientific doctrines and religious lore. This was done from a many-sided perspective, as he treated in them, along with the more philosophical and scientific doctrines cultivated by the Pythagoreans of the 6th to 4th centuries B.C., also the biographical and legendary tradition surrounding Pythagoras' own figure. Moreover, he wrote one more monograph in three books dealing exclusively with the doctrines of the 4th century Pythagorean Archytas (the most prominent 4th century Pythagorean who is widely known to have been Plato's friend), supplemented by an additional writing in one book commenting upon excerpts from Plato's *Timaeus* with regard to Archytas' philosophy, while an additional book contained a *Criticism of Alcmaeon's doctrines*, which Aristotle apparently viewed as compatible with those of the Pythagoreans, at least as far as the general idea of pairs of opposites was concerned, whereas no underlying implication

---

41 On the regular employ of Pythagoras' own name in Aristotle's early works, see Zhmud, *Pythagoras and the Early Pythagoreans*, 57 nn. 112–114; on the latter's writings devoted to Pythagorean themes and figures, see also the discussion in the following section.

236 ÁLVAREZ SALAS

of a school or personal affiliation with Pythagoras and/or other Pythagoreans is necessarily meant there for Alcmaeon himself.[42]

In particular, among Aristotle's works mentioned in the ancient lists, which record a lot of his written products that did not manage to survive as whole works until our times, the two Pythagorean items Πρὸς τοὺς Πυθαγορείους ("Against the Pythagoreans") and Περὶ τῶν Πυθαγορείων ("On the Pythagoreans") each in one book are featured (Diog. Laert. v 25), which were eventually conflated (perhaps around the 2nd century B.C.) into only one work in two books listed as Περὶ τῶν Πυθαγόρου δοξῶν ("On the doctrines of Pythagoras") in Ptolemy's catalogue of Aristotle's works,[43] but included in Hesychius' catalogue as Περὶ τῶν Πυθαγορείων in just one book,[44] apparently as a result of a further condensation of the previous two-book stage of this compilation. This same work is seemingly also mentioned by later authors under various titles, so that it may be deemed identical as well to the treatise Περὶ τῆς Πυθαγόρου φιλοσοφίας quoted by Aëtius and Stobaeus that was apparently constituted by at least two books (Arist. fr. 201 Rose), further to the Περὶ τῆς Πυθαγορικῶν δόξης (or Δόξαι τῶν Πυθαγορικῶν) from whose second book Alexander of Aphrodisias drew some information for his commentary (Arist. frr. 202–203 Rose); finally, it would be the same work as the Συναγωγή τῶν Πυθαγορείοις ἀρεσκόντων cited by Simplicius (Arist. fr. 200 Rose). Whatever the actual title and bulk of these works, the numerous references to them by a long series of witnesses from the 4th century B.C. onwards give proof of their Aristotelian genuine authorship, in spite of which they have even been suspected of being pseudepigraphic writings by skeptical scholars like Rohde and Rose, who hypercritically rejected as spurious all Aristotle's alleged treatises on Pythagorean matters along with all his remaining lost works. This attempt notwithstanding, the authenticity of such lost works on Pythagoreanism is confirmed beyond any reasonable doubt by Aristotle's own allusion to a more detailed exposition of his on the Pythagorean planetary system at *Metaph.* 986a 12: διώρισται δὲ περὶ τούτων ἐν ἑτέροις ἡμῖν ἀκριβέστερον, which suggest a separate writing likely to be identified with

---

42 For Aristotle's remarks on the close resemblance between the Pythagoreans' table of opposites and Alcmaeon's own doctrine, see *Metaph.* 986a22-986b4 (= Alcmaeon 24 A 3 DK = Alcmaeon 23 D5 + P1 LM); for the probable connection between Alcmaeon and Pythagoras at *Metaph.* 986a 29 f., see the preceding section.

43 Ptolemy al-Gharîb is meant, who preserved for us an abridged version of the lost catalogue of Aristotle's works drawn up by Andronicus of Rhodes, which is transmitted in an Arabic manuscript kept in Istanbul (Ms. Ayasofya 4833, f. 10a-18a).

44 Hesych. *Vit. Arist.* 109 Düring. This important list of Aristotle's writings is contained in the *Vita Hesychii*, also known as *Vita Menagiana* or *Vita Menagii*, which is available in Ingemar Düring, *Aristotle in the ancient biographical tradition* (Göteborg: Elanders, 1957), 82–89.

the work Alexander of Aphrodisias refers to as Δόξαι τῶν Πυθαγορικῶν in his commentary to this very passage.[45] Moreover, we have a quotation from Aristotle's treatise *On the Pythagoreans* in Apoll. *hist. mirab.* 6 (= Arist. fr. 191 Rose), presumably reached through Bolus, which provides a *terminus ante quem* for it somewhere in the 2nd century B.C., thus virtually excluding its being one of the Hellenistic pseudo-Pythagorean fabrications that arguably blossomed from the 1st century B.C. to the 1st century A.D.

In point of fact, the surviving quotations from these treatises—whose authenticity no serious scholar doubts today—allow us to ascertain that Aristotle collected and discussed in them a large mass of material regarding Pythagoras' life and the legend that had formed around him, as well as the body of doctrine he bequeathed to his followers for them to keep and follow, even though it might eventually have undergone developments and expansions at the hands of later Pythagoreans. At any rate, it is absolutely certain that the material gathered by Aristotle (or else by one of his collaborators in the Peripatos, presumably acting under his supervision and following his project) pertained not just to the superstitious injunctions and the rules governing the Pythagorean way of life included in Pythagoras' teaching, but it also concerned other pieces of information related to the more scientific or philosophical aspect of Pythagoreanism, as guaranteed by the quotations included in their own writings by the commentators of Aristotle's works.

However, even if space constraints will prevent me from discussing in detail all the passages where such doctrines, irrespective of their being usually transmitted under the collective label 'Pythagoreans' (either in Aristotle's extant works or in the related commentaries), are likely to go back to Pythagoras himself,[46] it will be useful to draw anyway the attention here to some of the surviving fragments from Aristotle's lost works, which clearly show that the Stagirite did not shrink at all from mentioning the Samian thinker by name, even in connection with philosophical or even scientific teachings. To begin with, there is a fragment retrieved from Aristotle's lost *Protrepticus* that runs like this:

---

45   Alex. Aphrod. *in Ar. metaph.* (1, 5) p. 30, 25 Bon. (= Arist. fr. 203 Rose).

46   It was already pointed out above (with regard to Arist. *Mag. mor.* 1182a 11 ff.) the likelihood of having Pythagoras himself be the founder of the number speculation usually linked with ancient Pythagoreanism; for a sympathetic treatment of this matter, see Kahn, *Pythagoras and the Pythagoreans*, 31 ff.; an optimistic attempt to vindicate most of the doctrines reported by Aristotle as Pythagoras' own teaching is made by Riedweg, *Pythagoras*, 105 ff.; one may also see below the discussion of the Pythagorean soul theory as handed down by Aristotle.

Τί δὴ τοῦτ' ἐστὶν τῶν ὄντων οὗ χάριν ἡ φύσις ἡμᾶς ἐγέννησε καὶ ὁ θεός; τοῦτο Πυθαγόρας ἐρωτώμενος, 'Τὸ θεάσασθαι' εἶπε 'τὸν οὐρανόν', καὶ ἑαυτὸν δὲ θεωρὸν ἔφασκεν εἶναι τῆς φύσεως καὶ τούτου ἕνεκα παρεληλυθέναι εἰς τὸν βίον.

For which among existing objects [sc. of thinking] has Nature along with God brought us into being? Pythagoras, when asked this question, answered: 'To observe the heavens', and used to say that he was an observer of nature, and that this was the reason why he had come into this life.[47]

This report, which by the use of the term οὐρανός in a sense—verging on that of the *terminus technicus* κόσμος as probably resemantized by Pythagoras himself[48]—such as Aristotle himself adopts in a whole set of passages from his *Physics* and *Metaphysics* where he discusses the principles postulated by the Pythagoreans to account for the generation of everything, including the οὐρανός itself "as it is called,"[49] not only creates a solid link with the tradition about the 'contemplative' life contained in the anecdote about Pythagoras as the inventor of the word φιλοσοφία that has been traced back to Heraclides of Pontus,[50] where θεωρία was the key word to disclose to the laymen the meaning

---

47 Iambl. *Protr.* 51, 6–10 Pistelli (= Arist. fr. 18 Rose). Translation is mine (after Düring). The idea attributed to Pythagoras in this fragment turns up likewise at Iambl. Protr. 52, 6–8 Pistelli (= Arist. fr. 20 Rose): Καλῶς ἄρα κατά γε τοῦτον τὸν λόγον Πυθαγόρας εἴρηκεν ὡς ἐπὶ τὸ γνῶναί τε καὶ θεωρῆσαι πᾶς ἄνθρωπος ὑπὸ τοῦ θεοῦ συνέστηκεν ("According to this argument [sc. to the answer given by Anaxagoras to the question: "Why would you choose to become a human being and be alive? To gaze at the heavens and the stars in it, as well as at the moon and the sun"], then, Pythagoras was right in saying that every man has been shaped by God in order to acquire knowledge and observe"). Translation after Zhmud with slight changes.

48 Aët. II 1, 1 (*Dox. Gr.* 327, 8) = Pyth. 14 A 21 DK = Pyth. 10c. D13 LM (cf. also Iambl. *VP* 162); for a reflection of the original Pythagorean notion of κόσμος in Plato *Gorg.* 506c-8a (especially 507e-508a), see Palmer, "The Pythagoreans and Plato," 205 f.; for further treatments of this subject, see Macris, "Pythagore," 831.

49 Arist. *Metaph.* 989b29-990a5 (= Anon. Pyth. 58 B 22 DK = Pyths. Anon. 17 D5 LM); further cosmological references to Pythagorean explanations of how the οὐρανός (≈ κόσμος ≈ τὸ πᾶν) rises out of numbers (or out of breath and void) are the following: *Metaph.* 986a2 f. (ὑπέλαβον ... τὸν ὅλον οὐρανὸν ἁρμονίαν εἶναι καὶ ἀριθμόν); *Metaph.* 1080b16 ff.; *Metaph.* 1090a30 ff.; *Phys.* 203a6 ff.; *Phys.* 213b22 ff. (cf. [*Pr.*] 910b36 ff.: ἢ ὅτι ἐν δέκα ἀναλογίαις τέτταρες κυβικοὶ ἀριθμοὶ ἀποτελοῦνται, ἐξ ὧν φασὶν ἀριθμῶν οἱ Πυθαγόρειοι τὸ πᾶν συνεστάναι;).

50 For φιλόσοφος/φιλοσοφία as a word coinage original with Pythagoras and with Heraclitus as its first witness, see Francesc Casadesús, "¿Escribió Heráclito la palabra *philosophous* en el fragmento DK B 35?," 144 ff.; a similar treatment of this issue with an insightful discussion of the sources going back to Heraclides can be found in Riedweg, *Pythagoras*, 120–128; for further discussion of Pythagoras' naming performances, see Macris, "Pythagore," 829 ff.

ARISTOTLE'S OUTLOOK ON PYTHAGORAS AND THE PYTHAGOREANS   239

lying in that then recent coinage.[51] It also brings Pythagoras into a lineage of research on nature based on 'gazing', to which, in addition to Thales,[52] especially Anaxagoras belongs, with whom the sage from Samos is closely paralleled in a conspicuous set of testimonies.[53]

Again, in a surviving fragment from his treatise *On Archytas' Philosophy*,[54] Aristotle recorded a specific philosophical doctrine, which he attributed to Pythagoras himself:

> Ἀριστοτέλης δὲ ἐν τοῖς Ἀρχυτείοις ἱστορεῖ καὶ Πυθαγόραν "ἄλλο" τὴν ὕλην καλεῖν ὡς ῥευστὴν καὶ ἀεὶ ἄλλο καὶ ἄλλο γιγνόμενον· ὥστε δῆλός ἐστι καὶ ὁ Πλάτων ταύτῃ τὰ ἄλλα ἀφοριζόμενος [*i.e.* τὰ αἰσθητά].

> Aristotle in his writing on Archytas reports that also Pythagoras called matter the 'other', on account of its flowing state and its ever becoming other. It is plain, then, that also Plato is applying to the 'others' [*i.e.* the perceptible objects] that same distinction.[55]

As is expected, this reference to a purported doctrine of Pythagoras that is remarkably similar to one of the main tenets of Plato's philosophy has aroused suspicions among modern scholars, who have been divided between those that squarely reject the report as unreliable and those that emendate the text to make it fit Zeller's (and Burkert's) pronouncement about Aristotle systematically avoiding Pythagoras' name in his published or, rather, extant whole writings.[56] While the former group accounts for the notice as a projection onto

---

51   Diog. Laert. I 12, Cic. Tusc. v 8 (= Heraclid. Pont. fr. 87–88 Wehrli; cf. also Iambl. *VP* 58); on this see Riedweg, *Pythagoras*, 121 f., 127 f.; Zhmud, *Pythagoras and the Early Pythagoreans*, 56 f., 429 f.

52   The earliest extant testimony on this aspect of Thales' interests is found at Pl. *Tht.* 174a-b.

53   On the tradition linking Pythagoras with Anaxagoras, see Zhmud, *Pythagoras and the Early Pythagoreans*, 43 f.; 47 f.; 56.

54   The precise work by Aristotle lying behind the vague reference to "matters pertaining Archytas" (ἐν τοῖς Ἀρχυτείοις) ought to be Περὶ τῆς Ἀρχυτείου φιλοσοφίας (or Περὶ τῆς Ἀρχύτου φιλοσοφίας) rather than Τὰ ἐκ τοῦ Τιμαίου καὶ τῶν Ἀρχυτείων (or Ἐκ τῶν Τιμαίου καὶ Ἀρχύτου).

55   Damasc. *In Parm.* 172.20 (= Arist. fr. 207 Rose). Translation is mine. This commentator introduces the quotation from Aristotle by referring to Plato equating 'others' and perceptible objects in the *Phaedo*: "Ἐν τε γὰρ τῷ Φαίδωνι οὕτως ὀνομάζει τὰ ἄλλα τὰ εἴδη, τὰ αἰσθητὰ λέγων "ἄλλα καὶ ἐν ἄλλοις." The passage meant thereby seems to be *Phd.* 83b: ὅτι δ' ἂν δι' ἄλλων σκοπῇ ἐν ἄλλοις ὂν ἄλλο, μηδὲν ἡγεῖσθαι ἀληθές· εἶναι δὲ τὸ μὲν τοιοῦτον αἰσθητόν τε καὶ ὁρατόν, ὃ δὲ αὐτὴ ὁρᾷ νοητόν τε καὶ ἀιδές.

56   In this case, however, Burkert himself (*Lore and Science*, 81) conceded the possibility of Pythagoras being mentioned by Aristotle: "If the doxography goes back, in general, to the Old Academy, it is possible that Aristotle too, either in an early work, or in an exoteric

Pythagoras of a later doctrine, *i.e.*, Plato's own, which the Neoplatonists would have thus uplifted to ancient lore, the latter dispose of Pythagoras' name by arbitrarily 'correcting' Πυθαγόραν to Πυθαγορείους,[57] so as to harmonize this passage with the dominant scholarly prejudice just recalled. However, neither of these two approaches proves necessary if we bear in mind that a) the notice being excerpted from a treatise devoted to the examination of Archytas' contributions,[58] it might well be a recollection by Archytas about Pythagoras old-fashionedly explaining how physical objects are generated by a process comparable to those clumsy cosmologic theories of the Pythagoreans Aristotle alludes to at several points of his extant works;[59] b) the problem of change having being debated vigorously by several Presocratic thinkers already in Pythagoras' own time and in the few previous and next generations—take for instance Epicharmus' so-called "growth argument," whereby bodily constitution is subject to an ongoing process of loss and repair as a result of growth and decay[60]— a statement by him on matter as 'changing' need not be deemed at

---

discussion, perhaps in a looser, dialogue form, adopted the Pythagoras of his colleagues. Maybe he was attempting a philosophical interpretation of a traditionary pronouncement of Pythagoras, in which the word 'other' (ἄλλο) occurred."

57 Huffman, *Archytas of Tarentum*, 590, claims that the "original reference to Pythagoreans has been corrupted in the course of transmission, so that it has become Pythagoras in Damascius. This is exactly the sort of change that is to be expected in the later tradition where Pythagoras himself becomes all important"; for a suitable criticism of this view, see Zhmud, *Pythagoras and the Early Pythagoreans*, 411 n. 97.

58 On this see above n. 54. Schofield, "Archytas," 81 f., who doubts the very existence of Aristotle's works on Archytas, also objects to the validity of the doctrine on change being attributed to Pythagoras on Archytas' authority; unfortunately, I cannot dwell here on Archytas' as recorder of ancient Pythagorean traditions and his probable role as one of Aristotle's main informants on Pythagorean matters (for the time being, I may refer to Huffman, *Archytas of Tarentum*, 51 ff.).

59 Some instances of references to such Pythagorean doctrines are Arist. *Metaph.* 1080b16-21 (= Anon. Pyth. 58 B 9 DK = Pyths. Anon. 17 D27 LM); Arist. *Metaph.* 1091a13-18 (= Anon. Pyth. 58 B 26 DK = Pyths. Anon. 17 D28 LM); Arist. *Phys.* 213b22-27 (= Anon. Pyth. 58 B 30 DK = Pyths. Anon. 17 D29 LM).

60 Our main sources for reconstructing Epicharmus' "growth argument" are Pl. *Tht.* 152d-e (= Epich. 23 A 6 DK = Dox. 1 T2 LM); Plut. *De sera* 15 p. 559 AB; *Anon. in Plat. Tht.* col. 71, 12 (= CPF III, p. 458–461 Bastianini-Sedley = Epich. 23 B 2 DK = Dram. 43 T8 LM = Epich. fr. 136 K.-A.); on this question, see Omar Álvarez Salas, "From Epicharmus's Theatrics to Zeno's Paradoxical 'Drama'," in *Philosopher Kings and Tragic Heroes. Essays on Images and Ideas from Western Greece*, ed. Heather Reid, Davide Tanasi (Sioux City, Iowa: Parnassos Press, 2016), 31–35; and Omar Álvarez Salas, "Philosophy on Stage and Performance in Argument: Epicharmus vis-à-vis Western Greek Intelligentsia," in *Politics and Performance in Western Greece*, ed. Heather Reid, Davide Tanasi, Susan Kimbell (Sioux City, Iowa: Parnassos Press, 2017), 179–183.

ARISTOTLE'S OUTLOOK ON PYTHAGORAS AND THE PYTHAGOREANS 241

all as unlikely; c) what is more, even if the assumption of Pythagoras setting forth a physical theory were not acceptable for Aristotle even in the context of a second-hand report, such an assertion might also have found a fitting place in the framework of a discussion of the eschatological doctrine associated with the Samian philosopher, where the recurrent metensomatosis of each individual soul was an orderly process, which caused anybody to become again and again 'other'.

Moreover, in other passages of Aristotle's lost treatises the display of superhuman powers by Pythagoras himself could apparently be dealt within the framework of a biographical context linking the superstitious and marvelous side of his legend with a report on his cultivation of scientific doctrines, as is strongly suggested, among other fragmentary material handed down to us, by a formulation like the following, which comes from an unidentified lost work, but that most likely belongs to the already discussed monograph *On the Pythagoreans*:

τούτοις δὲ ἐπιγενόμενος Πυθαγόρας Μνησάρχου υἱὸς τὸ μὲν πρῶτον διεπονεῖτο περὶ τὰ μαθήματα καὶ τοὺς ἀριθμούς, ὕστερον δέ ποτε καὶ τῆς Φερεκύδου τερατοποιίας οὐκ ἀπέστη.

Coming after them, Pythagoras, the son of Mnesarchus, at first devoted his efforts to the sciences and to the numbers, but afterwards he did not refrain from Pherecydes' manner of wonder-working.[61]

So far, there is nothing in the surviving evidence on Aristotle's treatment of Pythagoras, either in the extant or the lost works, that justifies viewing his attitude as skeptical (less still as hostile) vis-à-vis Pythagoras' own role in the production of philosophical or other doctrines. On the contrary, Aristotle can be seen to display everywhere a deep curiosity for every aspect of the Pythagorean tradition, where the legendary account of Pythagoras' arcane lore and extraordinary deeds was collected on a par with his philosophical and/or scientific contribution. This would have required from him a wide research carried out mostly on written accounts of various kind, produced either by members of the Pythagorean society itself and other direct witnesses or else by early antiquarians or collectors of ancient doctrinal opinions, such as were some of his fellow Peripatetics, among which Aristoxenus stands out as the main exponent, but without leaving out Heraclides, Dicaearchus and Eudemus.[62]

---

61   Apollon. *mirab.* 6 (= Arist. fr. 191 Rose = Pyth. 14 A 7 DK); translation is mine.
62   See Huffman, "The Peripatetics on the Pythagoreans," 275 ff. (on Aristoxenus 285–295); more specifically on Aristoxenus' role, see Zhmud, "Aristoxenus and the Pythagoreans," 223 ff.

This fact would betray more often than not a rather sympathetic interest of Aristotle in Pythagoreanism and thus even favor a more balanced judgment in his reports about it than has been acknowledged in modern scholarship. As a matter of fact, in the assessment of the Pythagorean body of doctrine that Aristotle put forth in some of his now lost works, the part due to the founder himself must have had a privileged place, as the quotations retrieved therefrom allow us to ascertain.

5

At this stage it becomes necessary for us to more fully substantiate a claim that rings as if running counter to the received modern opinion, according to which Aristotle would have refrained from mentioning Pythagoras' name because of the lack of any dependable information, inasmuch as this personage would have appeared to him more shadowy than any of the former's contemporaries. In fact, a view like this turns out to be a mere *petitio principii* as soon as a comparison is done with the references in the *Corpus Aristotelicum* to other thinkers active in about the same period. The frame of reference may be seen in the somewhat older Thales, whose identification as the first philosopher or wise man, which must have antedated Aristotle by a very long time, must have turned him quickly into an intellectual 'star' and entailed a host of allusions to his wisdom from every side. The antiquity of such a tradition is supported by Thales' 'official' nomination as σοφός under Damasias' archonship in Athens (582/1 B.C.)[63]—which may be related to his consistent inclusion in the several lists of the Seven Sages[64]— by his important role in the proto-doxographical accounts of the sophistic period (Hippias' or of other people),[65] as well as by the anecdotal tradition about his astronomical knowledge that is already settled down, *e.g.*, in Herodotus and in Plato.[66] In spite of such an impressive conspicuousness, Thales' own name appears in only five

---

63   Diog. Laert. I 22; one may speculate whether Thales' probable nomination as σοφός and his subsequent fame was anyhow connected with his celebrated astronomical exploit of predicting the total eclipse of the sun that was observable in Asia Minor on May 28, 585 b.C., when the Medes led by Cyaxares and the Lydians led by Alyattes were in the heat of battle and thereupon stopped fighting (Hdt. I 74).

64   Pl. *Prt.* 343a; Diog. Laert. I 41.

65   Arist. *De an.* A 2. 405a 19; Diog. Laert. I 24 (= Hippias 86 B 7 DK); both reports are about magnet having a soul according to Thales; for further pieces of information on Thales that were put together by Hippias, see below.

66   Hdt. I 74; Pl. *Tht.* 174a-b.

passages of Aristotle's extant works, namely twice in the *De anima* (at 405a19 ff., in a discussion about the soul's self-moving properties and at 411a7 f. about soul being mixed up in the All); again in the famous passage of Thales' 'investiture' as the first philosopher at *Metaph.* 983b20-984a3, with Aristotle inferring from the bare notice about a statement by Thales on original water a full-blown biological analogy of his own;[67] and twice more in the *Politics*, being the one at *Pol.* 1259a5-19 a savory second-hand anecdote—as confirmed by the expression Θαλῆς μὲν οὖν λέγεται—about Thales being constrained to make profits from his astronomical knowledge, whereas that at *Pol.* 1274a28 f. is a 'genealogical' report also from an intermediate and still less reliable source associating Thales with Onomacritus as would-be lawgivers and making of him the very teacher of Lycurgus and Zaleucus, which Aristotle himself doubts by pointing out the chronological incongruity this would imply.[68] It should not go without saying that the three more significant of these passages about Thales, those at *De an.* 405a19 ff. and at *De an.* 411a7 f., along with that at *Metaph.* 983b20-984a3 have been traced back conclusively to Hippias' *Anthology*,[69] whereas the two from the *Politics*, as shown above, belong in a parallel—albeit of unknown provenance and by far less dependable—tradition of anecdotal and genealogical compilations with no warrant at all.

The remaining two Milesians, the early 6th century Anaximander and Pythagoras' nearly exact contemporary Anaximenes, both of whom definitely enjoyed a much lesser popularity than his older countryman Thales as inspirational motives, are almost equally seldom mentioned in Aristotle's extant works, with just four occurrences each. In fact, Anaximander's name turns up at *Cael.* 295b12, at *Metaph.* 1069b22—the former passage concerning Anaximander's cosmological theory of the unsupported central earth, whereas the latter features him in a quick association with Empedocles' 'mixture'— and twice in the *Physics*: at *Phys.* 187a21 on the separation of the opposites from the One in Anaximander's theory, and at *Phys.* 203b14 on the immortality and indestructibility of his divine ἄπειρον.

---

67   Patzer, *Der Sophist Hippias*, 33–42, traced back this notice to a report that Hippias concocted by combining philosophical doctrines with poetical quotations from Homer and 'Orpheus' (cf. Hippias 86 B 6 DK) about Okeanos and Tethys.

68   Arist. *Pol.* 1274a28 ff.: τούτου [*sc.* Ὀνομακρίτου] δὲ γενέσθαι Θάλητα ἑταῖρον, Θάλητος δ' ἀκροατὴν Λυκοῦργον καὶ Ζάλευκον, Ζαλεύκου δὲ Χαρώνδαν. ἀλλὰ ταῦτα μὲν λέγουσιν ἀσκεπτότερον τῶν χρόνων λέγοντες.

69   On the notices about Thales' doctrines being ςollected by Hippias see especially Snell, "Die Nachrichten," 175 ff.; and Patzer, *Der Sophist Hippias*, 33–42.

For his part, Anaximenes is named at *Cael.* 294b13 along with Anaxagoras and Democritus in connection with the theory of the earth being supported by the air acting as a kind of 'shelf' (cf. Pl. *Phd.* 99b), whereas at *Metaph.* 984a5 he is included in a list of thinkers who posited only one material principle (with Anaximenes being put besides Diogenes of Apollonia as having propounded the priority of air over water as first principle among the simple bodies), and his name appears twice in the *Meteorologics* (at 365a18 and at 365b6) in a passage recording the three (scientific) explanations of earthquakes already put forth up to Aristotle's time.

By even the more rigorous critical standards, these figures cannot be regarded as sensitively more perspicuous than those concerning recollection of Pythagoras himself in Aristotle's extant works, let alone those found in his lost monographs. What is more, by taking into account the occurrences of the collective designation "Pythagoreans," which nothing entitles us to envisage as excluding in any way Pythagoras or any other member of the more ancient Pythagorean community,[70] the allusions to a certain knowledge of Pythagorean tenets in Aristotle's extant works outweigh by far those to the three Milesians put together. In fact, a quick consultation of an Aristotelian index gives the astonishing number of forty-six occurrences of a form of the adjective Πυθαγόρειοι (or Πυθαγορικός) presumably used with reference to a group of followers of Pythagoras. Here, however, it is important to stress that in just a very limited number of such instances (namely six in the whole *Corpus Aristotelicum*), the collective designation Πυθαγόρειοι is qualified by the attributive participle καλούμενοι,[71] which has been usually understood and translated as "the so-called Pythagoreans" and taken to convey an attitude of cautious reservation, similar in meaning to our "quotation marks," vis-à-vis an anonymous group of people—not inclusive of Pythagoras, nor of any other 6th century Pythagorean—that would have staked a (rather illegitimate) claim to that title.[72] Over against what we have shown so far to be the case as far as Aristotle's

---

70   I concur in this view with Zhmud, *Pythagoras and the Early Pythagoreans*, 57.

71   The passages in question are Arist. *Cael.* 284b 7; *Cael.* 293a 20; *Metaph.* 985b 23; *Metaph.* 989b 29; *Mete.*342b 30; *Mete.* 345a 13.

72   That was famously the thesis of Frank, *Plato*, vi, which was already refuted by Cherniss, *Aristotle's Criticism*, 385: "it has been suspected that by 'the so-called Pythagoreans' Aristotle meant to indicate that the doctrines in question were not those of genuine Pythagoreans but had in one way or another been fathered on the old sect. The use of the phrase, however, does not imply this subtlety."; in spite of this, it still comes up in a slightly modified form even in more recent scholarship, for instance in Carl Huffman, "Pythagoreanism," in *The Stanford Encyclopedia of Philosophy*, ed. Edward N. Zalta (2): "Aristotle's expression, 'so-called Pythagoreans,' suggests both that at his time this

ARISTOTLE'S OUTLOOK ON PYTHAGORAS AND THE PYTHAGOREANS 245

references to Pythagoras himself are concerned, the collective label οἱ (καλού-μενοι) Πυθαγόρειοι has been arbitrarily thought to indicate that Aristotle would have refused to take any responsibility for the attribution of specific scientific or philosophical doctrines to any single Pythagorean, least of all to Pythagoras himself,[73] whom he would have exclusively linked, as is usually claimed, to the esoteric side of the Pythagorean teaching that was mainly dealt with in his now lost monographs.

However, a number of objections to this common view may be raised legitimately and, at least in one particular instance, it can be proved conclusively that Aristotle must have been fully aware of the probable configuration of a specific doctrine through Pythagoras himself, in spite of the fact that it had become common Pythagorean lore by the 4th century B.C. This doctrine is the belief in the immortality and the transmigration of the soul or metempsychosis, with which Aristotle deals at *De an.* 407b20-26 in the framework of a broader survey of the connection between the soul and the body,[74] which the earlier psychological theories, by simply placing the former into the latter, with no regard for how each of them is constituted or under what circumstances their linking takes place, would have left mostly unaccounted for.[75] Specifically, the awkwardness of the particular instance lying in some "Pythagorean tales"— κατὰ τοὺς Πυθαγορικοὺς μύθους—is brought forth (Arist. *De an.* 407b22),[76] according to which the process whereby any chance soul enters any chance body and hangs around it for a lifetime, irrespective of the own kind or structure of

---

group of thinkers was commonly called Pythagoreans and, at the same time, calls into question the actual connection between these thinkers and Pythagoras himself."

73 The main supporter of such an extreme approach is Huffman, "Philolaus," 7.1: "Aristotle is emphatic that the [Philolaic] system dates after the time of Pythagoras, and second, his expression 'so-called Pythagoreans' is most reasonably understood to suggest that, although he knows that the name 'Pythagorean' is often given to Philolaus and his contemporaries, he can see little reason to connect the philosophical system they espouse to Pythagoras himself." A similar stand is taken by Primavesi, "Aristotle on the 'so-called Pythagoreans,'" 249 (upon which we shall return below).

74 This passage is usually collected under the anonymously transmitted Pythagorean doctrines: Anon. Pyth. 58 B 39 DK = Pyths. Anon. 17 D52 LM.

75 This first move against the Pythagorean doctrine of the soul is made at Arist. *De an.* 407b13-17: ἐκεῖνο δὲ ἄτοπον συμβαίνει καὶ τούτῳ τῷ λόγῳ καὶ τοῖς πλείστοις τῶν περὶ ψυχῆς· συνάπτουσι γὰρ καὶ τιθέασιν εἰς σῶμα τὴν ψυχήν, οὐθὲν προσδιορίσαντες διὰ τίν' αἰτίαν καὶ πῶς ἔχοντος τοῦ σώματος.

76 Arist. *De an.* 407b20-23: οἱ δὲ μόνον ἐπιχειροῦσι λέγειν ποῖόν τι ἡ ψυχή, περὶ δὲ τοῦ δεξομένου σώματος οὐθὲν ἔτι προσδιορίζουσιν, ὥσπερ ἐνδεχόμενον κατὰ τοὺς Πυθαγορικοὺς μύθους τὴν τυχοῦσαν ψυχὴν εἰς τὸ τυχὸν ἐνδύεσθαι σῶμα. Objections against that same theory—without explicitly calling it Pythagorean—are again put forth at Arist. *De an.* 414a20-25.

246   ÁLVAREZ SALAS

each, is described in terms such as "getting into (something)" (ἐνδύεσθαι) and "taking (someone) in" (δέχεσθαι).[77]

Interestingly, this language has strong overtones of putting on something as a garment or a disguise,[78] and it likewise has a ring of great antiquity that closely matches that of the description Herodotus (II 123) made of the soul's reiterative entrance each time into a new body in a famous passage dealing with the purported Egyptian origin of the Pythagorean and Orphic belief in the metempsychosis.[79] There, the historian sets out this doctrine by referring to the mechanism of transmigration through a verb of the same root as that later adopted by Aristotle, albeit with a different prefix attached to it, namely ἐσδύεσθαι (ἐσδύνειν) "to creep or crawl into," which has a similar although somewhat more restricted usage gamut as compared with ἐνδύεσθαι.[80] Moreover, the fact that Aristotle speaks in the passage at issue not of an account, but of some "Pythagorean tales" (Πυθαγορικοὶ μῦθοι) unavoidably takes us to think of the stories turning on the successive incarnations of Pythagoras' soul, which Heraclides of Pontus—who was first a member of Plato's Academy and then became an associate of Aristotle's Lyceum—set forth as a savory tale apparently told as a claim repeatedly made by Pythagoras himself: Τοῦτόν φησιν Ἡρακλείδης ὁ Ποντικὸς περὶ αὑτοῦ τάδε λέγειν, κτλ. "Heraclides of Pontus says that he [i.e. Pythagoras] used to recount the following about himself, etc."[81] No doubt,

---

77   Likewise, the construction ἐνδύεσθαι εἰς to mean the embodying process of a soul being reborn is employed twice by Plato (*Phd.* 82a; *Resp.* 620c).

78   Among the many instances, see Hom. *Il.* 2.42, 5.736; Soph. *Trach.* 759; Hdt. I 172, II 81; Ar. *Eccl.* 288. For an interesting treatment of the semantic sphere of the verb ἐνδύεσθαι "to put on clothing," see Francesca Alesse, "La dottrina pitagorica della metempsicosi nel *De Anima* di Aristotele," in *Tra Orfeo e Pitagora: origini e incontri di culture nell'antichità. Atti dei seminari napoletani 1996–98*, ed. Marisa Tortorelli Ghidini, A. S. Marino, A. Visconti (Naples: Bibliopolis, 2000), 409 ff.

79   For a similar take on the use of the verb ἐνδύεσθαι as a reflection of a very ancient ("proto-Pythagorean") tradition, see Gabriele Cornelli, "Aristotle and the Pythagorean Myths of Metempsychosis," *Méthexis* 28 (2016), 10 f. (author writes "The same verb is used by Herodotus ...," whereas Herodotus uses ἐσδύεσθαι).

80   For some examples of ἐσδύεσθαι, which lends itself well to figurative usages, see Hom. *Il.* 23.622; Soph. *OT* 1317.

81   Diog. Laert. VIII 4 (= Heraclid. fr. 89 Wehrli); for a recent assessment of metempsychosis as Pythagoras' own teaching that supported his claim to superior knowledge, see Caterina Pellò, "The Lives of Pythagoras: A Proposal for Reading Pythagorean Metempsychosis," *Rhizomata* 6 (2) 2018: 148 ff.; on Aristotle's invaluable testimony for the great antiquity (*i.e.* 6th century b.C.) of the Pythagorean belief in the immortality and transmigration of souls and of its being conceived as a 'tale' (μῦθος), see Cornelli, "Aristotle and the Pythagorean Myths of Metempsychosis," 5 ff.; likewise Alesse, "La dottrina pitagorica della metempsicosi nel *De Anima*," 408, who fittingly recalls Plat. *Gorg.* 493a; even if the Italiote storyteller who would have devised the symbolic designation for the appetitive part of the

it was the same doctrine that Dicaearchus, one of Aristotle's main collaborators in the Peripatos, seems to have identified as one of the central tenets of
Pythagoras' teachings that became most widely known,[82] but that he may have
also derided by having Pythagoras be once embodied as a beautiful courtesan
named Alco.[83] Again, this is in agreement with the fact that, somewhere in the
sixth century B.C., already Xenophanes had ridiculed Pythagoras' belief in the
transmigration of souls, as is plain from an elegiac fragment of his—Xenoph.
21 B 7 D K, upon which we shall return below—containing the oldest extant use
of the word ψυχή to designate the core element of individual identity, which
is capable of surviving longer than any single human (or animal) body and of
passing successively into other bodies.[84]

Likewise, already Plato in the *Phaedo* had brought this very belief to notorious philosophical display, while drawing the attention also to the theory of the
soul as *harmonia* purportedly held by the 4th century Pythagorean Simmias
of Thebes, which has sometimes been thought to be a faithful continuation
of a teaching that Philolaus would have imparted to him and to Cebes during
his exile among them.[85] The fact is that, while this theory is set out at Pl. *Phd.*
85e-86d, Philolaus is indeed explicitly named only at Pl. *Phd.* 61d-e in connection with a likewise presumably Pythagorean doctrine according to which the
body is a 'jail' (φρουρά) for the soul (Pl. *Phd.* 62b), from which it should not

---

     soul is usually identified with Philolaus—as Diels-Kranz printed the above extract in the
     chapter devoted to this thinker (Philol. 44 B 14 DK, over against its assignment to the
     doctrines of undetermined attribution collected under Pyths. 18 R4 LM; on this issue, see
     Palmer, "The Pythagoreans and Plato," 207 f.)—, it is nevertheless possible to catch here a
     hint of an older Pythagorean way of putting major teachings in figurative language, such
     as that associated with Pythagoras himself (see above, nn. 48–51).

82   Porph. *VP* 18–19 (= Pyth. 14 A 8a DK = Dicaearch. fr. 40 Mirhady = Pyth. 10a. P25 + Pyth. 10c.
     D5 LM); in Dicaearch. fr. 33 Wehrli only Porph. *VP* 18 is accepted as a verbatim quotation,
     on which see Zhmud, *Pythagoras and the Early Pythagoreans*, pp. 73–77; for the more com-
     prehensive editorial decision made by David Mirhady—in *Dicaearchus of Messana: Text,
     Translation, and Discussion*, ed. William W. Fortenbaugh, Eckart Schütrumpf, 1–142 (New
     Brunswick, N.J.: Transaction Publishers, 2001)—, see Burkert, *Lore and Science*, 122 f., and
     Huffman, "The Peripatetics on the Pythagoreans," 281 f.

83   Aul. Gell. *Noct. Att.* IV, XI, 14 (= Dicaearch. fr. 42 Mirhady = Dicaearch. fr. 36 Wehrli,
     Clearch. fr. 10 Wehrli); for a plausible explanation of the series of Pythagoras' reincarna-
     tions, including Alco, see Pellò, "The Lives of Pythagoras," 145 ff.

84   For a positive assessment of the role played by Pythagoras in the shaping of the ψυχή
     conceived as the nucleus of personal identity, see Jan N. Bremmer, "Ψυχή," in *A History
     of Ancient Greek. From the Beginnings to Late Antiquity*, ed. Anastasios-Fivos Christidis
     (Cambridge: Cambridge University Press, 2015), 1146 f.

85   For a discussion of the bearing of the *harmonia* theory of the soul on the original
     Pythagorean teaching, see Palmer, "The Pythagoreans and Plato," 212 f.

endeavor to deliver itself or run away before those who are in charge of us, *i.e.* the gods, decide that due time has come.[86] Attribution of this doctrine to the Pythagorean thinker in question seemed also supported by an extract from one of his works that is transmitted literally by Clemens, where the soul is said to be buried in the body (σῶμα) as if in a grave (σῆμα), but this fragment has been suspected of being a later forgery,[87] so that it is safer here to suspend judgment on this particular point. Whatever the original Pythagorean pertinence of this specific doctrine, the whole discussion about the nature and the fate of the soul that ensues in Plato's *Phaedo* may not be altogether unrelated to Pythagoras' and Philolaus' eschatological teachings, insofar as these appear likewise anonymously echoed with strong Pythagorean overtones elsewhere in Plato's works (Pl. *Crat.* 400b-c: σῶμα = σῆμα; Pl. *Men.* 81a-c: on immortal soul and its transmigration), once with explicit reference to an unnamed sage who theorized (or gave an allegorical interpretation of a myth devised by a clever Sicilian or Italiote)[88] about the soul being buried within the body like a dead man in a grave (Pl. *Gorg.* 493a-b).[89] In his turn, Aristotle must have been well acquainted with Philolaus' thought and writings, as is suggested not just by the discussion he makes of the theory of the soul as a *harmonia* at *De an.* 407b27-408a30, but also by the extensive treatment he devotes in several of his extant treatises to Pythagorean scientific doctrines, which have been found by Burkert and other scholars to correspond in the main to Philolaus' own theories and world picture and which Aristotle systematically scrutinizes from a critical

---

86   For a recent analysis of the Pythagorean overtones in Plato's treatment of the doctrine of the soul's immortality and its *post mortem* fate in the *Phaedo*, see Palmer, "The Pythagoreans and Plato," 210 ff.

87   Clem. *Strom.* III 17 (= Philol. 44 B 14 DK = Philol. 12 D30 LM); on the authenticity issue, see Gabriele Cornelli, *In Search of Pythagoreanism. Pythagoreanism as an Historiographical Category* (Berlin: De Gruyter, 2013), 108 ff.; *contra* Burkert, *Lore and Science*, 248 n. 47 and Huffman, *Philolaus of Croton*, 402 ff.; according to Athenaeus (IV 157 C), this same notion would have been attributed by the Peripatetic Clearchus (fr. 38 Wehrli) to the otherwise unknown Pythagorean Euxitheos.

88   Burkert, *Lore and Science*, 248 n. 48 insists on drawing a sharp line between the 'mythologer' and the exegete in Plato's passage at issue, even if it is quite possible that they are one and the same person, *i.e.* a Pythagorean who, like Philolaus, couched his teachings in mythical language.

89   An interesting examination of the probable reference in the indicated passage of the *Gorgias* to a Pythagorean doctrine regarding the twofold division of the soul into a part housing desires and a part controlling them is found in Palmer, "The Pythagoreans and Plato," 207 ff.; for a positive stand on the connection between Pl. *Gorg.* 493a and Philol. 44 B 14 DK, see Cornelli, *In Search of Pythagoreanism*, 107 ff. (see 101 ff. for a discussion of the Pythagorean background in Pl. *Men.* 81a-c).

ARISTOTLE'S OUTLOOK ON PYTHAGORAS AND THE PYTHAGOREANS   249

(but seemingly not hostile) point of view,[90] even though he references them under the characteristic collective label οἱ (καλούμενοι) Πυθαγόρειοι that we are discussing here.[91]

Furthermore, in order for us to clinch the present argument, it may be recalled that somewhere in the 6th century, nearly one and a half centuries before Aristotle's lifetime, Xenophanes, who was an almost exact contemporary and Ionian countryman of Pythagoras, wrote an elegy caricaturing the latter's belief in the transmigration of the souls through the example of a little dog being beaten and recognized by him as the bearer of a deceased friend's soul.[92] Therefore, when Aristotle objects at *De an.* 407b20-23 to the Pythagorean account of the soul passing from one body into another, it is just unlikely that he could simply be unaware of the ultimate origin in Pythagoras himself of a doctrine that his own associates Heracleides and Dicaearchus,[93] as is demonstrable on the basis of their above quoted fragments, were able to explicitly connect with the 6th century thinker.[94] We have to reckon here, as the above discussed evidences show, with a deliberate pretermission by Aristotle of (so to say) sensitive data or, better, with an instance of a well attested critical technique based on the replacement of an individual name by an anonymous collective label arguably for the purposes of scientific objectivity, which he would have probably inherited from previous doxographic accounts and then uplifted to a highly refined tool of systematic presentation.

---

90   The main passages here are *Phys.* 202b30 ff. (on the *apeiron*) and *Cael.* 293a17-b30 (on the cosmic system with the earth revolving around the central hearth and the celestial bodies producing the so-called harmony of the spheres); at *Metaph.* 985b 23–986a 21, as is often asserted, an account of Philolaus' theory of principles is given, along with an allusion to the Pythagorean world picture including the counter-Earth as tenth celestial body; for the conformity of such doctrines as reported by Aristotle with what is known about Philolaus' own system, see Burkert, *Lore and Science*, 236 ff.

91   A comparable perspective on this issue is found in Zhmud, *Pythagoras and the Early Pythagoreans*, 434.

92   Diog. Laert. VIII 36 (= Xenoph. 21 B 7 DK = Xenoph. D64 LM = Pyth. 10a. P32 LM); further instances of the early association of the belief in the immortality of the souls and in their transmigration to different bodies with Pythagoras are found in Ion of Chios 36 B 4 DK (= Pyth. 10a. P29 LM) and Hdt. II 123 (= Pyth. 10c. D4 LM); for a discussion of the testimonies on Pythagoras' contribution to the development of the free ψυχή conception, see Jan N. Bremmer, *The Rise and Fall of the Afterlife* (London-New York: Routledge, 2001), 2, 11 ff., 24 ff.; on the testimonial value for Pythagoras of Xenophanes' reference to metempsychosis, see also Cornelli, *In Search of Pythagoreanism*, 89 ff.

93   On Heracleides and Dicaearchus, see above (with nn. 81–83).

94   On the doctrine of the immortal soul and of its metempsychosis as one of the teachings that may be attributed with strong likelihood to Pythagoras himself, with a virtually exhaustive list of the studies devoted so far to this aspect, see Macris, "Pythagore," 832 ff.

6

What we have discussed so far regarding Aristotle's far-flung procedure not to single out the author of even widely known theories or teachings brings us to ask the question whether Aristotle himself, by resorting to such collective designations, was solely responsible for the choice not to name the particular Pythagorean thinker (either Pythagoras or someone else) who was at the origin of a specific doctrine, or instead to what extent he was relying on a historiographical strategy that had been gradually building up over time and was already available to him as a ready-made resource. To this effect, it is worth recalling the use by Plato of a classificatory technique that forestalls later doxographic practices, either of his own invention or based on previous attempts at developing critical categories, to refer to a group of thinkers whose doctrinal coherence comes to question at a given moment, bringing about thus an intellectual genealogy or pedigree, with respect to which he may want to induce his readership to take a circumspect stance.[95] While some of such instances provide an out-of-hand denomination for a conspicuously anonymous group of well-known followers of a historical or mythical leader, others may contain instead a more subtle although certainly biased reference to a single personage (on occasions two or more of them), who are thus sarcastically blurred by putting them on the same level as the people with an actual group of followers.[96] This is how the anonymous and phantasmagoric group of Heraclitean partisans depicted at *Theaet.* 179e-180b, which cannot be considered at all an actual group of disciples or followers of the Ephesian philosopher—as previously shown by me in a dedicated study[97]— but are nothing more than a literary fabrication by a playful Plato, emerge as the doxographic category of the "Heracliteans" on a par with similar labels employed by Plato to play up ideological affinities and, through them, to more easily disparage groups of people for

---

95   Pl. *Cra.* 409b (οἱ Ἀναξαγόρειοι); *Resp.* VII 530d (οἵ τε Πυθαγόρειοι, to compare with *Resp.* X 600a: οἱ ... Πυθαγόρειον τρόπον ἐπονομάζοντες τοῦ βίου); Plato often uses periphrastic prepositional syntagmata with a person or place name as a nucleus, like οἱ ἀμφὶ Πρωταγόραν (*Euthyd.*, 286c), with a spike in the *Theaetetus* (170 c: τις τῶν ἀμφὶ Πρωταγόραν; 179 d: οἱ γὰρ τοῦ Ἡρακλείτου ἑταῖροι; 179 e: τοῖς περὶ τὴν Ἔφεσον) and in the *Cratylus* (400c: οἱ ἀμφὶ Ὀρφέα; 440c: οἱ περὶ Ἡράκλειτον).

96   On this see Cambiano, "Tecniche," 61 ff. and Álvarez Salas, "Cratylus and the reception of Heraclitus," 246 ff.

97   Álvarez Salas, "Cratylus and the reception of Heraclitus," 239–247.

ARISTOTLE'S OUTLOOK ON PYTHAGORAS AND THE PYTHAGOREANS   251

the sake of a theorization actually alien to the original core ideas supported by those very same people.[98]

One such instance, among those collective expressions employed or more seldom coined by Plato to jestingly call forth the image of a definite 'school' out of a number of wholly unrelated personages or instead to stress seriously the solidary anonymity of an actual corporation or brotherhood, is provided by people referred to at *Resp.* x 600a-b. There a contrast is set off between, on the one side, the Ὁμηρίδαι, which look more like an hypothetical entity, namely some "admirers of Homer,"[99] as the context makes plain, and, on the other side, οἱ ὕστεροι ἔτι καὶ νῦν Πυθαγόρειον τρόπον ἐπονομάζοντες τοῦ βίου ("those coming after [Pythagoras] who even to this day call Pythagorean their way of life"), which in all likelihood are to be identified with at least a handful of real people—maybe identical with "the last of the Pythagoreans" (reportedly disciples of Philolaus and Eurytus) which Aristoxenus himself still came to know[100]— practicing the "way of life" instituted by the Master about one and a half centuries before Plato's time.[101]

A final and, in my view, definitive proof of Plato's recourse to the doxographic cliché above sketched as consisting in the adoption of a collective denomination to emphasize the doctrinal coherence of a real or alleged group, even if the specific teachings being attributed to them may be linked with a

---

98   For a choice of examples of this strategy, see above n. 95; further discussion of such a doxographical technique in Cambiano, "Tecniche," 65 ff., and Álvarez Salas, "Cratylus and the reception of Heraclitus," 251 ff., where it is shown how in such instances Plato's usage fluctuates between collective designations of the kind we are examining here— οἱ Ἀναξαγόρειοι, οἱ Πυθαγόρειοι, etc. and the more neutral periphrastic formulations quoted above.

99   These evanescent "admirers of Homer" are likely to be set apart from the real corporation of Homeric bards active in Chios, which first turn up at Pind. *Nem.* 2,1 (cf. Pl. *Ion* 530e and *Phdr.* 252b).

100   Diog. Laert. VIII 46 (= Aristox. Fr. 19 Wehrli = Pythag. 14 A10 DK = Pyth. 10b. T29 LM): τελευ-ταῖοι γὰρ ἐγένοντο τῶν Πυθαγορείων, οὓς καὶ Ἀριστόξενος εἶδε, Ξενόφιλός τε ὁ Χαλκιδεὺς ἀπὸ Θρᾴκης καὶ Φάντων ὁ Φλιάσιος καὶ Ἐχεκράτης καὶ Διοκλῆς καὶ Πολύμναστος, Φλιάσιοι καὶ αὐτοί. ἦσαν δὲ ἀκροαταὶ Φιλολάου καὶ Εὐρύτου τῶν Ταραντίνων.

101   A similar (albeit ironically tainted) reference to an anonymous group of followers or imitators of Pythagoras' lifestyle—insofar as they observed the rigorous silence or ἐχεμυθία he was said to impose on his would-be disciples (cf. Iambl. *VP* 226)—can also be found in Isocrates (*Bus.* 28–29 = Pythag. 14 A4 DK = Pythag. 10a. P18 + 10b. T12 LM): Πυθαγόρας ὁ Σάμιος ... ἔτι γὰρ καὶ νῦν τοὺς προσποιουμένους ἐκείνου μαθητὰς εἶναι μᾶλλον σιγῶντας θαυμά-ζουσιν ἢ τοὺς ἐπὶ τῷ λέγειν μεγίστην δόξαν ἔχοντας (note the verbal echo ἔτι καὶ νῦν κτλ. of the above quoted Pl. *Resp.* x 600b).

252 ÁLVAREZ SALAS

particular thinker, can be indicated in a well-known passage from the *Republic* (VII 530d):[102]

Κινδυνεύει, ἔφην, ὡς πρὸς ἀστρονομίαν ὄμματα πέπηγεν, ὡς πρὸς ἐναρμόνιον φορὰν ὦτα παγῆναι, καὶ αὗται ἀλλήλων ἀδελφαί τινες αἱ ἐπιστῆμαι εἶναι, ὡς οἵ τε Πυθαγόρειοί φασι, καὶ ἡμεῖς, ὦ Γλαύκων, συγχωροῦμεν.

It might well be, I said, that just as our eyes are shaped with a view to astronomy, so too our ears took shape with a focus on harmonic motion and that these sciences are like sisters to one another, as both the Pythagoreans say, and we concur with, Glaucon.

These anonymously construed Pythagoreans, whose very stance on scientific matters (namely regarding star-gazing and the musical theory upon which the harmony of the spheres is based) comes approvingly to quote in this passage, are nonetheless treated by Plato with calculated circumspection, insofar as he maintains a critical distance to them by artfully concealing the specific source thereby meant. Fortunately for us, this is revealed by a long quotation that was transmitted to us by Porphyry (with the first part being also preserved by Nicomachus) from the *incipit* of the Pythagorean Archytas' treatise Περὶ μαθηματικῆς ("On the mathematical science"):

περί τε δὴ τὰς τῶν ἄστρων ταχυτᾶτος καὶ ἐπιτολᾶν καὶ δυσίων παρέδωκαν ἀμὶν σαφῆ διάγνωσιν καὶ περὶ γαμετρίας καὶ ἀριθμῶν καὶ σφαιρικᾶς καὶ οὐχ ἥκιστα περὶ μωσικᾶς. ταῦτα γὰρ τὰ μαθήματα δοκοῦντι ἦμεν ἀδελφεά·

So then, they handed down to us a clear judgment regarding the speed of the stars, as well as regarding their risings and settings, and likewise regarding geometry and numbers and spherical [*i.e.* astronomy], and not least regarding music. For these sciences seem to be sisters.[103]

Besides the strikingly similar wording of the last sentence in Archytas' text and Plato's statement put in the mouth of 'Socrates': καὶ αὗται ἀλλήλων ἀδελφαί τινες

---

102 This passage was included in the commentary to Archyt. 47 B1 DK (= Pyths. R. 18 R1 LM); my translation.

103 Porphyr. *In Ptolem. Harm.* p. 56 Düring (= Archyt. 47 B1 DK = Archy. 14 D14 LM); my translation; the text is reproduced as in DK, who for the above quoted portion of the text follow mainly the version given by Nicomachus (*Inst. Arith.* I 3, 4 p. 6, 16 Hoche); for a discussion of the degree of fidelity displayed by either witness of Archytas' fragment, see Huffman, *Archytas of Tarentum*, 115 ff., 153 ff.

αἱ ἐπιστῆμαι εἶναι, which has an unmistakable ring of being a literal quotation from the former—with just the dialectal differences and the lexical replacement of the Platonic *terminus technicus* ἐπιστῆμαι for the stock Pythagorean word μαθήματα[104]—the whole educational and scientific discussion in which the Platonic passage appears links it firmly to the programmatic overview of the sciences set forth by the Pythagorean philosopher. Therefore, it is just unavoidable the conclusion that the unnamed Pythagoreans, whose saying is invoked as warrant at *Resp.* VII 530d (ὡς οἵ τε Πυθαγόρειοί φασι), are nothing more than a suitable anonymous mask concealing Archytas himself.[105] In its turn, this case makes plain that in approaching similar questions to those treated by Aristotle—who likewise resorts often to that same formula or a similar one to introduce a Pythagorean view, even though he is most likely relying on written accounts[106]—already Plato had recourse to the same doxographical technique that I have shown above to be displayed in a series of cases where the label οἱ Πυθαγόρειοι (which is quite seldom qualified, without any recognizable limiting nuance, by the participle καλούμενοι)[107] or some such collective designation (like οἱ περὶ τὴν Ἰταλίαν or τῶν δ' Ἰταλικῶν τινες)[108] turns up in the *Corpus Aristotelicum*. Such instances of anonymous reference to doctrines

---

104   Such a close correspondence between the texts of both authors led Huffman to acknowledge the authenticity of Archytas' fragment—over against Burkert's doubts (*Lore and Science*, 379 n. 46)—which he thus regards likewise as the source of Plato's quotation—Huffman, *Archytas of Tarentum*, 114.

105   In recognizing Archytas' above quoted passage as Plato's specific reference here, I also concur with Malcolm Schofield, "Archytas," in Huffman, *A History of Pythagoreanism*, 73 ff.

106   While the expression ὡς οἱ Πυθαγόρειοι φασιν appears at Arist. *An. post.* 94b 33, comparable syntagmata occur at the following points: *Cael.* 268a 10–11 (Καθάπερ γάρ φασι καὶ οἱ Πυθαγόρειοι); *Cael.* 284b 7 (καθάπερ οἱ καλούμενοι Πυθαγόρειοι [*sc.* φασιν]); *Cael.* 285b 25 (ὡς οἱ Πυθαγόρειοι λέγουσιν); *Cael.* 293a 20–21 (ἐναντίως οἱ περὶ τὴν Ἰταλίαν, καλούμενοι δὲ Πυθαγόρειοι λέγουσιν); *Cael.* 300a 16–17 (ὥσπερ τῶν Πυθαγορείων τινές [*sc.* φασιν]); *Eth. Nic.* 1106b 29–30 (ὡς οἱ Πυθαγόρειοι εἴκαζον); *Eth. Nic.* 1132b 22 (ὥσπερ οἱ Πυθαγόρειοι ἔφασαν); Arist. *Mag. mor.* 1, 33, 13, 6 (ὡς οἱ Πυθαγόρειοι ἔλεγον); *Metaph.* 1053b 12 (καθάπερ οἵ τε Πυθαγόρειοί φασι); *Mete.* 342b 30 (τῶν δ' Ἰταλικῶν τινες καλουμένων Πυθαγορείων ... λέγουσιν); *Mete.* 345a 13–14 (τῶν μὲν οὖν καλουμένων Πυθαγορείων φασί τινες); [*Oec.*] 1344a 10 (καθάπερ οἱ Πυθαγόρειοι λέγουσιν); *Phys.* 204a 32–33 (ὥσπερ οἱ Πυθαγόρειοί φασιν).

107   All six such instances—over against the forty remaining occurrences of the unqualified adjective Πυθαγόρειοι (or Πυθαγορικός) used with reference to a group of followers of Pythagoras—are recorded above (n. 71); Zhmud, *Pythagoras and the Early Pythagoreans*, 434, who suspends judgment about the οἱ καλούμενοι qualification, sees in Aristotle's Ἰταλικοί a designation for the Pythagoreans, specifically Philolaus and Archytas together with their respective circles of followers.

108   Arist. *Cael.* 293a 20 and *Meteor.* 342b30; these instances are to be compared with the similar examples from Plato listed above (n. 95).

held by then relatively well-known thinkers being employed by Plato either to stress the notion of a community following the stipulations of an internal code or set of rules,[109] or else to posit mischievously the existence of such a group through the use of a collective denomination—like "the Anaxagoreans" (οἱ Ἀναξαγόρειοι) mentioned at *Crat.* 409b,[110] or "the Heracliteans" (οἱ ... τοῦ Ἡρακλείτου ἑταῖροι or οἱ περὶ Ἡράκλειτον) that are jokingly called into being at *Tht.* 179d-e and *Crat.* 440c[111]—Aristotle is likely to have turned such expressions into more technical formulations that convey mostly a denotative sense, which proved to be at his hands a quite useful classificatory and descriptive tool. In the same manner as Plato, then, Aristotle may have had recourse to already available doxographical tags, sometimes devising himself some of them upon request, even though most of the time availing himself of traditional or ready-made categories. One of them was precisely that of the 'Pythagoreans', which was already current in proto-doxographical usage, as shown above, at least from Herodotus and Plato onwards and allowed him to encompass a whole intellectual lineage coming down from Pythagoras' time to the second half of the 4th century B.C.

Accordingly, all those attempts at accounting for the collective denomination "Pythagoreans" that, by tendentiously focusing exclusively on the "so-called" qualification occasionally attached to it, assign to that denomination the meaning and function of a restrictive or illegitimately applied tag, are likely to have missed the mark. This holds true even of the masterful analysis of the first part of chapter 5 of *Metaphysics* A (985b23-986a3), where οἱ καλούμενοι Πυθαγόρειοι are prominently featured, which was painstakingly and skillfully carried out in a recent scholarly study.[112] In fact, altogether disregarding the remaining five occurrences of the syntagma οἱ καλούμενοι Πυθαγόρειοι in the *Corpus Aristotelicum*, this scholar comes to regard the "so-called" qualification fastened there by Aristotle on the collective designation "Pythagoreans" as the upshot of a developmental outlook on Pythagoreanism as proceeding from primitive 5th century arithmology to Philolaus' more evoluted theory of

---

109 Cf. Pl. *Leg.* 782c: Ὀρφικοί τινες λεγόμενοι βίοι ἐγίγνοντο ἡμῶν τοῖς τότε ("those men of us who existed at the time lived what is called an Orphic life").

110 Notwithstanding, be aware of the fact that, some time before Plato, already the collective label "Anaxagoreans" (Ἀναξαγόρειοι) comes up together with "Pythagoreans" (Πυθαγόρειοι) in the Sophistic treatise, dated to c. 400 b.C., usually titled *Contrasting Arguments* (Δισσοὶ λόγοι, 90, 6, 8 DK), where both groups are presented as teachers of wisdom and excellence (on this see Zhmud, *Pythagoras and the Early Pythagoreans*, 47 n. 84).

111 For a thorough discussion of this issue, see Álvarez Salas, "Cratylus and the reception of Heraclitus," 247 ff.

112 Primavesi, "Aristotle on the 'so-called Pythagoreans'," 227 ff.

principles.[113] On this interpretation, the latter doctrine would hardly qualify in Aristotle's view as "Pythagorean" in a narrow sense, but then, realizing that this term had already wide currency, the Stagirite would have chosen to attach to it the limiting qualification "so-called."[114] This, however, is tantamount to a slightly modified revival of the biased interpretation Erich Frank set out in his now long deprecated monograph, according to which the doctrines that Aristotle attributes to the "so-called Pythagoreans" were not those of the true Pythagoreans (whoever they were and whenever they lived) but had been foisted somehow upon them, which was already refuted by Cherniss (with the carefully reasoned assent of Burkert) and which nobody may take seriously nowadays.[115]

7

After the survey conducted so far of Aristotle's references in his extant (and in the fragments of his lost) works to Pythagoras himself and to the doctrines he would have shaped, the allegedly total absence of this philosopher's name from the surviving whole works of Aristotle—purportedly due to the historical opaqueness surrounding such an enigmatic personage (as is often stressed in modern scholarship), which would have led him to talk in an anonymous way about the Pythagoreans—has turned out to be but a modern misconception or a *petitio principii*. Instead of that, the references to him alone have been shown to be on a par with the exiguous number of occurrences of Anaximander's and Anaximenes' (not to speak of Thales') own names in the extant whole works of Aristotle, as represented by the *Corpus Aristotelicum*. Thus, what has been mostly interpreted as an indication of an extremely cautious

---

113   Primavesi, "Aristotle on the 'so-called Pythagoreans'," 227–230, 246–249, especially 229 n. 10, where two *contra* references are (unknowingly) given: Cherniss, *Aristotle's Criticism*, 385 (see above, n. 72) and Burkert, *Lore and Science*, 30: "The doctrine of the Pythagoreans usually appears as an undifferentiated unity; or in any case there is no sure foothold for the modern attempts to discern various stages in its development."

114   Primavesi, "Aristotle on the 'so-called Pythagoreans'," 249: "Aristotle might have felt comfortable calling the *acusmata* Pythagorean, but he recognizes that Philolaus introduces some quite new material. Although this material is in a sense a development of earlier ideas, he has some hesitations about calling these new developments 'Pythagorean.' Since, however, he recognizes that many people describe it thus, he uses the phrase 'so-called Pythagoreans'." For a similar statement by Huffman, "Philolaus," 7.1, see above n. 73.

115   Frank, *Plato*, vi; a kindred approach to this issue by Huffman, "Pythagoreanism," (2), was already recalled above n. 72; for Cherniss's and Burkert's objections, see the references above (n. 72 and 113, respectively).

attitude vis-à-vis an elusive personage, whose own contribution to the scientific doctrines that were under discussion could not be ascertained by Aristotle himself, should be viewed instead as this philosopher's average treatment of the sages of old.

Moreover, even the collective label 'Pythagoreans' applied to the authors of some very definite and ancient doctrines, such as the arithmological symbolism described in the *Metaphysics* and especially the metempsychosis discussed in the *De anima*—as well as, to a lesser extent, also the cosmological theories reported in the *Metaphysics* and the *Physics*—may be seen as inclusive of the founder of the school himself, since early and dependable witnesses like Xenophanes, Ion of Chios and Herodotus associated him with a teaching on the *post mortem* fate of the soul (at least that of Pythagoras himself), and likewise some fellow Peripatetics of Aristotle, among which in particular Heracleides and Dicaearchus, as shown above, did not refrain from referring by name to the sage of Samos in this same connection.

As a necessary outcome of the evidences discussed above, an objective assessment of the sense carried by the verbal syntagma οἱ Πυθαγόρειοι (qualified or not by the participle καλούμενοι) and of its likely configuration at the hands of Aristotle himself, arguably on the basis of previous doxographic accounts (Plato's and of still earlier authors), discloses it as a wide-ranging resource in his own discussion of Pythagorean matters (of scientific import or not), at least in his extant works, and suggests that we have to do here with a conscious choice of his. While this decision by Aristotle was hardly aimed at pretermitting (so to say) classified information—as could be the case regarding personages with whom he was personally acquainted, like Plato and his other fellow Academics—we are tempted nonetheless to see in the replacement of an individual name by an anonymous collective tag an instance of an expository technique arguably employed by him for addressing a more objective criticism to the matters being examined. In fact, he is likely to have first gotten acquainted with it through Plato's equivocal approach to earlier thinkers, but then, probably following in the footsteps of other previous doxographic accounts, he would have upgraded it to a highly productive tool of systematic discussion.

Once the proto-doxographical character of designations like "Pythagoreans" or "Italiote (thinkers)" in the context of a criticism or a polemic conducted by Aristotle is thus recognized, because of the convenience of resorting in such instances to a collective label, a higher frequency of Pythagoras' own name in Aristotle's lost works of historical nature may be expected as normal. According to this *constat* about the Stagirite's own way of coping with such an instance, modern scholarship should more fairly adjust Pythagoras' image as mirrored in Aristotle's extant and lost works, so as to enable a more balanced and sympathetic account of him as an original and influential thinker.

Bibliography

Alesse, Francesca. 2000. "La dottrina pitagorica della metempsicosi nel *De Anima* di Aristotele." In *Tra Orfeo e Pitagora: origini e incontri di culture nell'antichità. Atti dei seminari napoletani 1996–98*, edited by Marisa Tortorelli Ghidini, A. S. Marino, A. Visconti, 397–412. Naples: Bibliopolis.

Álvarez Salas, Omar. 2017. "Philosophy on Stage and Performance in Argument: Epicharmus vis-à-vis Western Greek Intelligentsia." In *Politics and Performance in Western Greece*, edited by Heather Reid, Davide Tanasi, Susan Kimbell, 163–192. Sioux City (Iowa): Parnassos Press.

Álvarez Salas, Omar. 2016. "From Epicharmus's Theatrics to Zeno's Paradoxical 'Drama'." In *Philosopher Kings and Tragic Heroes. Essays on Images and Ideas from Western Greece*, edited by Heather Reid, Davide Tanasi, 25–44. Sioux City (Iowa): Parnassos Press.

Álvarez Salas, Omar, and Enrique Hülsz Piccone, eds. 2015. *El libro de Heráclito 2500 años después*. Mexico: UNAM.

Álvarez Salas, Omar. "Cratylus and the reception of Heraclitus' doctrine in Athens." In Álvarez and Hülsz, *El libro de Heráclito 2500 años después*, 239–268.

Bremmer, Jan N. "Ψυχή." In *A History of Ancient Greek. From the Beginnings to Late Antiquity*, ed. Anastasios-Fivos Christidis, 1146–1153.

Bremmer, Jan N. 2001. *The Rise and Fall of the Afterlife*. London-New York: Routledge.

Burkert, Walter. 1972. *Lore and Science in Ancient Pythagoreanism*. Translated by Edwin L. Minar. Harvard: Harvard University Press. [orig. publ. 1962. *Weisheit und Wissenschaft. Studien zu Pythagoras, Philolaos und Platon*. Nuremberg: Hans Karl.]

Cambiano, Giuseppe. 1986. "Tecniche dossografiche in Platone." In Cambiano, *Storiografia e dossografia nella filosofia antica*, 61–83.

Cambiano, Giuseppe, ed. 1986. *Storiografia e dossografia nella filosofia antica*. Turin: Tirrenia.

Casadesús, Francesc. "¿Escribió Heráclito la palabra *philosophous* en el fragmento DK B 35?" in *El libro de Heráclito 2500 años después*, ed. Álvarez and Hülsz, 127–151.

Cherniss, Harold Fredrik. 1935. *Aristotle's Criticism of Presocratic Philosophy*. Baltimore, MD: The John Hopkins University Press.

Christidis, Anastasios-Fivos, ed. 2015. *A History of Ancient Greek. From the Beginnings to Late Antiquity*. Cambridge: Cambridge University Press. [Two-part reprint of the corrected edition in one volume (2010); the first English language edition (2007) was translated from the original Greek, published as Χριστίδης, Αναστάσιος-Φοίβος

(Επιστημονική Επιμέλεια) (2001). *Ιστορία της ελληνικής γλώσσας. Από τις αρχές έως την ύστερη αρχαιότητα.* Θεσσαλονίκη: Κέντρο της Ελληνικής Γλώσσας. Ινστιτούτο Νεοελληνικών Σπουδών].

Classen, Carl-Joachim. 1965. "Bemerkungen zu zwei griechischen ,Philosophiehistorikern'," *Philologus* 109: 175–181.

Cornelli, Gabriele. 2016. "Aristotle and the Pythagorean Myths of Metempsychosis," *Méthexis* 28: 1–13.

Cornelli, Gabriele. 2013. *In Search of Pythagoreanism. Pythagoreanism as an Historiographical Category.* Berlin: De Gruyter.

Curd, Patricia, and Daniel W. Graham, eds. 2008. *The Oxford Handbook of Presocratic Philosophy.* Oxford: Oxford University Press.

Diels, Hermann and Walther Kranz, eds. 1951. *Die Fragmente der Vorsokratiker.* Berlin: Weidmann.

Diogenes Laertius. 2013. *Lives of Eminent Philosophers.* Edited with an introduction by Tiziano Dorandi. Cambridge: Cambridge University Press.

Diogenes Laertius. 1999. *Vitae Philosophorum.* Edited by Miroslav Marcovich. Stuttgart-Leipzig: Teubner.

Düring, Ingemar. 1957. *Aristotle in the ancient biographical tradition.* Göteborg: Elanders (repr. New York and London: Garland Publishing, 1987).

Fortenbaugh, William W., and Eckart Schütrumpf, eds. 2001. *Dicaearchus of Messana: Text, Translation, and Discussion.* New Brunswick, N.J.: Transaction Publishers.

Frank, Erich. 1923. *Plato und die sogenannten Pythagoreer.* Halle: Max Niemayer.

Frede, Michael. 2004. "Aristotle's Account of the Origins of Philosophy." *Rhizai: A Journal for Ancient Philosophy and Science* 1: 9–44 [reprinted in *The Oxford Handbook of Presocratic Philosophy*, ed. Curd and Graham, 501–529].

Huffman, Carl. 2019. "Pythagoreanism." In *The Stanford Encyclopedia of Philosophy*, edited by Edward N. Zalta. https://plato.stanford.edu/archives/fall2019/entries/pythagoreanism/.

Huffman, Carl. 2018. "Pythagoras." In *The Stanford Encyclopedia of Philosophy*, edited by Edward N. Zalta. https://plato.stanford.edu/archives/win2018/entries/pythagoras/.

Huffman, Carl. 2016. "Philolaus." In *The Stanford Encyclopedia of Philosophy*, edited by Edward N. Zalta. https://plato.stanford.edu/archives/sum2016/entries/philolaus/.

Huffman, Carl, ed.2014. *A History of Pythagoreanism.* Cambridge: Cambridge University Press.

Huffman, Carl. "The Peripatetics on the Pythagoreans." In Huffman, *A History of Pythagoreanism*, 274–295.

Huffman, Carl. 2005. "Two Problems in Pythagoreanism." In *The Oxford Handbook of Presocratic Philosophy*, edited by Patricia Curd and Daniel W. Graham, 284–304. Oxford: Oxford University Press.

Huffman, Carl. 2005. *Archytas of Tarentum: Pythagorean, Philosopher and Mathematician King*. Cambridge: Cambridge University Press.

Huffman, Carl. 1993. *Philolaus of Croton: Pythagorean and Presocratic*. Cambridge: Cambridge University Press.

Iamblichus. 1991. *On the Pythagorean Way of Life*. Text, Translations and Notes by John M. Dillon and Jackson P. Hershbell. Atlanta: Scholars Press.

Kahn, Charles H. 2001. *Pythagoras and the Pythagoreans. A Brief History*. Indianapolis/Cambridge: Hackett Publishing Company, Inc.

Laks, André, and Glenn Most, eds. 2016. *Early Greek Philosophy*, 9 vols. Harvard: Loeb Classical Library.

Long, Herbert S. ed. 1964 (repr. 1966). *Diogenis Laertii vitae philosophorum*. 2 vols. Oxford: Clarendon Press.

Macris, Constantinos. 2018. "Pythagore." In *Dictionnaire des philosophes antiques*, Vol. VII: D'Ulpien à Zoticus, edited by Richard Goulet, 681–850. Paris: CNRS Éditions.

Mansfeld, Jaap. 1986. "Aristotle, Plato, and the Preplatonic Doxography and Chronography." In Cambiano, *Storiografia e dossografia nella filosofia antica*, 1–60.

O'Meara, Dominic. 1990. *Pythagoras Revived: Mathematics and Philosophy in Late Antiquity*. Oxford: Oxford University Press.

Palmer, John. "The Pythagoreans and Plato." In Huffman, *A History of Pythagoreanism*, 204–226.

Patzer, Andreas. 1986. *Der Sophist Hippias als Philosophiehistoriker*. Munich: Karl Alber.

Pellò, Caterina. 2018. "The Lives of Pythagoras: A Proposal for Reading Pythagorean Metempsychosis." *Rhizomata* 6 (2): 135–156.

Philip, James A. 1963. "Aristotle's Sources for Pythagorean Doctrines." *Phoenix* 17, No. 4: 251–265.

Primavesi, Oliver. "Aristotle on the "so-called Pythagoreans": from lore to principles." In Huffman, *A History of Pythagoreanism*, 227–249.

Riedweg, Christoph. 2007. *Pythagoras. Leben, Lehre, Nachwirkung*. Munich: Beck.

Rose, Valentinus. 1886. *Aristotelis qui ferebantur librorum fragmenta*. Leipzig: Teubner.

Schofield, Malcolm. "Pythagoreanism: emerging from the Presocratic fog (*Metaphysics* A 5)." In Steel—Primavesi, *Aristotle's* Metaphysics *Alpha*, 141–166.

Schofield, Malcolm. "Archytas." In Huffman, *A History of Pythagoreanism*, 69–87.

Snell, Bruno. 1944. "Die Nachrichten über die Lehren des Thales und die Anfänge der griechischen Philosophie- und Literaturgeschichte," *Philologus* 96: 170–182. Reprinted in *Sophistik*, edited by Carl-Joachim Classen, 478–490. Darmstadt: Wissenschaftliche Buchgesellschaft, 1976.

Steel, Carlos, Oliver Primavesi, eds. 2012. *Aristotle's* Metaphysics *Alpha*. Oxford: Oxford University Press.

Zeller, Eduard. 1877. "Über die Benützung der aristotelischen *Metaphysik* in den Schriften der älteren Peripatetiker." In *Abhandlungen der Königlichen Akademie der Wissenschaften zu Berlin*, 145–167. Berlin: Akademie der Wissenschaften.

Zeller, Eduard. 1865. *Die Philosophie der Griechen in ihrer geschichtlichen Entwicklung.* Vol. 1. Leipzig: O. R. Reisland.

Zhmud, Leonid. 2012. "Aristoxenus and the Pythagoreans." In *Aristoxenus of Tarentum. Texts and Discussion*, edited by Carl Huffman, 223–250. New Brunswick, N.J.: Transaction Publishers.

Zhmud, Leonid. 2012. *Pythagoras and the Early Pythagoreans.* Oxford: Oxford University Press.

CHAPTER 8

Eleatic *Archai* in Aristotle: A Dependence on Theophrastus' *Natural History?*

Christopher Kurfess

In memoriam Keith Bemer

⁙

A little over a century ago, A. E. Taylor suggested that, of the many insights we owe to Aristotle and his school, the greatest may be their realization of "the importance of systematic historical research into the evolution of ideas and institutions." Blessed with an innate gift for detailed scientific study and the beneficiary of early medical and biological training, Aristotle, according to Taylor, established the framework for a grand research agenda to be pursued by his immediate followers and bequeathed to later thinkers:

> The earliest sketches of the history of Philosophy and Psychology are those contained in the present book [i.e., *Metaphysics* A] and in the first book of the treatise *de Anima*, respectively. The earliest outline of the history of Physics is similarly that given by Aristotle in the opening chapters of the first book of his "*Lectures on Physics*." The first separate and complete history of Physics was composed by Aristotle's pupil and immediate successor, Theophrastus, and the first history of Mathematics by another disciple, Eudemus, and it is principally to second or third hand epitomes and to later citations from these works that we are still indebted for our detailed knowledge of the development of early Greek science in both these departments.[1]

---

1 Taylor 1910, 29–30. Cf. Zeller 1931, 219–222; Jaeger 1962, 334–337. In a note (29 n. 1), Taylor elaborates: "The dependence of the epitome of physical theories known as the *Placita Philosophorum*, which has been preserved to us in a double form in the writings ascribed to Plutarch and in the *Eclogae* of Stobaeus, on the lost Φυσικαὶ Δόξαι of Theophrastus was established by Diels in the prolegomena to his *Doxographi Graeci*; the work of Eudemus is mainly known to

---

© KONINKLIJKE BRILL NV, LEIDEN, 2021 | DOI:10.1163/9789004443358_010

Taylor recognized that Aristotle was not the most sympathetic of critics, and that "if we relied on the letter of his statements about cruder and older philosophies, we should often be led astray."[2] But, he continues, "when we have ... made allowance, as it is usually easy to do, for this tendency to read his own system into the utterances of his predecessors, what he tells us is ... of the highest importance, and it is hardly too much to say that the first book of the *Metaphysics*, thus cautiously interpreted, is by far the most valuable single document for the history of early Greek philosophy."

With certain qualifications called for by the work of Harold Cherniss and others,[3] what Taylor described basically remains the standard view of Aristotle's impact on ἱστορία-writing and the later doxographical tradition. Under the direction and influence of the Master, Theophrastus and others are envisioned as carrying out a systematic program of documenting, critiquing, and appropriating the opinions and arguments of earlier thinkers in a wide array of disciplines.[4]

While Aristotle's influence on later thought can hardly be overstated, I propose in what follows that our understanding of his relationship with Theophrastus may require some revision. Contrary to the still widespread view that Theophrastus was simply (if industriously) working within the general outlines he inherited from Aristotle, there are reasons for thinking that in the case of Aristotle's discussions of Presocratic *archai*, the dependency may have worked the other way. As Pamela Huby, with an eye on the biological treatises, has aptly observed, "Theophrastus was only about thirteen years younger than Aristotle ... and is to be thought of as a colleague even more than as a pupil."[5] Taking that observation to heart, I wish to advance the notion that

---

us from the use made of it by the Neo-Platonic philosopher, Proclus, in his commentary on the first book of Euclid's Elements."

2   Taylor 1910, 32. Cf. Burnet 1930, 31–32; Jaeger 1947, 52–53.

3   Most notably, Cherniss 1935 showed that granting due allowance for Aristotle's handling of his predecessors is more involved than Taylor and others had acknowledged. McDiarmid 1953 aimed to apply Cherniss' approach to Theophrastus. More recent scholarship has also brought to light possible predecessors to the Peripatetics' doxographical efforts. See esp. Mansfeld 1986 for an account of earlier work and Mansfeld's own contributions, and Frede 2008 and Palmer 2008 for recent discussions.

4   Cf. Mansfeld 1999, 31: "it is clearly Aristotle's methodology as revised by Theophrastus that determines the layout of the *Placita*." A notable voice of dissent on this point is that of A. V. Lebedev, for whom "The Φυσικαὶ Δόξαι of Theophrastus as the *Urquelle* of all Pre-Platonic physical doxography is a myth" and Theophrastus "is at best a marginal source" for the *Placita* (2016, 574). For a recent, well-elaborated account of Peripatetic historiography, see Zhmud 2006, 117–165.

5   Huby 1985, 313. Huby suggests in her paper that Theophrastean material may have been incorporated into the later books of the *Historia Animalium* and the *Mirabilia* (without, it

ELEATIC *ARCHAI* IN ARISTOTLE

Theophrastus, in what would have been one of his earlier works, consulted by the 6th-century C.E. commentator Simplicius of Cilicia and referred to by him as the Φυσικὴ Ἱστορία or *Natural History*, provided an account of early thinkers' views on natural principles that Aristotle himself employed in composing the "historical" surveys found in the opening books of the *Physics*, *Metaphysics*, *de Anima* and elsewhere.

Since a proper argument for Aristotle's use of Theophrastus' text would require more discussion than is possible here, my aim on the present occasion is mainly to raise the issue. I hope that the possibility of such influence proves intriguing enough that others will test the hypothesis in their own readings of the texts in question. I shall focus below on three passages from Simplicius' commentary on Aristotle's *Physics* that form the basis for my suggestion. Each text affords us a view of Theophrastus' report of an Eleatic thinker's *archē* or "principle," and each is related to passages in Aristotle that may be better read as responding to the reports in Theophrastus than vice versa.

1   **Theophrastus on Xenophanes**

Our first text is a troublesome passage from early in Simplicius' commentary. A word must be said about its setting before we turn to the text itself. The passage comes at the beginning of a summary of early thinkers' views on the *archai* of natural things that Simplicius offers as a framework for his consideration of Aristotle's divisions of natural principles in the early chapters of the *Physics*. The bulk of the summary, which fills the better part of seven pages in Hermann Diels' edition of the commentary, is widely recognized as deriving from Theophrastus, framed by and with occasional remarks from Simplicius himself.[6]

There is, however, some dispute over exactly which of Theophrastus' works was involved. Diels, following Hermann Usener and followed by many (such as

---

should be noted, assuming Aristotle himself authored those works). Huby 2002 raises related questions with respect to the logical treatises.

6   Thus most of the summary (spanning *in Phys.* 22.22–28.31 Diels) is reproduced in Diels' collection of the fragments of Theophrastus' *Physicorum Opiniones* (see Diels 1879, 475–485, where fragments 1–5, 8 and 9 are all drawn from Simplicius) and even more fully, with an accompanying translation, under the heading "Doxography on Nature" in the recent collection of Theophrastean fragments by Fortenbaugh et al. (see FHSG frags. 224, 225, 226A, 227A, 228A, 229, and 230). A commentary by Han Baltussen on the doxographical fragments in FHSG is forthcoming. For a general orientation to Simplicius' use of Theophrastus, see Baltussen 2008, 54–68 and 88–106.

Taylor in note 1 above), believed the ultimate source for Simplicius' summary to be a doxographical work entitled Φυσικῶν Δόξαι or Φυσικαὶ Δόξαι in sixteen (or eighteen) books.[7] Peter Steinmetz has challenged this identification, arguing that the work employed was actually Theophrastus' *Physics* (i.e., Φυσικά).[8] Steinmetz's identification has been accepted by some, but others remain unconvinced.[9] While I count myself among the latter, I am not particularly concerned with that dispute here and I shall refer hereafter simply to the *Natural History*. In so doing, I regard the verbatim agreement between the report about Anaxagoras in the summary (at *in Phys.* 27.17–23) and the quotation later in the commentary (at *in Phys.* 154.17–23), introduced by the words γράφει δὲ οὕτως ἐν τῇ Φυσικῇ ἱστορίᾳ, as sufficient reason for thinking that the summary derives from a work that Simplicius knew as the *Natural History*.[10] Guided in what follows by Simplicius, I refrain from opining on the relationship between the *Natural History* and the Φυσικῶν (or Φυσικαὶ) Δόξαι (Simplicius nowhere cites such a title), but the *Natural History* would have to be distinct, on my reading, from the work that Simplicius refers to as Theophrastus' *Physics*, which Theophrastus seems to have composed with Aristotle's writings on natural science in hand.[11] The broader problem is complicated by the multiplicity of titles on

---

7   I say "ultimate source" because Diels believed that Simplicius was getting this information second-hand, but this is not true of all who trace the summary back to this work. Cf. Zhmud 2006, 157 with n. 163. For disagreement over the exact title of this work (which appears in Diogenes Laertius' list of titles as Φυσικῶν Δοξῶν α´–ις´), see Mansfeld 1992 (arguing for Φυσικαὶ Δόξαι, i.e., *Natural Opinions*) and Zhmud 2001, 227–232 (defending Φυσικῶν Δόξαι, i.e., *Opinions of the Natural Philosophers*). For a useful overview of the materials and issues relating to the various titles of Theophrastus' works on nature, see the commentary on FHSG frag. 137 in Sharples 1998, 1–13.

8   Steinmetz 1964, 334–351. Simplicius had quoted from Theophrastus' *Physics*, using that title, at *in Phys.* 9.7–10 (later recalling the same point, without specifying the work, at *in Phys.* 21.8–10) and at *in Phys.* 20.20–26. One might easily assume, since Simplicius does not expressly state that the material in the summary comes from a different work, that references to Theophrastus there are also from the *Physics*, but there is no necessity that it be so.

9   In favor of Steinmetz's identification, see Runia 1992, 117; Mansfeld 1999, 26; Lebedev 2016, 596. Against, see Zhmud 2001, 230–232. Cf. Sharples 1998, 2–13.

10 Simplicius refers to the same work at *in Phys.* 115.12 and 149.32 (on which see note 15 below). Note the uses, in the summary itself, of ἱστορία at *in Phys.* 22.29, 23.30, and 26.11, and of ἱστορεῖν at *in Phys.* 25.6, 26.7, and 28.30. On the verbatim agreement of *in Phys.* 27.17–23 and 154.17–23, cf. Sharples 1998, 9: "Theophrastus did indeed make similar points in more than one work, but it strains credulity to suggest that he discussed Anaxagoras in almost verbally identical terms in two different works *and* that Simplicius in the same commentary cited the same passage from two different Theophrastean works."

11 For citations of Theophrastus' *Physics*, see FHSG frags. 143, 144B, 146, 149, 153A, 153C, 176, and 238. In these cases, Simplicius is generally reporting Theophrastus' views on topics raised in Aristotle's works, including the *de Caelo* as well as the *Physics*. I incline therefore

ELEATIC *ARCHAI* IN ARISTOTLE

265

natural science ascribed to Theophrastus and by the fact that not all of our witnesses seem to have been as careful as was Simplicius about keeping the titles straight, so there is often room for doubt as to whether citations of the same or similar titles involve identical works or not.[12]

Despite some confusion over the work in question, there is little doubt that Theophrastus is responsible for most of the material in the summary. Simplicius explicitly names Theophrastus toward the start of the summary (at *in Phys.* 22.28–29, in discussing Xenophanes) and on four subsequent occasions.[13] Two later Peripatetics, Nicolaus of Damascus and Alexander of Aphrodisias, are also named in the summary, but they do not appear to be used as authorities of first resort. Each is named twice, but only as offering alternatives, and seemingly inferior ones, to Theophrastus' account.[14] Theophrastus, meanwhile, can be positively identified as the source of information in the summary even where he is not explicitly named.[15] The same does not appear to be true of the others.[16]

---

    toward viewing Theophrastus' *Physics* as a late effort addressed to the wider Aristotelian curriculum in natural science, and his *Natural History* as an early one, perhaps later incorporated or expanded into the doxographical work. The distinction between such a *Physics* and a *Natural History* is consistent with the evidence from Simplicius' colleague Priscian of Lydia; see FHSG frag. 137 1b, 5b (citing both Theophrastus' *Naturalis auditus* and his *Naturalis historia*) and cf. FHSG frag. 297, with 307A (ἐν τῷ πέμπτῳ τῶν Φυσικῶν, δευτέρῳ δὲ τῶν Περὶ ψυχῆς).

12   Cf., e.g., Simplicius' quotation of Theophrastus from "the beginning of his own *Physics*" (FHSG frag. 144B) with what Philoponus reports as given ἐν τῇ ἰδίᾳ Περὶ φύσεως πραγματείᾳ (144A), and the various texts that make up FHSG frag. 227, including what I would consider Simplicius' report from Theophrastus' *Natural History* (227A), a quotation by Alexander of Aphrodisias found ἐν τῷ πρώτῳ Περὶ τῶν φυσικῶν (227C), and references by Diogenes Laertius (227D) to both Theophrastus' *Summary* (ἐν τῇ Ἐπιτομῇ) and his *Physics* (ἐν τοῖς Φυσικοῖς).

13   At *in Phys.* 23.31 (discussing Thales), 25.6 (on Diogenes of Apollonia), 26.7 (on Plato), and 27.11 (on Anaxagoras' similarity to Anaximander).

14   Nicolaus at *in Phys.* 23.14–15 (on Xenophanes) and 25.8 (on Diogenes); Alexander at *in Phys.* 23.16 (on Xenophanes) and 26.13 (on Plato).

15   The account of Anaximander at *in Phys.* 24.13–21—which includes DK 12 B 1, the only quotation of Anaximander to survive—seems sure (*pace* Lebedev 2016, 597–598) to be drawn from Theophrastus, although he is not named in it (see Kahn 1994, 13–15). As already noted, the latter part of the account of Anaxagoras (*in Phys.* 27.17–23) matches verbatim *in Phys.* 154.17–23, explicitly attributed to Theophrastus' *Natural History*. The description of Anaximenes at *in Phys.* 24.29–31 likewise agrees with *in Phys.* 149.29–32, where Theophrastus is named and an abbreviated title is given (ἐν τῇ Ἱστορίᾳ). It may, moreover, be Theophrastus, rather than Aristotle (as assumed at Diels 1879, 475 and FHSG 407), who is the unexpressed subject of οὓς καὶ φυσικοὺς ἰδίως καλεῖ at *in Phys.* 23.22–23.

16   Diels' influential (but I think ill-founded) suggestion that Simplicius depended on Alexander for his Theophrastean material (cf. note 7 above) will be addressed below.

266   KURFESS

We may now turn to the text itself. Echoing the opening of the second chapter of Aristotle's *Physics*,[17] Simplicius' summary begins as follows:[18]

> [1] So it is necessary for the principle to be either single or not single, which is the same as to say that there are many, and if it is single, it must be either unmoved or in movement. And if it is unmoved it must be either unlimited, as Melissus of Samos seems to say, or limited, as Parmenides son of Pyres from Elea says; these men are not speaking about an element of natural (things), but about being as a whole.
>
> [2] That the principle is single, or that what is and the All is single and neither limited nor unlimited, neither in motion nor at rest, was, Theophrastus says, the supposition of Xenophanes of Colophon, the teacher of Parmenides; (though) he admits that the mention of this man's opinion belongs to another enquiry rather than to that concerning nature.
>
> [3] [For][19] Xenophanes said that this One and All is god. He shows that it is one from the fact that it is the most superior of all things: for if there were more than one, he says, it would be necessary that they should all alike possess superiority; and the most superior and best thing of all is god. [4] He showed that it did not come to be, from the necessity that what comes to be should come to be either from what is like or from what is unlike; a thing cannot be affected, he says, by what is like it, for it is no more appropriate for a thing to produce what is like it than to be produced by it; but if it were to come to be from what is not like it, being will come from not-being. And in this way he showed that it did not come to be and is eternal. [5] (He showed that) it is neither unlimited nor limited, because it is what is not that is unlimited, since it has neither beginning nor middle nor end, and it is things that are more than one in number that are limited by each other. [6] And in a similar way he removes from

---

17   *Phys.* 1.2 184b15–22: "It is necessary either that the *archē* be one or more than one; and if one, either unmoved, as Parmenides claims, and Melissus, or in motion, as the *physikoi* do, some asserting that air, others that water is the first *archē*; and if more than one, either limited or unlimited; and if limited and more than one, either two, or three, or four, or some other number; and if unlimited, either the way Democritus has it, one in kind, but differing in shape, or differing and even contraries in form."

18   Simpl. *in Phys.* 22.22–23.20, as translated in FHSG frag. 224, with material in brackets added. The numbering of the sections is that of Diels (see note 23 below).

19   Following Diels, FHSG ends the preceding sentence with δόξης and prints what follows as a separate paragraph. This ignores the particle γάρ (untranslated in FHSG), which links Xenophanes' speaking of the One as god with Theophrastus' admission that mention of this opinion belongs to another ἱστορία than that concerned with nature.

ELEATIC *ARCHAI* IN ARISTOTLE 267

it both movement and rest, for it is what is not that is unmoved, since neither does anything else enter it, nor does it approach anything else, and
it is things that are more than one that move, since one thing changes to
another. [7] So, when he says that it remains in the same place and does
not move,

> but always remains in the same place, not moving at all;
> nor is it fitting for it to go to different places at different times,

[DK 21 B 26]

he is not saying that it "remains" in the sense in which rest is opposed to
motion, but rather in that of "remaining" that transcends both motion
and rest.

[8] Nicolaus of Damascus, in *On the Gods*, records (Xenophanes) as
saying that the principle is unlimited and unmoved; Alexander, that it is
limited and spherical. [9] But that he shows that it is neither limited nor
unlimited is clear from what has been said; he speaks of it as limited and
spherical, on the other hand, because it is similar in every direction. And
he says that it thinks all things, saying

> but without toil it sways all things by the thought of its mind.

[DK 21 B 25]

Interestingly, given the general recognition of Theophrastus' role in Simplicius'
summary, scholars have regularly sought to relieve Theophrastus of responsibility for the portrait of Xenophanes with which Simplicius seems clearly to
credit him. Eduard Zeller, for instance, wished to confine Theophrastus' contribution to what is contained in section 2, implausibly taking Simplicius' report
of Theophrastus' admission "that mention of this man's opinion belongs to another enquiry than that concerning nature" as an indication that what follows
did not come from the same source, despite the fact that the arguments in sections 3, 5 and 6 address precisely the attributes mentioned in section 2, namely,
the god's being single (§ 3), neither unlimited nor limited (§ 5), and neither
in motion nor at rest (§ 6).[20] For the later sections, Zeller claimed, Simplicius
must have used the work now commonly known as *On Melissus, Xenophanes*

---

20   See Zeller 1881, 542–544. The argument presented in § 4 for the god's being ungenerated
      and eternal is admittedly not anticipated in § 2, but we would not necessarily expect
      these attributes to be mentioned there. In § 2, as in § 1 with Parmenides and Melissus,
      Simplicius' main concern is to report how a thinker stands with respect to the differentiae
      used in Aristotle's divisions of the *archai* of his predecessors (i.e., one/more than one;
      unmoved/in motion; limited/unlimited—see the passage quoted in note 17 above), so it
      is unsurprising that the description mentions only these specifically.

268 KURFESS

and Gorgias (MXG).[21] The most obvious problem with this idea is that, while the account in the third chapter of the *MXG* and the portrait of Xenophanes preserved in Simplicius are unmistakably related, the *MXG* does not supply, as Simplicius' source must have, the verses quoted in sections 7 and 9 describing the special immobility and the manner of thought of Xenophanes' god. (Simplicius' text is our sole source for these two fragments.)

Diels, sharing concerns about attributing the full portrait to Theophrastus, aimed to improve on Zeller by placing the words "and neither limited nor unlimited, neither in motion nor at rest" in section 2 in parentheses, as though they belonged not to Theophrastus but to Simplicius.[22] Though it would prove influential, Diels' proposal had problems of its own. In addition to reducing the scope of Theophrastus' contribution to such a degree that it might seem pointless for Simplicius to have cited him at all, it involved a still more complicated story about the constitution of Simplicius' text: as with Zeller's suggestion, Simplicius was supposed to have combined both Theophrastus and the *MXG*, but, according to Diels, Simplicius knew Theophrastus' text only from quotations in Alexander's *Physics* commentary, and his passage frequently interweaves or shifts between his sources without indicating the fact.[23]

While forcefully challenged as early as 1916 by Karl Reinhardt,[24] variations on these tactics have persisted. John Burnet, for instance, would claim,

---

21 See Zeller 1881, 544–547. Chapter 3 of the *MXG* presents a series of arguments for god's being (1) ungenerated; (2) eternal; (3) one; (4) in every way alike; (5) spherical; (6) neither infinite nor finite (οὔτ' ἄπειρον οὔτε πεπεράνθαι); and (7) neither moved nor unmoved (οὔτε κινεῖσθαι οὔτε ἀκίνητον). Curiously, the chapter does not actually name Xenophanes, but the parallels with Simplicius' passage make the identification reasonably certain. On the *MXG* author's habit of not naming the principal subjects of his discussions, see Kurfess (forthcoming).

22 This bracketing of καὶ οὔτε πεπερασμένον οὔτε ἄπειρον οὔτε κινούμενον οὔτε ἠρεμοῦν began with Diels 1879, 480, and (though the text appeared without parentheses in Diels 1882, 22) continued in Diels 1900, 36, in Diels 1901, 30, and in DK 21 A 30. Various subsequent studies followed Diels' lead (e.g., Kirk and Raven 1957, 167; KRS 167; Finkelberg 1990, 114; Lesher 1992, 212), but the bracketing is rightly resisted in FHSG and other recent works (e.g., Mansfeld 1987, 307 n. 68, citing the earlier examples of Reinhardt and Steinmetz; Barnes 2001, 43; and Graham 2010, 114–115).

23 Cf. Diels 1901, 31: "Simplicius ex Alexandro parum diligenter transscripsit primum Theophrasti ex Physicorum Placitis eclogam (fr. 5 Dox. p. 480), ubi etiam versus Xenophanis citati esse videntur, tum Aristotelis q. f. de MXG [cf. A 28] excerpta, et sunt quidem: § 1 paraphr. Ar. Phys. 184^b 15, § 2 Theophrastea admixta parenthesi ex Ar. de MXG; § 3 ex l. de MXG 977^a 14. 23–28, § 4 indidem 977^a 15–22; § 5 ind. 977^b 2–7; § 6 ex 977^b 8–12; § 7 Theophrastea admixto l. de MXG 977^b 17 sqq.; § 8 ex Alexandro ipso; § 9 Simplicii iudicium adiecto versu ex Theophrasteis Alexandri."

24 See Reinhardt 1916, 89–112. Reinhardt defends Simplicius' account as being both drawn from Theophrastus directly and a relatively trustworthy report, along with the *MXG*, of

ELEATIC *ARCHAI* IN ARISTOTLE

269

"Alexander used this treatise [i.e., the *MXG*] as well as the work of Theophrastos, and Simplicius supposed the quotations from it to be from Theophrastos too. Having no copy of the poems he was completely baffled, and until recently all accounts of Xenophanes were vitiated by the same confusion."[25] It is probably true that Simplicius did not have a copy of Xenophanes' poems,[26] but I see no indications in the text of his being "baffled." Rather, Burnet himself seems confused in believing that the *MXG* could be the source for quotations not found there. (Again, Simplicius is our sole source for DK 21 B 25 and 26.) In subsequent treatments of this material, scholars have tended to endorse one or another of the elements of these arguments while rejecting others, but a nearly universal trait is the adoption of some hypothesis which allows us to avoid making Theophrastus responsible for the arguments in sections 3–6.[27]

One may well wonder here why there has been such reluctance to attribute the latter portions of the account to Theophrastus. Read by itself, Simplicius' passage seems to present a perfectly coherent report. After reading (in § 1) that Parmenides and Melissus each held that there was a single, unmoved *archē*, which Melissus seemed to speak of as unlimited, Parmenides as limited—information generally agreed to come from Theophrastus, even if he has not yet been named—we are told (in § 2) that Xenophanes, said to be Parmenides' teacher, supposed the *archē* to be single, and, rather curiously, *neither* limited *nor* unlimited, and *neither* in motion *nor* at rest. We also learn that, just as

---

actual arguments by Xenophanes. I agree unreservedly with the first point, and am open to the second, without endorsing Reinhardt's further contention that those arguments must postdate Parmenides' poem.

25 Burnet 1930, 126. Cf. McDiarmid 1953, 90: "Simplicius confuses Theophrastus with the writer of the late treatise *De Melisso, Xenophane, Gorgia* and fails to see that the account of Alexander, to which he opposes this treatise, has been derived from Theophrastus." In fact, in claiming that the god is spherical and limited, it may be Alexander himself that was following the *MXG* author, who argues that sphericity entails limitedness (*MXG* 4 978a16–24).

26 Simplicius admits to having limited access to Xenophanes' verses at *in Cael.* 522.7 Heiberg (= DK 21 A 47).

27 Jaeger 1947, 214–215 n. 64 ("after quoting Theophrastus, Simplicius shifts to another source (from § 3 on), and this source is obviously the author of the *De Xenophane Melisso Gorgia*") effectively reverts to Zeller's position without attempting to address its inadequacies. More recently, cf. Kahn 1994, 13–14 (allowing, with Reinhardt, that Simplicius had direct access to Theophrastus, but suggesting that he ignored him in favor of the "transcendental interpretation" of the *MXG*); Mansfeld 1987, 305–307 (accepting Theophrastus as the direct source for §§ 1–2, including the words that Diels brackets, but not for what follows); Finkelberg 1990, 149 n. 106 (suggesting that Simplicius had a mutilated copy of Theophrastus, and relied on Alexander's (confused) report of Theophrastus for what was not preserved).

neither Parmenides nor Melissus were, according to the report, speaking about an altogether *natural* element, but about being in some more general sense, Theophrastus likewise admitted that mention of Xenophanes' opinion is more properly at home in another inquiry than that into nature.[28] This remark is given greater specificity in what follows (§3; note the "for" (γάρ), indicating the continuity of the thought, which had to be supplied in the translation above): Xenophanes was not concerned with nature exactly, but with something that he spoke of as god, which he showed, by proofs of a sort, to be one (§3), ungenerated (§ 4), neither limited nor unlimited (§ 5), and neither moved nor at rest (§ 6). Since "neither limited nor unlimited" and "neither in motion nor at rest" are unusual predicates, particularly liable to be misunderstood, additional clarification is given on these points (the latter in § 7, the former in § 9). Apart from the remarks in section 8 about Nicolaus and Alexander, which illustrate plainly the need for the additional clarification offered, and after which Simplicius seems to return to his earlier source for an additional point, with quotation, about the god's thought, there is no suggestion that Simplicius is using any source other than Theophrastus. What makes scholars think otherwise?

The problem, apparently, is that the portrait of Xenophanes presented in Simplicius' summary and in the third chapter of the *MXG* runs afoul of one or another deeply-held dogma about Xenophanes or his place in the development of early Greek thought, and scholars do not want to grant that portrait the authority that it would have if it were associated with Theophrastus. Specific arguments against the historicity of the portrait vary. For Zeller,

> The contents of the chapter [i.e., *MXG* 3] do not agree with what we know on ancient authority respecting Xenophanes. While Xenophanes himself declares the divinity to be unmoved, this work says it is neither moved nor unmoved; and while Aristotle assures us that Xenophanes gave no opinion as to the Limitedness or Unlimitedness of the One, both predicates are here expressly and categorically denied in respect to it.[29]

---

28   This is not, as Zeller would have it, an indication that Theophrastus said no more about Xenophanes in the work that Simplicius was consulting, but an acknowledgment (in language which incidentally supports the identification of that work as the *Natural History*) that Xenophanes was evidently engaged in a somewhat different enterprise than most of the figures Theophrastus would have been discussing, i.e., those whom he and Aristotle might call φυσικοί or φυσιολόγοι *sensu stricto*.

29   Zeller 1881, 547–548. Cf. Jaeger 1947, 52–54.

ELEATIC *ARCHAI* IN ARISTOTLE   271

Here we would do well to ask: What *do* we know about Xenophanes? Who are the ancient authorities that we can bring against the testimony of the *MXG* and Simplicius, ancient authorities themselves, and—more importantly— seemingly reliable ones? Zeller appeals to the declaration of "Xenophanes himself" that his divinity is unmoved, but the fragment he has in mind is none other than DK 21 B 26, which (again) is known only from the passage of Simplicius before us and is quoted with the specific caveat, seemingly Theophrastus' own, that "remaining" and "not moving" as spoken of there were not meant in the sense which Zeller gives to them.[30] Readers are free to view that caveat with suspicion, but dismissing it out of hand as crediting Xenophanes with "distinctions ... unknown before the time of Aristotle" is merely begging the question.[31] As for Aristotle's alleged assurance "that Xenophanes gave no opinion as to the Limitedness and Unlimitedness of the One," we shall see shortly that Aristotle's text is not so clear-cut.

For Diels, there was the concern that what Simplicius appears to present as Theophrastus' account of Xenophanes conflicted with Diels' own reconstruction of what Theophrastus had said about him. But one may reasonably doubt that we should put more faith in that reconstruction than in Simplicius' straightforward testimony.[32] Another line of argument offered against the portrait of Xenophanes in Simplicius and the *MXG* is that those texts "make him out to be a systematic thinker using logical argument of a type impossible before Parmenides, and that anything else that is known about him makes it extremely unlikely that the picture is a true one."[33] Again, there are varieties of this line of thought, some focused on the form of the arguments, others on the ideas employed,[34] but each is essentially an argument from silence. I would

---

30   With the caveat of § 7 cf. the distinction, in Ch. 5 of Theophrastus' own *Metaphysics*, between a "better" sense of ἠρεμία that may be ascribed to first principles and that which is a mere privation of movement.

31   See Zeller 1881, 547 n. 2.

32   See Mansfeld 1987 for many reasons to doubt Diels on this point.

33   Guthrie 1962, 368–369. Cf. Graham 2010, 95: "Some sources present him as making elaborate interlocking arguments for metaphysical theses much like Parmenides does (see esp. [*MXG* 3 and Simplicius]). Yet scholars have become deeply suspicious of these reports, which seem to have arisen fairly late in the tradition and not to be based on actual arguments from the texts of Xenophanes. If we rely on the fragments themselves (which are admittedly limited) we do not see signs of close argument."

34   E.g., Mansfeld 1988, 240 n. 6 suggests that the "sophisticated negative theology" of the portrait demands a late date, while Finkelberg 1990, 136–137, allowing that "there is nothing inherently improbable in assuming Xenophanes' use of logical proofs," takes the use of "the notions of being and not-being" in such arguments as "betraying their post-Parmenidean date." See Lesher 1992, 193–194 for an overview of such arguments.

agree that the presentations in Simplicius and the *MXG* must be reformulations of whatever was to be found in Xenophanes' verses, but I am also wary of asserting that any such arguments were "impossible before Parmenides." Given the state of our records for this early period of Greek thought, we cannot meaningfully substantiate such categorical claims. As important a figure in the history of philosophy as Parmenides was and remains, the notion that sophisticated argumentation was impossible before him seems highly dubious. Parmenides' verses may provide our earliest surviving example of an extended deductive argument, but that does not entail that Xenophanes did not reason along similar lines beforehand.[35]

To be clear, I should state plainly that I am not asserting that the arguments outlined in Simplicius and the *MXG* were genuinely Xenophanean. They may well be, but all I am claiming here is that there is no compelling reason to doubt that Simplicius, in sections 1–7 and 9 of the passage above, was faithfully reporting what he found in Theophrastus. Some possible grounds for lingering doubt will be addressed in connection with the other passages to be discussed, so we may now turn to them.

2 Aristotle on Xenophanes

In the fifth chapter of the first book of the *Metaphysics* Aristotle writes the following about the Eleatics:

> But there are some who declared about the whole that it is one nature, though not all in the same way, either in how good their thinking was or with respect to the nature. An account of them in no way fits into the present examination about causes (for they do not speak in the same way as some writers about nature, who set down being as one but generate things out of the one as from material, but in a different way, since those others add in motion when they generate the whole, but these people say that it is motionless). Nonetheless, it can find a home in this inquiry to this extent: Parmenides seems to take hold of what is one according to reason, Melissus of what is one in material (on account of which one says that it is finite, the other infinite). But Xenophanes, the first of these

---

35   It was with some justification that M. L. West could fault "the conventional approach to the study of the Presocratics" for its "exaggeration of the achievement and influence of individuals … and the implicit assumption that nobody contributed to the development of thought except the few whose writings survived them" (1971, 219).

ELEATIC *ARCHAI* IN ARISTOTLE

who made things one (for Parmenides is said to have become a student of his), made nothing clear, nor does he seem to have made contact with nature in either of these two ways, but gazing off into the whole heaven, he said that divinity was one. So these, as we say, must be dismissed from the present inquiry, two of them completely as being a little too crude, Xenophanes and Melissus, though Parmenides to some degree seems to speak with more insight; for since he thought it fit that besides being, nonbeing could not be in any way, he necessarily supposed that being is one and that there is nothing else (about which we have spoken more clearly in the writings about nature), but being forced to follow appearances, and assuming that what is one from the standpoint of reason is more than one from the standpoint of perception, he set down in turn two causes and two sources, a hot one and a cold one, as though speaking of something like fire and earth, and of these he ranks the hot one under being and the other under nonbeing.[36]

Several points here deserve noting. First, we may observe that Aristotle does *not* assure us, as Zeller claimed, "that Xenophanes gave no opinion as to the Limitedness or Unlimitedness of the One."[37] Zeller seems to finds such assurance in the words οὐδὲ τῆς φύσεως τούτων οὐδετέρας ἔοικε θιγεῖν, "the meaning of which," he says, "can only be that Xenophanes did not discuss those questions on which Parmenides and Melissus disagreed with one another."[38] This clearly reads more into Aristotle's words than is stated explicitly. When Aristotle says that Xenophanes "seems not to touch on either 'nature' of these," "seems" (ἔοικε) suggests a certain epistemological modesty on Aristotle's part at odds with Zeller's characterization, while "nature" seems more likely, given the passage up to this point, to refer to the distinction between Parmenides' One "according to reason" (κατὰ τὸν λόγον) and Melissus' One "in material" (κατὰ τὴν ὕλήν) than to the question of finitude. In any case, Aristotle does not assert that

---

36 *Metaph.* A.5 986b10–987a2 Ross, as translated in Sachs 1999, 13.

37 See above, with note 29. Zeller is insistent that Aristotle "does not merely assert that Xenophanes left it uncertain whether he conceived of the One as a formal or material principle, but that he refused to define it as limited or unlimited" (1881, 548 n. 1). Cf. Jaeger 1947, 53.

38 Zeller 1881, 548 n. 1. In fact the meaning of these words is not so clearly limited and has been much disputed; see Finkelberg 1990, 106–107 n. 13, with references. Ross 1924, 1:154 ("τῆς φύσεως τούτων οὐδετέρας, 'the nature of either of these causes'. With τούτων we must understand τῶν ἀρχῶν or τῶν αἰτιῶν") represents a common way of taking τούτων, but cf. Sachs' "these ... ways" in the translation quoted and "these [qualifications]" in Mansfeld 1987, 307.

Xenophanes was silent on these natures or that he refused to discuss them, but merely that whatever he said (perhaps unclearly and crudely) can be passed over in the present inquiry.

Nonetheless, Aristotle does describe Xenophanes as: (1) the teacher of Parmenides; (2) a monist whose One is especially alien to natural science; and (3) speaking of his One as "the god" (ὁ θεός). Since Simplicius credits Theophrastus with the same points about Xenophanes, Aristotle's passage is typically thought to have provided the points of departure for Theophrastus' description.[39] My proposal, bearing in mind the observation of Huby quoted earlier, is that the reverse may just as easily have been the case, and would, moreover, spare us the contorted readings of Simplicius' straightforward account. Indeed, Aristotle's text gives an overt indication of just such a dependency in the parenthesis in which Parmenides "is said" (λέγεται) to have been Xenophanes' pupil, revealing that Aristotle is drawing on some other account. The obvious agreements with Theophrastus make him a good candidate for Aristotle's source.[40] In addition, it seems more plausible to understand Aristotle's complaint that, in contrast to Parmenides and Melissus, Xenophanes "made nothing clear" (οὐθὲν διεσαφήνισεν), as Aristotle's reaction to a description of Xenophanes' One as "neither limited nor unlimited, neither in motion nor at rest," than to suppose that it was the basis for that statement by Theophrastus or some later author.[41] The same is true, I think, for the remarks about Parmenides' and Melissus' Ones. Aristotle takes it as given that Parmenides' One was limited while Melissus' was unlimited (expressed more reservedly at *in Phys.* 22.24–25 as what they *seemed* to say) and explains this difference by using the "according to reason"/"in material" distinction. Since that distinction does not feature in Simplicius' passage, it again appears more likely that Theophrastus' text served as the basis for Aristotle's, if one drew directly from the other.

---

39   This is a nearly universal and often tacit assumption among those who have compared these texts. A possible exception of which I am aware by way of a footnote (Mansfeld 1986, 50 n. 29) is Gigon 1969. According to Mansfeld, "Gigon attempts to explain the difficulties of Aristotle's larger and smaller dialectical surveys by means of the hypothesis that he used Theophrastus' doxographical work." I have not yet had the opportunity to study Gigon's paper and compare the bases for his suggestion with mine.

40   Recent studies, recognizing that Aristotle relied on earlier collections of material in *Metaph.* A, tend to identify that source as Hippias (see, e.g., Palmer 2008, 519–521 and Barney 2012, 88–92). Without disputing Aristotle's use of Hippias in certain instances, I submit that Theophrastus should be considered a candidate as well.

41   Cf. Zeller 1881, 543 n. 1; Jaeger 1947, 214–215 n. 64; and Guthrie 1962, 369, each assuming a progressive garbling of Aristotle's statement in later authors.

ELEATIC *ARCHAI* IN ARISTOTLE   275

Finally, we should take careful note of the wording of Aristotle's remark about Parmenides' argument at 986b28–30: "since he thought it fit that besides being, nonbeing could not be in any way, he necessarily supposed that being is one and that there is nothing else" (παρὰ γὰρ τὸ ὂν τὸ μὴ ὂν οὐθὲν ἀξιῶν εἶναι, ἐξ ἀνάγκης ἓν οἴεται εἶναι, τὸ ὄν, καὶ ἄλλο οὐθέν). As we shall see, this bears more than a passing resemblance to what is reported elsewhere as the version of Parmenides' argument given in Theophrastus' *Natural History*.

3   Theophrastus and Alexander on "Parmenides' Argument"

We have seen that Diels and others, looking to curtail the amount of Theophrastean material in Simplicius' account of Xenophanes, have advanced the notion that Simplicius knew Theophrastus' text only via Alexander's now lost commentary on the *Physics*. As already indicated, this is rather improbable. Simplicius certainly quotes Alexander often enough, and he may be in the background of even more of Simplicius' commentary than the many explicit references to him indicate,[42] but the summary from Theophrastus is introduced in reaction to the comments of the "exegetes of Aristotle," Alexander clearly among them, with the intention of providing a better and more complete division of the early opinions on natural *archai*.[43] Moreover, as Charles Kahn has observed, "The hypothesis that such abundant excerpts could have appeared in Alexander's lost commentary is not borne out by the same author's extant work on the *Metaphysics*."[44] Nevertheless, remarks from the commentary on *Physics* 1.3 have been cited as support for the idea that Simplicius relied on Alexander.[45] As recently translated by Huby, Simplicius writes:

---

42   For an overview of Simplicius' use of Alexander, see Baltussen 2008, 107–135 and Baltussen 2009, 128–132.

43   See *in Phys.* 20.28–22.21, where the content tagged by φησίν ὁ Ἀλέξανδρος at 22.1 may begin as early as 21.21 and may extend as far as 22.8, despite Diels' limiting the quotation proper to 21.35–22.1.

44   Kahn 1994, 14 n. 1. The hypothesis is especially weak in the case of Xenophanes, given that Aristotle does not mention him in the *Physics*. In his *Metaphysics* commentary, Alexander's acquaintance with Xenophanes does not appear to go beyond Aristotle's text.

45   See Diels 1879, 113, where *in Phys.* 38.18–28 and 700.18–19 are also cited in support of the purported dependency, and cf. Kahn 1994, 13 n. 2. Of *in Phys.* 700.18, Finkelberg 1990, 149 n. 106 rightly points out that "the mere mention of Alexander's name after Theophrastus' is not sufficient testimony to reliance on Alexander," but goes on to describe *in Phys.* 38.20 (mistakenly identified as *Phys. Opin.* frag. 6) and 115.11 as "undeniable" cases. I will focus only on the latter text in the main body of the paper, but the case for *in Phys.* 38.18–28 is much the same: each passage merely provides evidence that Alexander made some use of

The argument of Parmenides, as Alexander reports, Theophrastus sets out like this in the first book of his *Research concerning Nature*: 'What is other than Being is not: what is not is nothing: therefore Being is one', but Eudemus like this: 'What is other than Being is not: but also 'being' is used in one sense only: therefore Being is one'. I cannot say if Eudemus set this out anywhere else as clearly as this, but in his *Physics* he wrote the following about Parmenides, and it is perhaps possible to derive the stated conclusion: 'Parmenides does not appear to prove that Being is one, not even if anyone were to agree with him that "being" is used in only one way, unless as in the "what" category of each thing, as "man" of men. For when the accounts of each have been given the account of Being will be one and the same in all, just as the account of animal in all animals. ...[46]

Simplicius' quotation from Eudemus carries on until *in Phys.* 116.4, after which Simplicius remarks, "And having got so far about Parmenides, he [i.e. Eudemus] turned to Anaxagoras."[47] Huby summarizes this passage of Simplicius thus: "he quotes from Alexander the short statements of both Theophrastus and Eudemus of Parmenides' argument, admitting that he himself may not have full knowledge of Eudemus' work."[48] A note to the translation adds: "From what he says at 115,13–15 above, and later at 133,24–5, it is clear that Simplicius accepted that he did not have access to all Eudemus' works, and was happy to use Alexander as well."[49] We might also imagine that, should Simplicius not have had Theophrastus' text, he would have been equally happy to use Alexander as a source for Theophrastus, as Diels and others have supposed.

In weighing this evidence, it is important to be clear on precisely what Simplicius does and does not say. Critically, he does not say that he is without Theophrastus' work or that he relies on Alexander for Theophrastus' formulation of Parmenides' argument. What Simplicius ascribes to Alexander is the *parallelism*

Theophrastus. Neither passage, read with an awareness of its context, is strong evidence that Simplicius relied on Alexander for his reports of Theophrastus.

46   Simpl. *in Phys.* 115.11–20, as translated in Huby and Taylor 2011, 27. This is the source of *Phys. Opin.* frag. 7 and FHSG frag. 234, each of which gives no more than *in Phys.* 115.11–13 (and thus only part of Simplicius' first sentence).

47   Huby and Taylor 2011, 27. Simplicius goes on to relate Porphyry's remarks (*in Phys.* 116.6–18, which incorporate the earlier reports; note esp. εἴ τι παρὰ τὸ ὄν ἐστιν, ἐκεῖνο οὐκ ὄν ἐστι at *in Phys.* 116.10) before turning to Aristotle's own formulation (discussed below), and, finally, the relevant verses of Parmenides' poem (*in Phys.* 116.25–117.13).

48   Huby and Taylor 2011, 3.

49   Huby and Taylor 2011, 93 n. 93. Cf. Baltussen 2002, 135–136. On *in Phys.* 133.24–25, see note 52 below.

ELEATIC *ARCHAI* IN ARISTOTLE   277

of that version of the argument with what Alexander offers as Eudemus' version. Simplicius adds that he cannot confirm the latter formulation as Eudemus', but he does not quibble with the former. This might be taken to suggest that he *was* able to confirm Theophrastus' formulation. In any case, as we shall see below, Simplicius had already quoted Theophrastus' version of Parmenides' argument earlier in the commentary, without mention of Alexander.[50] Moreover, with respect to Eudemus, while Huby provides a charitable reading of Simplicius' expressions, it is not, I think, an entirely faithful one. In "admitting" that he "cannot say if Eudemus set this out anywhere else as clearly as this, but in his *Physics* he wrote the following, and it is perhaps possible to derive the stated conclusion," the point Simplicius is making, in his somewhat understated way, is that Alexander is paraphrasing rather than quoting Eudemus' exact words. To drive the point home, Simplicius provides an extended quotation from Eudemus (up to the point where Eudemus turns to Anaxagoras) that includes one of the premises ("that 'being' is used in only one way," μοναχῶς λέγεσθαι τὸ ὄν) but does not present the argument in the form that Alexander gives it.[51] Far from an admission that he was "happy to use" him, the passage is an example of Simplicius casting doubt on Alexander's literalness—and displaying his own scrupulousness.[52]

4 Aristotle on "Parmenides' Argument"

While the passage just quoted (i.e., *in Phys.* 115.11ff.) does not provide the evidence it is sometimes claimed to provide for Simplicius' reliance on Alexander,

---

50 This goes unnoted by Huby and unnoticed in most of the literature. Cf. the app. crit. for FHSG frag. 234 and Sharples 1998, 9, where the later parallels at *in Phys.* 118.2–3 and 134.11–12 are noted, but the earlier instance at *in Phys.* 103.9–11 is not. See note 59 for other instances not cited in FHSG.

51 Which is to say, on the model of Theophrastus' version of the argument. It appears that Alexander was assimilating Eudemus' account to Theophrastus' syllogism. The different translations of μοναχῶς above (as "in one sense only" in Simplicius' report of Alexander but "in only one way" in Simplicius' quotation of Eudemus) obscures slightly the common element in the two reports of Eudemus. Eudemus' second premise as Alexander presents it is ἀλλὰ καὶ μοναχῶς λέγεται τὸ ὄν ("but also 'being' is used in one sense only" in Huby's translation).

52 Cf. Barney 2009, 110: "Simplicius has a markedly agonistic relationship with the great Peripatetic exegete Alexander of Aphrodisias. His attitude to and use of Alexander is complex and ambivalent: Simplicius by turns appropriates, cites, praises, and strives to refute him." Simplicius' remarks at *in Phys.* 133.24–25 (see Huby's remarks above, with note 49) and *in Phys.* 1355.34–38 (see Baltussen 2002, 136) seem to be similar cases of drawing attention to Alexander's departures from literalness (n.b. τὴν λέξιν ταύτην at 133.24–25, τὴν γραφήν at 1355.34).

it does hold valuable information for our present purposes. In it, we learn both how Theophrastus reconstructed Parmenides' argument and where he wrote about it: the first book of his *Natural History*.[53] As mentioned above, Theophrastus' formulation is rather like what we saw Aristotle attributing to Parmenides in the *Metaphysics*. In writing παρὰ γὰρ τὸ ὂν τὸ μὴ ὂν οὐθὲν ἀξιῶν εἶναι, ἐξ ἀνάγκης ἓν οἴεται εἶναι, τὸ ὄν, καὶ ἄλλο οὐθέν ("for thinking that, apart from what-is, non-being is nothing, he supposes that what-is is of necessity one, and nothing else"), Aristotle seems to be stating more loosely what Theophrastus puts in bare-bones syllogistic form: τὸ παρὰ τὸ ὂν οὐκ ὄν· τὸ οὐκ ὂν οὐδέν· ἓν ἄρα τὸ ὄν ("What is apart from what-is is not a being; what is not a being is nothing; therefore what-is is one"). Theophrastus' formulation is also comparable to a separate Aristotelian version of Parmenides' argument in the *Physics*, which Simplicius quotes a little further on in the same discussion, describing it as equivalent to the preceding formulations:

> Aristotle, however, in what follows, seems to recall Parmenides' argument in this way: "If 'being' (or 'what-is') signifies one thing, and its contradiction cannot be at the same time, there will not be non-being at all." (*Phys.* 187a4–5) This also expresses the same notion as the preceding. For if "being" signifies one thing, what is apart from that is not a being and nothing. And if its contradiction is not co-existent, so that the same thing both is a being and not a being at the same time, it is evident that what is apart from being will not be a being, and what is not a being will be nothing.[54]

Simplicius does not name him here, but from his explanation it seems clear that it is Theophrastus' version of Parmenides' argument that is foremost in his mind when he compares Aristotle's version with "the preceding" ones. This is an easily overlooked, but, I believe, critically important point for grasping portions of Simplicius' ensuing discussion, with potentially dramatic

---

53   It is not obvious whether the words ἐν τῷ πρώτῳ τῆς Φυσικῆς ἱστορίας come from Alexander or are added by Simplicius himself. The latter may be more likely, since Alexander does not elsewhere refer to this title. Cf. FHSG frag. 227C in note 12 above.

54   Simpl. *in Phys.* 116.18–24, my translation after the colon. Beyond that point Huby's translation is unfortunately likely to mislead in several respects: 116.20–21 is not marked (nor translated) as a quotation of *Phys.* 187a4–5; οὗτος (sc. λόγος) in line 21 is taken as referring to Parmenides as a person rather than to Aristotle's wording of Parmenides' argument; and τοῖς προτέροις is treated as referring to Parmenides' predecessors rather than the preceding formulations of Parmenides' argument by Theophrastus and others.

ELEATIC *ARCHAI* IN ARISTOTLE

consequences for our understanding of the relationship between Aristotle's and Theophrastus' texts.

Plainly, Theophrastus and Aristotle present closely related accounts of Parmenides' argument. As with their accounts of Xenophanes, one might easily assume that this similarity is due to Theophrastus' dependency on Aristotle. In the passage just quoted, however, Simplicius seems to treat Theophrastus' as the prior formulation, explaining Aristotle's locutions by reference to Theophrastus'. This merits careful consideration, for it hints at the intriguing possibility that to Simplicius, with both Theophrastus' *Natural History* and Parmenides' poem at hand, it was evident—or obvious enough, at least, that he did not belabor the point—that Aristotle was directing parts of his critique of Parmenides in *Physics* I.3 not at the verses of Parmenides himself, but at Theophrastus' reconstruction of Parmenides' argument.

That possibility seems to grow more likely as one reads on in the commentary. Prior to his discussion of Parmenides' actual verses in a coda to the commentary proper (*in Phys.* 142.28–148.24), Simplicius regularly uses Theophrastus' version of Parmenides' argument when commenting on Aristotle's text, referring to the poem only incidentally.[55] Most conspicuously, after detailing the faults Aristotle finds with "Parmenides' argument," Simplicius states: "in this way the premises given by Theophrastus are rejected as being false, and as inconclusive, because while the conclusion that followed was 'what is apart from what-is is nothing', he added, 'therefore what-is is one'."[56] Although the verb here is passive, the words ὡς ψευδεῖς ... διελέγχεται clearly echo τὸ ψεῦδος ἐλέγχει ... ὁ Ἀριστοτέλης at *in Phys.* 117.14–15, leaving little doubt that it is Aristotle that Simplicius understands to be rejecting the premises as given by Theophrastus. Later, in commenting on the portion of the *Physics* that includes what Simplicius had earlier identified as Aristotle's way of recalling Parmenides' argument,[57] Simplicius again turns to Theophrastus to gloss Aristotle's reference to an argument "that all things are one, if 'being' signifies one thing" (*Phys.* 187a1–2), saying: "It is the argument of Parmenides, that all

---

55 At *in Phys.* 116.25–117.13 (immediately following the passage just quoted), Simplicius quotes DK 28 B 2.3–8 and DK 28 B 6 as verses corresponding to the Theophrastean/Aristotelian formulations of Parmenides' argument that he has been discussing. Thereafter, Simplicius treats the Theophrastean version of the premises (τὸ παρὰ τὸ ὂν οὐκ ὄν, τὸ οὐκ ὂν οὐδέν) as the standard articulation of Parmenides' thesis. Cf. *in Phys.* 117.17, 117.28–29, 118.28–30, 126.5–6, 133.32–134.1, 137.24–27 (and 236.7–10).

56 Simpl. *in Phys.* 118.2–5, translation modified from Huby and Taylor 2011, 29, which again obscures the sense somewhat.

57 That is, in commenting on *Phys.* 187a1–11, a portion of which (187a4–5) is quoted at *in Phys.* 116.20–21. See *in Phys.* 116.18–24, translated above, with note 54.

280 KURFESS

things are one, if 'being' signifies one thing. For other than it there will be nothing. As Theophrastus proposed: 'What is other than being is not. What is not is nothing'."[58] By referring repeatedly to Theophrastus' version of Parmenides' argument in order to explain Aristotle's criticisms, Simplicius appears to take for granted that certain of Aristotle's remarks are either inspired by or directly addressed to Theophrastus' formulations.[59]

5   "The Argument of Melissus"

A similar situation seems to have obtained with Melissus. As was touched upon above, what is identified at *in Phys.* 115.11–13 as the version of Parmenides' argument given in Theophrastus' *Natural History* not only resurfaces later in the commentary, but had actually appeared earlier.[60] Precisely the same wording featured in Simplicius' explication of Aristotle's judgment near the beginning of *Physics* 1.3 that the arguments of Melissus and Parmenides are unsound:

> But he [i.e. Aristotle] says that it is not difficult to refute the arguments, because he will show both that the premises are false and that the figures used in the combinations are not valid. He finds more fault with the argument of Melissus, as has been said earlier, either because, as well as the rest, he also says that Being is infinite, or because he too both seems to adopt false premises, and to put them together invalidly, when he says that *if what comes to be has a starting-point, what does not come to be does not have a starting-point*, when in negating the consequent he ought to say 'what does not have a starting point has not come to be'. For in this way the second mood of hypothetical syllogism is completed. Parmenides puts the premises in order, and adds to the premises not the deducible

---

58   Simpl. *in Phys.* 134.9–12, translation modified from Huby and Taylor 2011, 45. Among other alterations, I omit the words τὸ ὄν following ἕν in 134.10. Huby translates ἓν τὸ ὄν as "the one Being," but this conventionally translates τὸ ἓν ὄν, so scribal error seems more likely than Simplicius giving Aristotle's words a Neoplatonic spin.

59   Simplicius was not, it turns out, alone in this assumption. Theophrastus' formulation was also used as the standard version of "Parmenides' argument" by Themistius (see *in Phys.* 8.26–28, 12.12–13 Vitelli) and by Philoponus (see *in Phys.* 58.7–8, 62.7–8 Schenkl). Both authors are probably relying on Alexander, for neither seems to know quite where the formulation comes from, though Philoponus does associate it with Theophrastus (and, oddly, Plato) at *in Phys.* 62.6. See also Alex. Aphr. *in An. Pr.* 346.17–19 and 357.1–10 Wallies and *in Metaph.* 44.10–45.2 Hayduck.

60   See above, with note 50.

ELEATIC *ARCHAI* IN ARISTOTLE

conclusion but a different one when he says: 'what is other than Being is not-Being, what is not Being is nothing' and not adding 'other than Being is nothing' which follows, but 'Being, then, is one'.[61]

Here "Parmenides' argument" (i.e., Theophrastus' version of it) is preceded by a faulty inference ascribed to Melissus, the wording of which also deserves noting. Like "Parmenides' argument," the words in italics above serve as the standard version of Melissus' inference in Simplicius' discussion of Aristotle's criticisms.[62] The Greek corresponding to those words (εἰ τὸ γενόμενον ἀρχὴν ἔχει, τὸ μὴ γενόμενον οὐκ ἔχει ἀρχὴν, *in Phys.* 103.4–5) is, but for the final word, printed by Diels in expanded type, apparently indicating that he took this to be a quotation of *Phys.* 186a11–13 (εἰ τὸ γενόμενον ἔχει ἀρχὴν ἅπαν, ὅτι καὶ τὸ μὴ γενόμενον οὐκ ἔχει), part of the text on which Simplicius is here commenting. But it is an even closer match for, and thus presumably drawn from, language found in a lengthy paraphrase of Melissus' argumentation that immediately follows. Simplicius' text continues:

> But these things [sc. concerning Parmenides] will be put to the test later; for now let us look at the argument of Melissus, which he addresses first. Melissus used the axioms of the natural philosophers, and began his writing on coming to be and passing away thus: 'If there is nothing, what could be said about that as if it were existent? But if there is something, either it has come to be or it has always existed. ...'[63]

The full paraphrase, too long to quote here, extends to *in Phys.* 104.15 and outlines a series of deductions showing that what-is (1) always is, neither coming to be nor being destroyed; (2) is without beginning or end; (3) is unlimited;

---

61 Simpl. *in Phys.* 102.31–103.11, as translated in Huby and Taylor 2011, 15–16, italics added. Although the translation differs from that given on the later occasions, the wording of Parmenides' propositions at *in Phys.* 103.9–11 is identical to that at *in Phys.* 115.12–13, 118.4–5, and 134.11–12.

62 The corresponding (but verbally quite different) text of Melissus is DK 30 B 2, quoted by Simplicius at *in Phys.* 29.22–26 and 109.20–25. For subsequent occurrences of the phrasing of the inference in Simplicius' discussion, see note 65 below.

63 Simpl. *in Phys.* 103.11–17, translation modified from Huby and Taylor 2011, 16. Huby translates Νῦν δὲ τὸν Μελίσσου λόγον ἴδωμεν, πρὸς ὃν πρότερον ὑπαντᾷ in 103.13 with "Let us now look at the argument of Melissus, which he [i.e. Aristotle] earlier opposed." Graham 2010, 469 is similar and Harriman 2015, 23 is identical. Simplicius' point, however, seems to be that, in what follows in chapter 3, Aristotle takes up the argument of Melissus before that of Parmenides.

(4) is one; and (5) is unmoved in a number of other respects.[64] It is the second deduction of the paraphrase (where we find ἐπειδὴ τὸ γενόμενον ἀρχὴν ἔχει, τὸ μὴ γενόμενον ἀρχὴν οὐκ ἔχει at *in Phys.* 103.24) that seems to be the source for the phrasing given at *in Phys.* 103.4–5 (εἰ τὸ γενόμενον ἀρχὴν ἔχει, τὸ μὴ γενόμενον οὐκ ἔχει ἀρχήν) and employed repeatedly as the standard version of Melissus' inference in what follows.[65] Immediately following the paraphrase, Simplicius provides what looks like his own summary of the overall argument, precisely repeating (although reordering) the wording of the faulty inference found in the paraphrase.[66]

Because of the way it is introduced, the paraphrase was once taken as Melissus' own, and treated as the source for five independent fragments.[67] But while the first sentence(s) may preserve some of Melissus' actual wording,[68] Arnold Pabst demonstrated in 1889 that that was not generally true of the passage as a whole.[69] Following Pabst, whose conclusions were soon endorsed by Diels and Zeller, many scholars have assumed that Simplicius authored the paraphrase himself.[70] Others, however, have observed that this is not Simplicius' typical method,[71] and it may seem odd, moreover, for Simplicius to immediately summarize his own paraphrase. My suggestion, if it is not already obvious, is that the paraphrase, which Simplicius (despite having Melissus' own work) introduces as "the argument of Melissus" and follows with the remark "this is enough from Melissus with regard to Aristotle's refutation," comes from the same source as the formulation that Simplicius (despite having Parmenides' poem) treats as "the argument of Parmenides" and had paired with Melissus'

---

64 The beginning of the *MXG* features a comparable sequence, so that the paraphrase of Melissus here stands in a similar relation to the opening of *MXG* 1 as the account of Xenophanes treated above does to *MXG* 3.

65 Cf. *in Phys.* 104.18–19, 104.21–22, 104.29, 105.12–13, 105.24–25, 105.32, 107.18–19, and 108.13–14. In these texts, we generally find εἰ rather than ἐπειδή (only at 104.18) in the protasis and ἀρχήν regularly precedes οὐκ ἔχει (μὴ ἔχει at 104.29) in the apodosis.

66 "This much then is enough from Melissus with regard to Aristotle's refutation. His premises, speaking shortly, are like this: 'Being has not come to be. What has not come to be has no starting-point, since what has come to be has a starting-point. (τὸ μὴ γενόμενον ἀρχὴν οὐκ ἔχει, ἐπειδὴ τὸ γενόμενον ἀρχὴν ἔχει.) What does not have a starting point is infinite. The infinite could not be second alongside another, but [must be] one. And the one and the infinite is unchanging." (*in Phys.* 104.16–20, trans. Huby and Taylor 2011, 17, Greek added).

67 See Brandis 1813, 186–190 and Mullach 1845, 80–84.

68 So, e.g., Burnet 1930, 321. See Harriman 2015, 23–25 for a recent discussion.

69 See Pabst 1889, 17–29, and cf. Burnet 1892, 334–338.

70 See, e.g., Solmsen 1969, 8, KRS 392, Merrill 1998, 210–218, Graham 2010, 480, and Harriman 2015, 23.

71 See Burnet 1892, 337 and Fairbanks 1898, 282. Cf. Harriman 2015, 22.

ELEATIC *ARCHAI* IN ARISTOTLE

283

faulty inference just before the paraphrase. I propose, that is, that the paraphrase comes from Theophrastus.

Though unusual, this suggestion is not altogether new. Like Pabst, Burnet, in the first edition of his *Early Greek Philosophy*, had argued that the summary could not have been by Melissus. Unlike Pabst, Burnet did not think Simplicius had written it either. He remarked further:

> it is a striking fact that, just a little before, the faulty conversion of Melissos is quoted along with the syllogistic version of the argument of Parmenides, which undoubtedly comes from Theophrastos. It seems, then, most probable that here, as elsewhere, Simplicius had recourse to the extracts of Theophrastos preserved by Alexander, and that fr. 1–5 should be removed from editions of Melissos and inserted in the *Doxographi Græci*.[72]

Unfortunately, because Pabst's arguments for removing the text from editions of Melissus were so convincing, Burnet no longer thought it necessary to repeat his own arguments in later editions of his work.[73] As a result, his recommendation that the passage be assigned to Theophrastus disappeared from subsequent editions and seems to have been forgotten.

I propose that we revive Burnet's recommendation, but in a modified form, free from the notion that Simplicius knew Theophrastus only by way of extracts in Alexander. Accordingly, I would assign the paraphrase of Melissus, together with the account of Xenophanes and the "argument of Parmenides" discussed above, to Theophrastus' *Natural History*, on which Simplicius would be drawing directly. Though it may introduce complications to what we think we know about Xenophanes or the *MXG*, this seems the most straightforward reading of Simplicius' texts.

Furthermore, I propose that we be prepared to entertain the idea that Aristotle himself was working from Theophrastus' text. As he did with "Parmenides' argument," Simplicius, with access to documents that we lack, appears to have assumed that Aristotle's criticisms of Melissus were directed at what would have been, if the proposal above is correct, Theophrastus' formulations of Melissus' argument. Moreover, though it is less readily apparent, other

---

72 Burnet 1892, 337–338.

73 Thus a discussion spanning five pages in Burnet 1892 was replaced with a footnote (see Burnet 1930, 321, n. 4) beginning: "It is no longer necessary to discuss the passages which used to appear as frs.1–5 of Melissos, as it has been proved by A. Pabst that they are merely a paraphrase of genuine fragments."

commentators seem to have shared those assumptions.[74] One especially interesting text in this regard is Simplicius' description of Eudemus' reaction to Melissus' argument, which includes a quotation:

> Eudemus, however, says that even through these premises nothing else is proved except what was there originally, that Being is uncreated, for the valid conversion is: 'what does not have a starting-point is uncreated, and Being does not have a starting-point'. But it is said [by him] like this: 'it is not the case that *if what has come to be has a starting point, what has not come to be does not have a starting-point*; rather, what does not have a starting-point is uncreated. For it is in this way that the sequence of the negations comes about. So Being becomes uncreated for him. For it does not have a starting-point.'[75]

Apart from a slight change in word order (with ἀρχήν preceding rather than following οὐκ ἔχει, making it even closer to the language of the paraphrase) the words in italics here, which belong to Eudemus' own text, are identical with what appeared in italics in the quotation of *in Phys.* 102.31–103.11 above. This indicates that, as early as Eudemus, readers of Aristotle's *Physics* were treating Theophrastus' formulation, rather than the text of Melissus itself, as the relevant version of the "argument of Melissus" for discussing Aristotle's work. Coming from a contemporary of the men themselves, this is strong support for the suggestion that Aristotle had Theophrastus' text before him. Such a situation would, of course, readily explain the similarity that Diels observed between *Phys.* 186a11–13 and *in Phys.* 103.4–5.

If there is merit in them, these proposals raise interesting prospects for future study. Careful readings of the commentators, particularly Simplicius, in conjunction with Aristotle's texts and other sources for Theophrastus, may yield further material from the *Natural History* and related works.[76] Fresh

---

74 For the Parmenidean argument, see note 59 above. For echoes of what would be the Theophrastean version of Melissus' faulty inference in other commentaries, see Them. *in Phys.* 7.16–18 and 8.3–4 and Philop. *in Phys.* 51.8, 52.8–9, 53.3–4, 58.15, and 59.9. At *in Phys.* 50.30–51.6 Philoponus expresses an awareness that what he presents as "Melissus' argument" is not in fact Melissus', but does not seem to know, or care, whose formulation it is.

75 Simpl. *in Phys.* 105.21–27 [= Eudemus frag. 38 Wehrli], as translated in Huby and Taylor 2011, 18, italics added.

76 As some of the references pointed out above confirm (see note 15), Simplicius still has the *Natural History* at hand in the commentary to *Phys.* 1.4, when he moves on to Aristotle's discussions of the natural philosophers proper. See *in Phys.* 149. 5–11 (cf. FHSG frags. 225 and 226A), 149.29–150.1 (cf. FHSG frag.226A), and 154.14–23 (= FHSG frag. 228B).

ELEATIC *ARCHAI* IN ARISTOTLE   285

readings of Aristotle in light of what we can reconstruct of Theophrastus' work may allow us to better understand not only Aristotle's text and his problematic historical sense, but the roles that each played in the transmission of early Greek thought to later generations. I hope that the foregoing has cleared some of the ground for and helps to foster such readings.[77]

Bibliography

Baltussen, H. 2002. "Wehrli's Edition of Eudemus of Rhodes: The Physical Fragments from Simplicius' Commentary *On Aristotle's* Physics." In *Eudemus of Rhodes*, ed. I. Bodnár and W. W. Fortenbaugh, 127–156. New Brunswick: Transaction Publishers.

Baltussen, H. 2008. *Philosophy and Exegesis in Simplicius: The Methodology of a Commentator*. London: Duckworth.

Baltussen, H. 2009. "Simplicius and the Subversion of Authority." *Antiquorum Philosophia* 3: 121–136.

Barnes, J. 2001. *Early Greek Philosophy*. 2nd rev. ed. London: Penguin Books.

Barney, R. 2009. "Simplicius: Commentary, Harmony, and Authority." *Antiquorum Philosophia* 3: 101–120.

Barney, R. 2012. "History and Dialectic (*Metaphysics* A 3, 983a24-4b8)." In *Aristotle's Metaphysics Alpha (Symposium Aristotelicum XVIII)*, ed. C. Steel, 69–104. Oxford: Oxford University Press.

Brandis, C. A. 1813. *Commentationum Eleaticarum Pars Prima*. Altona: Hammerich.

Burnet, J. 1892. *Early Greek Philosophy*. 1st ed. London and Edinburgh: Adam and Charles Black.

Burnet, J. 1930. *Early Greek Philosophy*. 4th ed. London: Macmillan.

Cherniss, H. 1935. *Aristotle's Criticism of Presocratic Philosophy*. Baltimore: The Johns Hopkins Press.

Diels, H. 1879. *Doxographi Graeci*. Berlin: G. Reimer.

Diels, H. 1882. *Simplicii in Aristotelis Physicorum libros quattuor priores commentaria*. Berlin: G. Reimer.

Diels, H. 1900. *Aristotelis qui fertur De Melisso Xenophane Gorgia libellus*. Berlin: G. Reimer.

---

77 An early version of this paper was presented at the World Congress "Aristotle, 2400 Years" held in May 2016 at the Aristotle University of Thessaloniki. I am grateful to Pantelis Golitsis for questions on that occasion and to Petter Sandstad and Jim Lennox for comments afterward. Thanks are due also to Mathilde Brémond for comments on a later version and to the editors of the volume, both for inviting this contribution and for their cheerful patience while awaiting it.

Diels, H. 1901. *Poetarum Philosophorum Fragmenta*. Berlin: Weidmann.

DK = Diels, H. and W. Kranz. 1951. *Die Fragmente der Vorsokratiker*. 6th ed. Berlin: Weidmann.

Fairbanks, A. 1898. *The First Philosophers of Greece*. London: Kegan Paul, Trench, Trübner & Co.

Finkelberg, A. 1990. "Studies in Xenophanes." *Harvard Studies in Classical Philology* 93: 103–167.

FHSG = Fortenbaugh, W. W., P. M. Huby, R. W. Sharples, and D. Gutas. 1992. *Theophrastus of Eresus: Sources for his life, writings, thought and influence*. Leiden: Brill.

Frede, M. 2008. "Aristotle's Account of the Origins of Philosophy." In *The Oxford Handbook to Presocratic Philosophy*, ed. P. Curd and D. Graham, 501–529. Oxford: Oxford University Press.

Gigon, O. 1969. "Die der Vorsokratiker bei Theophrast und Aristotleles." In *Naturphilosophie bei Aristoteles und Theophrast*, ed. I. Düring, 114–123. Heidelberg: Lothar Stiehm Verlag.

Graham, D. W. 2010. *The Texts of Early Greek Philosophy: The Complete Fragments and Selected Testimonies of the Major Presocratics*. Cambridge: Cambridge University Press.

Guthrie, W. K. C. 1962. *A History of Greek Philosophy: I. The earlier Presocratics and the Pythagoreans*. Cambridge: Cambridge University Press.

Harriman, B. 2015. "The Beginning of Melissus' *On Nature or On What-Is*: A Reconstruction." *Journal of Hellenic Studies* 135: 19–34.

Hayduck, M. 1891. *Alexandri Aphrodisiensis in Aristotelis Metaphysica commentaria*. Berlin: G. Reimer.

Heiberg, I. L. 1894. *Simplicii in Aristotelis de Caelo commentaria*. Berlin: G. Reimer.

Huby, P. 1985. "Theophrastus in the Aristotelian Corpus, with particular reference to Biological Problems." In *Aristotle on Nature and Living Things: Philosophical and Historical Studies*, ed. A. Gotthelf, 313–325. Pittsburgh: Mathesis Publications.

Huby, P. M. 2002. "Did Aristotle Reply to Eudemus and Theophrastus on Some Logical Issues?" In *Eudemus of Rhodes*, ed. I. Bodnár and W. W. Fortenbaugh, 85–106. New Brunswick: Transaction Publishers.

Huby, P. and C. C. W. Taylor. 2011. *Simplicius: On Aristotle Physics 1.3–4*. London: Bristol Classical Press.

Jaeger, W. 1947. *The Theology of the Early Greek Philosophers*. Oxford: Clarendon Press.

Jaeger, W. 1962. *Aristotle: Fundamentals of the History of his Development*. 2nd ed. Translated by R. Robinson. Oxford: Clarendon Press.

Kahn, C. H. 1994. *Anaximander and the Origins of Greek Cosmology*. Corrected 2nd printing. Indianapolis: Hackett.

Kirk, G. S., and J. E. Raven. 1957. *The Presocratic Philosophers*. Cambridge: Cambridge University Press.

ELEATIC *ARCHAI* IN ARISTOTLE

KRS = Kirk, G. S, J. E. Raven, and M. Schofield. 1983. *The Presocratic Philosophers*. 2nd ed. Cambridge: Cambridge University Press.

Kurfess, C. forthcoming. "Being at Play: Naming and Non-Naming in the Anonymous *De Melisso Xenophane Gorgia*." In *Eleatic Ontology in the Hellenistic period and Late Antiquity*, ed. C. Kurfess and A. Motta.

Lebedev, A. V. 2016. "The Origin and Transmission of the Doxographical Tradition *Placita Philosophorum* (Arius Didymus, Ps.-Plutarch, Stobaeus, Theodoret, Nemesius, Porphyrius)." In *Indo-European Linguistics and Classical Philology*, ed. N. N. Kazansky, 573–633. St. Petersburg.

Lesher, J. 1992. *Xenophanes of Colophon: Fragments*. Toronto: University of Toronto Press.

Mansfeld, J. 1986. "Aristotle, Plato, and the Preplatonic Doxography and Chronology." In *Storiographia e dossographia nella filosophia antica*, ed. G. Cambiano, 1–59. Turin: Tirrenia Stampatori.

Mansfeld, J. 1987. "Theophrastus and the Xenophanes Doxography." *Mnemosyne* 40: 286–312.

Mansfeld, J. 1988. "*De Melisso Xenophane Gorgia*: Pyrrhonizing Aristotelianism." *Rheinisches Museum* 131: 239–276.

Mansfeld, J. 1992. "*Physikai doxai* and *Problēmata physika* from Aristotle to Aetius (and beyond)." In *Theophrastus: His Psychological, Doxographical, and Scientific Writings*, ed. W. W. Fortenbaugh and D. Gutas, 63–111. New Brunswick: Transaction Publishers.

Mansfeld, J. 1999. "Sources." In *The Cambridge Companion to Early Greek Philosophy*, ed. A. A. Long, 22–44. Cambridge: Cambridge University Press.

Merrill, B. L. 1998. *Melissus of Samos: A Commentary on the Sources and Fragments*. Ph.D. dissertation. University of Texas at Austin.

McDiarmid, J. B. 1953. "Theophrastus on the Presocratic Causes." *Harvard Studies in Classical Philology* 61: 85–156.

Mullach, F. G. A. 1845. *Aristotelis de Melisso, Xenophane et Gorgia Disputationes cum Eleaticorum Philosophorum Fragmentis*. Berlin: Besser.

Pabst, A. 1889. *De Melissi Samii Fragmentis*. Bonn.

Palmer, J. A. 1998. "Xenophanes' Ouranian God in the Fourth Century." *Oxford Studies in Ancient Philosophy* 16: 1–34.

Palmer, J. 2008. "Classical Representations and Uses of the Presocratics." In *The Oxford Handbook to Presocratic Philosophy*, ed. P. Curd and D. Graham, 530–554. Oxford: Oxford University Press.

Reinhardt, K. 1916. *Parmenides und die Geschichte der Griechischen Philosophie*. Bonn: F. Cohen.

Ross, W. D. 1924. *Aristotle's* Metaphysics. 2 vols. Oxford: Clarendon Press.

Ross, W. D. 1936. *Aristotle's* Physics. Oxford: Clarendon Press.

Runia, D. T. 1992. "Xenophanes or Theophrastus? An Aëtian *Doxographicum* on the Sun." In *Theophrastus: His Psychological, Doxographical, and Scientific Writings*, ed. W. W. Fortenbaugh and D. Gutas, 112–140. New Brunswick: Transaction Publishers.

Sachs, J. 1995. *Aristotle's* Physics*: A Guided Study*. New Brunswick, NJ: Rutgers University Press.

Sachs, J. 1999. *Aristotle's* Metaphysics. Santa Fe, NM: Green Lion Press.

Schenkl, H. 1900. *Themistii in Aristotelis Physica paraphrasis*. Berlin: G. Reimer.

Sharples, R. W. 1998. Theophrastus of Eresus: *Theophrastus of Eresus: Sources for his life, writings, thought and influence. Commentary Volume 3.1: Sources on Physics*. Leiden: Brill.

Solmsen, F. 1969. *The 'Eleatic One' in Melissus*. Amsterdam: North-Holland Publishing Company.

Steinmetz, P. 1964. *Die Physik des Theophrastos von Eresos*. Berlin: Gehlen.

Taylor, A. E. 1910. *Aristotle on His Predecessors, Being the First Book of His Metaphysics*. 2nd ed. Chicago: Open Court.

Vitelli, H. 1887. *Ioannis Philoponi in Aristoelis Physicorum libros tres priores commentaria*. Berlin: G. Reimer.

Wallies, M. 1883. *Alexandri in Aristoelis Analyticorum Priorium librum I commentarium*. Berlin: G. Reimer.

West, M. L. 1971. *Early Greek Philosophy and the Orient*. Oxford: Oxford University Press.

Zeller, E. 1881. *A History of Greek Philosophy from the Earliest Period to the Time of Socrates*. Vol. I. Translated by S. F. Alleyne. London: Longmans, Green and Co.

Zeller, E. 1931. *Outlines of the History of Greek Philosophy*. 13th ed., rev. by W. Nestle and translated by L. R. Palmer.

Zhmud, L. 2001. "Revising Doxography: Hermann Diels and his Critics." *Philologus* 145: 219–243.

Zhmud, L. 2006. *The Origin of the History of Science in Classical Antiquity*. Berlin: Walter de Gruyter.

CHAPTER 9

The Reception of Presocratic Flat Earth Cosmology in Aristotle, the Doxography, and Beyond

Dirk L. Couprie

1 Introduction

The Presocratic conception of a flat earth is not always easy to understand, because we are used to the idea of a spherical earth in a practically infinite universe. We may call this our spherical earth bias. On a flat earth, cosmological, temporal, geographic, and climatological aspects are different, and usually completely different, from what we are used to. Almost all of Presocratic cosmology we do not know from the works of the ancient Greek cosmologists themselves, but from its rendering in Aristotle and in the doxography. Aristotle was still involved in direct discussion with his predecessors who believed that the earth is flat. His presentation of flat earth cosmologists is mainly polemical. Since he wrote down his proofs of the sphericity of the earth, the spherical earth has become the obvious frame of reference for cosmologists and astronomers. The idea of a flat earth soon became obsolete and biased by the knowledge that the earth is spherical. Therefore, we must read the rendition of flat earth cosmology by later authors with extra caution. To these authors, the world-picture of a spherical earth was current practice. Their reception of the idea of the flat earth coincided with interpretation and was subject to various misunderstandings, due to the spherical earth bias. Modern scholars, too, can be shown to have occasionally fallen into the trap of spherical earth bias. Examples will be discussed below, especially in the sections *The Distance of the Heavens, The Tilt of the Celestial Axis*, and *The Alleged Tilt of the Earth*. After a short specification of what was meant by "a flat earth," I will successively examine some distinctive features of the Presocratic world picture of the flat earth and the main difficulties and misunderstandings inherent in its reception.[1]

---

1 This study has been written with the support of grant project GA ČR GA15-08890S. For the translation of the ancient texts, I borrowed freely from available editions but mainly from Daniel W. Graham, *The Texts of Early Greek Philosophy* (Cambridge: Cambridge UP, 2010) (= Gr). Other abbreviations used are: Dox = Hermann Diels, *Doxographi Graeci* (Berlin: Walter de Gruyter, 1879); DK = Hermann Diels and Walther Kranz, *Die Fragmente der Vorsokratiker*

© KONINKLIJKE BRILL NV, LEIDEN, 2021 | DOI:10.1163/9789004443358_011

2 A Specification of the Flat Shape of the Earth

When the ancient Greeks said that the earth is flat, they did not mean it in a mathematical way, since the surface of the earth shows mountains and valleys, land and sea. More specifically, the idea of the flat earth as somewhat concave does not seem to have been uncommon in Presocratic cosmology. It goes back as far as Anaximander's earth, shaped like a column drum. Hahn has convincingly shown how such drums were made slightly concave by a technique called ἀναθύρωσις.[2] A similar shape is also found in Anaximenes, where the setting sun is said to be hidden behind the higher parts of the earth.[3] It is attested for Archelaus, according to whom the earth is "lofty around the edge and hollow in the middle" (λίμνην (...) κύκλῳ μὲν οὖσαν ὑψηλήν, μέσον δὲ κοίλην),[4] for Democritus (κοίλην δὲ τῷ μέσῳ)[5] and Leucippus (κοίλην δὲ τῷ μεγέθει),[6] and for some anonymous thinkers: "They postulate (ποιήσαντες) walls in a circle [around the earth]."[7]

The idea of a somewhat concave earth is related to the observation that the inhabitable world (the οἰκυμένη) was situated around the basin of the Mediterranean Sea. Two other reasons are mentioned in the next lines of the just quoted text: "so that they may screen us against the vortex, as it whirls around outside the earth, and for all those (πᾶ[σ]ιν) who drive the heavenly bodies around in a circle overhead ([ὕ]π[ερ κε]φά[λ]ης)."[8] The same image survives even in Plato's *Timaeus* when he tells the story of the isle of Atlantis and

---

(Zürich/Hildesheim: Weidmann 1951[6]); KRS = Geoffrey S. Kirk, John E. Raven and Malcolm Schofield *The Presocratic Philosophers* (Cambridge: Cambridge University Press, 2009). All drawings in this chapter are made by the author.

2 Robert Hahn, *Anaximander and the Architects* (Albany: SUNY 2001), 169ff and 195–196.

3 Hippolytus, *Haer.* 1.7.6 = DK 13A7.

4 Hippolytus, *Hear.* 1.9.4 = DK 60A4(4).

5 Aët. 3.10.4–5 = DK 68A94.

6 Pseudo-Galen, *Hist. Phil.* 82, not in DK, but see Dox 633. The ingenious suggestion in Dmitri Panchenko, "The Shape of the Earth in Archelaus, Democritus and Leucippus," *Hyperboreus* 5, no 1 (1999): 22–39, that Archelaus, Leucippus, and Democritus meant that the earth is shaped like a shield with a convex upper side is not very convincing.

7 Graziano Arrighetti, *Epicuro Opere* (Torino: Giulio Einaudi, 1960), 233–234 (*Herculaneum Papyri*, 1042.8.vi), not in DK. In Gr (Axs 20), this text is placed under the name of Anaximenes. In Dirk L. Couprie, *When the Earth Was Flat* (New York: Springer, 2018), 121, I have argued that it can also be read as a polemic against an archaic conception of the paths of the heavenly bodies along the periphery of the earth between their setting and rising.

8 *Ibid.* The interpretation of these enigmatic words would go beyond the scope of this chapter. Here I quote the reading as in Arrighetti and Graham's translation. I intend to take a closer look at the wording, translation, and interpretation of this text in another publication, reading πά[λ]ιν instead of πᾶ[σ]ιν.

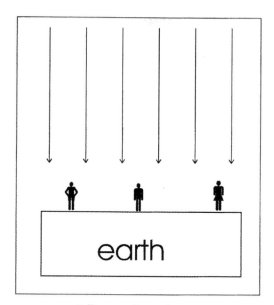

FIGURE 9.1 Falling on a flat earth

mentions "the land surrounding the Ocean, which may most rightly be called, in the fullest and truest sense, a continent."[9] This obviously presupposes the concept of a flat earth, as is fit for a story about a vanished mythical age. In Plato's *Phaedo*, Socrates talks about the place we live in as one of the many hollows in the spherical or dodecahedron-shaped earth and compares us, living around the Mediterranean Sea, with ants or frogs around a pond.[10]

3   Falling on a Flat Earth

On a flat earth, the direction of falling is perpendicular, in parallel lines towards the earth's flat surface, unless some additional cause forces falling objects into another direction (see Figure 9.1).

That falling is perpendicular to the earth's flat surface is not documented, but follows from common sense, because otherwise it would mean that

---

9   Plato, *Ti.* 24–25a.
10 Plato, *Phd.* 109a9–b4. For a comprehensive discussion of this text, see Dirk L. Couprie, *Heaven and Earth in Ancient Greek Cosmology: from Thales to Heraclides Ponticus* (New York: Springer 2011), ch. 17, "The Dodecahedron, or the Shape of the Earth According to Plato."

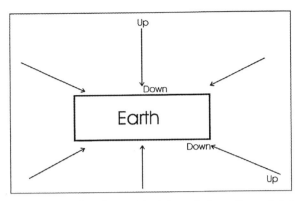

FIGURE 9.2 Alleged "centrifocal dynamics" on a flat earth (after Rovelli)

for most people things would fall at angles, which is obviously not the case. Therefore, Rovelli's drawing of what he calls "centrifocal dynamics" on Anaximander's earth is wrong (see Figure 9.2).[11]

That all falling is perpendicular is also implied in the question of why the earth does not fall. Aristotle investigates the answers his predecessors gave to this question, calling the answers more incomprehensible than the question itself: Xenophanes said that the earth extended downwards infinitely, but this is begging the question; Thales supposed that the earth floats on water, but this leads to the question of what the water rests upon; Anaximenes, Anaxagoras and Democritus thought that the earth settles on the air below it like a lid, but their argument concerns rather the size of the earth than its flatness; Empedocles argued that the heavenly vortex prevented the motion of the earth, but light and heavy existed before the vortex arose; Anaximander held that the earth remains at rest because it is equally related to the extremes and thus has no impulse to move, but this does not explain why the earth is in the center, and not, for example, fire.[12] According to Aristotle, Thales, Anaximenes, Xenophanes, Anaxagoras, and Democritus worried about the question of why the earth does not fall and thus they looked for something the earth could rest on. Obviously, they were not interested in the questions of why the earth does not move sideways or upwards. Anaximander and Empedocles, according to Aristotle, answered the broader question of why the earth stays in the center of the universe. There are reasons to doubt, however, whether Aristotle rightly

---

11 Carlo Rovelli, "Anaximander's Legacy." *Collapse: Philosophical Research and Development* 5 (2009): 50–71, at 55, Fig. 4.

12 Aristotle, *Cael.* 294a11–295b20.

RECEPTION OF PRESOCRATIC FLAT EARTH COSMOLOGY IN ARISTOTLE 293

ascribes the aforementioned argument to Anaximander. Simplicius suggests that Aristotle here attacks Plato's similar argument in the *Phaedo* and that Anaximander should belong to those who let the earth rest on air.[13]

If falling is always in one direction, it is also reasonable to ask: Why do the heavenly bodies not fall upon the earth? For Anaximander they are enclosed within heavenly wheels, and for Anaximenes they are nailed into the firmament, but the usual answer of the Presocratic cosmologists was that the heavenly bodies stayed in place because of the heavenly whirl, the vortex. However, the stone that fell from heavens in Aegospotami,[14] which is associated with Anaxagoras' opinion that the heavenly bodies were made of stony matter, undermined the theory of the vortex because, as Aristotle says, heavier bodies always move towards the middle of a vortex.[15]

4 Temporal Features

On our spherical earth, theoretically speaking, only places on the same meridian have the same time of the day, but apart from this every place on earth has its own local time.[16] On the Presocratic flat earth, however, differences in time cannot be accounted for; there it is always, for everyone everywhere, the same time.[17] When the sun rises, it rises all over the flat earth and a day is of equal length everywhere. Curiously, this consequence of the concept of a flat earth is mentioned only once in the doxography. According to Hippolytus, Archelaus used it in a misguided attempt to overcome this problem by arguing that the earth is not completely flat but slightly concave: "He gives as a proof of this concavity the fact that the sun does not rise and set at the same times at all places, which would inevitably be the case if the earth were flat."[18]

---

13 Simplicius, *in Cael.* 532,1–15, not in DK; cf. Plato, *Phd.* 198e3–109a8. See also: Radim Kočandrle, "The Stability of the Earth in Anaximander's Universe." *Ancient Philosophy* 37 (2017): 265–280.

14 See, e.g., Diog. Laërt. 2.10 = DK 59A1(10).

15 Aristotle, *Cael.* 295a13.

16 Nowadays this is regulated by means of the 24 time zones, within each of which it is supposed to be the same time.

17 In the Chinese *gai tian* system, dating from the Han period, this problem was ingeniously solved. See Christopher Cullen, *Astronomy and Mathematics in Ancient China: the Zhou bi suan jing* (Cambridge: Cambridge University Press, 1996), 52 and Figure 5. See also Couprie, *When the Earth Was Flat*, ch. 13.

18 Hippolytus, *Haer.* 1.9.4 = DK 60A4(4).

294   COUPRIE

However, on a concave earth the sun would be seen earlier by those in the occidental regions than by those in the oriental regions, which is the opposite of the actual state of affairs. Tannery already wondered how Archelaus could have drawn conclusions precisely opposite to those which he should have drawn.[19] Rather than concluding that Archelaus was stupid, we may suppose that Hippolytus was confused. When we read the argument in its context, it looks rather misplaced within a story about cosmogony and the origin of life on earth:

> He says that the heavens are inclined, with the result that the sun gave light on the earth, made the air transparent and the earth dry. For it was originally a marsh, being lofty around the edge and hollow in the middle. He gives as a proof of this concavity the fact that the sun does not rise and set at the same times at all places, which would inevitably be the case if the earth were flat. Concerning animals, he says that when the earth grew warm, first of all in its lower part, where hot and cold were blended, many kinds of animals appeared, including man.[20]

This text is clearly about cosmogony. It is stated that originally the sun was hidden behind the mountains that surrounded the earth and gave it its concave outlook. Due to the tilt of the heavens (more on this below) the sun began to shine on the earth and as the earth warmed up animal life was enabled to originate. The differences in time on earth have nothing to do with this story and were probably added by Hippolytus.

We should not be surprised that, apart from this dubious case, the argument of time differences does not appear in Presocratic cosmology. It is not so easy to apprehend time differences on earth when you cannot make a phone call to people in the far east or west, asking them what time it is. Characteristically, Aristotle did not mention the argument when he sought to prove the spherical

---

19   Paul Tannery, *Pour l'histoire de science Hellène: de Thalès à Empédocle* (Paris: Félix Alcan 1887), 288. See Panchenko, "Shape of the Earth," 23, for more scholars on this subject. The explanation in D.R. Dicks, *Early Greek Astronomy to Aristotle* (Ithaca, NY: Thames and Hudson, 1970), 77 is incomprehensible.

20   Hippolytus, *Haer.* 1.9.4–5 DK 60A4(4–5). Here I disagree with Panchenko, "Shape of the Earth," 25, who states that the southern region was most fit for generating life, because it was nearest to the sun. The text, however, speaks of "the lower region, *where the hot and the cold were blended.*" This description suits the subtropical climate of the lands around the Mediterranean Sea, which traditionally was the center of the flat earth. Panchenko's suggestion that in this text a convex instead of a concave earth is meant conflicts with Hippolytus' report that the earth is lofty around.

shape of the earth in *On the Heavens*. Similarly, the ancient Greek flat earth cosmologists did not address the problem of the differences in the duration of daylight at different latitudes. At least they did not recognize it as a problem in relation to the shape of the earth. Perhaps the reason was that the time differences of the latitudes between which they traveled were not considerable enough to be clearly identified.

It might be argued, however, that Homer's story of Odysseus in the land of the Laestrygonians, which is enigmatically said to be "where the paths of the night and the day are close together," already contains an allusion to northernly regions where in summer the nights are short.[21] Apart from this and as far as I know, the first time the issue of time differences is alluded to is by Herodotus, who has heard of people who live in the far north and sleep six months of the year, but he underlines that he does not believe a word of it.[22] Xenophanes is said to have discerned between "regions, sections, and zones (κλίματα, ἀποτομάι, ζώναι) of the earth," each having its own sun.[23] There is no indication, however, that this is intended as an allusion to time differences. The topic of differences in the duration of daylight is also not mentioned in the doxography on Parmenides, where he is said to have divided the *spherical* earth in five zones (ζώναι).[24] These zones were introduced to make a climatological differentiation between uninhabitable (cold or torrid) and inhabitable (temperate) parts of the earth. In Aristotle's *Meteorology*, the zones on earth are differentiated by being inhabitable or uninhabitable because of the temperature, but not in relation to differences in the duration of daylight.[25] Neither does Aristotle use the argument of time differences as proof of the earth's sphericity, which can be seen as an indication that even in his time it did not play a role in the discussion.

Later, Ptolemy used it both in a general way and more specifically in connection with the observation of eclipses:

> It is possible to see that the sun and moon and the other stars do not rise and set at the same time for every observer on the earth, but always earlier for those living towards the orient and later for those living towards

---

21   Homer, *Od.* 10.80–86.

22   Herodotus, *Hist.* IV.25.

23   Aët. 2.24.9 = DK 21A41a. Mario Untersteiner, *Senofane: Testimonianze e frammenti* (Milano: Bompiani, 2008), 83 (125) considers the word ζώναι not authentic, but rather as inserted by the doxographer.

24   Strabo, *Geogr.* 2.2.2 = DK 28A44a.

25   Aristotle, *Mete.* 391a31ff.

the occident. (...) If it were flat, the stars would rise and set for all people together and at the same time.[26]

For we find that the phenomena of eclipses taking place at the same time, especially those of the moon, are not recorded at the same hours for everyone (...); but we always find later hours recorded for observers towards the orient than for those towards the occident.[27]

Differences in duration of daylight are explicitly used as an argument for the sphericity of the earth by Cleomedes, who is also more specific on the use of eclipses to measure time differences:

If the earth were flat in shape (...), the sun's risings and settings, and thus also the beginnings of daytimes and nighttimes, would occur at the same time everywhere. But this does not in fact happen. (...) Daytimes would also turn out to be of equal length for everyone, although entirely the opposite is present in the phenomena.

The heavenly body that is eclipsed among the Iberians in the 1st hour is detected as undergoing an eclipse among the Persians in the 5th hour.[28]

Pliny adds the nice story of a messenger who ran the same way eastwards and westwards, but although the way eastwards was downhill this run lasted longer.[29]

5   The Distance of the Heavens

On an earth conceived of as flat, the heavenly bodies are close by. The ancient Greek flat earth cosmologists were well aware of this feature. They could not even imagine the enormous distances of the heavenly bodies that intrinsically belong to a spherical earth. Anaximenes is said to have used the image of heaven as a felt cap with the stars attached to it. Whatever its precise interpretation,

---

26   Ptolemy, *Alm.* 1.4. Panchenko, "Shape of the Earth," 24, mentions several other ancient authors who used this argument.

27   Ptolemy, *Alm.* 1.4. See also Strabo, *Geogr.* 1.1.12.

28   Alan C. Bowen and Robert B. Todd, *Cleomedes' Lectures on Astronomy* (Berkeley: The University of California Press, 2004), 66, 68, and 67 (Cleomedes, *Cael.* 1.5). Cf. Pliny, *HN* 2.72.

29   Pliny, *HN* 2.73. The same effect we now experience to an increased extent when flying by plane eastward or westward.

RECEPTION OF PRESOCRATIC FLAT EARTH COSMOLOGY IN ARISTOTLE

its implication is that of a nearby heaven.[30] According to Xenophanes, the heavenly bodies are incandescent clouds, comparable to St. Elmo's fire, while the sun is composed of tiny flares gathered together from moist evaporation.[31] The comparison of the heavenly bodies with clouds implies that they cannot be at a great distance. From Empedocles two contradictory reports have been handed down. Pseudo-Plutarch's version of Aëtius' text is: "Empedocles says the moon is twice as far from the sun as from the earth," while Stobaeus has: "Empedocles says the distance of the moon to the earth is twice that of the moon to the sun."[32] However, the obvious implication of either is that the moon and the sun are not far from the earth. Another report on Empedocles confirms this: "Empedocles says that the distance along the breadth [of the earth] is greater than the height from earth to heaven, which is its altitude above us (...)."[33] That the sun is not at a great distance from us when the earth is flat is easy to prove with the help of Thales' method to measure the height of a pyramid (see Figure 9.3).

The two triangles AGH and APQ are similar. If the length of the gnomon HG, the length of its shadow AG, and the length of the shadow of the pyramid AP until the point right below the top of the pyramid are known, it is easy to calculate the height of the pyramid QP.[34] Similarly, the perpendicular SX is the height of the sun above the flat earth. Since the triangles AGH and AXS are similar, we get: AG: HG = AX: SX. In Athens at noon at the summer solstice, the shadow (AG) is roughly a quarter of the length of the gnomon (GH). Accordingly, the distance AX must be also a quarter of the distance SX. The ancient Greeks could have made a rough estimation of the distance AX, say, 2,000 kilometers.[35] Then the height of the sun above the flat earth must be about 8,000 kilometers. Even with a mistake of some hundreds of kilometers in the estimate of AX, the result is that the sun must be quite close. The moon could not

---

30   See Hippolytus, *Haer.* 1.7.6 = DK 13A7(6), and cf. Dirk L. Couprie, "The Paths of the Celestial Bodies According to Anaximenes." *Hyperboreus* 21, no. 1 (2015), 5–32.

31   See Aët. 2.13.14 = DK 21A38, Aët. 2.18.1 = DK 28A39, and Aët.2.20.3 = DK 28A40.

32   See Dox 362, Aët. 2.30.1. In DK 31A61, Diels gives both versions and offers a kind of emendated text. For a thorough study of both versions, see Jaap Mansfeld, "Cosmic Distances: 'Aëtius' 2.31 Diels and Some Related Texts." *Phronesis* 45 (2000), 175–294, where Diels' emendation is called "questionable" (175) and Pseudo-Plutarch's version is argued to be the right one (184–185). See also Jaap Mansfeld & David T. Runia, *The Method and Intellectual Context of a Doxographer.* Aëtiana II.2 (Leiden: Brill 2009), 638.

33   Aët. 2.31.4 = DK 31A50. According to the remainder of this report, Empedocles concluded that the heavens (the κόσμος) is egg-shaped.

34   This is the method as described by Plutarch, *Conv. sept. sap.* 2 = DK 11A21.

35   The actual distance between Athens and the Tropic of Cancer is about 1,600 km as the crow flies.

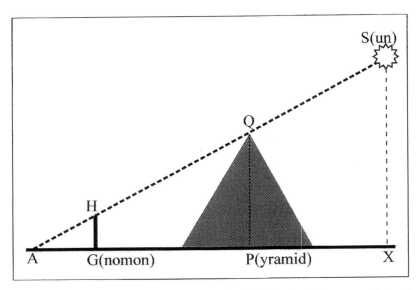

FIGURE 9.3 Measuring the height of a pyramid and the height of the sun on a flat earth (drawing not to scale)

be far beneath the sun, for otherwise, orbiting the earth, it would not be able to pass the rim of the earth.

Being at such a small distance from the earth, the sun must be very small, much smaller than the earth itself. Thales is said to have measured the visible diameter of the sun, which is about 0.5°, or 1/720th of its orbit around the earth.[36] The radius of the sun's orbit is the line AS, which can be calculated either with Pythagoras' theorem (about 8,250 kilometers), or by means of a comparison with AH, which can be measured with the help of a measuring cord. The orbit of the sun is then $2\pi \times 8{,}250$ = about 50,000 kilometers (taking $\pi = 3$), and the diameter of the sun 50,000/720 = about 70 kilometers.[37]

Virtually the same conclusion can be reached by means of an even more simple drawing. In Athens at noon at the summer solstice, the sun is about 76° above the southern horizon. Figure 9.4 shows that if there exists a place on the

---

36 See Diogenes Laërtius 1.24 = DK 11A1(24) and Apuleius, *Flor.* 18 = DK 11A19.

37 Detlev Fehling, "Das Problem der Geschichte des griechischen Weltmodells vor Aristoteles," *Rheinisches Museum für Philologie* 128 (1985), 209–210, argues that Anaxagoras made an estimation of the sun's diameter of about 250 km, based on reasonable suppositions ("eine Schätzung auf Grund vernünftiger Annahmen") without telling what these reasonable suppositions could have been.

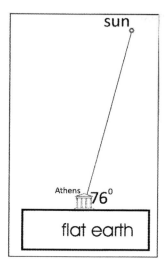

FIGURE 9.4 On a flat earth, the sun is nearby and rather small

flat earth where the sun at noon at the summer solstice stands in the zenith, the sun must be nearby and thus much smaller than the earth.

Aristotle was well aware of the fact that the sphericity of the earth had enormous consequences for the distances and sizes of the celestial bodies. They became as it were catapulted into space and must therefore be much larger than the earth. When he summarizes the conclusion from his polemical arguments against the opinions of the flat earth cosmologists and his own proofs of the sphericity of the earth, he writes:

> From these arguments we must conclude not only that the earth's mass is spherical, but also that it is not large (μὴ μέγαν) in comparison with the size of the other heavenly bodies (ἄστρα).[38]

The doxographers, accustomed as they were to the concept of the sphericity of the earth, did not always fully understand the implications of the concept of a flat earth. The doxography on Anaxagoras and the size of the sun is illustrative:

> Anaxagoras says that the sun is much bigger than (πολλαπλάσιον) the Peloponnesus.[39]

---

38 Aristotle, *Cael.* 298a18–21; see also 290b19: ἄστρων τὸ μέγεθος.
39 Aët. 2.21 = DK 59A72.

The sun exceeds (ὑπερέχειν) the Peloponnesus in size.[40]
He said the sun is greater than (μείζω) the Peloponnesus.[41]

Figures 9.3 and 9.4 illustrate that the sun cannot be *much* farther away and thus *much* bigger than the Peloponnesus, as the reports suggest. This was already stipulated by Dreyer: "Anaxagoras (...) was led to believe the sun to be (...) greater than the Peloponnesus, *and therefore not at a great distance from the earth.*"[42] The exaggeration of the doxographers, who are used to the concept of a spherical earth and its celestial consequences, is due to their knowledge of the enormous distance of the sun which was also the presupposition of Eratosthenes' famous calculation of the circumference of the earth.

Several modern scholars have argued that Anaxagoras measured the size of the sun at the opportunity of a solar eclipse.[43] Due to the spherical earth bias, they make a characteristic mistake. This can be best illustrated by a quotation from the article of Graham and Hintz: "*Assuming that the sun was far distant from the earth* and the moon relatively close, the sun's rays would approximate parallel lines and projecting a shadow roughly the size of the moon towards the earth."[44] As we have seen, Anaxagoras, believing that the earth is flat, could not possibly have assumed that the sun was far distant from the earth and that accordingly the rays of the sun were approximately parallel lines. What is evident for a modern astronomer, who is acquainted with the sphericity of the earth and the real distance of the sun, was not at all evident for an ancient Greek cosmologist who believed the earth was flat.

At first glance, Leucippus and Democritus seem to be an exception to the rule that says that a belief in the flat earth implies that the heavenly bodies are nearby, since they were said to hold that the universe is infinite, containing infinite worlds:

---

40   Hippolytus, *Haer.* 1.8.8 = DK 59A42(8).

41   Diog. Laërt. 2.8 = DK 59A1(8).

42   John L.E. Dreyer, *A History of Astronomy from Thales to Kepler* (Mineola, NY: Dover Publications, 1953), 31 (my italics). Fehling, *Problem*, 209, remarks on Pseudo-Plutarch's text: "ihm war das Richtige nicht groß genug."

43   Daniel W. Graham, and Eric Hintz, "Anaxagoras and the Solar Eclipse of 478 BC," *Apeiron* 40 (2007): 319–344. Earlier attempts in Martin L. West. *Early Greek Philosophy and the Orient* (Oxford: Clarendon Press 1971), 233 n.1, and Sider, David, "Anaxagoras on the Size of the Sun," *Classical Philology* 68 (1973), 128–129.

44   Graham and Hintz "Anaxagoras," 321 (my italics). Repeated in similar words in Daniel Graham, "Anaxagoras: Science and Speculation in the Golden Age," In *Early Greek Philosophy. The Presocratics and the Emergence of Reason*, ed. Joe McCoy (Washington, D.C.: The Catholic University of America Press 2013), 151, and in Graham, *Science*, 148.

He said there are numberless worlds (ἀπείρους δὲ εἶναι κόσμους) differing in size. In some there is no sun or moon, in some they are larger than ours, in some there are more of them. There are unequal distances between worlds, and in some places more, in some places less; some are growing, some are flourishing, and some are declining, and in some places they are being born, in other places they are failing. They perish when they collide with each other. Some worlds are devoid of animals, plants, and any moisture.[45]

As a result of our spherical earth bias and our knowledge of the dimensions of the universe, we are inclined to think that the "infinite worlds" are the stars. However, Furley has convincingly argued that this is not the case: "In the cosmology of classical antiquity (...) it was a matter of common agreement that the stars we see are part of our world: they are the boundary beyond which the infinite universe (if it is infinite) begins." And elsewhere: "What they saw in the night sky was not the beginning of the infinite universe: it was rather the boundary beyond which the infinite universe began."[46] In other words: Democritus' world (the earth and all the visible heavenly bodies) was bounded by the sphere of stars. The "infinite worlds" were beyond observation, they were merely a conclusion drawn from his speculations about space.

Let us conclude this section with an insoluble problem concerning the distances of the celestial bodies in the reports on Anaximander's cosmology. The reports in question read:

> Anaximander says there is a circle 28 times the size of the earth (...), and this is the sun.
> Anaximander says that the circle of the sun (...) is 27 times as big as the earth.
> The circle of the sun is 27 times as big as ⟨the earth, that of⟩ the moon ⟨18 times⟩.
> Anaximander says that the circle of the moon is 19 times as big as the earth.
> Anaximander says that the moon is a circle, 16 times the earth.[47]

---

45   Hippolytus, *Haer.* 1.13.2–4 = DK 68A40(2–4).

46   David Furley, *The Greek Cosmologists. Volume I: The Formation of the Atomic Theory and Its Earliest Critics* (Cambridge: Cambridge University Press, 1987), 136. See also David Furley, *Cosmic Problems. Essays on Greek and Roman Philosophy of Nature* (Cambridge: Cambridge University Press 1989), 2.

47   Respectively: Aët. 2.20.1 = DK 12A21, Aët. 2.21.1 = DK 12A21, Hippolytus, *Haer.* 1.6.5 = DK 12A11(5), Aët. 2.25.1 = DK 12A22, Pseudo-Galen, *Hist.* 67.1, not in DK, but see Georg Wöhrle,

302   COUPRIE

The usual interpretation is in one way or another a sequel to Tannery's suggestion that the numbers should be understood and completed as $3 \times 3 \times 3(+1)$ for the sun, $2 \times 3 \times 3(+1)$ for the moon, and $1 \times 3 \times 3(+1)$ for the stars.[48] In Kahn's words: "the essentially mathematical turn of Anaximander's mind" shows itself in "the speculative symmetry of his scheme," and even: "it is legitimate to consider Anaximander as the earliest known type of a mathematical physicist."[49] However, in any version of this interpretation, including my own, the numbers are much too big for what should be the case on a flat earth. It is hard to believe that Anaximander, who is said to have introduced the gnomon, would not have considered the consequences of its use as shown in Figure 9.3. It is a typical case of spherical bias that this problem has not been recognized earlier. We are so used to the idea that the heavenly bodies are at great distances that we inadvertently assume that the ancient flat earth cosmologists shared the same idea. With regard to the interpretation of Anaximander's numbers, we are in need of a completely new approach.[50]

6   The Distance of the Heavens and an Ancient Argument for the Flat Earth

In the previous section I argued that on a flat earth the sun must be close by and that Aristotle was well aware of the fact that, on the other hand, the sphericity of the earth implies that the sun must be very far away. Yet Aristotle seems to have fallen victim to the spherical earth bias when he tried to counter an argument for the flatness of the earth. The argument that can be attributed to Anaxagoras says that the rising and setting sun or moon are cut off at the horizon by a straight line, while it should be curved if the earth were spherical.[51] Curiously, Anaxagoras' argument is repeated several times by modern

---

     Die Milesier: Anaximander und Anaximenes (Berlin: Walter de Gruyter 2012), A1224; this last report is mostly neglected as mistaken.

48   Tannery, *Science hellène*, 91–92 and 119.

49   Charles H. Kahn, *Anaximander and the Origins of Greek Cosmology* (Indianapolis/Cambridge: Hackett Publishing Company, Inc., 1994), 92 and 97.

50   Perhaps the first half of Philip Thibodeau's article "Anaximander's Model and the Measures of the Sun and Moon," *Journal of Hellenic Studies* 137 (2017), 92–111, could be seen as a first attempt of such a new approach.

51   Aristotle mentions the argument in *Cael.* 294a1–4. Dmitri Panchenko, "Anaxagoras' Argument Against the Sphericity of the Earth," *Hyperboreus* 3 (1997): 175–178, has shown that it goes back to Anaxagoras.

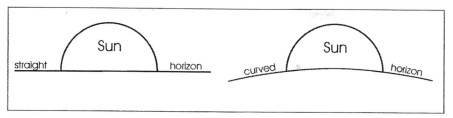

FIGURE 9.5 Anaxagoras' proof that the earth is flat

defenders of the flat earth, who obviously are not acquainted with its ancient origin.[52] The argument is illustrated in Figure 9.5.[53]
Aristotle clearly has difficulties in dealing with thiscurious argument. He says that its defenders:

> leave out of account the great distance of the sun from the earth and the great size of the circumference, which, seen from a distance on these apparently small circles appears straight.[54]

Heath calls Aristotle's attempt to refute the argument "confused."[55] More precisely, Furley puts his finger on the anachronism of the great distance of the sun: "it is not clear what this has to do with it."[56] Simplicius was the first to give the proper rebuttal:

> Perhaps one could say that if we were outside the earth and saw the sun partially obstructed by the earth, the sections would always appear to us to be curved (…). But now, since we are on the earth and we see the sun rising and setting because of the horizon (and the horizon is the plane extended through the surface of the earth and our eye), it results that the solar sphere is cut in a circle by the horizon; but a circle which is in the same plane as our eye is seen as a straight line.[57]

---

52 For example, in William Carpenter, *One Hundred Proofs That the Earth Is Not a Globe* (Baltimore: the author, 1885), 38, no. 47, and in several videos on the internet.
53 After Daniel W. Graham, *Science Before Socrates* (Oxford: University Press, 2013), picture on 129.
54 Aristotle, *Cael.* 294a5–7. For a detailed discussion of this argument, see Couprie, *Heaven and Earth*, 181–188.
55 T. Heath, *Aristarchus of Samos. The Ancient Copernicus*. Oxford: Clarendon Press 1913, 235.
56 Furley, *Greek Cosmologists*, 198.
57 Simplicius, *in Cael.* 520.5–8, not in DK.

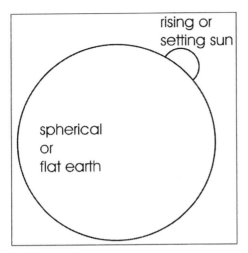

FIGURE 9.6 Seen from far above the earth's surface, the horizon that cuts the sun is curved irrespective of whether the earth is spherical or a flat disk

In other words, the same phenomenon of the straight horizon would occur both on a spherical and on a circular flat earth. It originates from our being, practically speaking, in the same plane as the earth's surface, and it will disappear when we are high above the earth. But then it does not differentiate between a spherical earth and a disk-shaped flat earth, as is shown in Figure 9.6. So, after all, Aristotle's conclusion is right that "this phenomenon offers (…) no cogent ground for disbelieving in the spherical shape of the earth."[58] But it does not offer cogent ground for disbelieving in the flat shape of the earth either.

7   The Tilt of the Celestial Axis

A typical issue in Presocratic cosmology is the tilt of the heavens, or the tilt of the cosmos, or the tilt of the stars, or the tilt of the celestial axis, or the tilt of the pole (or the Bears),[59] all of which amounts to the same

---

58   Aristotle, *Cael.* 294a8.
59   The Greek word ἄρκτος means bear and was also used as an indication of the celestial pole. The plural could be understood in flat earth cosmology as indicating the northern celestial pole (where the two constellations of the Great Bear and the Little Bear can be seen), or in spherical earth cosmology as indicating the northern and southern celestial poles.

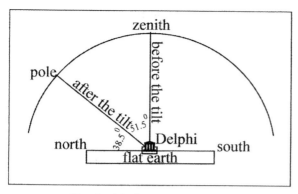

FIGURE 9.7 The tilt of the heavens

thing.⁶⁰ The idea was that the celestial axis ran from the celestial pole in the northern part of the heavens to the center of the flat earth, traditionally thought to be Delphi. Originally, this axis stood perpendicular and the pole coincided with the zenith of the earth's center, but somehow during the process of cosmogony the heavens had tilted (see Figure 9.7).

The original situation is rather graphically described in the doxography on Anaxagoras:

> Originally the stars (ἄστρα) moved as in a dome (θολοειδῶς) so that the always visible pole (πόλος) was right above (κατὰ κορυφήν) the earth, but later it inclined.⁶¹

In the original situation, the daily movements of the heavenly bodies around the pole were in circles parallel to the flat earth's surface (Figure 9.8, left). The sun and moon originally moved around the edge of the earth's surface. We may compare this with what an observer on the north pole of the *spherical* earth would see.⁶²

Archelaus imagined the original situation of the earth as a marsh surrounded by a rim of mountains that obscured the sun during the whole

---

60 This tilt is documented for Anaxagoras (Diog. Laërt. 2.9 = DK 59A1(9): tilt of the ἄστρα and the πόλος); Anaxagoras and Diogenes (Aët. 2.8.1 = DK 59A67: tilt of the κόσμος); Archelaus (Hippolytus, *Haer.* 1.9.4 = DK 60A4(4): tilt of the οὐρανός); and Empedocles (Aët. 2.8.2 = DK 31A58: tilt of τὰ ἄρκτα and the κόσμος).
61 Diog. Laërt. 2.9 = DK 59A1(9).
62 Cf. William A. Heidel, *The Heroic age of Science* (Baltimore: Williams & Wilkins Company, 1933), 122.

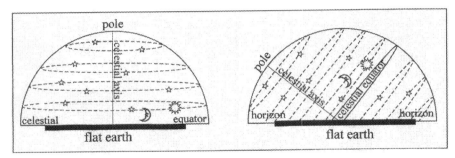

FIGURE 9.8   The daily paths of the heavenly bodies before and after the tilt of the heavens

year. The tilt of the heavens first made the sun shine on the earth and dry up the marsh:

> Archelaus says that the heavens (οὐρανός) are inclined and this is how the sun came to shine on the earth, made the air transparent, and the earth dry. For in the beginning the earth was a marsh, elevated at its periphery and hollow in the middle.[63]

It might be argued that the idea of a tilt of the heavens goes back to Anaximander:

> He says that at the coming to be of this cosmos that which since days of old is generative (τὸ ἐκ τοῦ ἀιδίου γόνιμον) of hot and cold was secreted (ἀποκριθῆναι) and from this (ἐκ τούτου) a sort of sphere of flame grew around the air about the earth like bark around a tree. This [sphere of flame grown around the air] subsequently broke off and was closed into individual circles to form the sun, the moon, and the stars.[64]

The simile of the bark around a tree reminds us of the image of the world tree, which in several ancient cultures was supposed to support the heavens and which was also associated with the axis of the heavens.[65] During the process of the origin of the world, the axis of the heavens, symbolized by the cosmic tree, broke off and tilted:

---

63   Hippolytus, *Haer* 1.9.4 = DK 60A4(4).
64   Pseudo-Plutarch, *Strom.* 2 = DK 12A10.
65   See, e.g., Wolfgang Beck, *Der Weltenbaum*. In *Mittelalter-Mythen 5 – Burgen, Länder, Orte*, ed. Ulrich Müller and Wolfgang Wunderlich (Konstanz: UVK Verlagsgesellschaft, 2008), 965–979.

Anaximander says the moon is a circle (...) like that of the sun, *lying aslant* (κείμενον λοξόν) [the plane of the earth] *as does the sun* (...)[66]

The doxographer obviously had in mind the obliquity (λόξωσις) of the ecliptic. The Greek word for the obliquity of the ecliptic is λόξωσις, whereas the word for the tilt of the heavens is ἔγκλισις. However, most scholars agree with Dicks that here the doxographer uses an anachronism: "the words κείμενον λοξόν are a late addition in the doxographic tradition, inserted by someone who was so familiar with the slanting ecliptic of late Greek astronomy that he could not conceive of its not being a well-known concept in this early period."[67] The discovery of the (obliquity of) the ecliptic is ascribed to Oenopides, who lived a century after Anaximander.[68] Therefore, in the context of Anaximander's cosmology, the words κείμενον λοξόν, said of the solar circle, must be interpreted and are usually understood as "lying aslant the plane of the earth," just like the circles of the stars (cf. Figure 9.8, right).[69]

The confusion between the tilt of the heavens and the obliquity of the ecliptic, which is actually a form of spherical earth bias, is a main source of misunderstanding, both in the doxography and in modern commentaries. The tilt of the heavens on a flat earth depends on where one thinks the center of the earth to be. In Delphi it is $51.5°$ in relation to its supposed original upright position. The ecliptic, on the other hand, is the yearly path of the sun among the stars. The obliquity of the ecliptic is always $23.5°$ in relation to the celestial equator, both before and after the tilt of the heavens. A typical recent instance of this confusion is in Dumont's edition of the Presocratics, commenting on the following text:

Diogenes and Anaxagoras said after the world was formed and brought forth living things from the earth, the world (κόσμος) somehow spontaneously tilted (ἐγκλιθῆναι).[70]

---

66   Aët. 2.25.1 = DK 12A22.

67   D.R. Dicks, "Solstices, Equinoxes, and the Presocratics," *The Journal of Hellenic Studies* 86 (1966), 35–36. And again in Dicks, *Early Greek Astronomy*, 45: "a familiarity with the concept of the celestial sphere and its main circles (...) is entirely anachronistic for his (sc. Anaximander's) time."

68   See Eudem. fr.94 Spengel = DK 11A17 and DK 41A7.

69   Cf., e.g., Charles H. Kahn, "On Early Greek Astronomy," *Journal of Hellenic Studies* 90 (1970), 102. I agree with his remark that "The ancient sources do not clearly distinguish such ἔγκλισις from the obliquity of the zodiac," but I disagree with his opinion that "an outright confusion of the two nowhere occurs." See also Martin L. West, *Early Greek Philosophy and the Orient*, Oxford: Clarendon Press, 1971, 85; Graham, *Texts*, translation of A xr25.

70   Aët. 2.8.1 = DK 59A67.

Dumont refers to the discovery of the obliquity of the ecliptic by Oenopides as though it were the same idea as the tilt of the cosmos.[71] However, the ecliptic has nothing to do with the tilt of the cosmos. Another example is Dicks, who, in spite of his critical remark quoted above, a few years later discusses the tilt of the cosmos and then adds that "this seems to be a recognizable attempt to account for the facts that the plane of the ecliptic is inclined to the plane of the equator."[72] Gershenson and Greenberg mention "the inclination of the cosmos" under the wrong head "On the inclination of the ecliptic."[73] The title of the relevant section of Aëtius is: "What is the reason the world is inclined?" Gershenson and Greenberg distort the meaning by adding "to the plane of the ecliptic."[74]

The same confusion is also not absent in the doxography. The previous quote on Anaxagoras and Diogenes continues: "The cosmos (...) inclined *towards its southern portion* (εἰς τὸ μεσημβρινὸν αὐτοῦ μέρος)." On a *spherical* earth, the celestial axis can be said to be tilted in relation to the north ecliptic pole by 23.5° "towards the southern portion of the cosmos" (see Figure 9.9), which is just another description of the inclination of the ecliptic. On a *flat* earth, however, the celestial axis does not run through the poles of the earth, but through its center, and the tilt of the heavens is naturally described as a tilt towards the north (see Figure 9.7). In other words, in his rendition of Presocratic flat earth cosmology, Aëtius was subject to a form of spherical earth bias.

And again, in his account on Empedocles Aëtius writes:

> Empedocles says that because the air yielded to the pressure of the sun, the pole(s) tilted (ἐπικλιθῆναι τὰς ἄρκτους), and the northern parts were raised, the southern lowered, and accordingly the whole world (κόσμος) tilted.[75]

Aëtius obviously has in mind the concept of a spherical earth within a *spherical* cosmos. That is why he can speak of the northern and southern parts of the cosmos. As already said, the words τὰς ἄρκτους are ambiguous. When we translate "the Bears" it indicates the (north) pole, but later, in spherical earth

---

71   Jean-Paul Dumont, *Les Présocratiques* (Paris: Gallimard, 1988), 1430, note 3 on page 648.

72   Dicks, *Early Greek Astronomy*, 59.

73   Daniel E. Gershenson and Daniel A. Greenberg, *Anaxagoras and the Birth of Physics* (New York: Blaisdell Publishing Company, 1964), 340–341.

74   Gershenson and Greenberg, *Anaxagoras*, 164 (no. 165) and 489, n. 165. For more examples, see Couprie, *Heaven and Earth*, 77.

75   Aët. 2.8.2 = DK 31A58.

cosmologies, it was used for the two celestial poles. On a flat earth, it is natural to speak of the celestial pole, in the singular, which is lowered *towards the north* (meaning the northern part of the earth), due to the tilt of the heavens.

8 The Alleged Tilt of the Earth

In the doxography on Leucippus and Democritus, not the heavens but the earth is said to be tilted: "⟨...⟩ the earth being tilted (κεκλίσθαι) towards the south."[76] Diels has tried to repair the mutilated text, suggesting an emendation between the angle brackets: τὴν δὲ λόξωσιν τοῦ ζῳδιακοῦ γενέσθαι ("the oblique path of the ecliptic is due to"). However, the obliquity of the ecliptic has nothing to do with an alleged tilt of the earth nor, for that matter, with a tilt of the heavens. The obliquity of the ecliptic is always 23.5° in relation to the equatorial plane, regardless of whether the heavens or the flat earth are assumed to be tilted. On a *spherical* earth, the obliquity of the ecliptic can be rendered as a 23.5° tilt of the earth in relation to the central perpendicular on the ecliptic plane (see Figure 9.9). This is the manner in which modern earth globes are usually placed. In other words, Diels was subject to a form of spherical earth bias, which resulted in an emendation which in German is called a "Verschlimmbesserung."

Two other texts also mention a tilt of the earth:

Leucippus says the earth tilts (παρεκπεσεῖν) towards the south.[77]
Democritus says because the southern part is weaker than its surroundings, as the earth grew it tilted (ἐγκλιθῆναι) toward the south.[78]

At first glance, we are perhaps inclined to say that for inhabitants of a flat earth the visual experience would be the same both after a tilting of the earth towards the south and after a tilting of the heavens towards the north. But when we visualize such a tilt of the earth in a picture (see Figure 9.10 on the right), we see there is a problem. Several scholars have been puzzled by this enormous dip of the earth. Panchenko, for example, remarks: "in general, the picture of a tilted earth hanging in the middle of the spherical cosmos is bizarre, to say the least."[79]

---

76   Diog. Laërt. 9.33 = DK 67A1(33).
77   Aët. 3.12.1 = DK 67A27.
78   Aët. 3.12.2 = DK 68A96.
79   Panchenko, *Shape of the Earth*, 29. Zeller already wondered why, with such a huge dip of the earth, all the water does not accumulate in the southern regions: Eduard Zeller and

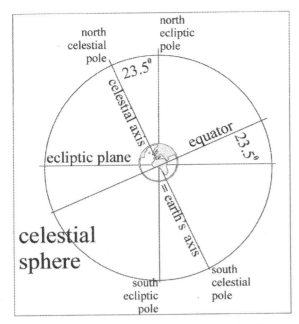

FIGURE 9.9 The tilt of a spherical earth equals the obliquity of the ecliptic

This supposed tilt of the earth is in flagrant contradiction with Aristotle's report:

> Anaximenes, Anaxagoras, and Democritus say flatness is the cause of [the earth's] staying in place. It does not cleave the air beneath it but covers it like a lid.[80]

Aristotle would not have written that Democritus' flat earth "does not cleave the air but covers it like a lid" if he would have known of such an enormous dip of Democritus' earth.[81] Moreover, he mentions Democritus in one breath with Anaxagoras, who taught the tilt of the *heavens*. When we look more

---

Wilhem A. Nestle, *Die Philosophie der Griechen in ihrer geschichtliche Entwicklung. 1. Teil, 2. Hälfte: Allgemeine Einleitung, Vorsokratische Philosophie* (Leipzig: O.R. Reisland, 1920⁶), 1108 n. 6.

80 Aristotle, *Cael.* 294b13–21 = DK 13A20.
81 Cf. Georg Wöhrle, *Anaximenes aus Milet. Die Fragmente zu seiner Lehre* (Stuttgart: Franz Steiner Verlag, 1993), 75: "Die Neigung der Erdscheibe wäre so beachtlich, daß man sich kaum (…) vorstellen kann, wie sie noch auf dem Luftpolster schwimmen könnte und wieso die Bewohner der Erde von dieser Neigung nicht das geringste verspüren."

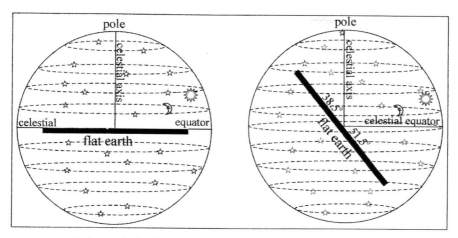

FIGURE 9.10 Before and after the supposed tilt of the earth

carefully at the texts, the context appears not to be a cosmological at all, but climatological:

> ⟨...⟩ the earth being tilted toward the south. The region toward the north is always snowy, cold, and frozen.[82]
>
> Leucippus says the earth tilts (παρεκπεσεῖν) towards the south because of the rarity [of the air] of the southern regions, whereas the northern regions are compacted because they are frozen by frosts, while the contrary regions are fiery.[83]
>
> Democritus says because the southern part is weaker than its surroundings, as the earth grew it tilted (ἐγκλιθῆναι) toward the south. For the northern regions are intemperate, the southern temperate; hence this region is heavy, where there is a greater abundance of flora, as a result of the growth.[84]

Perhaps the doxographers had in mind this text of Aristotle:

> Many of the ancient cosmologists are convinced that the sun does not travel under the earth, but rather around the earth and that (northern) region, and it disappears and causes night *because the earth is high toward the north.*[85]

---

82   Diog. Laërt. 9.33 = DK 67A1(33).
83   Aët. 3.12.1 = DK 67A27.
84   Aët. 3.12.2 = DK 68A96.
85   Aristotle, *Mete.* 354a28–32 = DK 13A14. Graham translates "this region," but meant is the northern region mentioned just before.

However, Aristotle is not referring here to a dip of the earth, but to its northern mountain ranges, from which the greatest rivers flow, as KRS already remarked.[86] On the basis of these considerations, we may conclude that, due to a spherical earth bias, the doxography was mistaken on the alleged dip of the earth in Leucippus and Democritus and that the atomists taught a tilt of the heavens, just like the other Presocratic flat earth cosmologists.

In modern commentaries, the confusion caused by the spherical earth bias continues. Repeatedly, the dip of the earth is equated with the tilt of the heavens or even with the inclination of the ecliptic. Gershenson and Greenberg, for instance, assert that in a dialogue which is ascribed to Plato, two boys, disputing the cosmologies of Anaxagoras and Oenopides, discuss "the inclination of the earth."[87] Neither Anaxagoras nor Oenopides speaks of an alleged tilt of the earth. It is clear from the context that these young men were talking about the circles of the heavenly bodies and probably also about the obliquity of the ecliptic, which is said to have been Oenopides' discovery. Dreyer makes it even worse when he reads the alleged dip of the atomists' earth back into the cosmologies of Anaxagoras and Empedocles. On Anaxagoras he wrote: "The inclination of the axis of the heavens to the vertical *was caused by a spontaneous tilting of the earth towards the south*," and on Empedocles: "The north pole of the heavens must therefore originally have been vertically above the earth, *until the latter was tilted so as to bring the northern end up and the southern end down*."[88] Similarly, KRS, commenting on Anaxagoras and Diogenes, state that "the earth, which is a circle, presumably a round disc, is tilted (…)."[89] The doxography on Anaxagoras, Empedocles, and Diogenes clearly testifies that not the earth but the heavens tilted (or the cosmos, or the stars, or the celestial pole).

9 Geographical and Climatological Issues

The ancient Greeks imagined their flat earth circular, as Herodotus relates when he describes the ancient maps:

---

86 KRS 157.

87 Gershenson and Greenberg, *Anaxagoras*, 59.

88 Dreyer, *History*, 31 and 26 (my italics).

89 KRS 446, cf. Aët. 2.8.1 = DK 59A67. For more examples, see Couprie, *When the Earth Was Flat*, 77.

RECEPTION OF PRESOCRATIC FLAT EARTH COSMOLOGY IN ARISTOTLE 313

> I laugh to see how many have ere now drawn maps of the earth (...). They draw the earth round as if fashioned by compasses, encircled by the river Ocean, and Asia and Europe of like size.[90]

Agathemerus seems to report another view:

> The ancients drew the inhabited earth (οἰκουμένη) as round, with Greece in the center and Delphi in the center of Greece (...). Democritus (...) first that the earth (γῆ) is oblong, with its length one and a half times its breadth.[91]

Here probably the words οἰκουμένη and γῆ have changed places, since the first is the ancient Greek word for the inhabited earth, which was considered oblong, and the second is the word for the earth, which the ancients considered round (see Figure 9.11).[92]

In accordance with Herodotus' words "Asia and Europe of like size," my reconstruction of the oldest maps shows only two continents, "Europe occupying the northern and Asia the southern segment," as Heidel says.[93] The grey circle that forms the periphery of the earth represents the mountains that keep the water of the Ocean inside.

As we have seen, the celestial axis was thought of as tilted and running through the flat earth's center, Delphi. Accordingly, the doxography on the Presocratic flat earth cosmologies does not speak of the earth's poles, but only of the celestial pole or poles. The subpolar point, where the celestial pole is in the zenith, probably was thought to fall outside the disk of the earth (see Figure 9.12). When an observer goes toward the north or the south, the pole is seen under another angle. The only way to cope with this phenomenon is that on a flat earth the stars are not far away.

Due to the spherical earth bias, Cleomedes no longer understands this when he writes, obviously presupposing that the stars are very far away: "If the earth's

---

90   Herodotus, *Hist.* IV 36 = DK 12A6.

91   Agathemerus, *Geogr.* 1.1.2 = DK 68B15.

92   Cf. William A. Heidel, *The Frame of the Ancient Greek Maps. With a Discussion of the Discovery of the Sphericity of the Earth* (New York: American Geographical Society, 1937), 12 n.22: "It is quite certain that the continental mass, not to speak of the οἰκουμένη, was not circular, though the map probably was in the earlier times."

93   Heidel, *Frame*, 12. See also Hugo Berger, *Die Geographie der Ionier* (Leipzig: Verlag Von Veit & Comp., 1903), 81.

FIGURE 9.11 The circular flat earth

shape were flat, the pole would be seen by everyone at an equal distance from the horizon."[94]

Heidel has argued that we might speak of the "Ionian equator and tropics," which run elsewhere than we are used to on a spherical earth. As seen from Delphi, the "Ionian equator" is the line from where the sun rises to where it sets at the equinoxes. This line runs approximately through the Pillars of Hercules in the west and Miletus in the east. The points of sunrise and sunset at the summer and winter solstices define the "Ionian tropics" (see Figure 9.11). The oblong region between these "tropics" is roughly the inhabitable zone, the οἰκουμένη of the flat earth, and consists mainly of the lands around the Mediterranean Sea.[95] On a flat earth, the northern regions are the colder ones, until

---

94   Bowen and Todd, *Cleomedes*, 67 (Cleomedes, *Cael.* 1.5).
95   Heidel, *Frame*, 20 and 54.

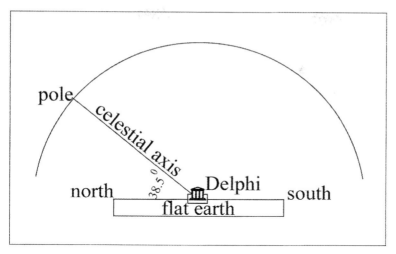

FIGURE 9.12 The position of the celestial pole on a flat earth

one comes to those lands where it is too cold to live; the southern regions are the warmer lands, until one comes to the lands where people are burnt black by the sun. This is the way the doxography speaks about the geography and climates of the Presocratic flat earth. For example, in the last lines of the reports on Leucippus and Democritus, already quoted in the previous section:

1. (…) the northern regions are compacted because they are frozen by frosts, while the contrary regions are fiery.[96]
2. (…) For the northern regions are intemperate, the southern temperate.[97]

The cause of these climatological differences from north to south is the tilt of the heavens in relation to the surface of the flat earth. It was even suggested (perhaps by the doxographer) that the very reason for this tilt was the providence of nature, in order to make some parts of the earth temperate and thus inhabitable:

> (…) the world (κόσμος) somehow spontaneously inclined (…), perhaps by providence, that some regions of the world (κόσμος) might be uninhabited, some inhabited on the basis of cooling, heating, and moderation.[98]

---

96 Aët. 3.12.1 = DK 67A27.
97 Aët. 3.12.2 = DK 68A96.
98 Aët. 2.8.1 = DK 59A67.

The word "uninhabited" makes it clear that by "regions of the world (κόσμος)," the regions and climates of the earth (γῆ) that lie beneath the celestial regions are meant.[99]

10   The Milky Way and the Cause of Lunar Eclipses

This last section covers a problem in Anaxagoras' astronomy that at first sight has nothing to do with the flat earth. Pseudo-Plutarch's version of Aetius' report on the explanation of lunar eclipses says:

> Plato, Aristotle, the Stoics and the mathematicians agree (...) that eclipses of the moon occur when it enters the earth's shadow, when the earth comes between the sun and the moon.[100]

In Stobaeus' version, however, the name of Aristotle has been replaced by those of Thales and Anaxagoras, and he adds a quotation of Theophrastus:

> Thales, Anaxagoras, Plato, and the Stoics agree with the mathematicians (...) that eclipses of the moon occur when it enters the earth's shadow, when the earth comes between the sun and the moon.
>
> Theophrastus says that Anaxagoras held that eclipses also occur when bodies underneath the moon happen to obstruct it.[101]

I think that Pseudo-Plutarch's text is right, and that Stobaeus, having read in Theophrastus that Anaxagoras explained lunar eclipses by bodies underneath the moon, inserted his name in the line before as well, thus making him the defender of two different theories of eclipses of the moon.[102] However, Hippolytus also credits Anaxagoras with the discovery of the true cause of eclipses of the moon, which is the earth's shadow:

---

99   This is also the implication of Mansfeld & Runia, *Doxographer*, 409, who remark that "E[usebius] changes the order (...) so that the temperate climate is in between the hot and the cold."

100   Pseudo-Plutarch *Plac.*2.29.6, see Dox 360= DK 59A77.

101   Stobaeus, *Ecl.* 1.26.3(6 and 7), see Dox 360.

102   The defense of the opposite, as in Mansfeld & Runia, *Doxographer*, 187, I do not find convincing.

RECEPTION OF PRESOCRATIC FLAT EARTH COSMOLOGY IN ARISTOTLE 317

> (Anaxagoras says) the moon is eclipsed when the earth blocks it (...). He first correctly explained eclipses and illuminations (φωτισμούς).[103]

This attribution is repeated in most modern commentaries and standard works. Most recently, it has been presented as Anaxagoras' great discovery in Graham's *Science Before Socrates*.[104] But Hippolytus also wrote, between the just quoted lines:

> There are below the stars certain bodies invisible to us which are carried around with the sun and the moon. (The moon is eclipsed when the earth blocks it), or sometimes one of the bodies below the moon.[105]

It sounds strange that Anaxagoras is said to have discovered the real cause of lunar eclipses and at the same time would have undermined his discovery by giving an additional – and wrong – explanation. Accordingly, several scholars have tried to find a rationalization for the introduction of invisible heavenly bodies as a secondary cause of lunar eclipses.[106] Even more strange is that, immediately after the above quoted lines, Hippolytus ascribes to Anaxagoras quite another theory of the earth's shadow, which is completely incompatible with his alleged discovery of eclipses of the moon as caused by the earth's shadow:

> The Milky Way is the reflection of the light of stars that are not illuminated by the sun.[107]

The ascription of the explanation of the Milky Way to Anaxagoras goes back to Aristotle, who also refers to the optical theory that is behind it:

> The schools of Anaxagoras and Democritus maintain that the Milky Way is the light of certain stars. The sun, they say, in its course beneath the earth, does not shine upon some of the stars; the light of those upon

---

103 Hippolytus, *Haer.* 1.8.9 = DK 59A42(9).
104 See Graham, *Science*, especially 122–134.
105 Hippolytus, *Haer.* 1.8.6 and 9 = DK 59A42 (6 and 9).
106 See H.W. Schaefer, *Die astronomische Geographie der Griechen bis auf Eratosthenes* (Flensburg: Schulprogramm des Flensburger Gymnasiums, 1873), 19; Franz Boll, "Finsternisse," in August Pauly & Georg Wissowa, *Real-Encyclopädie der classischen Altertumswissenschaften* VI.2 (Stuttgart: J. B. Metzler, 1909), 2351; Heath, *Aristarchus*, 80; Peter J. Bicknell, "Lunar Eclipses and 'Selenites'," *Apeiron* 2, no. 1 (1967): 16–21; Graham, *Science*, 128–130.
107 Hippolytus, *Haer.* 1.8.10 = DK 59A42(10).

which the sun does shine is not visible to us, being obscured by its rays, while the Milky Way is the light peculiar to those stars which are screened from the sun's light by the earth.[108]

This explanation of the Milky Way is about the best documented astronomical theory of Anaxagoras.[109] Yet, it is either neglected in modern handbooks,[110] apparently because it sounds so strange to us, or the point of its inconsistency with the explanation of lunar eclipses is missed by those who discuss it.[111] The idea behind this theory of the Milky Way is, as Alexander of Aphrodisias explains,[112] that lights appear brighter in a dark environment. That is why the stars in the band of the earth's shadow – the Milky Way – light up more than the stars outside that shadow. This explanation of the Milky Way, strange as it may seem to us, makes some sense within the context of Anaxagoras' conviction that the earth is flat: When the earth is flat, the stars cannot be far away, as we saw above, so that the earth's shadow can reach them. The explanation of lunar eclipses as caused by the earth's shadow, on the contrary, does not go very well together with the concept of a flat earth. Aristotle gives as his main empirical argument for the sphericity of the earth that during eclipses the boundary of the earth's shadow on the moon is always convex, which could not be the case when the earth was flat.[113] Moreover, the shadow of the earth on the moon is conical, while it must be widening when the earth is flat, as shown in Figure 9.13.

Since the two theories of the earth's shadow – as cause of the Milky Way and as cause of eclipses of the moon – are incompatible, we must choose which

---

108   Aristotle, *Mete.* 345a25–31 = DK 59A80.

109   Aristotle's report is repeated at least six times in the doxography; see Gershenson and Greenberg, *Anaxagoras*, 333.

110   KRS do not have any text at all about Anaxagoras and the Milky Way, and Gr (Axg 297) has only Hippolytus' report.

111   See, e.g., Tannery, *Science hellène*, 279; Theodor Gomperz, *Griechische Denker I* (Leipzig: Veit & Comp., 1896), 179; Gershenson and Greenberg, *Anaxagoras*, 42–43; William K.C. Guthrie, *A History of Philosophy II: The Presocratic Tradition from Parmenides to Democritus* (Cambridge: Cambridge University Press, 1965), 309; D. O'Brien, "Derived Light and Eclipses in the Fifth Century." *Journal of Hellenic Studies* 88 (1968), 114–127, 125; Graham, *Science*, 131–133. Three positive exceptions are Heath (1913, 84 and 85), Fehling, *Problem*, 211, and D. Panchenko, "Anaximandros von Milet," in H.J. Gehrke (ed.), *Die Fragmente der griechischen Historiker Part V*, Die Geographen. Published by Brill online 2013, http://referenceworks.brillonline.com/browse/fragmente-der-griechischen-historiker-v. These authors mention the discrepancy but do not choose between the two incompatible theories of the earth's shadow.

112   Alexander of Aphrodisias, *in Mete.* 37.23 = DK 68A91.

113   See Aristotle, *Cael.* 297b23–31.

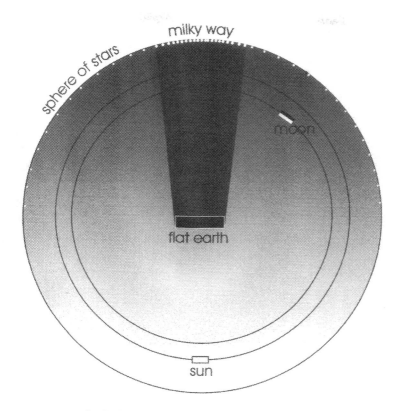

FIGURE 9.13   The shadow of the earth causing the Milky Way

one was held by Anaxagoras. All the evidence points to the theory of the Milky Way, which is the best documented and matches best with the concept of a flat earth. The theory of invisible bodies causing lunar eclipses is completely compatible with the idea that the Milky Way results from the shadow of the earth. What results is a unifying theory of eclipses (including star occultations) all caused by heavenly bodies between the earth and the eclipsed object. In eclipses of the sun and star occultations, the interfering object is the moon and in eclipses of the moon it is an invisible heavenly object. We may conclude that for Anaxagoras the shadow of the (flat) earth had nothing to do with lunar eclipses, since its task was to cause the Milky Way, and that invisible heavenly bodies were the only cause of eclipses of the moon.

This example illustrates, as did the various previous ones, that when studying Presocratic flat earth cosmology, not only in its representation in Aristotle and the doxographers, but also in modern interpretations and translations, we should always beware of anachronisms in order to avoid fundamental misunderstandings. These misunderstandings do arise not in the least because of our own preconceived ideas, and especially because of the spherical earth bias, a lack of understanding of what the concept of a flat earth actually was about.[114]

Bibliography

Arrighetti, Graziano. 1960. *Epicuro Opere*. Torino: Giulio Einaudi.

Beck, Wolfgang. 2008. *Der Weltenbaum*. In *Mittelalter-Mythen 5 – Burgen, Länder, Orte*, edited by Ulrich Müller and Wolfgang Wunderlich. Konstanz: UVK Verlagsgesellschaft.

Berger, Hugo. 1903. *Die Geographie der Ionier*. Leipzig: Verlag Von Veit & Comp., 1903.

Bicknell, Peter J. 1967. "Lunar Eclipses and 'Selenites'." *Apeiron* 2, no. 1: 16–21.

Boll, Franz. 1909. "Finsternisse." In *Real-Encyclopädie der classischen Altertumswissenschaften VI.2*, edited by August Pauly & Georg Wissowa, 2330–2363. Stuttgart: J. B. Metzler.

Bowen, Alan C. and Robert B. Todd. 2004. *Cleomedes' Lectures on Astronomy*. Berkeley: The University of California Press.

Carpenter, William. 1885. *One Hundred Proofs That the Earth Is Not a Globe*. Baltimore: the author.

Couprie, Dirk L. 2011. *Heaven and Earth in Ancient Greek Cosmology: from Thales to Heraclides Ponticus*. New York: Springer.

Couprie, Dirk L. 2015. "The Paths of the Celestial Bodies According to Anaximenes." *Hyperboreus* 21: 5–32.

Couprie, Dirk L. 2018. *When the Earth Was Flat: Studies in Ancient Greek and Chinese Cosmology*. New York: Springer.

Cullen, Christopher. 1996. *Astronomy and Mathematics in Ancient China: the Zhou bi suan jing*. Cambridge: Cambridge University Press.

Dicks, D.R. 1966. "Solstices, Equinoxes, and the Presocratics." *The Journal of Hellenic Studies* 86, 26–40.

Dicks, D.R. 1970. *Early Greek Astronomy to Aristotle*. Ithaca, NY: Thames and Hudson.

Diels, Hermann. 1879. *Doxographi Graeci*. Berlin: Walter de Gruyter.

Diels, Hermann and Walther Kranz. 1951⁶. *Die Fragmente der Vorsokratiker*. Zürich/Hildesheim: Weidmann.

---

114   The issues of the Milky Way and lunar eclipses, as well as the related problem of the explanation of the phases of the moon according to Anaxagoras are extensively discussed in Couprie *When the Earth Was Flat*, chapters 9 and 10.

Dreyer, John L.E. 1953. *A History of Astronomy from Thales to Kepler*. Mineola, NY: Dover Publications.

Dumont, Jean-Paul. 1988. *Les Présocratiques*. Paris: Gallimard.

Fehling, Detlev. 1985. "Das Problem der Geschichte des griechischen Weltmodells vor Aristoteles." *Rheinisches Museum für Philologie* 128: 195–231, 209–210.

Furley, David. 1987. *The Greek Cosmologists. Volume I: The Formation of the Atomic Theory and Its Earliest Critics*. Cambridge: Cambridge University Press.

Furley, David. 1989. *Cosmic Problems. Essays on Greek and Roman Philosophy of Nature*. Cambridge: Cambridge University Press.

Gershenson, Daniel E. and Daniel A. Greenberg. 1964. *Anaxagoras and the Birth of Physics*. New York: Blaisdell Publishing Company.

Gomperz, Theodor. 1896. *Griechische Denker I*. Leipzig: Veit & Comp.

Graham, Daniel W. 2010. *The Texts of Early Greek Philosophy*. Cambridge: Cambridge University Press.

Graham, Daniel W. 2013. "Anaxagoras: Science and Speculation in the Golden Age." In *Early Greek Philosophy. The Presocratics and the Emergence of Reason*, edited by Joe McCoy, 139–156. Washington, D.C.: The Catholic University of America Press.

Graham, Daniel W., 2013. *Science Before Socrates*. Oxford: University Press.

Graham, Daniel W. and Eric Hintz. 2007. "Anaxagoras and the Solar Eclipse of 478 BC." *Apeiron* 40: 319–344.

Guthrie, William K.C. 1965. *A History of Philosophy II: The Presocratic Tradition from Parmenides to Democritus*. Cambridge: Cambridge University Press.

Hahn, Robert. 2001. *Anaximander and the Architects*. Albany: SUNY.

Heath, Thomas. 1913. *Aristarchus of Samos. The Ancient Copernicus*. Oxford: Clarendon Press.

Heidel, William A. 1933. *The Heroic Age of Science*. Baltimore: Williams & Wilkins Company.

Heidel, William A. 1937. *The Frame of the Ancient Greek Maps. With a Discussion of the Discovery of the Sphericity of the Earth*. New York: American Geographical Society.

Kahn, Charles H. 1970. "On Early Greek Astronomy." *Journal of Hellenic Studies* 90, 99–116.

Kahn, Charles H. 1994. *Anaximander and the Origins of Greek Cosmology*. Indianapolis/Cambridge: Hackett Publishing Company, Inc.

Kirk, Geoffrey S., John E. Raven and Malcolm Schofield. 2009. *The Presocratic Philosophers*. Cambridge: Cambridge University Press.

Kočandrle, Radim. 2017. "The Stability of the Earth in Anaximander's Universe." *Ancient Philosophy* 37: 265–280.

Mansfeld, Jaap. 2000. "Cosmic Distances: 'Aëtius' 2.31 Diels and Some Related Texts." *Phronesis* 45:175–294.

Mansfeld, Jaap & David T. Runia. 2009. *The Method and Intellectual Context of a Doxographer* (Aëtiana II.2). Leiden: Brill.

O'Brien, Dennis. 1968. "Derived Light and Eclipses in the Fifth Century." *Journal of Hellenic Studies* 88, 114–127.

Panchenko, Dmitri. 1997. "Anaxagoras' Argument Against the Sphericity of the Earth." *Hyperboreus* 3, 175–178.

Panchenko, Dmitri. 1999. "The Shape of the Earth in Archelaus, Democritus and Leucippus." *Hyperboreus* 5, no 1: 22–39.

Panchenko, Dmitri. 2013. "Anaximandros von Milet," in H.J. Gehrke (ed.), *Die Fragmente der griechischen Historiker Part V*, Die Geographen. Published by Brill online, http://referenceworks.brillonline.com/browse/fragmente-der-griechischen-historiker-v.

Rovelli, Carlo. 2009. "Anaximander's Legacy." *Collapse: Philosophical Research and Development* 5: 50–71.

Schaefer, H.W. 1873. *Die astronomische Geographie der Griechen bis auf Eratosthenes.* Flensburg: Schulprogramm des Flensburger Gymnasiums.

Sider, David. 1973. "Anaxagoras on the Size of the Sun." *Classical Philology* 68: 128–129.

Tannery, Paul. 1887. *Pour l'histoire de science Hellène: de Thalès à Empédocle.* Paris: Félix Alcan.

Thibodeau, Philip. 2017. "Anaximander's Model and the Measures of the Sun and Moon." *Journal of Hellenic Studies* 137: 92–111.

Untersteiner, Mario. 2008. *Senofane: Testimonianze e frammenti.* Milano: Bompiani.

West, Martin L. 1971. *Early Greek Philosophy and the Orient.* Oxford: Clarendon Press.

Wöhrle, Georg. 1993. *Anaximenes aus Milet. Die Fragmente zu seiner Lehre.* Stuttgart: Franz Steiner Verlag.

Wöhrle, Georg. 2012. *Die Milesier: Anaximander und Anaximenes.* Berlin: Walter de Gruyter.

Zeller, Eduard and Wilhem A. Nestle. 1920[6] . *Die Philosophie der Griechen in ihrer geschichtliche Entwicklung. 1. Teil, 2. Hälfte: Allgemeine Einleitung, Vorsokratische Philosophie.* Leipzig: O.R. Reisland.

CHAPTER 10

Elements and Their Forms: The Fortunes of a Presocratic Idea

Tiberiu Popa

1 Introduction

The notion that utterly different phenomena can be explained through the operations of a handful of fundamental principles must have been from the outset as aesthetically seductive as it was theoretically fruitful. And yet, there is a measure of salutary messiness about several treatments of simple stuffs, whether those stuffs are genuinely elementary or whether they are (as in Plato and Aristotle) further analyzable into basic constituents. What I mean is that a number of influential ancient theories of matter, formulated roughly over the span of a century, do not depend strictly on positing elements or quasi-elementary simple stuffs as well as their countless mixtures. They also involve substances—forms of air, forms of fire etc.—which occupy a zone largely intermediary between simple elements and mixtures: not just pure and simple air or earth etc., but dry and static air, the thickest water, the strongest fire, forms of earth that are soluble, and so on. They rarely command much attention, but generally demonstrate an explanatory prowess which cannot be ignored. The goal of this chapter is twofold.

(a) It highlights the importance of the forms of simple bodies in several ancient theories of matter, an importance not always fully appreciated in recent scholarship. Well aware that this topic can stretch its tendrils out in too many philosophical directions, I will focus firmly on discussions of elemental and quasi-elemental varieties, and will provide only general outlines of the contexts in which they occur. The chapter is divided into three main sections: Diogenes of Apollonia—with some observations on Anaximenes; early Hippocratic works, with emphasis on *Regimen*; later, especially Aristotle's, treatments of forms of elements and non-elementary simple bodies.

Forms of air are essential to Diogenes of Apollonia's—original or refurbished—monism, in particular to the differentiations undergone by his *aēr*; forms of air may have been instrumental also in the position previously defended by Anaximenes. Similar elemental forms are mobilized in early Hippocratic works which perhaps bear the imprint of Diogenes' method,

© KONINKLIJKE BRILL NV, LEIDEN, 2021 | DOI:10.1163/9789004443358_012

especially in *Regimen* I, where various kinds of water and fire are said to generate different types of human constitutions and of mental and temperamental dispositions, a typology crucial in turn to dietetics. Plato's brand of geometric atomism relies both on varieties of (atomic or composite) triangles and on *eidē* of polyhedral bodies corresponding to earth, water, air and fire. He puts them to work, among other things, in explaining dispositional properties, for instance, in the section of the *Timaeus* devoted to pathology (82a-83a). Forms of earth and of water help Aristotle make the transition from a purely theoretical approach to elements and simple bodies to a more applied study of the homoeomers and of the emergence of material properties and higher-level dispositions (e.g., in the context of his biology). Finally, Theophrastus' *On Fire* provides an interesting segue to Aristotle's discussion by distinguishing forms of fire and by connecting structural features (such as the tenuous or dense texture of flames) with capacities of fire, in ways reminiscent of earlier authors. My study does not claim to be exhaustive; I remain open to the possibility that further authors can be added to the *dramatis personae* listed here, and in fact a few other thinkers make episodic or cameo appearances in these pages.

(b) The overall nature of the varieties of water, earth etc. at the heart of the theories explored here, as well as their functions (e.g., accounting for material dispositions like solubility or for higher order dispositions like perceptiveness) and, in some cases, the inferential methods and the technical terminology used—all of these point to continuity in the history of this idea. The doctrinal differences between the texts analyzed in this chapter and the details of the explanatory mechanisms they propose should, of course, be taken into account in any such comparison; but the possible common points should not be ignored either, if we are to capture the full significance of those (quasi)elemental forms. In the absence of overt acknowledgements, it is often impossible to establish with certainty the precise lineage or avatars of such ideas. Besides, it is quite possible that the same author, e.g. the author of *Regimen*, could have been inspired by the methods and doctrines of several *phusiologoi* in his handling of the notion of elemental varieties. It is equally possible that the influence might have been direct, through acquaintance with earlier works, or indirect, through summaries and compilations, or that it could have been more diffuse, insofar this idea may have become a sort of common currency during the last decades of the 5th century BCE. I will, then, have to settle here for a broad historical trajectory rather than for exact filiation. With this caveat in mind, let me start by evaluating the role of elemental variation in the natural theory of Diogenes of Apollonia, the first author who, as far as I can tell, gave prominence to this notion.

ELEMENTS AND THEIR FORMS: THE FORTUNES OF A PRESOCRATIC IDEA 325

2 Diogenes[1]

2.1 *Differentiations of the Elementary Air*

Diogenes took *aēr* to be the single element (DK64B2) and an animating principle (B4).[2] It is at the same time a ubiquitous (and eternal, A5, B7, B8) divinity and intelligence or *noēsis* (B4, B5; cf. A19). Air is not immutable, as Empedocles' four elements are;[3] it changes continually, giving rise to all recognizable aspects of the world. Diogenes' references to the alterations affecting air are made both in the context of his proof that everything emerges from one common substratum (otherwise things would be mutually impassible, B4) and in his discussion about the differences between species and between individuals belonging to the same species.[4] Frequent changes affecting air have led to the

---

1 Most scholars agree, with various degrees of confidence, that he wrote sometime during the second half of the 5th century BCE. See, e.g., André Laks, *Diogène d'Apollonie. La dernière cosmologie présocratique* (Lille: Presses Universitaires de Lille, 1983), xx, who suggests that Diogenes flourished after Anaxagoras; cf. André Laks and Glenn W. Most, *Early Greek Philosophy*, vol. II, part 1 and vol. VI, part 1, (Cambridge, MA and London: Harvard University Press, 2016), 218; James Longrigg, "Elements and After: A Study in Presocratic Physics of the Second Half of the Fifth Century," *Apeiron* 19, no. 2 (1985): 100–101: "... it may safely be assumed that he was active philosophically between 440 and 423 B.C."; and Richard D. McKirahan, *Philosophy Before Socrates. An Introduction with Texts and Commentary*. 2nd edition (Indianapolis and Cambridge: Hackett, 2010), 345, who points out that "He was probably active in the two decades after 440, which would place him later than Empedocles and Anaxagoras and contemporary with Melissus and Leucippus."

2 In his important reconsideration of accepted views about material monism, Daniel W. Graham, *Explaining the Cosmos. The Ionian Tradition of Scientific Philosophy* (Princeton and Oxford: Princeton University Press, 2006), 290, notes that the Milesians advocated a type of theory he calls Generating Substance Theory: "There is one original stuff, which is transformed by a process such as condensation into other basic substances which make up the cosmos." While admitting he cannot completely disprove that Diogenes was a reviver of an earlier version of material monism (MM), Graham argues that it is more plausible to consider Diogenes a genuine material monist, developing "a theory according to which there is only one substance, air, which by altering or changing its states, can appear as a plurality of substances. (...) Hence MM is a neo-Ionian theory using Eleatic principles to modify and reconceive the principles of cosmology."

3 On the nature of these four elementary stuffs—in their pure state and when mixed with each other—in Empedocles' doctrine and on whether 'roots' (*rhizōmata*) should be considered an unqualified synonym for 'elements' (*stoicheia*), see Timothy J. Crowley's convincing reevaluation of this influential Presocratic theory, especially in the first major section of his chapter ("Aristotle, Empedocles, and the Reception of the Four Elements Hypothesis," in this volume). Crowley offers a helpful analysis of the (im)permanence of the four Empedoclean elements and their relation with the cosmic sphere, in light of Aristotle's comments (for this aspect, see mainly the second section of Crowley's chapter).

4 Aristotle agrees in broad outline with this principle in *Gen. corr.* (1.6.322b11-18 =A7). On this, see Laks, *Diogène d'Apollonie*, 84–85.

present condition (*ta ... nun eonta*) of our *kosmos*—one of potentially infinitely many *kosmoi*. Diogenes implicitly assumed an initial, pre-cosmic stage when the air was perfectly homogeneous, irreducibly simple and in continuous motion, gradually giving way to compounds and complex structures in which air assumes various qualities and allows for the generation of the world in its current state.[5] He notes emphatically that air still goes through successive and cyclical transformations (B2) and that eventually everything will be converted back into air.

The qualities exhibited by the kinds of this first principle are responsible for the formation of different parts of the world, most notably of living beings in their wondrous morphological, physiological and behavioral diversity. The mechanism is not fully elucidated, but mixing is mentioned in the extant fragments and testimonia on several occasions (e.g. *misgesthai*, B2; cf. *mixin* in A32 and B9, *krasin* in A19). Yet, the nature of mixtures constituting various materials or tissues can only be one facet of Diogenes' explanatory apparatus, since, unlike Empedocles, for example, he does not rely in final analysis on (re)combinations of elementary simple stuffs.[6] Water and earth (mentioned in B2) and all other substances, however combined, owe their essential as well as accidental properties in part to the forms (*tropoi*, B5) of air from which they emerge and possibly also to the way in which they emerged from those forms (e.g., through condensation of a certain intensity or type).[7]

Although air encompasses—and indeed *is*—everything (*panta ta onta ... to auto einai*, B2), there are no two things that are identical manifestations of this universal principle. The multiplicity of stuffs and organic and inorganic things in the cosmos is explainable in terms of the virtually unlimited range of properties that mark the instantiations of this element:

> And there is not a single thing which does not share in this [i.e. air]. But not a single thing shares in it similarly to anything else, but there are many forms (*polloi tropoi*) both of air itself and of intelligence; for it is manifold, warmer and colder, drier and moister,[8] more static and having

---

5 A6 (Pseudo-Plutarch, *Miscellanies* 12) comes close to offering a cosmogonic account.

6 For an illuminating study of the complexities (and, in some respects, ambiguities) of Empedocles' theory, see Crowley's chapter in this volume.

7 I take it that "in its own nature" (*tēi idiai phusei*, B2) indicates the ultimate nature of things, everything being essentially air, in contrast to accidental properties that make things in the ordered world appear different from each other.

8 That this list starts with warm, cold, dry and moist is hardly surprising. On the place of these qualities in early Greek thought, the classic study is: G.E.R. Lloyd, "The Hot and the Cold, the Dry and the Wet in Greek Philosophy," *The Journal of Hellenic Studies* 84 (1964): 92–106.

ELEMENTS AND THEIR FORMS: THE FORTUNES OF A PRESOCRATIC IDEA 327

sharper movement, and many other differentiations can be found in it, including innumerable (*apeiroi*) differentiations both of flavor and of color. (B5)

In this context, "forms" appears to cover all substances and things, including and chiefly the kinds of air mentioned here. The notion of variety introduced by *polloi tropoi* is further underlined, with no fear of tautology, by the repeated use of the adjective *polutropos*, "multiform" or "manifold." The first of three occurrences of *polutropos* (and virtual synonyms like *tou plētheos tōn heteroiōseōn*, "the multitude of alterations") in this relatively short fragment applies to air and echoes the immediately preceding *polloi tropoi*. The adjectives listed in this passage must therefore point to forms of air,[9] understood as more basic modifications of elemental air than, say, earth, water, gold or animals and their parts. The whole fragment is intended to spell out the idea that multiplicity is explainable through alterations of the one fundamental substance, air, and, along with A19 (see below), suggests that (basic) forms of air constitute an intermediary between pure and simple air and the observable things that make up the world.

Before attempting to further clarify the nature of those forms of air and their explanatory functions, let me briefly comment on the structure of the entire fragment (B5), which throws into sharp relief the centrality of this notion in Diogenes. It opens with a teleological manifesto,[10] followed by a claim about everything's participation in the one element or god. The remainder of this fragment deals with the causes underlying the differentiation from homogeneous air. The scope of the first statements on differentiation is universal: "And there is not a single thing which does not share in this [i.e. air]. But not a single thing shares in it similarly to anything else ..." Everything owes its existence and its specific nature to the more basic differentiations (*heteroiōsies*) which affect air itself, those forms of air being, again, an intermediary between the undifferentiated air and the many stuffs and structured things which are the furniture of the world.

The next segment of Diogenes' brief but significant discussion about *heteroiōsis* focuses on the realm of life. It starts (a) with an explanation for

---

9   Their comparative forms hint at different degrees for each quality.
10   On teleology in Diogenes, see Laks, *Diogène d'Apollonie*, xxviii and André Laks, "Speculating about Diogenes of Apollonia," in *The Oxford Handbook of Presocratic Philosophy*, eds. Patricia Curd and Daniel W. Graham (Oxford, New York: Oxford University Press, 2008b), 358 (Laks distinguishes between teleology proper and noetics), and Graham, *Explaining the Cosmos*, 286.

differences in the souls of animals (differences between distinct kinds of animals and between individuals within a certain kind) based on fluctuations in one particular quality of air: warmth.[11] The second set of statements regarding the realm of life (b) is somewhat more general, referring not just to what can be seen as pertaining to the soul (behavioral dispositions and intelligence,[12] *diaitan ... noēsin*), but also to appearance or shape (*idean*). Perhaps that is why the earlier reliance on the functions of warmth is now replaced with a reference to multiple differentiation (*polutropou eousēs tēs heteroiōsios*), including variations in heat, but not only. Thus the distinctive properties of all things depend partially (besides mixture) but crucially on corresponding forms of air and on their respective affections. This dependence can be detected in B5 at three levels: our entire *kosmos*; the realm of life in general; the souls of human beings and of non-human animals. My preliminary conclusion based on this brief analysis of the structure of B5 is that, while everything is conditioned by intelligence or thinking (*noēsis*) as an attribute of air, it also depends, at a more strictly material level, on the many forms (*tropoi*) of air, that is, on the countless alterations that affect the one element. This turns out to be, accordingly, one of the dominant aspects of his cosmology.

2.2 *Diogenes on the Relation between Different Orders of Properties*

There is another methodological function of the *tropoi* of air that invites attention. Judging by the surviving evidence, parts of Diogenes' work dealt in some detail with the causal connections between (a) elemental varieties (implicitly with their basic capacities or dispositional qualities: hot, moist etc.) and (b) higher level dispositions (way of life, intelligence, and so on). As we have already seen, he argues in B5 that the multitude (*plētheos*) of differences in physical aspect (*idea*), general behavior or way of life (*diaitan*) and intelligence (*noēsin*) are produced by many forms (*poloi tropoi*) of air distinguishable in virtue of qualities which range from the air's level of moisture to its degree of mobility. The numerous kinds of animals (*polutropa ... ta zōia*) are due to the manifold differentiation of air.[13]

---

11 "The heat is not the same in any two animals, since it is not the same even among human beings, but it differs, not much, but in such a way as to be to resemble each other (*alla diapherei mega men ou, all'hōste paraplēsia einai*)." The implication here seems to be that differences in the intensity of the heat of *aēr* are more pronounced between distinct species and more attenuated between individuals belonging to the same kind.

12 Or, more broadly, perception or even modes of awareness: André Laks, *Diogène d'Apollonie*, 2nd edition (International Pre-Platonic Studies, Vol. 6, Sankt Augustin: Academia Verlag, 2008a), 85.

13 *Polutropou eousēs tēs heteroiōsios* (B5), a genitive absolute indicating cause.

ELEMENTS AND THEIR FORMS: THE FORTUNES OF A PRESOCRATIC IDEA   329

What is missing here is a clear account of how that causation is played out. Fortunately, we have Theophrastus' *On the Senses* (39–45=A19); according to this important summary, Diogenes builds a fairly elaborate theory about the nature and workings of mind and perception, and about the causes of pleasure and pain. While the details of such operations are sometimes left disappointingly vague, the main aspects of this investigation are reasonably clear. The method employed is multipronged: anatomical structures (e.g. long and thin passageways) are invoked to account for degrees of perceptive acuity—as are quantitative factors.[14] These two aspects are occasionally combined to sketch mechanical explanations; for example, towards the end of A19 children are said to be prone to an impulsive, unstable behavior because a large amount of air is expelled through narrow passages. Besides, certain types of blockage can prevent air from flowing freely through passages and impair our mental capacities permanently or temporarily.[15]

These structural factors are certainly important to Diogenes' causal explanations of higher order dispositions, but there is another decisive condition for the coming about of capacities of a certain nature and intensity, according to A19, namely the *sort of air* prevalent in the mixture or blend[16] which constitutes our bodies. As in *Regimen*, which will be discussed later in this chapter, the more basic material dispositions of our ingredients and their mixtures in our bodies, together with structural features like the ones just mentioned above, determine a variety of higher level capacities; in this case (A19), courage (*tharsos*), health (*hugieian*) or tendency to fall ill under certain conditions or to experience pain (*lupēn*), (un)intelligence (*phronein, aphrona*), being prone to fits of anger (*orgila ... oxurropa*), and forgetfulness (*lēthēs*). It makes no small difference if the air is pure or mixed. Pleasure is produced by the fact that a considerable amount of air mixes (*misgētai*) with blood and makes it lighter; pain arises precisely in the absence of such mixture. When combined with moisture,[17] air inhibits intelligence and sharp

---

14   A small amount of air in the head, being less contaminated than a large amount, is a necessary condition for a keen sense of smell. (A19).

15   The author of *Regimen*, who may have been a contemporary of Diogenes and may have been exposed to his ideas, deals with the physical basis of temperamental dispositions—quick temper, indolence etc., caused in part by the excessive amount of water in the composition of the body (1.36) as an impediment for the movement of fire (a source of perceptiveness).

16   *Tēi krasei, tēn krasin* (cf. *sugkrēsis* in *Regimen* 1.36).

17   Moist air can be conceived probably both as a basic modification of 'pure' elemental air (like in the enumeration of forms of air in B5) and as a mixture of 'pure' air and moisture (like here, in A19).

memory.[18] The presence of fine air in the composition of a body is a condition for keen eyesight; pure and dry air is necessary for (clear) thinking, *phronein*. The reasoning behind these connections between two orders of dispositions (material vs mental etc.) is not consistently clear, but we can detect at least some discreet hints. The high mobility of air, for example, seems to correspond to quick thought; moisture, on the other hand, prevents air from pervading the entire body and slows down its flow, which explains why children are comparatively "slow" (*nōthē*). Pleasure is associated with lightness, pain with heaviness. Purity (and dryness) of air is linked with clarity of mind, and so on. Hot air (in B5) sustains life in general,[19] as warmth and breathing are readily connectable with the functioning of many kinds of organisms. In sum, the numerous forms of air posited by Diogenes play a major explanatory role by causally connecting two orders of capacities or dispositional differentiae.[20]

This inferential device is also central to medical theories articulated probably around the same time as, or soon after, Diogenes' work. Before turning my attention to them, let me indulge in a final speculation. How indebted was Diogenes to Anaximenes in this regard? Hippolytus' doxographic synopsis of Anaximenes' view of nature (*Refutation* 1.7.1–9 = DK13A7; cf. 13A5) reports on the form or character (*eidos*) of air and on its transformations.[21] Hippolytus may not have followed Anaximenes' own terminology here, although several parts of 13A7 could be quotes from the Milesian thinker,[22] but even if the word *eidos* was in fact chosen by Anaximenes, it was very probably not used there to mark

---

18   This is probably borrowed from Heraclitus (22.B36, where soul is equated with air, and B117); see also *Regimen* (e.g., 1.32).

19   It may also be that heat is not a modification of air simply, but an inherent attribute of pre-cosmic unmodified air and of the state to which everything will return eventually, as Laks (1983, 9 and 2008b, 357) suggests.

20   Exactly how those forms are generated is by no means obvious. In McKirahan's view (*Philosophy Before Socrates*, 347), the differentiation of air becomes more intelligible if we suppose that Diogenes' theory imported and made the most of the concept of void: "I find it most plausible that Diogenes followed Leucippus in accepting the existence of void and that one of the main functions of void in his theory was to provide a basis for the differentiation of air, so that (as for the Atomists) void makes plurality and change possible." This interpretation is supported, I think, by Diogenes Laertius' (A1; cf. A5, A6, A10) report on what appear to be early atomistic tenets. Diogenes of Apollonia, then, seems to have selected those principles of Leucippus' theory that he regarded as reconcilable with his natural philosophy, but did not go as far as to adopt the notion of indivisibly small discrete particles.

21   That synopsis is based on Theophrastus' summary (Laks and Most, *Early Greek Philosophy*, II.1, 338 ff.).

22   See Daniel W. Graham, *The Texts of Early Greek Philosophers. The Complete Fragments and Selected Testimonies of the Major Presocratics* (Cambridge: Cambridge University Press, 2010), 78, 80 and 92.

ELEMENTS AND THEIR FORMS: THE FORTUNES OF A PRESOCRATIC IDEA 331

a division into kinds of air, as is the case with Diogenes' *tropoi*. Even so, the question could be asked whether Diogenes' discussion about the forms of air might still have been shaped by Anaximenes' influence. I am inclined to answer in the affirmative, but, given the relative scarcity of information at our disposal regarding the details of Anaximenes' theory, my answer can only be tentative. In so far as air appears different (*diaphoron*) by transitioning from a uniform and imperceptible substance to various stuffs which are perceptible, owing to their specific properties, this account bears some resemblance to Diogenes' passage that we know as DK64B5. The very examples listed by Hippolytus (differences in *aēr* with respect to heat,[23] moisture, mobility: *tōi thermōi, tōi noterōi kai tōi kinoumenōi*), too, are reminiscent of B5, and the fact that they are enumerated in the same order further reduces the chances of a pure coincidence. Hippolytus' notes on Anaximenes indicate an intermediary stage between perfectly homogeneous air and the generation of stuffs (and composite structures made of those stuffs). I take McKirahan's comment (2010, 49) to highlight this very possibility: "Air can take on different appearances, and when conditions are right it even becomes different types of substances." This being said, the probable *difference* between the two authors' approaches to the nature of those transformations and to the status of the underlying *archē* is equally notable. While resorting to the same basic mechanism of condensation and rarefaction, Diogenes is mainly interested in alterations (*heteroiōsies*) of one substratum, which never and nowhere fails to maintain its essential nature. The passage from Hippolytus offers a rather different angle, placing the emphasis squarely on the coming to be (*ginomena, ta gegonota, ginesthai* etc.) of various things from air, and, besides, it may not be the case that for Anaximenes air is a permanent substratum, rather than one stage in successive transformations of matter.[24]

3   Hippocratic Writers

3.1   *Varieties of Air—and Other Stuffs—in Some of the Early Hippocratic Works*

Diogenes of Apollonia is not the only author in the second half of the 5th century BCE to build a cosmology in which processes of differentiation rely on

---

23   Cold and heat are the result of structural properties and of degrees of density (B1, a passage from Plutarch's *On the Principle of Cold* 7). What is contracted and condensed or concentrated (*to ... sustellomenon ... kai puknoumenon*) is cold, and what is rare and loose (*to d'araion kai to chalaron*) is hot.

24   On this see Graham, *Explaining the Cosmos*, 45–84 and Graham, *The Texts of Early Greek Philosophers*, 92.

distinctions between elemental varieties and to outline the development of organisms in terms of the formation and acquisition of increasingly complex capacities, from the powers of simple stuffs to mental abilities. The author of *Regimen*, an early Hippocratic and arguably late Presocratic work, paints an even richer picture of such elemental varieties and of their theoretical and practical significance. Before analyzing some of the most relevant passages in *Regimen* and the methodological aspects they share with Diogenes' approach, let me consider briefly and more generally the impact that Diogenes' philosophical outlook may have had on early Greek medicine.

Whether Diogenes himself was a physician is debatable. His account of the veins,[25] with all its shortcomings, is quite an exploit and his physiology of perception and cognition betrays some interest in the morphology and workings of the human body. Positions among scholars differ, however: McKirahan (*Philosophy Before Socrates*, 345–6), for instance, is more open to this possibility, while Láks[26] seems somewhat more skeptical that the Diogenes mentioned by Galen (*On Medical Experience* 22.3) and by Pseudo-Galen (*History of Philosophy* 119) is our Presocratic thinker. There is more agreement, on the other hand, on the likely imprint that Diogenes' theory left on a few medical treatises.[27]

The chronology of both Presocratic and Hippocratic works is fraught with difficulties, but, if Diogenes and the authors of *Breaths, Regimen, The Sacred Disease*, and *Airs, Waters, Places* flourished during the second half of the 5th c. BCE,[28] then it is at least conceivable that those Hippocratic authors may have been familiar with Diogenes' ideas—and perhaps also that the latter, in turn, might have been aware of certain contemporary Hippocratic tenets and methods. The author of *Breaths* stressed the basic unity of diseases: they all result ultimately from variations in winds (*pneumata*) and thus in air (*phusa* inside our bodies, *aēr* outside). Like the author of *The Sacred Disease*, he does not articulate a cosmology of his own and provides no clear treatment of how elements may be altered or transformed. He demarcates kinds of air (*diapherei … aēr aēros, Breaths* 6.12–16) which have distinct effects on the health of different

---

25 In Aristotle, *Hist. an.* III.2=B6, comparable with Ch. 11 of *On the Nature of Man*; cf. *The Sacred Disease* 6 ff.

26 *Diogène d'Apollonie*, xxvi.

27 See, e.g., McKirahan, *Philosophy Before Socrates* quoted above, and Graham, *The Texts of Early Greek Philosophers*, 457; cf. W.H.S. Jones, trans. notes, *Hippocrates*, vol. I (Cambridge, MA, London: Harvard University Press, 1957), 133.

28 Jacques Jouanna, *Hippocrates*, translated by M.B. DeBevoise (Baltimore and London: Johns Hopkins University Press, 2001), 412, cf. 375.

ELEMENTS AND THEIR FORMS: THE FORTUNES OF A PRESOCRATIC IDEA 333

individuals and species. Changes in air or wind are more pronounced during the transition from one season to another: in winter, air, which is essentially thin (*leptos*), becomes thick and cold (*puknon kai psuchron*), whereas in summer it tends to be gentle and calm (*prēu kai galēnon*). A precise mechanism for those changes is not described here, but it may be that structural changes and increases in density underlie qualitative changes (from hot to cold, from watery to fiery) that can be beneficial or harmful (*Breaths* 8.28–39). Air can also be pure or corrupted by pollutions (*miasmasin*, *Breaths* 6.19), which implies that admixture is *one of* the reasons for the qualitative variation of air—a view shared by Diogenes.

The purity of air is also a key factor in the pathology of *The Sacred Disease* (19.10–21).[29] Air is the cause of consciousness and bestows intelligence, a claim echoing the defining functions of air in Diogenes. It needs, therefore, to reach the brain before spreading through the body; otherwise, it may lose its sharpness (*mēketi einai akribēs*) by being mixed with the moisture from the flesh and the blood. Radical changes in the air (notably during the transition from one season to another, 20.29–33) produce correspondingly drastic changes in the brain.

A more nuanced treatment of the relation between the powers of different kinds of air or winds, waters etc. and the way in which disease is generated is the focus of much of *Airs, Waters, Places*, probably by the same author as *The Sacred Disease*.[30] The causal link between the material properties of different sorts of water, air or soil, on the one hand, and health, appearance, temperament, and intelligence, on the other, is repeatedly established and lavishly illustrated. Sources of water facing towards the sunrise are clear, smell sweet, are soft and overall delightful; they are conducive to good complexion, clear voice, better temper, and keen intelligence, compared to less fortunate people who get their water from sources exposed to the north winds (Ch. 5, 11 ff.). As in *Breaths*, distinctive qualities are due (a) to structural features and (b) to mixing and separation, causes which are sometimes intermingled in the account of *Airs, Waters, Places*. Rain water is described (*Airs* ..., 8.3–10) as the lightest,

---

29   If a cold and moist environment instigates the excessive production of phlegm in a body, discharges of phlegm can block the passageways through which air courses. Explanations of this sort, based on anatomical structures and obstructions are employed also in Diogenes' attempt at the physiology of perception (A19) and in *Regimen* (see 1.36 on blockages which compromise the mobility of fire and produce undesirable temperamental propensities).

30   On the different powers (*dunamias, dunamis*) of water, see, for example, *Airs, Waters, Places* I.9–22.

the sweetest, the finest (*leptotata*) and the most clear; low density and the other properties are the outcome of evaporation, a process in which the brine is separated from the finest and lightest part. On the other hand, rain water is also liable to become foul because it is a blend from many sources (*hoti apo pleistōn sunēktai kai summemiktai*), and when it rises, attracted by the sun's heat, it goes through additional combinations and separations; the dark part becomes mist, while the lightest and most clear part is concocted by the sun and becomes sweet (8.25–35; cf. 8.53–57). Water can also be saturated with salt or alum. When different sorts are mixed, the strongest confers its attributes to the mixture (9.10–14).

The first two chapters of *Regimen* II discuss differences between the natures and powers of winds (*pneumatōn phusin ... kai dunamin* 11.38) in terms that are quite similar to *Airs, Waters, Places*. Yet, it is in the first book of this hybrid medical-philosophical treatise that we find an impressively elaborate cosmology, including careful distinctions between kinds of water and of fire and between their effects on our physical, mental and temperamental qualities. The systematic study of the material constitution of the *kosmos* in *Regimen* I and the fact that this book is so manifestly imbued with Presocratic tenets should entitle us to consider this early Hippocratic treatise itself to be inscribed in the Presocratic tradition. If so, its possible exposure to Diogenes' speculations (with respect both to the role of cosmic teleology and to that of elemental variations) can be regarded as an interaction *within* the boundaries of Presocratic thought.

3.2   *Elemental Varieties in* Regimen

The author of *Regimen* (likely a near-contemporary of Diogenes) does not argue for monism in his work devoted largely to dietetics; rather, fire and water are the two elementary components of the bodies of all animals—and in fact of the entire universe[31] (see the end of Ch. 3: *autarkea esti pasi dia pantos*). They operate only in combination with each other; otherwise fire alone would be ineffective due to a lack of nourishment provided by water, and water

---

31   H.W. Miller, "The Concept of *Dynamis* in De victu," *Transactions and Proceedings of the American Philological Association* 90 (1959): 149, and, more recently, Catalin Enache, "*The Typology of Human Constitutions in Hippocrates'* De victu 1, 32," *Wiener Studien* 124 (2011): 39, n. 2, adopt the same reading, which seems to be favored by most scholars. For an alternative view, see Hynek Bartoš, *Philosophy and Dietetics in the Hippocratic* On Regimen (Leiden: Brill, 2015), 77, who believes that the *Regimen*'s references to air, *pneuma* and earth may indicate additional elements, besides fire and water.

ELEMENTS AND THEIR FORMS: THE FORTUNES OF A PRESOCRATIC IDEA   335

would lack the mobility imparted by fire. Fire is hot and dry, water is cold and moist (Ch. 4), but the two elements also lend each other certain properties: fire can be moist (but never cold), while water can be dry (but not hot). The constant changes of the elements (*aiei alloioumena*, 4.11) and sundry structural transformations lead to the generation of numerous variations of fire and of water: moist fire, dry water, rare fire, etc. These forms of fire and water and their mixtures generate an extraordinary variety (*pollas kai pantodapas ideas*, 4.7–8) of seeds and animals with their specific capacities.

The ontological and cosmological landscape unfolding in *Regimen* 1, then, includes (a) two material principles with their specific basic powers, (b) types of fire and water that are *not* introduced as mixtures, as well as (c) mixtures of fire and water of varying degrees of complexity.[32] The earliest references to forms of water and fire are found in Chs. 7, 9 and 10: fine water (*hudatos leptou*), air-like fire (*puros ... ēeriou*), and the hottest and strongest fire (*thermotaton kai ischurotaton pur*). Such distinctions are crucial to the author's discussion about *phronēsis* in Ch. 35, where several degrees and kinds of (un)intelligence are presented as manifestations of corresponding blends of forms of fire and of water. To take an example, the significant presence of the moistest fire and the driest water in someone's constitution is a condition *sine qua non* for a soul that is highly intelligent and has the best memory; the sketchy rationale is that what is most self-sufficient (*hekateron de houtōs autarkestaton*) is also most capable to carry out a certain task.

Elemental varieties also serve as both underlying causes and classifying criteria in the typology of human natures in Ch. 32. This chapter explores the connections between six human physical constitutions and the seasons in which certain diseases can occur or can be intensified because of the onset (*ephodos*) of fire or water, that is, the prevalence of elemental powers, like dry and hot (in summer) or moist and cold (in winter).[33] If a body is mostly cold

---

32   A more detailed analysis of the role of elemental variations in *Regimen* 1 can be found in Tiberiu Popa, "Observing the Invisible: *Regimen* 1 on Elemental Powers and Higher Order Dispositions," *The British Journal for the History of Philosophy* 22, no. 5 (2014b): 888–907. Enache's "The Typology of Human Constitutions" deals in particular with Ch. 32 of *Regimen* 1, and distinguishes between principal and secondary variations based on their frequency in that chapter and on the perceived importance to the six human constitutions.

33   Besides genetic factors, age is an important aspect too, according to *Regimen* 1.33: the constitution of children is moist and warm, of adolescents dry and warm, of adults dry and cold and of the elderly moist and cold.

and moist, winter can accentuate its properties and compromise its 'chemical' balance. The passages that outline the six physical constitutions list or describe: (a) a mixture of specific varieties of fire and water; (b) the general *phusis* of an individual whose body is characterized by that blend (e.g. moist and warm); (c) the conditions under which dispositions—such as being vulnerable to disease in spring—can be manifested; (d) the diet that can offset the impact of a certain season. Here are some of those human constitutions in broad outline:

1. the finest water and the rarest fire; the healthiest condition; immune to harmful effects from major changes in the seasons; lasting good health;

(...)

4. the moistest fire and the thickest water; moist and warm constitution; tendency to be sick especially in spring (excess of moisture) and in autumn (moderate amount of dryness); the youngest are the least healthy; catarrhs are likely; a proper regimen is recommended;

5. the strongest fire and the finest water; dry and warm nature; the onset of fire (i.e. warm weather) tends to cause illness, especially during prime age; cooling food and exercises can help;

6. the rarest fire and the driest water; dry and cold nature; liable to fall ill in autumn; healthiest in childhood; a warming and moistening regimen is appropriate.

In the first case a blend of the finest (*leptotaton*) water and of the rarest (*araiotaton*) fire is necessary, though not sufficient, for the healthiest constitution. The explanation (*dia tade*) is that these particular varieties of water and fire cannot be contributing causes for the onset of a disease during the transition from one season to another. We can infer that the physical properties implied in 'finest' and 'rarest,'[34] preclude an unduly high intensity in these elemental forms. In many cases, however, the reason for the author's choice of a certain form of fire or water to explain tendencies regarding morbidity or temperament etc. is left to the reader's intuition.

---

34 I mentioned the role played by this quality in exploring (micro)structural features in several theories, e.g., in Diogenes' cosmology and in *Airs, Waters, Places* (*tou hudatos to te leptotaton kai kouphotaton*, Ch. 8). See also Empedocles' earlier references to 'rare' and 'thick' elements (in Theophrastus' summary in *De sensu* I.11), and, in later literature, with Aristotle's use of *leptomeres* in *Gen. corr.* II.2.330a2, in his discussion about the four basic contraries, and with Theophrastus' use of *leptomeresteron* in *De igne* (e.g., 270.29).

ELEMENTS AND THEIR FORMS: THE FORTUNES OF A PRESOCRATIC IDEA 337

How elemental varieties emerge is not spelled out either. 'Rare' (*araion*) or 'fine' (*lepton*) fire and water are probably taken to be the result of physical or (micro)structural modifications. Perhaps the rarest fire (*araiotaton*, Ch. 32, 148.3) consists of particles which are interconnected only very loosely. References to 'portions' or 'parts' of water (*mereōn*, end of Ch. 10; *moiran*, Ch. 7; *merea*, Ch. 25), suggest a corpuscular theory of matter looming in the background of these inferences and demonstrations, and of the accompanying dietetic prescriptions.

There is, finally, a striking asymmetry between the frequency of the comments on those elemental variations as genetic determinants or as key factors in our development, and the absence of any explicit clarification of their status. In Joly's view,[35] the *Regimen's* appeal to forms of fire and water reflects the influence of Anaxagoras' 'everything in everything' principle, since our medical author assumes the presence of the dry in water and of the moist in fire.[36] I cannot detect any plausible evidence, however, that any forms of fire or water are meant to be considered mixtures. Taking into account the context and the terminology used in *Regimen* I, it is more likely that these are intermediaries between plain elementary water and fire and mixtures. Some varieties have distinctive microstructural peculiarities, others—just different degrees of contamination by a quality belonging principally, but not exclusively, to the other element (moist or dry, but never hot or cold). Moist is an essential property of water ('dry water' certainly does not imply the complete absence of moisture) and it can be an accidental property of fire.

The influence of *Regimen* on later philosophical theories was likely significant. In a groundbreaking study on the philosophical legacy of this work, Bartoš[37] argues that "... not only Plato, but also his disciple Aristotle knew *On Regimen* and read it closely" and that "... already in Aristotle's time *On Regimen* stood as a standard point of reference in the discussion of the nature of man."[38] This influence probably extends to Plato's and Aristotle's approaches to (quasi)elemental forms.

---

35   Robert Joly, in collaboration with Simon Byl (ed., trans., comm.), *Hippocrate, Du régime. Corpus Medicorum Graecorum* (Berlin: Akademie Verlag, 1984), 30.

36   Joly, *Hippocrate, Du régime*, 25–34, provides a comprehensive synopsis of possible Presocratic influences on *Regimen*.

37   *Regimen*, 230–91.

38   *Regimen*, 288.

4 Later Treatments Of (Quasi)Elemental Variation

4.1 *Plato on Varieties of Triangles and of Simple Bodies*

Among the inquiries into forms of simple bodies Plato's is certainly the most explicitly and carefully articulated. Since it has also been the most widely discussed, I will only offer a general contour of it, to set the stage for my discussion of Aristotle's approach to this topic. Plato's theory of matter is an atomism of sorts,[39] with a strong Pythagorean flavor; still, his cosmology and, particularly, his conception of (quasi)elemental transformations are profoundly original. After dealing with the nature and interactions of the four simple bodies,[40] whose corresponding 'molecular' shapes are determined in part by two types of right-angled triangles (isosceles in the case of earth; half-equilateral for water, air and fire), Plato argues that the four simple bodies come in numerous varieties. The idea is brought up at 57c-d, but developed in earnest at 58c-61c. The first mention of these *genē* of earth, water etc. alerts us to the difference in size between the triangles constituting the four types of simple bodies: the invisibly small (56b-c) cubes collectively called 'earth', the octahedra we call 'air', the icosahedra that constitute 'water', and the tetrahedra we commonly refer to as 'fire'. There are as many (dimensional) kinds of triangles as there are forms within each of the four main types of simple bodies[41] (*hosaper an ēi tan tois eidesi genē*, 57c).[42] The varieties of earth, fire etc. are endless, because the combinations of triangles of different sizes among themselves and with each other are infinite.

The elements are the triangles, more exactly those half-equilateral and isosceles right-angled ones that are not analyzable into smaller triangles. This, then, cannot also be said about the four primary bodies, but there is a partial correspondence between variations in size of the two types of triangles

---

39   The last few decades have seen the publication of several comprehensive studies and running commentaries, including: Luc Brisson, *Le même et l'autre dans la structure ontologique du* Timée *de Platon* (Paris: Éditions Klincksieck, 1974); Thomas K. Johansen, *Plato's Natural Philosophy. A Study of the* Timaeus-Critias (Cambridge: Cambridge University Press, 2004); Sarah Broadie, *Nature and Divinity in Plato's* Timaeus (Cambridge: Cambridge University Press, 2012).

40   On Plato's debt to Empedocles, with respect to his selection of the four simple bodies, see e.g. section VI of Crowley's chapter in this volume.

41   Perhaps the implication is that the larger triangles are analyzable into smaller ones, as Cornford demonstrates persuasively: Francis M. Cornford, *Plato's Cosmology* (London and Henley: Routledge & Kegan Paul, 1937, reprinted 1977), 232–38.

42   *Eidē* are divided into *genē* here, but the two terms are used interchangeably in most of this section of the *Timaeus* on (quasi)elemental varieties.

and the variations of the simple bodies (for example, the cubes that make up 'earth' coming themselves in many sizes). This dissimilarity, caused both by the sizes of atomic or composite triangles and by admixtures in different proportions (e.g. water containing traces of fire), is intended to fulfill several functions. Most generally, it helps Plato to bolster his view that the world is a plenum (the smallest interstices being filled by the smallest bodies) and to make the transition from a theoretical exposition of the nature of the simplest bodies to the actual diversity revealed by an empirical approach to the stuffs that make up the physical world. The four generic types of polyhedra corresponding to earth, water, air and fire are not considered by Plato sufficient to explain the virtually infinite (57d) variety of compounds with their specific qualities, unless we also grant the existence of endless forms for the four simple bodies.

The study of the material properties continues at 61c-68d, where varieties of simple stuffs are occasionally mentioned, as e.g. at 66d (*ta gēs hudatos te genē*), and where Plato is concerned mainly with perceptible qualities; earlier, at 58c-61c, his focus was on what Aristotle will call "more proper (or: inherent) qualities,"[43] like being liquefiable or solidifiable. Some perceptible properties, such as heat (61e-62a), are explained by the shapes of the basic bodies (the pyramids or tetrahedra which constitute fire are pointy, can penetrate more easily and so must be responsible for our sensation of hot) and by the way in which they are organized in compounds (smoothness is caused by uniformity and density, 63e-64a).[44] Plato may well have taken a page from the natural philosophy of the earliest atomists here, major differences notwithstanding.

The causal connection between physical makeup and dispositions does not stop there in the *Timaeus*. Plato's comments on the etiology of diseases repeatedly muster his earlier claims about elemental triangles and about primary stuffs—and their variations. In good Greek medical tradition, going back to Alcmaeon, equilibrium is the name of the game. If one of the four primary bodies figures disproportionately in the composition of a body, Plato contends, the outcome will be some sort of disease with its specific set of symptoms (excess of fire will lead to persistent fever etc., 86a). Agitation in a body's composition and structure, resembling the disorderly movement in the Receptacle, prevents the organism from reaching a stable balance and leads to a sort of elemental civil war. The nature of the triangles themselves is decisive too, in so far as it is a determining, though not unique, factor for our life

---

43   *Oikeioterois pathesin, Mete.* IV.8.385a5.

44   See also his comments on being soluble by water or fire and on the liquefiability of various forms of earth (*gēs eidē*) at 60d-e.

span (89bc). In this context, varieties of the four primary stuffs are invested with special significance. The fundamental mechanism underlying a disease is, again, some sort of imbalance and conflict in our physical constitution; this condition, however, can be exacerbated by lack of 'chemical' uniformity, i.e., by conglomerations of distinct varieties of earth, water etc. Good health, on the other hand, is dependent on the sort of triangles involved in certain physiological processes that cause growth (*auxēsis*, 82d), namely, the triangles that are necessary ingredients in the smoothest and oiliest organic stuffs that can penetrate the dense texture of the bones and nourish the marrow. In sum, the causal connection between compositional and structural peculiarities, on the one hand, and material dispositions (hot, hard) as well as higher order capacities (robustness, being prone to fall ill under certain conditions, etc.) is one of the main functions of (quasi)elemental varieties in Plato. It is in fact a methodological feature shared with other thinkers, including Diogenes and the author of *Regimen*, as well as Aristotle.

4.2   *Aristotle on Forms of Earth and of Water*

Aristotle's theory of (quasi)elemental transformation, his conception of uniform mixture, and his sophisticated treatment of material capacities mark some of the major differences between his theory of matter and those of earlier authors. Yet, for all his radical innovations and despite his virulent rejection of Plato's geometric atomism, he speaks quite liberally of forms of earth and of water. His former mentor's use of the expressions "forms of water" and "forms of earth," especially in *Timaeus* at 58c–61c, must have influenced Aristotle's terminology in *Mete.* IV; the more distant antecedents of this notion, as mobilized in *Mete.* IV, however, should probably be sought in late Presocratic and early medical theories, even if he offers no explicit acknowledgement.

As with Plato, for Aristotle earth, water, air and fire[45] are not truly elements (a title that goes to the four basic contraries—hot, cold, moist and dry); rather, they are the simplest stuffs or bodies in the sublunary realm.[46] The forms (*eidē*) of earth and water function in Aristotle as a hinge between (1) the elements

---

45   Crowley's chapter "Aristotle, Empedocles, and the Four Elements Hypothesis" (included in this volume), takes a fresh look at Aristotle's view of the merits and limitations of Empedocles' theory of matter, including the nature of the four elementary stuffs.

46   His theory of the elements and of the four quasi-elementary stuffs is less straightforward than it is generally taken to be. On some of the problems involved in Aristotle's view of these concepts, see Tiberiu Popa, "Aristotle on Pure and Simple Stuff," *Rhizai, Journal for Ancient Philosophy and Science* VII (2010): 29–61.

ELEMENTS AND THEIR FORMS: THE FORTUNES OF A PRESOCRATIC IDEA   341

and the simple bodies considered abstractly, and (2) the more applied study of the constitution and properties of the homoeomers in *Mete.* IV 1–11,[47] a study that forms the scientific foundation for several key aspects of his biological studies.[48] Here are a few examples from *Mete.* IV:

a.   Water and forms of water (*hudōr kai hudatos eidē*) are dried, as are things that possess water whether extraneous or innate (…). The following are forms of water (*hudatos d'eidē*): wine, urine, whey, and in general things that have no sediment or little sediment without viscosity. (5.382b10-16)[49]

b.   … [E]arthenware and certain kinds of stones that come to be when earth is burned by fire, such as millstones, are insoluble, whereas soda and salt are soluble by moisture—not by all, but by cold. Hence, they are melted by water and by forms of water (*hudati kai hosa hudatos eidē*), but they are not melted by olive oil. (6.383b11-15)

c.   Since the nonuniform bodies are constituted by another cause, whereas the matter from which these are constituted is the dry and moist, and therefore water and earth (for each of these has the very conspicuous potency of one or the other of those), while the productive potencies are heat and cold (for heat and cold constitute and solidify bodies from the dry and moist), let us grasp which sorts of uniform bodies are forms of earth, which of water, and which are compounds (*poia gēs eidē kai poia hudatos kai poia koina*).[50] (10.388a20-26)

In *Mete.* IV 'water' tends to be used interchangeably with 'moist,' and 'earth' with 'dry' for the reason he conveys in this very passage from Ch. 10. As the discussion in the fourth book revolves around the composition and the defining capacities of organic and inorganic uniform materials, earth and water are expectedly the protagonists. *Most* uniform stuffs—from copper to bone and from milk to wood—are compounds, uniform mixtures of earth and water

---

47   The somewhat ambiguous status of the homoeomers is discussed, among the more recent studies on Aristotle's theory of matter, in Marwan Rashed (ed. trans. comm.), *Aristote: De la Génération et la Corruption* (Paris: Les Belles Lettres, 2005), especially cxxvi ff.

48   See especially *Part. an* II and *Gen. an.* II and V.

49   These passages are translated by Mary Louise Gill, James Lennox and myself.

50   The distinction between the roles played by two basic active potencies (the hot and the cold) and by the passive ones (the moist and the dry) is made explicitly at the very beginning of *Mete.* IV (378b10-14) and is central to much of that treatise. On this topic, see Tiberiu Popa, "Aristotle on the Powers of Thermic Equilibrium," in *Heat, Pneuma and Soul in Ancient Philosophy and Science*, edited by Hynek Bartoš and Colin Guthrie King (Cambridge: Cambridge University Press, 2020), 202–216.

(occasionally of air,[51] possibly of fire as well),[52] present potentially in different proportions and having undergone various agencies (*ergasiai*) of the active properties, hot and cold.[53] However, not all homoeomers are taken to be compounds. Some forms of earth and water can indeed be mixtures in which one ingredient is vastly predominant, but at least in some instances Aristotle clearly speaks of uniform stuffs made of only one element, as in Ch. 10 (388b12-24),[54] where he distinguishes solids composed only of earth both from solids that contain only water (e.g., ice) and from solids which are largely earthy but from which moisture has not evaporated completely.[55]

I cannot embark here on an excursus about the possible difficulties confronting Aristotle, whose references to pure stuffs may run afoul of his claims elsewhere that the four simple bodies in the sublunary realm are always mixed.[56] I would like to consider another problem, instead: what could account, in Aristotle's view, for the fact that different materials can be forms of the same simple stuff, e.g. earth, while being characterized by distinct

---

51   Air is mentioned sometimes as an ingredient (existing *dunamei*, we should assume) in oil or wood, as at 7.383b25, 7.384b16-18.

52   No distinction between forms of air or of fire, however, is made in *Mete.* IV, but the first three books of *Mete.* distinguish between two forms of exhalations or *anathumiaseis*, one of which is said to be fiery. They have a rather unclear status in the larger context of Aristotle's discussion of elements, quasi-elements and homoeomers. Olympiodorus' comments on the exhalations are useful, even if not fully convincing; see, e.g., 16.15–22 in Christina Viano, *La matière des choses. Le livre IV des* Météorologiques *d'Aristote et son interprétation par Olympiodore* (Paris: J. Vrin, 2006). On the nature of the exhalations, see also Popa, "Aristotle on Pure and Simple Stuff."

53   See especially *Mete.* IV.1–3.

54   Additionally, in Ch. 5 of *Mete.* IV (5.382b13-15) we are told that forms of water contain little or no sediment (*hupostasin*); in Ch. 6, watery stuffs (*hosa ... hudatos*, 6.383a7) are distinguished from compounds of water and earth (*hosa de koina gēs kai hudatos*, 6.383a14). This probably indicates that the watery stuffs discussed there contain either no earth or only an extremely small proportion of earth, whereas in compounds of earth and water, there is a more significant amount of earth even in liquids like new wine. Other Aristotelian works too suggest that not all homoeomers are mixtures; in *Part. an.*, for example, we read at 11.2.649a30-31: "... [C]old solidifies those things composed of water alone (*hosa ... hudatos monon*), whereas fire solidifies those things composed of earth (*hosa de gēs*)." In any case, Aristotle never completely dispels the ambivalence of the expressions 'forms of water' and 'forms of earth' in *Mete.* IV, expressions covering somewhat confusedly the category of pure stuffs (forms of unmixed earth and of unmixed water) as well as that of mixtures in which one ingredient is overwhelmingly predominant.

55   Rather than using *eidē* (*hudatos, gēs*), Aristotle prefers here to use the adjective *elikrinēs* (pure), and *hosa* ("as many as") followed by the genitive *gēs*, the latter formulation (*hosa gēs, hosa hudatos*) is found in much of Book IV.

56   On this topic, see Popa "Aristotle on Pure and Simple Stuff."

ELEMENTS AND THEIR FORMS: THE FORTUNES OF A PRESOCRATIC IDEA   343

dispositional differentiae? Aristotle is silent on this, but part of the answer can be found perhaps in the positions of those forms along the dry-moist and hot-cold continua. That is to say, salt, baked clay, amber etc. are *eidē gēs* in the sense that they are all clustered closer to the cold and dry extremes than to the hot and moist extremes, but likely at 'coordinates' that do not coincide with those of (theoretical) pure and simple earth. Besides, what Aristotle says about the physical structure of the forms of earth seems to offer a few useful hints. Mainly but not only in Ch. 9 of *Mete.* IV, the explanations of the behavior of uniform stuffs is centered on *poroi*[57] or invisible channels that pervade solid bodies. The microstructure[58] of a solid uniform body is responsible for some of its dispositional properties and can be revealed by those dispositions.[59] Soda, for example, is shot through with *poroi* (9.385b23)—in a way in which earthenware is not; as a consequence, soda is easily soluble in water. This physical organization of earthy solids could explain, therefore (together with the position of the forms of earth along the dry-moist and hot-cold continua), why different forms of earth such as clay, soda and salt, while consisting of only one simple body, can nonetheless exhibit strikingly different qualities.

---

57   Among the more helpful recent studies on the place of the *poroi* in Aristotle's inquiry into the nature of the homeomers, see Eric Lewis, trans., notes. *Alexander of Aphrodisias—On Aristotle's* Meteorology *4* (Ithaca, NY: Cornell University Press, 1996), 3–9; Luigi Pepe, "Motivi centrali del IV libro dei *Meteorologica*," in *Aristoteles Chemicus,* edited by Cristina Viano (Sankt Augustin: Academia Verlag, 2002), 31–33; Viano, *La matière des choses,* 71–72.

58   Foreshadowing Theophrastus (on whom—see below), Aristotle occasionally seems inclined to give corpuscularian accounts, despite his commitment to continua and cognate concepts. He speaks, quite remarkably, of *ogkoi* of water, which may be *theoretically* infinitely divisible but not physically, and thus cannot enter the minuscule openings in certain types of solid uniform bodies, such as earthenware (8.385a30; 9.385b20). Williams and Chalmers address from different angles the corpuscularian or granular aspect of Aristotle's theory of matter: C.J.F. Williams, trans. comm. *Aristotle's* De Generatione et Corruptione (Oxford: Oxford University Press, 1982), 13, 28, 65–68; Alan Chalmers, *The Scientist's Atom and the Philosopher's Stone. How Science Succeeded and Philosophy Failed to Gain Knowledge of Atoms* (Dordrecht, Heidelberg, London, New York: Springer, 2009), 65–69. Density too plays an important role in some of Aristotle's scientific theories, not only because thickening is crucial to explaining the main types of concoction or *pepsis* (*Mete.* IV.3), but also because it can help us to differentiate among uniform stuffs and to establish what causes their capacities. Theophratsus' *De igne* offers a number of parallels to *Mete.* IV with respect to the presumed revelatory role of density.

59   On the nature of Aristotle's inferences from the expected behavior of uniform materials to their constitution (and on the relevance of those inferences to his philosophy of science), see Tiberiu Popa, "Scientific Method in Aristotle's *Meteorology* IV," *History of Philosophy of Science* 4, no. 2 (2014a): 306–34.

As far as the theoretical *functions* of this notion of *eidē gēs/hudatos* are concerned, the distinction between forms of water and of earth is instrumental (a) in demarcating types of homeomers,[60] and (b) in properly explaining the emergence of dispositional qualities.[61] Microstructural characteristics (*poroi* of a certain diameter—allowing water or only fire in etc., distributed uniformly or by fascicles, arranged lengthwise or in some other manner),[62] along with a particular 'chemical' composition (e.g., predominance or exclusivity of earth), explain some of the more proper or intrinsic (*oikeioterois, Mete.* IV.8.385a5) dispositions explored in Book IV: fragility, flammability, etc. As in Diogenes, in *Regimen* and in Plato's *Timaeus*, more basic properties underlie higher order dispositions. In the context of *Mete.* IV.1–11 alone this means that, say, the hardness necessary for the presence of certain types of *poroi* or the ratio between water and earth necessary for the formation of concatenations (*haluseis,* 9.387a11-15) in viscous liquids under certain thermic conditions are more fundamental properties on which other properties (solubility, fragility, viscosity, etc.) depend. This being said, as *Mete.* IV.12 reminds us,[63] Aristotle's '(bio)chemistry' is a worthwhile enterprise not just in its own right but also, and eminently, in virtue of its relevance to his biology.[64] The tight connection between these two new scientific domains is revealed, among other things, by the causal-explanatory relation between the basic material qualities (fluid, solidifiable by cold, etc.) of the organic uniform stuffs, and a higher order of dispositions (timid, prone to outbursts of rage, intelligent, etc.).[65] In this regard, as well as in its appeal to structural characteristics, Aristotle's systematic distinction between forms of simple bodies recalls earlier efforts to explain the enormous range of properties in the physical world and to account for the emergence of more complex capacities.

---

60 See the section on *diairesis* in Tiberiu Popa, "Scientific Method in Aristotle's *Meteorology* IV."

61 The most helpful study on this topic is James G. Lennox, "Aristotle on the Emergence of Material Complexity: *Meteorology* IV and Aristotle's Biology," *History of Philosophy of Science* 4, no. 2 (2014): 272–305.

62 See especially in Chs. 8 and 9 of *Mete.* IV.

63 See Mary Louise Gill, "The Limits of Teleology in Aristotle's *Mete.* IV.2," *History of Philosophy of Science* 4, no. 2 (2014): 335–50 for an important reassessment of *Mete.* IV.12.

64 The extent to which Aristotle's biological corpus is indebted to his 'chemistry' is the main object of the investigation in Lennox, "Aristotle on the Emergence of Material Complexity."

65 *Part. an.* II.4 is perhaps the most celebrated illustration of such causal links in Aristotle, who claims that the material dispositions of blood are responsible for cognitive and temperamental dispositions.

ELEMENTS AND THEIR FORMS: THE FORTUNES OF A PRESOCRATIC IDEA 345

4.3 *Fiery Disposition*

There is a curious sequel to Aristotle's story in Theophrastus. If Aristotle finds it unnecessary or maybe theoretically inconvenient to mark out different kinds of fire, his close collaborator devotes much of his *On Fire* to exactly this task.[66] Fire is unlike earth, water and air because its (self)generation depends on a suitable substratum that serves as fuel. Being less autonomous, it seems not to be considered an element or a simple body proper. Theophrastus is not consistent on this point, however, and his overall position, for all his detailed descriptions and causal accounts, is hard to capture. In Ch. 6 of his treatise, for example, fire is regarded as different from heat, whereas elsewhere, e.g., in Chs 36–44, 'fire' and 'heat' are mentioned alternatively as if they were synonymous.[67] If Theophrastus' 'metaphysics' of fire is intractably opaque, his inquiry into the typology of this substance and its workings is clearer and occasionally fascinating.

His discussion is not just about fire pure and simple and about its interactions with other stuffs, but also and mainly about the many forms that fire assumes. In Ch. 4 he distinguishes between several types of fire (*pleious*) reducible to two basic categories: fire as we know it from experience (it originates in a substratum etc.), and a hypothetical fire understood as a first body and a sort of principle (*prōton ... kai hoion archēn*).[68] If the latter is a real aspect of the cosmos, although this cannot be ascertained, it must be basically unmixed and pure heat (*amikton thermotēta kai katharan*), in contradistinction to fire or flame in the sphere of the earth, which is mixed, *memeigmenē*, and always in the process of becoming. Theophrastus adds in the next segment (Ch. 5) that, if the sun is a type of fire (*puros tis idea*),[69] we should assume that it is significantly different from the sort of fire with which we are familiar.

---

66 The extent to which Theophrastus followed or departed from Aristotle's view of the nature of fire has been discussed in Victor Coutant, (trans. comm.) *Theophrastus, De igne. A Post-Aristotelian View of the Nature of Fire* (Assen: Royal Vangorcum, 1971), xvii-xx; István M. Bodnár, "Theophrastus' *De igne*: Orthodoxy, Reform and Readjustment in the Doctrine of Elements," in *On the Opuscula of Theophrastus*, edited by William W. Fortenbaugh and Georg Wöhrle (Stuttgart: Franz Steiner Verlag, 2002), 75–90; A.M. Battegazzore, *Teofrasto—Il Fuoco* (Sassari: Edizioni Gallizzi, 2006), 67, 124–25 and 171–72; Marlein Van Raalte, "The Nature of Fire and Its Complications: Theophrastus' *De Igne* 1–10," *Bulletin of the Institute of Classical Studies* 53 (2010): 47–97.

67 The relation between fire and smoke is equally ambiguous; see Coutant, *Theophrastus*, xx; cf. *On Fire* 7.

68 Among the more recent studies on that hypothetical fire, see van Raalte, "The Nature of Fire and Its Complications."

69 Its heat is mixed with air, we read in Ch. 44, and is characterized by gentleness and fineness (*malakotēti kai leptotēti*), while the heat of fire is hard and burning (*sklēra kai perikaēs*).

His emphasis in *On Fire*, however, is decidedly on the forms of fire accessible to our experience. Ch. 9 underlines the most characteristic properties (*idiaitatas dunameis*) and the multiform nature (*polueides*) of fire; no other simple body is so polymorphic or so irregular in its capacities (*outh' houtō polueides out' anōmalon tais dunamesin*), so diverse in its own nature (*autēi tēi phusei diaphoron*), and so pervasive. The many varieties of fire are marked out by several sets of complementary criteria:[70] (a) the natural and artificial modes in which they are produced (by striking, rubbing, compressing), (b) the substratum or fuel involved, (c) the medium (according to Ch. 40, the difference (*diaphora*) between kinds of fire and heat can be determined by the dry or moist substance in which it occurs) and (d) the resulting structural characteristics and corresponding *dunameis* or dispositional properties (e.g. penetrating or destructive forces).

Theophrastus shares with the other authors I have discussed in this chapter a strong interest in the (micro)structures that underlie such properties, in the related notion of density and in its correlation with force. Ch. 12 (cf. Ch. 34) calls our attention to the proportion—expressed, expectedly, in non-mathematical terms—between intensity (e.g. of the light of a lantern) and degrees of concentration. Charcoal is earthy and dense, hence the fire fueled by it will be compact and will generate very intense heat (Ch. 36). Reeds produce a fire that is fine (because they are light) and compact (because they are continuous). The sun can set things alight (Ch. 73) because of the fine particles constituting it (*leptomereia*) and because it is more continuous (*suneches … mallon*) than fire as we know it; the sun's fire possesses a higher penetrating power owing to its compactness or concentration and fineness (*tōi athroismōi kai tēi leptotēti*).

Thus, even more than Aristotle in *Mete.* IV, Theophrastus tends to utilize a handful of concepts which are at least compatible with, if not expressions of, a corpuscularian theory of matter, although one that is not fully elaborated or unified. Particles of water can be too large (*megalomeres*) to penetrate certain *poroi* (Ch. 42),[71] which is why moist heat fails to melt things; or, according to Ch. 45, this inability of heat is due to the fact that water particles are both too soft and too large (*dia tēn malakotēta kai megalomereian*). On the contrary, the stone from which quicklime is produced can dissolve into fine particles (*eis lepta*), as the heat consisting itself of fine particles can be dispersed into small portions (*eis de mikra to leptomeresteron*), due to its capacity to penetrate other bodies thoroughly. At the same time, a fire whose texture is of this nature

---

70   See also Ch. 57: *diaphorai de ginontai pleious tou puros.*

71   *On Fire* may betray the influence of Aristotle's *Mete.* IV in this regard. This mechanism was also described by Plato in the *Timaeus* (60d-e).

ELEMENTS AND THEIR FORMS: THE FORTUNES OF A PRESOCRATIC IDEA 347

(see Ch. 65, *mikromerēs agan*) can be weak (*asthenes*) and easy to extinguish. We can see, then, that varieties of fire are explained not only by appeal to the processes of mixing (as e.g. in Ch. 43 and in the earlier sections dealing with various sorts of fuels), but also by elucidating the structural basis of the dispositional qualities of fire and heat (penetrating power, weak force, (in)ability to melt etc.), a method that is also central to the other theories explored here.

5   Conclusion

It has become clear by now, I hope, that what is shared by these various authors, from Diogenes of Apollonia to Theophrastus, is not merely the idea that simple stuffs—whether elementary or analyzable into elements—can have many forms, distinguishable by qualitative differentiae, which are often taken to be the result of structural peculiarities. Those elementary and quasi-elementary simple bodies also fulfill comparable *functions*, chiefly that of causal factors explaining[72] (1) the capacities of the stuffs which furnish the universe and (2) the nature of our physical, mental, and temperamental dispositions. I have avoided, however, offering an account that is unduly unifying, given the considerable differences between these authors' doctrinal backgrounds and their stated or, more often, implicit goals. One of the most challenging aspects in the philosophical treatments of this notion, incidentally, is the lack of *explicit* theoretical elaboration in the relevant texts, with the exception of Plato's *Timaeus*, and so grasping those implicit goals has been one of my main objectives here.

I have also tried to be conservative in marking possible and probable influences, which, as I suggested before, can be direct (acquaintance with original texts), indirect (access to doxographic works) or quite diffuse—in so far as this conceptual and methodological continuity may well have been based in part on a sort of intellectual common currency. I have not ventured to identify the origins of this idea. It can be argued perhaps that a rudimentary version of it can be traced back to Anaximenes. What I believe is safe to claim, however, is that already during the second half of the fifth century BCE elemental varieties were regarded as a key explanatory device. They were enlisted in order to argue coherently from material monism (in the case of Diogenes' *aēr*) and from material dualism, so to speak (water and fire in *Regimen* I), to the emergence of a world order whose parts can display exceedingly different properties. It

---

72   I should add: together with other explanatory factors, such as *mixtures* of elements, of forms of simple bodies, and of compounds. In fact, as we have seen, forms of earth, etc. can sometimes refer to mixtures as well.

was almost a matter of theoretical necessity for Diogenes, for whom qualitative distinctions, resulting from structural changes and fluctuations in density, mark the transition from pre-cosmic and undifferentiated air to the world as we know it. It was a matter of theoretical convenience for the author of *Regimen*; in principle, he could have relied strictly on mixtures of water and fire in various proportions to explain the wide range of qualities recognizable in the *kosmos*. Instead, he opted also for forms of water and fire to articulate a more refined ontology, which he found more congenial to explaining the complexities of human nature and, in final analysis, to advocating his brand of dietetics.

For Plato, the forms and kinds (*eidē, genē*) of fire, air, water and earth are an effective instrument in proving that the world is a plenum, in articulating his view of the transformation of the four primary stuffs, and in his etiology of diseases. He spoke of varieties both of (elementary and composite) triangles and of polyhedra corresponding to the simple bodies, and assigned them a transitional role; as Zeyl[73] puts it, his account "(...) provides the link between the four primary bodies so far abstractly discussed, and the stuffs that make up the mid-sized objects of our everyday experience." For Aristotle, the forms of earth and water play an important part in his '(bio)chemistry', that is, in the division of homoeomers (not all of them mixtures) into overlapping kinds and in the inference of the composition of uniform materials from their expected behavior or dispositional differentiae. While Aristotle did not discuss forms of fire, Theophrastus readily assumed this task; varieties of fire are essential to his discussion about the capacities of this subtle stuff whose status remains rather equivocal in *On Fire*.

Whatever its precise historical trajectory, this concept, in its different guises, has its roots in early Greek philosophy. Its impact was profound and enduring and its place in several seminal theories of matter deserves our renewed attention and scrutiny. After all, the claims and the arguments that express conceptions of elementary stuffs are often the nexus between cosmologies and ontological theories, and, therefore, can offer an especially profitable angle for the study of several ancient philosophical doctrines.

Bibliography

Bartoš, Hynek. 2015. *Philosophy and Dietetics in the Hippocratic* On Regimen. Leiden: Brill.

---

73   Donald J. Zeyl, *Plato*: Timaeus (Indianapolis, Cambridge: Hackett, 2000), lxxii.

ELEMENTS AND THEIR FORMS: THE FORTUNES OF A PRESOCRATIC IDEA   349

Bartoš, Hynek and King, Colin Guthrie. ed. 2020. *Heat, Pneuma and Soul in Ancient Philosophy and Science*. Cambridge: Cambridge University Press.

Battegazzore, A.M. 2006. *Teofrasto—Il Fuoco*. Sassari: Edizioni Gallizzi.

Bodnár, István M. 2002. "Theophrastus' *De igne*: Orthodoxy, Reform and Readjustment in the Doctrine of Elements," in *On the* Opuscula *of Theophrastus*, edited by William W. Fortenbaugh and Georg Wöhrle, 75–90. Stuttgart: Franz Steiner Verlag.

Brisson, Luc. 1974. *Le même et l'autre dans la structure ontologique du* Timée *de Platon*. Paris: Éditions Klincksieck.

Broadie, Sarah. 2012. *Nature and Divinity in Plato's* Timaeus. Cambridge: Cambridge University Press.

Chalmers, Alan. 2009. *The Scientist's Atom and the Philosopher's Stone. How Science Succeeded and Philosophy Failed to Gain Knowledge of Atoms*. Dordrecht, Heidelberg, London, New York: Springer.

Cornford, Francis M. 1937 (reprinted 1977). *Plato's Cosmology*. London and Henley: Routledge & Kegan Paul.

Coutant, Victor. (trans. comm.) 1971. *Theophrastus, De igne. A Post-Aristotelian View of the Nature of Fire*. Assen: Royal Vangorcum.

Curd, Patricia and Graham Daniel W. 2008. *The Oxford Handbook of Presocratic Philosophy*. Oxford, New York: Oxford University Press.

Enache, Catalin. 2011. "*The Typology of Human Constitutions in Hippocrates'* De victu 1, 32." *Wiener Studien* 124: 39–54.

Gill, Mary Louise. 2014. "The Limits of Teleology in Aristotle's *Meteorology* IV.2." *History of Philosophy of Science* 4, 2: 335–50.

Graham, Daniel W. *Explaining the Cosmos*. 2006. *The Ionian Tradition of Scientific Philosophy*. Princeton and Oxford: Princeton University Press.

Graham, Daniel W. *The Texts of Early Greek Philosophers*. 2010. *The Complete Fragments and Selected Testimonies of the Major Presocratics*. Cambridge: Cambridge University Press.

Johansen, Thomas K. 2004. *Plato's Natural Philosophy. A Study of the* Timaeus-Critias. Cambridge: Cambridge University Press.

Joly, Robert, in collaboration with Byl, Simon (ed., trans., comm.). 1984. *Hippocrate, Du régime*. *Corpus Medicorum Graecorum*. Berlin: Akademie Verlag.

Jones, W.H.S. (trans. notes) 1957. *Hippocrates*, vol. I. Cambridge, MA, London: Harvard University Press.

Jones, W.H.S. (trans. notes) 1959. *Hippocrates*, vol. II. Cambridge, MA, London: Harvard University Press.

Jouanna, Jacques. 2001. *Hippocrates*. Translated by M.B. DeBevoise. Baltimore and London: Johns Hopkins University Press.

Laks, André. 1983. *Diogène d'Apollonie. La dernière cosmologie présocratique.* Lille: Presses Universitaires de Lille.

Laks, André. 2008a. *Diogène d'Apollonie*, 2nd edition (International Pre-Platonic Studies, Vol. 6). Sankt Augustin: Academia Verlag.

Laks, André. 2008b. "Speculating about Diogenes of Apollonia," in Patricia Curd and Daniel W. Graham, *The Oxford Handbook of Presocratic Philosophy*, 353–364. Oxford, New York: Oxford University Press.

Laks, André and Most, Glenn W. 2016. *Early Greek Philosophy*, vol. II, part 1 and vol. VI, part 1, Cambridge, MA and London: Harvard University Press.

Lennox, James G. trans. comm. 2001. *Aristotle—On the Parts of Animals.* Oxford: Oxford University Press.

Lennox, James G. 2014. "Aristotle on the Emergence of Material Complexity: *Meteorology* IV and Aristotle's Biology." *History of Philosophy of Science* 4, 2: 272–305.

Lewis, Eric. trans., notes. 1996. *Alexander of Aphrodisias—On Aristotle's* Meteorology 4. Ithaca, NY: Cornell University Press.

Lloyd, G.E.R. 1964. "The Hot and the Cold, the Dry and the Wet in Greek Philosophy." *The Journal of Hellenic Studies* 84: 92–106.

Longrigg, James. 1985. "Elements and After: A Study in Presocratic Physics of the Second Half of the Fifth Century." *Apeiron* 19, 2: 93–115.

McKirahan, Richard D. 2010. *Philosophy Before Socrates. An Introduction with Texts and Commentary.* 2nd edition. Indianapolis and Cambridge: Hackett.

Miller, H.W. 1959. "The Concept of *Dynamis* in *De victu.*" *Transactions and Proceedings of the American Philological Association* 90: 147–64.

Pepe, Luigi. 2002. "Motivi centrali del IV libro dei *Meteorologica*," in *Aristoteles Chemicus,* edited by Cristina Viano, 17–34. Sankt Augustin: Academia Verlag.

Popa, Tiberiu. 2010. "Aristotle on Pure and Simple Stuff." *Rhizai, Journal for Ancient Philosophy and Science* VII: 29–61.

Popa, Tiberiu. 2014a. "Scientific Method in Aristotle's *Meteorology* IV." *History of Philosophy of Science* 4, 2: 306–34.

Popa, Tiberiu. 2014b. "Observing the Invisible: *Regimen* I on Elemental Powers and Higher Order Dispositions." *The British Journal for the History of Philosophy* 22, 5: 888–907.

Popa, Tiberiu. 2020. "Aristotle on the Powers of Thermic Equilibrium," in *Heat, Pneuma and Soul in Ancient Philosophy and Science*, edited by Hynek Bartoš and Colin Guthrie King, 202–216. Cambridge: Cambridge University Press.

Rashed, Marwan (ed. trans. comm.). 2005. *Aristote: De la Génération et la Corruption.* Paris: Les Belles Lettres.

Van Raalte, Marlein. 2010. "The Nature of Fire and Its Complications: Theophrastus' *De Igne* 1–10." *Bulletin of the Institute of Classical Studies* 53: 47–97.

Viano, Cristina. ed. 2002. *Aristoteles Chemicus*. Sankt Augustin: Academia Verlag.

Viano, Cristina. 2006. *La matière des choses. Le livre IV des* Météorologiques *d'Aristote et son interprétation par Olympiodore*. Paris: J. Vrin.

Williams, C.J.F. trans. comm. 1982. *Aristotle's* De Generatione et Corruptione. Oxford: Oxford University Press.

Zeyl, Donald J. 2000. *Plato*: Timaeus. Indianapolis, Cambridge: Hackett.

CHAPTER 11

Aristotle, Empedocles, and the Reception of the Four Elements Hypothesis

Timothy J. Crowley

The claim that seems first to have been put forward by Empedocles of Acragas, that there are four elements, of which all sensible things are made, and that these are fire, air, water, and earth, was an extraordinarily resilient one. A history of its reception would be a history dealing with over two thousand years of natural philosophy, if it began with Empedocles himself in the 5th century BC, and finished, say, in the 17th century, with the Irish scientist Robert Boyle's broadside against the four elements theory, and contemporary element theory in general, in his *Sceptical Chymist* (1661).[1] An adequate history might be expected to begin even earlier, and end later,[2] much later, indeed, if one includes in the history the somewhat related career of the four humours.[3]

Fortunately, that is not the task I set for myself here. My aim is much more limited. I am going to consider, rather, nothing beyond approximately the first century of the reception of the four elements hypothesis. To be more specific, I will be looking at its reception, or what seems to me to be some of the significant aspects of its reception, in the work of Aristotle. In particular, I want to try to see how much we can discover about the reception, and contemporary status, of the four elements hypothesis from an examination of Aristotle's

---

1 *The Sceptical Chymist* (London, 1661), in T. Birch (ed.), *The Works of the Honourable Robert Boyle, vol. 1* (London, 1772). On Boyle, see, for instance, Chalmers 2016, and Clericuzio 2000, 103-148.

2 See Guthrie 1965, 141-3. Guthrie finds evidence of advocacy of the four elements hypothesis in the late 18th c. (143, n. 1); Jane Marcet's *Conversations on Chemistry* indicates that the hypothesis continued to be generally accepted well into the 19th c.; see Rossotti 2006, 4, n. 1.

3 For Wright 1981, 26-7, the theory of four humours is an adaptation of Empedocles' theory of elements; see also Nutton 2004, 81. But while the four humours may seem obviously related to the four elements, this appears not to be the case initially, in Polybus' *Nature of Man*, where the four humours first appear (Hipp. *Nat. Hom.* 4.1). Not until Galen, indeed, is there an explicit correspondence between the four elements and the four humours; see Jouanna 2012a, 339. For some idea of the hold that humoral medicine had on Western medical practice even into the 19th c., and humoral psychology beyond that, see Arikha 2007. The influence of the four humours is in fact still today apparent in South Asia, in Unani medicine ('Unani' being Arabic for 'Ionian'); see Bala 2007, 64.

© KONINKLIJKE BRILL NV, LEIDEN, 2021 | DOI:10.1163/9789004443358_013

ARISTOTLE, EMPEDOCLES, AND THE FOUR ELEMENTS

remark at *Metaphysics* Alpha, that Empedocles "was the first to speak of the four so-called elements of the material kind" (1.4, 985a32). It seems to me to be important, in any attempt to assess the early reception of Empedocles' elements, to try to grasp the significance of what Aristotle is saying here. That, in any case, is what I shall try to do in what follows.

1

Let's begin, then, by attempting to get clear about the sort of originality that Aristotle intends to attribute to Empedocles, when he says that Empedocles "was the first to speak of the four so-called elements (τὰ λεγόμενα στοιχεῖα) of the material kind". In the very next line he identifies these four as fire, air, water, and earth (1.4, 985b1-2). So, it seems, we have it on Aristotle's authority that Empedocles identified fire, air, water, and earth as the στοιχεῖα, the elements, or principles, and, moreover, that he was the first to do so.[4]

Perhaps the first thing to do is to point out that Aristotle is not crediting Empedocles with terminological novelty. Empedocles did not call fire, air, water, and earth στοιχεῖα. The use of the term στοιχεῖον in the sense of 'element' or 'principle of nature' is generally accepted to be a later innovation.[5] Now this is well known, and is not typically deemed to be of great significance, or in any way an impediment to understanding Empedocles. Indeed, that Empedocles did not use the term seems often to be treated as a mere historical accident, as if, incidentally, the word στοιχεῖον, in the appropriate sense, wasn't yet available to Empedocles; as if, had the word been available to him, he would have used it, to refer to fire, air, water, and earth. In other words, there appears often to be an assumption that Empedocles set out a theory of four elements, and simply used a different term for 'elements'—namely, 'roots', ῥιζώματα (DK31B6).[6] Thus Ross writes, "Empedocles' own word for elements was ῥιζώματα".[7] The assumption here is that, in discussions of Empedocles' physics, the term that would later be used for 'elements', i.e., στοιχεῖα, or rather, the sense of this term,

---

4 See, e.g., Diels 1899, 15; Burnet 1892, 228; Kahn 1960, 121; Longrigg 1976, 429, n. 44.

5 One usually credited to Plato; see Diels 1899, 17; Burkert 1959, 167–97 at 174–6; but cf. Crowley 2005. Gallavotti 1975, 164-5 thinks it not improbable that Empedocles used the term στοιχεῖα at B7, as Hesychius seems to report; but in any case he doesn't think the term would have yet had for Empedocles a technical significance.

6 Sedley 2007, 33, n. 7 suggests 'rootings' as a more literal rendering of ῥιζώματα; cf. Wright 1981, 164.

7 Ross 1924, vol. 1, 138. Likewise Zeller 1883, 56. See also Lloyd 1970, 40, Vlastos 1975, 68, n. 7, Longrigg 1976, 420, Barnes 1982, 309, Inwood 2001, 37, Graham 2006, 39, 103, 195, Preus 2015, 142.

can readily be read into the term that Empedocles actually used, i.e., ῥιζώματα, 'roots'. But this is an assumption that we might well afford to treat with some caution.

Now, in raising this note of doubt, I do not mean to suggest that we should eschew talk of 'elements' when we talk of Empedocles' fire, air, water, and earth, and talk only and exclusively of 'roots'. This is indeed a move that we sometimes see adopted, motivated no doubt by a worry that to speak in terms of στοιχεῖα, 'elements', would be anachronistic.[8] But while such a move may be useful to signal that Empedocles doesn't use the term στοιχεῖα, it may well be more misleading to insist on referring to fire, air, water, and earth as Emped- ocles' 'roots', than to talk about them as his 'elements'.[9] The issue here is not so much whether it is anachronistic or not to talk about Empedocles' fire, air, water, and earth as his 'elements'. If we take as central to the later use of the term στοιχεῖον in the sense of 'element', that is, its use in physical contexts, the notion that a στοιχεῖον is a basic constituent of bodies (*Metaph.* v.3, 1014a26- 34), then it seems that Empedocles does have such a notion in mind, for he does deploy fire, air, water, and earth as the constituents of bodies. He does so, for instance, at B21 (especially 21.13–14; see also B23).[10] Empedocles holds that everything that comes to be is a mixture of these four. As such, these four things, insofar as they are constituents of compound bodies, are elemental, or at least candidates for elemental status, and so we might call them 'elements', indeed, 'Empedocles' elements'.[11]

That, then, is not the issue. The issue here, rather, is whether or not the term ῥιζώματα, as Empedocles uses it, does more or less the same job as στοιχεῖα will do for later writers, such that it is appropriate to think that, in effect, ῥι- ζώματα, as Empedocles uses it, and στοιχεῖα are more or less interchangeable. And there is some reason to think they are not. For one thing, while the term ῥιζώματα itself suggests something of an organic or botanic vitality, which may indeed evoke the idea of a principle or origin, that from which other things grow,[12] it is not clear that this can also capture the notion central to the term

---

8   Wright 1981 and Inwood 2001 show clear preference for 'roots' over 'elements', see, for instance, Inwood 31, n. 66. Curd 1998, 155f uses the term 'roots' exclusively throughout her discussion of Empedocles.

9   On this point I side with Sedley 2007, 33, n. 7; in fact the point can be put in even stronger terms (see below).

10 See Lloyd 1970, 39–41, and Longrigg 1976, 429.

11 A nice antidote to fear of anachronism in using terms of later coinage when interpreting earlier philosophers is proffered by Barnes 1982, 475.

12 LSJ, s.v., ῥίζα. Cf. Hesiod's use, *Theog.* 728, with West's comments, 1966, 361. See also Hershbell 1974, 152, Longrigg 1976, 423, with n. 17, Wright 1997, 165.

ARISTOTLE, EMPEDOCLES, AND THE FOUR ELEMENTS

στοιχεῖον, that is, the most basic, simplest constituent of bodies (*Metaph.* v.3, 1014a26-34).[13] Moreover, in the surviving fragments, Empedocles uses the term ῥιζώματα but once as a generic term for fire, air, water, and earth (B6). It does not seem, in other words, to be a devoted generic or 'technical' term adopted by Empedocles to refer to fire, air, water, and earth, one that effectively plays the role of, or can readily be replaced by, a later term like στοιχεῖα.[14] Arguably it would not be characteristic of Empedocles to employ a technical term for specific uses.[15] These two points might already seem to count against both those who wish to say that Empedocles' word for στοιχεῖα or 'elements' is ῥιζώματα, as well as those more overly conscientious scholars who disdain to use the term 'elements' with regard to Empedocles, insisting upon the use of 'roots' instead.

But there is another point which is more pressing. On the one occasion when Empedocles uses the phrase 'the four roots of all things', he names these roots not as 'fire', 'air', 'water', and 'earth', but personifies them as the divinities Zeus, Hera, Nestis and Aidoneus (Hades) (B6).[16] There is no doubt, of course, that these divinities refer to fire, air, water, and earth. But likewise there is no doubt that their divine status ought to be taken seriously, and not as a mere poetic gesture. In the context of Presocratic physics, it is not unusual to find the basic principles ascribed with divine status, an ascription that captures their ungenerated and imperishable attributes. By perhaps the late 5th c. or so, however, things appropriately called στοιχεῖα are taken to be inanimate material entities, and not divinities (see, e.g., Plato's *Laws* 889b1f.).[17] Now this general observation in itself may introduce further hesitancy regarding a ready identification of the ῥιζώματα with στοιχεῖα. But this general observation is not the pressing point here; the point is rather more specific to the context of Empedocles' poem.

---

13   Kirk, Raven and Schofield 1983, 286, insist, without supporting argument, that "the name ['roots'] marks them as basic and mutually irreducible elements from which all other things are formed". Likewise Inwood 2001 sees no issue with the term's ability to do double duty: 'roots', he says "is chosen to highlight their permanence and their joint role as the causes and components of other things", 37. But compare Hershbell 1974, 153.

14   For Gallavotti 1975, 173, ῥιζώματα is used here in a figurative, not a technical, sense.

15   Guthrie 1965 remarks that "Empedocles has no fixed terminology", 141; see also Longrigg 1967, 4, and 1976 428, n. 39; see also Sedley, 2007, 33, n. 7. Empedocles doesn't even stick to calling his elements 'fire', 'air', 'water', and 'earth'; he refers to them like so, all four together as a group, on only two occasions, B17.18 and B109 (αἰθήρ replacing ἀήρ); in other fragments he calls them by different names; see Wright 1981, 22-3.

16   See previous note. There is some controversy about which divinity corresponds to which root; for the history of the debate, see Guthrie 1965, 144-146; and esp. Kingsley 1995, 13-68, with Picot 2000. See also Palmer 2009, 262, n. 4.

17   See Sedley 2013, 346f. Cf. Lloyd 2003, 24.

For, it seems, it makes a significant difference as to whether we understand fire, air, water, and earth as the completely separate and independent principles effected under the rule of Strife (νεῖκος), in which state their true nature is revealed, or as being regarded as mixed together, culminating in the complete uniformity of the Sphere or σφαῖρος, under the rule of Love (φιλία) (see B17, esp. 17.1–8, 16–20; B27, 28; see also A27). Indeed, as Primavesi has argued, it is under the former, but not the latter, condition, when each is separated into a purified, unmixed mass, that fire, air, water, and earth enjoy the status of divine beings.[18] In particular, they are, in this state, the 'long lived gods' to which Empedocles refers at B21.12. The σφαῖρος is a god too (B31), but at the opposite end of the cycle, when Love is ascendant; it ceases to exist when the cycle passes to Strife—and hence, like the other 'long lived gods', it is not eternal.[19]

But what this may well indicate is that 'roots', ῥιζώματα, is, after all, a term with a sense or a use that is pertinent not to the 'elemental' status of fire, air, water, and earth, that is, when they are mixed together in compound bodies, but rather to the status of fire, air, water, and earth as the four pure masses that are fully formed at the end of the rule of Strife. Again, it is only in that purified state that fire, air, water, and earth are (or 'learn to be', B35.14) immortal, and as such divine; and, as noted, the one occurrence of 'roots' with reference to fire, air, water, and earth involves the use of divine names for these entities (B6).

If this reading is correct, then it would be a mistake to say, without qualification, that fire, air, water, and earth are divine; and likewise a mistake to use the term 'roots' as a generic term for Empedocles' fire, air, water, and earth.[20] The 'roots' are these entities under one aspect only, in their state as separate, pure, independent entities prior to the rule of Love.[21] It would seem, then, to be misleading not merely to insist upon talking of 'roots' instead of 'elements', when discussing Empedocles' fire, air, water, and earth; it is also misleading to suggest that ῥιζώματα and στοιχεῖα, 'roots' and 'elements', are interchangeable

---

18 Primavesi 2009, 252f.

19 Primavesi 2009, 255-6. See also Inwood 2001, 51, 57, 59. As Primavesi (253-5) argues, the length of time that the four pure masses exist in that state is not instantaneous, as, for instance, O'Brien takes it, 1969, 1, 57 (also Barnes 1982, 309), but lasts as long as the Sphere lasts. Cf. Aristotle, *Ph.* VIII.1, 252a7-10.

20 See Primavesi 2009, 273, n. 64.

21 Insofar as it recognises the mutability of the elements, this reading of Empedocles is in line with Osborne 1987, 41-2, and Palmer 2009, 279-298; it may in fact possibly defuse the apparently contradictory status that Empedocles gives to fire, air, water, and earth, that is, as being eternal and unchanging, and yet as being also subject to generation and corruption; see Aristotle *Gen. et corr.* 315a3-19 and discussion in s. 11 below, with n. 35.

ARISTOTLE, EMPEDOCLES, AND THE FOUR ELEMENTS

terms, the former simply being the term Empedocles used, due to the unavailability of the latter.

2

The next point to make is that Aristotle presumably does not intend to suggest at 985a32 that Empedocles' claim to originality lies in his selection of fire, air, water, and earth as his principles and elements. For Empedocles does not introduce as a principle anything that his predecessors had not already considered as a possible principle (see, e.g., *Ph.* II.1, 193a22). Admittedly, at an earlier point in *Metaphysics* Alpha, Aristotle seems to indicate that there is something novel about Empedocles' addition of *earth* to the principles that others had already identified, namely water, air, and fire (1.3, 984a5-9). Elsewhere, however, Empedocles is singled out for making *water* a fourth principle, as others had already named earth, and fire and air, among their principles (*Gen. corr.* II.1, 329a1-2). This blatant contradiction would seem to suggest that Aristotle is not intending in either place to make an historical claim about how Empedocles arrived at these four principles.[22] It is certainly not in naming water as a principle that Empedocles' originality lies, no more than in naming earth.[23]

Perhaps, then, what Aristotle thinks is significant about Empedocles is not the specific identity of Empedocles' principles, for these entities are familiar candidates; but rather the very fact that Empedocles insists upon *four*, and only four, of them. For many scholars, this is indeed the substance of Aristotle's claim for the originality of Empedocles. For Guthrie, for instance, the novelty that Aristotle credits to Empedocles is precisely that "for the first time the four take the rank of genuine *archai*: none is prior to any other, nor is there anything else more fundamental."[24] Others recognised them indeed; but they

---

22 Cherniss 1935, 399 suggests Empedocles added *air* to the three others, already evident in Heraclitus (DK22B31, B36); but see Longrigg 1976, 424, and Wright 1981, 27, 29.

23 Earth is somewhat unusual in that, as Aristotle notes, none of the monists named earth as their principle, even though the view that all things come from earth is an old and popular belief (1.8, 989a5-12). But it was named by those positing more than one principle. Xenophanes, for instance, named earth and water, B29, B33, cf. B27; Aristotle often says Parmenides named earth as one of his principles or causes, alongside fire (*Metaph.* 1.3, 984b4, 1.5, 986b34, *Ph.* 1.5, 188a20, *Gen. et corr.* 1.3, 318b6, 330b14). Ion of Chios is likely the one to whom he is referring at *Gen. et corr.* II.1, 329a1-2, who named three principles, fire, earth and air; see Rashed 2005, 152.

24 Guthrie 1965, 142. Cf. Kahn 1960, 153: "The system which recognizes these four, and these four alone, is the innovation of Empedocles", also 149, 150. See also Ross 1924 (I),

either made one of them more fundamental than the others, as, for instance, air is for Anaximenes; or they posited a principle other than these four that is more fundamental, and from which they are derived, such as the ἄπειρον of Anaximander. Or, as in the cases of his contemporaries Anaxagoras, Melissus and Diogenes of Apollonia, the four are merely listed among other phenomena, such as clouds, stones, and, as Diogenes puts it, "all the rest that are seen to exist in this cosmos" (see, respectively, 59B16, 30B8, 64B2). Empedocles' originality, on this reading, is that there are no more—and no less—than four principles, and that his four have equal status as principles.

And yet perhaps even this is not entirely without some precedent. The earliest texts of Greek literature already recognise a rudimentary four-fold division of the cosmos,[25] a division which, as Kahn puts it, "can be assimilated to the classic doctrine of the elements," and indeed might perhaps help to explain the apparently rapid acceptance of Empedocles' tetrad.[26] Now to this one might respond as Aristotle did, to those who tried to downplay the originality of Thales by pointing to the use of water in the ancient poetic or mythical cosmogonies of Homer, Hesiod, and Orpheus (*Metaph.* 1.3, 983b27-30).[27] One might point out, that is, that there is a very great difference between what Empedocles is proposing, and what can be found in Homer and Hesiod.[28]

On the other hand, however, Empedocles has predecessors who are clearly engaged in the same sort of enterprise as he is, and in their investigations the identification of *four* principles or forces seems also to be found. Ionian speculation may have been generally of a monist bent, but there we do find appeal to four forces, namely the opposites hot and cold, dry and wet (see, e.g., Heraclitus (B126)).[29] It has been suggested that Empedocles arrived at his four 'roots' by 'hypostasizing' these contraries.[30] Then again, in his choice of four as the number of his elements, one cannot discount Pythagorean influence.[31]

138, Cornford 1935, 162, Longrigg 1976, 429, Wright 1981, 26f., Kirk, Raven and Schofield 1983, 286.

25   See, for instance, Homer, *Il.* 15.187ff., 18.483; Hesiod *Theog.* 106-7, 736-7.

26   Kahn 1960, 152; see full discussion in Kahn, pp. 133-154. See also Wright 1981, 28-29.

27   For Ross 1924 (1), 130, Aristotle has in mind Plato's remarks in the *Theaetetus* about Homer being the source for Presocratic doctrines, but compare Snell 1944, 170-82.

28   As Kahn 1960 himself notes, 137. On Aristotle's conception of the difference between Thales and his predecessors, see Frede 2004, 28-33.

29   See Lloyd 1964, and Wright 1981, 26, and 1997, 165.

30   For this interpretation of Empedocles, see Burnet 1892, 228, and Kirk and Raven 1957, 119, 329; but cf. Longrigg 1976, 424-5, Guthrie 1965, 142, n. 2, Wright 1981, 27.

31   Ross 1924 (1), 138, Guthrie 1965, 141. For Empedocles' Pythagorean background, see Diog. Laert. 8.54-5, with Inwood (2001), 10. Epicharmus may have recognized four elements too, choosing water, earth, breath, and snow, see Ross 1924 (1), 138.

ARISTOTLE, EMPEDOCLES, AND THE FOUR ELEMENTS

Now one might again object that to point to such apparent precedents is merely to note that Empedocles' insistence on, and conception of, four elements or principles, as well as his selection of fire, air, water, and earth, is informed by a background of speculation.[32] Aristotle, of all people, so the objection might continue, would have been well placed to appreciate this, and yet, evidently, this does not, in Aristotle's eyes, take away from Empedocles' originality.

This objection, however, begs the question, insofar as it assumes that, as far as Aristotle is concerned, Empedocles' originality does in fact rest with the identification of four basic and irreducible principles. But this is an assumption that would appear to be undermined immediately by Aristotle himself. For in the very next line after telling us that Empedocles was the first to speak of the four so-called elements, Aristotle points out that Empedocles doesn't use these elements as four, but as two. For he opposes fire to the others, as if earth, water and air were 'of a single nature' (ὡς μιᾷ φύσει, *Metaph.* I.4, 985a33-b1; see also *Gen. corr.* II.3, 330b19). This would seem to indicate that these elements are not, after all, of equal power, at least as far as Aristotle is concerned.[33]

The issue is further complicated by the action, already adverted to above, of the two further principles in Empedocles' physics, Love and Strife (φιλία and νεῖκος). Indeed, just before crediting Empedocles with being the first to speak of the four elements, Aristotle explains how, under the influence of Love, the elements combine into a unity, the Sphere (σφαῖρος); and that, under the influence of Strife, they are separated out again (*Metaph.* I.4, 985a23-29, with I.3, 984a9-11). Moreover, elsewhere (*Gen. corr.* I.1, 315a3-19), Aristotle takes it that the elements throw off their differentiae when united by Love in the Sphere—and thereby cease to be.[34] But if the elements can cease to be in the Sphere, and come to be out of it again, then they are not truly eternal, and Empedocles seems to be contradicting himself.[35] In particular, this raises for Aristotle the question as to whether the four elements are indeed genuinely elemental, or whether the Sphere is more fundamental, a question Aristotle admits he cannot answer (*Gen. corr.* I.1, 315a19-25). If that is the case, then the claim that, in Aristotle's eyes, Empedocles' innovation was to insist upon fire, air, water, and

---

32   Ross 1924 (1), 138, Guthrie 1965, 141, 142, n. 2; and 1962, 122f., 313. Cf. Wightman 1951, 15.

33   Burnet 1892 wonders where Aristotle gets this idea, and reiterates that fire "has no preeminence over the rest: all are equal" 231. But see Wright's support for Aristotle's interpretation, 1981, 24-5, and Palmer 2009, 315.

34   For a defence of Aristotle's interpretation here, see Wright 1981, 35-6, Osborne 1987, 33, 41-4, and esp. Palmer 2009, 289-298. For critique of Aristotle's reading, see Curd 1998, 161f.

35   See Philoponus, *in De Gen. et Cor.* 19.3-10 (31A41), 20.6-9; see also n. 21 above.

earth as four genuine ἀρχαί, equal in power and irreducible to each other or to anything else, seems extremely dubious. For Aristotle evidently does not think that Empedocles uses them as four distinct principles; and, in any case, Empedocles seems to posit a more fundamental principle from which they come to be. If he treats his principles in this way, then it would appear that Empedocles does not yet fully understand what a principle, or element, is (see also *Gen. corr.* I.8, 325b19-25).[36]

3

So what is Aristotle saying, then, when he says that Empedocles is the first to speak of the four so-called elements of bodies? Let's look again at the context, in particular at the preceding discussion. For when he says that Empedocles was the first to speak of four so-called elements, this is actually the second time in the space of a few Bekker lines that Aristotle credits Empedocles with originality (I.4, 985a29-33). His other original contribution, according to Aristotle, is with regard to the recognition of the moving cause, that is, the cause of moving things, and bringing things together. Now, of course, Aristotle is not saying Empedocles is the first to introduce such a cause. Hesiod was already groping towards such a cause (984b23), and indeed Aristotle says that every thinker before Empedocles touched upon this cause, as well as the material cause (985a10-13). Empedocles is said, rather, to be the first to provide a more advanced version of the moving cause, given that he posited two opposed principles of motion, Love and Strife (985a29-31). Nevertheless, although an improvement on his predecessors, Aristotle criticises Empedocles for an inadequate and inconsistent use of these principles (985a22-23; see also I.8, 989a19-26).

Now the point of looking at what Aristotle says about Empedocles as regards the moving cause is that it may help us understand Aristotle's thinking about the attribution of historical or philosophical priority, and thus what he intends when he says Empedocles is 'first' to speak of this or that; and, thus, what is, and what is not, intended when he says that Empedocles was the first to speak of the four so-called elements. The discussion here is part of Aristotle's enquiry at the beginning of the *Metaphysics* into the extent to which his predecessors recognised the causes of things, in particular the extent to which they recognised the four causes, the material, formal, moving, and final

---

36 See Longrigg 1967, 3-4 for an attempt to defend Empedocles from the charge.

ARISTOTLE, EMPEDOCLES, AND THE FOUR ELEMENTS

causes, as set out in his *Physics* (1.3, 983a26-b6; see *Ph.* 11.3). This is not intended as an exercise in the history of philosophy for its own sake, but as a way of reaffirming his view that there are four causes, and no more (1.3, 983b5-6, 1.5, 986a13, 1.7, 988a18-23, b16-18).[37] His concluding statement at the end of Book Alpha is that, indeed, his predecessors did try to seek the causes he identified in the *Physics*, and only these kinds of cause (1.10, 993a11-13). But he adds that they talked about the causes in a vague or confused way (a13; see also 988a22-23)—in his memorable image, like untrained fighters who sometimes land a blow (985a13-15).[38] Indeed, he adds, they don't quite understand what they are saying (985a16, cf. 993a22-24). So in one sense they hit upon all the causes that Aristotle recognises; but in another sense they failed to grasp any, because they failed to state them clearly (993a13-15, 22-24).

Thus when Aristotle states that Empedocles is the first to offer a more sophisticated account of the moving cause, we ought to understand that Empedocles' notion of the moving cause, while an improvement on his predecessors', is still somewhat ill expressed, and is still some distance from Aristotle's notion (1.8, 989a25-6). Accordingly, then, given this context, and a clearer appreciation of what Aristotle is doing in this part of the *Metaphysics*, when Aristotle names Empedocles as the first to speak of the four so-called elements, we ought presumably to understand the significance of Empedocles' innovation in a similar manner.

The point Aristotle is making, then, is perhaps something like this: Empedocles hits the mark in naming the four so-called elements, but, as Aristotle immediately makes clear, he fails to treat them as proper principles. There is still some distance between Empedocles' grasp of the principles of matter and Aristotle's. Nevertheless, Empedocles is on the right track. He offers a decisive advance upon his predecessors; what is crucial, however, as the context makes clear, is that it is an advance in the direction of Aristotle's own conception of the principles. For Aristotle has no interest in recording originality or innovation in the history of philosophy *per se*; he is interested rather in the question as to whether one's originality anticipated later theories, in particular, his own. His history of philosophy is a motivated account, marking stages in the development of philosophy towards his own position.

Perhaps the difficulty, then, with assessing Aristotle's claim at 985a32 about the priority of Empedocles with regard to fire, air, water, and earth, is one that arises because we have been looking from the wrong direction. Aristotle says

---

37   Ross 1924 (1), 128. This is one of the aims of Alpha, but not the only one; see Frede 2004, 12f.
38   Aristotle even allows that Empedocles and Anaxagoras stumbled, unknowingly as it were, upon the final cause; 1.7, 988b8-11.

Empedocles was the first, and we naturally look to see what others did, or did not do, before him, to judge the claim for priority or originality, to determine precisely wherein the originality lies. But then we find that the claim for originality is somewhat attenuated: some of his predecessors chose as their principles one or more of fire, air, water and earth; and even the choice of four principles is not an unqualified novelty. And so we might be tempted to say that Aristotle identifies Empedocles as the first to see that fire, air, water, and earth are four genuine principles, equal in power and irreducible to each other or to anything else. But in fact Aristotle himself blocks this reading. What needs to be emphasised, then, is that Aristotle's account of the history of philosophy is not retrospective but, we might say, prospective; he is looking back from his own position for evidence that his predecessors hit upon any of his four causes (and no further cause). And, tracing the line of inquiry backwards, he finds that the first to speak of fire, air, water, and earth as the material elements of things, the first, that is, to say that everything consists of an organised mixture of fire, air, water, and earth, or the first to come appreciably close to saying something like this, such that we can conjecture that this is what he intended to say, is Empedocles.[39] This is a novelty worth highlighting as a 'first' precisely because it is the earliest anticipation of Aristotle's own view. But it is not yet Aristotle's own view; Empedocles, after all, does not treat fire, air, water, and earth as four genuine elements or principles of matter.

4

This, then, is what I suggest Aristotle intends when he says that Empedocles was the first to name fire, air, water, and earth as the material elements of bodies. Now this interpretation is not without consequence for the issue of the reception, and status, of Empedocles' natural philosophy in the 4th century. This is because it is a reading that opens up the possibility that the four elements hypothesis, as understood by Aristotle's contemporaries, is not necessarily a hypothesis that would have been immediately associated with Empedocles.

Consider again what Aristotle is doing when he tells us that Empedocles was the first to speak of the four elements fire, air, water, and earth. As I have argued, he intends to highlight that something approaching his own theory of matter can be traced back to Empedocles, as part of his overall project of

---

39 On attending to the intent, rather than the expression, of Empedocles, see *Metaph.* I.4, 985a4-5 (A39), and *Cael.* III.6, 305a1-4 (A43A.).

ARISTOTLE, EMPEDOCLES, AND THE FOUR ELEMENTS   363

reaffirming his own view that there are four, and only four causes. In other words, Aristotle is sharing the fruits of his research into the history of the material cause. Presumably, then, when he is informing his audience of this point, he is telling them something that they might not have been expected to know, namely, that Empedocles was the first to name fire, air, water, and earth as the elements of bodies.

But we might be persuaded to go further, and suggest that it was not well known that Empedocles held the view that fire, air, water, and earth are the four elements of bodies, let alone that he was the first to do so. This, at least, seems to be a plausible reading of the following passage from Aristotle's *Topics*. "One should collect premises from written works," Aristotle writes, and "make marginal notes on the opinions of particular people, for example, that it was Empedocles who said that there are four elements of bodies" (*Top.* 1.14, 105b12-18; trans. Smith).[40] The reason why one would make such a note about, say, Empedocles, is that, in an argument over the elements of bodies, one's opponent might concede that there are four, if told that a famous or reputable philosopher, such as Empedocles, had held this view. Empedocles was well known, it seems, but not well read. Aristotle seems to be suggesting that he knows this point about Empedocles because he has access to, and has read, Empedocles' book, and has duly noted it. Aristotle was known, of course, to place, for the time, an unusual emphasis on collecting and reading books.[41] It is notable indeed that, whereas his treatment of Plato's views can often be brief and paraphrastic, he regularly quotes from Empedocles, and other Presocratics, sometimes at some length (e.g., B84 at *Sens.* 2, 437b11f.). As Natali points out, what we might reasonably infer from this is that, whereas Plato's texts were presumably readily available to Aristotle's audience, the work of Empedocles was not.[42]

Now to give this as an example of something that one has read, and might wish to make a note of, for later use in argument, would seem to be a good indication that it was not, after all, common knowledge that Empedocles named fire, air, water, and earth as the four elements of bodies, let alone that he was the first to do so. What we might also infer from the use of this example is that an argument or debate over the number, and perhaps too the nature, of the elements or constituents of bodies could be won if one pulled out the trump

---

40   Smith 1997.

41   Natali 2013, 20, 157.

42   Natali 2013, 98-9. Indeed, Hussey 1995, 546 suggests that the writings of Empedocles, as well as Parmenides and perhaps Democritus, "probably would have been intended for restricted audiences from the start".

card of Empedocles' authority. This imagined scenario invites the speculation that such disputes were reasonably frequent, and moreover, it seems, were often conducted in ignorance of the view of Empedocles on the matter. After all, Aristotle's point here is about examining written sources in order to strengthen one's arguments; in particular, to find and record persuasive nuggets of information of which one's opponent can be expected to be unaware.

Admittedly this may seem quite a lot to hang on one example. But perhaps there is some corroborating evidence in the Hippocratic treatise *The Nature of Man*, credited to Polybus, and written perhaps in the last decades of the 5th century.[43] For there is clear reference here to public disputations over the constituents of bodies, particularly the human body, that were going on at the time.[44] Moreover, it seems the protagonists in these disputations apparently did not invoke the authority of Empedocles, at least not explicitly. Indeed, this point is all the more striking considering, firstly, that all four elements are mentioned in the first chapter, and secondly, Polybus himself will proceed to name as constituents of bodies the four humours (Hipp. *Nat. Hom.* 4.1). Yet no connection is made here between the four humours and the four elements.[45] Polybus is concerned rather with criticizing monists, that is, those who attempt to explain the body in terms of *one* of earth, water, air, and fire. The possibility of a theory that makes more than one of these elements the constituents of body—or all four, as with Empedocles—is not entertained. It is clear, too, that Polybus is referring to monists among his own contemporaries: he is talking of people who hold such views *now*, and whose debates one could attend, and not of people who held such things in the past.[46]

Clearly, then, among Polybus' contemporaries, and significantly he makes clear he is not talking of the physicians (*Nat. Hom.* 2.1), there are those who say that water is the sole constituent of the body; others air, or fire, or earth (1.1-2). The four elements are all present and accounted for, but they are not spoken of as a quartet, and Empedocles—without reference to whom one might have thought it difficult to speak, near the end of the 5th century, about fire, air, water, and earth—is absent.[47] Together with the evidence of the *Topics*,

---

43 For Polybus' authorship, see Aristotle, *Hist. an.* III. 3, 512a12–513a7; for date of the *Nature of Man*, see Craik 2015, 212.

44 Lloyd 1978, 38, Craik 2015, 210.

45 See Jouanna 2012a, 336, and n. 3 above. Jouanna 2012b does think, however, that the *Nature of Man*'s humoral theory was "indirectly influenced by Empedoclean philosophy" 230. Cf. Rashed 2005, xxxv. Note that the term 'humour' (χυμός) does not actually appear in this treatise.

46 Lloyd 1970, 61, Huffman 1993, 294.

47 Empedocles, of course, is typically thought to be a major background influence on the Hippocratic writings (see Jouanna 1961), but there is only one explicit reference to him,

ARISTOTLE, EMPEDOCLES, AND THE FOUR ELEMENTS

this seems to give encouragement to the claim towards which we are moving, namely, that, in Aristotle's time, while the four elements hypothesis is well known, its origin with Empedocles is not, nor even the specific views of Empedocles on the elements. With this in hand, let's look again at Aristotle's remark at 985a32, to see if we seem to find support for this claim.

5

Let's start by drawing attention to what is perhaps the least contentious point that emerges from Aristotle's remark about Empedocles at 985a32. It is this: the remark minimally implies that others, after Empedocles, also say that fire, air, water, and earth are the elements or constituents of things. This, after all, is generally what we intend when we recognise someone to be the first to do or say something. For, obviously, to be identified as the first to do or say something, it is necessary that there be others who come after, who do or say more or less the same thing. So there were others, presumably, who came after Empedocles, who also spoke about what Empedocles was the first to speak about, namely, the four elements fire, air, water, and earth. As he puts it at *De Generatione et Corruptione* II.7, there are "those who speak as Empedocles does" (334a26-7), that is, about the elemental composition of bodies.

Moreover, it would seem clear that, unlike Empedocles, these people actually did use the term στοιχεῖα with reference to fire, air, water, and earth. In fact, the very phrase that Aristotle uses here, τὰ ὡς ἐν ὕλης εἴδει λεγόμενα στοιχεῖα τέτταρα, "the four so-called elements of the material kind" would seem itself clearly to point towards this conclusion. If fire, air, water, and earth are τὰ λεγόμενα στοιχεῖα, the 'so-called elements', or 'the things that are called στοιχεῖα', then the very least we can infer from this is that there are people who call these things στοιχεῖα. Whatever further significance Aristotle's use of this phrase may have, and, as we shall note in a moment, commentators have often invested in it a great deal of significance, his use of the phrase τὰ λεγόμενα στοιχεῖα at 985a32 confirms this much at least; that Empedocles spoke of things that later came to be called, by some people, στοιχεῖα, and indeed are presumably still called, by some people, presumably contemporaries of Aristotle, στοιχεῖα. But who are these people? By whom are fire, air, water, and earth called the στοιχεῖα?

---

at *On Ancient Medicine* 20, and this is a brief and rather hostile dismissal of the sort of 'philosophical medicine' that he and others espouse.

The temptation to say that they must be self-professed followers of Empedocles ought, I think, to be resisted.[48] For if it were only 'neo-Empedocleans', those who took themselves to be followers of Empedocles, and were known to be so, that identified such things as fire, air, water, and earth as elements or principles, then this fact, that Empedocles was the first to say such things are elements, or principles, would hardly need pointing out. In fact, it would render the remark rather trivial, as Aristotle would be saying that Empedocles was the first to name as elements of bodies the things that his followers call elements. This tells us little.

Compare the use of the similar phrase τὰ καλούμενα στοιχεῖα near the beginning of *Physics* I.4, where Aristotle is distinguishing the doctrines of Anaxagoras and Empedocles. They are similar, he says, insofar as they both separate things out from a mixture (μῖγμα), but whereas the former separates out an infinite number of things, Empedocles separates out "only the so-called elements" (τὰ καλούμενα στοιχεῖα μόνον, 187a20-26). Now if τὰ καλούμενα στοιχεῖα were to be completed as "by Empedocles' followers", then what Aristotle would appear to be saying at *Physics* I.4 is: "Empedocles separates out only the things that Empedocles' followers call 'elements'". This in the context would be a peculiarly uninformative claim to make, as it would leave one at a loss to specify precisely *what* Empedocles separates out from the mixture, and why his doctrine differs from that of Anaxagoras on this point—unless one knows already what it is that Empedocles, and his followers, identify as the elements.

On the other hand, if one does not already know what Empedocles identifies as the elements, but one does know to what Aristotle is referring by the phrase τὰ καλούμενα στοιχεῖα, then one will learn from this passage what Empedocles identifies as his elements or principles. This, indeed, seems to me to be the function of Aristotle's use of the phrase τὰ καλούμενα, or λεγόμενα, στοιχεῖα. It would be no good, for instance, to say "Empedocles separates out the στοιχεῖα", nor, indeed, to say "Empedocles was the first to speak of the four στοιχεῖα", that is, without qualifying στοιχεῖα with the participles καλούμενος or λεγόμενος. This is because it would be too vague. For it appears that Aristotle's contemporaries used the term στοιχεῖον for a whole range of entities other than fire, air, water, and earth, incorporeal as well as corporeal. There is, for instance, some evidence in Aristotle that the Platonists call their incorporeal principles στοιχεῖα (*Metaph.* XIV.1, 1087b9-10, b12-13; cf. XIII.6, 1080b6-7, XIII.7, 1081b32,

---

48 Aristotle refers to "followers of Empedocles" (οἱ περὶ Ἐμπεδοκλέα) at *Cael.* III.7, 305b1, and *Gen. et corr.* I.1, 314a21. Rashed 2005, takes Aristotle to be thinking of followers of Empedocles throughout the *De Generatione et Corruptione*; see xxxv, and his explanation of τὰ καλούμενα στοιχεῖα, at 129.

XIV.3, 1091a9-10). And in his definition of στοιχεῖον at *Metaphysics* Delta, Aristotle notes that the most universal things, for instance, the genera, are called στοιχεῖα (στοιχεῖα τὰ γένη λέγουσί τινες, 1014b10-11).[49] Aristotle himself is often rather catholic in his use of the term στοιχεῖον with reference to the material principles of his predecessors. He uses στοιχεῖα, for instance, for Anaxagoras' principles (τὰ γὰρ ὁμοιομερῆ στοιχεῖα, *Cael.* III.3, 302a31, III.4, 302b13; cf. also *Metaph.* I.8, 989a31f.), and also the atoms of Democritus (see, e.g., *Gen. et corr.* I.1, 314a18-20, *Ph.* III.4, 203a20, *De an.* I.2, 404a4-5; cf. also *Metaph.* I.4, 985b5). Even when speaking of Empedocles, he on occasion refers to Love and Strife as στοιχεῖα (e.g., *Metaph.* XIV.4, 1091b12, and *De an.* I.5, 410b6).

When Aristotle uses the phrase τὰ καλούμενα or τὰ λεγόμενα στοιχεῖα, however, he always has a particular set of corporeal elements in mind, and these are fire, air, water, and earth. Aristotle's aim or intention when using the phrase, presumably, is to underline that what he is talking about, when he uses the phrase, are the things commonly called 'elements', namely, fire, air, water, and earth. Clearly Aristotle's use of this phrase, then, ought to be recognised as an excellent resource when discussing the reception of the four elements theory in the work of Aristotle and his contemporaries. But it seems to me that the potential usefulness of this resource has been obscured by the prevalence of the view that Aristotle is using the participle λεγόμενος, or καλούμενος, to signal misuse of the term qualified, i.e., στοιχεῖα. In other words, there is a widespread assumption that the participle carries a negative or sceptical connotation, corresponding somewhat to the attributive use of the English participial adjective 'so-called'.[50] Thus fire, air, water, and earth are *merely* 'so-called' elements, as opposed to genuine elements.[51]

But this presumption reveals a far too narrow conception of the kinds of things the participle καλούμενος is capable of doing when it qualifies a term. For, just as the English participial adjective 'so-called' need not always be used to indicate impropriety, so also this is not the only function that the participle καλούμενος performs—if indeed it ever does perform it. And in fact it is not at

---

49   Here it is usually thought that Aristotle has in mind Plato, or Platonists, and Pythagoreans; Ross 1924 (I), 295. Cf. *Metaph.* I.5, 986a1; III. 3, 998b9-11; VII.2, 1028b25-8; XII.1, 1069a26-28.

50   Something is a 'so-called *x*' in the attributive use when it is "called or designated by this name or term, but not properly entitled to it or correctly described by it", OED, s.v., 'so-called'.

51   This is by far the most common explanation of Aristotle's use of the phrase τὰ καλούμενα στοιχεῖα. Explicit commitment to this explanation can be found in Burnet 1892, 230, n. 3; Diels 1899, 25; Joachim 1922, 137; Ross 1936, 484; Düring 1943, 124; Kahn 1960, 120; Sokolowski 1970, 269f.; Williams 1982, 152; Graham 1987, 476, n. 5, and 2006, 39; Longrigg 1993, 151; Crubellier 2000, 142; and Rashed 2005, 152-3.

368   CROWLEY

all clear that καλούμενος does perform this function; certainly it is difficult to discover precedents for the understanding of the participle καλούμενος that the prevailing explanation of τὰ καλούμενα στοιχεῖα requires.[52]

It seems to make more sense, then, to think that the phrase τὰ καλούμενα στοιχεῖα is being used here, at *Physics* I.4, because Aristotle is confident that, when he uses this phrase, his audience will immediately know just what it is that Empedocles separates out from the mixture. For Aristotle, I suggest, uses the phrase τὰ καλούμενα στοιχεῖα (and τὰ λεγόμενα στοιχεῖα) as a way of fixing the reference to the four elements of bodies, fire, air, water, and earth. But for this to be the case, the 'so-called elements' must be the things that are quite generally called 'elements', regardless of whether or not Empedocles, or anyone else, chooses them as his elements. It might seem reasonable to infer, then, from Aristotle's statement at 985a32, that such things as fire, air, water, and earth have become, by Aristotle's time, the sort of things that are often or frequently identified as the elements and principles of things. And, indeed, the view that fire, air, water, and earth are the material constituents of things would appear to be already fairly common by Plato's time.

Take what Plato says in the *Timaeus*, for instance. Plato has the main spokesman of the dialogue, Timaeus, criticise the view that fire, air, water, and earth are the most basic constituents of things, because they can be further analysed into more fundamental elements or στοιχεῖα (48b-c). Now presumably the reason why Plato is eager to criticise this view is that it is a common or popular view, perhaps the most popular view, regarding the material constituents of the world that is to be found among his own contemporaries.[53] For the most significant feature of the *Timaeus* passage, for our present purposes, is that it seems these four elements are commonly or popularly called ἀρχαί and στοιχεῖα. Indeed, what irks Timaeus here is precisely that people tend to call fire, air, water, and earth the ἀρχαί and στοιχεῖα of everything. Timaeus will agree that fire, air, water, and earth are constituents of bodies, but he wants to deny that they deserve to be called the ultimate or most elemental constituents, the στοιχεῖα, of bodies.[54] What is at issue,

---

52   For further discussion, see Crowley 2008, esp. 233-240.

53   Cf. *Ti.* 49b. Further evidence in Plato's works that fire, air, water, and earth are popularly regarded as the material constituents of things is available at *Phlb.* 29a, *Crat.* 408d, *Prt.* 320d. See also Hershbell 1974, 154, and Crowley 2005, 278f.

54   It is often held that Plato himself introduced the term στοιχεῖον in the sense of 'element' (Diels 1899, 17; Burkert 1959, 174-6); if that is so, then Plato cannot be saying that some people call fire, air, water, and earth στοιχεῖα. But see Crowley 2005.

ARISTOTLE, EMPEDOCLES, AND THE FOUR ELEMENTS

in other words, has to do with contemporary usage of the terms ἀρχαί and στοιχεῖα.[55]

What Aristotle seems to be saying, then, at 985a32, is that Empedocles was the first to say something that is now, in Aristotle's time, fairly common, that is, that fire, air, water, and earth are the στοιχεῖα, the material constituents of bodies. But, in acknowledging this, and keeping the *Topics* evidence in mind, we need to be very cautious about concluding that it is the four elements theory of Empedocles, or the 'Empedoclean theory of elements', that has evidently become a familiar or popular natural philosophy in 4th c. Athens. That is, the identification of Empedocles as the first to say that there are four elements, and that these are fire, air, water, and earth, hardly seems sufficient to commit everyone else who says this to the Empedoclean theory of elements. To put it in a nutshell: To say that someone was the first to name x, y, and z 'F' certainly implies that others, who came later, also said that the x, y, and z are F; but it does not follow that these others necessarily share or agree with the original conception either of x, y, and z, or of the way in which x, y, and z are F. It does not follow, in other words, that those who hold that fire, air, water, and earth are the material constituents of things share, or would share, if they were to become aware of it, Empedocles' conception of the nature of fire, air, water, and earth.

Consider again, for instance, how, as we noted above, immediately after crediting Empedocles with the introduction of the four so-called elements, Aristotle points out that Empedocles doesn't use the elements as four, but opposes fire to the others, as if there were just two elements (*Metaph.* I.4, 985a33-b1). If indeed it is common among some of Aristotle's contemporaries to speak of fire, air, water, and earth as the elements of things, it might seem a reasonable conjecture, then, that Empedocles' use of the four elements differs in this respect to the common conception. For Aristotle is saying, in effect, that Empedocles is the first to speak of the four so-called elements, but, he adds immediately, he doesn't speak of them in the way we might expect, or, perhaps, in the way that people who speak of these things use them today, because he opposes three of them, as if they were one, to the fourth. Aristotle's repetition of this point at *De Generatione et Corruptione* II.3 adds support to this conjecture (330b19-21). For here he says that *some* (ἔνιοι) say that there are four elements, for instance, Empedocles; but he then specifies that Empedocles alone reduces them to two, setting fire against the others.

---

55   I disagree with Burkert 1959, 176, then, who does not think that *Ti.* 48b is of relevance for the question of the usage of στοιχεῖον.

370   CROWLEY

6

One must be wary, then, of inferring that, if there are people who say that fire, air, water, and earth are the constituents of things, and who duly call these things ἀρχαί and στοιχεῖα, then these people, while not consciously following Empedocles, are, after all, without realising it, following Empedocles. Aristotle's purpose, when he credits Empedocles as the first to speak of the four so-called elements, is not to reveal to people, who now speak of the four so-called elements, that they thereby hold a theory that is rightly to be credited to Empedocles, and as such they are, without realising it, really Empedocleans. On the contrary, it seems plausible, from what Aristotle says, to think that there is a theory, or hypothesis, that fire, air, water, and earth are the elements of bodies; and this theory of the four elements, which seems to be a common or popular theory already by the time Plato wrote the *Timaeus*, is similar to, but somewhat independent of, the Empedoclean natural philosophy.

Now one might well object that, if we look again at Plato's *Timaeus*, then surely we must concede that this work is heavily influenced by Empedocles;[56] and that, if Plato has a target when he criticises the elemental status of fire, air, water, and earth, one would most naturally assume that the target is, in fact, Empedocles.[57] But, in general, the fact is that in the *Timaeus* we find no explicit reference to Empedocles or his writings; no quotations, not even paraphrases, are in evidence; and stylistic or verbal echoes of Empedocles cannot be affirmed with any certainty.[58] Certainly, we might readily concede, Plato does have a view in mind that can be traced back to Empedocles; for, as Aristotle tells us, Empedocles is the first to speak of the four so-called elements. And perhaps Plato himself is aware that it is, ultimately, a view that can be traced to Empedocles.[59] But it seems to me that there is an important sense in which it

56   For Taylor 1928, the *Timaeus* is Plato's attempt to graft Empedoclean biology and medicine onto Pythagorean mathematics; see also Taylor 1926, 436. Cf. Cornford 1935, v-x, for rejection of Taylor's interpretation. Cornford, however, like many others, maintains that Empedocles is a continuous presence in the *Timaeus*; see also Guthrie, 1965, vol. 2, 237-8, O'Brien 1969, 144-5, Gregory 2000, 37-9, and 2008, xvi, xviii, 137.

57   See, for instance, Vlastos 1975, 68, Zeyl 2000, 37, n. 51, Polito 2013, 128 131. Cf. Taylor 1926, 436, n. 1.

58   See Hershbell 1974, 146, 151, 165. Hershbell's deflationary discussion of the question of Empedocles' influence on the *Timaeus* remains valuable. Cf. also Kingsley 1995, who, while insisting that Plato knew Empedocles' work very well (114), nevertheless admits that establishing Plato's "direct indebtedness" to Empedocles is "far from simple or straightforward", 142; and Johansen 2004, 5.

59   There is no question, of course, about Plato's general awareness of Empedocles, and his doctrines; see, e.g., *Meno* 76c (A92), *Tht.* 152e (the only two occasions where Plato

ARISTOTLE, EMPEDOCLES, AND THE FOUR ELEMENTS

may be going beyond the evidence, indeed misleading, to say, for instance, that when Plato criticises the view that fire, air, water, and earth are the elements and principles in the *Timaeus*, he must have specifically Empedocles, or even Empedocleans, in mind. If this is a view that is, as it were, 'in the air', then it is not necessary to conclude that Plato is directly attacking Empedocles.[60] Again, the reason why Plato's character Timaeus attacks this four elements theory is presumably because it is a popular view that he regards as mistaken.

A similar point, perhaps, may be made for the critique of the natural philosophy that underlies the atheist thesis in Book x of the *Laws*. On the face of it, it may seem that Plato, or his spokesman, the Athenian, must have had Empedocles in mind, for he outlines a physics based on fire, air, water, and earth, which, together with nature and chance, is said to be sufficient to explain all things—the earth and the heavenly bodies, and all plant and animal life (889b-c).[61] But, despite the foundation of this argument on the four elements, it is even less certain, indeed unlikely, that Plato is attacking Empedocles here. What Plato is attacking, rather, is a concoction of different views, or perhaps something like a "climate of opinion".[62] Or indeed the critique might be taken as evidence of an established atheist movement in contemporary Athens, a group who, of course, to avoid prosecution for impiety, anonymously publish and circulate texts that set out their views.[63] In any case, the *Laws*

---

mentions Empedocles by name), *Phd.* 96a-b (A76), *Grg.* 493a, *Soph.* 242c-e (A29). Aristophanes' speech at *Symp.* 189c-193d is often thought to be based on, indeed a parody of, Empedocles; see, e.g., O'Brien 1969, 227-9; but see also Guthrie 1965, 205, n. 2, and esp. Allen 1991, 31, n. 52.

60   As Hershbell 1974 points out, "the discussion of the four elements in the *Timaeus* is in a language and conceptual scheme far removed from that of Empedocles' roots ... it is possible that Plato is drawing on [a] common tradition, and not directly on Empedocles at all," 153-4.

61   For Taylor 1928, 19, in *Laws* X "Empedocles more than anyone else is plainly aimed at"; Curd (1998), 159 reckons the theory that the Athenian describes is "probably" that of Empedocles.

62   Saunders' phrase 1970, 409. Saunders thinks it "almost impossible" to identify a single thinker or school as the target here, likewise Stalley 1983, 168. Mayhew 2008, 79, points out that, on the atheist thesis so summarised, fire, air, water, and earth need not even be assumed to be the four basic elements, as they are for Empedocles, and concludes that Plato has no particular figure in mind; see also England 1921, 453. Guthrie 1978 thinks Plato is thinking of the great Sophists and their followers, who were drawing opportunistically from Presocratic natural philosophy, 361-2. Cf. Bury 1967 who takes Plato to be summarising Atomism, n. 1 at 889c. See also Popa 'Elements and their Forms: The Fortunes of a Presocratic Idea', in this volume, for the similar suggestion that certain views regarding the elements may have formed a 'sort of intellectual common currency'.

63   Sedley 2013 makes a strong case for this last possibility, notably making no reference to Empedocles at all.

may well offer further evidence that a four elements hypothesis could have been proposed in 4th and late 5th century Athens without it necessarily implicating Empedocles.

7 Conclusion

The four elements hypothesis, the hypothesis that the basic constituents of things are fire, air, water, and earth, proved very successful, and much of this success can be explained by a sense of familiarity. The notion of four divisions of the world was familiar from the poets; and the identity of the elements themselves was familiar from the speculations of preceding thinkers.[64] There was also, of course, an observational or empirical plausibility to the hypothesis.[65] But what I have suggested here is that there is evidence that the hypothesis was so successful that it was held by many who were not in any sense Empedocleans, or followers of Empedocles, or who may well have had little idea that the first thinker to put forward the hypothesis was in fact Empedocles. Indeed, the evidence suggests that we need to separate the question of the reception of the four elements hypothesis from the question of the reception of *Empedocles'* four elements theory. A careful look at what Aristotle, and Plato, has to say about fire, air, water, and earth compels us to accept that it was a common, popular view that fire, air, water, and earth are the elements of all things. When Aristotle says that Empedocles posited the four so-called elements, or that was he was the first to do so, he is not saying, as would be redundant, that Empedocles posited the Empedoclean elements, or was the first to do so. Rather, he clearly intends to point out that the hypothesis that the fundamental constituents of bodies are fire, air, water, and earth, which is a familiar hypothesis in the 4th century, was, as a matter of fact, held by Empedocles, indeed, Empedocles was the first to posit it. Moreover, the priority of Empedocles is worth pointing out, if indeed it is has become relatively common, among a significantly broad selection of Aristotle's contemporaries, to speak of fire, air, water, and earth as the elements or principles; and if, moreover, Empedocles' priority is not well known. But, and this is crucial, once Empedocles' theory is delineated by Aristotle for the benefit of his audience, it appears that it is best understood to be a *version* of a view that was already common or popular by Plato's time, namely, that fire, air, water, and earth are the elements of bodies.

---

64 See above, s. 11.
65 Wright 1981, 27-8.

ARISTOTLE, EMPEDOCLES, AND THE FOUR ELEMENTS

For Empedocles' version is a version that Aristotle rejects; Aristotle, it turns out, will offer his own version.[66]

Bibliography

Allen, R.E. 1991. *The Dialogues of Plato, Vol. II: The Symposium* Translated with Comment. New Haven: Yale University Press.

Arikha, N. 2007. *Passions and Tempers: A History of the Humours.* New York: HarperCollins.

Bala, P. 2007. *Medicine and Medical Policies in India: Social and Historical Perspectives.* Lanham: Lexington Books.

Barnes, J. 1982. *The Presocratic Philosophers.* London: Routledge. 1st ed.1979.

Burkert, W. 1959. "Στοιχεῖον. Eine semasiologische Studie." *Philologus*, 103: 167–97.

Burnet, J. 1892. *Early Greek Philosophy.* 4th edition, 1930, reprint of the 3rd edition, 1920. London: Adam and Charles Black.

Bury, R.G. 1967. *Plato Laws.* Loeb Classical Library. London: Heinemann/Cambridge (Mass.): Harvard University Press.

Chalmers, A. 2016. "Robert Boyle's Corpuscular Chemistry: Atomism before its Time." In *Essays in the Philosophy of Chemistry*, edited by E. Scerri and G. Fisher. Oxford: Oxford University Press.

Cherniss H. 1935. *Aristotle's Criticism of Presocratic Philosophy.* Baltimore: Johns Hopkins Press.

Clericuzio, A. 2000. *Elements, Principles and Corpuscles: A Study of Atomism and Chemistry in the Seventeenth Century. International Archives of the History of ideas, 171*: Dordrecht: Kluwer Academic Publishers.

Cornford, F. M. 1935. *Plato's Cosmology: The Timaeus of Plato.* London: Routledge and Kegan Paul.

Craik, E. M. 2015. *The Hippocratic Corpus: Content and Context.* New York: Routledge.

Crowley, T. J. 2013. "*De Generatione et Corruptione* 2.3: Does Aristotle Identify the Contraries as Elements?". *The Classical Quarterly* 63.1: 161–182.

Crowley, T. J. 2008. "Aristotle's 'So-Called Elements'." *Phronesis* 53.3: 223–42.

Crowley, T. J. 2005. "On the Use of *Stoicheion* in the Sense of 'Element'." *Oxford Studies in Ancient Philosophy* 29:367–94.

Crubellier, M. 2000. "*Metaphysics*Λ 4.". In *Aristotle's* Metaphysics *Lambda*, edited by Michael Frede and David Charles. Oxford: Clarendon Press.

Curd, P. 1998. *The Legacy of Parmenides: Eleatic Monism and Later Presocratic Thought.* Princeton, NJ: Princeton University Press.

---

66   See Crowley 2013 for a fuller defence of this claim.

Diels, H. 1899. *Elementum*. Leipzig: Teubner.

Düring, I. 1943. *Aristotle's* De Partibus Animalium: *Critical and literary Commentaries*. Göteberg: Elanders Boktyckeri aktiebolag.

England, E.B. 1921 *The Laws of Plato*, 2 vols. Manchester: Manchester University Press.

Frede, M. 2004. "Aristotle's Account of the Origins of Philosophy." *Rhizai* 1: 9–44.

Gallavotti, C. 1975. *Poema fisico e lustrale: Empedocle*. Milan: Mondadori.

Graham, D.W. 2006. *Explaining the Cosmos: The Ionian Tradition of Scientific Philosophy*. Princeton, NJ: Princeton University Press.

Graham, D.W. 1987. "The Paradox of Prime Matter." *Journal for the History of Philosophy* 25: 475–90.

Gregory, A. 2008. *Plato: Timaeus and Critias*. Introduction and Notes by A. Gregory, translated by Robin Waterfield. Oxford: Oxford University Press.

Gregory, A. 2000. *Plato's Philosophy of Science*. London: Duckworth.

Guthrie, W.K.C. 1978. *A History of Greek Philosophy, Volume V: The Later Plato and the Academy*. Cambridge: Cambridge University Press.

Guthrie, W.K.C. 1965. *A History of Greek Philosophy, Volume II: The Presocratic Tradition from Parmenides to Democritus*. Cambridge: Cambridge University Press.

Guthrie, W.K.C. 1962. *A History of Greek Philosophy, Volume I: The Earlier Presocratics and the Pythagoreans*. Cambridge: Cambridge University Press.

Hershbell, J. P. 1974. "Empedoclean Influences on the *Timaeus*." *Phoenix*, 28.2: 145–166.

Huffman, C. 1993. *Philolaus of Croton: Pythagorean and Presocratic*. Cambridge: Cambridge University Press.

Hussey, E. 1995. "Ionian inquiries: on understanding the Presocratic beginnings of science." In *The Greek World*, edited by A. Powell. London: Routledge.

Inwood, B. 2001. *The Poem of Empedocles*. Text and Translation with Introduction. Toronto: University of Toronto Press.

Joachim, H.H 1922. *Aristotle On Coming-to-be and Passing-away* A Revised Text with Introduction and Commentary. Oxford: Clarendon Press.

Johansen, T. K. 2004. *Plato's Natural Philosophy: A Study of the* Timaeus-Critias. Cambridge: Cambridge University Press.

Jouanna, J. 2012. *Greek Medicine From Hippocrates to Galen: Selected Papers*. Edited by P. Van Der Eijk. Leiden: Brill.

Jouanna, J. 2012a. "The Legacy of the Hippocratic Treatise *The Nature of Man*: The Theory of the Four Humours." in Jouanna 2012.

Jouanna, J. 2012b. "At the Roots of Melancholy: Is Greek Medicine Melancholic?" In Jouanna 2012.

Jouanna, J. 1961. "Présence d'Empédocle dans la Collection hippocratique." *Lettres d'Humanité*, 20: 452–63.

Kahn, C. H. 1960. *Anaximander and the Origins of Greek Cosmology*. New York: Columbia University Press.

ARISTOTLE, EMPEDOCLES, AND THE FOUR ELEMENTS

Kingsley, P. 1995. *Ancient Philosophy, Mystery, and Magic: Empedocles and the Pythagorean Tradition*. Oxford: Clarendon Press.

Kirk, G.S., and J.E. Raven. 1957. *The Presocratic Philosophers: A Critical History with a Selection of Texts*. Cambridge: Cambridge University Press, 1971 reprint with corrections.

Kirk, G.S., and J.E. Raven and M. Schofield. 1983. *The Presocratic Philosophers: A Critical History with a Selection of Texts*. Cambridge: Cambridge University Press, 2nd edition.

Lloyd, G.E.R. 2003. *In the Grip of Disease*. Oxford: Oxford University Press.

Lloyd, G.E.R. 1978. *Hippocratic Writings*. London: Penguin.

Lloyd, G.E.R. 1970. *Early Greek Science: Thales to Aristotle*. New York: Norton.

Lloyd, G.E.R. 1964. "The Hot and the Cold, the Dry and the Wet in Greek Philosophy." *The Journal of Hellenic Studies*, Vol. 84: 92–106.

Longrigg, J. 1993. *Greek Rational Medicine: Philosophy and Medicine from Alcmaeon to the Alexandrians*. London: Routledge.

Longrigg, J. 1976. "The 'Roots of All Things'." *Isis* 67:3: 420–438.

Longrigg, J. 1967. "Roots." *The Classical Review*, New Series Vol. XVII, No. 1: 1–4.

Mayhew, R. 2008. *Plato: Laws* 10. Translation and Commentary. Oxford: Clarendon Press.

Natali, C. 2013. *Aristotle: His Life and School*, edited by D.S. Hutchinson. Princeton, NJ: Princeton University Press.

Nutton, V. 2004. *Ancient Medicine*. London: Routledge.

O'Brien, D. 1969. *Empedocles' Cosmic Cycle*. Cambridge: Cambridge University Press.

Osborne, C. 1987. "Empedocles Recycled." *The Classical Quarterly*, 37: 24–50.

Palmer, J. 2009. *Parmenides and Presocratic Philosophy*. Oxford: Oxford University Press.

Picot, J.-C. 2000. "L'Empédocle magique de P. Kingsley." *Revue de Philosophie Ancienne,*18: 25–86.

Polito, R. 2013. "Asclepiades of Bithynia and Heraclides Ponticus: medical Platonism?" In *Aristotle, Plato and Pythagoreanism in the First Century BC* edited by M. Schofield. Cambridge: Cambridge University Press.

Preus, A. 2015. *Historical Dictionary of Ancient Greek Philosophy*, 2nd edition. New York: Rowman and Littlefield.

Primavesi, O. 2009. "Empedocles: Physical and Mythical Divinity." In *The Oxford Handbook of Presocratic Philosophy* edited by P. Curd & D.W. Graham. Oxford: Oxford University Press.

Rashed, M. 2005. *Aristote De la Génération at la Corruption: Texte et Traduction*. Paris: Les Belles Lettres.

Ross, W. D. 1936. *Aristotle's Physics: A Revised Text with Introduction and Commentary*. Oxford: Clarendon Press.

Ross, W. D. 1924. *Aristotle's Metaphysics: A Revised Text with Introduction and Commentary*, 2 Vols. Oxford: Clarendon Press.

Rossotti, H. 2006. *Chemistry in the Schoolroom: 1806: selections from Mrs. Marcet's 'Conversations on Chemistry'* Bloomington, In: Authorhouse.

Saunders. T.J. 1970. *Plato: The Laws* Translated with an Introduction. London, Penguin.

Sedley, D. 2013. "The Atheist Underground." In *Politeia in Greek and Roman Philosophy* edited by V. Harte and M. Lane. Cambridge: Cambridge University Press.

Sedley, D. 2007. *Creationism and its Critics in Antiquity*. Berkeley and Los Angeles, University of California Press.

Snell, B. 1944. "Die Nachrichten liber die Lehre des Thales und die Anfange der griechischen Philosophic- und Literaturgeschichte." *Philologus* 96: 170–182.

Smith, R. 1997. *Aristotle: Topics I and VIII*. Translated with commentary. Oxford: Clarendon Press.

Sokolowski, R. 1970. "Matter, Elements, and Substance in Aristotle." *Journal of the History of Philosophy*, Vol. 8: 263–288.

Stalley, R.F. 1983. *An Introduction to Plato's Laws*. Oxford: Blackwell.

Taylor, A.E. 1928. *A Commentary on Plato's* Timaeus. Oxford: Clarendon Press.

Taylor, A.E. 1926. *Plato: the Man and his Work*. London: Methuen. 7th ed. 1960.

Vlastos, G. 1975. *Plato's Universe*. Oxford: Clarendon Press.

West, M.L. 1966. *Hesiod: Theogony* Edited with prolegomena and commentary. Oxford: Clarendon Press.

Williams, C.J.F. 1982. *Aristotle's De Generatione et Corruptione*. Translated with notes. Oxford: Clarendon Press.

Wightman, W. 1951. *The Growth of Scientific Ideas*. New Haven: Yale University Press.

Wright, M.R. 1997. "Empedocles." In *Routledge History of Philosophy vol. 1: From the Beginning to Plato*, edited by C.C.W. Taylor. London: Routledge.

Wright, M.R. 1981. *Empedocles: The Extant Fragments*. New Haven: Yale University Press.

Zeller, E. 1883. *Outlines of the History of Greek Philosophy*, 13th ed. Revised by W. Nestle, trans. By L.R. Palmer. New York: Meridian Books.

Zeyl, D. J. 2000. *Plato: Timaeus*. Indianapolis: Hackett.

CHAPTER 12

The Aristotelian Reception Of Heraclitus' Conception of the Soul

Liliana Carolina Sánchez Castro

The first book of *De Anima* contains one of the largest catalogues that Aristotle made of his predecessors' opinions.[1] In the case of this particular treatise, the task justifying the invitation of all these ancient views is to have a point of departure for the investigation he is about to start on the soul. By gathering this gallery of "proto-psychologists", Aristotle pretends to perform a sifting procedure on their views in an effort to separate what they might have gotten right from that about which they were most certainly wrong (*DA* 403b23). Thus, the wrong paths can be avoided, but at the same time the truths contained in those opinions can be successfully used to contribute to Aristotle's current treatment of the soul.

In that context, one would expect that a figure like Heraclitus might have something important to say about the soul. This is a reasonable hope, given that among the early thinkers he was one of those who was most concerned with what we normally suppose to be the arena of psychology; he is also one of the very few early thinkers from whom we have fragments containing the word "soul" (Nussbaum 1972a 6; Laks 1999 253). In fact, given these facts, and maybe many others, it is not strange that Heraclitus has been called "the first great psychologist" (Dilcher 1995 69).[2] However, what Aristotle retains from Heraclitus as a psychologist is very limited. We have just one mention of the Ephesian in the first book of *De Anima*. Furthermore, this one direct reference

---

1 This paper was inspired by the ideas of the second half of the seventh chapter's argument of my PhD thesis, published in its original version by the National University of Colombia (Sánchez 2016, 241). However, this article has been completely rewritten, and contains new (and possibly radically different) claims about the Aristotelian reception of Heraclitus' view of the soul. I have to express my gratitude to the Research Foundation of the State of São Paulo (FAPESP), that made possible this work with the fund granted in the process n. 2016/ 05333-6. I want to express my gratitude to Chelsea Harris, who kindly helped me to correct many mistakes of the paper.

2 See also, Nussbaum 1972a 15; Kahn 1979 127; Hussey 1999 101; Betegh 2007 4.

© KONINKLIJKE BRILL NV, LEIDEN, 2021 | DOI:10.1163/9789004443358_014

consists of scarcely five lines, which are enchained with other presences in the middle of the *kinestist catalogue*.[3]

The lack of direct allusions to Heraclitus in the context of *De Anima*, however, did not represent an insurmountable obstacle for the Aristotelian interpretation. As a matter of fact, it may be the case that those few lines constitute the first instance of a whole tradition that could play an important role in the posterior reception of Heraclitus as a psychologist.[4] The scarcity may also respond to the fact that Aristotle is interested neither in *all* the ancient opinions on the soul, nor in its totality. His dialectical method, in fact, prevents him from doing so.[5] This is why it is necessary to specify what type

---

3 The *Kinetist Catalogue* is a list of ancient thinkers located at the end of the second chapter of *De Anima I* (405a8-405b10). One of the particularities that this precise passage exhibits is that, different from the other appeals to early thinkers, there is a connection between the opinions that Aristotle presents here. This macrotextual continuity is promoted by the product of an initial revision on ancient opinions (404a1-404b30), from where Aristotle is no longer just thinking in terms of motion and sensation as classificatory items. Rather, he is going to examine the early opinions at the light of the characteristics of the principle (ἀρχή) held by his predecessors: self-motion and subtlety, and further sensation is going to be explained as a sort of material continuity. Thus, those thinkers of the *Kinetist Catalogue* are enchained by the fact that the soul is going to be identified with the principle, and on that ground motion and sensation are explained. A second feature that must be remarked is that all these opinions are presented in a very compressed way, exhibiting a sort of inferential process from the part of Aristotle that need to be disclosed, which is going to be the target of my reading. The most important feature, finally, is that the *Kinetist Catalogue* is going to be, in fact, the anticipatory indicator of the central criticism Aristotle is going to perform on the Presocratics' views, namely, the refutation of the conception of the soul as self-moving (Viano 1996 58-64).

4 On the influence of the first book of *De Anima* in the subsequent psychological doxography, see Viano, *ibid*, 51.

5 The dialectical procedure is not a random discussion. In the *Topics* (105b12) and in the *Rhetoric* (1378a27) there are references to the διάγραφαι, which must have been a kind of collection of opinions ordered according to the subject of discussion or the argumentative topics where they are supposed to be useful (see, Smith 1997 90; Sánchez 2016 102). If this is the case, it means that the opinions that are employed in a particular treatise are carefully selected to suit the argumentative purpose (*Top.* 163b4). Besides this, Aristotle himself at times states that not all material is of interest to him, and that not all the opinions should be analyzed in the same way (Viano 1996, 53; Baltussen 2000 48). In the case of *De Anima*, for example, it is clear that not every single occurrence of the word ψυχή is useful for him: otherwise, Anaxagoras could stray far from the scope of his subject, and Homer needed to be an important reference. And it is clear that the opinions Aristotle is inviting correspond with his classificatory tools. It is therefore reasonable to think that he is manipulating the ancient views on the soul in the measure that they fit into his categories, and that he is most probably not taking into account celebrated views that do not relate to his objective. On the use of dialectics in scientific research, see Bolton 1999 79.

THE ARISTOTELIAN RECEPTION OF HERACLITUS' CONCEPTION

of hermeneutical benefit Aristotle obtained from Heraclitus. By doing so we may be in position to understand how this particular interpretive tradition on the Ephesian thinker is built, and if it can somehow be helpful to learn about Heraclitus' thinking.

1 The Testimony

At the beginning of the second chapter of *De Anima I*, Aristotle declares his interest in reviewing his predecessors' opinions for the purposes of his own research on the soul. In this context he sets out his first dialectical tool: two criteria inherited from ancient thinkers (but also from common sense), to establish a difference between what we consider to be ensouled and that which we do not. Those criteria are motion and perception (*DA* 403b26).[6]

From this point on, Aristotle is going to look for those characteristics in early thinkers' views. That examination, as it goes on, progressively incorporates additional elements: (i) that which moves must be in motion (*DA* 403b29); and (ii) that the soul must exist or be a first principle or the first principles (*DA* 404b8). These two features become entwined at a certain point in time in the dialectical survey; there were thinkers who believed that what produces motion, by virtue of this very fact, must be deemed to be a first principle (*DA* 405a3; see also Viano 1996 64).

At this point in the dialectical inquiry, the *kinetist catalogue* is introduced. This list of thinkers not only demonstrates that they all ascribed to a conception of the soul as a dynamic principle; most of them also allegedly thought that the soul was made from what counted for them as the first principle(s). In this way, then, Aristotle can use these opinions too as if they also meant that the soul was a principle of knowledge and perception. In this context we find the mention of the Ephesian:

(A) [DK22A15; LM R43] καὶ Ἡράκλειτος δὲ τὴν ἀρχὴν εἶναί φησι ψυχήν, εἴπερ τὴν ἀναθυμίασιν, ἐξ ἧς τἆλλα συνίστησιν· καὶ ἀσωματώτατόν τε καὶ ῥέον ἀεί·

---

6 "κινήσει τε καὶ τῷ αἰσθάνεσθαι". Nevertheless, in a further amplification of this latter criterion, Aristotle refers to "τὸ γινώσκειν καὶ τὸ αἰσθάνεσθαι" (*DA* 404b9). The term "sensation" can be understood as used in a large sense to cover also cognitive faculties. But there is an additional explanation: in the dialectical survey, and further in Book III, Aristotle points out that there were ancient opinions on the identity between perception and thought (*DA* 427a21). We must therefore accept that this category is going to be exploited by Aristotle bearing in mind that this conceptual refinement was not yet available. On this subject, see Laks 1999 255.

τὸ δὲ κινούμενον κινουμένῳ γινώσκεσθαι· ἐν κινήσει δ' εἶναι τὰ ὄντα κἀκεῖνος ᾤετο καὶ οἱ πολλοί.

ARISTOTLE, *De Anima* 405a25-29

Heraclitus too says that the soul is the first principle, if indeed it is the exhalation from which what exists is constituted; and that it is the most incorporeal and is always in flux. And what is in motion is known by what is in motion; he thought, as did many others, that what exists is in motion.

The description given of the alleged Heraclitean view of the soul integrates all the elements that Aristotle has been collecting through his dialectical examination. First of all, from the first line it is clear that the Ephesian is taken here to be one of the thinkers who identified the soul with the first principle. Secondly, this first principle, and consequently the soul, is the most incorporeal and restless phenomenon. And, in the third place, it is a cognitive principle in virtue of its own motion. For Aristotle, then, Heraclitus held a conception of the soul as material and automotive.

Such views of the Presocratics have made Aristotle the target of so much criticism. It has been said that this way of presenting ancient opinions complies more with Aristotle's desire to find a sort of anticipation for his own views than a philosophical interest (Cherniss 1935 xii; Kirk 1970 176); it has also been hypothesized that he is making a conscientious biased reading in order to make Presocratics vulnerable to his further criticism (Dilcher 1995 161). Be that as it may, I prefer to leave aside exegetical approaches of this kind, in order to try to conduct an analysis of the very testimony Aristotle offer us.

The passage can be divided into two sections. This division corresponds to two different moments at the macrotextual level, which can be separated in the syntactical sequence. So, we get:

(1) Heraclitus too says that the soul is the first principle, if indeed it is the exhalation from which what exists is constituted;

(2) and that it is the most incorporeal and is always in flux. And what is in motion is known by what is in motion; he thought, as did many others, that what exists is in motion.

The division proposed, rather than simply adhering to a syntactical feature, can help us to separate two different problems that we need to address with Aristotle's testimony on Heraclitus' view on the soul: (i) the fact that the soul is a principle; and (ii) its dynamic characteristic and capacity.

THE ARISTOTELIAN RECEPTION OF HERACLITUS' CONCEPTION 381

2   The Soul as First Principle

The first part of the text we are going to analyze seems to be, *prima facie*, what was closest to Aristotle's view of Heraclitus. This fact could be extracted from the observation that there is an evident direct attribution of an opinion to the Ephesian, which Aristotle expresses by referring to the reported speech (*DA* 405a25-27):

(*1*)   Heraclitus too says that (1.1) the soul is the first principle, if indeed it is (1.2) the exhalation from which what exists is constituted;

If the reported speech is removed, we are left with the result that the *basic claim*, which is attributed to Heraclitus, is (1.1) "the soul is the first principle". Nevertheless, we can notice that the reported speech in this case does not exactly function as a philological indication of a quote. This is evident from the fact that what I called the *basic claim* is, actually, the apodosis of a conditional. This hypothetical period as a whole, in its turn, serves as the direct object of the verb φησι. The protasis of the conditional is introduced by the conjunction εἴπερ (together with its relative clause), which is not just an indication of the hypothetical period but also an indication of doubt. If this is so, then, what Aristotle is reporting in this passage, as Heraclitus' opinion, is in fact his own inference (Hicks 1907 231).

So, we now have to explain how Aristotle's hermeneutical apparatus operates. If we extract the content of the protasis, we get (1.2) "the exhalation is constituted from what exists". This is a first principle in Presocratic cosmologies, where whatever counts as the origin from where what exists is constituted, this is said to be a first principle.[7] Now, putting all the elements in place, we may reconstruct Aristotle's inference as follows:[8]

> The exhalation is the first principle (1.2)
> The soul is exhalation (*)
> The soul is the first principle (1.1)

That Aristotle's goal was to understand Heraclitus as saying that the soul is composed of what the Ephesians thought was the first principle, is not

---

7   On the type of monism that the early Greek philosophers may profess, see Kahn 1979 132 and Polansky 2007 79. For a different perspective, recognizing that the concept must be alien for Heraclitus, see Mouraviev 2008ᵃ 141.

8   The syllogistic form of this reasoning, with this reconstruction, has been noticed by Hicks 1907 231 and Mouraviev 2008ᵃ 13 n.1 also. Nevertheless, the first scholar to point to the syllogistic form of the passage was Simplicius (*In DA*, XI 31, 27).

surprising. It was in fact anticipated in the dialectical process that was conducted on the ancient views just before the introduction of the *kinetist catalogue* (*DA* 404b8; 404b30). What should be a matter of interest is whether Aristotle is entitled to proceed in that way. In order to evaluate whether this is so, we need to trace Aristotle's steps back to the point of departure.

Returning now to the protasis: we have said that Aristotle was employing as input the declaration that for Heraclitus (1.2) "the exhalation is the first principle". This statement has given rise to at least two discussions: the first one is connected with the presence of the term ἀναθυμίασις; the other one has to do with the legitimacy of the first principle ascribed to Heraclitus.

The term ἀναθυμίασις provoked some debate among Heraclitean scholars, the fundamental reason for this being that this word (and the verb ἀναθυμιῶνται) are not attested in the Greek corpus before Aristotle.[9] Yet, the idea of an exhalation is very common both in Aristotelian and also in Presocratic thought; its traces in the testimonies of the *corpus heracliteum* have been attested to the point that it is natural to encounter the label "doctrine of exhalations" in almost every Heraclitean study. In the testimony we are concerned with, the term is crucial since, to reiterate, the statement where this word is embedded is the point of departure of Aristotle's inference that the soul is made up of the first principle for Heraclitus.

The terminological issue is, nevertheless, not sufficient reason to withdraw the claim that Aristotle possibly composed his inference from a truly Heraclitean view. The exhalation theory seems to be inferred from Heraclitus' cosmological statements, for which we depend highly on Aristotelian doxography. In these texts we found testimonies of the process of interchange between material masses. From there it has been argued that these interchanges involve an exhalation detached from the cosmic elementary masses, which is the active principle for the process to be performed.[10] Now, if this is so, Aristotle must be

---

9   On the term ἀναθυμίασις, see: Cherniss 1935 298 n. 31; Kirk 1954 368; Kahn 1979 259; Mouraviev 2006ᶜ 20; and Sánchez 2016 250. A few scholars believe that the term must be authentic Heraclitean, such as Hicks 1907 231; and Dilcher 1995 64.

10 The transmission of the theory from doxography is difficult (Kirk 1954 186 n. 1 and 275). The main testimony for the "exhalation doctrine" comes from Diogenes Laertius's account of Heraclitus, and from the quotation context of B6 in Aristotle's *Meteorologicae*. Nevertheless, it should be noted that what is retained as Heraclitean in B6 is no more than a single statement: that the soul is new every day. The sources for the exhalation theory were gathered together by Marcovich 2001 305; and Mouraviev (between his testimonies D63 and D75). Mouraviev's grouping shows very clearly the prime role that Aristotle and Theophrastus play in ascribing this theory to Heraclitus (2008ᵃ 36). On this topic, see also Dilcher 1995 166. There are, however, two other occurrences of the idea of exhalation in the extant fragments: in fragment B7, when Aristotle talks about the sense of smell in

THE ARISTOTELIAN RECEPTION OF HERACLITUS' CONCEPTION 383

transcribing in alien words a Heraclitean idea, given that the process of exhalations does play a major role in Aristotle's meteorological explanations, and we may suppose that this is a vocabulary he feels more comfortable with (Kahn 1979 333 n. 362; Betegh 2007 19). This is far from an oddity. It is, after all, not the first time we have found these kinds of hermeneutical strategies performed by Aristotle in his treatises when he is dealing with foreign opinions.[11] In fact, it responds to the exigencies of his own dialectical method.

But, how exactly those exhalations are present in the *corpus heracliteum* is a very good question to address. Actually, it is hard to say. The alleged "doctrine of exhalations" is primarily reconstructed either from the quotation context of the genuine fragments, or from doxography (or from both), for the occurrence of the word is meant to be external. In most of these cases, we find that the tradition ascribing this idea to Heraclitus is Aristotelian or dependent on an Aristotelian tradition. Even if we do accept this, there is still another obstacle to overcome. In our celebrated protasis, Aristotle reports that this exhalation is the first principle (1.2), which does not exactly fit with the information we have of the Heraclitean first principle in the extant fragments.[12] Paradoxically, nor is it consistent with Aristotle's own account elsewhere of Heraclitus' first principle (*Met.* 984a7). In fact, in all the Greek commentaries and paraphrases of the *DA*, it is apparent that the interpreters have problems in accepting the accuracy of Aristotle's account of the Heraclitean first principle and that they tend to doctor the passage through its exegesis:

– καὶ Ἡράκλειτος δὲ ἦν ἀρχὴν τίθεται τῶν ὄντων, ταύτην τίθεται καὶ ψυχήν· πῦρ γὰρ καὶ οὗτος. τὴν γὰρ ἀναθυμίασιν ἐξ ἧς τὰ ἄλλα συνίστησιν οὐκ ἄλλο τι ἢ πῦρ ὑποληπτέον, τοῦτο δὲ καὶ ἀσώματον καὶ ῥέον ἀεί.

THEMISTIUS, *In DA*, v.111 13 26-28

De Sensu (443a21); and in fragment B98, where we find the verbal form θυμιῶνται, and souls are said to be nourished by exhalations in Hades. Those fragments, however, are not unanimously considered as (totally) authentic by critics (Kahn 1979 256; Marcovich 2001 418).

11 One of the most celebrated Aristotelian lexical actualizations occurs in the *Metaphysics* (985b4-20 [DK67A6; LM D31]). There we find an explanation of the "characteristics" or *differences* (διαφοράς) that the atoms exhibit: they are *disposition* (ῥυσμός), *contact* (διαθιγή) and turn (τροπή). Aristotle translates them into *shape* (σχῆμά), *order* (τάξις) and *position* (θέσις). On this procedure performed on Democritus' theory, see Sánchez 2016, 149.

12 It is possible, however, that Aristotle was not sure about this. As Mouraviev says: "L'incertitude d'Aristote démontre en tout cas que le texte d'Héraclite *n'était pas suffisamment explicite à son gout pour qu'on puisse y identifier un principe quelconque de façon univoque*, il montre, autrement dit, que c'était une notion que l'Éphesien soit ignorait, soit rejetait" (2008a 141).

Also Heraclitus states the first principle for existing things as he does for the soul too; this is fire. For one must suppose that the exhalation from which the other existing things are constituted, is nothing different to fire, and it is incorporeal and in constant flux.

- Ἡράκλειτος δὲ πῦρ, εἴπερ ἐξ ἀναθυμιάσεως αὐτὴν ἔλεγεν, ἐξ ἧς καὶ τἄλλα συνίστησι, καὶ ἀσώματόν τε καὶ ῥέον ἀεί.

  SOPHONIAS, *In DA*, XIV 26–27

Heraclitus [says it is] fire, if indeed he said that it came from the exhalation from which also the other existing things are constituted, and the most incorporeal and always in flux.

This perturbation in the Aristotelian tradition needs to be explained. The two passages above are an important barometer of the situation, since they are both paraphrases: it could be argued, however, that even if a paraphrase is meant to run close to the original texts, still it entails a great charge of exegesis. But the interventions in these texts seem to carry more than just an exegesis; they appear *prima facie* to be what the authors believed to be necessary inclusions in order to correct unforgivable omissions at the light of tradition.

However, there may be a stronger reason beyond the Heraclitean tradition received by writers in Late Antiquity to explain why they needed to regain "fire" at that point in their exegesis. As we saw in the examination of Aristotle's testimony on Heraclitus, there were two characteristics of the first principle, the exhalation, which were important in explaining the psychic operations: the subtlety and the constant flux. It seems to be Aristotle himself who instructs his commentators to go in the direction of fire by establishing precisely those characteristics to the soul constituent:

(B) ἐπομένως δὲ τούτοις καὶ τὴν ψυχὴν ἀποδιδόασιν· τὸ γὰρ κινητικὸν τὴν φύσιν τῶν πρώτων ὑπειλήφασιν, οὐκ ἀλόγως. ὅθεν ἔδοξέ τισι πῦρ εἶναι· καὶ γὰρ τοῦτο λεπτομερέστατόν τε καὶ μάλιστα τῶν στοιχείων ἀσώματον, ἔτι δὲ κινεῖταί τε καὶ κινεῖ τὰ ἄλλα πρώτως.

ARISTOTLE, *De Anima*, 405a3-7

According to those [features], they give an account of the soul: for— not irrationally—they supposed that what is motor by nature [must be counted] among the principles. Hence it seemed to some of them that it was fire, for it is the most fine grained and quite incorporeal of the elements; further, it is moved and also moves mainly the other things.

As is evident, Aristotle explicitly connects the attributes of subtlety and motion with fire in his dialectical survey; it is important to remark that these attributes can also be attributed to the air (*DA* 405b17). But, besides the fact that is Aristotle who gives the interpretative clue, he does so at the point when he is introducing the *kinetist catalogue* where Heraclitus' view on the soul can be found. Although the first thinker who is going to be presented in the *catalogue* is Democritus, and he held the soul to be fire according to the *De Anima's* testimony, one might hope to see those references point in general to the "more coherent materialist model", whichever it (or they) may be (Viano 1996 64). That is why there is no direct connection with Heraclitus' strange "exhalation" from Aristotle's side; the paraphrasers, on the other hand, were just tracking the soul's characteristics back in the dialectical process and, so, employing the explanation Aristotle gave in order to make Heraclitus' statement clearer, they perhaps felt the necessity to make explicit the presence of fire.

This can be a reasonable supposition. However, this does not explain all the cases we find in the exegesis of *De Anima*. The commentaries, for example, too, mention fire, but they do not abandon the concept of exhalation:

> — περὶ δὲ Ἡρακλείτου συλλογιζομένῳ ἔοικεν, οὐχ ὡς σαφῶς λέγοντος πῦρ ἢ ἀναθυμίασιν ξηρὰν τὴν ψυχήν, ἀλλ' ὡς τοῦ πυρὸς πρὸς τῷ λεπτομερεῖ καὶ τὸ εὐκίνητον ἔχοντος καὶ τῷ κινεῖσθαι τὰ ἄλλα κινοῦντος, καὶ διὰ ταῦτά [τε] τῇ ψυχῇ προσήκοντος ὡς διὰ παντὸς τοῦ ζῶντος ἰούσῃ σώματος καὶ ὡς τῷ κινεῖσθαι κινητικῇ καὶ ἔτι ὡς γνωστικῇ.
>
> SIMPLICIUS, *In DA*, XI 31, 27–31

> He seems to be drawing inferences about Heraclitus, but not as he was saying clearly that soul was fire or dry exhalation, but given that fire was easily mobile as well as fine-grained and, by moving, moved other things, so it was fitted to be soul, since it permeated all living bodies, it originated motion by moving itself, and besides it is cognitive.[13]

Simplicius seems to be following Aristotle's advice in including fire in the testimony in function of the characteristics depicted for the Heraclitean first principle. But, as we can see in the lines extracted from his commentary, from very old times a great part of the specialized critic has solved the problem appealing to a "dry" and/or a "fiery" exhalation.[14] This almost automatic link seems

---

13   Translation by Ursom, modified (1995 50).
14   For examples of the acceptance of this supposition, see Lasalle 1858 327; Kirk 1954 340, 375 and 396; Zeller and Mondolfo 1961 88; Nussbaum 1972ᵃ 7; Conche 1986 454; Marcovich

to come, among the contemporary scholars, from understanding the πρηστήρ of fragment B31 as fire (in light of fragment B36), and from the statement in fragment B118 that a dry soul is wiser than a humid one. But it is hard to find in the extant fragments a literal declaration as such. Taking such an omission with this identification performs a semantic equivalence between the foreign term "exhalation" with the more familiar "fire". Although it is perfectly possible, given the actual state of the corpus, it does not explain exactly where the "exhalation" comes from. So the Aristotelian hermeneutical effort continues to be occluded.

There is, however, another possibility. When reconstructing Aristotle's inference, I briefly mentioned that the protasis of the conditional was introduced by the conjunction εἴπερ. Additionally, I stressed the point of departure of the inference as the proposition (1.2) "the exhalation is first principle". Let us take another look at it.

The enclitic particle περ has the function of reinforcing a specific semantic nuance; it is stressing a hypothetical hue, that of doubt. It could also be the case that the interpretive procedure Aristotle is conducting with Heraclitus was motivated more by a difficulty in understanding, or a low quality source, than a deliberate aim to distort. If this is so, the information available to him was not that (1.2) "the exhalation is the first principle" but that (*) "the soul was an exhalation".

We already know that the term ἀναθυμίασις is completely lacking in the extant fragments (we were advised even that the word was coined by Aristotle's times). Indeed, we do know that the attribution of an exhalation theory to Heraclitus is supported mainly by testimonies coming from an Aristotelian tradition, so we have to consider the fact that much of the exegetical aim we are trying to reconstruct is consolidated in that theory. We suppose that Aristotle is employing the term in order to translate some Heraclitean idea, and that he is being very careful in doing so by saying that the exhalation was for the Ephesian the constituent of what exists (1.2). We may have a sound hypothesis for explaining that.

The whole tradition supporting the idea of an exhalation in Heraclitus' thought is believed to be part of Heraclitean cosmogony and meteorology. Nevertheless, by looking for that in the extant fragments, we can try to figure out what may have been Aristotle's source.

2001 361; and Polansky 2007 79. For a broader perspective, bearing in mind the different interpretive traditions, see Kahn 1979 47; Mouraviev 2008ᵃ 166.

(a) [DK22B36; LM D100] ψυχῇσιν θάνατος ὕδωρ γενέσθαι, ὕδατι δὲ θάνατος γῆν γενέσθαι· ἐκ γῆς δὲ ὕδωρ γίνεται, ἐξ ὕδατος δὲ ψυχή.

CLEMENT of Alexandria, *Stromata*, 6 ii 17 2–3

For souls it is death to become water, for water it is death to become earth; from earth water arises, and from water soul.

(b)[DK22B31a; LM D86] πυρὸς τροπαὶ πρῶτον θάλασσα θαλάσσης δὲ τὸ μὲν ἥμισυ γῆ, τὸ δὲ ἥμισυ πρηστήρ.

CLEMENT of Alexandria, *Stromata*, 5 xiv 104 3–4

The reversals (changes) of fire: first sea, but of sea half is earth, half *prester*.

(c) [DK22B76b] πυρὸς θάνατος ἀέρι γένεσις καὶ ἀέρος θάνατος ὕδατι γένεσις.

PLUTARCH, *De E*, 392c9-10

The death of fire is birth for air, and the death of air is birth for water.

The idea of a cycle of transformation of matter cannot always be found in Heraclitus' fragments in the same form, and maybe this is also the cause for their being not exactly consistent. Besides, there is a high probability that we are looking at some allegorical uses in the terminology, which should prevent us reading the terms in exactly the same way and for looking for a straight consistency. For example, it is clear that we are looking at statements carrying some cosmological explanations of the transformation between elements, transformations that we can encounter with the term "reversal" τροπή, but also with the terms "death" (θάνατος) and "birth" (γένεσις). This particular linguistic feature could provide an explanation for the inconsistency exhibited by the fragments and give us a path to follow.

Consider this. There is an oddity included in text (b): it seems that "fire" is being considered at a different ontological level from that of the other elements; in Marcovich's words "it does *not* interfere in the rest of the saying" (2001 284). Although my interpretation differs very much from Marcovich's, I agree with the fact that we can read a clear caesura there. This conclusion can be taken from the position of the correlative particles μέν ... δέ, which seem to be distributing two elements that count as subclasses of πυρὸς τροπαί.[15] So, "fire" is the origin of the process, but is not an elementary mass *tout court*. If "fire" is held here not as an ordinary elementary mass, but something similar

---

15   On the style and parallelisms that exhibit this fragment, see Mouraviev 2006[b] 52.

to a basis of those elements, we can explain why "fire" is not part of the cycle in this fragment, but rather the origin of the cycle; so, fire never is annihilated, because is subsisting in everything, no matter what change occurs.

The idea of "fire", not as a material element but an allegorical label for the metaphysical ordering principle sometimes also expressed by the word λόγος is not unusual (see, for example, fragment B30 or B90). In text (c), on the contrary, it seems that "fire" is one of the elementary masses. We can notice that the language of text (b) exhibits a more allegorical tendency than the others; for example, where it is considering "water" as an elementary mass involved in cosmic transformations, the mass is referred to as "sea". This particular use of language, together with the apparently different ontological status for "fire", warns against a hasty interpretation of the term πρηστήρ. As a matter of fact, the most widespread tendency in Heraclitean studies is to associate πρηστήρ directly with "fire", when is not the case that it is indeed another name for "fire".

Text (a) raises additional questions. In the first place, it is very strange to encounter the term "soul" as an elementary mass in material cosmological transformations. We can try to provide an explanation by reverting to an allegorical interpretation of language used in the text (b). But, in that case, what corresponds with "soul"?

One possibility is to establish links among the elements in these three fragments to see if there are matches that help make explicit what the allegorical language carries. We can be sure that in any of these accounts at least three items are involved:

(a) Earth, water, soul
(b) Sea, earth, πρήστηρ
(c) Fire, air, water

We do not have a problem with "earth", for the same term has always been employed. "Water", on the other hand, must correspond with "sea". "Soul", then, must match with πρήστηρ (Betegh 2007 15). If the equivalences work, on the one hand, this will somehow explain why Aristotle excluded "fire", as the constituent principle of the "soul", in his account of *De Anima*, if his source about the soul exhalation was carrying this type of information. On the other hand, it can also make explicit the reason why he is so confident in ascribing to Heraclitus a material conception of the soul. But in order to argue in favor of any of these exegetical roads, the referent of πρηστήρ must be disclosed.

I have said that a full identification of πρηστήρ with "fire" is not completely satisfactory given the occurrence of the latter at a different ontological level in text (b): if is a τροπή of fire, as the sea is, then it cannot be exactly "fire" (*pace*

THE ARISTOTELIAN RECEPTION OF HERACLITUS' CONCEPTION 389

Kirk 1951, 39).[16] In fact, it is not clear exactly what this term means—neither for us today, nor for the ancients. Aristotle, for example, refers to a strange atmospheric phenomenon where a cloud is inflamed, and then colored, by the action of a subtle wind (*Meteor.* 371a16). Most modern interpreters understand it as a fiery event (Kirk 1954 331; Bollack-Wismann 1972 134; Kahn 1979 139); some others avoid translating it because of the uncertainty (Marcovich 2001 284; Mouraviev 2006ᵃ 88). Nevertheless, what seems clear from Aristotle's description is that the πρηστήρ is an atmospheric event, which involves mainly air.[17] If this is so, the occurrence of this term may be hiding an important element missing in Heraclitus' meteorological statements (a) and (b), but which is present in (c); that is, "air". Text (c), however, has been contested as a possible stoic fabrication made of fragment (a), which is how the occurrence of "air" in Heraclitus' cosmology is traditionally explained. But, if πρηστήρ can somehow be replacing "air" in an allegorical way in fragment (b), then we can be persuaded that it comes from the sea (or is generated from water). If this is the case in fragment (a), then it was substituted by the term "soul", which also comes from water. So, in both cases, this πρηστήρ seems to be something rising from the humid elementary mass, something ethereal, an exhalation.[18]

My interpretation, then, does not see in B36 an immediate reversal (τροπή) from water to fire, without an intermediary element (which must be "air" from B31). Nevertheless, it is impossible to obviate the fact that the phenomenon

---

16   And there are some doctrinal challenges that this identification cannot overcome. For example, how is it that "fire", the constituent of everything, can be annihilated in the cosmic process? Or how is that it is preferable to have a dry soul than a humid one if it is necessary that fire changes into water in the cosmic cycle, mostly in light of fragment B77 when this "dying" of the fire into water is expressed in terms of "pleasure" (τέρψις)? (Nussbaum 1972ᵇ 158; Marcovich 2001 361). Moreover, how can we deal with the strange idea of a wet fire if soul is to be understood as fire? (Betegh 2007 17).

17   "Tout comme le mot *mer* désigne ici l'élement liquid, le mot πρηστήρ doit designer l'élément gazeux et/ou igné, Étymologiquement ce mot derive de πρήθω «s'allumer, brûler (sous l'action d'un souffle) et est un quasi-doublet de αἰθήρ (qui lui dérive de αἴθω «allumer, brûler») et désignait aussi les fulgurations" (Mouraviev 2006ᶜ 39).

18   My interpretation, then, does not see in B36 an immediate reversal (τροπή) from water to fire, without an intermediary element (which must be "air" from B31). This idea has been defended before, but also has been attacked on the grounds of a possible stoic intrusion (Kirk 1954 340). Against the idea that the presence of "air" could mean a stoic interference, see Polito 2004 158; and Betegh 2007 16 n. 25. On the possible Heraclitean conception of an ethereal soul, that I share, see Gilbert 1907 46 n.1; Hicks 1907 231; and Kahn 1979 154 and 240–259. Mouraviev seems to share this opinion, although he is very careful in remarking that this identification between soul and air probably was not explicit in Heraclitus (2008ᵃ 167).

προστήρ designs somehow involves fire or light. Maybe it is the case that the reference is a mixture of both air and fire, which is probably the less dogmatic solution for an issue about which it is impossible to have certainty.[19] Whatever the case, we can proceed without a high level of accuracy on the point, given that both "air" and "fire" are dynamic and subtle elements.

So, are we now in a position to say that this exhalation is the constituent of what exists? Maybe we are, if we commit to the idea that those elementary masses are the primary material constituents of the world. And it happens, or at least it seems to be the case in Heraclitus, that these elementary masses must be the material principles if the conformation of things in the natural world responds to the process of material exchanges provoked initially by fire that we have in fragments (a), (b) and (c). In a way, everything is made from exhalations (1.2). But, as we have seen, there is support for calling that exhalation principle the "soul".[20]

I think I have shown that there is a possibility that the exhalation theory hides some truly Heraclitean idea, even in foreign terms. If this is so, we are in a position to argue that the point of departure from Aristotle's inference was, in fact, a proposition similar to the one we marked as a missing premise, that is, "the soul is an exhalation"(*).[21] So he is, indeed, entitled to say that this exhalation is the principle (or at least, part of it) proposed by Heraclitus to explain the world.

The result obtained in the last section, moreover, seems to be ratified by Philoponus. For it is true that, contrary to this passage, the paraphrasers and Simplicius prefer to include the missing and familiar Heraclitean fire, or refer to a "dry exhalation". Nevertheless, Philoponus makes a mention of fire, but rescues the concept of exhalation:

> — Εἴρηται πολλάκις ὅτι ἀρχὴν ἔλεγεν εἶναι τῶν ὄντων οὗτος τὸ πῦρ, πῦρ δὲ οὐ τὴν φλόγα· ὡς γὰρ Ἀριστοτέλης φησίν, ἡ φλὸξ ὑπερβολή ἐστι πυρός· ἀλλὰ πῦρ ἔλεγε τὴν ξηρὰν ἀναθυμίασιν· ἐκ ταύτης οὖν εἶναι καὶ τὴν ψυχὴν ὡς εὐκινήτου καὶ λεπτομερεστάτης.
>
> PHILOPONUS, *In DA*, xv 87, 10–13

---

19   This is Betegh's position (2007 22). For another "hybrid" position, this time adding water to the equation as well, Reinhardt 1916 194; Walzer 1964 52 n.2; and Viano 1996 67.

20   I agree with Betegh's claim that, even if the use of the exhalation theory seems to be very well consolidated in the Heraclitan tradition, "not all of Aristotle's own theory of exhalations can be ascribed to Heraclitus" (2007 20); in any case, we do not need the whole Aristotelian theory in order to understand the exegetical procedure, but the concept that works as a hermeneutical tool.

21   *Pace* Dilcher 1995 64, who says that Aristotle's uncertainty is based, not on "the equation of soul with ἀναθυμίασις, but on the exhalation being an ἀρχή".

THE ARISTOTELIAN RECEPTION OF HERACLITUS' CONCEPTION

> It has often been said that he said that fire was the principle of things, indeed fire, not flame; for as Aristotle himself says, the flame is an excess of fire. It is rather that he calls dry exhalation to fire; of this, then, soul is composed, too, since it moves easily and consists of very fine particles.[22]

If the commentators were so sure that the first principle for Heraclitus was fire, how can we explain Philoponus' insistence on clarifying that point? The exegete explains that exhalation has a dynamic capacity and the subtle material constitution required to move, and in consequence to know. But Philoponus also wanted to show that he is aware of the fact that "fire" is an equivocal term, and he thinks that Aristotle is trying to avoid a misunderstanding. So, in a certain way, he might find a reason to avoid a drastic intervention in the text. Nevertheless, the fact that Philoponus remained loyal to Aristotle's terminology is evidence that for the commentators (or at least, for some of them) the problem is not a question of access to reliable sources, or accuracy in presenting Presocratic quotes *tout court*. What we are witnessing here is that Philoponus understood the importance of the concept of exhalation in the very structure of Aristotle's reasoning.

3   The Operations of the Soul

The commentators' texts provide us with a lot more information that we need to trace back, for they all establish a direct link between the characteristics of the soul exhalation with the psychic operations in the very comment of Aristotle's account on Heraclitus' principle. In order to understand the implications that this link may have, we need to go back to the second part of the *De Anima's* testimony. Then, we can continue to analyze which other elements Aristotle puts forward, in order to reconstruct his exegetic procedure on Heraclitus' view. Let us recall the second division proposed for the text (*DA* 405a27-29):

(2)   and that it is the most incorporeal and is always in flux (2.1). And what is in motion is known by what is in motion (2.2); he thought, as did many others, that what exists is in motion (2.3).

If we concentrate on the information provided by the syntax of the whole testimony, we have another idea attributed to Heraclitus, that is, that the principle is the more incorporeal thing and that it is restless. Then, we find two clauses

---

22   Translation by van der Eijk 2005 108, slightly modified.

that seem to be contributing information to explain this inferential process. Although the very disposition of the wording is going to demand that some connections are established, which are not explicit in the text of the testimony, we can reconstruct the steps in Aristotle's hermeneutical effort.

The reasoning to be conducted, though, depends on the acceptance of a general premise, functioning as a sort of hermeneutical tool Aristotle is employing to understand his predecessors:

The similar knows the similar.

The most primitive version of this statement in the *De Anima* can be found in the announcement of the dialectical survey. Aristotle says there that, besides the fact that we have inherited from the ancient thinkers motion and sensation as characteristics of the soul, they also bequeath us that "what is not in motion cannot move another thing" (*DA* 403b29). This is a sort of negative version of the like-to-like principle that Aristotle is explicitly ascribing to his predecessors, and that he is stating as one of the starting points of his examination of their doctrines. We find it again, for example, in the words of Empedocles (*DA* 404b13 [DK 31B109]), and it is recalled too from Plato's *Timaeus* (*DA* 404b17). Both of these mentions support as further evidence that the tool comes from the predecessors themselves, and that Aristotle is entitled to apply it to the analysis of the ancient views (Sánchez 2016 256).

We can be confident that Aristotle is using this idea in the *De Anima* also as a principle applied to Heraclitus' thought, as it is clear from the occurrence of the same idea in the testimony. However, the presence of this hermeneutical tool is shaped according to the content of the view he is going to analyze (Hicks 1907 231). So, the structure of the reasoning can be presented as follows:

What is in motion is known by what is in motion (2.2)
Everything is in motion (2.3)
The first principle is the most incorporeal and restless thing (2.1)
The soul is the first principle, an exhalation (1.1) + (*)
The soul knows everything (**)

This part of the testimony seems to be the carrier of a different interpretive process Aristotle did on Heraclitus' thought, in order to include it in his research on the soul. The proof is that, in this occasion, the point of departure is going to be the Heraclitean characteristics of the principle, and consequently, of the soul; this point of departure is already exhibiting an exegesis performed with the aid of the like-to-like principle. Nevertheless, I will argue that despite all these elements coming from outside Heraclitus' account itself, maybe here we are looking at some other Heraclitean material.

If we consider closely the clause immediately following the καὶ, we need to read the adjectives as being related to some noun. The place to find that noun must be the conclusion of what I called the inferential process, that is, "the soul is the first principle" (1.1). In fact, given that what we have there is a nominal phrase, and given that we cannot make any distinction regarding gender, we are authorized to predicate both adjectives over "soul" and "first principle". But the fact that the accusative must be dependent on something, that is the substantive clause, those characteristics must refer to the soul and, by extension, to the first principle. So, one of the reasons Aristotle had to ascribe to Heraclitus the view that "the soul is first principle" (1.1) is that the soul, which happens to be the first principle, is "the most incorporeal and restless thing" (2.1). The question is how much information is being incorporated to Aristotle's hermeneutical process by this procedure.

I would say that for us, *prima facie*, it is not that clear. In order to connect the attributes of incorporeity and mobility to the first principle, we need to proceed having in mind some suppositions shared by the early thinkers (or at least, that Aristotle supposed to be shared by his predecessor in some general way). For example, one of the characteristics that Aristotle finds in his dialectical survey, and which was not stated from the beginning, is that all the ancient thinkers held that the first principle was the most incorporeal thing, the most subtle body (*DA* 405a5; 405b11). This distinctive quality is important for two reasons in understanding the information that is being added by the second part of the testimony: on the one hand, it is fitting that a material first principle and ultimate constituent of all things is also the most incorporeal thing; on the other hand, since the most appropriate condition for a body is that it be mobile, then its power to imprint motion can be explained in a mechanistic way. Thus, what we have here is that the attributes predicated to the soul elicit an interesting combination between an element that has been produced by the dialectical manipulation of the ancient views (subtlety)[23] and something that has been reported in the tradition as truly Heraclitean (the flux doctrine). For these reasons, this is an important place to observe how Aristotle put together concepts for his hermeneutical purposes and, in general, to understand his hermeneutical device to understand earlier thinkers.

---

23   In the testimony we found the superlative ἀσωματώτατόν. Saying that something is "the most incorporeal thing" does not mean that it is absolutely incorporeal, but rather that is the subtlest. See, Hicks 1907 231; Cherniss 1935 295 n. 20; Bodéüs 1993 100 n. 3.

To my knowledge, the incorporeity is not attested in any of the extant Heraclitean fragments as a characteristic of the first principle, or of fire itself. In fact, Aristotle was the one who has extracted the feature of the incorporeity, as attributed to the soul, not from Heraclitus, but from the previous dialectical process, which included several names. So, the role of incorporeity in this reasoning is perhaps explained by the fact that Aristotle is trying to give further information about the principle in question, that is, the exhalation, in order to make clear how it could work in the psychological context.

At the same level of the characteristic of subtlety we encounter the flux theory, which has traditionally been celebrated as a Heraclitean doctrine, but also highly criticized as non-Heraclitean. For this reason, the flux theory entails similar difficulties to the "exhalations doctrine": in this case, though, it is hard to establish it in Heraclitus' fragments under a single interpretation on the testimonies side (Mouraviev 2008 193). So, the flux doctrine was conserved and transmitted as shaped in function of the contexts where it is embedded. In the case we are examining, the flux doctrine is connected both with the soul-first principle and with its cognitive strength, which is what we see in the Aristotelian testimony. But, luckily on this occasion it is not the Aristotelian tradition that seemed to give birth to the idea, but rather older vestiges.

The most ancient testimonies carrying the attribution of the flux theory to Heraclitus are, however, as much contested as Aristotle is by the expert criticism. Nevertheless this interpretive tradition can probably be counted among the most successful ones in the Heraclitean transmission: Plato.[24] The case of Plato's testimony on Heraclitus in particular is bittersweet: on the one hand, it is one of the earliest sources on the Ephesian, which in a certain way is an important criterion for reconstructing Presocratic thought from vestiges; but, on the other hand, it is difficult to determine how good Plato's source was, given that the direct material he provides on Heraclitus is "virtually non-existent" (Kirk 1954 13): he did not quote; he appropriates theories with the aid of his own dialectical device. Nevertheless, we have passages that established pretty much the same links between the elements of the exegetical process as Aristotle. Just to give an example:

---

24   Although several editors and scholars recognize the difficulty, none of them disagree on the fact that this precise platonic interpretation is the most celebrated in the Heraclitean tradition. On the trajectory of this interpretation, see: Kirk 1951 35; 1954, 366; Zeller and Mondolfo 1961 39; Kahn 1979 147; Bodéüs 1993, 98 n. 5; Dilcher 1995 163; Sánchez 2016 242; Laks and Most 2016 115. There are even people who say that besides the extreme interpretation of the flux theory, the Platonic (and the Aristotelian) testimony can be accepted. See, for example, Hussey 1999, 99; Sánchez 2016 252.

THE ARISTOTELIAN RECEPTION OF HERACLITUS' CONCEPTION

— ὅσοι γὰρ ἡγοῦνται τὸ πᾶν εἶναι ἐν πορείᾳ, τὸ μὲν πολὺ αὐτοῦ ὑπολαμβάνου-
σιν τοιοῦτόν τι εἶναι οἷον οὐδὲν ἄλλο ἢ χωρεῖν, διὰ δὲ τούτου παντὸς εἶναί
τι διεξιόν, δι' οὗ πάντα τὰ γιγνόμενα γίγνεσθαι· εἶναι δὲ τάχιστον τοῦτο καὶ
λεπτότατον. οὐ γὰρ ἂν δύνασθαι ἄλλως διὰ τοῦ ὄντος ἰέναι παντός, εἰ μὴ
λεπτότατόν τε ἦν ὥστε αὐτὸ μηδὲν στέγειν, καὶ τάχιστον ὥστε χρῆσθαι
ὥσπερ ἑστῶσι τοῖς ἄλλοις.

PLATO, *Cratylus*, 412d1–d8

Those who think that the universe is in motion believe that most of
it is of such a kind as to do nothing but give away, but that something
penetrates all of it and generates everything that comes into being. This,
they say, is the fastest and smallest thing of all; for if it were not the smallest, so that nothing could keep it out, or not the fastest, so it could treat
all other things as though they were standing still, it wouldn't be able to
travel through everything.[25]

The invitation in this passage could be contested by the fact that there is evidently no mention of Heraclitus there.[26] This is true. However, the same is
also true of the pieces of Aristotelian testimony that can be discerned in this
passage: the statement that everything is in motion is ascribed to more people
(2.3), and the incorporeity is a concept invited by Aristotle. Now, this passage
of the *Cratylus* in particular was taken from the application, by Socrates, of
the flux theory to the analysis of names in order to persuade Hermogenes that
there is some natural correction in the constitution of names: here we support
the general attribution to a group of people (they must be early thinkers) of
a conception of a flowing cosmos, an idea that is based on the supposition
of a very subtle principle as the ultimate cause of the world.

There has been some controversy surrounding the question as to whether
the information that could be extracted from the dialogue can carry some authentic Heraclitean material. The famous sentence "πάντα χωρεῖ καὶ οὐδὲν μένει"
[*Cratylus* 402a8; DK22A6; LM R29], on which this very interpretation rests, is not
accepted as an example of Heraclitus' *expressima verba*. What prevents the specialized criticism from accepting Plato's testimony in the flux doctrine is, rather,
the absence of stability that this interpretation introduces into the world, which
seems to be contrary to Heraclitus' claims on identity and the regularity of the
Cosmos (Kirk 1951 35; Marcovich 2001 212). This interpretation of flux theory

---

25   Translation by Reeve 1997 130.
26   Sedley, for example, links the passage with Anaxagoras (2003 118).

thus is also considered Plato's own conscientious fabrication, in order to argue the impossibility of knowing things in the sensible world (Kirk 1954 15).

These suspicions may be the subject of contemporary criticism, but it does not seem that the ancient writers were of the same opinion. For example, while explaining the passage, Philoponus elicits the main role of the flux doctrine by saying:

– Δεῖ ὑπερβιβάσαι τὴν λέξιν, ἵνα σαφέστερον γένηται τὸ λεγόμενον, οὕτως· ἐν κινήσει δὲ εἶναι τὰ ὄντα κἀκεῖνος ᾤετο καὶ οἱ πολλοί, τὸ δὲ κινούμενον κινουμένῳ γινώσκεσθαι. ἐπεὶ γὰρ ἐν κινήσει τὰ ὄντα ὑπελάμβανον εἶναι, διὰ τοῦτο ἐκ τοῦ κινητικωτάτου τὴν ψυχὴν ἔλεγον· δεῖ γὰρ τὸ κινούμενον κινουμένῳ γινώσκεσθαι· τῷ γὰρ ὁμοίῳ τὸ ὅμοιον. ὅτι δ' οὐκ ἀνήρηται ἐκ τῶν ὄντων ἡ στάσις, ⟨ὡς⟩ οὗτοι ὑπελάμβανον, δείκνυσι καὶ ἐν τῷ Θεαιτήτῳ καὶ πολλαχοῦ ὁ Πλάτων καὶ ὁ Ἀριστοτέλης καὶ ἐν τῇ Περὶ οὐρανοῦ καὶ ἐν τοῖς Μετὰ τὰ φυσικά. εἰ γὰρ μὴ εἴη, φασί, στάσις ἐν τῷ παντί, ἀδύνατον ἀεὶ κίνησιν εἶναι· αὐτὸ γὰρ τοῦτο τὸ ἀεὶ κινεῖσθαι μονή τίς ἐστι καὶ στάσις· εἰ δὲ ἀναιρεθείη ἡ στάσις, συναναιρεθήσεται καὶ ἡ κίνησις· εἰ γὰρ μὴ στάσιν σχοίη ἐν τῇ κινήσει τὸ κινούμενον, οὐ κινηθήσεται δηλονότι.

PHILOPONUS, *In DA*, xv 87, 30–88, 8

We should transpose the words here, so that their meaning becomes clearer, in the following way: he, as well as the majority of people, thought that things are in motion, and that what is moved is known by what is moved. Since they supposed that things are in motion, they said that this is why the soul is made up of what is most easily moved; for what is being moved must be known by what is being moved; for like is known by like. Yet he did not abolish stability from the realm of things that exist, as they supposed, and this is shown both by Plato in the *Theaetetus* and in many other places and by Aristotle in *On the Heavens* and in the *Metaphysics*. They say that if there were no stability in the Universe, it would be impossible for there always to be movement; for the very fact of there always being movement is a kind of constancy and stability; and if stability were abolished, movement would be abolished as well; since, if what is moved does not have stability in its movement, it will obviously not be moved.[27]

As has been said, for Philoponus the flux theory has a major role in the account Aristotle presents of Heraclitus: on the one hand, it fits well with the like-to-like principle, which is employed as a hermeneutical tool for the analysis of

---

27   Translation by van der Eijk 2005 108.

THE ARISTOTELIAN RECEPTION OF HERACLITUS' CONCEPTION   397

early views in general; on the other hand, it provides a justification for the particular constitution of the soul in material terms. But what is most important in this passage of the commentary is that Philoponus seems to anticipate the objection made to the flux theory as an annihilator of stability in the world. Philoponus, thus, provides an explanation seeking to redeem the flux theory in the particular way Plato uses it, in order to make sense of Aristotle's reasoning.

Moreover, Philoponus' rescue mission could be explained in light of more substantial evidence. It cannot be denied that the idea circulated as Heraclitean, mostly accompanied (as is *Cratylus'* case) with the celebrated image of the river. The river statements consist basically of two fragments: B12[28] and B91.[29] The particularity of the Heraclitean occurrences of the river image, which can contribute to this case, is not the link with flux theory, though it helps. What is rather going to be decisive to us, vis-à-vis Philoponus' explanation is what the wording and context of fragment B12 can provide:

– [DK22B12; LM D65a, D102 and R51] Περὶ δὲ ψυχῆς Κλεάνθης μὲν τὰ Ζή-νωνος δόγματα παρατιθέμενος πρὸς σύγκρισιν τὴν πρὸς τοὺς ἄλλους φυσι-κοὺς φησιν ὅτι Ζήνων τὴν ψυχὴν λέγει αἰσθητικὴν ἀναθυμίασιν, καθάπερ Ἡράκλειτος. βουλόμενος γὰρ ἐμφανίσαι ὅτι αἱ ψυχαὶ ἀναθυμιώμεναι νο-εραὶ ἀεὶ γίνονται, εἴκασεν αὐτὰς τοῖς ποταμοῖς, λέγων οὕτως· 'Ποταμοῖσι τοῖσιν αὐτοῖσιν ἐμβαίνουσιν ἕτερα καὶ ἕτερα ὕδατα ἐπιρρεῖ· καὶ ψυχαὶ δὲ ἀπὸ τῶν ὑγρῶν ἀναθυμιῶνται.' ἀναθυμίασιν μὲν οὖν ὁμοίως τῷ Ἡρακλεί-τῳ τὴν ψυχὴν ἀποφαίνει Ζήνων, αἰσθητικὴν δὲ αὐτὴν εἶναι διὰ τοῦτο λέγει ὅτι τυποῦσθαί τε δύναται τὸ μέρος τὸ ἡγούμενον αὐτῆς ἀπὸ τῶν ὄντων καὶ ὑπαρχόντων διὰ τῶν αἰσθητηρίων καὶ παραδέχεσθαι τὰς τυπώσεις. ταῦτα γὰρ ἴδια ψυχῆς ἐστι.

ARIUS DIDYMUS APUD EUSEBIUS, *Praep. Evang.* XV 20, 2

On the soul of Cleanthes, setting out the doctrines of Zeno for comparison with the other natural philosophers, says that Zeno affirms that the soul is a percipient exhalation, just like Heraclitus: for, wishing to manifest that souls by being exhaled are always becoming intelligent, likened them to rivers speaking like this: *Upon those who step into the same rivers*

---

28 The connections between the B12 and Aristotle's account are numerous, which leads to think that the source of the *De Anima* could be some similar to this fragment, if not the statement itself. See, Dilcher 1995, 64; Colvin 2005 266.

29 However, there are editors, such as Marcovich, who do not recognize two different fragments, but two sources referring to the same fragment (2001 206). I am going to follow this advice for methodological reasons, but the main focus is going to be just fragment B12.

different and again different waters flow; and souls also are exhaled from moisture. Then Zeno, similarly to Heraclitus, shows the soul to be an exhalation, and for this reason he says that it is perceptive, for the part of it rising from what exists through and underlies the sense organs can be impressed and receive impressions. For these are particularities of the soul.

The fragment just quoted is transmitted in a Stoic context. What is particularly interesting in this case is that we have a sort of analogy fabricated by Cleanthes between Heraclitus and Zeno's thought,[30] on which it is possible to base the hidden premise of the inferential process I have argued that Aristotle was making on the grounds of Heraclitean thought. However, here the very content of the Aristotelian premise is explicitly attributed to Heraclitus. In fact, this is the point over which the comparison is going to be performed: for both of them, Heraclitus and Zeno, "soul is an exhalation" (*). The other important feature that this fragment exhibits for the argument is that this context is also on the same page as the frame of the cosmological fragments, particularly in B36, where "soul" strangely was included as one of the elementary masses. Comparatively speaking, indeed, in fragment B12, "soul" is produced from the moist element, and what is more important is not called "fire", but "exhalation".

Although in a very first moment the whole statement was retained as a fragment (Diels 1951 154), there is a consensus among contemporary scholars in terms of avoiding considering the second part of the statement as genuinely Heraclitean (καὶ ψυχαὶ δὲ ἀπὸ τῶν ὑγρῶν ἀναθυμιῶνται).[31] The reasons that justify this decision are mostly of a stylistic order. Nevertheless, it should be considered that the idea that the exhalation, of which the soul consists, comes from the humid elementary mass could be found in other Heraclitean fragments (Kahn 1979 259). Moreover, as we have seen, the second part of the statement seems to give some basis to the Aristotelian interpretation. Of course this could not be used as an argument to prove that these words were genuinely written by Heraclitus'; this second part may somehow have been transmitted

---

30   On Cleanthes as an interpreter of Heraclitus, see Dilcher 1995 178 and Colvin 2005 258.

31   This very last statement was removed by some editors and interpreters such as Bywater 1877 17; Burnet 1920 100; Kirk 1954 367; Kahn 1979 52; Marcovich 2001 194; and Colvin 2005 258. There are, nevertheless, those who retain it, not without expressing some doubts, like Reinhardt 1916 61; Capelle 1924 121; Diels and Kranz 1951 154; Walzer 1964 53; Mondolfo 1966 32; von Arnim 1968 117; Bollack and Wismann 1972 87; Conche 1986 452; des Places 1987 352 n.2; Dilcher 1995 183 and Mouraviev 2006ᵃ 43. There is just one case where both parts are retained as genuine: the flux part [D65b] and the exhalations part [D102] (Laks and Most 2016 190). For a complete study on this fragment, see Mouraviev 2008ᵇ 4.

in a distorted form, but has the very same Heraclitean parfum that Aristotle also was detecting. Despite whether the second part of the fragment B12 is or is not Heraclitus' own words, I think taking seriously the presence of this statement inside the fragment (and reading it together with B36) provides a path to an interpretation built on a reasoning very similar to Aristotle's exegesis, and may possibly be supported by a similar source too.

What this fragment, and particularly the context of its quotation, shares with the *Cratylus'* testimony is important for this case; on the other hand, the flux theory, or the image of the river, is not. What matters is, rather, that the Heraclitean saying and the flux theory are, both of them, included in a context of epistemological concerns (Sánchez 2016 255). Even if the perceptive process that is explained in terms of impressions is clearly ascribed in the fragment to Zeno and not to Heraclitus, the characteristic of percipience is a constant in the analogy: it seems to be that both Heraclitus and Zeno thought that the soul was percipient, but they differ with regard to the explanation. The characterization of the soul as a cognitive principle, however, is not our current concern. Aristotle seems to be doing the same as the *Cratylus* and Cleanthes: the second part of the testimony focuses on the cognitive capacity that the soul may have.

4 Conclusion

To recapitulate: in the first part of the testimony, we had a proposition (a premise, in fact) without the testimony that was crucial in order to understand Aristotle's possible interpretive path, that is, that "the soul was an exhalation" (*). Then, in the second part of our testimony, we again had a missing proposition, but this time we reconstructed it at the locus of a conclusion, namely, "the soul knows everything" (**). If the second part of the testimony intends to be part of the same exegetical process as the inference conducted at the very beginning, we may then suppose that the resulting conclusion was what motivated Aristotle's hermeneutical effort.

If this explanation is correct, then Philoponus seems to be the person who understood perfectly the objective of the Heraclitean view in the *De Anima*. Aristotle was applying his exegetical apparatus not to force Heraclitus to hold a materialistic view of the soul or to make him a relativist; Aristotle was motivated in his exegesis by the aim of trying to explain how it was that Heraclitus made the soul a cognitive principle. And there are no grounds for thinking this was not a truly Heraclitean idea (Kahn 1979 127; Dilcher 1995 75; Betegh 2007 4), even if his own explanation could not be proved to be given in physiological terms by Heraclitus himself (Laks 1999 254).[32] Perhaps, the physiological terms were there gravitating around the fragments and the context of their quotations, and all that was missing was that they needed to be put together. This could be the Heraclitean material we are seeking in the *De Anima* passage, and the physiological account could be Aristotle's exegetical product.

As far as we have analyzed, Aristotle's hermeneutical process does not seem to be just the product of an exacerbated refutational or distorting aim. It seems, rather, that Aristotle arrived at the conclusion that, for Heraclitus, the soul existed in the first principle because it was a necessary condition for cognition. However, the emphasis was not directly on particular conditions or some kind of material continuity, but on the continuity of motion. And motion is the important feature that the first principle and what exists share, which has to be the fundamental trait of the soul according to Heraclitean thinking that Aristotle included in his dialectical survey (Sánchez 2016 241). Then, Heraclitus' relevance, despite the scarcity of the lines devoted to him, is not trivial. All the elements analyzed here are going to be fundamental for one of the main targets of a further analysis: Aristotle's sifting of his predecessors' views concerning the soul—i.e., that it moves because it is itself in motion. But this will have to be the subject of subsequent research.

Bibliography

Arnim, J. Von. ed. 1968b. *Stoicorum veterum fragmenta*, vol. 1. Leipzig: Teubner.

Baltussen, Hans. 2000. *Theophrastus against the Presocratics and Plato: Peripatetic Dialectic in the* De Sensibus. Leiden: Brill.

Baltussen, Hans. 1999. "Peripatetic Dialectic in the *De Sensibus*". In: *Theophrastus*, edited by Fortenbaugh and Gutas, 1–19. London: Transaction Publishers, Rutgers University Studies in Classical Humanities.

Betegh, Gábor. 2007. "On the Physical Aspect of Heraclitus' Psychology". *Phronesis*, Vol. 52, No. 1, pp. 3–32.

Bodéüs, Richard. 1993. *Aristote: De l'âme*. Paris: Flammarion.

Bollack, Jean and Wismann, Heinz. 1972. *Héraclite ou la separation*. Paris: Les éditions de minuit.

Bolton, Robert. 1999. "The Epistemological Basis of Aristotelian Dialectic". In: *From Puzzles to Principles*, edited by May Sim, 57–106. New York: Lexington Books.

---

32   Betegh is against this position (2007 4). Although I have shown that a physiological account on Heraclitus soul is possible, I am not sure that this comes directly from Heraclitus hand. I think, rather, that this interpretation is the one founded by the Aristotelian tradition.

Burnet, John. 1920. *Early Greek Philosophy*. London: A & C Black.

Burnet, John. ed. 1967. *Platonis opera i*. Oxford: Clarendon Press.

Bywater, I. ed. 1877. *Heracliti Ephesii Reliquiae*. Oxonii: Typhographeo Clarendoniano.

Capelle, W. 1924. "Heracliteum". En: *Hermes* 59, H. 1 (Mar. 1924), pp.121–123.

Cherniss, Harold. 1970. "The Characteristics and Effects of Presocratic Philosophy". In: *Studies in Presocratic Philosophy 1*, edited by Furley and Allen, 1–28. London: Routledge.

Cherniss, Harold. 1935. *Aristotle's Criticism of Presocratic Philosophy*. Baltimore: John Hopkins.

Colvin, Matthew. 2005. "Heraclitus and Material Flux in Stoic Psychology". In: *Oxford Studies in Ancient Philosophy* xxviii (Summer 2005), pp. 257–272.

Conche, Marcel. ed. 1986 *Héraclite: Fragments*. Paris: Presses Universitaires de France.

Cooper, J. & Hutchinson, D. eds. 1997 *Plato: Complete Works*. Indianapolis: Hackett.

Diels, H. and Kranz, W. eds. 1951 *Die Fragmente der Vorsokratiker*. Berlin: Weidmannsche Verlagsbuchhandlung.

Dilcher, Roman. 1995. *Studies in Heraclitus*. Hildesheim: George Olms.

Eijk, Philip van der. 2005. *Philoponus: On Aristotle's* On the Soul *1.1–2*. Ithaca (NY): Cornell University Press.

Fobes, F. H. ed. 1967. *Aristotelis meteorologicorum libri quattuor*. Cambridge (Mss): Harvard University Press.

Fortenbaugh, W. and Gutas, D. eds. 1992 *Theophrastus: His Psychological,Doxographical, and Scientific Writings*. London: Transaction Publishers, Rutgers University Studies in Classical Humanities Vol. 5.

Furley, D. & Allen, R. E. eds. 1970. *Studies in Presocratic Philosophy 1: The Beginnings of Philosophy*. London: Routledge.

Gilbert, Otto. 1907. *Die meteorologischen Theorien des griechischen Altertums*. Leipzig: Teubner.

Hayduck, M. ed. 1897. *Ioannis Philoponi in Aristotelis de anima libros commentaria, CAG 15*. Berlin: Reimer.

Hayduck, M. 1883. *Sophoniae in libros Aristotelis de anima paraphrasis*, CAG 23.1. Berlin: Reimer.

Hayduck, M. 1882. *Simplicii in libros Aristotelis de anima commentaria, CAG 11*. Berlin: Reimer.

Heinze, R. ed. 1899. *Themistii in libros Aristotelis de anima paraphrasis, CAG 5.3*. Berlin: Reimer.

Hicks, R. D. ed. 1907 *Aristotle: De Anima*. Cambridge: Cambridge University Press.

Hussey, Edward. 1999. "Heraclitus". In: Long, *The Cambridge Companion to Early Greek Philosophy*, pp. 88–112.

Kahn, Charles. ed. 1979 *The Art and Thought of Heraclitus*. Cambridge: Cambridge University Press.

Kirk, G. S. 1970 "Popper on Science and the Presocratics". In: *Studies in Presocratic Philosophy 1*, edited by Furley and Allen, 154–177. London: Routledge.

Kirk, G. S. 1951. "Natural Change in Heraclitus". In: *Mind*, New Series, Vol. 60, No. 237 (Jan., 1951), pp. 35–42.

Kirk, G. S. ed. 1954. *Heraclitus: The Cosmic Fragments*. Cambridge: Cambridge University Press.

Laks, André. 1999. "Soul, Sensation, and Thought". In: *The Cambridge Companion to Early Greek Philosophy*, edited by Long, 250–270. Cambridge: Cambridge University Press.

Laks, André & Most, Glenn. eds. 2016. *Early Greek Philosophy: Early Ionian Thinkers 2*. Cambridge (Mss.): Harvard University Press.

Laks, André & Most, Glenn. 2016. *Early Greek Philosophy: Later Ionian and Athenian Thinkers 2*. Cambridge (Mss.): Harvard University Press.

Lasalle, Ferdinand. 1858. *Die Philosophie Herakleitos des Dunklen von Ephesos*. Berlin: Verlag von Franz Duncker.

Long, A. A. ed. 1999 *The Cambridge Companion to Early Greek Philosophy*. Cambridge: Cambridge University Press.

Mansfeld, Jaap. 1999. "Sources". In: *The Cambridge Companion to Early Greek Philosophy*, edited by Long, 22–44. Cambridge: Cambridge University Press.

Marcovich, Miroslav. ed. 2001. *Heraclitus: Greek text with a short commentary*. Sankt Agustin: Akademia Verlag.

Mondolfo, Rodolfo. 1966 *Heráclito: textos y problemas de su interpretación*. Traducción de Oberdan Caletti. México: Siglo XXI editores.

Mouraviev, Serge. ed. 2008ª. *Heraclitea III.2 Recensio: Placita*. Sankt Agustin: Akademia Verlag.

Mouraviev, Serge. 2006ª. *Heraclitea III.3.B/i Recensio: Fragmenta*. Sankt Agustin: Akademia Verlag.

Mouraviev, Serge. 2006ᵇ. *Heraclitea III.3.B/ii Recensio: Fragmenta*. Sankt Agustin: Akademia Verlag.

Mouraviev, Serge. 2006ᶜ. *Heraclitea III.3.B/iii Recensio: Fragmenta*. Sankt Agustin: Akademia Verlag.

Mouraviev, Serge. 2008ᵇ. "Héraclite. Les fragments du fleuve: F12. Le context: T261". In: *Revue de Philosophie Ancienne*, XXVI, n. 2, pp.

Nussbaum, Martha. 1972ª. "Ψυχή in Heraclitus, I". In: *Phronesis 17*, No. 1, pp. 1–16.

Nussbaum, Martha. 1972ᵇ. "Ψυχή in Heraclitus, II". In: *Phronesis 17*, No. 2, pp. 153–170.

des Places, Édouard s.j. 1987. *Eusèbe de Césarée: La preparation évangélique*. Paris: Du Cerf.

Polansky, Ronald. 2007. *Aristotle's De Anima*. Cambridge: Cambridge University Press.

Polito, Roberto. 2004. *The Sceptical Road: Aenesidemus' appropriation of Heraclitus*. Leiden-Boston: Brill.

Primavesi, Oliver. ed. 2012. "Text of *Metaphysics A* (and of the corresponding parts of *M4-5*". En: *Aristotle's* Metaphysics *A*, edited by Steel, 465–516. Oxford: Oxford University Press.

Reeve, Ch. 1997. *Cratylus*. In: *Plato: Complete Works*, edited by Cooper & Hutchinson, 102–156. Indianapolis: Hackett.

Reinhardt, Karl. 1916. *Parmenides und die Geschichte der Griechischen Philosophie*. Bonn: Friedrich Cohen.

Sánchez Castro, Liliana Carolina. 2016. *Traditio Animae: la recepción aristotélica de las teorías presocráticas del alma*. Bogotá: Universidad Nacional de Colombia.

Sánchez Castro, Liliana Carolina. 2012. "La filosofía heraclítea interpretada por Platón". En: *Ideas y Valores*, vol. LXI, No. 150 (Dic. 2012), pp. 229–244.

Sedley, David. 2003. *Plato's Cratylus*. Cambridge: Cambridge University Press.

Sieveking, W. ed. 1972. *Plutarchi Moralia Vol. 3*. Leipzig: Teubner.

Sim, M. ed. 1999 *From Puzzles to Principles: Essays on Aristotle's Dialectic*. New York: Lexington Books.

Smith, Robin. 1997. *Aristotle: Topics Book I and VIII*. Oxford: Clarendon Press.

Steel, C. ed. 2012. *Aristotle's* Metaphysics *A: Symposium Aristotelicum*. Oxford: Oxford University Press.

Viano, Cristina. 1996. "La doxographie du *De Anima* (i, 2–5) ou le contre-modèle de l'âme". In: *Corps et âme*, edited by Viano, 51–80. Paris: Vrin.

Viano, C. ed. 1996. *Corps et âme: sur le* De Anima *d'Aristote*. Paris: Vrin.

Walzer, R. 1964. *Eraclito*. Hildesheim: Georg Olms Verlagsbuchhandlung.

Zeller, E. & Mondolfo, R. 1961. *La filosofia dei greci nel suo sviluppo storico, parte prima: presocratici, vol. IV: Eraclito*. Firenze: La Nuova Italia.

CHAPTER 13

Mixing Minds: Anaxagoras and Plato's *Phaedo*

Iakovos Vasiliou

The longest and most well-known discussion of Anaxagoras in Plato occurs in Socrates's "autobiography" in the *Phaedo* (96a ff.).[1] Anaxagoras' positing of Nous as a cause and arranger of the universe generates a hope in Socrates that he will, at long last, learn a teleological account of the cosmos and what goes on in it rather than the typical mode of explanation among philosophers of nature (i.e. those we call "Presocratics") in terms of mere material causes.[2] According to the *Phaedo*, despite Anaxagoras's mention of Nous and its functions, Anaxagoras ends up appealing to the same old material causes and thus makes no use of his potentially groundbreaking insight that Nous is the real cause of things. Unsurprisingly, Plato thinks that Anaxagoras's philosophy makes deep and fundamental mistakes, but I shall argue that Plato's engagement with him is more serious and that his debt to him in the *Phaedo* is more substantial and widespread than typically thought.[3] It has been noticed by scholars, of course, that the sort of cosmology and philosophy of nature Socrates claims to have sought from Anaxagoras in the "autobiography," comes to fruition in Plato's *Timaeus*.[4] But I shall argue that even if a cosmology and natural philosophy that does justice to Anaxagoras's initial insights must wait for the *Timaeus*, Plato is already employing Anaxagorean ideas in the *Phaedo*, suitably modified of course, with respect to the *mikrokosmos*: the compound of body and soul that is the individual human being.

---

1   "Autobiography" is in scare-quotes since, of course, Plato puts these autobiographical remarks into the character Socrates's mouth and therefore their veracity is doubtful. See McCabe 2000, 155.

2   For an interpretation of Plato's relationship to Presocratic natural philosophy more generally, see Gregory, "Plato's Reception of Presocratic Philosophy" in this volume.

3   Tzamalikos 2016, 527–536, is devoted to a comparison of the views of Plato and Anaxagoras. His discussion ranges widely over the Platonic corpus but does not address the issues I am most concerned with; the interpretations are often weakened, in my view, by overly psychologizing readings.

4   See Sedley 2007, 93–95, who argues further that the myth at the end of the *Phaedo*, which he describes as a sketch of "what Anaxagoras *should* have said," is a precursor to the account that Plato will later supply in the *Timaeus*. On Anaxagoras and Plato's *Timaeus*, see also, Wright's "Presocratic Cosmology and Platonic Myth" and Gregory's "Plato's Reception of Presocratic Philosophy," both in this volume.

© KONINKLIJKE BRILL NV, LEIDEN, 2021 | DOI:10.1163/9789004443358_015

MIXING MINDS: ANAXAGORAS AND PLATO'S *PHAEDO* 405

For Plato in the *Phaedo* the constitution of an individual soul, meaning whether it is corporeal or incorporeal, is contingent and a matter of degree. Surprising though it sounds, Plato holds that an individual's soul can be more or less corporeal: the incorporeality of any given individual soul is an end and an achievement, not a metaphysical fact about its nature. It is important in this context to recall that nature functions in at least two ways in Greek philosophy: in one, the nature of a thing is a fixed, unchanging essence; but in another sense, the nature of a thing is the best state of that thing, something to be achieved or realized, as in the idea that a human being's nature consists in being virtuous. Socrates argues that in life, and especially so in the lives of most people, the soul is mixed and combined with the body. The soul is not simply born *in a body*—that is, embodied—but it is actually, to varying degrees, *bodily* and it can be so even after biological death, i.e., even after the soul has been separated from a particular body and so is no longer *embodied*.

To be in its best state, which is of course being wise as a true philosopher seeks, the soul needs to be separated not only from the body in which it is incarnated, but also from the bodily as such, in order to be like and so to know its proper objects, the Forms. What makes the soul itself more or less bodily is how one lives one's life. As we shall see, the argument for this is presented mostly in the sections of the dialogue known as "Socrates' Defense" (63b-69e) and the "Affinity Argument" (78b-84b). Anaxagoras uniquely among the natural philosophers holds that Nous orders the cosmos. His idea that Nous is "most pure and unmixed" (B12) is important to Plato in this context not because Plato agrees that an individual's mind/soul simply *is* unmixed but because he believes that its being unmixed is the *best* way for it to be and, further, that, once embodied, it needs to effect its own separation from the bodily.[5] I shall argue that Plato uses Anaxagorean ideas about Nous, separation, and mixture and adapts them to explain the relationship between soul and body within an explicitly teleological framework—the very framework that he has Socrates notoriously criticize Anaxagoras for ignoring during his "autobiography." In the *Phaedo's* account, Plato will describe the soul's proper role of ruling and ordering the individual human with a view towards the best. Let's begin by turning to the criticisms leveled against Anaxagoras in the "autobiography."

---

5 The soul in the *Phaedo* is equivalent to the mind or, in the terms of later dialogues, the rational part of the soul. In the *Phaedo*, perception, appetites, and similar activities are all attributed to the body; for some discussion, see Vasiliou 2012.

1 Socrates's "Autobiographical" Disappointment with Anaxagoras

Socrates explains that as a young man he was interested in investigations into nature and occupied himself with—to use slightly anachronistic language—studying material causes to explain why and how things are as they are. Dissatisfied with the adequacy of these explanations for reasons I shall not explore here, Socrates heard someone reading from a book of Anaxagoras, who claimed that Nous both ordered and was responsible for all things (97c1-2; cf. B12). Socrates then assumed that if mind orders and is responsible (αἴτιος, 97c2, c4) for all things, it must do so by deciding what is the best way for things to be. Thus, the search for the cause of why things are or come to be the way they are would be found in an investigation into the way it is best for those things to be: "If then one should wish to discover the cause of each thing, in what way it comes to be or perishes or is, it is necessary to discover about it what was the best way for it to be, or to be affected by another, or to act" (97c6-d1). Furthermore, if one knew the best way for things to be, one would also know the worse;[6] for it is part of "the same knowledge" (97d4-5). Once Socrates gets hold of Anaxagoras's books, however, reading them "as quickly as possible" so that he could learn what is best and worse "as quickly as possible" (98b4-6), he is sorely disappointed: for, he claims, Anaxagoras made "no use" of mind, but instead referred as causes to air, ether, water and many different and strange things (98b8-c2).

Socrates then offers an illuminating example: his own decision to remain in prison, and suffer the penalty the Athenian jury imposed, rather than escape into exile.[7] The mistake Anaxagoras makes in his use of Nous would be like attributing the "cause" of Socrates' sitting in prison to his bones and sinews, and their capacity to bend and flex, rather than to Socrates' *decision* that it would be unjust for him to escape from prison and that virtue requires that he remain and suffer the penalty. Socrates repeatedly emphasizes that decisions about the best are the causes of things, explaining how, first, "it seemed to be better to the Athenians" (Ἀθηναίοις ἔδοξε βέλτιον εἶναι)" to condemn him and then, "it seemed better to me in turn" (ἐμοὶ βέλτιον αὖ δέδοκται)" to remain in prison and pay the penalty (98e2-5). Furthermore, Socrates adds, he could have taken his "sinews and bones" off to Megara or Boeotia carried there "by a belief about the best," (ὑπὸ δόξης φερόμενα τοῦ βελτίστου) "if I had not thought it more just and

---

6 Despite the awkwardness in English, what is here opposed to the "best" is "the worse" not "the worst." The idea is presumably while there is one best state, there are innumerable conditions that fall short of it, all of which are clearly worse.

7 A reasonably clear reference to the argument in Plato's *Crito*.

MIXING MINDS: ANAXAGORAS AND PLATO'S *PHAEDO* 407

more noble" (εἰ μὴ δικαιότερον ᾤμην καὶ κάλλιον) not to escape but to remain (99a1-4). Finally, Socrates acknowledges that while he would not be able to act (or sit!) without bones and sinews, it would be absurd to treat bones and sinews as the cause or explanation of his actions rather than his "decision about the best" (τῇ τοῦ βελτίστου αἱρέσει) (99a8-b1).

A couple of points here are important for my purposes. First, decision, as an act of mind, is more than something that is simply *for* an end; it is also an efficient cause. The decision *causes* Socrates to remain rather than to escape *because* he decides that remaining is better (more just) than escaping.[8] Second, Socrates sanctions a direct parallel between Anaxagoras' cosmic Nous and his own individual mind. Presumably, just as his own mind's decision about the best is the proper cause of his actions, so Anaxagoras should have explained how the cosmic Nous' decisions about the best were the explanations of its actions in the universe (see, 97e-98b).

Despite this criticism, the conclusion that Socrates/Plato read Anaxagoras and then simply tossed him aside as just another mistaken figure in "inquiry about nature" (περὶ φύσεως ἱστορίαν) (96a7) is inaccurate. Anaxagoras is singled out here for a reason. Uniquely among the Presocratics, he posits a single, rational force—Nous—as what guides and directs the formation of the universe. The rough outline of the Anaxagorean account is clear, even if the details remain subject to intense scholarly dispute. In the beginning the cosmos is an undifferentiated, thoroughly mixed mass that contains everything within everything (B1), so that no quality or kind is perceptually distinguishable. For Anaxagoras, as for arguably all of the Presocratics, there is no clear idea of a substance with inherent qualities. Rather, there are mixtures of stuffs: some cold, some hot, some wet, some dry, some yellow and so on. Nous, by generating motion in a vortex, begins to separate out identifiable qualities and stuffs until we get the differentiated, macroscopic world of our perceptual experience, with objects that sort into kinds with various qualities.[9] This process of separation is still going on.

---

8   In this sense the sought-after *aitia* here is distinct from Aristotle's final cause. In Aristotle, nature is an end and for something: so roots are for nourishment, flat teeth in the back of the mouth are for grinding, and so on (e.g., see *Phys* II.1–2 and II.7–8). These sorts of teleological causes or explanations, however, are simply part of nature and no mind or designer is involved; they are therefore distinct from the "efficient cause." The proper parallel in Aristotle would be his discussion of deliberation (*bouleusis*) and decision (*prohairesis*), *Nicomachean Ethics* III.2–3, VI.2.

9   It is a matter of dispute whether the primordial mixture contains only opposite qualities or also certain basic stuffs—like flesh, gold, bone. It certainly contains "seeds," although

408 VASILIOU

Plato likes the idea of Nous, unmixed, pure, guiding and steering all things, presumably as a result of decisions it makes about what is best. Of course it is the last part—the decision about what is best—that goes missing in the account. On my view, Plato is arguing about how to generate a soul in the best condition, namely, wise, which will be done by purifying and separating it from the corporeal with which it is mixed during its embodiment (i.e. life), so that it will be in a condition to grasp the Forms.

2   Anaxagoras' Philosophy

I am not aiming to provide an original reading of the fragments of Anaxagoras, and I hope that my argument does not rely on contentious interpretations of them. Furthermore, I will not try to assess the extent to which Socrates' criticism in the "autobiography" is accurate. Rather, my goal is to show how pervasive Anaxagorean themes are in the *Phaedo*, and, with attention to that, to provide a new interpretation of Plato's understanding of the soul. There is, I will argue, a thorough engagement with Anaxagorean themes, which goes beyond the infamous criticism of him in the "autobiography" we have just considered. Nous is the most important element in the Anaxagorean picture. On most interpretations, it is a unique sort of stuff that permeates and controls all things. The key role it plays in Anaxagoras' philosophy is to meet the Parmenidean requirement of explaining motion and change. What is the agent of change? Nous is described as:

> [...] unlimited and self-ruling and mixed with no thing but alone itself by itself (ἄπειρον καὶ αὐτοκρατὲς καὶ μέμεικται οὐδενὶ χρήματι, ἀλλὰ μόνος αὐτὸς ἐφ᾽ ἑαυτοῦ ἐστιν) [...] for it is the finest of things and the purest and has every knowledge about everything, and greatest power (ἔστι γὰρ λεπτότατόν τε πάντων χρημάτων καὶ καθαρώτατον, καὶ γνώμην γε περὶ παντὸς πᾶσαν ἴσχει καὶ ἰσχύει μέγιστον) [...] (B12).

Anaxagoras is of course speaking of a cosmic Mind or Nous, as is recognized in the description of Anaxagoras' position in 97ff., but he speaks also of "greater and smaller" *nous* (B12) and of *nous* as present in some other things as well (B11).[10] Plato, I shall argue, borrows and transforms some of these ideas and

---

what these are is also a matter of contention. See, especially, Sedley 2007, chap. 1, Curd 2007, Sider 2005, and, most recently, Marmodoro 2017, chap.'s 2, 3, and 5.

10   See Sider 2005, 139–140; Curd 2007, 202.

applies them to the soul/mind of individuals in line with how we have seen Socrates use the example of the decisions of his own mind as examples of proper explanations.

Here there are a couple of ideas that will loom large in the *Phaedo*: (1) the idea of a thing's being "itself by itself." As we shall see, gathering the soul together itself by itself is one of the goals of the practice of a genuine philosopher; (2) the idea that the soul/mind ought to be "most pure" and "unmixed."[11] We shall see that the purity of the soul is something to be achieved; (3) finally the idea that it is the soul/mind (not the body) that both knows things and is stronger, more long-lasting, than the composite body, which is liable to dissolution.

Before turning to the *Phaedo*, I should say something brief about the relationship between incorporeality and immortality. These two ideas are clearly distinct. In Homer's description of the underworld in Book XI of the *Odyssey*, souls are depicted as apparently immortal but also clearly corporeal (they are visible and resemble their fully corporeal selves) although the souls are clearly separable from their organic bodies, which were burned. On a "harmony theory" where the soul consists in a harmonious, attuned relationship among the bodily parts, such as is described by Simmias in the *Phaedo* itself (85e-86d), the soul is clearly *incorporeal*; it is in fact the only time Plato uses *asômatos* for the soul outside of the pseudo-Platonic *Epinomis*. But on this view, as Socrates points out, the soul is clearly inseparable from the body, and thus *a fortiori* not immortal. Plato seems to conclude, however, not only in the *Phaedo* but also in the *Phaedrus, Timaeus, Republic* 10, and *Laws* 10, that an individual's soul (or at least a part or aspect of it) is immortal.[12] My contention is that while for Plato the soul may just be, by nature, *immortal* (and so it cannot be destroyed) it is not similarly by nature *incorporeal*, but may be, at different times in differing degrees, corporeal. Of course, Plato also holds that the best way for a human being's soul to be is incorporeal, but we will learn in the *Phaedo* that this requires significant effort on the part of the individual.

While Anaxagoras seems to some scholars to be reaching toward the notion of an incorporeal substance, there is overwhelming agreement that he does not think of Nous as an incorporeal substance.[13] The key element of

---

11   See *Cratylus* 413c. Aristotle too attributes to Anaxagoras the view that nous is "unmixed," and endorses it: see *De Anima* III.4, 429a18-20; *Physics* VIII.5, 256b24-27.

12   The *Symposium* is sometimes considered to conflict with this, given that it says that mortal creatures participate in immortality via reproduction. But it never explicitly says that the human *soul* is mortal; just that human beings are.

13   Kirk, Raven, and Schofield (1983), 364: "Anaxagoras in fact is striving, as had several of his predecessors, to imagine and describe a truly incorporeal entity. But as with them, so still with him, the only ultimate criterion of reality is extension in space. Mind, like

Anaxagoras' theory, however, that influenced both Plato and Aristotle, is Nous' purity, where this consists in its being unmixed with anything else. Now this is part of the singular nature of Nous, since for Anaxagoras "all things were together" (B1). It was and is the action of Nous generating rotation that separated off and ordered the cosmos (B4, B9, B12), differentiating macroscopic "objects," including not only things like hair or nails, but colors, hot and cold, wet and dry, and so on. As we have seen, Socrates complains that this process is described in a mechanical way (via rotation) acting on material elements, despite the idea that Anaxagoras says that Nous is controlling and ordering the universe (cf. *Cratylus* 400a8-10). But for our purposes, it is important that on Anaxagoras' view, every portion of everything, no matter how small, contains some smaller bit of everything else. So ice contains some bit of hot as well as cold, although cold dominates; any bit of white also contains a bit of black, although in a white object, white dominates, and so on. At the end of the essay, I will connect a problem that arises for Anaxagoras' metaphysics with one that concerns Plato's account of soul in the *Phaedo*.

3 Socrates' Defense

In a section of the text typically labeled "Socrates' Defense" (63e8-69e5), Socrates is called upon to defend his claim that a true philosopher ought to welcome death most of all. I shall focus on this argument and the closely related "Affinity Argument" a little further on in the dialogue (78b-84b). I shall show that the Affinity Argument, although ostensibly another argument for the immortality of the soul, is better understood as primarily about issues raised in the Defense concerning what the soul is like rather than whether the soul is immortal. We shall see that both of these arguments provide examples of how the mind can direct the separation or mixture of its own corporeal and incorporeal parts according to its conception of what is best. Socrates clearly gives an account for a human being of what is best and what is worse—precisely what he claims

---

everything else, is corporeal ...". McKirahan (1994), 219–220, has a similar view. Barnes (1982), 406–407, denies that Anaxagoras was not "hinting at mental incorporeality" but is rather wrestling with how to continue to hold that Mind, like everything else, is a material "stuff" but one with unique properties. Sedley (2007), 12: "But it seems clear to me that his device of making mind "unmixed" is as close an approximation to the now familiar separation of the incorporeal from the corporeal as was conceptually possible in the first half of the fifth century B.C." Curd (2007), 200–201, argues against thinking of Nous as a material stuff rather than a force, akin to Love and Strife in Empedocles. Guthrie (1965), by contrast, holds that Anaxagoras' Mind is incorporeal.

MIXING MINDS: ANAXAGORAS AND PLATO'S *PHAEDO* 411

Anaxagoras fails to do with respect to cosmic Nous—while nevertheless employing the basic Anaxagorean ideas of Nous as what effects a crucial separation and differentiation.

The Defense is explicitly about what a true philosopher (lover of wisdom) *ought to think* (63e9-10, 64a4, 64b4-5, 64b9). Moreover it is conducted with a view to the restricted audience of those present, especially Simmias and Cebes ("let us talk among ourselves and let's say goodbye to them (i.e. to the many, 64b2)" (64c1)).[14] The argument begins at 64c with a definition of death. Socrates says that death is the "separation" (ἀπαλλαγή) of the body and the soul, after which the body is apart, separated "itself by itself," and the soul is apart, separated "itself by itself."[15] Let's call this "Thanatos-separation," or "T-separation" for short, as referring to biological death. (*Whether* the soul can exist "itself by itself" is precisely the point that Cebes will challenge at 70a.) A body without a soul is of course inanimate and lifeless.[16]

Socrates immediately follows his definition of death with a description of the true philosopher in two parts: (1) 64d2-65a8 concerns the philosopher's attitude towards pleasure; (2) 65a10-66a10 concerns the philosopher's attitude toward the object of his love, wisdom and its acquisition. In (1) we learn that the philosopher is least concerned with food, drink, sex, or clothing, except insofar as they are necessary (64e1). Presumably the reference to "necessity" here is to the idea that to deny oneself all food, drink, clothing (in many places in the world), and sex (on the level of the species, if not the individual), would result in death and so violate the religious prohibition on suicide.[17]

---

14   Pakaluk 2003, 97, notes the limited audience.

15   This is a loaded term with religious connotations of "deliverance," "release from bondage," etc.

16   We might note that this is, according to Sarah Broadie 2001, what marks the difference between Plato and Descartes: the Platonic soul, unlike the Cartesian mind, *animates* the body. This is no doubt correct, but, in contrast with the position defended here, she does not hold there is any difference in the nature of Plato's soul and Descartes' mind; both are immortal, incorporeal entities. See, most recently, Ebrey 2017 for a defence of the ascetic reading, and a critique of Woolf and Pakaluk.

17   A question that arises here is whether the philosophers' stance towards bodily pleasure is properly described as asceticism (namely, the view that one should avoid bodily pleasure as much as possible), as most scholars have thought, or what I would call "indifferentism" (namely, to express an attitude of indifference towards the body and its pleasures). See Woolf 2004, who seems to assimilate the ascetic "stance" to a matter of "behavior" and the evaluative "stance" to a matter of attitude. This leads him to sharply separate behavior and attitude (119, 121–2), which then leads him to think there is a problem in the account in the *Phaedo*. I think that behavior and attitude are more intimately linked in Plato; attitude causes behavior and then behavior reinforces attitude, much the way habituation operates in Aristotle *NE* II.4 or, for that matter, in the *Republic*.

Socrates says that this makes it plain that the philosopher "differs from the rest of humanity" in that the philosopher "separates" or "frees" (ἀπολύων) the soul from association with the body "as far as possible," with the result that most people think of philosophers as "close to dead."[18] It is clear that this separation of soul and body is something brought about by a form of life, by one's attitudes and behaviors towards bodily pleasures.[19] For reasons that will become apparent, let us call it *katharsis*-separation" (or "K-separation" for short).[20]

In the second part of the Defense, Socrates turns to the philosopher's pursuit of wisdom. He explains that the senses are not adequate for grasping the truth; when the soul tries "to consider something with the body" it ends up deceived by it (65a-b). Socrates' select audience happily grants without argument that the true objects of knowledge are not sensibles but transcendent Forms (65d-e). Furthermore they readily agree that these are not grasped by the senses in any case but are grasped "most purely" (65e7) by reasoning and intellect alone itself by itself when it has been separated as far as possible (ἀπαλλαγεὶς ὅτι μάλιστα) from the senses and the whole body (66a1-5).

So, in sum, the philosopher disdains the body as a distraction that pulls him away from achieving knowledge and truth insofar as he experiences bodily pleasure and desire. Moreover, he is not taken in by the alleged information that the body provides about the world (i.e. the testimony of the senses), because the senses are unreliable and incapable of grasping the most genuine objects of knowledge, the Forms.[21]

---

18 Recall Callicles' remark in the *Gorgias* (492e5) that a person who was not interested in or in need of any bodily pleasure (and so had extremely limited appetites) would be like a "stone or a corpse."

19 This is true whether or not this attitude is better described as "asceticism" or "indifferentism."

20 In the idea of K-separation, I think we get the two main strands of pre-Platonic influence in the *Phaedo*: *katharsis* and related words playing off religious imagery, which I will say nothing about here, and vocabulary around separation, combination, mixture, blending, and so on, which I will argue owes much to Anaxagoras.

21 Since what I am calling "K-separation" involves both a separation from the pleasures/desires of the body and from the "information" provided by the body, this suggests that the ascetic reading is not correct and that indifferentism is a more accurate account of what Socrates is advocating for the true philosopher. For while ascetism is possible with respect to bodily desires, it does not make much sense to "deny one's senses" and, for example, to make as little use of them as possible by avoiding hearing or seeing anything as far as possible, the way one might abstain completely from sex or alcohol. In fact, the Recollection Argument precisely *relies on the senses* to "trigger" the process of recollecting the Forms; see too the argument about "summoners" in *Republic* 7 (523a-525a).

MIXING MINDS: ANAXAGORAS AND PLATO'S *PHAEDO* 413

A question now arises: what is the difference between T-separation and K-separation? Perhaps the difference is merely one of degree, so that T-separation maximally achieves what K-separation can only somewhat achieve. This is the conclusion of Michael Pakaluk:

> We might imagine, too, that part of Plato's purpose in introducing the imagery of purification into SD [Socrates' Defense] [...] is to suggest that separation in this life differs only in degree from death. [...] In linking the practice of death to the notion of purification, then, Socrates evidently means to suggest that dying is a matter of reaching an extreme degree of a state already attained ... (2003, 101).

On this view, death effects a complete separation, leaving body and soul each itself by itself. The philosopher does this to a limited extent by living a certain way, but there is really no difference in kind in what is accomplished by the philosopher's practice (K-separation) in contrast to what is accomplished by biological death (T-separation). The philosopher simply hankers after something that, were it not for a religious prohibition, he would do himself.

But there is more going on here, as is foreshadowed from the very opening of the defense when the idea is first introduced that engaging in philosophy is in fact practicing for death and that genuine philosophers look forward to death (64a):

> Simmias laughed at this and said: "Yes by Zeus, Socrates, you've made me laugh, even though I wasn't much inclined to laugh just now. I suppose that most people, on hearing this, would think it very well said of philosophers [...] that they are, indeed, verging on death, and that it has not escaped their notice, at any rate, that this is what philosophers deserve to undergo."[22]
>
> [Socrates replies] "And they would speak the truth, Simmias, except for the part about its not escaping their notice; because it has escaped their notice in what sense true philosophers are verging on death and deserving of it, and what sort of death they deserve [...]" (64a10-b9).

What immediately follows is a definition of death as T-separation. But what Socrates goes on to describe in some detail is what the many fail to understand, namely, what sort of "death," that is what sort of separation of body and soul,

---

22   Again, think of Callicles' remark.

philosophers strive for *while alive*—that is, K-separation. If T-separation is, for everyone, the complete separation of the body from the soul with the result that every soul finally achieves wisdom, then it would be true that only the philosopher would look forward to it. But why would the philosophers work so hard to bring about the second-rate K-separation that comes from the indifference to bodily pleasure and rejection of the testimony of the senses? It seems odd to strive and to practice in order to separate the soul from the body while alive, when this will be done once and for all soon enough at death. Why not just volunteer for a lot of dangerous missions and sea-voyages, so one can die and get to knowledge as soon as possible?

The answer is that T-separation and K-separation are not in fact different in *degree* but in *kind*. Further, it is the successful achievement of K-separation that determines the nature of T-separation. This will turn out to include not only the post-mortem fate of one's soul, as everyone understands once they reach the upcoming "Affinity Argument," but also the physical/metaphysical condition of one's soul. The whole point of K-separation is that it is a necessary preliminary for T-separation's having the philosopher's desired result. This explains why the many also fail to understand "what sort of death (i.e. what sort of T-separation) philosophers deserve."[23]

Let's look at the textual evidence that supports this interpretation, beginning with the structure of the rest of the argument of the Defense. After concluding that the purest wisdom and knowledge is attained by the soul acting by itself, unsullied by any participation with the body, in pursuit of the genuine "things that are" (i.e. the Forms) (65e6-66a10), Socrates then goes on to provide an account of what ought to be said to anyone who is a prospective "genuine" philosopher (66b3-67b2). This speech sums up the conclusions of how the body, with its pleasure, pains and desires, on the one hand, and its deceptive senses on the other, distract, distort and impede the philosopher's search for genuine knowledge. The philosopher will never get knowledge so long as "we

---

23   It is true that T-separation and K-separation have something in common. Death presumably provides one with some K-separation by force insofar as your disembodied soul no longer has sense experience or bodily pleasure. (I owe this objection to Terry Irwin.) But a soul that has not practiced K-separation while embodied will yearn to be reincarnated as quickly as possible—and will indeed get its wish, see 81d9-e2. And this is my main point: T-separation without prior K-separation becomes a different sort of event, even if it is true that a soul is temporarily deprived of sense experience and bodily pleasure. In what is an apt metaphor, T-separation goes nowhere (or not very far!) without proper, prior K-separation.

MIXING MINDS: ANAXAGORAS AND PLATO'S *PHAEDO* 415

have a body, and our soul is kneaded together" (συμπεφυρμένη) "with an evil thing of this sort (i.e. the body)" (66b5-6).[24]

The proper response to being in this contaminated state, Socrates explains, is to bring about K-separation as far as possible. In this life we will be "closest to knowing" if we avoid associating with the body as far as possible and thereby avoid being "filled up with/infected by" (ἀναπιμπλώμεθα) the nature of the body and remaining pure "until god himself frees/delivers us" (i.e. until T-separation) (67a5-6).

> In this way, pure, being separated from the folly (ἀφροσύνης) of the body, we will, as is probable, be with such [people; i.e., pure ones] and we will know through us ourselves the genuine whole; and this, probably, is the truth, for it is never ever permissible for the impure to lay hold of the pure (μὴ καθαρῷ γὰρ καθαροῦ ἐφάπτεσθαι μὴ οὐ θεμιτὸν ᾖ) (67a7-b2).

Here in this overtly religious language the difference between K-separation and T-separation is made clear. Without having properly K-separated one's body and soul, T-separation has no chance of yielding wisdom and knowledge. Why won't T-separation accomplish the separation by itself? While death is a separation of the soul itself by itself from the body itself by itself (as was said at 64c), without K-separation, which "purifies" the soul, the soul that is "itself by itself" will in fact be "mixed together with" and "contaminated by" the body and thus, given the stricture above that the "impure cannot lay hold of the pure," it (the soul) will never be able to know the pure objects of knowledge (i.e. the Forms).[25]

Confirmation of this occurs in what follows. Socrates says that his journey "there" (i.e. to the underworld) may be made "with good hope by any other man who considers his intellect (τὴν διανοίαν) as prepared, just as having been purified" (67c1-3). In other words, T-separation is not sufficient, unless it is preceded by K-separation. I argue that purification is no mere metaphor. As will become increasingly clear, purification is a matter of achieving an incorporeal soul, which will be of like kind to the Forms; what is bodily cannot, as such, grasp Forms. Purification will be accomplished by a separating out of the incorporeal soul from the soul/body mixture.

---

24   Burnet 1911, presumably followed by Rowe 1993, points out that this word contrasts with "most pure" in 65e6.

25   This is Plato's common way of expressing the mind "touching" or "grasping" (ἅπτω, ἐφάπτω) the Forms; see, e.g., *Rep* 490a8-b7; 611b-612a; *Symp* 211d8-212a7; *Phd.* 79c8, 79d6.

We are being shown an important truth about the soul: its incorporeality is contingent. Plato is clear that the Forms are incorporeal, knowable objects that exist "outside" the universe. The soul must be "like" them or as like them as possible in order to know them. The fact that this is a matter of degree shows the contingent, transitional composition of the soul and thus the significance of K-separation. As on Anaxagoras' account of the universe, the embodied soul will remain all mixed together with the bodily unless the person's mind acts to direct the human being towards a particular kind of life that effects the soul's separation from the bodily.

There is further evidence that K-separation is just this sort of process in what follows next:

> Doesn't purification turn out to be just what's been said for a while now in the argument: the parting (τὸ χωρίζειν) of the soul from the body as far as possible, and the habituating of it to assemble and gather itself togeth-er (συναγείρεσθαι τε καὶ ἀθροίζεσθαι) by itself, away from the body in every way, and to live, as far as it can, *both in the present and in the hereafter*, released from the body, as from bonds? (67c5-d2).[26]

Notice here clear reference to the significance of the habituation that is K-separation, which is necessary if the soul is to be separated from body not only in this life, but also in the hereafter.[27] It is only *after* this speech that Socrates once again refers to death, defining it as "the release and separation of the body and the soul" (67d4-5). But he does this not to say that K-separation and T-separation are basically the same, differing only in degree, but to show how they differ in kind. The philosopher will not only be more prepared for and positive about the prospect of T-separation than others, but T-separation will in fact be a different event for him insofar as he has already engaged in K-separation.

Thus, as Socrates said at the start of the Defense (64b), the many are ignorant of (1) the way philosophers are "nearly dead" (i.e. in virtue of their practice of K-separation); (2) the way they deserve to be (i.e. the key role of

---

26   Rowe 1993 on c7-8 ("assemble and gather itself together"): "is a picturesque way of describ-ing the process by which the philosopher distances himself from sensations—some of which, at least, may be located anywhere in the body." Rowe thus takes *pantochthen* as "in every part" rather than "in every way," but I think Plato is preparing the ground for the idea of separating the soul not only from *the* body, but from *body*.

27   This leaves open the possibility, which will be affirmed in the upcoming Affinity Argument, that the soul may still be mixed together with body after T-separation.

MIXING MINDS: ANAXAGORAS AND PLATO'S *PHAEDO* 417

K-separation in achieving wisdom, the aim of the philosopher); and, finally, (3) about the kind of death a philosopher deserves. The phrase "the kind of death a philosopher deserves" obviously does not refer to what we colloquially mean when we say that someone did not deserve, for example, a violent death. It is a metaphysical claim: the kind of death a philosopher is worthy of is a *pure* one, one in which his soul, already purified by living the sort of life he has, is then separated not only *from the body* to which it has been attached but also, because of his practice, *from the bodily as such*, which does not happen to non-philosophers. So, while the "practice of the philosopher" is *for* death (i.e. the right kind of death), the *practice* of a philosopher, that is, the practice he engages in, is K-separation.

Thus, the embodied mind of an individual needs to direct itself (and its body) to live a certain life in order to attain its best state: purity. This plays with the Anaxagorean picture, according to which cosmic Nous begins in a pure state; for Plato, a human being begins incarnated life in the mixed state, more akin to the starting point of the cosmos in Anaxagoras, and then, as on Anaxagoras's picture, Nous initiates the process of separation, only now the separation is of itself from the corporeal because of its own decision and understanding about what is the best way for it to be (namely, separated) and, as we shall see further in the Affinity Argument, what are worse ways (namely, mixed with the bodily). Furthermore, in Anaxagoras's philosophy, the cosmic separation is a matter of degree—it is more separated now than it was and will be further differentiated in the future (as Nous continues the rotation of the universe). For Plato, as we have seen and will see further in what follows, K-separation is also a matter of degree, although it is effected by living according to what is best (i.e. as a genuine philosopher) and not by a mechanical process of rotation.

4   The Affinity Argument (78b–84b)

One of the infamous weaknesses of the so-called "Affinity Argument" as an argument for the immortality of the soul is that it relies on a tenuous and poorly defended analogy between soul and Forms. In brief, Socrates argues that the division between Forms and sensibles and between soul and body are analogous. The body, like sensibles, is visible and changeable; the soul, like Forms, is invisible, and so, Socrates tries to conclude, also unchanging and immortal. Socrates seems to recognize the argument's weakness when he concedes that the soul is only "most similar" to what is divine, immortal, and unchanging, that is, the Forms (80b). The language and content of Socrates' Defense, however, reemerges forcefully in the "Affinity Argument" (78b-84b).[28] Rather than see it as a weak argument for immortality, we ought to understand it as adding a coda, as it were, to the two initial arguments for the immortality of the soul, in which we find a more elaborated version of the idea first discussed in Socrates' Defense, as we have seen, that the soul's incorporeality is contingent and a matter of degree.

If we properly understand the importance of K-separation for Socrates' Defense, we should not expect the soul's incorporeality to be a determinate issue. This in turn ought to make us less surprised at the tenuous nature of the analogy between soul and Forms, since it will not be true that *all* souls will simply be like Forms, invisible and pure and unchanging. The souls of those who have not practiced K-separation will be impure, changing, and, as we shall see, sometimes so corporeal they are visible.

Consider the following passage:

> If it [the soul] is separated purely, while dragging along with it nothing of the body (μηδὲν τοῦ σώματος συνεφέλκουσα), inasmuch as it did not associate with it willingly during life, but fleeing it, having also gathered itself into itself (συνηθροισμένη αὐτὴ εἰς ἑαυτήν), inasmuch as it always practiced this [it has practiced for death.] (80e2–5).

The practice referred to is, unsurprisingly, philosophy. A soul that has adequately practiced K-separation drags "nothing of the body" with it at T-separation. This suggests, what Socrates makes explicit next, that if a person has *not* practiced K-separation, at T-separation his soul *will* drag something of the body with it.

> Whereas if it [the soul] is separated from the body when it has been polluted and made impure, because it has always been with the body, has served and loved it, and been so bewitched by it, by its passions and pleasures, that it thinks nothing else real save what is corporeal (σωματοειδές)—what can be touched and seen, drunk and eaten, or used for sexual enjoyment—yet it has been accustomed to hate and shun and tremble before what is obscure to the eyes and invisible, but intelligible

---

28   As Pakaluk 2003, 109, recognizes. While Pakaluk refers to and even quotes many of the key passages in the Affinity Argument that I will discuss as exemplifying "K-separation," he does not remark on them except to say that they are similar to the language of the Defense and to conclude, rightly, that this further shows that the Defense does not merely precede the other arguments, but provides context for them.

MIXING MINDS: ANAXAGORAS AND PLATO'S *PHAEDO* 419

and grasped by philosophy; do you think a soul in that condition will be separated (ἀπαλλάξεσθαι), unsullied and itself by itself (αὐτὴν καθ'αὑτὴν εἰλικρινῆ)?

> 81b1–c2; GALLOP, slightly modified

Here Socrates adds details to what happens in the most typical situation when T-separation occurs without prior, adequate K-separation, thus giving an account of "the worse" as he demanded of a proper explanation in the "autobiography."[29] The result is that the soul, while separated from the body in one sense—it leaves a corpse behind—is not separated from the bodily as such, thus it is not separated "in purity," and so cannot gather itself by itself, which is a necessary condition for its being free of the bodily and of its achieving wisdom by knowing the Forms. Socrates says that such a soul is "permeated with the corporeal" (διειλημμένην ... ὑπὸ τοῦ σωματοειδοῦς) (81c4) and because of how the person has led his life, i.e. by not practicing K-separation and caring about and serving the body, it has become "of like nature" (σύμφυτον) (81c6).[30] In extreme cases of love of the body, the souls become visible and hang around the graves of the body (as ghosts) (81c-e). This is no mere image on my account: Plato is explaining the contingent incorporeality of the soul.

> Because each pleasure and pain fastens it [the soul] to the body with a sort of rivet (ὥσπερ ἧλον ἔχουσα), pins it there, and *makes it corporeal* (ποιεῖ σωματοειδῆ),[31] so that it takes for real whatever the body declares to be so [i.e. via the testimony of the senses]. Since by sharing opinions and pleasures with the body it is, I believe, forced to become of like character and like nurture to it, and to be incapable of entering Hades in purity; but it must always exist contaminated by the body, and so quickly fall back into another body, and grow in it as if sown there (ὥσπερ σπειρομένη ἐμφύεσθαι) and so have no part in communion with the divine and pure and uniform (μονοειδοῦς).
>
> 83d4–e3; GALLOP trans., slightly modified

---

29 See 97d, 98b, and discussion above.

30 I think this gives yet more evidence that the ascetic reading is wrong. K-separation is a kind of "practicing" (μελετή) or exercise of bodily activities in the proper way.

31 Hackforth 1955 simply does not translate this phrase and does not comment, meanwhile on 67c at 52, n.3, he says, ignoring the present passage: "This is perhaps the most materialistic language used by Socrates about the soul in the whole dialogue. Taken literally, it would imply the spatial diffusion of a sort of vital fluid throughout the body; but of course it must not be taken literally, but rather as a vivid metaphor to bring out the completeness of the soul's detachment."

If read without prejudice, this passage makes it plain that the nature of the soul is determined by the sort of life one lives. Living the life of attention to the body, both to its pleasures and pains and to the testimony of the senses, makes one's soul corporeal. K-separation differs deeply from T-separation; without it one's soul will be bodily so that upon T-separation it will remain corporeal, be unable to examine and grasp what is "unlike it"—namely, the incorporeal Forms—and will quickly be reincarnated. The philosophers, who have engaged in K-separation, will by contrast forever exist "completely without bodies" (114c3-4).[32]

With this understanding of soul in the *Phaedo* and its participation and role in K-separation, let us turn back to Anaxagoras, beginning with attention to the first time he is mentioned in the dialogue, some 25 Stephanus pages before the "autobiography," during the "Cyclical Argument."

5 The Cyclical Argument (70c–71e)

Outside of Socrates' autobiography, Anaxagoras is mentioned in only one sentence much earlier in the dialogue, in the midst of the so-called "Cyclical Argument." This argument is the first argument responding to Cebes' challenge that once the soul and body are separated, the soul will no longer be "anything anywhere." Appreciating what has been said about K-separation and T-separation will be key to understanding the otherwise puzzling question of why Anaxagoras would be mentioned here.

The argument seeks to establish that the living come back from the dead. It begins by discussing contraries—the beautiful and ugly, the just and unjust, and so on—claiming that the contraries come to be from one another. There is a glaring shift from discussion of contrary properties as such to discussion of comparatives in order to make the principle about coming-to-be plausible. So, it is not that the beautiful comes to be from the ugly, but that anything that comes to be more beautiful must have been less beautiful before, anything

---

32   Although, as I have shown, in these passages Plato explicitly describes the soul as heavy, ponderous, corporeal, visible, etc., most scholars have downplayed these descriptions because they are inconsistent with the idea that the soul is an incorporeal entity and so, they must be merely metaphorical and/or ironical; see, e.g., commentary in Hackforth 1955, Gallop 1975, and Rowe 1993. But I have argued that K-separation is a serious and distinct practice and the dismissal of these passages would make a mess of the K-separation/T-separation distinction; for K-separation would not be effecting any real separation. But that is contrary to what Socrates says, and also contrary to the parallel with Anaxagoras's philosophy. I shall come back to this in the final section of the paper.

MIXING MINDS: ANAXAGORAS AND PLATO'S *PHAEDO* 421

that has come to be larger must come to be from being smaller, and so on. Socrates' next point is that there is a process connecting the two contraries, sometimes named but frequently nameless. As an example he mentions, strikingly, "separation and combination" (διαχρίνεσθαι καὶ συγκρίνεσθαι) (71b6), notions that are, of course, central both to Anaxagoras' thought and the process of K-separation.

When Socrates turns to the contraries of significance, being alive and being dead, it is often remarked that he drops the comparatives, so important for making the central principle plausible, since it seems manifestly false that people come to be strong, full stop, from being weak, beautiful from being ugly, etc.[33] Further, one might think, Socrates could not leave the comparatives in because being "more alive" or "more dead" does not even make sense.[34] But we have seen, in the context of Socrates' Defence, being "more alive" or "more dead" *does* make sense: by practicing K-separation the philosopher explicitly is and seeks to be "more dead" during life; the lover of the appetites and senses, by contrast, will be "more alive"—that is, her soul will be more mixed with the bodily.

What is significant now, however, is that, in a short coda to the main argument, Socrates makes the dialogue's first mention of Anaxagoras. He says that there is further evidence that the claim that the living come from the dead is correct in the fact that there must be a balance between the two processes of becoming, so that they go round in a circle, or else "all things would ultimately have the same form, be affected in the same way, and cease to become" (72b4-5). (Now, this claim, for us knowledgeable Platonists, is quite striking, and I'll come back to it briefly below.)[35]

Socrates then elaborates as follows:

> If, for example, there was such a process as going to sleep, but no corresponding process of waking up, you realize that in the end everything would show the story of Endymion to have no meaning. There would be no point to it because everything would have the same experience as he, [namely] be asleep. *And if everything were combined and nothing separated, the saying of Anaxagoras would soon be true, that "all things [are] together."* In the same way, my dear Cebes, if everything that partakes of

---

33   See Hackforth 1955, 64; Hackforth's criticism rebutted by Gallop 1975, 108, followed by Rowe 1993, 156.

34   See, e.g., Gallop 1975, 107.

35   Gallop 1975, 112, asks: "Is it being suggested that a perpetually dormant universe is inconceivable? If it is, Socrates does not say why he finds it so." See also Bostock 1986, 54.

life were to die and remain in that state and not come to life again, would not everything ultimately have to be dead and nothing alive? Even if the living came from some other source, and all that lived died, how could all things avoid being absorbed in death? (72b7-d3; Grube trans., modified).

If we read through the paragraph, skipping the sentence in bold, it reads perfectly smoothly and the argument's analogy between sleeping and dying is complete and cogent without it. There are at least two oddities about the striking reference to Anaxagoras at this point.[36] First, why mention separating and combining? The analogy of sleeping and waking is more apt and clearer for the argument at hand. But separating and combining are key both to T-separation and K-separation: combination of body and soul is what makes for human life; separation of body and soul at death, if properly preceded by the practice of a philosopher, enables the soul to realize its true, incorporeal and wise nature. This leads to the second oddity: Plato is quoting what is apparently the first sentence of Anaxagoras' book and what Anaxagoras takes to be the *initial* state of things in the universe.[37] On Anaxagoras' account, which would presumably be familiar to the reader—and is explicitly familiar to Socrates, who, as I mentioned, we later find out eagerly read all of Anaxagoras' books (98b)—the world is *first* all mixed together and *then* the action of Nous differentiates the elements in the cosmos via separation. But Socrates' use (or, perhaps I should say, misuse) of Anaxagoras here understands the mixed state as the *end* point. Why does the state of everything mixed together carry the negative valence here, on a par with everything dying or everything going to sleep? It makes perfect Platonic sense if we recall the mixed state of soul and body, which most people take to be "life." The Cyclical Argument, after all, concerns the cycle of souls that are reincarnated. We understand from the Defense (and with hindsight from the later Affinity Argument) that these souls are not those of the true philosophers who have engaged in K-separation. Anyone whose soul is mixed together with the body will in fact be reincarnated. The remedy for

---

36   Neither of which, so far as I know, has been remarked upon.

37   Commentators universally mention this, but no one remarks on the fact that the argument presents Anaxagoras's starting point of the universe as the absurd *ending* point of it. Burnet 1911, adds: "There is similar jesting in the use of the phrase ["all things together"] in *Gorg.* 465d3," but the jest is not similar. There Socrates is referring to the necessity that soul/mind distinguish between *technai*, like medicine and gymnastics, and pseudo-*technai*, like cookery and cosmetics. The reference to Anaxagoras works by saying that without nous (the soul), the body controlling itself (465d1) would be unable to distinguish what, for example, tastes delicious from what is genuinely healthy, and so all the *technai* and pseudo-*technai* would be one undifferentiated mass.

MIXING MINDS: ANAXAGORAS AND PLATO'S *PHAEDO* 423

this is the appropriate separation of soul from body, specifically K-separation while alive.[38] For Anaxagoras, the motion initiated by Nous (and still ongoing) continues to separate and differentiate objects in the world via a mechanical, rotating process. For Plato, by contrast, incarnation in the sensible world is something to be avoided: the aim is to escape the mortal coil and return (cf. *Phaedrus*) to the realm of the Forms. Contrary to scholars' objections, then, it is not that Plato fails to conceive of the possibility of a static situation in which everything were "dead." Rather, such a static state of an incorporeal soul in timeless contemplation of unchanging Forms *is* the ultimate aim. Recall the Platonic-sounding sentence I mentioned earlier: if the processes in question were simply linear and not cyclical then "all things would ultimately have the same form, be affected in the same way, and cease to become" (72b4-5). This is a wonderful description of the world of Forms, which the philosopher's purified and separated mind will join.

So, what we are getting in the Cyclical Argument is an account of the world of becoming, which borrows in a startling way from Anaxagorean cosmology. Anaxagoras' account begins with the universe in the mixed state (B1), and then Nous separates out elements (B12, 13, and 14). By Plato's lights in the *Timaeus* and *Laws*, that is exactly wrong. But it *isn't* wrong for the *mikrokosmos*: in our embodied life as human beings, our souls are all mixed together with body.[39] It is the task of the philosopher's life, using his mind, to separate out his incorporeal soul by leading a certain kind of life. Now the "life" to which the philosopher is heading, ideally, is a life apart from any cycles or becoming at all—it is pure being. But nous/the soul does not begin its earthly life in that state; it is a goal-directed achievement, which is not attained by most people. Nevertheless the view shares with Anaxagorean philosophy the idea that the ultimate good is separation not mixture effected by *nous*.

Plato (like Aristotle) thus admires and in a way agrees with the Anaxagorean idea that mind is unmixed and pure (and perhaps incorporeal, as some think Anaxagoras' Nous is). Further Plato holds that mind is what effects the necessary separation; T-separation (biological death) does not accomplish that by itself. Plato has taken Anaxagoras' idea of the unmixed nature of mind and, instead of making it a starting point, makes it an end, a *telos*. Nous/the soul takes

---

38   What's more, as Plato makes clear in the *Timaeus* and *Laws* 10, the initial state is for pure, incorporeal and immortal soul to exist itself by itself, before it is mixed with the corporeal, which comes into existence later. So the mixed state is not, cosmologically speaking, the initial state, but a later state. In this way too, Plato turns Anaxagoras on his head.

39   Of course the *Timaeus* presents the whole cosmos as originating from a mind, the Demiurge, imposing order on a chaotic "receptacle;" but I cannot pursue this here.

as its own end achieving its own incorporeality, for this is precisely the *best* state for it to be in. Now we see that Plato is providing an account of the human being and of why one would lead a certain kind of life and seek a certain sort of separation of the body from the soul, using Anaxagorean concepts, but with a clear teleological structure, which turns out to be very similar to what Socrates seeks, but complains he does not get, from Anaxagoras in the "autobiography." Furthermore, in the arguments' vivid descriptions of what happens to the soul that has led life without K-separation, and therefore has been made corporeal, we have an account of not only what the best life is—the life of pursuit of wisdom and indifference to bodily appetites and avoidance of thinking that genuine knowledge can come from the senses—but also of the worse: bodily indulgence and trust in the senses that leads one to have a mixed and therefore corrupted and impure soul.

6 Coda: A Metaphysical Problem for Anaxagoras and Plato

I have focused in this paper on a particular aspect of what the soul is like in the *Phaedo*, namely whether it has a corporeal or incorporeal constitution. I have argued that while the best way for it to be is incorporeal, when embodied it is mixed to varying degrees with the corporeal depending on the sort of life a person leads. So we can see the adoption and modification of what is basically an Anaxagorean scheme, shifted from the cosmos at large to the *mikrokosmos* of the human being. At the birth of the individual, similar to the primordial mixture at the birth of the Anaxagorean universe, both body and soul are mixed together.[40] It is up to mind (in the individual) or Cosmic Mind for the universe to begin the process that leads to separation and differentiation of the elements. While, according to Socrates' complaint, Anaxagoras's Mind accomplishes this without out any discussion of how and why a certain separation and differentiation is best (and why others may be worse), the *Phaedo* provides an account of the best and worse ways for a human being to separate (or not) his incorporeal soul from its body and corporeal elements. We should note here that just because the process of separation is directed via a decision by mind about what is best does not mean and provides no evidence for the view that Plato conceives of this separation "metaphorically" or "ironically" and not literally. After all, Plato clearly does not deny that the material universe is subject to

---

40 Of course, on Anaxagoras' account Nous is alone, unmixed (B12). Plato is also going to need an original, unmixed incorporeal soul, as we shall see below.

MIXING MINDS: ANAXAGORAS AND PLATO'S *PHAEDO*

material processes—of course it is, just as are our bodies. His objection is to the idea that such material causes, on their own, provide an adequate *explanation* of how and why things are the way they are. In the *Timaeus*, there will be plenty of corporeal and quasi-corporeal processes created and described, but the crucial difference is that they have been brought about ultimately by a Mind (the Demiurge) aiming at the best. Thus, I see no reason to deny that Plato thinks of the soul/body mixture that is our embodied life as a literal description of our physical state of being.

Moreover, a notorious problem afflicts our understanding of how separation into qualities and basic stuffs occurs on the Anaxagorean account. Anaxagoras seems clearly to rely on a "Principle of Preponderance" to explain ordinary macroscopic objects being as they are. According to Anaxagoras, if something is perceptibly gold and yellow, for example, it is because gold and yellow have come to predominate at this location, having been separated by Nous from the primordial mixture of everything in everything. So, in B1: "Anaxagoras says that the homogenous stuffs, unlimited in amount, are separated off from a single mixture" (ἐξ ἑνὸς μίγματος), "with all things being in everything but each being characterized by what predominates."[41] The idea that all qualities and things begin jumbled together and are then separated might initially seem coherent enough, but it becomes much less clear when we recall that Anaxagoras also holds that everything is in everything and that there is no least bit of a thing to which this principle does not apply. Thus, everything is susceptible to further division *ad infinitum*, and each divided bit itself contains everything (B1, B3, and B6).[42] It is difficult to understand how these different claims can cohere in the end. In particular, what does it mean for, say, gold to dominate (in a piece of gold) despite each bit of gold containing everything else in it (hair, nails, flesh, black, hot, and so on)? We must, it seems, think of bits of pure gold, which come to dominate (for example, by being more numerous than) the other bits. But this also must be wrong: for it is central to the account that everything (except Nous) is mixed with everything else and everything contains a portion of everything (B4, B6, B11). If everything contains a portion of everything—so there is no portion of a pure anything—it is difficult to understand in what sense any macroscopic object can have, say, "more gold." The responses to this

---

41   Curd 2007, 15, translation. See also B12 (Curd 2007, 24, translation): "Nothing else is like anything else, but each one is and was most manifestly those things of which there are the most in it."

42   Scholars interpret this in a variety of ways, see the following note. By "bit" I do not necessarily mean particle, but it could be some "drop" of a liquid or bit of paste or even just something occupying a portion of space.

426   VASILIOU

puzzle are legion, but fortunately I do not need to adjudicate among them for my purposes.[43] I simply want to call attention to the fact that on my interpretation Plato faces a very similar problem with respect to the soul. And, if I am right about the influence of Anaxagorean ideas, this should come as little surprise.

If the soul has become corporeal, even to the point of being visible (81c-d), presumably there must be, as it were, "incorporeal bits" mixed together with the corporeal bits. As we have seen, it is the process of K-separation to separate these and to make the soul "pure." The process of K-separation, however, must rely on the idea that the incorporeal bits or parts of the soul can be extracted from the mixture with the corporeal, generated through appetite and sensation. The presumption must be, then, that there was, at some point, pure, incorporeal soul, that was, at some point, mixed with the corporeal and which now, via K-separation and T-separation, can be separated. Like the fragments of Anaxagoras, the *Phaedo* provides no details on what the corporeal/incorporeal mixture is like. In any case, in other dialogues, such as the *Timaeus*, we learn that the (purely) incorporeal preceded the creation of the corporeal: mind, and apparently one immortal mind, the Demiurge, *made* the corporeal.[44] So, the Platonic view must be, crudely, that there are incorporeal "bits" of soul in our currently mixed, embodied souls, which, via a proper K-separation directed by the soul/mind itself, can be separated out from the corporeal elements and gather themselves together (the soul being "itself by itself") so that, at death, the soul can escape "pure," without corporeal elements, and thus remain in eternal contemplation of the Forms. So, just as the Anaxagorean would seem to require some pure portions or bits of things in order

---

43   See, as a sample, Schofield 1980, Inwood 1986, Barnes 1982, Matthews 2002, Sider 2005, Sedley 2007, Curd 2007. Marmodoro 2017, chap. 4, surveys the problems with all of the proffered solutions. She argues that we should not conceive of the "everything in everything" principle on the model of *containment*, but *compresence*—so it is not as though in any bit of yellow there is also, say, black, but that everywhere yellow is, so is black. Marmodoro argues (chap. 3) that Anaxagoras' metaphysical account is one of "gunk." While her arguments are persuasive on their own, she concedes that the problem discussed above concerning how any quality could come to predominate is not one that is solved by supposing compresence of gunk is denser in some areas then others (see, especially, 96–98).

44   The Demiurge, of course, did not make *everything*. The Demiurge did not make the Forms nor the Receptacle, from which eventually the four elements and the corporeal world were fashioned. Similarly, in Anaxagoras, Nous did not make the primordial mixture nor give it the powers it apparently has. Sedley 2007, 23–25, likens Nous to a cosmic farmer, who organizes and utilizes certain given materials, like soil, light, water, seeds, and so on, to generate a desired outcome.

for certain qualities to predominate, so too does the *Phaedo* with respect to the incorporeal soul. Plato will make this explicit, however, only in later dialogues like the *Timaeus* and *Laws*.[45]

Bibliography

Archer-Hind, Richard D. 1883. *The Phaedo of Plato*. London: MacMillan and Company.

Barnes, Jonathan. 1982. *The Presocratic Philosophers*, rev. ed. London: Routledge & Kegan Paul Ltd.

Bluck, Richard S. 1955. *Plato's Phaedo*. London: Routledge & Kegan Paul Ltd.

Bostock, David. 1986. *Plato's Phaedo*. Oxford: Oxford University Press.

Broadie, Sarah. 2001. "Soul and Body in Plato and Descartes." *Proceedings of the Aristotelian Society* 101.3: 295–308.

Burnet, John. 1911. *Platonis Opera Phaedo*. Oxford: Oxford University Press.

Bury, Robert G. 1932. *The Symposium of Plato, 2nd ed*. Cambridge: Cambridge University Press.

Curd, Patricia. 2007 *Anaxagoras of Clazomenae*. Toronto: University of Toronto Press.

Ebrey, David. 2017. "The Asceticism of the Phaedo: Pleasure, Purification, and the Soul's Proper Activity." *Archiv für Geschichte der Philosophie* 99.1: 1–30.

Gallop, David. 1975. *Plato Phaedo*. Oxford: Oxford University Press.

Gerson, Lloyd P. 1987. "A Note on Tripartition and Immortality in Plato." *Apeiron* 20.1: 81–96.

Gerson, Lloyd P. 1986. "Platonic Dualism." *The Monist* 69: 352–69.

Guthrie, William K.C. 1965. *A History of Greek Philosophy*, Volume Two. Cambridge: Cambridge University Press.

Kirk, Geoffrey.S., Raven, John E., and Schofield, Malcolm. 1983. *The Presocratic Philosophers,* 2nd ed. Cambridge: Cambridge University Press.

Hackforth, Reginald. 1955. *Plato's Phaedo*. Cambridge: Cambridge University Press.

Inwood, Brad. 1986. "Anaxagoras and Infinite Divisibility." *Illinois Classical Studies* 11: 17–33.

Marmodoro, Anna. 2017. *Everything in Everything: Anaxagoras' Metaphysics*. Oxford: Oxford University Press.

---

45 I have benefitted from comments by Tad Brennan, Charles Brittain, Friedemann Buddensiek, Matt Evans, Brad Inwood, Terence Irwin, Eric Kenyon, Wolfgang Mann, Phillip Mitsis, Gisela Striker, Rosemary Twomey, Nancy Worman, and audiences at Cornell University, Columbia University, Universität Frankfurt am Main, and Aristotle University of Thessaloniki.

Matthews, Gareth. 2002. "On the Idea of There Being Something of Everything in Everything." *Analysis* 62 (1): 4–10.

McCabe, Mary Margaret. 2000. *Plato and his Predecessors: The Dramatisation of Reason.* Cambridge: Cambridge University Press.

McKirahan, Richard. 1994. *Philosophy Before Socrates.* Indianapolis: Hackett Press.

Pakaluk, Michael. 2003. "Degrees of Separation in the *Phaedo*." *Phronesis* 48.2: 89–115.

Rowe, Christopher J. 1993. *Plato Phaedo.* Cambridge: Cambridge University Press.

Sedley, David. 2007. *Creationism and its Critics in Antiquity.* Berkeley: University of California Press.

Schofield, Malcolm. 1980. *An Essay on Anaxagoras.* Cambridge: Cambridge University Press.

Sider, David. 2005. *The Fragments of Anaxagoras*, 2nd Edition. Sankt Augustin: Academia Verlag.

Tzamalikos, Panagiotes. 2016. *Anaxagoras, Origen, and Neoplatonism: The Legacy of Anaxagoras to Classical and Late Antiquity.* Berlin: DeGruyter.

Vasiliou, Iakovos. 2012. "From the Phaedo to the Republic: Plato's Tripartite Soul and the Possibility of Non-Philosophical Virtue." In *Plato and the Divided Self*, edited by Rachel Barney, Tad Brennan, and Charles Brittain, 9–32. Cambridge: Cambridge University Press.

Woolf, Raphael. 2004. "The Practice of a Philosopher." *Oxford Studies in Ancient Philosophy* 26: 97–129.

CHAPTER 14

Platonic Reception – Atomism and the Atomists in Plato's *Timaeus*

Barbara M. Sattler

1 Introduction

Still today our model of how one philosopher should discuss the thought of another is largely founded on the conception that Aristotle had of the matter: Aristotle established that the thinker in question is usually named,[1] and his position briefly sketched, before the position and the arguments for it are evaluated.[2] But this is not how the Presocratics themselves usually react to each other; rather this is a mode of dealing with other philosophical positions that only gradually developed in ancient times.

Plato's treatment of his predecessors is especially interesting for the development of a model for philosophical reception, since we find him to be an important point of transition from a Presocratic way to an Aristotelian way of dealing with preceding thinkers: he seems to be the first philosopher who provides us with sketches of something like a history of philosophy (without, however, necessarily giving the names of his predecessors) and we find different forms of explicit and implicit reception of his philosophical predecessors. In this paper I will focus on Plato's reception of the atomists Leucippus and Democritus in the *Timaeus* as an interesting case study of *one way* in which Plato engages his predecessors. The atomists are a particularly interesting case because (unlike various other thinkers with whom Plato engages philosophically) they are conspicuously unnamed – a fact for which I will be offering a novel explanation, if only tentatively.

---

1 The thinker discussed is, however, not always named; sometimes Aristotle simply talks about "some people". This can be seen – to give just two examples from natural philosophy, the field on which the latter part of this paper will concentrate – in his discussion of the pangenesis theory in *Generation of Animals* 1,17–18, which only talks of "some" (*tines*) thinkers holding this theory; or in his account of being faster at the beginning of *Physics* VI,2 which he claims to be "in conformity with an account of faster given by some (*tines*)".

2 This is not to claim that Aristotle always evaluates positions of other thinkers in an unbiased way, but simply that he established a model of reception that is still important for us today.

© KONINKLIJKE BRILL NV, LEIDEN, 2021 | DOI:10.1163/9789004443358_016

I will start the paper with an outline of the Aristotelian way of engaging with other philosophers before I describe briefly the manner in which the Presocratics seem to react to each other. Against this background, I will then characterize different ways in which Plato reacts to his predecessors before I look in more detail at his reception of the atomists, especially at his reception of their natural philosophy.

2 Different Forms of Philosophical Reception in the Presocratics, Plato, and Aristotle

2.1 *Aristotle*

With Aristotle and his school, the philosophers reacted to are usually named and their positions with respect to a certain problem are discussed, at least in their essential outlines. We are given an evaluation of each position in such a way that it is clear what insight should be retained from it (if any), what should be rejected, and why.[3] And, to a large extent, we today still attempt to follow the example of this Aristotelian way of dealing with other philosophers in a discussion.

With Aristotle this way of dealing with preceding positions seems to be, at least to a certain degree, also a reaction to Plato:[4] one likely reason for the fact that Aristotle spends much more time than any of the thinkers before him arguing in detail against preceding positions is that he comes from Plato's Academy and thus seems to be forced to show why he does not think that Plato, at least with respect to the fundamental outlines of his position, is right. Aristotle seems to be the first well-documented example in Western philosophy of somebody thoroughly trained in one school who then goes off to found another, competing school.[5] And Plato was clearly seen as an authority by many

---

3 Obviously, a much more fine-grained account of Aristotle's way of reacting to his predecessors could be given in individual cases than I have space to do here (see, for example the more elaborate structure of his reception of Parmenides in *Physics* I, 2 and 3).

4 This does not mean, of course, that all discussion of his predecessors derives in some way from Aristotle's reaction to Plato, but only that Aristotle's emphasis on discussing his predecessors and the general model of reception he develops seem to be based on his reaction to Plato, see below.

5 Student-teacher relationships are, of course, used as a frequent pattern in doxography – starting right with Thales and Anaximander. . And there are anecdotes about alleged relationships that seem less obvious to us now, like Diogenes Laertius's claim that Parmenides was originally influenced by the Pythagorean Ameinias, DL IX, 3, 21. However, such student-teacher relationships often seem to have been used simply as a pattern for presenting the history of philosophy, and it is unclear how much we can indeed trust these stories. In any

PLATONIC RECEPTION

philosophers at the time Aristotle starts out his own writing so that Aristotle indeed had to argue against Plato in order to introduce his own position. If Aristotle has to make it clear in which aspects and why he differs from his teacher, it seems natural that this may also have prompted Aristotle to lay down in detail how his own position relates to that of his other predecessors, the Presocratics.

Let us now consider briefly the manner in which the Presocratics react to each other before we look at the different ways in which Plato engages with his predecessors.

2.2 *The Presocratics*

The Presocratic thinkers only rarely react to each other by quoting or naming each other. Accordingly, the traces of influence are often not very clear. Sometimes they may take up a 'signature word' from a predecessor, for example, some scholars think that Parmenides's usage of the word *"palintropos"* in fragment 6 is suggestive of Heraclitus:[6]

> [...] οἱ δὲ φοροῦνται
> κωφοὶ ὁμῶς τυφλοί τε, τεθηπότες, ἄκριτα φῦλα,
> οἷς τὸ πέλειν τε καὶ οὐκ εἶναι ταὐτὸν νενόμισται
> κοὐ ταὐτόν, πάντων δὲ παλίντροπός ἐστι κέλευθος.
> [...] they [the double-headed mortals] are carried along
> Both deaf and blind, dazzled, undiscriminating hordes,
> For whom being and not-being are the same
> And not the same, and the path of them all is backward turning (fragment 6, lines 6b-9).

The double-headed mortals assume there to be what Parmenides considers a *palintropos keleuthos*, a path that is turning backwards. This has been understood as taking up Heraclitus's talk about *palintropos harmoniê* in fragment 51,[7] a harmony that is turning backwards, as in a bow and lyre:

> οὐ ξυνιᾶσιν
> ὅκως διαφερόμενον ἑωυτῶι ὁμολογέει· παλίντροπος
> ἁρμονίη ὅκωσπερ τόξου καὶ λύρης.

---

case we do not get any detailed criticism of the arguments of one of these alleged teachers by one of these alleged students.

6 So, for example, Hussey 1973, pp. 86–88 and Osborne 2006, p. 235–236 (though Osborne thinks that it is more likely that Heraclitus is here reacting to Parmenides).

7 If it is indeed *palintropos* in Heraclitus and not *palintonos*, back-stretched, as is claimed by Kirk, Raven, and Schofield 1983, pp. 192-193.

> They do not apprehend how being brought apart it is being brought to-
> gether with itself: there is a backward turning connection, as in a bow
> or lyre.

Even if Parmenides has taken up the word *"palintropos"* from Heraclitus, this still leaves open the question in which way Parmenides means to react to Heraclitus in fragment 6. There is a wide range of possibilities: is he simply claiming that Heraclitus is wrong in the passage where he uses the image, and that it is only the double-headed mortals who in fact understand the path of all things to be *palintropos*? Or is it an attempt to correct Heraclitus? Perhaps Parmenides claims that Heraclitus is right in introducing the idea of certain things being *palintropos*, but that he did not get the sample of things right or the right realm where this applies? Using the word *palintropos* in his fragment, if it is indeed meant to refer to Heraclitus, is like shouting "Heraclitus!" – without providing a statement that would make a clear claim about Heraclitus.

To what extent then can we say that the Presocratics react to each other's *philosophy*? I think this happens in at least two ways: they answer questions raised in the tradition and they take over arguments from earlier thinkers. For example, Anaximander and Anaximenes give different answers to what seems to have been a question put forward by Thales – whether there is one basic kind of stuff that can explain the infinite plurality of phenomena. Post-Parmenidean thinkers like Empedocles, Anaxagoras, and the atomists seem to take up the Parmenidean argument against generation in fragment 8 and answer the challenge it puts forward to natural philosophy by explaining all generation in terms of rearrangement of basic elements.[8] In this way, different Presocratic thinkers participate in a philosophical discussion without, however-er, usually naming the other parties in this debate; a form of reception that we can still sometimes see in Plato.

The exception to this is Heraclitus who famously criticizes some of his predecessors by name – in fragment B40 he names Pythagoras and Xenophanes (as well as Hesiod and Hekataios) in order to scorn them by claiming that learning many things does not teach intelligence; otherwise it would have taught them. In fragment B81 he refers to Pythagoras as "originator of imposters", and in fragment B129 we are told that Pythagoras of all men gathered most inquiries and made his own wisdom simply by selecting from the writing of others.[9] So not

---

8 For a discussion of the atomists's reaction to the Parmenidean argument, see Sattler 2020, chapter 4.

9 Diels/Krantz, however, classify fragment 129 under "Zweifelhafte, falsche und gefälschte Fragmente".

PLATONIC RECEPTION

only does Heraclitus name some of his predecessors explicitly, we also see him unambiguously criticizing his predecessors for merely being aware of many things without deriving any real knowledge from this. While this seems indeed to be a new way of engaging with preceding philosophers, we do not, however, thereby learn anything about Pythagoras's and Xenophanes's specific positions in the way Heraclitus understood it (apart from the fact that he took Pythagoras's position to be eclectic without adding anything interesting of his own).

2.3   *Plato*

Plato seems to be one of the first or even the first philosopher to provide something like an overview of the history of philosophy up to that point: in his *Sophist,* 242c-243a he gives an overview of the position of Parmenides and those philosophers so far who tried to determine how many and what kinds of Beings (*onta*) there are (*posa te kai poia*). It follows a basic scheme, an example of which we can see also at the beginning of Aristotle's *Physics*, which starts with an account of how many basic principles his predecessors assumed.[10] We find a similar scheme in Isocrates's *Antidosis* 268 – a scheme which seems to go back ultimately to Gorgias. What distinguishes Plato from Gorgias and Isocrates is that he uses this overview of different positions in a philosophically productive way: he employs it to show the basic philosophical problems these positions bring with them and eventually to help establish a positive account. By contrast, what scholars have identified as a comparable organization in Gorgias's treatise *On Nature or On what is not* is used there as a tool for skepticism – a way to establish universal scepticism against any kind of ontology – and in Isocrates as a way to show that these ontological accounts are mere speculation, which "do not profit anyone" (Isocrates, *Antidosis* 269).[11]

With Plato, we find a wide variety of ways in which he reacts to his philosophical predecessors.[12] And with some predecessors Plato deals in a way that prepares Aristotle's approach: he names the philosopher in question, presents

---

10   Cf. also *Metaphysics* A 3,983b19-20, where *to plethos kai to eidos* seems to correspond to Plato's *posa te kai poia* in the *Sophist.*

11   For a more detailed discussion of how Plato's account relates to what scholars have understood as first histories of philosophy in Gorgias, Hippias, and Isocrates, see Sattler in preparation.

12   This is only to look at Plato's reception of preceding philosophers. We may have reasons for counting some of the sophists discussed by Plato among these philosophers, but whatever the truth is on this point, it seems that Plato deliberately treats the teachers of rhetoric very differently from those predecessors he considers to be genuine philosophers. For a systematic account of his reception of the Presocratics, see Sattler in preparation.

the position, and discusses the problems and merits of the position. Of all the predecessors who play a role in his dialogues, the one to whom Plato gives pride of place is of course Socrates, the main interlocutor in the early and middle dialogues.[13] Plato seems to have taken up at least Socrates's deep care for ethics and his interest in definitions (whether or not they ultimately understood the same by what we call definition).

As for his Presocratic predecessors, with some Plato just takes up a single idea, while with others he discusses the whole of their basic foundation. For example, in the *Phaedo* Plato reacts to Anaxagoras by referring to the single, but well-recognizable claim of Anaxagoras that *nous* is the cause and order of all things. Without really discussing any of the arguments for this position, Plato attempts to show that on Anaxagoras's account *nous* does in fact not do any work, since Anaxagoras ultimately gives materialistic explanations of natural phenomena. If *nous* were indeed active, according to Plato, it would be the basis for explaining why it is good that natural phenomena are the way they are. In contrast to his treatment of Anaxagoras, Plato not only discusses one central assumption of Parmenides, but also gives an elaborate discussion of the main gist of Parmenides's arguments that there is only one Being.[14]

But whether Plato discusses only one central idea or the whole of the core assumptions of a preceding thinker, the Presocratic philosopher Plato engages with is usually clearly referred to – often by directly naming the thinker in question, sometimes with the help of a geographical hint, or a playful 'nickname'.[15] The exception to this rule is his treatment of the atomists Leucippus and Democritus, with respect to whom Plato is surprisingly silent.[16] It seems clear that Plato takes up central assumptions from the atomists, at least

---

13 This exceptional status holds whether or not Socrates is seen as a mouthpiece of Plato's own ideas in Plato's dialogues.

14 In the *Sophist*, which shows the most elaborate discussion of Parmenides's doctrine, we find in fact different forms of engagement with Parmenides's position that also exhibit different degrees of seriousness and accuracy – some are dealing with Parmenides' historic position, while others only deal with some form of monism or other.

15 An example of the geographical hint is Plato's mention of "Sicilian Muses" in *Sophist* 242d, which many scholars understand as referring to Empedocles; an example of a nickname is Plato's reference to Zeno as "Eleatic Palamedes" in *Phaedrus* 261d: after Palamedes had been named as one who gave instructions for rhetoric in 261b, Plato now refers to the "Eleatic Palamedes" who makes the same appear similar and dissimilar to the listener and who shows that the art of *antilogikê* is not restricted to the courts and public assemblies.

16 For the purposes of this paper, I am not going to attempt to distinguish between the positions of Leucippus and of Democritus.

PLATONIC RECEPTION

assumptions about the material world in his *Timaeus*.[17] But nowhere in his works does he name them, nor does he give any geographical or other hint that he is talking about them. His reception of the atomists consists simply in taking over some central insight without making their influence in any way explicit, which is out of line with how he deals with ideas of other Presocratic thinkers. Plato names Anaxagoras, Empedocles, Heraclitus, and Parmenides, among others, so why not also the atomists? Why do we find such a different treatment in their case?

This is one of the big puzzles that the secondary literature on the relation between Plato and the atomists continues to ponder: almost all scholars agree that Plato takes up central features of atomism from Leucippus and Democritus in his *Timaeus*;[18] indeed, with respect to their basic account of the ultimate parts of the physical world, it sometimes seems hard even to distinguish Plato and the atomists.[19] But why then does Plato not name the atomists, if he is indeed so close to them? Before we try to answer this question, let us first have a look at the extent to which Plato does indeed take over important atomistic assumptions. For my discussion I will focus on the *Timaeus* where the overlap between Plato's and the atomists' position seems to be most striking. I will not be able to take into account other dialogues of possible interest for his reception of the atomists, as for example, the *Sophist*,[20] the *Protagoras*, or the *Philebus*, and thus will also not discuss whether Plato may refer to an atomistic theory of pleasure there.[21]

---

17   Only a few scholars have diverged from this consensus: Taylor 1928 attempts to show that any possible influence we may see of Democritus in Plato's *Timaeus* ultimately stems from a common Pythagorean source (Pythagoreanism is the main source of influence Taylor sees at work in the *Timaeus*), though he does allow for some influence of Leucippus. And Friedländer 1975, p. 336 claims that Democritus is only one of a series of natural philosophers whom Plato integrates and that Plato's reception does not concern any particular doctrine but "die gesamte ältere Naturphilosophie".

18   And this is not just our modern impression; rather we also find it in Aristotle, who sometimes treats Plato in the same breath as Democritus.

19   For example, the famous passage 187a1-3 in Aristotle's *Physics* 1.3 is commonly read in the literature as referring to the atomists Leucippus and Democritus; however, ancient commentators and more recently Sedley 2007 have read it is a reference to Platonic atomism.

20   McCabe 2000 and others have suggested to understand some of the insults of the idealists towards their opponents in the *Sophist* and the attack against the earth-bound giants as references to the atomists (pp. 75, n. 61, and 77, n. 65).

21   I will briefly say something about Plato's polemic against materialism in the *Laws* below, but will not be able to discuss whether Plato in his treatment of how the states on earth came into being in *Laws* III was influenced by Democritus's cultural history, as, for example, Wilamowitz-Moellendorf 1919, p. 657 assumes.

436 SATTLER

3 Plato's Reception of the Atomists

3.1 *The Atomistic Base in Plato's* Timaeus

For the atomists as well as for Plato's *Timaeus* our sensible world is made up of ultimate smallest building blocks. The combination and rearrangement of these explains the different sensible phenomena, their coming into being, changing, and passing away. But to what extent should we count this assumption in Plato as a reception specifically of Leucippus and Democritus? Could it be just in general an atomistic position not necessarily tied to taking up anything from these two thinkers?[22]

I do not want to take a view here on the controversial idea of Pythagorean atomism.[23] But I think it is reasonable to ask whether there may have been some more general atomistic inclinations around. If all we understand by atomism is that there are some ultimate building blocks of the sensible world, Plato may perhaps have taken up such a simple atomistic foundation in a general sense; i.e. a position assuming that there are most basic elements of the sensible world that cannot be broken down any further. Such an assumption, however, need not have been tied to Leucippus and Democritus in particular; rather, it may just have been one possible position to explain the world in contrast to assuming the world to consist of something that is always further divisible (in the way it was depicted as problematic by Zeno in his first two paradoxes of motion and probably most famously formulated in a positive way later on in Aristotle's account of continua).[24]

However, Plato does indeed take up much more from Leucippus and Democritus than a vague idea of basic building blocks; it seems to me that the following points are fairly clearly adopted from Leucippus and Democritus:

---

22 Some scholars are reluctant to talk about atomism in Plato, because they assume that an atomistic position necessarily has to include a notion of a void, while, as we will see below, Plato excludes that there is any void in the created cosmos. However, I do not share this view, since think the features named in the main text in the following are features characteristic of an atomistic position (moreover, the receptacle takes over some of the important functions of the atomistic void, see Sattler, manuscript).

23 This idea was originally introduced by Tannery 1877, and defended prominently in the English speaking world by Cornford, who also saw Zeno's paradoxes of motion as a reaction to Pythagorean atomism. For the dismissal of this idea see especially Booth 1957; Furley 1967, pp. 44–56; Owen 1957–8; and Barnes 1982, p. 291.

24 If we keep atomism that general, however, we may want to count the Pythagoreans as atomists of a sort again, since their basic elements – that is, numbers – seem to fit this profile.

PLATONIC RECEPTION   437

(a)   For the atomists as well as for Plato, the ultimate elements are neither any one of the traditional four elements on its own, fire, air, water, and earth individually, nor all of them together, as they seem to have been for preceding Presocratics. Rather, the traditional 'elements' themselves rest on something more basic and much more abstract – bodily atoms in the case of the atomists, two kinds of basic triangles that then form tetrahedra, octahedra, icasohedra and cubes, respectively, in the case of Plato.

(b)   While the basic elements constitute the perceptible world, they are not themselves perceptible. We do not perceive atoms – the individual atom is not a possible object for our senses – but only a certain arrangement of them. According to Plato, the basic elements as such are too small to be perceived by us (56c). And this is also the way the atoms of the atomists are usually understood: we do not perceive atoms because of their smallness.[25]

(c)   The features of the arrangement of atoms that we perceive are different from those of individual atoms. For example, according to Democritus, we perceive something as sweet or coloured, while the atoms themselves possess neither sweetness nor colour.[26] And while we perceive different forms of air for Timaeus, the underlying atoms are just a bunch of geometrical octahedra.[27] So the whole possesses different feature than its parts.

      Once enough of the basic elements aggregate so that they actually constitute a perceptible mass, what we see is not a bunch of these basic elements, but something quite different – sensible phenomena. As with Leucippus and Democritus, so also in the *Timaeus*, what we perceive is not the basic elements of the world, but only a bunch of

---

25   See, for example, Aristotle, *On Generation and Corruption* 326a24-25. There is, however, another line of doxography that claims more generally that atoms are simply not of the right size for perception according to the atomists; so in principle there could also be atoms that are too big for us to be perceived, see Aetius DK 68 A43 and Dionysius *ap.* Eusebius, DK 68 A 47.

26   With Democritus this is probably most clearly expressed in the following fragment: "By convention sweet and by convention bitter, by convention hot, by convention cold, by convention colour; but in reality atoms and void" (Sextus, *Against the mathematicians*, VII. 135, also in Diogenes Laertius and Galen, DK68 B9).

27   See, for example, *Timaeus* 58d where it is claimed that there are many different kinds of air (such as aether or gloom) "which are formed by the inequality of the triangles" – so differences among the basic triangles (here in size) lead to what we perceive as different kinds of air; see also 57c-d.

438   SATTLER

them together that appear as the physical phenomena to which we are accustomed.

(d)   Imperceptible differences in shape or behavior on the level of atoms are translated into perceptible physical differences on the phenomenal level.[28] For example, with Democritus we derive sweetness from round atoms and sour tastes from large shapes with many angles.[29] And with Plato the fineness of the edges of the basic tetrahedra, the sharpness of their angles, and the swiftness of their motions lead to the piercing experience of fire.[30]

(e)   In both accounts of natural philosophy we find what we could call a predecessor of space as one basic metaphysical kind – the void with the atomists, the receptacle with Plato.[31] And both the void and the receptacle share crucial features –they are indeterminate, they do not possess any of the qualities physical things possess, and they are thus imperceptible. Yet, they are real and necessary to explain motion.[32]

(f)   Plato's *Timaeus* as well as the atomists employ what we can call a "saving the phenomena" principle: both assume that while the basic metaphysical basis is of a genuinely different kind from the observable phenomena, it nevertheless can explain these phenomena as they present themselves to us.[33]

(g)   There is a like-to-like sorting principle: in the *Timaeus* the sorting motion of the traces of the elements in the receptacle is illustrated with the help of the image of a winnowing basket:

---

28   Both Plato and the atomists seem to agree that causal explanations cannot be given in terms of the hot and the cold, as some previous thinkers did, but rather in terms of shape, see Simplicius, *Commentary on Aristotle's De Caelo* 564, 24ff. However, Plato and the atomists do not agree which of the shapes are responsible for what. The clearest example is the mobility and productiveness of heat and combustion that we find with fire – according to Democritus this is grounded in a spherical shape, while for Plato it is based on the shape of a pyramid; see Aristotle's *De Caelo* 306b30ff.

29   A135, Theophrastus, *De Sensu* 65–67; cf. also DK 68 A 129.

30   *Timaeus* 61e. Plato's account of phenomenal qualities also includes the interactions between the different mathematical solids. While physical features are derived from the basic polyhedra for Plato, the ultimate building blocks are the basic triangles. Thus Plato seems to divide up different features of the atoms and connect some with the triangles, others with the four geometrical bodies.

31   For a defense of understanding Plato's receptacle as a basis for space, see Sattler 2012.

32   See also Natorp 1890, p. 517f. and Hammer-Jensen 1910, p. 100–103.

33   For a discussion of how we should understand the principle of "saving the phenomena" with Plato and the atomists and the exact status of the observable phenomena for both positions, see Sattler, 2020, chapters 1, 4, and 6.

PLATONIC RECEPTION

διὰ δὲ τὸ μήθ' ὁμοίων δυνάμεων μήτε ἰσορρόπων ἐμπίμπλασθαι κατ'οὐδὲν αὐτῆς ἰσορροπεῖν, ἀλλ' ἀνωμάλως πάντῃ ταλαντουμένην σείεσθαι μὲν ὑπ' ἐκείνων αὐτήν, κινουμένην δ' αὖ πάλιν ἐκεῖνα σείειν· τὰ δὲ κινούμενα ἄλλα ἄλλοσε ἀεὶ φέρεσθαι διακρινόμενα, ὥσπερ τὰ ὑπὸ τῶν πλοκάνων τε καὶ ὀργάνων τῶν περὶ τὴν τοῦ σίτου κάθαρσιν σειόμενα καὶ ἀνικμώμενα τὰ μὲν πυκνὰ καὶ βαρέα ἄλλῃ, τὰ δὲ μανὰ καὶ κοῦφα εἰς ἑτέραν ἵζει φερόμενα ἕδραν·

[B]ecause it [the receptacle] was filled with powers that were neither alike nor evenly balanced, there was no equipoise in any region of it; but it was everywhere swayed unevenly and shaken by these things, and by its motion shook them in turn. And they, being thus moved, were perpetually being separated and carried in different directions; just as when things are shaken and winnowed by means of winnowing-baskets and other instruments for cleaning corn, the dense and heavy things go one way, while the rare and the light are carried to another place and settle there.

PLATO, Timaeus 52e1–53a2, CORNFORD's translation

This description of the sorting motion corresponds to the one expressed in Democritus DK 68 B 164:[34]

καὶ γὰρ ζῷα, φησίν, ὁμογενέσι ζῴοις συναγελάζεται ὡς περιστεραὶ περιστεραῖς καὶ γέρανοι γεράνοις καὶ ἐπὶ τῶν ἄλλων ἀλόγων ὡσαύτως. ⟨ὡς⟩ δὲ καὶ ἐπὶ τῶν ἀψύχων, καθάπερ ὁρᾶν πάρεστιν ἐπί τε τῶν κοσκινευομένων σπερμάτων καὶ ἐπὶ τῶν παρὰ ταῖς κυματωγαῖς ψηφίδων· ὅπου μὲν γὰρ κατὰ τὸν τοῦ κοσκίνου δῖνον διακριτικῶς φακοὶ μετὰ φακῶν τάσσονται καὶ κριθαὶ μετὰ κριθῶν καὶ πυροὶ μετὰ πυρῶν, ὅπου δὲ κατὰ τὴν τοῦ κύματος κίνησιν αἱ μὲν ἐπιμήκεις ψηφῖδες εἰς τὸν αὐτὸν τόπον ταῖς ἐπιμήκεσιν ὠθοῦνται, αἱ δὲ περιφερεῖς ταῖς περιφερέσιν ὡς ἂν συναγωγόν τι ἐχούσης τῶν πραγμάτων τῆς ἐν τούτοις ὁμοιότητος.

Animals flock together with animals of the same kind, doves with doves and cranes with cranes and similarly with other irrational creatures, and so with non-living things too, as one can see in the case of seeds in a sieve and pebbles on a beach. In the one lentils are sorted out by the swirl of the sieve to lie together with lentils, barley with barley, and wheat with wheat, and in the other oblong pebbles are pushed by

---

34   Cornford 1997, pp. 200–201 objects that winnowing baskets only separate different qualities (heavy and dense), not, as in the Democritean picture, different sizes. However, while the sorting is indeed due to differences in density and weight in *Timaeus* 53a–b, these are connected to different shapes, as becomes clear in 56a-b. And Morel 2017, p. 12 refers to Leucippus DK67 A1 for a cosmic sorting that is based on differences in weight.

the motion of the waves into the same place as oblong and round into
the same place as round, as if that sort of similarity of things had a kind
of attractive force.

> DK 68 B 164, SEXTUS, *Against the mathematicians* VII, 116–18, translation
> by TAYLOR

For Democritus as well as for Plato, basic sorting processes come about in
the world due to a metaphysical like-to-like principle that shows itself in two
different versions: in Democritus animals of the same kind flock together by
themselves, while similar inanimate things, such as lentils and pebbles of similar size, are brought together by the motion of something external, like the
motions of a sieve or a wave. These two different versions work for different
things in Democritus, whereas Plato takes up these two versions as two different forces that are at work at the same time for the same elemental sorting
process: one force is internal to the like things gathering together with like –
the attraction between like traces in the *Timaeus*[35] –the other force is external – the motions of the receptacle in the *Timaeus*. But the result is the same
in both thinkers – some kind of basic order such that similar elements end up
close together.

(g) One point that may be of special interest for natural philosophy is the
notion of necessity in play. In fragment 2 of Leucippus we find the following:

> οὐδὲν χρῆμα μάτην γίνεται, ἀλλὰ πάντα ἐκ λόγου τε
> καὶ ὑπ' ἀνάγκης.
> Nothing happens in vain, but everything from reason and by necessity.
> DK 67 B2

Prima facie the two principles due to which everything happens according
to Leucippus seem to correspond exactly to the two basic causes according to
which the cosmos is set up in the *Timaeus*: on the one hand we have what is
made by reason;[36] on the other hand we have what is caused by necessity, a
form of mechanistic causation,[37] what is due to the materials with which the
demiurge has to work.

---

35 See, for example, 52e-53a and also 57c-58a.

36 Leucippus talks of *logos* here, while in the *Timaeus* the basic principle is referred to as
    nous; however, what is done according to this principle in the *Timaeus* is that the demi-
    urge bestows *logos* and *metron* on to what is given to him.

37 Atomistic necessity is usually also understood as mechanistic. However, see Barnes 1984,
    pp. 141–58 for the claim that our fragment could be compatible with teleological thinking
    as well as dismiss any teleology.

PLATONIC RECEPTION 441

There are at least four problems, however, with seeing this division between reason and necessity in the *Timaeus* as directly influenced by Leucippus: (1) It is not clear whether for Leucippus *logos* and *anagkê* are also two different kinds of causes, or whether he counts them as the same principle – after all, in the fragment just quoted, Leucippus talks about reason "and" necessity, not reason "or" necessity, so it is not clear whether he intends to contrast these two principles.[38] And even if *logos* and *anagkê* do not refer to the same principle, it would be unclear whether reason is really understood in a similar way by Leucippus and Plato. (2) In the set-up of the cosmos in Plato's *Timaeus*, *anagkê* is persuaded by reason; thus it is brought in line with reason as much as possible (but not the other way round) – a relationship in no way hinted at in Leucippus. (3) In contrast to Plato, the atomists do not employ teleological causation, that is, causation which aims at making something so that it achieves a certain (often, the best) end, see below. It is teleological causation which for Plato is connected with reason as a cause. (4) We find a positive formulation of this cause or these causes only in this very fragment of Leucippus, but nothing like it in Democritus. According to Aristotle, Democritus "reduces to necessity all the operations of nature".[39] Apart from necessity, we are not given any positive reasons or causes with Democritus, but rather *ou mallon* arguments – there is no more reason to assume F than not-F.[40]

However, even if we do not find both basic principles of the *Timaeus* with the atomists, the notion of necessity employed by the atomists seems to have been at least an important influence for Plato's account of *anagkê* in the *Timaeus*. Morel has argued that Democritus's understanding of necessity "could have served as a relevant paradigm" for the notion of necessity we find in the *Timaeus*: not with regard to its status (since it is only a secondary cause in Plato, but the only principle in Democritus), but with respect to the way it is characterized – in that it is seen as possessing a causal power that is compatible with things happening at random.[41] And for both thinkers, necessity is a

---

38   Indeed Morel 2017, p. 4–5 understands reason and necessity in Leucippus as referring to one and the same principle.

39   Aristotle GA 789b2-3; cf. also Taylor 1999, pp. 188–189.

40   Different conclusions are drawn from such *ou mallon* arguments in different testimonies, see Sattler 2020, chapter 4. For example, since there is no sufficient reason according to Democritus to assume that all atoms have a particular shape, he assumes that they are of all possible shapes.

41   2017, p. 8; cf. also Morel 2002, pp. 133 ff. However, Friedländer 1975, p. 335 claims that it is an "Irrtum, dass sich Platon mit Blick auf den Bereich der Ananke mit seinem großen Antipoden Demokrit auseinandersetze".

principle that can be seen as a force, as something that brings about changes or motions.[42]

It has also been suggested that the image of an element (*stoicheion*) – a term which Plato uses for his "atoms" – is originally derived from Democritus.[43] Democritus may have employed the image of the *stoicheion* in order to show that there is something more basic than what we immediately perceive: in the same way in which the syllables we hear consist of something smaller that we do not immediately hear, namely individual letters, so the phenomena we perceive consist of something smaller that is not perceived, namely atoms. However, given the fragmentary character of Democritus's work, it seems it cannot be decided with certainty whether the atomists did indeed use this term and metaphor.[44]

3.2 *Plato's Changes to the Atomistic Theory*

In general, we can say that Plato systematizes the atomistic base and provides it with a mathematical underpinning, which helps to show the universe to be intelligible. As with other Presocratic predecessors, so also with the atomists,

---

42   For Democritus see Ps-Plutarch 1.26.2 and Taylor 1999, p. 190–195; for Plato see *Timaeus* 47e ff.

43   This idea was first introduced by Diels 1899. On pp. 13ff. he suggests that the comparison of basic elements with the notion of '*stoicheia*' comes from Democritus who compared the atoms with letters of the alphabet and the complexes they form with syllables. Diels eventually concludes that Democritus was probably the first to use the example of the letters "um an der unendlichen Kombinationsfähigkeit der Buchstaben die unendliche Mannigfaltigkeit der Atomverbindungen zu demonstrieren, ohne jedoch die Metapher zum Begriff zu verdichten und wahrscheinlich auch ohne das Wort stoicheia zu verwenden". In this account of Diels it remains unclear, however, in how far Democritus can he be said to be the father of this idea, if Democritus neither used the word nor the concept.

44   The passages Diels 1899 refers to (Aristotle *Metaphysics* 985b4ff (DK 67A6) and *De gen et corr.* 315b6 ff.) do not in fact mention Democritus using the term *stoicheia*. The second passage claims that tragedy and comedy are made of the same letters, without, however, clarifying whether this was an example used by Democritus or supplied by Aristotle. Simplicius in his *Commentary on Aristotle's De Caelo* 295.1 ff., DK 68 A 37 claims that for Democritus out of the different forms and shapes and sizes of the atoms, "as though out of letters (*stoicheia*)" what appears is generated – but again there is no claim that Democritus himself used the metaphor of *stoicheia*. Taylor's 1928 objection, however, that atomists would not have invented this comparison since they assumed an infinity of atoms, which would not fit with a finite alphabet, also does not seem to be conclusive. For it could still be a useful comparison for them in order to show that there is something more basic than what we immediately perceive and, as Diels claims, in order to illustrate how the plurality of phenomena can be explained in terms of atoms that are all qualitatively equal and only different in size and shape.

PLATONIC RECEPTION   443

he uses them as a productive starting point in such a way that he not only takes up some of their assumptions, but also modifies them to some degree, while also disagreeing with other core points. Let us first look at his modifications, i.e., at those changes Plato introduces that still take place within an atomistic framework, before we look at crucial points in which he clearly distances himself from atomism.

3.2.1 Modifications of the Atomistic Theory

(a)   On Plato's account, the shapes of the basic building blocks are not any old shapes,[45] but certain geometrical shapes, triangles, that make up the so-called Platonic solids. In this way Plato introduces mathematical structure into the atomistic framework.

(b)   What accounts for the infinite diversity of the phenomena in Democritus and Leucippus are the infinitely many shapes of the atoms.[46] By contrast, instead of accounting for "every sort of diverse appearance" with the help of infinitely many shapes of atoms, Plato assumes only two basic kinds – two kinds of triangles that cannot be reduced to each other – by which the basic bodies are bound;[47] all phenomena can be explained as variations of these two forms. In addition, to make sure that he can explain the richness of the phenomenal world, Plato employs triangles of different sizes, so that we get varieties within each element (57c–d). From a systematic point of view, explaining the phenomenal world with only two kinds of forms can be seen as a rather remarkable improvement on the atomistic account.[48]

---

45   While for the atomists the *ou mallon* principle seems to be the reason why they allow for all kinds of shapes for the atoms, Plato does not use the *ou mallon* principle to account for their shapes.

46   See, for example, Aristotle, *De. gen. et cor.* 315a34-b15.

47   53d–54b; cf. also Aristotle, *De Caelo* 325b25ff. These basic triangles – the fairest ones – are the foundation for the most beautiful solids, which form the basis of the four elements. Thus, we see teleological reasoning informing the specific assumption of the basic building blocks.

48   While Morel's claim (2002, p. 130) seems right that Aristotle does not present Plato's position as a correction and refutation of Democritus (in fact, in 316a Aristotle even claims that Plato with his two-dimensional atoms gets into more problems that Democritus with his atomistic bodies), the reduction in the number of basic shapes seem to be a clear case of correction on Plato's part. This is not to deny, of course, that the atomists too had already employed some principle of explanatory economy in their theory when they reduced all properties to only three kinds – *schêma, taxis,* and *thesis* (see Aristotle, *Metaphysics* A, 4, 985b13-15). Nevertheless, the atomists assumed infinitely many *schêmata*, see *De gen. et corr.* 315b11.

(c) For the atomists, the atoms are the basic building blocks and as such indivisible and impenetrable. By contrast, Plato leaves it open in the *Timaeus* whether what he names as the basic building blocks, the two kinds of triangles, are indeed the ultimate building blocks, or whether they themselves can be divided further, into lines or even points.[49]

(d) For Plato the immediate appearances of the aggregates of the basic building blocks are the four elements, which then account further for different perceptibles, while Democritus straightaway talks about sweetness and coldness as appearances.

(e) Plato does not simply assume that just any kind of differences in shape on the atomistic level translates into perceptible physical differences. Rather, Plato looks for abstract similarities between geometrical shapes and physical phenomena that would explain the possibility of such transformations. For example, pointedness is a feature of acute angles and also of a piercing experience in the physical world. Accordingly, the pointedness of acute angles is assumed to belong especially to tetrahedra, and the fact that tetrahedra constitute the basic bodies constituting fire then explains why fire is acute. We experience this acuteness as burning, as the fire cuts through other things.

The atomists may in fact have been open to these five modifications, as they leave the basic assumption of atoms and their interaction untouched.

3.2.2 Disagreement with the Atomists

Besides the modifications of the atomistic framework named, there are also a couple of points where Plato straightforwardly seems to disagree with the atomistic theory of Leucippus and Democritus. And in contrast to the modifications just looked at, these changes would undermine some of the most basic assumptions of the atomists:

3.2.2.1 *Teleology*

For Plato, *ou mallon* reasoning, which is employed by the atomists, is not sufficient for an explanation of the cosmos. Instead he thinks that an explanation of the cosmos requires teleological reasoning, which he understands as reasoning that explains why it is best for something to be the way it is.[50] For Plato,

---

49 53d. While the atomists leave it open what shapes exactly the atoms possess, it is clear that they are bodies, see, for example, Aristotle *De gen. et corr.* 315b29-30 (Aristotle there takes Plato simply to assume planes as indivisible magnitudes, leaving out that Timaeus is in fact hedging on whether these are the ultimate building blocks).

50 See, for example, *Phaedo* 97c-99b, and cf. Sattler 2018.

PLATONIC RECEPTION

teleological reasons are sufficient reasons (while mechanistic reasons are only necessary). Accordingly, arguing that there is no more reason to assume F than not-F, as we see the atomists do with their widespread *ou mallon* principle, does not fit Plato's commitment to teleology.[51]

Assuming teleology also has implications for the concrete content of natural philosophy, according to Plato. For example, teleological reasoning tells us that, contrary to the assumption of the atomists, there are not innumerably many worlds but only one.[52] And for the universe as a whole this means that it is created by an all good demiurge who makes everything as good as possible.[53]

3.2.2.2   *No Void*

For Plato there is no void in the world once ordered by the demiurge. It seems to be in play in the beginning, "before" the demiurgic activity takes place. But it is clearly abandoned once the world as a whole is ordered, because a densely

---

51 Morel 2017, p. 1 even assumes that since Democritus is one of the main proponents of necessary causes, he is also one of the main targets of Plato's critique of mere necessary causes and that Plato focuses on Democritean necessity in order to show that we need something else over and above it, namely teleological causes.

52 *Timaeus* 31a and 55c-d. In the second passage, however, he allows that there could be five worlds, the number given by the Platonic bodies. Broadie 2012, p. 3, n.8 understands the argument against infinitely many worlds in the second passage to refer to the atomists, while Taylor 1928, p. 378 has seen it as a reference to the Pythagoreans. Morel 2017, p.2 thinks that we cannot decide between the atomists and the Pythagoreans and that there is no reason to assume that Timaeus does feel compelled here "to make any fine distinctions between his opponents".

53 McCabe 2000, pp. 178–193 distinguishes between two kinds of teleology in Plato's discussion of *Philebus* 28–29: one concerning the process of the world's having reached the current state (against the assumption of chance ruling) and one concerning the current orderly state of the world (against the assumption of the world being disorderly). She thinks that the first, by assuming a divinity external to the world bringing it about, may be vulnerable to a Democritean objection – that also causes within the world and chance may have brought about the current order; and that Socrates is only going for the second in the *Philebus*. Interestingly, Plato assumes both kinds of teleology in the *Timaeus*, and may even be understood to infer the teleology of the process of the cosmos coming into being from its current teleological order, 28b-29a. We find a description of the kind of order achievable without any *nous* or *logos* at work at *Timaeus* 52d-53b – the dense and heavy traces of the elements gather in one place, the rare and light ones in another so that there are different regions tied to the four different elements. But we are explicitly told that this basic like-to-like regionalization is still without proportion (*alogôs*) and measure (*ametrôs*). So Plato's answer to the Democritean objection seems to be that there can be some kind of order due to mere chance and necessity within the world, but unless *logos* and *metron* are bestowed upon the basic elements by divine reason in the process of the world formation, we cannot explain the mathematically expressible order of the whole cosmos that we experience now.

packed universe without any void is responsible for ensuring that there will be constant motion in the universe.[54] However, Plato also seems to respond to the same problem that the atomistic void does, namely that in order to guarantee the possibility of motion of the basic bodies there has to be something *in which* they can move, something that itself cannot be a body in the way the bodies in it are because then there would be two bodies in the same place. Plato's answer to this problem is the receptacle, a new metaphysical kind, that is neither something straightforwardly intelligible nor sensible. The atomistic void also seems to have been introduced as a metaphysical principle with the atomists and functions as a predecessor to a notion of space.[55] However, the receptacle, while also fulfilling a spatial function, is clearly not a void, as it is moved and moves the elemental traces in turn.

3.2.2.3   *The Intelligibility of Motion*

For Plato there is chaotic motion of the elements before creation, but the demiurge bestows regular motions onto the cosmos. The atomists, by contrast, assume chaotic motions of the atoms in and outside their cosmoi throughout all time, which nevertheless somehow lead to the more regular motions of the phenomena we perceive. But the atomists do not show motion itself to be intelligible in the way Plato does, for example with the regularity of the heavenly motions which follow the intellectual motions of the World Soul and proceed along circles set up according to mathematical proportions. The intelligibility of motion simply does not seem to be a point of concern for the atomists, and their theory does not provide any resources for understanding motion as in itself intelligible.[56]

3.2.2.4   *Transformation of the Basic Bodies*

Both the atomists and Plato explain various sensible qualities in terms of basic three-dimensional bodies – the atoms with Leucippus and Democritus, the four geometrical bodies with Plato. However, for Plato these three-dimensional basic particles are not indivisible, as they are for the atomists, but can break down further so as to turn into each other. In fact, this possibility of

---

54   58a-c; see also Sattler 2012, pp. 172–173 on this point.

55   Melissus introduced the void in an ontological context as a possible 'entity' (fr. B7) but only to reject its existence, while the Pythagoreans introduced it in a cosmological context; see Sattler, manuscript, chapter 3.

56   The theory of Leucippus and Democritus can explain the cause of the motion of the perceptible phenomena, but not of the atoms themselves.

PLATONIC RECEPTION

transformation is an important advantage of his theory, [57] since it can explain the phenomena we (allegedly) perceive: that water can turn into air, air into fire, and so forth.

3.3 Why are the Atomists Not Named?

While Plato disagrees strongly with some assumptions of the atomists and modifies others, we have seen that he also takes over core features of the atomic theory in his *Timaeus*. But yet nowhere in the Platonic corpus does he explicitly refer to Leucippus and Democritus, neither directly nor by nickname. How then should we understand his reception of the atomists?

There is a long tradition, recently taken up by Brisson[58] for example, that Plato does not name the atomists in order to hide his deep debt to them. And an anecdote in Diogenes Laertius suggests that Plato was intellectually not up to getting into an intellectual fight with Democritus, which allegedly meant he could not even name Democritus:

> Aristoxenus in his *Historical Notes* affirms that Plato wished to burn all the writings of Democritus that he could collect, but that Amyclas and Clinias the Pythagoreans prevented him, saying that there was no advantage in doing so, for already the books were widely circulated. And there is clear evidence for this in the fact that Plato, who mentions almost all the early philosophers, never once alludes to Democritus, not even where it would be necessary to controvert him, obviously because he knew that he would have to match himself against the prince of philosophers, for whom, to be sure, Timon has this meed of praise: Such is the wise Democritus, the guardian of discourse, keen-witted disputant, among the best I ever read.
>
> DIOGENES LAERTIUS, book IX, 40; translation by HICKS

However, the principle of charity asks us to see whether there may not be a reason for not naming the atomists other than moral or intellectual deficits on Plato's side. After all, Plato does not hide his debt to Parmenides or Socrates. I think in the end the absence of an explicit reference to the atomists has to be accounted for by a set of different explanations: it seems to be due to (1) the time and circumstances in which Plato is writing; (2) the set-up of the *Timaeus*, which is the dialogue where he is most indebted to the atomists; and

---

57   Even if the transformation is restricted to fire, air and, water; earth is excluded from this process of transformation for mathematical reasons (56d).

58   Brisson 2016, pp.32–33.

finally (3) the kind of reception Plato seems to think to be appropriate for the atomists given their basic metaphysical assumptions. This last point will bring us back to the different kinds of receptions we find in Plato. Let me go through each of these three points in turn:

(1)   A few scholars have argued that it is possible that Plato may not have known Democritus as a person or his work for chronological reasons.[59] That seems highly unlikely to me, at least if we stick to the usual dating of Democritus, according to which he lived sometime between 470/460 and 380/370.[60] Thus Democritus's life seems to have overlapped with Plato's life and there is reason to assume that Democritus's works were very well known in the later part of his lifetime; as we just saw, also Diogenes Laertius reports that Democritus's books circulated widely.

If we take the time and circumstances in which Plato is writing as one possible factor, it seems more likely to me that not naming Democritus and Leucippus is due to a general dislike we seem to find in Plato of naming philosophers who were at least for some time contemporaries of his (even if the *Timaeus* was probably composed after Democritus had already died).[61] Furthermore, Plato may have felt

---

59   So Taylor 1928, pp. 3 and 84 (though he thinks that Plato may allude to the atomism of Leucippus who was older and is seen to be a pupil of Parmenides by Taylor); cf. also Thesleff 1986; against this assumption, see Zmuhd 1997, p. 131, n.1. Other scholars have suggested that Socrates, though also a contemporary of Democritus, did not know him; so Gigon 1972, pp.154–155. Similarly, Diogenes Laertius, who claims in IX,7,36 that while Democritus knew Socrates, Socrates did not know him, which could explain why Democritus cannot be referred to in a dialogue that features Socrates as a speaker. However, Plato also lets Socrates meet Parmenides, even though according to Diogenes Laertius's own dating of Parmenides, such a meeting would in fact not have been possible (our dating of Parmenides stands on uncertain grounds – it either relies on the alleged meeting of Socrates and Parmenides sketched in Plato, in which case Parmenides is supposed to have lived sometime between 515 and 445 BCE; or it follows Diogenes Laertius, in which case Parmenides is assumed to have lived sometime between 540 and 470 BCE and could not possibly have met Socrates). Nikolaou 1998 even suggest that Socrates *could* not have known Democritus for *chronological* reasons, but this assumption is in conflict with all that we know about Socrates's and Democritus's dates of life.

60   Apollodorus of Athens tells us that he was born in the 80th Olympiad (460–457 BC); Thrasyllus places his birth in 470 BC.

61   Plato does, however, name contemporaries like Gorgias and Isocrates – this may be due to their being introduced as a sophist and a rhetorician, respectively, rather than as philosophers properly speaking. Furthermore, both Gorgias and Isocrates are at least to some degree also criticized for their positions, while the atomists in the *Timaeus* would have to be mentioned primarily for what they get right – but what they get right holds true for Timaeus simply because it is the truth, not because it was suggested by anybody. Cf. also Natorp 1890, p. 530: "Platon nennt in der Regel nur, wen er bekämpft; mit Demokrit findet er sich von vornhinein auf einer Bahn; er überholt ihn, ohne von ihm ausgegangen zu

PLATONIC RECEPTION

that he does not have to name the atomists, because their position is so well-known at that time that everybody knows what basis he is building upon.

(2) The *Timaeus* does not name any predecessors, and Timaeus's monologue would not have fitted such a discussion of earlier positions in the way in which, for example, the dialogues that Socrates and the Eleatic Stranger conduct with Theaetetus do.[62] For Timaeus presents his cosmology as an unbroken monologue from a single perspective, the perspective of the demiurge (and his helper gods). The unified perspective as such excludes any detailed discussion of earlier theories and thus may make it feel inappropriate for Timaeus to name any predecessors. And the perspective of divine reasoning would obviously be spoiled by having it interspersed with explicit arguments for or against earlier Presocratic theories, like the atomistic theory.[63]

(3) Finally, while Plato is heavily influenced by the atomists, he believes they failed to understand the most important thing, namely that what truly *is* is only intelligible, not bodily. Parmenides already realized that what truly is does not belong to the sensible realm,[64] and thus got the basic metaphysical assumption right, according to Plato. The atomists, by contrast, as hard core materialists, were correct in some respect – namely, in their basic assumptions about the set-up of the physical world. But they were wrong in the all-decisive point when they assumed that everything can be reduced to a material base. From a Platonic perspective, the atomists can be seen as mistaking the atoms for what truly is *tout court*, not just understanding them as what underlies the sensible world. If we look at Plato's *Laws*, we see that one of the positions we most have to take care to fight against is materialism. Accordingly, Plato has to make sure that nobody could accuse him of taking over materialism from the atomists with the *Timaeus* and that he is not seen as an atomist qua materialist himself.[65] We may think that Plato could have explicitly clarified the differences between him

---

sein; und so fehlt ihm die dringende Veranlassung, sich in einer mehr direkten Weise mit ihm auseinanderzusetzen".

62 Furthermore, if Broadie 2012 is right that the *Timaeus* wants to get a general research project started as a group enterprise (in which Plato welcomes better suggestions from others), then the individual name is not as important for such a common enterprise.

63 I owe this point about the divine perspective to Sarah Broadie.

64 For a defence of this reading, see Sattler 2011.

65 Cf. also Ferwerda 1972, p. 359.

and the atomists. However, even such a discussion would still be substantial (disagreeing with them on the main metaphysical point while agreeing with them on core points concerning the sensible world) and would have given the atomists a prominence Plato seems wary to risk given their thoroughgoing materialism. If we compare Plato's reception of the atomists with his reception of Anaxagoras, we see that he takes over many more central claims of the atomists than of Anaxagoras, so that a brief discussion of one central theorem in the way in which we find it with Anaxagoras in the *Phaedo* would not have sufficed.

Thus despite all their points of agreement with respect to the physical world, the metaphysical *disagreement* between them is of a character, for Plato, that is much more important than the agreements. This disagreement about what truly *is* is so deep that it, among the other things mentioned above, seems to have prevented him from even naming them. Naming the atomists, while being so heavily influenced by them in his natural philosophy, may have given them the same status as Parmenides within Plato's work. But this is not something that would fit the overall Platonic project in the *Timaeus* in which Plato takes into account the works of necessity that contribute to the universe's material constitution as part, but only part, of an overall account of the world as most beautiful and intelligible, ordered by reason.[66]

Bibliography

Barnes, Jonathan. 1982. The *Presocratic Philosophers*, revised edition, London.

Barnes, Jonathan. 1984. "Reason and Necessity in Leucippus", in: Linos Benakis (ed.), *Proceedings of the First International Congress on Democritus* (Volume 1), Xanthi 1984, pp. 141–58.

Broadie, Sarah. 2012. *Nature and Divinity*, Cambridge: CUP.

Booth, N.B. 1957. "Were Zeno's Arguments Directed against the Pythagoreans?" in: *Phronesis* 2: 90–103.

Brisson, Luc. 2016. *Lectures de Platon*, Paris : J. Vrin.

Cornford, Francis M. 1997. *Plato's Cosmology. The Timaeus of Plato. Translated with a Running Commentary*. Indianapolis: Hackett Publishing.

---

66   This paper came into existence as a talk at the conference "Philosophy in the Making: Early Receptions of and Reactions to Presocratic Thought" at Stanford University. I want to thanks Alan Code for encouraging me to write the paper and the other participants of the conference for useful feedback. Thanks also to Sarah Broadie, Michael Della Rocca, Verity Harte, and Pierre-Marie Morel for helpful comments on the written version.

PLATONIC RECEPTION

Diels, Hermann. 1899. *Elementum, Eine Vorarbeit zum Griechischen und Lateinischen Thesaurus*, Leipzig: Teubner.

Ferwerda, Rein. 1972. "Democritus and Plato", in *Mnemosyne* 25.

Friedländer, Paul. 1975. *Platon* Bd. III, Berlin.

Furley, David. 1967. *Two Studies in the Greek Atomists*, Princeton: Princeton University Press.

Gigon, Olof. 1972. "Platon und Demokrit", in: *Museum Helveticum* 29.

Hammer-Jensen, Ingeborg. 1910. "Demokrit und Platon", *Archiv für Geschichte der Philosophie* 23, 1910.

Hussey, Edward. 1973. *The Presocratics*, New York.

Kirk, G. S., Raven, J. E. and Schofield, M. (ed.). 1983. *The Presocratic Philosophers*, second edition, Cambridge: CUP.

McCabe, Mary Margaret. 2000. *Plato and his Predecessors: The Dramatisation of Reason*, Cambridge: CUP.

Morel, Pierre-Marie. 2002. Le *Timée*, Démocrite et la nécessité, in M. Dixsaut, A. Brancacci (ed.), *Platon, source des présocratiques. Exploration*, Paris: Vrin, 129–150.

Morel, Pierre-Marie. 2017. "Necessity in Democritus and the *Timaeus*", talk at the conference "Plato's *Timaeus* I" at Brown University and Providence College, April 7–9.

Natorp, Paul. 1890. "Demokrit-Spuren bei Platon", *Archiv für Geschichte der Philosophie* 3.

Nikolaou, Sousanna-Maria, 1998. *Die Atomlehre Demokrits und Platons Timaeus*, Stuttgart und Leipzig.

Osborne, Catherine. 2006. "Was there an Eleatic Revolution in philosophy", in: *Rethinking Revolutions through Ancient Greece*, ed. by Simon Goldhill and Robin Osborne, Cambridge: CUP.

Owen, G.E.L. 1957. "Zeno and the mathematicians", in: *Proceedings of the Aristotelian Society* 58, 1957–8.

Sattler, Barbara. 2011. "Parmenides' System – the Logical Origins of his Monism", in: *Proceedings of the Boston Area Colloquium in Ancient Philosophy* Vol. XXVI.

Sattler, Barbara. 2012. "A Likely Account of Necessity, Plato's Receptacle as a Physical and Metaphysical Basis of Space", in: *Journal of the History of Philosophy* 50: 159–195.

Sattler, Barbara M. 2018. "Sufficient Reason in the *Phaedo* and its Presocratic antecedents" in: *Plato's* Phaedo. *Selected Papers from the Eleventh Symposium Platonicum*, ed. by Gabriele Cornelli, Francisco Bravo, and Tom Robinson, International Plato Studies, St. Augustin: Academia Verlag, 239–248.

Sattler, Barbara M. 2020. *The Concept of Motion in Ancient Greek Thought – Foundations in Logic, Method, and Mathematics*, Cambridge University Press, 2020.

Sattler, Barbara M. *Conceptions of Space in ancient Greek Thought*, monograph manuscript, in preparation for the CUP series *Key Themes in Ancient Philosophy*.

Sattler, Barbara M. "Platonic history of philosophy", article in preparation.

Sedley, David. 2007. *Creationism and its critics in antiquity*, Berkeley: University of California Press.

Tannery, Paul. 1877. *Pour L'Histoire de La Science Hellène*, Paris.

Taylor, A. E. 1928. *A commentary on Plato´s Timaeus*, Oxford: Clarendon Press.

Taylor, C.C.W. 1999. *The atomists Leucippus and Democritus, Fragments, A Text and Translation with a Commentary*, Toronto.

Thesleff, Holger. 1986. "Plato and Literature" in: *Literatur und Philosophie in der Antike*, ed. Heikki Koskenniemi, Turku.

Wilamowitz-Moellendorf, Ulrich von. 1919. *Platon* I, Berlin: Weidmann (1st edition).

Zmuhd, Leonid. 1997. *Wissenschaft, Philosophie und Religion im frühen Pythagoreismus*, Berlin: Akademie Verlag.

CHAPTER 15

Presocratic Cosmology and Platonic Myth

Rosemary Wright

The beginnings of cosmological theory, with the accompanying arguments, hypotheses and speculations, are to be found in the evidence from the Presocratics, a general term for the early Greek philosophers of the 6th and 5th centuries BCE. Although the last of these are contemporary with Socrates, they are classed together with their predecessors because of their common interests, in particular in cosmological problems involving theories concerned with matter, space and time. The fragmentary nature of the Presocratic inheritance excludes any definitive conclusions concerning their beliefs and arguments, whereas the survival of the complex and extensive Platonic texts presents their own difficulties, in particular that they are composed mostly in the form of dialogues spoken by Socrates as the main *persona*. From these texts it is practically impossible to attribute particular theses to Plato himself in separation from the characters in the dialogues. In addition, *continuous* texts are sometimes found within his dialogues or at their ends in the form of mythical narratives, which previously, but less so more recently, were glossed over by scholars as unphilosophical, and even somewhat embarrassing. Yet it is in these myths that interest in the Presocratic legacy may be traced, and assessed as contributing to the development of some key issues in Plato's own ways of thinking. To this end the arguments for Presocratic 'reception' in Platonic myth in the present paper are developed through the following sections: *I*: a general view of Plato's citation of the Presocratics; *II*: Plato's conflicting views on myths in their contexts variously as ethically misleading, educationally helpful or as appropriate objects of *doxa* ('opinion'); *III*: the relevance of Presocratic cosmology to Platonic myth; *IV*: the eschatological myths with their corresponding cosmologies in *Gorgias, Phaedo, Republic* and *Phaedrus*; and *V*: the particular case of the *Timaeus* myth.

1 Plato and the Presocratics

To put the subject in context a reminder is helpful of the comparatively few occasions when Plato cites a particular Presocratic by name in the established *corpus*. This is not a lengthy procedure as Plato rarely mentions individuals

---

© KONINKLIJKE BRILL NV, LEIDEN, 2021 | DOI:10.1163/9789004443358_017

directly, and, when he does, the reference is brief, and often with a touch of irony. Thales, the first Presocratic, is introduced as one of the seven sages in *Hippias Major* and *Protagoras*, in *Theaetetus* there is the anecdote about him falling into a well while star-gazing, contrasted with the mention in *Republic* of Thales as an example of an inventor of useful devices.[1] Plato only indirectly brings in the other two Milesians, Anaximander and Anaximenes, in Socrates' philosophical biography at *Phaedo* 99c. With Pythagoras there is the single citation of him as passing on a 'way of life', and Pythagoreans being still conspicuous for what they call the Pythagorean *bios*. Earlier, in the discussion of the higher education of the philosopher-rulers, the subjects astronomy and harmonics, 'sister sciences' for the Pythagoreans, are to be included. In harmonics it is said that the Pythagoreans rightly investigate the numbers that are to be found in audible consonances, but they do not make the ascent to tackling the problems themselves. The individual Pythagorean Philolaus is introduced in *Phaedo* in connection with Simmias and Cebes as taking a stand against suicide, and in the discussion of soul as 'harmony'.[2]

Heraclitus appears in the Platonic *corpus* in *Symposium* 187a in the speech by Eryximachus on the subject of Eros, who gives a typically pedantic interpretation of Heraclitus' fragment 51 on the παλίντονος ἁρμονίη of the bow and lyre. *Hippias Major* (289a) discusses fragment 82 of Heraclitus on the ratios of individual wisdom: 'as monkey is to man so is man to god', and, at *Republic* 498a, there is a strange simile to the effect that philosophy should not be practised in the manner of Heraclitus' cosmic fire, alternately kindling and quenching (fr. 30), but as being a continuous activity. Plato is said to have been tutored in the work of Heraclitus by Cratylus, although the dialogue involving Cratylus only deals with the one phrase πάντα ῥεῖ ('everything is in flux') from the 'river' fragment.[3]

In this round-up of the surprisingly few named Presocratics in the Platonic *corpus* belongs the speech of the Eleatic Visitor to Athens in the *Sophist* (242c-243a). This gives a general indication of Plato's attitude to the Presocratics, being gently ironic, but with an underlying seriousness:

> We are told a myth ⟨about how many things there are and what they are like⟩ as if we were children ... Our Eleatic tribe, starting from Xenophanes and even earlier, mythologises about what are called all things – that

---

1 *HippM* 281c, *Prot* 343a, *Theaet* 174–5, *Rep* 600a; at *Laws* 10.899b there is the quotation 'everything is full of gods', not attributed here, but generally accepted as from Thales.
2 *Rep* 600b, 530d, 531c; *Phaedo* 61d6-16.
3 DK 22.91. This famous saying is taken up in *Theaetetus, at 152e, and 180d-83e.*

PRESOCRATIC COSMOLOGY AND PLATONIC MYTH

they are just one. Later some Ionian and Sicilian Muses thought it safe to weave both views together and say that what there is *is* both many and one, bound by Strife and Love. The more stringent of the Muses say that in moving apart the many are brought together, the more relaxed softened the position that this is always the case, saying that, at one time, the whole is one and loving under Aphrodite, and, at another time there are many, and mutually hostile, because of some sort of Strife.

The one mention of Xenophanes in Plato is in this context, in which he is put at the beginning of the 'Eleatic tribe', saying that 'all things are one' (or, Plato adds, 'this may come from someone earlier still'). The *Sophist* passage also brings in the cryptic sayings of Heraclitus under the heading of the Ionian Muse, enigmatically expounding his fragment 51, that in moving apart the many are brought together.[4] In contrast, Empedocles' poetry is that of the Sicilian Muse, positing one and many, not however simultaneously as with Heraclitus, but in succession as a result of the agency of Love and Strife. Both Heraclitus and Empedocles are here opposed to the Eleatic 'tribe' (ἔθνος), who maintain that all things are one thing. Anaxagoras is not mentioned in this context as a pluralist, and Democritus not at all. Empedocles however is main-stream, and in another citation of Empedocles (at *Meno* 76c) Plato also takes him seriously in a discussion of his theory of the mechanics of vision.

In a different scenario, a lengthy discussion on pluralists and monists between Socrates and Theaetetus puts Protagoras with Heraclitus and Empedocles (and going back to Homer on Tethys)[5] with those who believe in many things that are continually moving, and sets against them Parmenides, Melissus 'and the rest of them' who are monists, holding to a universe that is one and unmoved. It is here (*Theaetetus* 183e) that Socrates claims, in his youth, to have met Parmenides as an old man, and found him to be noble, revered and awe-inspiring. This tribute obviously sets the scene for the dialogue *Parmenides*, which features 'father Parmenides', aged 65, distinguished-looking and highly respected, with a sharp intellect shown in his devastating critique of the Platonic theory of forms. The bulk of that dialogue then passes to Zeno, in his one appearance in Plato. Significantly Zeno first gives the young Socrates a demonstration of the long and arduous training in dialectic necessary for the true philosopher, before he can strike out independently.

---

4   Cf. the six arguments put forward by Marcovich *Heraclitus* pp 119, 125–6.
5   Tethys was wife of Oceanus in Homer, and mother-source of the main rivers.

Anaxagoras is not mentioned here in *Theaetetus* or in the *Sophist* passage with the other Presocratics, but he appears comparatively frequently elsewhere. There is the famous reference from *Apology* (26d) of his writings (βι-βλία) on sale in the ἀγορά, in which the sun and moon are said to be just stones, along with other atheistic views on natural phenomena. In *Phaedo* (98d) Socrates discusses at length 'some book' of Anaxagoras on physical causation, in the context of the true reason why Socrates has not tried to escape but is sitting in prison, and (at 72c) 'everything mixed together' (ὁμοῦ πάντα) is cited. The 'everything mixed together' quotation is repeated in *Gorgias* (at 465d) to show that such a mixture would be the case if soul did not govern body, a view that the respondent Polus was well acquainted with. Anaxagoras appears again in *Cratylus*, in a discussion about the moon's light in relation to the sun, but more importantly on mind as self-ruling, and also ordering and sustaining everything else (*Cratylus* 400a, 409b, 413c). At *Phaedrus* (270a) Anaxagoras is said to have influenced Pericles with his 'ethereal speculation', in particular on the nature of mind, a subject on which, Plato adds, Anaxagoras had a great deal to say. In these passages Plato shows himself well versed in the main theories of Anaxagoras – the original mixture of 'all things together', mind (νοῦς) as self-ruling, as well as arranging and governing everything else, and his views about the planets. On the whole he is treated here with respect even though Socrates objects to his calling sun and moon merely stones, and giving an inadequate account of physical causes. Anaxagoras however, does not appear in the two main passages on Plato's predecessors, those in *Sophist* and *Theaetetus*, perhaps because he cannot be so easily classified with them. Plato would not have come across Anaxagoras personally in his time in Athens (for Anaxagoras died probably shortly before Plato's birth). Democritus however may well have been in the vicinity of Athens at the turn of the century (given his dates as approximately 460–375 BCE), yet Plato never mentions *him* by name. Obviously, the atomic theory is present behind the theory of elements in *Timaeus*,[6] but Plato may be so unsympathetic towards Democritus and his outright materialism that he has no wish to acknowledge his contribution to the history of philosophy.[7]

---

6 See Sattler, "Platonic Reception: Atomism and the Atomists in Plato's *Timaeus*" in this volume.

7 The only passage in which Plato specifically acknowledges a theory of atomic type preelements (and its unacceptable consequences) is at *Laws* book 10 (892e) where the Athenian Visitor is faced with the dangerous challenge of a young and clever atheist, clearly a follower of Democritus, who believes that soul and gods are *derived* from elements, and are subsequent to them.

PRESOCRATIC COSMOLOGY AND PLATONIC MYTH 457

To summarise Plato's selection of specific Presocratics: The only Milesian mentioned is Thales, as a sage from the past, literally star-gazing, but also an inventor. Pythagoras and Pythagoreans are connected with astronomy and harmonics, as well as a way of life. Xenophanes is a precursor of the Eleatics, to be followed by Parmenides and Melissus, with Zeno as a practitioner of dialectic. Anaxagoras is recalled for his theory of an original 'mixture of all things', and also for finding in νοῦς an all-powerful agent of control in the cosmos. Heraclitus and Empedocles are seen as pluralists contrasting with the Eleatics, Heraclitus mainly for 'everything in flux' and a simultaneous one and many, whereas Empedocles supposes one and many in succession. Anaximander, Anaximenes and Democritus do not appear as such in the *corpus*.

The relevant conclusion from this survey of Plato on the Presocratics is that Plato rarely names his predecessors, and when he does the reference is brief, often slightly ironic, and related to the topic in hand. But the absence of a fuller documentation is no evidence for Plato's ignorance of their work. He had been tutored in Heraclitus by Cratylus, Anaxagoras' writings were well known, Democritus had been in Athens, and Plato had visited the centres of western philosophy in south Italy and Sicily. He was an expert on the Eleatics, and would know of the Pythagoreans in particular from his friend, the mathematician Archytas from Tarentum. He chose to have the *Timaeus* myth delivered by another (probably fictitious) south Italian, 'most skilled in astronomy' (ἀστρονομικώτατος). Although in *Timaeus* there is still no Presocratic named, nevertheless there is some justification for the work being called 'a Presocratic prose hymn'.[8]

2   Plato on the Use and Abuse of Myth

Plato's approach to myth is ambiguous. Traditional myths, especially as found in Homer and Hesiod, have for Plato an educational use, to be told to children, as stories in which a false account is given, but with some truth in it, part playful and part serious, and children love hearing them. Such a dichotomy between fact and fiction was already in Hesiod's *Theogony*, where the poet attributes the inspiration for his account of the emergence of the known world to the nine Muses. He describes the goddesses as appearing to him on Mount Helicon, and offering him gifts: the staff which assures his authority as minstrel, the breath of divine voice, and the subject of his poem. The resulting account

---

8   Shorey (1933) p.284. See further on section IV below.

of the emergence of the world and the settlement within it of divine, human and natural features will be a combination of lies and truth, for, as the Muses say, 'we know how to relate many false things that resemble what is real, but, when we wish, to tell the truth'.[9] Plato therefore regards Hesiod-type 'lies that are like the truth and with some truth in them' in two ways: on the one hand the myth-making of poets and orators is to be condemned as using persuasion and emotional appeal rather than correct teaching methods which foster reason, but, on the other hand, where we are dealing with the unknowable, myth-makers may produce something useful if their skilful verbal images bring the false close to the true.[10] When the innate falsehood is put into words and made as like the truth as possible, the result may be positively beneficial. There is however a danger with the 'falsehood like the truth' (τὸ ὡς ἀληθῶς ψεῦδος); this appears as a result of the recipient being deceived by what is plausible, or from blind ignorance with regard to the topics that are rated most highly. As such this 'falsehood like the truth' is said to be utterly abhorrent to gods and men, and inflicts lasting harm on the soul, the most important part of ourselves, in its most important concerns.[11]

In the education of children, as set out in *Republic*, a distinction is made between *logoi* that are myth-like, and those that are truer; and this distinction is found again in the education of the citizens themselves as set out in *Laws*.[12] One reason why the narrative structures that are characteristic of myth, if used with caution, might be helpful in preparing the way for more demanding topics is that they stay in the memory. We feel at home with what we are used to, just as we remember what we learned when young although we may forget recent events.[13] In the Atlantis myth of *Critias* for example Plato uses the attractive characteristics of myth – vivid, enjoyable narrative and memorable

---

9   Hesiod *Theogony* 27–28.

10 *Rep* 382d; the condemnation of the myth-making of the poets follows here and in books 3 and 10. Cf. similar criticism of the orators at *Pol* 304c and *Prot* 328c-29b where Protagoras' myth, reinforced by *logos*, is unable to deal with Socratic *elenchos*.

11 *Laws* 887d, 890b-d; *Rep* 377a, and the whole argument 382a-e.

12 *Rep* 522a, *Laws* 71b-e.

13 Cf. *Tim* 26b: 'It's true what people say, that what we learned as children stays with us; I'm not sure I could remember everything we said yesterday, but I'd be surprised if I forgot what I was told long ago'. But also *Rep* 377a: 'A myth that is *kalos* we must accept, one that is not is to be rejected. And the myths that are accepted we shall ask the nurses and mothers to tell to their children, and mould their souls with myths more than their bodies with hands; but most of the myths they now tell are to be thrown out'. Also 382d: In the myths to be rejected 'isn't it the case that, through not knowing the truth about the past, we make the false as like the true as possible, and so produce something useful?' The question is clearly applicable Plato's own (abandoned) myth of Atlantis in *Critias*.

PRESOCRATIC COSMOLOGY AND PLATONIC MYTH

detail – to bolster the plausibility of his own invention. The enjoyment derived from myth is often under-rated in the complex theorising of its status, but it is there from the beginning. When for example in the *Odyssey* the minstrel Demodocus sings as a set piece the tale of Hephaestus' entrapment of Aphrodite and Ares, Odysseus 'was delighted in his heart to hear it, as were all the Phaeacians'.[14] In this tradition Plato can play down his long narrative of massive structures and careful details in *Timaeus* as merely entertainment, light relief from the hard work of metaphysics and devoid of truth, and yet present it as a contribution, possibly the best yet, to the ongoing debate about the formation and structure of the physical world.

On the down-side children (and the unphilosophical) are to be protected from being led astray on the most important topics by the plausibility and attractiveness of traditional stories, which is why poets, Homer and Hesiod in particular, are censored and banished from the education syllabus of *Republic* and *Laws*. There is moral danger in the enjoyment of traditional epic, yet, in a lighter vein, Plato views not only his own physical theories as relaxation from metaphysics, but, with a certain irony, presents the philosophies of his predecessors as nursery stories. Socrates downgrades Protagoras' famous *dictum* 'everyone is the measure of everything' to a *mythos*, as well as that of Theaetetus that 'knowledge is perception'. More to the point, as was shown in the last section, the Visitor in *Sophist* treats all the Presocratics as myth-makers when, in their cosmologies, they tell stories to us as if we were children, about wars, births, marriages and the like. The Visitor also reports the great disputes between the Materialists and the Eleatics in terms of the violent battles between the gods and the giants, and Heraclitus' insight into perpetual change as a derivation from the mating of the ever-flowing rivers Oceanus and Tethys, the eldest of the Titans in Hesiod's *Theogony*.[15] The greatest achievements of earlier thinkers are viewed as little more than glorified story-telling. Faced with a sophist like Thrasymachus, an unscrupulous Callicles or a hard-hitting atheist, the philosopher needs his working tools of critical enquiry, assessment of evidence, verification and demonstrable proof. Would not someone who is going to give an account of the origins and structure of the physical world need these same tools? But Plato regards the study of natural science, as with eschatology, as a myth-making exercise, in which continuous narrative is more appropriate than cut and thrust argument.

This view of the Presocratics, given in the *Sophist* as (mere) story-tellers, may be ironic, but appears basically unfair. The Presocratics themselves saw

---

14   Od 8.365-7.
15   *Theaet.* 164d, 180c-d, *Soph* 242c-d, 246a.

themselves as *replacing* the traditional myths with a new account of the way things are. Xenophanes castigates Homer and Hesiod for attributing to the gods everything that is blameworthy and disgraceful among humans (fragment 110 – 'theft and adultery and mutual trickery'), and giving them human attributes in their own image, whereas there is one god, 'not at all like mortals in body or mind', who with no effort 'keeps everything moving by the thinking of his mind' (fragments 23 and 25). Furthermore, there are natural explanations for supposedly divine attributes, as with the rainbow and other meteorological phenomena (fragments 30 and 32). Heraclitus similarly disparaged Homer and Hesiod (fragments 40, 57, 42, 56), based his own *logos* on natural philosophy, and required a revision of the status of Zeus (fragments 1, 50, 32, 53, 102, 67), as well as an honest acceptance of the rituals of Dionysus (fragment 15). Parmenides puts his account of the natural world in the 'Way of Opinion' as opposed to the 'Way of Truth', Empedocles then reworked the former theology by identifying gods with his four basic elements, since the divine pair, Zeus and Hera, are now the basic elements of fire and air (fragment 6). The atomists completely rejected the primacy of the divine, and viewed gods and soul not as primary, but as derivative, as secondary formations of basic atoms moving in void.

As well as being useful in the education of children for the pleasure of the tale and the imprint on the memory, story-telling could be part of the higher education provided by the sophists in Athens, and an element of their showmanship. When Protagoras is challenged by Socrates to justify his claim to teach virtue as the necessary qualification for citizenship, he offers both myth and argument. The story-telling approach is more popular, so he launches into the tale of Prometheus and Epimetheus, who are responsible for the advance of technology and the distribution of civic virtue, but Socrates can counter the torrent of Protagoras' myth with a mere brief yet devastating question.[16] Aristophanes, in the *Symposium*, gives a story that is humorous with an underlying seriousness about the early race of men, women and 'androgynes' as his contribution to the speeches on *Eros*, and Diotima herself is represented as making a key point with her myth of the parentage and true character of *Eros*.[17] Elsewhere in the dialogues Plato uses Socrates himself as the mouthpiece for a range of shorter accounts, some as narratives and some as what might be called 'thought experiments'. In *Republic* there is the well-known device of the 'ship of state' where mutinous (and ignorant) sailors take control, with

---

16   *Protagoras* 319a-329b.
17   *Symposium* 189c-193e, 203b-204b.

PRESOCRATIC COSMOLOGY AND PLATONIC MYTH 461

disastrous results, and the 'allegory of the cave' provides an illustration of the distorted priorities of the uneducated. Also in *Phaedrus* there are stories for the discovery of writing, the cicadas who live for the moment, and the myth of Boreas. Examples of myths as 'thought experiments' come with Socrates saying 'let's suppose' that Patroclus is brought back to life, or that we had Gyges' ring to make us invisible.[18] Less attractive is the re-working of Hesiod's 'myth of the metals' in *Republic* III, put forward by Socrates with considerable reluctance. In this the point is made that citizens are inherently comparable to gold, silver and bronze, and, with rare exceptions, should stay in their natural class, and not expect to be promoted. Finally there is the 'puppet story' in *Laws*, recommended by the Visitor, which illustrates humans as puppets whose strings are manipulated by the gods.[19]

3   **Presocratic Cosmology**

This study of the wide variety of material that Plato treats as myth, including the contrast and alignment of myth with argument (*logos*) and truth, its usefulness, attractiveness and dangers, is a necessary preliminary to understanding the reception of Presocratic cosmology in Platonic myth. The other requirement is to attempt to ascertain what is meant by 'Presocratic cosmology', and to collate the appropriate inheritance available to Plato.

The preliminary to questions of space and time is an understanding of what there actually *is*, as the basic 'stuff' of the universe. The early Greek philosophers viewed the problem as the search for a 'first principle' which became known as *archē* ('beginning') and *stoicheion* (element), indicating what there was in the past and continues to exist in the present in a fundamental form. Anaximander from Miletus began the enquiry in the sixth century BCE. According to Aristotle he posited *to apeiron* ('the limitless'), an attempt at a new language for a new idea, to represent what is neutral, without limit in space or time, or defined by any quality, And for the first time it was recognised that a lack of temporal limit works both ways. Eternity means no beginning as well as no end, a blow to the standard contemporary religion of gods who were thought to have been born, but are then *athanatoi* – 'deathless'. From

---

18   The 'revival' of Patroclus, *Laws* 944a; Gyges' ring: *Rep* 359d. In a sense the whole of the city in *Republic* is a 'thought experiment' presented in terms of both myth and *logos*, and 'made in heaven' cf. *Rep* 369a.

19   *Rep* 414d-415d where Socrates expresses great reluctance to introduce the principle of class distinctions; humans as puppets at *Laws* 644d.

the *apeiron* Anaximander suggested that a 'seed' (*gonimon*) arose, from which opposite qualities, viewed as 'things', emerged, and eventually produced a cosmos. The concept of *apeiron* was so neutral as to be almost meaningless, and Anaximander's successors, Anaximenes and Heraclitus, preferred a *characterised* substance for a basic principle. Anaximenes defined his principle as air (*aēr*), all-pervading, and as 'breath', essential for life. And by a *process* of thickening and thinning individual objects show their differences. Heraclitus followed Anaximander in explaining a diverse world in terms of an underlying principle in constant movement, but he gave it the quality of fire.[20] Its perpetual motions and transformations, in different placings and at different times, were predicated as essential for the maintenance of the whole.

The search for a single entity such as air or fire or the characterless *apeiron* to explain permanence through change was brought to a halt by the logic of Parmenides. His spokesperson, an unnamed goddess, argued that it was not sufficient to proclaim what things are made of and how they seem to change, but first a more basic principle needed to be established to meet her 'hard-hitting challenge'. However, as soon as her own premises of only '*esti*' ('it is', 'there is being') was compromised in the smallest degree in the assumption of *two* principles, a cosmology (labelled 'deceptive and untrue') could be constructed. From such a pair, which she named as fire (light) and night, came the first understanding of a theory of elements: 'the whole is full of light and unclear night, both equal, since nothing is without either' (fr. 9). In the neighbouring island of Sicily Empedocles picked up on this concession, and, despite appearances, reduced everything to a proportionate mixture of *four* basics – earth, air, fire and water: 'These are the only real things, but, as they run through each other, they become different objects at different times, yet are throughout forever the same' (fr. 17.34–35).

There were two diametrically opposed reactions to Empedocles' theory of everything being made from four basic elements, one was to suggest that 'everything is in everything', the other that there is both one thing and nothing. Anaxagoras proposed maximum plurality and diversity in his first blunt statement: 'all things were together' (fr.1), followed by: 'everything is in everything' (fr. 6). Scorning a theory of elements or variations of a basic substance to explain the wide variety of phenomena, the claims of Anaxagoras that (i) everything is in everything, (ii) all was there in the beginning, and (iii) that the universe is ever-expanding built into a theory similar to that of a 'microdot'

---

20   Heraclitus fr.30 'This cosmos, the same for all, no one of men or gods have made, but it ever is and will be ever-living fire, kindling in measures and being quenched in measures'.

which explodes into a 'separating-out' in a continually expanding universe. The second reaction to Empedocles' four elements came from the atomists, who posited an infinite number of characterless atoms (*a-toma*, i.e. 'uncuttables') in incessant movement in an infinite expanse of void.[21]

The first Greek understanding of cosmic *space*, as found in the Homeric poems, is a simplistic portrayal of the earth as a circular flat disk, around which flows the freshwater river Ocean; the vault of the sky above is a hemisphere, below stretches the depths of Tartarus. Air at ground level appears as mist or fog, and above is the bright blue cloudless sky, the home of the gods. At night this region twinkles with complex star formations, which alternate with the sun in rising from and setting into Ocean. The post-Homeric poet Hesiod used a genealogical model of matings and births to explain meteorological formations and the arrangement of creatures on the earth. Of particular interest is his naming of the vague initial area as *Chāos*, a word that connects with 'yawning' and 'chasm', a fair attempt to describe what there was before anything else.[22]

Anaximander recast the *Chāos* as *to apeiron*, neuter and negative, with no internal limiting factor (*peras*), but expressed as a vast characterless origin of all things, extending endlessly in space and time. Within it rose a 'seeds' of opposites, hot and cold, dry and wet in particular, the hot rising to form a flame that split off into the circles of sun, moon and stars, the cold concentrated as central earth. The war of attrition between opposites was thought to balance out to give the repeated sequences of bright days and dark nights, hot, dry summers and cold, wet winters. Anaximander also came to two remarkable conclusions – the first that the earth does not 'fall down' because it is freely suspended in a central position with no reason to go one way or another, and, secondly, that the earth could not be flat but three-dimensional, and he concluded that it had the shape of a cylinder with life on the surface opposite to ours, literally 'antipodes', with feet opposite each other on the facing surfaces. The world structure grew like an organism from a seed, but when established followed simple mathematical laws.[23] Anaximenes gave to the limitless cosmos of his predecessor the attribute of air/breath extending outwards as sky,

---

21   The contrast is between 'is' for atom and 'is not' for void, one as real as the other.

22   From Chaos the mists of Tartarus emerged, and Hesiod attempts to measure the height above and the depths below with a heavy bronze anvil, falling 9 days and nights, reaching earth on the tenth, and, if it fell from earth, would fall another 9 nights and days, and come to Tartarus on the tenth., *Theogony* 721–5.

23   He used a simple (wrong) calculation connected with the powers of 3, for moon, star and sun 'rings' as 9, 18 and 27.

and being also the air that is breathed, essential to human life and *psychē*.[24] The structure of a universe with a central *earth*, surrounded by *water* as sea, with *air* and *fire* (home to sun, moon and stars above) came to be the accepted pattern of the universe, the 'whole', with the four elements of Empedocles standardised as its material.[25]

The 'hard-hitting' arguments of Parmenides' goddess brought the ongoing Presocratic practice of devising a cosmology to an abrupt halt, and henceforth his arguments had to be taken into account. If a basic 'is' (*esti*) is accepted, then logically its opposite ('is not', *ouk esti*) is to be rejected. Applied temporally *esti* rules out *ouk esti* and with it a beginning from, or destruction into, what is not; spatially *esti* is complete with no gaps of *ouk esti* internally or at the periphery, so movement, change and plurality are also ruled out. Parmenides went on to construct his own (false) cosmology by showing that with minimum change (two things rather than one) a cosmos could be generated. Then Empedocles posited *four* entities – earth, air, fire and water – and gave to each the characteristics of Parmenides' *esti*, namely being unchanging, ungenerated and indestructible. He went further, and identified Parmenides' *ouk esti* spatially, taking this to mean there could be no *kenon*, 'empty space'. As a *plenum* (i.e. a 'full'), what there is occupies all available territory, so that there is no place for nothing. However, outside this *plenum* there does exist what in later terminology was called *argē hylē*, 'inert matter'. The response of the atomists to these earlier theories was to proclaim that 'is not' exists as firmly as 'is': no-thing is as real as thing, and what 'things' are *atoma* (unlimited numbers of uncuttable units), moving at random through an infinite extent of space. According to this theory, the present galaxy arose as a consequence of the rotation of a group of atoms, and it was obvious that other world orders would be forming and disintegrating elsewhere. Infinite emptiness has no centre, and there was a puzzle to counter the suggestion of a boundary to the cosmos: suppose you

---

24   *Psychē* ('soul'), the 'shade' that leaves the body for Hades at death now gains a role in life here as the principle of life, thought and emotion.,

25   The combination of the universe as a living complex structured according to mathematical rules also characterised the ongoing cosmology of the Pythagoreans, and the Pythagorean Philolaus took the momentous step of moving the earth from its central position and replaced it with a central fire, the 'hearth of the cosmos', with a 'counter-earth' revolving round it, the earth beyond that, and then sun, moon and planets, with the fixed stars at the periphery. It was the Pythagoreans too, with their interests in mathematics, music and astronomy, who posited the 'harmony of the spheres'. Since sun, moon and stars move in fixed circles at varying speeds, sounds would inevitably arise, and in harmony according to the mathematical distances and musical ratios. On this cf. Aristotle *De Caelo* 290b.

PRESOCRATIC COSMOLOGY AND PLATONIC MYTH 465

went to the edge and stretched out a hand or stick – if it is obstructed you are not at the edge and have to go further, and if there is no obstruction there is no boundary.[26]

The question of cosmic *time* for the Presocratics was connected with that of spatial limit in that beginnings and ends were complementary. As the cosmos might be bounded or boundless in space so its birth would be complemented by its destruction in time, or, logically, there would be no beginning or end. The *apeiron* proposed by Anaximander was taken to be always existing, but from it emerged at one stage the 'seed' from which the present world order developed. Similarly the 'air' posited by Anaximander had no beginning or end but still was involved in the world that developed from the initial 'whirling', identified with the air and breath that keeps things alive within it. In the case of the 'ever-living fire' of Heraclitus the fire could be 'quenched' into water and earth and ignited back again, but there was an overall balance secured by *logos*.[27]

Once again Parmenides attacked his predecessors' ways of thinking with a strong and logical denial of any temporal beginning or end: 'How could 'what is' later perish? How could it come into existence? ... generation is extinguished and destruction incredible'.[28] He was answered in different ways. Anaxagoras countered with the affirmation of a universal Mind (*Nous*) controlling generation; this was not thought to be divine or moral or teleological, but it does have knowledge and power, and ensured an ordered cosmos from an initial rotation.[29] For Empedocles the four elements are ever-existing, but, in their interchange within the *plenum*, 'as they run through each other they become

---

26 The most detailed version of the puzzle comes at Lucretius 1.968–73, where the imagery of a Roman declaration of war is used, where an official went to the limit of home territory and threw a spear from there into enemy territory. The question of *movement* in space was raised in the four famous 'paradoxes' of Zeno of Elea, the young defender of Parmenides, referred to as 'crossing the stadium', the flying arrow', Achilles and the tortoise, and 'the moving blocks': cf. the summary at Aristotle *Physics* 239b and its commentary in Simplicius. These 'paradoxes' have a long history of later engagement with spatial and temporal infinitesimals.

27 Fr.30: 'This cosmos, the same for all, no one of men or gods has made, but it always was and is and will be – everliving fire, kindling in measures and extinguished in measures'. The divine is then to be understood in this way: fr. 67'God – day night, winter summer, war peace.

28 Cf. fr.8.22-5. Another argument is added, later known as 'the principle of sufficient reason': 'If it did come from nothing, what compulsion was there for it to arise later rather than earlier? Therefore, it must be all at once or not at all'.

29 Fr.8: 'All that has life Mind controls, and Mind controlled the rotation of the whole, so as to make it rotate from the beginning. First it began the rotation from a small area, but now rotates over a wider area *and will continue to rotate ever more widely*'.

different objects at different times, yet are forever the same' (fr.17.27–35). The direction of movement was determined by opposed principles of attraction and repulsion (which he called Love and Strife), and this results in parts of elements moving together into constructs or separating. In addition Empedocles introduced the notion of *cyclic* time. The foundations for this assumption were in the obvious turnings of night and day and the seasons of the year, with the possibility of a Great Year, when sun, moon and five planets return simultaneously to a similar earlier position against the background of the fixed stars.[30] The ordering of large-scale cyclic events underlying Empedocles' cosmology has been much debated, but it would seem that variations were possible within a general pattern of all the elements coming together under the force of attraction and forming a 'harmonious sphere' (which he called 'god'), and then being pulled apart by a separating force, in which our present world formation should probably be placed. For individuals the Pythagoreans also had the idea of 'life cycles' when the soul was thought to migrate through a series of mortal lives, and these lives might even be repeated in exact detail in endless repetition.[31]

These pluralists had recognised just the one world order in which we live, but the atomists took the arguments to their logical conclusion. If, as they believed, there is an infinite amount of material and an infinite extent of space, then it is likely that there will be innumerable world-orders (*kosmoi*) arising and disintegrating within it at different times and in different places. Their presentation is of 'whirls' starting up randomly in space and attracting more and more matter; the initial dense mass cools from a great heat and the resulting cosmic clumps are transformed into galaxies.[32]

4 Eschatological Myth in *Gorgias, Phaedo, Republic* and *Phaedrus*

The three previous sections outlined the Presocratic tradition of cosmological theory, supported by hard argument and in a competitive spirit, and also

---

30 The awareness of such a cycle for the totality of the planets goes back to observations recorded in ancient Egypt and Mesopotamia.

31 The extreme example is recorded (almost as a sick joke) by Eudemus: If you believe what the Pythagoreans say, everything comes back in the same numerical order, and I shall deliver this lecture to you with my staff in my hand as you sit there in the same way as now, and everything else shall be the same'. (*Physics* fr.51). The Stoic theory of *ekpyrōsis,* a periodic world conflagration was a development from Heraclitus's dominance of fire and these theories of eternal recurrence.

32 For the details see Diogenes Laertius 9.31–32 on Democritus.

PRESOCRATIC COSMOLOGY AND PLATONIC MYTH

Plato's attitude to myth as shifting, and, in different contexts, considered alternatively harmful or useful. When his dialogues deal with subjects for which there can be no proof or certainty, then as now, for example, on the origin and structure of the cosmos, the early history of the human race, and what awaits us after death, he is in the region of *doxa* rather than *alētheia*. Here he abandons the dialogue form, and, despite his denigration of Presocratics as (merely) story-tellers, makes up myths himself, and presents them as continuous narratives told in the *persona* of Socrates. Eschatology in this form is given at the end of arguments in *Gorgias*, *Phaedo* and *Republic*, and in a central section of *Phaedrus*.

4.1   Gorgias (523a–527a)

Book XI of Homer's *Odyssey* is the earliest and most famous Greek representation of a journey to the realm of the dead, and there are Homeric echoes throughout Plato's account at the conclusion of the *Gorgias*. Plato starts with the Homeric *dasmos* of the three regions allotted to Zeus, Poseidon and Pluto, followed by two decisions of Zeus: to make the judgment of human souls at death as fair as possible by removing fore-knowledge of the time of death, and having the soul presented before the judge alone, naked and vulnerable, still showing any defects belonging to the body, as well as weals and scars imprinted by perjury and wrong-doing. The Homeric tradition saw life here on earth as the true existence,[33] with a general drabness *post mortem* for the vast majority of the shades in Hades. There individuals could be distinguished only by the recognisable likeness of their shade to their former selves, the *memory* they held of great deeds in their past, and the *anticipation* of future fame on earth, through their own renown praised in song and the heroism of their descendants. The details of Plato's geography of the region here are vague. From the area of judgment some bad souls who are still capable of improvement are sent to a place for a time to undergo punishment and then are released, whereas those who are incurable act as a warning to others, 'hung up' for ever in the prison-house of Hades. But there are also the Isles of the Blessed for the rare souls who have lived 'in purity and truth', not taking part in politics, but most often devoted to philosophy.

This account is called by the narrator Socrates a *mythos* for the listener, but a true *logos* for himself. The adaptation of the Homeric *katabasis* ensures a serious assessment after death of the past moral life of each soul. Minos is now

---

33   Cf. the opening of the *Iliad*, where the souls go to Hades but the warriors themselves (αὐτοί) are left on the battlefield.

the supreme judge (assisted by Rhadamanthus and Aeacus), not just making shadow judgments as in Homer, but actually sentencing the souls before him, to temporary or permanent horrors, or to happiness in the Isles of the Blessed. The crucial new move is that an *individual* assessment is essential: 'the dead must be judged'.[34] This is deemed necessary as the appendix to the inconclusive argument with Callicles that it is better to be wronged than to act unjustly, and, if there is wrong-doing, to make amends in this life rather than suffer torment after death.

4.2   Phaedo (*107c–115a*)

The *Phaedo* myth is more sophisticated and philosophically interesting as the focus shifts from the likely destiny of someone like Callicles to that of Socrates himself, discussing immortality on his last day on earth. The extraordinary details in the myth that follows the four proofs that the soul is immortal are downplayed – not suitable for anyone of intelligence, but, given that the soul *is* immortal, the general tenor is suitable and worth risking.[35]

The first point Socrates makes in the main narrative is a *Presocratic* one – that the earth is spherical. This assertion starts with Anaximander: 'the earth stays aloft, not supported by anything, but staying where it is because it is the same distance from everything' (DK 12A11). For Anaximander the earth would be cylindrical in shape, like a column section, the two plane surfaces being literally *antipodes* (i.e. feet opposite). It did not move because of the 'principle of sufficient reason', namely that if there is no reason to move in one direction rather than another, it stays where it is.[36] A spherical earth is also attributed to Parmenides and Empedocles but Pythagoras may have been the first. His mathematical mind realised that a body 'held aloft' and equidistant from every part of a surrounding sphere would itself be spherical, and this then was the shape of the earth. Later Pythagoreans posited a central fire, but the model at first is geocentric, with sun, moon, and stars all being spherical, rotating beneath a fixed heaven around the stationary earth. The myth then continues to emphasise the smallness of the Mediterranean, humans living round it like frogs round a pond. This is in a hollow of the true earth – we think the

---

34   *Gorgias* 523d: τεθνεῶτας δεῖ κρίνεσθαι.

35   *Phaedo* 114d.

36   So Plato, *Phaedo* 108e: 'If the earth is a sphere in the middle of the heaven, it does not need air or anything else like that to stop it falling, but the uniformity of the *ouranos* in every direction and the equilibrium of the earth is reason enough to hold it in place, for anything in a state of equilibrium placed in the centre of what is uniform will not incline in one direction more than another, but stays where it is without inclining'.

PRESOCRATIC COSMOLOGY AND PLATONIC MYTH

air above is *aither*, when there is a further layer, with our sea to air equivalent to air in relation to *aither*, which is the true heaven, full of wonders. There is also a description of the great rivers of the earth, including Acheron flowing into the Acherusian lake, and it is there that the souls of the dead arrive and stay for times of varying lengths, before being judged and sent again into the generation of the living. Here there is another Pythagorean tenet, shown to be well-known in fragment 7 of Xenophanes, and adapted by Empedocles (in his fragment 115) in the wandering of the *daimōn* – that the majority of souls are re-formed and 'born again' in some way in a mortal life. The exceptions for Plato are the truly wicked who stay in Tartarus, and the truly good, purified by philosophy, who live for ever in 'fairer mansions'.

4.3   Republic (*614b–621d*)

The account of the journey of the soul after death (known as the 'Myth of Er') comes at the end of the ten books of *Republic*, and, like the eschatological myths of *Phaedo* and *Phaedrus*, is connected with (attempted) logical proofs for the immortality of the soul. Once this immortality is conceded, the details can be elaborated on in a *mythos*. The account related here in *Republic* by the Pamphylian Er starts much like that in *Gorgias* with a judgment with three outcomes – of eternal punishment for the incurably wicked, of temporary ten-fold punishment for those who earn release, and a period of happiness for the good. The last two groups return to a meadow through an opening up from the earth or down from the sky to a place where random lots will be cast for the next life on earth, and choices made accordingly. Here Er had a vision of the whole structure of the cosmos as a 'spindle of Necessity', in which the heavenly bodies turned in a series of 'whorls' of different widths, fitting together exactly, with the largest at the extremity and earth at the centre.

The recordings of celestial phenomena had been long established in the first scratched texts of Sumeria, in the cuneiform tablets in the libraries of Babylon and in Egyptian hieroglyphs. By the mid-eighth century BCE the path of the sun through the zodiac, the phases of the moon, and planetary move-ments were recorded on a regular basis, along with the calculations of the solar year. *Presocratic* cosmology started on the eastern coast and was brought to the west with Pythagoras and his followers, where their interests in astronomy, mathematics and music flourished. One of the most important of these was Philolaus of Croton who substituted a central fire for the geocentric theory and introduced 'counter-earths'. Plato's version in *Republic* ignores these two features and keeps to a standard traditional Presocratic version of the earth as central, and rotating round it would be the moon and sun, the planets Hermes, Aphrodite, Ares, Zeus and Kronos, and the outer rim of the stars. In addition, in

Plato's myth, there is the appropriate Siren standing on each 'whorl'; the moon with a shorter perimeter for each revolution would have fewer vibrations in its movement and so produce a lower note, the outer planets with more distance to travel at a faster speed would give off higher notes. Once the lengths and speeds were assumed to be proportionate, the sum of the sounds emitted would then be proportionate according to the octave. So arose 'the harmony of the spheres'. The reason that this is not heard (which may well go back to Pythagoras himself) is that it is there all the time, with no contrasting silence, and our experience is like those living near to a blacksmith's forge who are accustomed to the sound of the anvil, and so do not notice it. Plato here adapts and elaborates, without acknowledgment, the earlier theory of the 'harmony of the spheres' for his own context and purpose.

4.4   Phaedrus (246a–257a)

The *Phaedrus* myth occurs within the dialogue rather than at the end, as with *Gorgias, Phaedo* and *Republic*, but it connects, like *Phaedo* and *Republic*, with a proof for the soul's immortality. The soul is compared to a composite winged chariot, with the charioteer driving two horses, one white, upright, self-controlled and obedient, the other black, difficult to control, and 'a haphazard collection of limbs'. There is also, in the myth, a place for the souls (a 'plain of truth') where souls are judged and move on in a complex time scale involving thousands of years. Philosophers and philosopher-lovers may escape after three times one thousand years, the rest submit to judgment which may involve punishment in an underworld prison or they may be raised by *Dikē* to enjoy a time above in the *ouranos*. Every thousand years the exercise is repeated and here there follows a reincarnation in a range of human lives, strictly classified from philosophers down to tyrants into nine groups; the next time round there might be incarnation as an animal. Such a theory of reincarnation clearly follows Pythagorean beliefs (mocked by Xenophanes, fragment 7), and is possibly influenced by Empedocles' account of the *daimōn* (fragments 115, 127 and 146).

The *Phaedrus* myth also has a vision of the *ouranos* which differs from that in *Republic*. It is Presocratic in recasting the cosmos as spherical, but more original in its Platonic detail, with Olympians as charioteers encircling the circumference of the whole, observing Platonic forms as intelligible objects of true knowledge. Other souls follow different gods according to their inclination, the best staying with Zeus to be philosophers and leaders. These gods are not explicitly related to planets or zodiac signs but would still seem to be implicated in the continuous repetitive circular movements of heavenly bodies, while in some way enjoying the observance of τὰ ἐκεῖ, 'the things out there' – Platonic

PRESOCRATIC COSMOLOGY AND PLATONIC MYTH 471

Forms now occupying the ἀργη ὕλη ('idle matter') which Empedocles supposed to be external to the whole, and surrounding it.

5 The *Timaeus* Myth

Paul Shorey called the cosmic myth in Timaeus 'Plato's Presocratic prose poem', and its importance requires separate treatment. Modern introductions to the main editions of Timaeus give numerous generalisations about Presocratic influences but with no specific citations in the commentaries. In the ancient satiric tradition, following a common practice of philosophical invective, there had been the charge that Plato had copied out the whole Timaeus from a Pythagorean source. In modern scholarship the citing of Presocratic attributions vary. Archer-Hind for example saw Heraclitus, Parmenides and Anaxagoras as key contributors to Plato's account, and curtly dismissed Empedocles. For Taylor, Plato 'grafted Empedoclean biology onto Pythagorean mathematics', whereas Cornford's view was that Plato borrowed something from every Presocratic of importance. But these editors do not elaborate on their claims or give any supporting references in their commentaries. With more recent publications on Plato's Timaeus by Andrew Gregory (2000), Johansen (2004) and Broadie (2012), it seems that the Presocratic ingredients in the myth of Plato's natural philosophy merit further study.

So how is *Timaeus*, dominated by its cosmic myth, a 'Presocratic' prose poem? No Presocratics are named, and, as we have seen, Plato is rarely explicit about his predecessors, but it is hard to read the work without being reminded of earlier versions of the subject-matter, and viewing the result as *both* the climax of previous thinking about natural philosophy, *and* Plato's own contribution to contemporary discussions involving Eudoxus and other mathematicians, astronomers and cosmologists who frequented the Academy and the intellectual centres in western Greece in the mid-360s BCE. From the *Presocratic* point of view there are specific antecedents in various topics. For example, the contrast in *Timaeus* between 'being' and 'becoming' could be seen as a reconciliation of theoriesof Parmenides and Heraclitus; the material of the cosmos fuses the original mixture of Anaxagoras, the four elements of Empedocles and atomic theory into Pythagorean mathematical structures; the organising principle of the Δημιουργός has antecedents in the λόγος of Heraclitus, the δόξα of Parmenides and the νοῦς of Anaxagoras; while the parallel of macro/microcosm is a Presocratic given. Also relevant are the rethinking of the meaning of divinity, from Xenophanes' 'one god' to Empedocles' 'holy mind', the understanding of the world as both a technical construct and a living animal, and the need to explain further the details of the structure and movement of the heavenly bodies that began with the Milesians. This wealth of material may be studied in four parts: (i) science as myth in *Timaeus* as a continuation of the Presocratic concept of *doxa*; (ii) the function of Plato's craftsman-god and Presocratic causes of change and (iii) the constituents of matter and its antecedents; finally, in *VI*, there is the relation of macrocosm to microcosm, and *vice-versa*, in *Timaeus* and the Presocratics.

5.1 *Myth and* Doxa

There are some topics of study where there can never be certainty, in the past as now. These include pre-history, the nature of divinity, the origins of the human race, and eschatology. Some advances might be made, but the material is ultimately unverifiable, and so these are areas in which myth was rife. For Plato the dialogues *Gorgias, Phaedo, Republic* and *Phaedrus* included myths on what might happen to the soul after death but, given the nature of the subject, nobody *knows*, and there could only be degrees of probability. Surprisingly, perhaps, Plato puts science into this category. The account by the narrator, named as Timaeus from Sicily, of the latest developments in cosmology, astronomy, harmonics, mathematics, medicine, biology and chemistry is presented as a kind of story-telling, a relaxation from the hard toil of dialectic and metaphysics – so *Timaeus* 59c: 'when someone sets aside λόγοι about τὰ ὄντα, and mythologises in his spare time, he gains pleasure with no regrets ...', and this is tied in with human limitations: [29d] 'I who speak and you who judge – we are only human and should accept the likely myth (τὸν εἰκότα μῦθον) and seek no further'. In such statements the whole concept of an explanation of the cosmos being for Plato no more than a 'likely story' reiterates the contrast between certain knowledge and unverifiable opinion which marks the Presocratic beginnings of epistemology and scepticism. This goes back to Xenophanes, who recommends that what he says should be accepted as 'opinions like the truth' (fragment 35), and in fragment 34:

> No man has seen anything clearly nor will anyone *know* about gods and what I say about everything, for if by chance one should speak about what has come to pass, even as it is, still he himself would not *know*, but opinion (δόκος) is spread over all.

And similarly fragment 18:

> Gods, of course, did not reveal everything to mortals from the beginning, but in time by searching they improve their discoveries.

PRESOCRATIC COSMOLOGY AND PLATONIC MYTH

As Lesher has explained in the introduction to his Xenophanes edition, we have here an Ionian φυσιόλογος ('physiologist') imbued with the spirit of Ionian ἱστορία ('enquiry'), not expecting certainty but making ongoing improvements. Heraclitus too says that φιλόσοφοι ('philosophers') must be ἵστορες ('enquirers'), researching many subjects, 'divers' into truth, and diggers for gold in the earth (fragments 22, 35, DL 2.22). Related to this is the tradition that the works of individual Presocratics were almost all given the title of inquiry Περὶ Φυσέως ('Concerning Nature'), in that scientific spirit through the ages which expects that advances in research can, and are likely to be, bettered in time. That is why the *Timaeus* account could be called a 'myth'. As we have seen, Plato has a similar attitude to his eschatological myths in *Gorgias* (527a), in *Phaedrus* (246c): 'the reality only a god could tell, the likeness is less ambitious, and possible for humans', and *Phaedo* (114d): 'This, or something like it, is I think a suitable *doxa* ('opinion') and worth risking'.

But, as a preliminary to his account, the spokesman Timaeus has another reason for calling it *doxa*. He picks up the distinction, made first in *Republic* book 5, between what always exists and has no *genesis*, and what is always in a state of *genesis* and never actually *is*. The former is apprehended by νόησις and λόγος ('understanding' and 'reason'), the latter by δόξα and αἴσθησις ('opinion and perception') (*Timaeus* 27d-28a). He continues that, *if* we are going to talk about the whole heaven (ὁ πᾶς οὐρανός), or κόσμος, or whatever, the first question is whether it has always existed, having no beginning of genesis, *or* γέγονεν, does it belong with genesis, dependent on an ἀρχή, a first principle? The answer is γέγονεν, in the perfect tense – it belongs and has belonged with generation, for it is visible and tangible and has σῶμα ('body'), and all such are αἴσθητα, the object of δόξα. This distinction, between what always is, and what belongs with generation, recalls the language of Parmenides and Heraclitus, and both can be accepted in Plato's scheme. What there is, for Parmenides, is without generation or destruction, unique, unchanged and complete (fragment 8.3-6), whereas Heraclitus has continuous generation – the flowing river is a permanent state of affairs, summed up in fragment 84a: 'changing it rests'. Timaeus' account can have it both ways within the framework of model and copy, facing up to Parmenides' sense of the fundamental *irrelevance* of the physical world to truth and logic. Plato's model belongs with the eternal and unchanging, the present cosmos is a copy of it in the realm of generation and change, and the related *logoi* are similarly contrasted, for as being is to genesis so is truth to opinion. As humans therefore we have to accept the εἰκότα μῦθον ('the likely story'), and not look beyond it (*Tim* 29d). Socrates agrees, and Timaeus launches into his long account, bringing in the god (ὁ θεός) as the craftsman responsible for the construction in time and space of the perceptible copy of the eternal model.

5.2 *The Craftsman God and the Causes of Change*

The god is good, without φθόνος ('envy'), and he is said to be both αἰτία ('cause') and ἀρχὴ κυριωτάτη ('supreme first principle') of generation and the cosmos. In his goodness, and desiring the best possible outcome, he constructs νοῦς within ψυχή and ψυχή within σῶμα, so that, according to the εἰκὼς λόγος, the likely account, it must be said in truth 'that this *kosmos* is generated as ζῷον ἔμψυχον ἔννουν (*a living thing with soul and nous*) because of the providence (πρόνοια) of the god (30c). Presocratic antecedents here immediately spring to mind. Xenophanes had railed against anthropomorphic gods, and the tales of their theft, adultery and mutual deceit, setting in their place one god, unlike men in body and thought, seeing, thinking and hearing as a whole, unmoving and effortlessly 'shaking' everything with 'the thought of his mind'. There was also the 'one wise' of Heraclitus, which can be called Zeus in terms of primacy and power, but not in any anthropomorphic sense. Heraclitus introduced *theos* into his new philosophy of nature as a means of *explaining* the crucial identity of opposites, as in fragment 67: 'God: day-night, winter-summer, war-peace ...', and it was *logos* that brought with it the implications of speech and explanation, as well as of thought, wisdom and unity 'steering all through all' (fragments. 50, 41, 108). This notion of a divine intellectual dynamism that controls and maintains the whole cosmic structure was also picked up by Empedocles in his fragment 134 with the non-anthropomorphic φρὴν ἱερή, darting through the cosmos with swift thoughts' (fragments. 28, 29 and 134). Anaxagoras went further in having a cosmic intelligence called νοῦς responsible for all generation, movement, change and order in the cosmos. In his long fragment 12 on this the language is theological, but the word θεός is avoided. This νοῦς is unlimited and self-controlling, finest, purest, strongest, having knowledge of and controlling everything. 'And all that was and is and will be, mind put into a κόσμος'. The problem with this cosmic νοῦς for Plato (as it was for Socrates, *Phaedo* 98b) was that it is non-teleological. It provided explanations for physical structures and cosmic order, the 'how?', but not the 'why?' There are antecedents for the Demiurge of the *Timaeus* in the primacy and power and ordering of Anaxagoras' νοῦς, but there is nothing in the Presocratic here about 'goodness', and everything being 'for the best'.

In his excellent book on Plato's *Philosophy of Science* (p.268) Andrew Greogory argues that, in the absence of the understanding of the principles of gravity, force and natural law, Plato used *teleology* to give stability to the random movement of matter. In the *Republic* (509b) Plato had given to *the Form of the*

PRESOCRATIC COSMOLOGY AND PLATONIC MYTH

Good responsibility for the very existence of being and of our knowledge of it, but, in the narrative myth of the *Timaeus*, it is *the goodness of god*, working for the best, that establishes the stability of the cosmos. Aristotle saw the search for such an explanation as the great problem in Presocratic philosophy: what is the *cause* of generation and change? In his history of the Presocratics in *Metaphysics* Alpha he complains of their failure to recognise a motive cause. It was ignored by the Milesians, he says; but there was some answer in the 'lisping expression' of Empedocles, that, in a sense, good and evil (as Love and Strife) were motive principles. Following him, Anaxagoras, 'like a sober man among his rambling predecessors' says Aristotle, had νοῦς as ἀρχή, the source of change and movement, responsible for 'arranging things rightly'. But even so Anaxagoras used νοῦς as ἀπὸ μηχανῆς θεός, dragging it in whenever he was at a loss to say *why* something is necessarily the case (985a18). Parmenides, continues Aristotle, 'forced to take the sensible world into account', had, in the *Doxa*, set up the minimum of two principles, light as fire and dark as earth. Parmenides also had ἔρως in some sense as primary (which perhaps had an antecedent in Hesiod's *Theogony*, and may have affected Empedocles' choice of *Philia*) and, as well as ἔρως, there is 'the goddess (ἡ δαίμων) in the middle' steering all things. The verb here, κυβερνάω, recalls the function of *logos*, the one wise in Heraclitus (fr.41) which 'steers' everything through everything'. For Heraclitus ὁ θεός encompasses the opposites (fr.67), and, manifested as fire, is φρόνιμος, with the divine attribute of eternal life (fr.30), controlling, as well as being part of, the exchange of the world masses of fire, water and earth.

Aristotle does not mention Heraclitus in this context in *Metaphysics* Alpha, but he does bring in the atomists Leucippus and Democritus in the list of Presocratics looking for a cause of change, and reports that for them it was the three differences in the atoms themselves (of shape, order, and position) which explain everything, but they were 'as lazy as the rest' when it comes to detailed explanations of efficient (or final) cause. Plato makes no mention of atomists in the *Timaeus*, although they are relevant to his account of basic matter; even here the three differences of shape, order and position may have contributed to the idea of triangular shapes accounting for phenomena in their order and position.

One further principle that may have contributed to the original 'sorting out' of natural features is that of 'like to like'. This principle is active in Empedocles' cosmology when parts of the same element tend to come together when not constrained into compounds by Philia, so fr.37 'earth increases its own bulk, and air increases air', and fr.62.6: 'fire, as it tended to reach its like', sent up primitive shapes. This is also the case in atomic theory, where similar atomic groupings come together in the vortex. Democritus uses the illustration of the sieve (fr.

164) which sorts out similar grains – barley to barley and wheat to wheat, and this is close to the 'winnowing' instrument used for grain at *Timaeus* 52e which brings solid and heavy together, separated from the porous and the light in the ordering of matter in space. Moreover, the mechanical movement of air and water in Plato's illustration of the device of the 'fish-trap' (*Timaeus* 78a-e) also recalls Empedocles' clepsydra simile (fr.100) for the continuous movement of air and blood in respiration.

5.3   *The Constituents of Matter*

The first task of the Δημιουργός ('craftsman god') is to fashion the world body and the world soul. With a side-swipe at the atomists, it is claimed to be 'more correct' to have just one world, μονογενής, rather than many, continuous in past, present and future, in the spherical whole of a *plenum*, with no void. This single whole is a divine object, and, recalling descriptions by Xenophanes and Empedocles, it is non-anthropomorphic, not needing eyes or ears or hands or feet or internal organs. So Xenophanes had described the one god in fragments. 23 ('one god, not like mortals in body or mind') and 24 ('as a whole he sees, hears and thinks'), and Empedocles similarly in fragments 27–29 on the σφαῖρος κυκλοτερής ('rounded sphere'). Timaeus then proceeds to give the recipe for world-body and world-soul.

The new way of thinking that was common to most of the Presocratics was to find a non-mythical origin for the cosmos, and for the supply and maintenance of life within it, with *arguments* supporting the conclusions reached. So we have the well-known tradition of the life-giving, omni-present 'water' of Thales, Anaximander's warring opposites arising from τὸ ἄπειρον (the 'indefinite'), Anaximenes' 'thickening' and 'thinning' of the basic air, Heraclitus' transformations of the dominant fire through water and earth, Anaxagoras' 'mixing of all things', and the random movement of discrete atoms from Leucippus and Democritus. Parmenides, in the *Doxa*, first struggled with the idea of 'element' in the distinction of two equal 'forms' – light and dark night, permanent and unchanging, which could account for phenomena according to their *proportions* as the constituent parts of any particular compound (fragments 8.56–9 and 9). Empedocles followed this maxim, but realised that a minimum of *four* basic corporeal entities would be needed to account for the variety of θνητά, – the temporary arrangements of parts brought into compounds, without being subject to change themselves. It is this theory of four 'elements' that the craftsman god in Plato's *Timaeus* initially adopts for the construction of the body of the world. Individual artefacts are held together by the *proportion* of the elements within them, in much the same way as Empedocles earlier had ratios of his 'roots' explaining characteristic structures, as with bone in fragment 96

PRESOCRATIC COSMOLOGY AND PLATONIC MYTH

(which is 8:2:4 parts of earth, water and fire), and his craftswoman goddess Aphrodite was said to have produced a variety of forms of life from these same elemental 'roots' (frs 71 and 73). Similarly, the god of the *Timaeus* constructs the body of the world from Empedocles' four elements, held together in proportion, and it is explained that the ratios were such that earth (dry and cold) related to water (cold and wet) as air (wet and hot) to fire (hot and dry) on the pattern of the mutual relation of the cubes – 1: 3: 9: 27 (*Tim* 31c). This also begins to look like Pythagorean number theory.

In the next section of Timaeus' account a third entity is introduced into his scheme, that of the so-called 'Receptacle' or 'Place', acting as female mother to the father-god, and providing for the birth of the 'child', the human soul and body. Here now it is argued that for the structure of this body Empedocles' four 'roots' of earth, air fire and water are not elemental enough to account for what Plato takes as obvious transformations. They need to be broken down further, and these 'elements of elements' turn out to be triangles. Two basic right-angled triangles, scalene and isosceles, could be built up into the four solids of the polyhedra of fire, air, water and earth, with a fifth, the icosahedron, for the whole. The forming and re-forming of the minute triangles into and out of their basic units in unceasing movement within the *plenum* was then explained by the revolution of the whole, by the inequalities of their size and by the tendency towards natural place – of fire and air outwards, water and then earth to the centre.

So how much of this is due to Presocratics? to Pythagoras, Pythagoreans and/or Philolaus in particular? On the negative side the *Timaeus* universe has no central fire or counter-earth (as it did for Philolaus), but is firmly geocentric. The 'harmony of the spheres', which featured in the Myth of Er in the *Republic*, is notably absent from Timaeus' account, although it does have the calculation of the perfect year, (τελεῖον ἐνιαυτόν 39d), which is in Philolaus and earlier, for the return of the planetary movements to a previous position. And, later, in the discussion of human biology, Plato follows Philolaus (and further back to Alcmaeon) in locating reason in the head rather than the heart.

Early Pythagoreans held that number was the basis of all things, but were clearly embarrassed by the discovery of irrational numbers. In concentrating more on the magnitudes of geometry than of arithmetic they could however work on this problem, so there may well have been Pythagorean origins for the explanation in *Timaeus* of the two kinds of triangles as 'elements of elements', and the construction of solids from them. Again, although Plato here abandoned the 'harmony of the spheres', he is clearly with the Pythagoreans in the fusion of astronomy, mathematics and harmonics in the construction of the world soul. In a complex passage in the *Timaeus* (35c-36d) the god acts like a metallurgist, pouring into a bowl and mixing three ingredients–called intermediate sameness, intermediate difference and intermediate existence; then he hammers out a strip from the resulting mixture, marks it in proportions with a complex of harmonic scales, splits the strip down the middle and makes one the band of the Same for the fixed stars, and then the band of the Other within it moving in the opposite direction for the orbits of sun, moon and planets. The complexity of the harmonic scales used in this construction derives from the basic Pythagorean tenet that the seemingly mystic beauty of music depends on rigid and discoverable numerical ratios. This also connects with the education syllabus for the philosopher-rulers in Plato's *Republic*, which advanced from the study of plane surfaces to solid, and then to that of solids in motion (astronomy) and finally to harmonics, a syllabus directly attributed to the Pythagoreans. Here, at *Timaeus* 36e, the statement that the οὔρανος partakes of λόγισμος and ἁρμονία connects directly with Aristotle's report on the Pythagoreans (*Metaphysics* 983b1) that 'the whole heaven is harmony and number'.

6   Reciprocal Links of Macrocosm and Microcosm

The final topic on Plato's connection with the Presocratics is that of the macro/microcosm link. The atomist Democritus was the first to call the individual a 'microcosm' (μικρὸς κόσμος, fr.34), drawing attention to the analogy between a living creature (ζῷον) as a cosmos of atoms and void in miniature, and cosmos as a large-scale ζῷον. This analogy is found throughout Presocratic philosophy, and pervades Plato's *Timaeus*. The individual could be regarded as an ordered system comparable to the whole in its composite matter and psychic principle, and, conversely, the cosmos is viewed as a great organic structure, a massive expansion of a similar elemental arrangement infused with vital, and sometimes also rational and controlling powers. So water for Thales is the source which nourishes and maintains animate life, and also explains the world's stability. Anaximander had global opposites acting and reacting on each other like quarrelsome human neighbours 'punishing and making reparation to one another'. Anaximenes is more explicit in his one fragment: 'As our soul, which is air, maintains us, so breath and air surround the whole κόσμος'. For Heraclitus the all-pervading, ever-living *logos* which is fire, god, and the one wise, controls the cycle of the changes of the world masses, but also has a similar function in the 'turnings' in human life, in cooperation with the individual from fire to water to earth and back again.

Parmenides in the *Doxa* had said that if the minimum of two principles are allowed (fire as light and night as dark) then a world could be constructed from

PRESOCRATIC COSMOLOGY AND PLATONIC MYTH

them, and also the individual human *nous*. Anaxagoras similarly has universal and human *nous* controlling the cosmos in its separations and arrangements from the original mixture, and accounting for human rationality. Empedocles in particular insists that the same four elements constitute the whole and the individual, and that what are recognised as the most powerful, human emotions, loving and hating, are at work in macrocosm and microcosm alike. So in fragment 20: 'this is well known in the mass of mortal limbs' and fr.22, more poetically: 'all these – sun and earth and sky and sea – are one with the parts of themselves that have been separated from them and born in mortal things. In the same way those that are ready to combine are made similar by Aphrodite ... and those that are most hostile grieve deeply at their generation in strife',

In the *Timaeus*' account the macro/microcosm link is explicit. The lesser gods, imitating their own father and maker, borrowed *from the cosmos* portions of fire, earth, water and air for human bodies (42e), and human souls came from the same mixture as the world soul, albeit from the less pure residue. When inserted into the bodies at birth it is difficult at first for the baby to control the circles of the soul. It takes time to learn to walk, to get the soul structure to control the arms and legs initially, and then to learn to speak. With the subsequent development of reasoning powers from the child to the adult human being, our whole life becomes a struggle to stabilise the revolutions of soul within the body. Here surely the *Timaeus* echoes one of the most intriguing of the Presocratics, Alcmaeon, when he says in his second fragment that

Τοὺς ἀνθρώπους διὰ τοῦτο ἀπόλλυσθαι, ὅτι οὐ δύνανται τὴν ἀρχὴν τῷ τέλει προσάψαι.

People die because they cannot join the beginning to the end.

Appendix

On the Composition of *Timaeus* as Immediately Following *Republic* and before *Parmenides*

In or around the year 365 BCE Plato sailed back to Greece from Sicily, after engaging with the philosophies there and in south Italy, meeting up again with Archytas, and becoming involved in Sicilian politics. On his return to Athens he met with Eudoxus (who also knew Archytas) working in or with the Academy, Speusippus presumably was there, engaged in his number theories, and the young Aristotle had recently arrived. It was a time when mathematics, astronomy, harmonics and cosmology were subjects of the greatest interest, and the main topics of conversation. Plato himself raised the question of the retrograde planetary movements, which Eudoxus eventually solved, along with the problems of doubling the cube and the method of exhaustion; and it is likely that Aristotle started then on a first version of *Metaphysics Lambda*, his own essay on cosmology and the divine, which he later partially altered as a result of Eudoxus' research on planetary movement.THE It was in this atmosphere, and around this time, that Plato surely wrote *Timaeus*, as his contribution to the contemporary debates, and as a sequel to *Republic*. There had been some problems with the *Republic*: the experiment of educating a philosopher-ruler had been a failure in Sicily, and how was the ideal body politic, set up initially as a myth-type 'thought experiment', going to work in practice? The 'theory of forms' had been accepted as a given in *Republic* (as earlier in *Phaedo*) and may well have needed further explanation. The body-soul tensions, the evidence for a tri-partite soul and the eschatology were not altogether convincing, and the cosmology of the Myth of Er needed revising in the light of contemporary research. All these topics are addressed in *Timaeus*, continuing from *Republic* and to some extent updating it. The summary of the 'Myth of Atlantis', which precedes the cosmology, shows the idealised *polis* in action, represented by the early citizens of Athens defending the Mediterranean lands from external attack. There is a basic introduction to, and clearer explanation of, the theory of forms which had been casually accepted in *Republic* with the question: 'Shall we proceed as usual and begin by assuming the existence of a single nature or form for every set of things which we call by the same name?' (596a5). In *Timaeus* (51b) there is a start from more basic questions: 'Is there a form of fire? Are the only things which exist those which we see or otherwise perceive through the body, having reality of that kind? Is there nothing at all besides these anywhere?' Then a more sympathetic body/soul relationship is presented in *Timaeus*, and the cosmology of the Myth of Er is considerably expanded and revamped throughout. So Plato insists that *Timaeus* should be taken as an immediate sequel to *Republic*. To this end he links the introduction of *Timaeus* to the content and conversation of *Republic five times* with the word 'yesterday', χθές. 'The guests of yesterday' are mentioned in the very first sentence, the 'hospitality of yesterday' is recalled (at 17b), the main part of the discussion 'delivered yesterday' in *Republic* is summarised (17c-19a), concluding with Socrates' words 'may we say then that we have gone through again at least the main points of what was said yesterday' (19a), and, at 20b, there is 'yesterday's request' for an account of the *politeia*. The five repetitions of 'yesterday' as the time between the two works may not be exact, but it surely means that *Timaeus* follows closely on *Republic*, – not, as is generally accepted, after a 20 year gap and at least six dialogues later. Plato could hardly be more explicit. Furthermore, the topics of theory of forms, transmigration of souls and cosmology bind *Timaeus* closely to *Republic*, to the earlier *Phaedo*, and also to *Phaedrus* which is near to it in style, in the length of the set speeches (more prominent than dialogue) and in the elevated language of its myth. I would suggest that it is after these three dialogues that Plato gave up on the continuation of

PRESOCRATIC COSMOLOGY AND PLATONIC MYTH

Timaeus into *Critias*, changed tack completely with *Parmenides*, and honoured two of the greatest Presocratics, father Parmenides and Zeno, by making them spokesmen for his new interest in logic and epistemology.

Bibliography

Archer-Hind, R.D. 1888. *The Timaeus of Plato*, repr. New Hampshire: Ayer.

Brisson, L. 1974. *Le Même et l'Autre*, Paris: Klincksieck.

Brisson, L. with F.W. Meyerstein. 1995. *Inventing the Universe*, New York: SUNY.

Broadie, S. 2012. *Nature and Divinity in Plato's Timaeus*, Cambridge: CUP.

Cooper, J. ed. 1997. *Plato, Complete Works* Indianapolis: Hackett.

Cornford, F.M. 1935. *Plato's Cosmology*, London: Routledge.

Coxon, A.H. 1986. The fragments of Parmenides, Assen: Van Gorcum.

Cherniss, H. 1957. 'The Relation of the *Timaeus* to Plato's Later Dialogues', repr in Allen ed. *Studies in Plato's Metaphysics*, (1965) London: Routledge, 339–78.

Curd, P. 2007. *Anaxagoras of Clazomenae*, Toronto: *Phoenix Presocratics.*

Field, G.C. 1930. *Plato and his Contemporaries*, London: Methuen.

Gill, C. 1980. *Plato: The Atlantis Story*, Bristol: Bristol Classical Press.

Graham, D.W. 2010. *Texts of Early Greek Philosophy* Cambridge: CUP.

Gregory, A. 2000. *Plato's Philosophy of Science*, London: Duckworth.

Gregory, A. 2003. 'Eudoxus, Callipus and the Astronomy of the *Timaeus*' in *Ancient Approaches to Plato's Timaeus*, eds. Sharples and Sheppard, London: *BICS*, 28.

Hershbell, J. 1974. 'Empedoclean Influences on the *Timaeus*', *Phoenix* 28, 145–56.

Huffman, C. 1993. *Philolaus of Croton*, Cambridge: CUP.

Huffman, C. 2008. 'Two problems in Pythagoreanism', *Oxford Handbook of Presocratic Philosophy*, eds Curd and Graham, Oxford: OUP, 284–304.

Johansen, T.K. 2004. *Plato's Natural Philosophy: A Study of the Timaeus-Critias*, Cambridge: CUP.

Lee, H.D.P. 1971. *Plato, Timaeus and Critias, translated*, Harmondsworth: Penguin.

Lesher, J. 1992. *Xenophanes of Colophon*, Toronto: *Phoenix Presocratics.*

Marcovich, M. 1967. *Heraclitus: Greek Text with Commentary*, Los Andes UP: Merida.

McCabe, M.M. 2000. *Plato and his Predecessors*, New York: CUP.

Owen, G.E.L. 1953 'The Place of the *Timaeus* in Plato's Dialogues', repr in Allen ed. *Studies in Plato's Metaphysics*, 1965 London: Routledge, 313–38.

Owen, G.E.L. 1983. 'Philosophical Invective', Oxford Studies in Ancient Philosophy, 1:1–25.

Robinson, T.M. 1992 'Plato and the Computer', *Ancient Philosophy* 12.2: 375–82.

Shorey, P. 1933. *What Plato Said*, Chicago: Chicago: UP.

Taylor, A.E. 1928. *A Commentary on Plato's Timaeus*, Oxford.

Vlastos, G. 1975. *Plato's Universe*, Oxford: Clarendon Press.

Wright, M.R. 1981. *Empedocles: the extant fragments*, New Haven: Yale; (1995) Bristol CP.

Wright, M.R. 1995. *Cosmology in Antiquity*, London: Routledge.

Wright, M.R. 2000. ed., *Reason and Necessity: Essays on Plato's Timaeus*, London: Duckworth.

Index

Tables, figures, and boxes are indicated by an italic *t, f,* and *b* following the page numbers

Acheron   468–469
Aeacus   467–468
Aeschylus   146–147, 148
aether/aither   58–59, 469
Aëtius
   doxography on the moon's light by   102
   doxography on solar eclipses by   102,
     105–106
   doxography on lunar eclipses by   102–103,
     105–106
   lost doxography on Empedocles   139–141
   subject to spherical earth bias   307–309
Affinity Argument. See *Phaedo*
Agathemerus   313
Aïdoneus as one of Empedocles' *rhizomata*
   and paired with Persephone   138–142
aition/aitia   47–48, 53–54, 57–58, 195,
   204–205
Alcidamas the rhetor   130–131, 230–231
Alcmaeon   130–131, 227–230, 235–236,
   339–340, 477, 479
Alco the courtesan   246–247
Alexander of Aphrodisias   209–210, 227–228,
   233–234, 236–237, 265, 267, 268, 275
Amyclas the Pythagorean   447
anagke, necessity. See Leucippus *and*
   Democritus
anathumiasis, exhalation. See Heraclitus
Anaxagoras
   "all things together"   421–423, 462–463
   bifurcation of nature   77–78
   causes of eclipses   94, 316–317
   criticized in Plato's *Phaedo*   58–59, 86,
     406, 456
   earth as lid on the air below   292–293
   flat earth   302–303*f*
   heavenly bodies made of stony
     matter   293
   heliophotism in   93–94, 107–109
   mechanical metaphors avoided by   51–52
   Milky Way explained by   317–319
   nous in the thought of   404, 405,
     408–409, 474

Presocratic natural philosopher according
   to Plato   46, 49
"principle of preponderance" used
   by   425–426
size of the sun and moon   94–95, 299–300
tilting of the celestial pole   305, 307–308
tilting of the earth   312
vortex theory of   56
Anaximander
   apeiron as source of all things   ix–x,
     49–50, 73–74, 461–462
   biological metaphors used by   51–52
   celestial tilt   306–307
   circular motion   65
   cosmology of   463–464
   flat, round earth   56
   earth shaped like a column-drum   290
   earth motionless amid
     extremes   292–293
   heavenly bodies contained in
     wheels   293
   natural reciprocity   73–74
   poetic language of   ix–x
   in Plato's *Phaedo*   453–454
   principle of indifference   96–97
   sizes of the sun and moon relative to the
     earth   301–302
   time in the thought of   464–465
Anaximenes
   air as underlying nature of all things   74,
     461–462
   in Aristotle   244
   concave earth   290
   Diogenes' theory of *aer* as influence
     on   330–331
   earth as lid on the air below   292–293
   elemental varieties   347–348
   and heaven   293, 296–297
   heliotropism and *antiphraxis*
     theories   104–105
   and Plato's *Phaedo*   453–454
   Thales and Anaximander's ideas reworked
     by   73–74

Antilochus of Lemnos   231
Antiphon the Seer   231
Antiphon the Sophist   83–84
 hedonism   82–83
 heritability test of   35–36
 human nature defined by   82
 justice by nature and justice by
  law   82–83
antiphraxis. See eclipses
Aphrodite   454–455, 458–459, 469–470,
  476–477, 478–479
apodeixis
 Aristotle's theory of   193–195,
  199–200, 218
 epideixis different from   197
 in Herodotus   197
 in Hippocratean writers   198
 in Plato   199, 210–211
 Pythagorean use of numbers in   200,
  205–207
Apollodorus of Athens   231–233, 448n60
archē/arkhe
 internal principle of motion   3–4, 33–35
 principle not needing
  demonstration   195, 204, 208–209
Archelaus   290, 293–294, 305–306
Archytas of Tarentum   209–217, 235–236
Ares   469–470
Aristarchus of Samos   99, 105
Aristaeus   228–229n17
Aristophanes   67–68, 146–147, 460–461
Aristotle
 De Anima   379–391
 De caelo   64–66
 causal hierarchy recognized by   203–204
 on demonstration   193–195, 199–200, 218
 on the earth not falling   292–293
 on Empedocles' cosmic cycle   162–167
 Empedocles criticized by   359, 369
 on Empedocles' theory of
  elements   357–360, 372
 and *endoxa*   1–2
 heavenly bodies larger for spherical
  earth   299
 and Heraclitan theory of the *psuche*   7–8
 and the history of philosophy   222–223
 the "like to like" principle in   392
 Magna Moralia   227

Metaphysics   36
Meteorology   295, 340
Nicomachean Ethics   201–202, 407n8
 and paradoxes of motion of Zeno of
  Elea   vii–viii
phuseôs epistêmês in   1–2
Physics. See Physics
Posterior Analytics   193–194
 and pre–Platonic philosophy   221–222
Prior Analytics   200–201, 214–215
Protrepticus   237–238
 purposive *phusis*   87–88
 and Pythagoreanism   226, 234–238,
  241–242
On the Pythagoreans   117, 120–121
 reception of Presocratics conditioned by
  Plato   430
 setting/rising sun/moon   303–304
 and spherical earth   97, 289
ta legomena stoicheia used for set of four
  corporeal elements   365
 and Theophrastus on the "Argument of
  Melissus"   280
 and Theophrastus on "Parmenides'
  Argument"   277
 Theophrastus' *Physica* used in his
  historical surveys   262
 Theophrastus used on Xenophanes and
  the Eleatics   272
 theory of matter   340
Topics   199, 363, 364–365, 369, 378–379n5
Aristoxenus of Tarentum
 Pythagorean material in   227–230,
  241–242, 251
 and Plato's dependence on
  atomists   447
Asclepius of Tralles   227–228
Atlantis   290
atomists   466. *See also* Plato and *Timaeus*

Babylonians   65, 93, 103–104, 212–213,
  469–470
Berosus   98
Bolus of Mendes   236–237
Boreas   460–461
Boyle, Robert   352
Brotinus   130–131
Bryson/Bryas   228–229n17

INDEX

Callicles 83–85, 459, 467–468
cause and effect, asymmetry of 204–205
cave, allegory of the 460–461
Cebes of Thebes 59, 207–208, 247–249, 411,
  420, 421–422, 453–454
Chaos 463–464
Charondas 228–229
Chilon 230–231
Cicero 61–62
Claudius Ptolemy. *See* Ptolemy
Cleanthes 397–398
Clement of Alexandria 117, 247–249
Cleomedes 296, 313–314
Cleinias of Tarentum 447
Copernicus, Nicolaus 106–107
Cratylus, Platonic dialogue
  Heraclitean material in 395–396
  nature and form paired in 27–28
  relativism of Protagoras in 80–81
  speculative etymology of *selene* in 107
Cylon of Croton 231

Damasias 242–243
Delphi 113, 122–124, 304–305, 307, 313–314
demiurge. See *Timaeus*, Platonic dialogue
Democritus
  concave earth 290
  earth as lid on the air below 292–293
  infinite worlds theory 300–301
  "like-to-like" principle in 57, 439–440,
    475–476
  mechanical metaphors avoided by 51–52
  necessity in the thought of 441–442
  ou mallon principle in 444–445
  and Plato 434–435, 448
  purposive *phusis* in 78–79
  reality defined by 78–79
  stoicheion in the thought of 442
  tilting of the earth 309–311
  vortex theory of 56
Demodocus 458–459
demonstration. See *apodeixis*
Descartes, Rene vii
deuteros plous. See Socrates
Dicaearchus of Messana 119–120,
  246–247, 249
Diogenes of Apollonia
  aer in the thought of 325–330

and Anaximenes 244, 330–331
celestial tilt 307–308
and early Greek medicine 331–333
kubernan and *kratein* used by 49–50
Diogenes Laertius 115–117, 130–131
Diotima 460–461
doxography. *See also* Aëtius, eclipses, *and*
  heliotropism
  Aristotle and Theophrastus first
    practitioners of 97–98
  "Preplatonic" 223–224
  and "schools" of philosophy 224,
    250–255
  on the shape of the earth 98

eclipses
  and Anaxagoras 94, 106–107
  antiphraxis theory of 94–95, 103
  doxography on lunar
    eclipses 102–103, 316
  doxography on solar eclipses 102
  in Pythagorean system of
    Philolaus 105–106
  in Thucydides 96
einai in Presocratic writers ix–x
Eleatic Visitor 454–455
Empedocles of Agrigentum/Acragas
  abiotic stages in the cosmic cycle
    of 158–160
  aiones as time units in cosmic cycle
    of 170
  anthropogony conceptualized by 61–62
  and Aristotle 361
  biographical tradition on 130–131
  and bone formation 37–38
  and celestial tilt 308
  clepsydra simile in 475–476
  and cyclic time 465–466
  earth as motionless in the heavenly
    vortex 292–293
  and the Florentine scholia 162–172
  and four elements of equal status 352,
    357–358, 462, 464–465
  heavenly bodies near the earth according
    to 296–297
  intermediate times in the cosmic cycle
    of 162–163
  Katharmoi 119–121

INDEX

Empedocles of Agrigentum/Acragas
(cont.)
the "like-to-like" principle in the
cosmogony of 475–476
and *logoklopia* 130–131
Love and Strife in the theories of 132–
134, 153–154, 163–165
main division of the fragments
of 118–120
and the moving cause 360–361
Neoplatonizing view of the cosmic cycle
of 132–133
ontological problem of Parmenides solved
by 182–183
orthos logos in the thought of 180–181
and Parmenides 77–78, 114–115
Peri Phuseos/Physica 119–120, 121–122
and the *phren hiera* 474
Pythagorean number theory received
by 113–183
Pythagorean *tetraktys* used by 122–128
rhizomata used by. See *rhizomata*
and Sextus Empiricus 179–180
the Sicilian Muse 434–435n15, 455
six fundamental principles of 179–180
Sphairos in the cosmic cycle of 132–133,
153–155, 167, 172, 176–177
stoicheion as "element" absent from the
works of 353–354
structure of the cosmic cycle
of 153–160, 160t
texts not readily available to Aristotle's
contemporaries 362–363
timetable of the cosmic cycle of 162–182
zoogonic stages of the cosmic cycles
of 154–158
endoxa 1–3, 97–98, 194
Ennius 61–62
enthymeme in Aristotle 199
Epicharmus 239–241, 358n31
Epicurus and Epicureans 98–431
Epimenides of Cnossus 227–228,
228–229n17
Epimetheus 460–461
Eratosthenes of Cyrene 99–100
Eryximachus 454
eschatology in myth. *See* relevant dialogues
of Plato

Euclid of Alexandria 212–213, 217–218, 261
Eudemus of Rhodes 105, 209–210, 261,
276, 284
Eudoxus of Cnidos 64
Euripides 18
Eurytus 227–228, 251
Eusebius 139–141

flat earth theory 289–316
flux theory. *See* Heraclitus
Forms, Platonic theory of 27–28, 455,
479–481

Galen of Pergamum 332
Galilei, Galileo 106–107
Geminus of Rhodes 100–101
geometric atomism in Plato 323–324, 340
Glaucon 252
Gorgias, Platonic dialogue. *See* Plato
Gorgias of Leontini 17, 223–224, 433,
448–449n61
Great Year 465–466, 477
Gyges 460–461

Hades. *See* Aidoneus
Hecataeus of Miletus 432–433
heliophotism
and Anaxagoras 106–109
and Berosus 98
doxographical tradition on 102
in Empedocles 95–96
in Parmenides 92–95
in Philolaus 96, 106
in Thales and Pythagoras 103
Hephaestus 52–53n19, 458–459
Hera, as one of Empedocles' *rhizomata* and
paired with Zeus 138–142
Heraclides of Pontus 238–239, 246–247, 249
Heraclitus
"all is steered through all" 49–50
criticizing predecessors 432–433
cycle of transformation of matter
attributed to 387
exhalations, doctrine of 382–387, 390–391
fire as basic principle of
universe 461–462
heliotropism and *antiphraxis* theories
absent in 104–105

INDEX

487

Homer and Hesiod disparaged
by   459–460
the Ionian Muse   455
logos in   x–xi, 76, 77
nature as unification of opposites used by
Plato   87
theos in the thought of   474
palintropos harmonia in   431–432
philosophoi characterized by   473
phusis as *harmonia*   76–77
and Plato   454
soul in the thought of   379–380,
399–400
psychologist   377–379
flux theory in the thought of   380, 384,
391, 393–399
Hermogenes of Athens   395
Herodotus of Halicarnassus
apodeixis used by   197
circular maps described in   312–313
on *metempsychosis*   246–247, 256
time differences in the north   295
Hesiod of Ascra
excluded from Presocratic natural
philosophy   51
genealogical method of   463
Heraclitus critical of   432–433
"myth of the metals" in   460–461
Plato's attitude towards Hesiod–type
myths   457–458
Xenophanes critical of   75
water in the cosmogony of   358
Hippasus of Metapontum   126–128, 130–131
Hippias of Elis   223–224, 242–243
Hippocrates of Chios   211–212
Hippocratic writers
aer in   332–334
Airs, Waters, Places   333–334
"all is steered through all"   49–50, 337
On Breaths   332–333
exclusion from Presocratic natural
philosophy   53–54
human constitutions in   335–336
On the Nature of Man   364–365
and Plato   53–54
On Regimen   334–337
On the Sacred Disease   333
Hippolytus of Rome   131–133

Homer
corporeal souls in the underworld of the
Odyssey   409
cosmic space in   463
exclusion from Presocratic natural
philosophy   51, 55
Hades in the *Odyssey*   467
and "like to like" theory   56–57
northern regions described in   295
and *phusis*   55
Xenophanes critical of   74–75
water in the cosmogony of   358
Homeridae, admirers of Homer   251
humours, theory of four   352, 364

Iamblichus
"Catalogue of Pythagoreans" in   228–229
mathematikoi and *akousmatikoi* among
Pythagoreans   195–196
numbers among Pythagoreans   205
Pythagorean doctrine and school
incoherently described by   227–228
Ion of Chios   249n92, 256, 357n23
Isles of the Blessed   467–468
Isocrates   433, 448–449n61

Kant, Immanuel   vii
katharsis-separation. See *Phaedo*
Kepler, Johannes   106–107
kinetist catalogue   377–378n3, 379. *See also*
Aristotle, *De Anima*
kratein   49–50, 51–52
kubernan   49–50, 51–52, 474–475

Laestrygonians   295
Laws, Platonic dialogue
natural things in   28–29, 31–33
criticism of Presocratic cosmology
in   60–61
criticism of contemporary views on
stoicheia in   371–372
"puppet story" in   460–461
Leucippus
concave earth in   290
infinite worlds theory of   300–301
mechanical metaphors avoided by   51–52
necessity in the thought of   440–442
ou mallon principle used by   63, 444–445

488 INDEX

Leucippus (cont.)
    and Plato 434–435, 448
    among Pythagoreans 227–228,
        228–229n17
    tilting of the earth 309–311
    vortex theory of 56
Lobon of Argos 119–120, 128–129n80
logistike 212–214, 215–216
Love, universal force in Empedocles. *See*
    Empedocles
Lucretius 61–62, 464–465n26
Lycurgus 242–243

material cause 360, 362–363, 404, 406,
    424–425
material dualism 347–348
material monism 325–326n2, 347–348
Melissus of Samos 17, 266, 269, 272, 280,
    358, 455
metempsychosis 120–121, 245–247
Metrodorus of Lampsacus 102
mikrokosmos or microcosm 58, 404, 423,
    424–425, 471–472, 478
Milesian thinkers as a group 73
Milky Way, the 316
Minos 467–468
monists 357n23, 364, 455
moving cause 360–361
Myth in Plato. *See* Plato
Myth of Atlantis. *See* Atlantis
Myth of Er. *See Republic*

natural philosophy, as defined in this
    book 2–3
nature. See *phusis*
Neanthes of Cyzicus the Elder 130–131
Neo-Platonists 132–133
Nēstis 138–142
Nicolaus of Damascus 265
Nicomachus of Gerasa 228–229
nous in Plato 29, 49

Oceanus, deity and river 144–146n155,
    290–291, 313, 455n5, 459, 463
Ocellus Lucanus 151–152
Oenopides of Chios 307, 308, 312
On Ancient Medicine 19–20, 25
Onatas 231

Onomacritus 242–243
Orphic poets and Orphism, 51, 225–226,
    246–247, 358
orthos logos 179
ousia in Aristotle 35–36, 37–38

Pachymeres, George 150
paradeigma 28
paradoxes of motion, four vii–viii
Parmenides
    cosmogony of 475–476
    cosmology of 49–50, 92–93, 462,
        464–465
    critical of all natural philosophy 92–93
    and Empedocles' theory of
        principles 113–114, 462
    extended deductive argument of 271
    and Heraclitus 77, 431–432
    limited, unmoved *arche* in the thought
        of 269
    phusis as the "activity" of nature
        in 77–78
    search for Truth ix
    spherical earth 93, 295
Patroclus 460–461
Pausanias, pupil of Empedocles 121–122,
    143, 144
pēgē/paga
    in Empedocles 144–149
    in the *Oath* of the Pythagoreans 135–136
peri phuseos
    book title 17, 46n13, 48–49, 50–51, 473–474
    catalogue of questions generated
        by 22–23
    defining the scope of Presocratic
        philosophy 16–17
    genre of writing 19
    meaning of *peri phuseos skopein* in
        Phaedrus 270cd 52–53, 55
    meaning of *peri phuseos historian* in
        Phaedo 96a8 46–48, 52–53, 55
    inquiry into the way form functions as
        mover and end in Aristotle 36–37
    with limiting genitive 21–23
    phusis meaning approach rather than
        subject matter in formula 23
    meaning and common usage of in
        Classical philosophy 13

INDEX

straightforward explanation of 15
straightforward explanation of by
reference 16–21
Persephone. *See* Nestis
Phaeacians 48–49n9, 459
Phaedo, dialogue of Plato
eschatological myth in 468
"Affinity Argument" in 417
(in)corporeality of the soul in 405,
406–424
"Cyclical Argument" in 420
katharsis-separation in 412, 413–417
"like to like" principle in 56–57
peri phuseos historian in 46–48, 52–53
Presocratic doctrine of flat, round earth
in 55–56
Presocratic natural philosophy in 44
purification of the body to grasp the
Forms 415–416
Thanatos-separation in 411–412, 413–417
Phaedrus, Platonic dialogue
eschatological myth in 470
peri phuseos skopein in 52–53
Pherecydes of Syros 241
Philebus, Platonic dialogue
Presocratic cosmology in 48–49
Presocratic multiplicities criticized
in 62–63
Philia in Empedocles' cosmic cycle. *See*
Empedocles
Philo of Alexandria 132
Philolaus of Croton
antiphraxis theory and heliophotism
in 96
astronomical phenomena explained
by 105–106
body as "jail" for the soul 247–249
Democritus contemporary with 231–233
musical scale in 66–67, 207–208
Parmenides' bifurcation of nature
replicated in 77–78
Pythagorean cosmology and number
philosophy 225–226
Pythagorean mathematics in 205–207,
215–216
"unlimited" and "limiters" in 208–209
Philoponus, John 390–391, 396–398
philosophos phusis 27

phusike 14–15, 31, 33
phusiologos / *phusikos*
Aristotle uses to name his
predecessors 14–15, 50–51, 92
meaning in Presocratic natural
philosophy 46
practitioner of *phusike* in Aristotle 14–15,
50–51
phusis. See also under names of philosophers
aenaos phusis in the Pythagorean *Oath* 136
and *anagke* 21–22
in Antiphon 82–84
in Aristotle 3–4, 30, 87–88
"corrupted" by Sophists 79–85
in Democritus 78–79
dunamis (dispositional) account of 24–
25, 26, 74–75
earliest recorded use of 55
and efficient causation 30
in Euripides 18
genesis (genetic) account of 24–25,
74–75
as *harmonia* in Heraclitus 76–77
and *historia* 46–48
nomos phuseos advanced by Callicles in
Plato's *Gorgias* 83–84
origin and growth of the universe
74–75
in Parmenides 77–78
in Plato 4, 27–29, 47, 72, 85–86
purposive and prescriptive in earliest
Greek philosophers 71, 72–79, 87
in the Presocratics 3, 48–50
"the primary substance" to Ionians 16
private not universal and
necessary 83–84n29
in Protagoras 80–82
and *techne* 30–31
unified ancient Greek conception
lacking 71
used absolutely 21–22
in Xenophanes 74–75
Physics, Aristotelian treatise
natural and non-natural things
distinguished in 33–35
"natural science" about "natural
things" 31–32
Pindar 26

490 INDEX

Plato
and Anaxagoras 434
and Archytas 210–211
asymmetry of cause and effect recognized
by 204
atomists in the thought of 429–430,
436–447, 475
causal connection between physical
makeup and dispositions 339–340
Cratylus. See *Cratylus*
Gorgias 83–84, 467
and Heraclitus 394–396
Hippias Major 453–454
Laws. See *Laws*
"like to like" principle used by 56–58
macrocosm-microcosm analogy
in 54, 58
matter, theory of 338–339
Meno 193–194, 370–371n59, 455
and motion, intelligibility of 446
and multiplicities 62
and myth 457
ou mallon principle rejected by 444
and Parmenides 434, 455
Phaedo. See *Phaedo*
Phaedrus. See *Phaedrus*
Philebus. See *Philebus*
Philolaus' account of chords criticized
by 207–209
and Presocratic natural philosophy 44–
46, 55–58
Presocratic reception in Platonic
myth 457–461
Presocratics named by 453
Protagoras 81–82, 83–84, 435, 453–454,
460–461n16
Pythagoras rarely mentioned by 221–222,
453–454
Republic. See *Republic*
"school" labels used to play up ideological
affinities by 250–254
Sophist 28–29, 83–84, 454–455
soul as immortal, corporeal 409
spherical earth and cosmos in the thought
of 96–97
Symposium 409n12, 454, 460–461
Theaetetus 64, 80–81, 199, 200, 396, 449,
453–454, 455–456, 459

Timaeus. See *Timaeus*
transformation of basic bodies in the
thought of 446
universal *plenum* in the thought
of 338–339, 348
void absent in the thought of 445
Pliny the Elder 296
Plutarch of Chaeronea
Anaxagoras' heliotropism in 107–109
and Empedocles 117, 121–122, 132–133, 179
The Face on the Moon 107–108, 159–160
Polybus, pupil of Hippocrates 352n3,
364–365
Polycrates of Samos 195–196
poroi 342–344, 346–347
Porphyry of Tyre 252
Posidonius of Apamea or
Rhodes 99–100, 135
Presocratics, *passim*
"first wave" of Greek thinkers 1
language used in new ways and new
words invented by x
and myth 457–460
philosophoi as self-identification by x–xi
physiologoi in Aristotle 1
relationships with each other x–xi
terminology used by viii–ix
prester, kind of elemental fire 385–386,
388–390
Proclus Lycaeus the Successor 132–133,
211–212, 261
Prometheus 460–461
Protagoras, Platonic dialogue. *See* Plato
Protagoras of Abdera 80–82, 455, 459,
460–461
Pseudo-Plutarch
Placita philosophorum 139–141, 316
De Homero 139–141
Pseudo-Aristotelian *On Melissus, Xenophanes
and Gorgias* 267
Pseudo-Galen 332
Pseudo-Platonic *Epinomis* 409
psuche 7–8, 29, 52–53, 60
Ptolemy 101, 295–296
Pythagoras of Samos
arete first treated by 231–233
Aristotle names twice 227–228
astronomical expertise of 105–106

INDEX 491

incarnation of Hyperborean
Apollo 120–121, 182
matter called "other" by 239–241
"originator of imposters" in
Heraclitus 432–433
Plato names once 453–454
and Pythagoreanism 225–226
theorem of 298
wise man to the people of Italy 230–231
word *philosophia* invented by 238–239
Pythagoreanism and Pythagoreans
Aristotle regularly refers to 244–245,
255–257
mathematikoi and *akousmatikoi*
among 195–196
nonempirical belief first divided into two
types 200
number speculation by 231–234
Oath of 135–153, 169
Plato's possible adherence to 66–67
regular circular motion in 65
shadowy nature 221–222, 225
"so-called" in Aristotle 244–245,
254–255
tetraktys used by 122–124, 125–128

Rawls, John vii
Republic, dialogue by Plato
eschatological "Myth of Er" 469, 477
guardians showing unity of opposites in
their natures 86–87
mythoi and *logoi* distinguished
in 458–459
philosophos phusis in 27
phusis and injustice connected by
Thrasymachus 84–85
purposive *phusis* used by Socrates 85
"ship of state" in 460–461
Rhadamanthus 467–468
rhizomata, technical term of Empedocles
and *paga* in Pythagorean *Oath* 135–136
"elemental network" in Empedocles
135–136, 137–143
presence on divine and organic
levels 142
stoicheia not an equivalent for 354–357
deities according to Empedocles 137,
355–357

scientific method in ancient Greece 91–92,
193–194
Seven Sages, the 242–243, 453–454
Sextus Empiricus 56–57, 179–181
Simmias of Thebes 247–249
Simplicius of Cilicia
archai of early thinkers catalogued
in 263, 266
archaic or poetic language of earlier
writers noted ix
Empedocles characterized as a
Pythagorean by 114–117, 132–134
Empedocles' fragments 117, 128–129
Parmenides' fragments vii–viii, 117
Theophrastus used for
Empedocles 115–117
Theophrastus used for Melissus 282
Theophrastus used for Xenophanes 267
Sirens 122–124n55, 469–470
Socrates
Anaxagoras as interest viii–ix, 86, 406
"autobiography" in Plato's *Phaedo* 44,
58–60, 67–68, 86, 406
deuteros plous of 44, 59–60
between Presocratics and Classical
philosophers viii–ix
"Socrates' Defense" 410
Sophist. See Plato
Sophists 79–89, 223–224
Sophocles 18n26, 26
Sophron of Syracuse 125–126
Speusippus 113–114, 201–202n33, 479–481
Sphairos in Empedocles' cosmic cycle. *See*
Empedocles
spherical earth bias 289
Spinoza, Baruch vii
Stobaeus 139–141
Stoics 98, 102, 316, 465–466n31
Strasbourg Papyrus of Empedocles vii–viii,
128–129, 157–158, 159–160, 181
Strife, in Empedocles' cosmic cycle. *See*
Empedocles
Suda 119–120, 151
sullogismos 200–201, 214–215
Syrianus of Alexandria 132–133

"table of opposites" 194, 201–203, 210
Tartarus 463, 468–469

Telauges 130–131, 151
Tethys 242–243n67, 455, 459
tetraktys
    defined 66–67, 231–233
    double 124n61, 169–170, 172–174, 177–179
    etymology of 122–128
    in the Pythagorean *Oath* 136–137, 169
    timetable of Empedocles' cosmic cycles
        provided by 148–153
Thales of Miletus
    in Aristotle's works 242–243
    astronomical expertise of 103–105
    earth floating like a raft on a primeval
        sea 98, 103–104, 292–293
    first recorded *physiologos* 73
    in Plato 453–454
    solar eclipse first predicted by 103–104
    sun measured by 298
    water as common nature transformed into
        all things 73
Thanatos-separation, term for biological
    death. See *Phaedo*
Theon of Smyrna 122–124, 125
Theophrastus of Eresos
    On Fire 345
    first historian of physics 261
    "Parmenides' Argument" in 275
    On Physical Doctrines 115–117, 222
    On the Senses 329
    title of his work used by Simplicius 264
    Xenophanes' *arche* in 266
Thrasymachus. See *Republic*
Thucydides 96, 108–109
Timaeus, Platonic dialogue
    aitiai and *sunaitiai* in 58
    astrological knowledge in 65
    atomists not named in 449
    atomist doctrines adopted by Plato
        in 436
    demiurge in 28, 424–425, 426–427, 440,
        472–476
    human body and disease treated in 54
    infinite *kosmoi* criticized in 63
    the "like-to-like" principle in 57–58,
        438–440
    logos and *doxa* distinguished in 472
    microcosm and macrocosm linked in 479

myth in 471–478
number and matter related in 67
peri phuseos in 13
phusis in 28
planets' orbits in 66–67
purposive features of cosmogony in 86
Pythagorean fusion in the world soul
    in 477–478
Republic written right before 479–481
Receptacle/Place in the cosmogony
    of 477
"saving the phenomena" principle 438
spherical conception of cosmos
    in 96–97
stoicheia in 368–369, 370–371
zoogony in 61–62
Timon of Phlius 447

world tree, the 306–307

Xenocrates of Chalcedon 113–114, 124n59
Xenophanes of Colophon
    anthropomorphic gods 474
    arche as a god 269
    doxa in the fragments of 472–473
    divine nature 74–76
    earth infinitely extending
        downward 292–293
    heavenly bodies as incandescent
        clouds 296–297
    heliotropism and *antiphraxis* theories not
        known to 104–105
    Heraclitus critical of 432–433
    Homer and Hesiod in the thought of
        74–75, 459–460
    phusis in the thought of 74–75
    separate sun for each zone of earth 295
    and Theophrastus 263
    transmigration of souls 246–247,
        249, 256
    Plato mentions once 454–455

Zaleucus 228–229, 242–243
Zalmoxis 227–228, 228–229n17
Zeno of Citium 98, 106–107, 397–398, 399
Zeno of Elea vii–viii, 436, 455, 457,
    464–465n26, 479–481

Printed in the United States
By Bookmasters